The Exegetical Guide to the Greek New Testament

Volumes Available

Matthew	Charles L. Quarles
Luke	Alan J. Thompson
John	Murray J. Harris
Romans	John D. Harvey
Ephesians	Benjamin L. Merkle
Philippians	Joseph H. Hellerman
Colossians, Philemon	Murray J. Harris
Hebrews	Dana M. Harris
James	Chris A. Vlachos
1 Peter	Greg W. Forbes

Forthcoming Volumes

Mark	Joel F. Williams
Acts	L. Scott Kellum
1 Corinthians	Jay E. Smith
2 Corinthians	Colin G. Kruse
Galatians	David A. Croteau
1–2 Thessalonians	David W. Chapman
1–2 Timothy, Titus	Ray Van Neste
2 Peter, Jude	Terry L. Wilder
1–3 John	Robert L. Plummer
Revelation	Bruce N. Fisk

"Like other volumes in the EGGNT series, this work on Hebrews is both less than a commentary and more than a commentary. After years of close study of the Greek text of Hebrews, Dana Harris provides, in largely classical categories, a most detailed and informed grammatical analysis of this book—a boon to students and pastors everywhere. This is an inescapably important tool for the next generation of those who teach and comment on Hebrews."

—D. A. Carson, emeritus professor of New Testament, Trinity Evangelical Divinity School

"Harris is to be commended for the excellent way in which this volume on Hebrews fulfills the goals of the Exegetical Guide series. Her analysis of grammatical issues is appropriately thorough. She handles controversial questions with fair and balanced judgment. Furthermore, she writes in a clear and engaging style. Students of Hebrews are in her debt for the wealth of linguistic and syntactical information that this book puts at their fingertips."

—Gareth Lee Cockerill, emeritus professor of New Testament and biblical theology, Wesley Biblical Seminary

"Dana Harris offers a concise, elegant explanation of the Greek text of Hebrews as she elucidates complex exegetical decisions and explains the theological issues at play in the vocabulary, syntax, and grammar discussions. She provides readers with exegetical options before describing her position, helping the reader engage the text directly. Harris underlines connections between individual verses and the wider themes and literary style within the letter, so that readers see both the forest and the tree. The section 'Homiletical Suggestions' following each passage provides an excellent bridge between detailed exegesis and sermon outlines that will preach. Scholars and preachers alike will benefit greatly from this wonderful resource."

—Lynn H. Cohick, provost and dean, professor of New Testament, Denver Seminary

"Dana Harris knows Hebrews research, and, having taught the fundamentals of Greek grammar for years, she excels at making the intricacies of Koine Greek accessible. These competencies are brought together admirably in the Hebrews volume of the EGGNT. The pulling together of insights from the best grammars and lexicons, combined with the 'Further Study' bibliographies on each unit, makes this tool a gold mine of information on the book."

—George H. Guthrie, professor of New Testament, Regent College

"This substantial volume not only provides a careful and reliable guide to the structural and grammatical analyses of Hebrews, but also makes a strong and compelling case for the importance of a close study of the Greek text in the appropriation of its message and significance. Written by a Hebrews scholar who is a well-informed linguist and an experienced Greek teacher, this volume belongs on the shelf of every Greek student and conscientious pastor alike."

—David W. Pao, Chair of the New Testament Department, professor of New Testament, Trinity Evangelical Divinity School

"In an era lacking major commentaries on Hebrews, Dana Harris provides students and scholars of Hebrews with a commentary that takes seriously the complexities of this striking Greek composition. She offers important grammatical insights alongside perceptive theological commentary. This commentary by Harris attends to the complexity of the Greek text of Hebrews, offering significant insights on the grammar and syntax of the text. But she does not stop there. This volume also provides answers to pressing theological questions with Hebrews, making it an indispensable resource for students, scholars, and pastors alike."

—Madison N. Pierce, assistant professor of New Testament, Trinity Evangelical Divinity School

EXEGETICAL GUIDE TO THE GREEK NEW TESTAMENT

HEBREWS

Dana M. Harris

EXEGETICAL GUIDE TO THE GREEK NEW TESTAMENT

HEBREWS

Andreas J. Köstenberger
Robert W. Yarbrough
General Editors

B&H ACADEMIC
Nashville, Tennessee

Exegetical Guide to the Greek New Testament: Hebrews

Published by B&H Academic
Nashville, Tennessee

ISBN: 978-1-4336-7627-7

Dewey Decimal Classification: 227.87
Subject Heading: BIBLE. N.T. HEBREWS—STUDY AND TEACHING /
BIBLE. N.T.—CRITICISM

Printed in the United States of America

3 4 5 6 7 8 9 10 • 26 25 24 23 22
VP

To my students who have experienced the richness and beauty of Hebrews and who have journeyed with me into the promised rest, and, especially, to our Pioneer, who has gone before us, intercedes for us, and awaits us in the heavenly Zion, to our Priest who offered himself up as the sacrifice that enables us to come before the throne with cleansed consciences and worshipful hearts, to Jesus, our Great Shepherd, be all glory and honor—amen!

Contents

Hebrews

Acknowledgments

It has been a great joy and a privilege to study, teach, and preach through Hebrews for many years! I am thankful for eager students at Trinity Evangelical Divinity School, whose enthusiasm and insightful questions have increased my love for and sharpened my understanding of this wonderful epistle. I am especially grateful for those students who have wrestled with the often complex Greek in Hebrews with joy and perseverance. I am also thankful for the opportunity to teach through Hebrews in several home fellowships—to interact with the Word of God together with the people of God is a great honor.

I want to thank the many people who have supported me and prayed for me during the long season spent working on this book—the beloved people of God at Church of the Redeemer in Highwood, Illinois, and at St. Barnabas in Cambridge, UK. In both places, I am very thankful for biweekly home fellowships and for dear brothers and sisters who did not get tired of hearing the same prayer request over and over. Several people deserve special mention for their continued prayer, including Sharon Sheehan, Ingrid Faro, Michele and Dan Becker, Helen Bass, and Rick and Judy Bayley. Their friendship and sense of humor have been great blessings to me. I am also grateful for the support of my family.

I also want to thank dear colleagues at Trinity Evangelical Divinity School and Tyndale House. I have appreciated their enthusiastic support of my love for Hebrews. Special thanks goes to several graduate assistants whose help was tremendously valuable: Madison Pierce, Julia Lindenlaub, Jennifer Guo, and Johanan Kumar. I especially appreciate the 2017 fall sabbatical granted to me by Dean Graham Cole and the Board of Regents of Trinity Evangelical Divinity School, during which time I was able to make substantial progress on this book.

Finally, I want to thank Audrey Greeson, project manager at B&H Academic, for her cheerful patience as this project took longer than anticipated, and Bob Yarbrough, general editor of the Exegetical Guide to the Greek New Testament series, whose mentorship and friendship go back many years and whose willingness to read chapters along the way was greatly appreciated.

I am grateful to so many others, but especially to my Lord and Redeemer, Jesus.

Publisher's Preface

It is with great excitement that we publish this volume of the Exegetical Guide to the Greek New Testament series. When the founding editor, Dr. Murray J. Harris, came to us seeking a new publishing partner, we gratefully accepted the offer. With the help of the coeditor, Andreas J. Köstenberger, we spent several years working together to acquire all of the authors we needed to complete the series. By God's grace we succeeded and contracted the last author in 2011. Originally working with another publishing house, Murray's efforts spanned more than twenty years. As God would have it, shortly after the final author was contracted, Murray decided God wanted him to withdraw as coeditor of the series. God made clear to him that he must devote his full attention to taking care of his wife, who faces the daily challenges caused by multiple sclerosis.

Over the course of many years, God has used Murray to teach his students how to properly exegete the Scriptures. He is an exceptional scholar and professor. But even more importantly, Murray is a man dedicated to serving Christ. His greatest joy is to respond in faithful obedience when his Master calls. "There can be no higher and more ennobling privilege than to have the Lord of the universe as one's Owner and Master and to be his accredited representative on earth."[1] Murray has once again heeded the call of his Master.

It is our privilege to dedicate the Exegetical Guide to the Greek New Testament series to Dr. Murray J. Harris. We pray that our readers will continue the work he started.

B&H Academic

1. Murray J. Harris, *Slave of Christ: A New Testament Metaphor for Total Devotion to Christ* (Downers Grove, IL: InterVarsity Press, 1999), 155.

General Introduction to the EGGNT Series

Studying the New Testament in the original Greek has become easier in recent years. Beginning students will work their way through an introductory grammar or other text, but then what? Grappling with difficult verb forms, rare vocabulary, and grammatical irregularities remains a formidable task for those who would advance beyond the initial stages of learning Greek to master the interpretive process. Intermediate grammars and grammatical analyses can help, but such tools, for all their value, still often operate at a distance from the Greek text itself, and analyses are often too brief to be genuinely helpful.

The Exegetical Guide to the Greek New Testament (EGGNT) aims to close the gap between the Greek text and the available tools. Each EGGNT volume aims to provide all the necessary information for understanding the Greek text and, in addition, includes homiletical helps and suggestions for further study. The EGGNT is not a full-scale commentary. Nevertheless, these guides will make interpreting a given New Testament book easier, in particular for those who are hard-pressed for time and yet want to preach or teach with accuracy and authority.

In terms of layout, each volume begins with a brief introduction to the particular book (including such matters as authorship, date, etc.), a basic outline, and a list of recommended commentaries. At the end of each volume, you will find a comprehensive exegetical outline of the book. The body of each volume is devoted to paragraph-by-paragraph exegesis of the text. The treatment of each paragraph includes:

1. The Greek text of the passage, phrase by phrase, from the fifth edition of the United Bible Societies' *Greek New Testament* (UBS^5).[1]
2. A structural analysis of the passage. Typically, verbal discussion of the structure of a given unit is followed by a diagram, whereby the verbal discussion serves to explain the diagram and the diagram serves to provide a visual aid illumining the structural discussion. While there is no one correct or standard

1. The English translation from the Christian Standard Bible (CSB) has been added below each Greek phrase to help readers form a bridge between the Greek text and the following analysis. Please note that the CSB uses bold text for OT quotations.

way to diagram Greek sentences, the following format is typically followed in EGGNT volumes:

a. The original Greek word order is maintained.
b. When Greek words are omitted, this is indicated by ellipses (. . .).
c. The diagramming method, moving from left to right, is predicated on the following. In clauses with a finite verb, the default order is typically verb-subject-object. In verbless clauses or clauses with nonfinite verb forms, the default order is typically subject-(verb)-object. Departures from these default orders are understood to be pragmatically motivated (e.g., contrast, emphasis, etc.).
d. Indents are used to indicate subordination (e.g., in the case of dependent clauses).
e. Retaining original word order, modifiers are centered above or below the word they modify (e.g., a prepositional phrase in relation to the verb).
f. Where a given sentence or clause spans multiple lines of text, drawn lines are used, such as where a relative pronoun introduces a relative clause (often shifting emphasis).
g. Underline is used to indicate imperatives; dotted underline is used to indicate repetition (the same word or cognate used multiple times in a given unit); the symbol ⁝ may be used where an article is separated from a noun or participle by interjected material (such as a prepositional phrase).
h. In shorter letters diagrams are normally provided for every unit; in longer letters and Revelation, ellipses may be used to show less detail in diagramming (keeping larger blocks together on the same line) in order to focus primarily on the larger structure of a given unit; in the Gospels and Acts, detailed diagrams will usually not be provided, though less detailed diagrams may be used to illustrate important or more complex structural aspects of a given passage.

3. A discussion of each phrase of the passage with discussion of relevant vocabulary, significant textual variants, and detailed grammatical analysis, including parsing. When more than one solution is given for a particular exegetical issue, the author's own preference is indicated by an asterisk (*). When no preference is expressed, the options are judged to be evenly balanced, or it is assumed that the text is intentionally ambiguous. When a particular verb form may be parsed in more than one way, only the parsing appropriate in the specific context is supplied; but where there is difference of opinion among grammarians or commentators, both possibilities are given and the matter is discussed.
4. Various translations of significant words or phrases.
5. A list of suggested topics for further study with bibliography for each topic. An asterisk (*) in one of the "For Further Study" bibliographies draws

attention to a discussion of the particular topic that is recommended as a useful introduction to the issues involved.

6. Homiletical suggestions designed to help the preacher or teacher move from the Greek text to a sermon outline that reflects careful exegesis. The first suggestion for a particular paragraph of the text is always more exegetical than homiletical and consists of an outline of the entire paragraph. These detailed outlines of each paragraph build on the general outline proposed for the whole book and, if placed side by side, form a comprehensive exegetical outline of the book. All outlines are intended to serve as a basis for sermon preparation and should be adapted to the needs of a particular audience.[2]

The EGGNT volumes will serve a variety of readers. Those reading the Greek text for the first time may be content with the assistance with vocabulary, parsing, and translation. Readers with some experience in Greek may want to skip or skim these sections and focus attention on the discussions of grammar. More advanced students may choose to pursue the topics and references to technical works under "For Further Study," while pastors may be more interested in the movement from grammatical analysis to sermon outline. Teachers may appreciate having a resource that frees them to focus on exegetical details and theological matters.

The editors are pleased to present you with the individual installments of the EGGNT. We are grateful for each of the contributors who has labored long and hard over each phrase in the Greek New Testament. Together we share the conviction that "all Scripture is inspired by God and is profitable for teaching, for rebuking, for correcting, for training in righteousness" (2 Tim 3:16 CSB) and echo Paul's words to Timothy: "Be diligent to present yourself to God as one approved, a worker who doesn't need to be ashamed, correctly teaching the word of truth" (2 Tim 2:15 CSB).

Thanks to Michael Naylor, who served as assistant editor for this volume.

Andreas J. Köstenberger
Robert W. Yarbrough

2. As a Bible publisher, B&H Publishing follows the "Colorado Springs Guidelines for Translation of Gender-Related Language in Scripture." As an academic book publisher, B&H Academic asks that authors conform their manuscripts (including EGGNT exegetical outlines in English) to the B&H Academic style guide, which affirms the use of singular "he/his/him" as generic examples encompassing both genders. However, in their discussion of the Greek text, EGGNT authors have the freedom to analyze the text and reach their own conclusions regarding whether specific Greek words are gender specific or gender inclusive.

Abbreviations

For abbreviations used in discussion of text-critical matters, the reader should refer to the abbreviations listed in the Introduction to the United Bible Societies' *Greek New Testament*.

*	indicates the reading of the original hand of a manuscript as opposed to subsequent correctors of the manuscript, *or* indicates the writer's own preference when more than one solution is given for a particular exegetical problem, *or* in the "For Further Study" bibliographies, indicates a discussion of the particular topic that is recommended as a useful introduction to the issues involved
§, §§	paragraph, paragraphs

Books of the Old Testament

Gen	Genesis	Song	Song of Songs (Canticles)
Exod	Exodus	Isa	Isaiah
Lev	Leviticus	Jer	Jeremiah
Num	Numbers	Lam	Lamentations
Deut	Deuteronomy	Ezek	Ezekiel
Josh	Joshua	Dan	Daniel
Judg	Judges	Hos	Hosea
Ruth	Ruth	Joel	Joel
1–2 Sam	1–2 Samuel	Amos	Amos
1–2 Kgs	1–2 Kings	Obad	Obadiah
1–2 Chr	1–2 Chronicles	Jonah	Jonah
Ezra	Ezra	Mic	Micah
Neh	Nehemiah	Nah	Nahum
Esth	Esther	Hab	Habakkuk
Job	Job	Zeph	Zephaniah
Ps(s)	Psalm(s)	Hag	Haggai
Prov	Proverbs	Zech	Zechariah
Eccl	Ecclesiastes	Mal	Malachi

Books of the New Testament

Matt	Matthew	1–2 Thess	1–2 Thessalonians
Mark	Mark	1–2 Tim	1–2 Timothy
Luke	Luke	Titus	Titus
John	John	Phlm	Philemon
Acts	Acts	Heb	Hebrews
Rom	Romans	Jas	James
1–2 Cor	1–2 Corinthians	1–2 Pet	1–2 Peter
Gal	Galatians	1–3 John	1–3 John
Eph	Ephesians	Jude	Jude
Phil	Philippians	Rev	Revelation
Col	Colossians		

Dead Sea Scrolls

1QM	War Scroll
1QS	Rule of the Community
4Q Deut	4Q Deuteronomy
4Q Flor	4Q Florilegium
4Q Test	4Q Testimonia
11Q Melch	11Q Melchizedek
CD	Damascus Document

General Abbreviations

1 Clem.	1 Clement
1 En.	1 Enoch
ABD	*The Anchor Bible Dictionary*, 6 vols., ed. D. N. Freedman (New York: Doubleday, 1992)
ABR	*Australian Biblical Review*
abs.	absolute(ly)
acc.	accusative
act.	active (voice)
adj.	adjective, adjectival(ly)
adv.	adverbial(ly)
anar.	anarthrous
Ant.	Josephus, *Jewish Antiquities*
aor.	aorist

apod.	apodosis
appos.	apposition, appositive, appositional
Aram.	Aramaic
art.	article, articular
AsJT	*Asia Journal of Theology*
AsTJ	*Asbury Theological Journal*
AThR	*Anglican Theological Review*
attrib.	attributive
Attridge	H. W. Attridge, *The Epistle to the Hebrews*, Hermeneia (Philadelphia: Fortress, 1989)
aug.	augment/augmented
AUSS	*Andrews University Seminary Studies*
Barclay	W. Barclay, *The New Testament: A New Translation* (London: Collins, 1968–69)
Bauckham, *Cloud*	Richard Bauckham, Daniel Driver, Trevor A. Hart, and Nathan MacDonald, eds., *A Cloud of Witnesses: The Theology of Hebrews in Its Ancient Context,* Library of New Testament Studies 387 (London: T&T Clark, 2008)
Bauckham, *Theology*	Richard Bauckham, Daniel Driver, Trevor A. Hart, and Nathan MacDonald, eds., *The Epistle to the Hebrews and Christian Theology* (Grand Rapids: Eerdmans, 2009)
BBR	*Bulletin for Biblical Research*
BDAG	*A Greek-English Lexicon of the New Testament and Other Early Christian Literature*, rev. and ed. F. W. Danker (Chicago/London: University of Chicago, 2000), based on W. Bauer's *Griechisch-Deutches Wörterbuch* (6th ed.) and on previous English ed. W. F. Arndt, F. W. Gingrich, and F. W. Danker. References to BDAG are by page number and quadrant on the page, *a* indicating the upper half and *b* the lower half of the left-hand column, and *c* and *d* the upper and lower halves of the right-hand column.
BDF	F. Blass and A. Debrunner, *A Greek Grammar of the New Testament and Other Early Christian Literature*, trans. and rev. by R. W. Funk (Chicago: University of Chicago, 1961)
Beale and Carson	G. K. Beale and D. A. Carson, eds., *Commentary on the New Testament Use of the Old Testament* (Grand Rapids: Baker, 2007)

BGk.	Biblical Greek (i.e., LXX and NT Greek)
BGk. hapax	Biblical Greek hapax
Bib	*Biblica*
BibInt	*Biblical Interpretation*
BJRL	*Bulletin of the John Rylands University Library of Manchester*
BR	*Biblical Research*
BRev	*Bible Review*
Bruce	F. F. Bruce, *The Epistle to the Hebrews*, New International Commentary on the New Testament, rev. ed. (Grand Rapids: Eerdmans, 1990)
BSac	*Bibliotheca Sacra*
BT	*Bible Translator*
BTB	*Biblical Theology Bulletin*
Burton	E. de W. Burton, *Syntax of the Moods and Tenses in New Testament Greek*, 3rd ed. (Edinburgh: T&T Clark, 1898)
c.	circa (Lat.), about
Campbell, *Basics*	Campbell, Constantine R. *Basics of Verbal Aspect in Biblical Greek* (Grand Rapids: Zondervan, 2008)
Campbell, *VA*	Campbell, Constantine R. *Verbal Aspect, the Indicative Mood, and Narrative: Soundings in the Greek of the New Testament*, Studies in Biblical Greek 13 (New York: Peter Lang, 2007)
Cassirer	H. W. Cassirer, *God's New Covenant: A New Testament Translation* (Grand Rapids: Eerdmans, 1989)
CBQ	*Catholic Biblical Quarterly*
CEV	Contemporary English Version (1995)
cf.	*confer* (Lat.), compare
CGk.	Classical Greek
ch(s).	chapter(s)
circum.	circumstantial
CJT	*Canadian Journal of Theology*
Cockerill	Gareth Lee Cockerill, *The Epistle to the Hebrews*, New International Commentary on the New Testament (Grand Rapids: Eerdmans, 2012)
comp.	comparative, comparison
cond.	condition(al)

conj.	conjunctive, conjunction
consec.	consecutive
contemp.	contemporary/contemporaneous
correl.	correlative/correlation
CSB	Christian Standard Bible (2017)
cstr(s).	construction(s), construe(d)
CTJ	*Calvin Theological Journal*
CTM	*Concordia Theological Monthly*
CTQ	*Concordia Theological Quarterly*
CTR	*Criswell Theological Review*
CurBR	*Currents in Biblical Research*
CurBS	*Currents in Research: Biblical Studies*
CurTM	*Currents in Theology and Missions*
dat.	dative
DBI	*Dictionary of Biblical Imagery,* ed. L. Ryken, J. C. Wilhoit, and T. Longman III (Downers Grove, IL: InterVarsity Press, 1998)
dbl.	double
decl.	declension, decline
def.	definite
delib.	deliberative
dem.	demonstrative
deSilva	David A. deSilva, *Perseverance in Gratitude: A Socio-Rhetorical Commentary on the Epistle "to the Hebrews"* (Grand Rapids/Cambridge: Eerdmans, 2000)
Did	*Didaskalia*
dimin.	diminutive
dir.	direct
DJG	*Dictionary of Jesus and the Gospels*, 2nd ed., ed. J. B. Green, J. K. Brown, and N. Perrin (Downers Grove, IL: InterVarsity Press, 2013)
DLNT	*Dictionary of the Later New Testament and Its Developments*, ed. R. P. Martin and P. H. Davids (Leicester/Downers Grove, IL: InterVarsity Press, 1997)
DNTB	*Dictionary of New Testament Backgrounds*, ed. Craig A. Evans and Stanley E. Porter (Leicester/Downers Grove, IL: InterVarsity Press, 2000)

DPL	*Dictionary of Paul and His Letters*, ed. G. F. Hawthrone, R. P. Martin, and D. G. Reid (Downers Grove, IL: InterVarsity Press, 1993)
DSS	Dead Sea Scrolls
ed(s).	edited by, edition(s), editor(s)
EDNT	H. Balz and G. Schneider, eds., *Exegetical Dictionary of the New Testament*, 3 vols. (Grand Rapids: Eerdmans, 1990–93)
e.g.	*exempli gratia* (Lat.), for example
Ellingworth	Paul Ellingworth, *The Epistle to the Hebrews*, New International Greek Testament Commentary (Grand Rapids: Eerdmans, 1993)
emph.	emphasis/emphatic
encl.	enclitic
Eng.	English
epex.	epexegetic(al), epexegetical(ly)
esp.	especially
ESV	English Standard Version (2001)
ET	English translation
et al.	*et alii* (Lat.), and others
ETL	*Ephemerides Theologicae Lovanienses*
etym.	etymology, etymologically
EvQ	*Evangelical Quarterly*
EVV	English versions of the Bible
ExpT	*Expository Times*
Fanning	Buist Fanning, *Verbal Aspect in New Testament Greek* (Oxford: Oxford University Press, 1991)
fem.	feminine
f(f).	and the following (verse[s] or page[s])
fig.	figurative(ly)
fr.	from
freq.	frequent(ly)
fut.	future
gen.	genitive
Gk.	Greek
GNB	Good News Bible (1976)

GNT	Good News Translation (1992)
Guthrie	George H. Guthrie, *The NIV Application Commentary: Hebrews* (Grand Rapids: Zondervan, 1998)
Guthrie, "Hebrews"	George H. Guthrie, "Hebrews," in G. K. Beale and D. A. Carson, eds., *Commentary on the New Testament Use of the Old Testament* (Grand Rapids: Baker/Nottingham: Apollos, 2007), 919–95.
Harris	M. J. Harris, *Prepositions and Theology in the Greek New Testament* (Grand Rapids: Zondervan, 2012)
Heb.	Hebrew, Hebraism
HeyJ	*Heythrop Journal*
HGk.	Hellenistic Greek
hort.	hortatory
HTR	*Harvard Theological Review*
HUT	*Hermeneutische Untersuchungen zur Theologie*
HvTSt	*Hervormde Teologiese Studies*
ibid.	*ibidem* (Lat.), in the same place
IBS	*Irish Biblical Studies*
IDBSup	*Interpreter's Dictionary of the Bible (Supplement Volume)*
i.e.	*id est* (Lat.), that is
impers.	impersonal(ly)
impf.	imperfect (tense)
impv.	imperative (mood), imperatival(ly)
incl.	including, inclusive
indecl.	indeclinable
indef.	indefinite
indic.	indicative (mood)
indir.	indirect
inf.	infinitive
ingr.	ingressive
instr.	instrument, instrumental(ly)
Int	*Interpretation*
iter.	iterative
interr.	interrogative
intrans.	intransitive(ly)

ISBE	G. W. Bromiley, et al., eds., *The International Standard Bible Encyclopedia*, 4 vols. (Grand Rapids: Eerdmans, 1979–88)
iter.	iterative
JB	*Jerusalem Bible*
JBL	*Journal of Biblical Literature*
JETS	*Journal of the Evangelical Theological Society*
JJS	*Journal of Jewish Studies*
Jos.	Josephus
JSNT	*Journal for the Study of the New Testament*
JSNTSup	*Journal for the Study of the New Testament Supplement Series*
JTI	*Journal of Theological Interpretation*
JTS	*Journal of Theological Studies*
KJV	King James Version (= "Authorized Version," 1611)
Koester	Craig Koester, *Hebrews: A New Translation with Introduction and Commentary*, Anchor Bible (New York: Doubleday, 2001)
Lane	William L. Lane, *Hebrews*, 2 vols., Word Biblical Commentary 47 (Dallas: Word, 1991)
Lat.	Latin
LEB	Lexham English Bible
Lincoln	Andrew Lincoln, *Hebrews: A Guide* (London: T & T Clark, 2006)
lit.	literal(ly)
LN	J. P. Louw and E. A. Nida, eds., *Introduction and Domains*, vol. 1 of *Greek-English Lexicon of the New Testament Based on Semantic Domains* (New York: United Bible Societies, 1988)
locat.	locative, locatival(ly)
LQ	*Lutheran Quarterly*
LSJ	H. G. Liddell and R. Scott, *Greek-English Lexicon* (Oxford: Clarendon, 1996)
LTJ	*Lutheran Theological Journal*
LXX	Septuagint (=Greek Old Testament)
Macc	Maccabees
masc.	masculine

Mason	Eric F. Mason and Kevin B. McCruden, eds., *Reading the Epistle to the Hebrews: A Resource for Students* (Atlanta: SBL, 2011)
McKay	K. L. McKay, *A New Syntax of the Verb in New Testament Greek: An Aspectual Approach* (New York: Peter Lang, 1994)
Metzger	B. M. Metzger, *A Textual Commentary on the Greek New Testament* (Stuttgart: Deutsche Bibelgesellschaft; New York: United Bible Societies, 1994; original ed.,1971, based on UBS^3)
mg.	margin
MH	J. H. Moulton and W. F. Howard, *Accidence and Word-Formation*, vol. 2 of *A Grammar of New Testament Greek*, ed. J. H. Moulton (Edinburgh: T&T Clark, 1939)
mid.	middle
mng.	meaning
Moule	C. F. D. Moule, *An Idiom Book of New Testament Greek*, 2nd ed. (Cambridge: CUP, 1960)
Moulton	J. H. Moulton, *A Grammar of New Testament Greek*, vol. 1, *Prolegomena*, 3rd ed. (Edinburgh: T&T Clark, 1908)
MSG	*The Message*
MSJ	*The Master's Seminary Journal*
ms(s).	manuscript(s)
MT	Masoretic Text
n.	note
NA^{28}	*Novum Testamentum Graece*, 28th revised edition, Edited by Barbara Aland and others, © 2012 Deutsche Bibelgesellschaft, Stuttgart.
NAB	New American Bible
NASB	New American Standard Bible (1995)
NDBT	*New Dictionary of Biblical Theology*, ed. T. D. Alexander and B. S. Rosner (Downers Grove, IL: InterVarsity Press, 2000)
NEB	New English Bible (1970)
neg.	negative, negation
Neot	*Neotestamentica*
NET	New English Translation Bible (2005)
NETS	New English Translations of the Septuagint (2007)

neut.	neuter
NIDB	*New Interpreter's Dictionary of the Bible*, ed. Katherine Doob Sakenfield, 5 vols. (Nashville: Abingdon, 2006–2009)
NIDNTT	*The New International Dictionary of New Testament Theology*, 3 vols., ed. C. Brown (Grand Rapids: Zondervan, 1975–78)
NIDNTTE	*New International Dictionary of New Testament Theology and Exegesis*, 5 vols., ed. M. Silva (Grand Rapids: Zondervan, 2014)
NIV	New International Version (2011)
NJB	New Jerusalem Bible (1985)
NKJV	New King James Version
NLT	New Living Translation (2015)
nom.	nominative
NovT	*Novum Testamentum*
NovTSup	*Novum Testamentum* Supplements
NRSV	New Revised Standard Version (1990)
NSBT	New Studies in Biblical Theology
NT	New Testament
NT hapax	New Testament hapax legomenon
NTS	*New Testament Studies*
obj.	object(ive)
Odes Sol.	Odes of Solomon
opt.	optative
orig.	origin, original(ly)
OT	Old Testament
p(p).	page(s)
pace	(from Lat. *pax*, peace) (in stating a contrary opinion) with all due respect to (the person named)
par(s).	parallel(s), parallelism
pass.	passive (voice)
periph.	periphrastic
pers.	person(al)
pf.	perfect(ive)
pl.	plural

pluperf.	pluperfect
Porter, *Idioms*	S. E. Porter, *Idioms of the Greek New Testament* (Sheffield: JSOT Press, 1992)
Porter, *VA*	S. E. Porter, *Verbal Aspect in the Greek of the New Testament, with Reference to Tense and Mood*, Studies in Biblical Greek 1 (New York: Peter Lang, 1989)
pos.	positive
poss.	possessive
postpos.	postpositive
pred.	predicate, predicative
pref.	prefix
prep.	preposition(al)
pres.	present
Presb	*Presbyterion*
prog.	progressive
pron.	pronoun, pronominal
prot.	protasis
PRSt	*Perspectives In Religious Studies*
Pss. Sol.	Psalms of Solomon
ptc.	participle, participial(ly)
ptcl.	particle
QR	*Quarterly Review*
qual.	qualitative
quan.	quantitative(ly)
R	A. T. Robertson, *A Grammar of the Greek New Testament in the Light of Historical Research*, 4th ed. (Nashville: Broadman, 1934)
rdg(s).	(textual) reading(s)
REB	Revised English Bible (1990)
ref.	reference
refl.	reflexive
rel.	relative
rep.	repetition
ResQ	*Restoration Quarterly*
rev.	revise(d), reviser, revision
RevExp	*Review and Expositor*

RSV	Revised Standard Version (1952)
RTR	*Reformed Theological Review*
Runge	Steven E. Runge, *Discourse Grammar of the Greek New Testament: A Practical Introduction for Teaching and Exegesis* (Peabody, MA: Hendrickson, 2010)
SBJT	*Southern Baptist Journal of Theology*
SBLDS	*Society of Biblical Literature* Dissertation Series
SBLMS	*Society of Biblical Literature* Monograph Series
SBLSP	*Society of Biblical Literature* Seminar Papers
SE	*Studia Evangelica*
Sem.	Semitic, Semitism
sg.	single/singular
Sib. Or.	Sibylline Oracles
sim.	similar(ly)
Sir	Sirach/Ecclesiasticus
SJT	*Scottish Journal of Theology*
SNTSMS	Society for New Testament Studies Monograph Series
SR	*Studies in Religion*
ST	*Studia Theologica*
STL	Second Temple literature
subj.	subject(ive)
subjunc.	subjunctive
subord.	subordinate, subordination
subst.	substantive
suf.	suffix
superl.	superlative
SwJT	*Southwestern Journal of Theology*
T	N. Turner, *A Grammar of New Testament Greek*, vol. 3, *Syntax* (Edinburgh: Clark, 1963)
TBT	*The Bible Today*
TCNT	Twentieth Century New Testament
TD	*Theology Digest*
TDNT	*Theological Dictionary of the New Testament*, 9 vols., ed. G. Kittel and G. Friedrich, trans. G. W. Bromiley (Grand Rapids: Eerdmans, 1964–74)
temp.	temporal(ly)

Them	*Themelios*
TD	*Theology Digest*
Thompson	James W. Thompson, *Hebrews*, Paideia (Grand Rapids: Baker, 2008)
Thompson, *Philosophy*	James W. Thompson, *The Beginnings of Christian Philosophy: The Epistle to the Hebrews*, *CBQ* Monograph Series 13 (Washington, DC: Catholic Biblical Association of America, 1982)
TJ	*Trinity Journal*
TLG	Thesaurus Linguae Graecae
TNIV	Today's New International Version
tr.	translate(d), translator, translation(s)
trans.	transitive
TS	*Theological Studies*
TTE	*The Theological Educator*
Turner, *Grammatical*	N. Turner, *Grammatical Insights into the New Testament* (Edinburgh: T&T Clark, 1965)
Turner, *Style*	N. Turner, *Style*, vol. 4 of *A Grammar of New Testament Greek*, ed. J. H. Moulton (Edinburgh: T&T Clark, 1976)
Turner, *Syntax*	N. Turner, *Syntax*, vol. 3 of *A Grammar of New Testament Greek*, ed. J. H. Moulton (Edinburgh: T&T Clark, 1978)
TynBul	*Tyndale Bulletin*
UBS^5	*The Greek New Testament*, ed. B. Aland, K. Aland, J. Karavidopoulos, C. M. Martini, and B. M. Metzger, 5th rev. ed. (Stuttgart: Deutsche Bibelgesellschaft; New York: United Bible Societies, 2014)
untr.	untranslated
v., vv.	verse(s)
var(s).	variant (form[s] or reading[s])
vb(s).	verb(s)
VE	*Vox Evangelica*
viz.	*videlicet* (Lat.), namely
voc.	vocative
vol(s).	volume(s)
vs.	versus

Wallace	Daniel B. Wallace, *Greek Grammar beyond the Basics: An Exegetical Syntax of the New Testament* (Grand Rapids: Zondervan, 1996)
Wis	Wisdom of Solomon
Witherington	Ben Witherington III, *Letters and Homilies for Jewish Christians: a Socio-Rhetorical Commentary on Hebrews, James and Jude* (Downers Grove, IL: IVP Academic, 2007).
WTJ	*Westminster Theological Journal*
WUNT	Wissenschaftliche Untersuchungen zum Alten und Neuen Testament.
WW	*Word and World*
Z	Max Zerwick, *Biblical Greek Illustrated by Examples* (Rome: Pontifical Biblical Institute, 1963)
ZG	M. Zerwick, *A Grammatical Analysis of the New Testament*, trans. Mary Grosvenor (Rome: Pontifical Biblical Institute, 1988)
ZNW	*Zeitschrift für die Neutestamentliche Wissenschaft und die Kunde der Älteren Kirche*

Hebrews

Introduction

AUTHORSHIP

Unlike other parts of the New Testament, there is no clear early tradition about the authorship of the book of Hebrews. A long tradition has maintained that the apostle Paul wrote Hebrews. Yet many early church leaders doubted this. The ascription to Paul in the KJV (not in early mss.) was added nearly 1,500 years after Hebrews was written. Even so, it is likely that the author of Hebrews was part of Paul's circle (e.g., "our brother Timothy" in 13:23). Since Timothy was close to Paul, we can infer that the author of Hebrews was known by Paul, if not also close to him.

There are compelling reasons to reject Pauline authorship. First, the author considers himself as one to whom the gospel was delivered by others, a so-called second-generation believer (2:3–4), a claim that Paul would not make (see, e.g., Gal 1:12). Second, there are noticeable differences in both the Greek style (quite literary) and the vocabulary (distinctive) in Hebrews and the Pauline epistles. There is no opening salutation in Hebrews, unlike every Pauline epistle. Additionally, Hebrews uses distinctive imagery, such as an anchor or a ship drifting away, not found in Pauline epistles. The common Pauline designation "Christ Jesus" does not occur in Hebrews. Finally, Hebrews is one extended argument that mixes exposition and exhortation in ways that are unparalleled in Pauline writings.

Perhaps most important, there are clear differences in theology between Pauline epistles and Hebrews. For example, Hebrews focuses on the priestly and cultic significance of Jesus's death (a once-for-all sacrifice), whereas Paul focuses on the legal and forensic implications (vicarious substitutionary atonement). Hebrews focuses on Jesus's exaltation, whereas Paul focuses on his resurrection. Clearly these different emphases are complementary and not contradictory, yet they are significant. Another theological difference concerns the understanding of God's Word. In Pauline epistles, Scripture (the OT) is an authoritative, written source that provides evidence or support for his claims, often introduced with the formulaic γέγραπται. In Hebrews, however, the author introduces Scripture with speaking verbs, suggesting that God's words recorded in Scripture are still speaking today.

In addition to Paul, there have been many other candidates suggested for authorship, including Luke, Clement of Rome, and Barnabas. Perhaps most compelling is Martin Luther's suggestion of Apollos, whose known background appears to align well with an author profile that can be derived from Hebrews itself. Even so, there is no extant evidence that Apollos wrote Hebrews. Whoever wrote Hebrews was well educated and well known by the recipients of the letter. He (based on the personal pronoun used in Heb 11:32) was clearly a superb exegete of the Jewish Scriptures and was likely a Hellenistic Jew, who relied on the Septuagint, or the Greek translation of the Hebrew Scriptures. (The term *Septuagint* is best understood as shorthand for a complicated textual tradition of the translation of the Hebrew Scriptures.) He was a creative theologian, a gifted preacher, and a devoted pastor who cared deeply for his flock. Although he was assuredly known by the epistle's recipients, it is perhaps best to conclude with Origen (c. 185–253), "Who the author of the epistle is, God only knows."[1]

AUDIENCE

Despite the lack of an opening salutation, the final greeting in Hebrews 13 indicates that a specific group was addressed. The addressees were apparently second-generation believers (2:3), who had endured hardships for the gospel (10:32–35). Like the author, the recipients of this epistle had extensive knowledge of the OT, likely also via the Septuagint. They may also have been Hellenistic Jews.

Like much else about Hebrews, the location of the recipients is unknown, but Rome is plausible. There was a significant Jewish population in Rome in the first century. Christianity may have come to Rome as the result of Jews from Rome who came to Jerusalem for Pentecost and were converted there (Acts 2:5–12, 40–41). It can be inferred from the temptation not to meet together (Heb 10:25) that the group addressed was part of a larger network of house churches.

HISTORICAL SETTING AND DATE

The epistle itself is described as a "message of exhortation" (13:22), which coheres well with the five so-called warning passages in Hebrews (2:3–4; 3:12–4:11; 6:4–8; 10:26–32; 12:25–29) as well as key theological and Christological doctrines presented as the basis of this exhortation. Perhaps the key purpose of Hebrews is to urge perseverance and faithfulness. The recipients had already faced significant persecution (10:32–34; 12:4), and were apparently facing more.

The traditional view has been that the recipients were Jewish followers of Jesus who were tempted to return to Jewish beliefs and practices, although this is not mentioned explicitly in the letter. Even so, there are good reasons for this view. The Romans accepted Judaism as a legitimate religion (*religio licita*). At first, Romans did not distinguish between Judaism and Christianity; followers of Jesus were considered to be Jewish. As time went on, however, Christianity was recognized as a separate religion, one that was viewed as superstitious and dangerous. By the time of Nero and the fire

---

1. This citation is originally from Origen's Homilies on Hebrews, which is no longer extant, but which is preserved in Eusebius, *Ecclesiastical History* 6.25.13-14.

that burned Rome in AD 64, it was clear that Romans (at least Nero) distinguished Jews from Christians. Hebrews, therefore, likely reflects the temptation by Jewish followers of Jesus to pull back from Christianity and to retreat to the relative safety of Judaism.

There is no consensus regarding the date of Hebrews. Perhaps the biggest question is whether Hebrews was written before or after the temple was destroyed in AD 70. The temple is not directly mentioned in the epistle, yet given the author's intent to show the obsolescence of the earthly tabernacle (and by extension the temple) and its sacrificial system, it seems improbable that he would have failed to refer to the temple's destruction if it had already occurred, as this would have been a key part of his argument. Thus, it is probable that the letter was written before AD 70. Additionally, the reference to Timothy (13:23) indicates that the letter was written during Timothy's lifetime. This could suggest a time of composition in the late 50s or 60s. No major doctrine is at stake over this issue, and Hebrews may have been written later. The epistle, however, is quoted by Clement of Rome probably around AD 95, so it could not have been written after that time.

THE KEY ARGUMENT OF HEBREWS

The opening verses of Hebrews (1:1–4) are essential for understanding the entire epistle. The first four verses of Hebrews 1 are often referred to as the prologue, or exordium, which established audience expectations and prepared it for the upcoming message. Key themes developed in the epistle are anticipated in the exordium. Moreover, within the exordium, verses 1:1–2a are especially important, as they offer a hermeneutical key for understanding all of Hebrews. This verse and a half reveals both continuity and discontinuity in God's revelation—the continuity of God's continual speaking contrasts with the discontinuity of the time, manner, and content of God's speaking through the prophets vs. now through the Son, who is God's full and final revelation. The old order is associated with multiplicity and repetition; the new order is associated with the singular and unique Son.

Throughout Hebrews, the author presents numerous OT institutions, such as the Levitical priesthood and sacrifices, the Mosaic covenant, or the tabernacle, often noting their repetitious or incomplete nature. Then the author systematically shows how Christ corresponds to each of these OT institutions and yet surpasses them. Moreover, there is something provisional or anticipatory already within these OT institutions. Christ thus reveals God's true intention for these institutions and their perfection in his person and work. This is often indicated by means of κρείττων ("better" or "superior"), used fourteen times in Hebrews. For example, Jesus is "superior to" angels (ch. 1). He is also better than Moses (ch. 3), the promised rest (ch. 4), the Levitical priesthood (ch. 7), the Mosaic covenant (ch. 8), and the Levitical sacrifices (chs. 9–10). A corresponding theme is that with this final revelation in the Son, there is also greater responsibility and accountability for those who have received it. Moreover, the Son has appeared in the "last days"—the time between Jesus's exaltation and his second coming. During the present age, while it is still called "today," believers must encourage one another and persevere. Only those who remain with the Son will experience the promised rest in the age to come.

THE USE OF THE OT IN HEBREWS

The prevalence of the OT in Hebrews is obvious and often intimidating. The number of OT citations is disputed (around thirty-five), since the same passage is sometimes quoted more than once. Additionally, there are numerous allusions or references to OT events beyond direct citations. In general, the author draws on the Pentateuch for illustrative points and the Psalms for key Christological claims.

The author employs numerous exegetical techniques to appropriate the OT, including a type of *midrash* that quotes a long Scripture passage (e.g., Psalm 95), explains key points, and applies the passage's significance to the contemporary audience. He also uses *gezera shawa* ("rule of equivalence," or verbal analogy) and *qal wahomer* ("light and heavy," or *a fortiori* arguments).

Typology is also prevalent in Hebrews. A *type* is a past event, person, or institution that manifests in some way God's purposes and plans and that in some way corresponds to a subsequent event, person, or institution that more fully reveals God's purposes and plans, especially in the person of Jesus Christ/the kingdom of God. The term *typological trajectory* is my attempt to describe how the author of Hebrews appropriates and develops some typologies that are already significantly established within the OT (e.g., entering the land as a type of entering God's rest) to show their eschatological culmination in Christ. Specifically, a typological trajectory describes the pattern in Hebrews wherein the author uses a psalm that provides a (later) theological reflection on an (earlier) event recorded in the Historical Books (often the Pentateuch). Examples include the use of Psalm 95 to discuss the wilderness generation's failure to enter the land (Exodus 17 and Numbers 14, 20) and the use of Psalm 8 to reflect on God's original intentions for humanity (Genesis 1–2). By intentionally choosing later theological reflections on earlier historical events, the author can establish a typological trajectory from *within* the OT that points beyond itself toward its fulfillment in Christ.

THE STRUCTURE OF HEBREWS

There is no consensus on an approach or a structure for Hebrews; for many, the structure of Hebrews remains an unsolved problem. (See the extensive discussions in the recommended commentaries.) There is little debate on smaller units in Hebrews; indeed, there is near consensus on some units (e.g., 2:1–4; 5:1–10; 7:1–10; 12:18–24). Yet the lines between exposition and exhortation are not clearly drawn in Hebrews. Many have attempted to determine Hebrews's structure based on core OT citations, such as the numerous Psalm citations. No consensus has emerged from these attempts, however. Other approaches to the structure of Hebrews divide between thematic (e.g., Bruce, Hughes), rhetorical (e.g., Attridge, Koester, Witherington), and linguistic/discourse analysis approaches (Guthrie, Vanhoye).

Contributing to the difficulty is the fact that key points are often briefly introduced (e.g., "high priest" in 2:17–18) before they are extensively developed (e.g., 5:1–10; 7:1–10). The author achieves cohesion, however, through the use of numerous rhetorical devices, such as *inclusio* (the repetition of a word or cognate at the beginning and end of a section), chiasmus (the development and inversion of key points), hook words

(words used in one section that are repeated at the beginning of a new section), or the concentration of words (e.g., "angels" in Heb 1). Additionally, there is extensive parallelism between key sections in Hebrews (e.g., between Heb 4:14–16 and 10:19–23).

OUTLINE

I. Introduction: God's Final Revelation, the Son (1:1–4)
II. The Son: The Superior Mediator and the Perfect Human Being (1:5–2:18)
   A. The Son's Superiority to the Angels (1:5–14)
   B. First Warning: Heed the Revelation that Comes through the Son (2:1–4)
   C. The Humility and Glory of the Son, the Perfect Human Being (2:5–9)
   D. The Suffering, Solidarity, and Victory of the Son (2:10–16)
   E. The Perfected Son, the Merciful and Faithful High Priest (2:17–18)
III. The Son: His Faithfulness and Mercy (3:1–5:10)
   A. The Apostle of Our Confession, Even More Faithful than Moses (3:1–6)
   B. Second Warning: Listen to God's Voice While It Is Still Possible (3:7–19)
      1. The Lesson of the Wilderness Generation from Psalm 95 (3:7–11)
      2. The Psalm Applied to the Epistle's Audience (3:12–19)
   C. The Sabbath Rest of God That Remains (4:1–11)
   D. The Penetrating Nature of God's Word (4:12–13)
   E. Jesus the Son, the Great High Priest (4:14–16)
   F. The Son's Suffering as Qualifications for His Merciful Priesthood (5:1–10)
IV. Perseverance in the Promises (5:11–6:20)
   A. Prelude: It's Time to Grow Up and Move On to Maturity (5:11–6:3)
   B. Third Warning: There Is Only One Way to Be Renewed (6:4–8)
   C. The Conviction of Better Things (6:9–12)
   D. The Unchangeable Nature of God's Purposes (6:13–20)
V. The Son: The Superior High Priest (7:1–10:18)
   A. The New Order of Priesthood (7:1–28)
      1. Melchizedek and the Order of His Priesthood (7:1–10)
      2. The Aaronic and Melchizedekian Priesthoods Contrasted (7:11–19)
      3. The Superiority of the New Priesthood (7:20–28)
   B. The New Covenant (8:1–13)
      1. The Superior Ministry of Jesus (8:1–6)
      2. The Superior Covenant (8:7–13)
   C. The New Sanctuary and Sacrifice (9:1–10:18)
      1. The Limitations of the Old Order (9:1–10)
      2. The Eternal Redemption of the Son (9:11–14)
      3. The Mediator of the New Covenant (9:15–22)
      4. The Perfect Sacrifice (9:23–28)
      5. Shadow and Reality, Sacrifice and Obedience (10:1–10)
      6. The Finality of Christ's Sacrifice and Priesthood (10:11–18)

VI. Perseverance and Faith (10:19–12:29)
  A. Present Exhortations Based on Christ's Eternal Redemption (10:19–39)
    1. Approaching God's Throne and Meeting Together (10:19–25)
    2. Fourth Warning: The Reality of God's Judgment (10:26–31)
    3. Bold Perseverance in the Midst of Suffering (10:32–39)
  B. Past Examples of Faith in God's Promises (11:1–12:3)
    1. The Nature of Faith (11:1–3)
    2. Preflood Faith (11:4–7)
    3. The Faith of Abraham and Sarah (11:8–12)
    4. The City of God and True Homeland (11:13–16)
    5. The Faith of the Patriarchs (11:17–22)
    6. The Faith of Moses (11:23–28)
    7. Faith during the Exodus and Conquest (11:29–31)
    8. A Multitude of Examples that Culminate in the Perfection Achieved by Christ (11:32–40)
    9. The Example Par Excellence: Jesus (12:1–3)
  C. Pressing on to the Future Consummation (12:4–29)
    1. Discipline and Legitimate Children (12:4–11)
    2. The Necessity of Community (12:12–13)
    3. The Shortsightedness of Esau (12:14–17)
    4. Earthly Sinai and Heavenly Zion Contrasted (12:18–24)
    5. The Fifth Warning: Don't Miss God's Final Word (12:25–29)
VII. Exhortations and Offerings (13:1–21)
  A. Moral Exhortations for God's People (13:1–6)
  B. Remembering Church Leaders (13:7–19)
  C. Final Benediction (13:20–21)
VIII. Epilogue (13:22–25)

RECOMMENDED COMMENTARIES

The following six commentaries are cited regularly in this volume of EGGNT, all of which interact extensively with the Greek text of Hebrews.

Attridge, H. W. *The Epistle to the Hebrews*. Hermeneia. Philadelphia: Fortress, 1989.

Bruce, F. F. *The Epistle to the Hebrews*. New International Commentary on the New Testament. Rev. ed. Grand Rapids: Eerdmans, 1990.

Cockerill, Gareth Lee. *The Epistle to the Hebrews*. New International Commentary on the New Testament. Grand Rapids: Eerdmans, 2012.

Ellingworth, Paul. *The Epistle to the Hebrews*. New International Greek Testament Commentary. Grand Rapids: Eerdmans, 1993.

Koester, Craig. *Hebrews: A New Translation with Introduction and Commentary*. Anchor Bible. New York: Doubleday, 2001.

Lane, William L. *Hebrews 1–8*; *9–13*. Word Biblical Commentary. Dallas: Word, 1991.

If you are considering purchasing a commentary on Hebrews, Cockerill has a good balance between interaction with technical syntactic and textual questions and pastoral application of Hebrews for today. His work also considers both Greco-Roman and OT backgrounds and parallels for Hebrews. Attridge deals extensively with Greco-Roman backgrounds and parallels, but is less helpful for theological issues. Bruce's commentary offers consistently solid interpretations, but is less detailed than the others. Ellingworth offers the most extensive treatment of syntax, but is less focused on backgrounds and theology. Koester is the most helpful for the use of ancient rhetoric in Hebrews and has helpful summaries of Hebrews's history of interpretation. Lane offers the most extensive bibliography and OT backgrounds for Hebrews.

There are also a number of good articles that are helpful for studying Hebrews.

General Introduction or Overview

*Bruce, F. F. "The Structure and Argument of Hebrews." *SwJT* 28 (1985): 6–12.

Ellingworth, Paul. "Hebrews and the Anticipation of Completion." *Them* 14 (1988): 6–11.

*Glaze, R. E., Jr. "Introduction to Hebrews." *TTE* 32 (1985): 20–37.

Hagner, Donald A. "Interpreting the Epistle to the Hebrews." Pages 217–42 in *The Literature and Meaning of Scripture*. Edited by Morris A. Inch and C. Hassell Bullock. Grand Rapids: Baker, 1981.

Isaacs, Marie E. "Why Bother with Hebrews?" *HeyJ* 43 (2002): 60–72.

Niehof, Thomas J. "Balancing the Spiritual Diet: Suggestions for Preaching from the Book of Hebrews." *CTJ* 47 (2012): 248–56.

The Theology of Hebrews

Bruce, F. F. "Kerygma of Hebrews." *Int* 23 (1969): 3–19.

Ellingworth, 62–77.

Harrison, E. "Theology of the Epistle to the Hebrews." *BSac* 121 (1964): 333–40.

*Ladd, George Eldon. "Hebrews." Pages 617–33 in *A Theology of the New Testament*. Edited by Donald A. Hagner. Rev. ed. Grand Rapids: Eerdmans, 1994.

*Lindars, Barnabas. *The Theology of the Letter to the Hebrews*. New Testament Theology. Cambridge: Cambridge University Press, 1991.

MacLeod, David J. "The Doctrinal Center of the Book of Hebrews." *BSac* 146 (1989): 291–300.

Matera, Frank J. "The Theology of the Epistles to the Hebrews." Pages 189–208 in Mason.

Schreiner, Thomas R. Pages 435-499 in *Commentary on Hebrews*. Biblical Theology for Christian Proclamation. Nashville: Holman Reference, 2015.

Thompson, James. "The Underlying Unity of Hebrews." *ResQ* 18 (1975): 129–36.

Vos, Geerhardus. *The Teaching of the Epistle to the Hebrews*. Edited and rewritten by Johannes G. Vos. Grand Rapids: Eerdmans, 1956; Eugene, OR: Wipf and Stock, 1998.

Williamson, Ronald. "Hebrews and Doctrine." *ExpT* 81 (1970): 371–76.

I. Introduction: God's Final Revelation, the Son (1:1–4)

STRUCTURE

The prologue (or *exordium*) of Hebrews constitutes one carefully constructed sentence in the Gk. (a "periodic" sentence; BDF §§458, 464; e.g., 2:1–4; 3:12–15; 4:12–13; 5:1–3; 6:4–6; 7:1–3, 20–22, 26–28; 12:18–24) that centers around three main clauses. The structure of the first clause highlights both discontinuity and continuity between God's former revelation and his final revelation in the Son. The second clause lists seven attributes of the Son, and the third highlights his exalted status. Thus the prologue previews key themes in the epistle: the Son's superiority, his completed work, and his exaltation. Although some suggest that these vv. reflect an early hymn, most commentators rightly view these vv. as the author's own composition and an indication of his rhetorical skill.

Discontinuities are indicated by four contrasting cstrs. (indicated by the boxes in the structural analysis). Arrows indicate that the first two clauses modify υἱῷ in v. 2, whereas the third rel. clause points forward to ἐκάθισεν, which is modified by the preceding three ptcs.

1 Πολυμερῶς καὶ πολυτρόπως
πάλαι
ὁ θεὸς
λαλήσας
τοῖς πατράσιν
ἐν τοῖς προφήταις
ἐπ' ἐσχάτου τῶν ἡμερῶν τούτων
2
ἐλάλησεν
ἡμῖν
ἐν υἱῷ,

ὃν ἔθηκεν κληρονόμον πάντων,
δι' οὗ καὶ ἐποίησεν τοὺς αἰῶνας·

3 ὃς ὢν ἀπαύγασμα τῆς δόξης
καὶ χαρακτὴρ τῆς ὑποστάσεως αὐτοῦ,

φέρων τε τὰ πάντα τῷ ῥήματι τῆς δυνάμεως αὐτοῦ,
καθαρισμὸν τῶν ἁμαρτιῶν ποιησάμενος
ἐκάθισεν ἐν δεξιᾷ τῆς μεγαλωσύνης ἐν ὑψηλοῖς,

4 τοσούτῳ κρείττων γενόμενος τῶν ἀγγέλων
ὅσῳ διαφορώτερον παρ' αὐτοὺς
κεκληρονόμηκεν ὄνομα.

VERSE 1

Πολυμερῶς καὶ πολυτρόπως πάλαι
Long ago . . . at different times and in different ways.

The advs. πολυμερῶς and πολυτρόπως are both BGk. hapax. Πολυμερῶς means either "in various parts" (BDAG 847a) or "many times" (ESV, NIV). Πολυτρόπως indicates "in many ways" (BDAG 850c), perhaps alluding to theophanies, dreams, visions, oracles, and so on. These advs. indicate God's partial revelation before his complete revelation in the Son. The adv. πάλαι ("long ago" or "in the past" [most EVV]; "formerly" [BDAG 751b]) contrasts a point in the past with the pres.

ὁ θεὸς λαλήσας τοῖς πατράσιν ἐν τοῖς προφήταις
God spoke to the fathers by the prophets

Λαλήσας is the nom. sg. masc. of the aor. act. ptc. of λαλέω; the vb. is followed by the dat. τοῖς πατράσιν. The ptc. modifies ἐλάλησεν in v. 2; ὁ θεός is the subj. of both vbs. An aor. ptc. that precedes an aor. vb. may indicate an antecedent action (Z 261; Moule 99; Wallace 624). (See discussion of ἐλάλησεν in v. 2.) The phrase ἐν τοῖς προφήταις is instr.

The author's rhetorical skill is evident in the alliteration of π sounds: πολυμερῶς, πολυτρόπως, πάλαι, πατράσιν, προφήταις, which brings about "aural cohesion" (Cockerill 89). Similar examples of alliteration and other rhetorical devices are freq. in Hebrews.

VERSE 2

ἐπ' ἐσχάτου τῶν ἡμερῶν τούτων
In these last days,

Ἐσχάτου (gen. sg. neut. of ἔσχατος, -η, -ον) functions as a subst. ("the end"). Ἡμερῶν is a partitive gen., modified by the dem. adj. τούτων in the pred. position (R 700–701). The temp. use of ἐπί reflects a Heb. (BDF §234[8]). The entire prep. phrase (or closely related vars.) is common in Jewish apocalyptic writings. It is sim. used in the LXX (e.g., Num 24:14, Mic 4:1; see Lane 1:5, Attridge 39). In Hebrews, this time period begins with Christ's exaltation and ends with the final subjugation of all things under his feet (2:8).

ἐλάλησεν ἡμῖν ἐν υἱῷ
he has spoken to us by his Son.

Ἐλάλησεν (followed by the dat. ἡμῖν) is the main vb. for vv. 1–2. The anar. subst. has a qual. force (Z 171; Wallace 245), stressing the "essential character of the one who is Son" (Lane 1:5; cf. Koester 177). This force is freq. in Hebrews (e.g., 1:5; 3:6; 5:8). Additionally, the art. is often omitted following the prep. (BDF §255). The tr. "a Son" (NET; NRSV) misses this qualitative nuance. Many EVV (ESV; NASB; NIV) make explicit what is inferred by adding "his" (or "His") before "Son." The prep. ἐν may be instr., paralleling its use in v. 1, or more probably locat. (Lane 1:11), indicating the realm of God's final revelation "in the Son."

Together with v. 1, this clause highlights both continuity and discontinuity in divine revelation. Λαλήσας and ἐλάλησεν stress God's consistent self-revelation throughout salvation history. Hebrews associates this revelation with speaking vbs. (e.g., λαλέω, λέγω), not writing vbs. (e.g., γράφω), as in the Pauline epistles. Discontinuity includes: (1) God's former (πάλαι) revelation and his speaking "in these last days"; (2) the "fathers" vs. the pres. audience (and subsequent readers); (3) *many* prophets vs. the *one* Son; and (4) the many forms, times, and ways of God's previous revelation vs. the definitive, final revelation in the Son. The multiplicity of former revelations vs. the singularity of the Son is a primary hermeneutical key in Hebrews and indicates that God's former revelation can only be fully understood through the Son.

ὃν ἔθηκεν κληρονόμον πάντων
God has appointed him heir of all things

Ἔθηκεν is 3rd sg. aor. act. indic. of τίθημι, "appoint" (most EVV). This is the first of three rel. clauses that describe the Son. The rel. pron. ὅν is the obj. of the vb., and κληρονόμον (κληρονόμος, -ου, ὁ, heir [BDAG 548b]) is the obj. complement (T 246; Wallace 186). The subj. of the vb. is ὁ θεός (v. 1). This clause alludes to Ps 2:8, where the Davidic heir is promised the nations as his inheritance; Hebrews extends this eschatologically to "all things" (πάντων). This clause introduces the important theme of inheritance in Hebrews (e.g., 1:4, 14; 6:12; 9:15; 11:7, 8; 12:17; cf. Rom 8:17; Gal 4:7). See For Further Study 4 (Inheritance in Hebrews).

δι' οὗ καὶ ἐποίησεν τοὺς αἰῶνας·
and made the universe through him.

This second rel. clause also describes the Son. Καί functions as an adjunctive ("also"). The subj. of ἐποίησεν remains ὁ θεός. Αἰῶνας (αἰών, -ῶνος, ὁ) could be understood temp. ("age," "eternity"). Based on its LXX usage (BDAG 33a; T. Holtz, *EDNT* 1:44b–46c; BDF §4[2]; §141), however, the pl. has a spatial mng., as most EVV reflect (e.g., "world" [ESV, NET], "universe" [NIV]).

These two rel. clauses underscore the Son's deity by presenting his eschatological role as heir of "all things" and his protological role as the agent through whom the universe was made (see also John 1:3; 1 Cor 8:6; Col 1:16). By placing the eschatological first, Hebrews indicates that the Son is the ultimate goal of creation. These rel. clauses begin a list of seven Christological affirmations about the Son.

VERSE 3

ὃς ὢν ἀπαύγασμα τῆς δόξης καὶ χαρακτὴρ τῆς ὑποστάσεως αὐτοῦ
The Son is the radiance of God's glory and the exact expression of his nature,

This is the third rel. clause concerning the Son. As the arrows on the structural analysis indicate, the first two clauses modify υἱῷ in v. 2, whereas this third rel. clause points forward to ἐκάθισεν, which is modified by the three preceding ptcs. This shifts the focus onto the Son, who is the subj. of ἐκάθισεν (v. 3) and κεκληρονόμηκεν (v. 4). In most EVV, v. 3 begins a new sentence. The nom. ὅς suggests to some that the author drew on preexisting hymnic sources (e.g., Attridge 41), but the unique vocabulary and tight structuring of these first four vv. more likely reflect the author's own composition (Cockerill 91; Koester 179; Lane 1:7).

Ὤν (nom. sg. masc. of pres. ptc. of εἰμί) is the first of three ptcs. that describe the person and work of the Son. Ἀπαύγασμα (-τος, τό, "radiance," "effulgence" [BDAG 99b; G. Kittel, *TDNT* 1:507–8; NT hapax]) could indicate an act. *radiance* of God's glory (like the sun) or a pass. *reflection* (like the moon). Most EVV (except GNB, NJB, NRSV) and commentators adopt an act. sense. Δόξα, -ης, ἡ, "glory" (BDAG 257b) is an essential attribute of God (extensively developed in the OT; see G. Kittel, *TDNT* 2:232–55), which is made explicit in many EVV (e.g., "God's glory"). Δόξης is likely a descriptive gen. (Wallace 79–81), although it is possibly a gen. of quality or attrib. gen. (R 496; "glorious radiance"). Thus the Son perfectly radiates God's own glory.

The act. sense of ἀπαύγασμα complements the pass. sense of χαρακτήρ (-ῆρος, ὁ; "representation" [BDAG 1078a; NT hapax]). This word denotes an impress or imprint of a coin (G. Kelber, *TDNT* 9:418–23). Together these nouns emphasize the Son as the perfect image of God (see also John 1:18; 2 Cor 4:4; Phil 2:6; Col 1:15). The descriptive gen. ὑποστάσεως (ὑπόστασις, -εως, ἡ; "essence," "real being" [BDAG 1040d]) modifies χαρακτήρ to indicate that the Son represents the very essence or being of God. The difficulty in translating this rare word (three of the five NT occurrences are found in Hebrews [3:14; 11:1]) is indicated by the range of trs. in EVV ("nature" [ESV], "essence" [NET], "being" [NIV]), although "essential being" (Ellingworth 99) renders the Gk. well. See For Further Study 78 (Ὑπόστασις).

φέρων τε τὰ πάντα τῷ ῥήματι τῆς δυνάμεως αὐτοῦ
sustaining all things by his powerful word.

Φέρων is the nom. sg. masc. of the pres. act. ptc. of φέρω, "bear," "sustain" (BDAG 1052a). The ptc. is the second ptc. modifying ἐκάθισεν. The postpos. τέ joins the first two ptcs. and "indicates a somewhat closer unity than does καί" (R 1178). After describing the essential nature of the Son, the author here declares his sustaining relationship to τὰ πάντα ("universe" [BDAG 784b]). A sim. idea occurs in Col 1:17. The Son, the goal and agent of creation, is the one who carries creation to its intended goal.

In Hebrews, ῥῆμα (-ατος, τό) is used exclusively of God speaking (e.g., 6:5; 11:3; 12:19; Ellingworth 101), although any significant distinction between ῥῆμα and λόγος must be inferred from context (W. Radl, *EDNT* 3:210d). The dat. is instr. ("by" [most EVV]). Δυνάμεως is an attrib. gen., "his powerful word" (NIV, NRSV). "The ambiguity as to whether it is the Son's or God's word only highlights the close identity between the two" (Cockerill 95), although the context suggests the Son's word is in view.

καθαρισμὸν τῶν ἁμαρτιῶν ποιησάμενος
After making purification for sins,

Καθαρισμός, -οῦ, ὁ ("purification" [many EVV; BDAG 489b]) occurs only here and in 2 Pet 1:9 (there tr. "cleansing" in the CSB). Used in the LXX for ritual cleansing (e.g., Exod 30:10), this word in Hebrews indicates cleansing from sin through Christ's death (F. Hauck and R. Meyer, *TDNT* 3:423–31), and introduces a major focus of Hebrews (esp. chs. 9–10). Ἁμαρτιῶν is a gen. of separation. Ποιησάμενος (nom. sg. masc. of the aor. mid. ptc. of ποιέω), the third ptc., is either temp. ("after making purification") or causal ("because he made purification"), modifying ἐκάθισεν. The previous use of ποιέω suggests an interesting par.; the one through whom the world was made is the one who has made purification for sin (see Daniel J. Ebert IV, "The Chiastic Structure of the Epistle to the Hebrews," *TJ* 13 [1992]: 170–71). The mid. voice "calls attention to the subj." (R 804; cf. T 56) rather than the action. The gradual loss of the mid. in BGk. likely explains the var. rdgs. (δι' ἑαυτοῦ in D² Hᶜ K L 0243 and numerous minuscules or δι' αὐτοῦ in 𝔓⁴⁶ D* and a few other mss.), which appear to clarify that Jesus made purification "*through* himself" *for* us (e.g., ἡμῶν in א² D¹ and numerous early mss.). In these variants, the shorter rdg. is better attested and best explains the variant rdgs. (see Metzger 592; Ellingworth 101).

ἐκάθισεν ἐν δεξιᾷ τῆς μεγαλωσύνης ἐν ὑψηλοῖς
he sat down at the right hand of the Majesty on high.

The three preceding ptcs. anticipate ἐκάθισεν (3rd sg. aor. act. indic. of καθίζω, "sit down" [BDAG 491d]). The aor. is best understood as global, viewing the action in its entirety or as a summary (Wallace 557). The fact that the Son is sitting indicates that he has finished his work of purification and anticipates the later contrast between the perfect high priest and the Levitical high priests (Heb 10:11–14). The adj. δεξιᾷ (dat. sg. fem. of δεξιός, -ά, -όν, "right") assumes the substan. χείρ. Objects of prep. freq. omit the art. To sit at one's right hand indicates "supreme authority and highest honor" (Lane 1:16; see esp. Harris 106–7). This phrase alludes to Ps 110:1, the most freq. cited OT text in the NT (e.g., Rom 8:34; Eph 1:20; Col 3:1). In Hebrews, Ps 110:1 is alluded to or cited in 1:13; 8:1; 10:13; 12:2.

The poss. gen. μεγαλωσύνης ("Majesty") functions as a circumlocution for God (BDAG 623c; cf. Heb 8:1). The subst. pl. adj. ὑψηλός (-ή, -όν, "high") indicates heaven (BDAG 1044d) and introduces the epistle's focus on Christ's exaltation. This likely explains why Christ's resurrection is not prominent in Hebrews—exaltation assumes resurrection. Moreover, the Son's exaltation anticipates the eventual subjugation of all things to him, another important theme in Hebrews. This is the seventh statement about the Son in vv. 1–3. These seven statements anticipate the seven OT passages cited in vv. 5–14.

VERSE 4

τοσούτῳ κρείττων γενόμενος τῶν ἀγγέλων
So he became superior to the angels,

The dat. of the correl. adj. τοσοῦτος (-αύτη, -οῦτον; "so great, so large, so much" [BDAG 1012c]) is "used to indicate the extent to which the comparison is true" (Wallace 166) and modifies κρείττων (nom. sg. masc., "better"; comp. form of ἀγαθός; also κρείσσων [BDAG 566a]), which is further modified by the gen. of comp. τῶν ἀγγέλων. This cstr. is rare in the NT. Κρείττων is a key word in Hebrews (6:9; 7:7, 19, 22; 8:6[2x]; 9:23; 10:34; 11:16, 35, 40; 12:24) that stresses the Son's superiority; thirteen of the nineteen NT occurrences of this word are found in Hebrews (see Andreas J. Köstenberger, "Jesus, the Mediator of a 'Better Covenant': Comparatives in the Book of Hebrews," *Faith and Mission* 21, no. 2 [2004]: 30–49; Lane 1:*cxxix–cxxx*). The aor. ptc. of γίνομαι modifies κεκληρονόμηκεν and indicates an antecedent action. By virtue of his finished work of purification for sins, the Son has become so much better than angels, as indicated by the name that the Son inherits.

Although mention of angels might suggest a problem with angel worship, the association of angels with the mediation of the law is in view here, as Heb 2:1–4 makes clear (cf. Acts 7:53; Gal 3:19). The comp. stresses the superior mediation of Christ. The comp. to angels in v. 4 is expanded in Heb 1:5–14.

ὅσῳ διαφορώτερον παρ' αὐτοὺς κεκληρονόμηκεν ὄνομα
just as the name he inherited is more excellent than theirs.

The position of κεκληρονόμηκεν and its obj. ὄνομα at the end of this clause is emph. (BDF §473[2]). The pf. tense, following the two aor. vbs. in vv. 2–3, also indicates emph. (e.g., "intensified," Campbell, *VA* 201). Parallel to τοσούτῳ, the dat. correl. adj. ὅσῳ (ὅσος, -η, -ον; [by] "as much as" [BDAG 729c]) emphasizes the "degree of difference" (R 532) between the Son and angels and modifies the comp. of the adj. διάφορος (-ον; "superior" [NET, NIV], "outstanding," "more excellent" [ESV; BDAG 240a]). παρά + acc. indicates "more than" (BDAG 758a; BDF §185.3; §236). The correl. adjs. and the prep. phrase modify ὄνομα; "as the name he has inherited is more excellent than theirs" (NRSV). The rare cstrs. in this v. reveal the author's "excellent Greek" (Lane 1:17). His rhetorical skill is indicated by the *inclusio* formed with κεκληρονόμηκεν and κληρονόμον (v. 2).

Although many commentators (e.g., Cockerill 98; Koester 182; Lane 1:25) understand the "name" to be "Son," Guthrie ("Hebrews" 925b) presents a compelling case for viewing "the Name," formerly used in the OT for "God" or "Lord," as "an honor conferred by God on the Messiah as the Davidic heir at the establishment of his throne and in association with God himself." See also the discussion by Richard Bauckham, "The Divinity of Jesus Christ in the Epistle to the Hebrews" (Bauckham, *Theology* 15–36).

FOR FURTHER STUDY

1. The Structure and Function of the Exordium (1:1–4)

*Black, David Alan. "Hebrews 1:1–4: A Study in Discourse Analysis." *WTJ* 49 (1987): 175–94.

*Mackie, Scott D. "Confession of the Son of God in the Exordium of Hebrews." *JSNT* 30 (2008): 437–53.

MacLeod, David J. "The Finality of Christ: An Exposition of Hebrews 1:1–4." *BSac* 162 (2005): 210–30.

Moss, Candida R. "Standing at the Foot of the Staircase: Christology and Narrative Structure in the Prologue to Hebrews (Heb 1:1–4)." Pages 319–33 in *Portraits of Jesus: Studies in Christology*. Edited by Susan E. Myers. WUNT 2/321. Tübingen: Mohr Siebeck, 2012.

*Smillie, G. R. "Contrast or Continuity in Hebrews 1.1–2?" *NTS* 51 (2005): 543–60.

*Webster, John. "One Who Is Son: Theological Reflections on the Exordium to the Epistle to the Hebrews." Pages 69–94 in Bauckham, *Theology*.

2. Ancient Rhetoric and Hebrews (1:1–2)

Cockerill, 11–16, 60–77.
*Koester, 79–96.
*Koester, Craig R. "Hebrew, Rhetoric, and the Future of Humanity." *CBQ* 64 (2002): 103–23.
*Lane, 1:*lxxv–lxxx*; 1:5–7.
Lincoln, 9–22.
*Löhr, Hermut. "Reflections of Rhetorical Terminology in Hebrews." Pages 199–210 in *Hebrews: Contemporary Methods—New Insights*. Edited by Gabriella Gelardini. Biblical Interpretation Series. Leiden: Brill, 2005.
Martin, Michael W., and Jason A. Whitlark. "Choosing What Is Advantageous: The Relationship between Epideictic and Deliberative Syncrisis in Hebrews." *NTS* 58 (2012): 379–400.
Olbricht, Thomas H. "Hebrews as Amplification." Pages 375–87 in *Rhetoric and the New Testament: Essays from the 1992 Heidelberg Conference*. *JSNTSup* 90. Sheffield: JSOT Press, 1993.
Small, Brian C. "The Use of Rhetorical *Topoi* in the Characterization of Jesus in the Book of Hebrews." *PRSt* 37 (2010): 53–69.
Thompson, James W. "Argument and Persuasion in the Epistle to the Hebrews." *PRSt* 39 (2012): 361–77.
Walters, J. R. "The Rhetorical Arrangement of Hebrews." *AsTJ* 51/2 (1996): 59–70.
*Watson, Duane F. *DLNT* 1041–51.
———. "Rhetorical Criticism in Hebrews and the Catholic Epistles since 1978." *CurBS* (1997): 175–207.
Witherington, 33–59.

3. The Word of God in Hebrews (1:1–2)

Koester, 115–18.
*Peterson, David. "God and Scripture in Hebrews." Pages 118–38 in *Trustworthiness of God: Perspectives on the Nature of Scripture*. Edited by Paul Helm and Carl R. Trueman. Grand Rapids: Eerdmans, 2002.
Schenck, Ken. "God Has Spoken: Hebrews' Theology of the Scriptures." Pages 321–336 in Bauckham, *Theology*.

4. Inheritance in Hebrews (1:2)

Caulley, Thomas Scott. *NIDB* 3:42–43.
DBI 420–21.
Foerster, W. *TDNT* 3:758–69.
*Fuller, Ruth M. *DLNT* 1038–41.
Hammer, Paul. *ABD* 3:415–17.
Hirsch, Frank E., and Donald K. Kim. *ISBE* 2:823–25.
NIDNTTE 2:693–701.

HOMILETICAL SUGGESTIONS

God's Revelation: Continuity and Discontinuity (1:1–2)

1. Continuity: The God Who Speaks (vv. 1–2a)
2. Discontinuity
   (a) Timing: Past vs. Present
   (b) Audience: Ancestors vs. "Us"
   (c) Extent: Partial vs. Complete
   (d) Mediator: Multiple vs. Singular

Seven Christological Statements about the Son (1:2–4)

1. The heir of all things (v. 2)
2. The agent of creation (v. 2)
3. The radiance of God's glory (v. 3)
4. The perfect image of God's essence (v. 3)
5. The one who sustains the universe by his word (v. 3)
6. The one who has made purification for sins (v. 3)
7. The exalted one who sits at the right hand of God (v. 3)

The True Heir (1:2, 4)

1. The Heir of All Things: The Origin and Goal of Creation (v. 2)
2. The Name Inherited: The Son's Person and Work Superior to Angels (v. 4)

II. The Son: The Superior Mediator and the Perfect Human Being (1:5–2:18)

A. THE SON'S SUPERIORITY TO THE ANGELS (1:5–14)

STRUCTURE

Seven OT citations, called a *catena* (Lat. = "chain"; also called "chain quotations"), present seven scriptural affirmations that ground the opening declarations about the Son. Attempts to find a tight correlation between these declarations and the scriptural citations are not convincing (e.g., J. P. Meier, "Structure and Theology in Hebrews 1, 1–14," *Bib* 66 [1985]: 168–89). The catena consists of three paired OT quotations joined by hook words, following exegetical techniques found in Qumran (e.g., 4QFlor and 4QTest) and rabbinic exegesis, called *haraz* (see Herbert W. Bateman IV, *Early Jewish Hermeneutics and Hebrews 1:5–13: The Impact of Early Jewish Exegesis on the Interpretation of a Significant New Testament Passage* [New York: Lang, 1997]; cf. Rom 9:25–29; 10:18–21; 11:8–10; 1 Pet 2:8–10). Each pair stresses the Son's superiority to angels: the first pair outlines the Son's unique relationship to the Father; the second, the subservient ministry of angels vis-à-vis the Son; the third, the Son's eternality. The three pairs culminate in a citation from Ps 110:1. Five of the seven OT quotations are from Psalms, reflecting the Psalter's importance in Hebrews. The catena is structured about three occurrences of λέγω; the arrow indicates a temp. clause dependent on λέγει.

This opening exposition about the Son (1:5–14) is followed by the exhortation (2:1–4), which is then followed by further exposition about the Son (2:5–18)—a freq. pattern in Hebrews.

5 Τίνι γὰρ εἶπέν ποτε τῶν ἀγγέλων·
υἱός μου εἶ σύ,
ἐγὼ σήμερον γεγέννηκά σε;
καὶ πάλιν·
ἐγὼ ἔσομαι αὐτῷ εἰς πατέρα,
καὶ

αὐτὸς ἔσται μοι εἰς υἱόν;
6 ὅταν δὲ πάλιν εἰσαγάγῃ τὸν πρωτότοκον
εἰς τὴν οἰκουμένην,
λέγει·
καὶ προσκυνησάτωσαν αὐτῷ πάντες ἄγγελοι θεοῦ.
7 καὶ πρὸς μὲν τοὺς ἀγγέλους
λέγει·
ὁ ποιῶν τοὺς ἀγγέλους αὐτοῦ πνεύματα
καὶ τοὺς λειτουργοὺς αὐτοῦ πυρὸς φλόγα,
8 πρὸς δὲ τὸν υἱόν·
ὁ θρόνος σου ὁ θεὸς εἰς τὸν αἰῶνα τοῦ αἰῶνος, καὶ
ἡ ῥάβδος τῆς εὐθύτητος ῥάβδος τῆς βασιλείας σου.
9 ἠγάπησας δικαιοσύνην καὶ
ἐμίσησας ἀνομίαν·
διὰ τοῦτο ἔχρισέν σε ὁ θεὸς ὁ θεός σου ἔλαιον ἀγαλλιάσεως
παρὰ τοὺς μετόχους σου.
10 καί·
σὺ κατ᾽ ἀρχάς, κύριε, τὴν γῆν ἐθεμελίωσας,
καὶ ἔργα τῶν χειρῶν σού εἰσιν οἱ οὐρανοί·
11 αὐτοὶ ἀπολοῦνται,
σὺ δὲ διαμένεις,
καὶ πάντες ὡς ἱμάτιον παλαιωθήσονται,
12 καὶ ὡσεὶ περιβόλαιον ἑλίξεις αὐτούς,
ὡς ἱμάτιον καὶ ἀλλαγήσονται·
σὺ δὲ ὁ αὐτὸς εἶ καὶ
τὰ ἔτη σου οὐκ ἐκλείψουσιν.
13 πρὸς τίνα δὲ τῶν ἀγγέλων εἴρηκέν ποτε·
κάθου ἐκ δεξιῶν μου,
ἕως ἂν θῶ τοὺς ἐχθρούς σου ὑποπόδιον τῶν ποδῶν σου;
14 οὐχὶ πάντες εἰσὶν λειτουργικὰ πνεύματα
εἰς διακονίαν ἀποστελλόμενα
διὰ τοὺς μέλλοντας κληρονομεῖν σωτηρίαν;

VERSE 5

Τίνι γὰρ εἶπέν ποτε τῶν ἀγγέλων·
For to which of the angels did he ever say,

The postpos. *γάρ* further explains the Son's superiority with regard to angels (v. 4). The prologue is also linked to the catena by hook words, such as ἄγγελοι and υἱός. The interr. pron. τίς functions subst. as the obj. of εἶπεν (on the dat. dir. obj. with speaking vbs., see R 539; Wallace 171–73). The aor. is summary (BDF §332). The implicit subj. is God, drawing on the opening declaration of God's speaking (made explicit in many EVV). Τῶν ἀγγέλων is partitive, denoting the class from which τίνι derives (see BDF

§164[1]; Moule 42–43; T 208–10). Its placement at the end of the clause is emph. (BDF §473 [1]). When the encl. ptcl. ποτέ ("once," "formerly") is used with τίς "in rhetorical questions that expect a neg. answer" (BDAG 856d), it means "ever" (most EVV).

Angels were highly esteemed in Jewish thought; hence, their inferiority to the Son underscores the Son's supremacy. Angels are portrayed positively in Hebrews, challenging the claim that Hebrews confronts angel worship (so Cockerill 101 n. 6) or an angel Christology (Attridge 53). Although angels collectively were called "sons of God" (e.g., MT Job 2:1; 38:7 and LXX Gen 6:2, 4; Ps 28 [ET 29]:1), an individual designated "Son of God" does not occur before Jesus's incarnation (Bruce 53; Lane 1:26); thus the sg. τίνι is significant (Cockerill 103). The rhetorical question introduces the first pair of OT citations and is repeated in v. 13, forming an *inclusio* that brackets the catena.

υἱός μου εἶ σύ, ἐγὼ σήμερον γεγέννηκά σε
You are my Son; today I have become your Father,

The first citation of the first OT pair is from Ps 2:7, a Davidic psalm considered messianic before the first century (e.g., Pss. Sol. 17:26). This v. is cited at Jesus's baptism (Matt 3:17//Mark 1:11//Luke 3:22) and transfiguration (Matt 17:5//Mark 9:7//Luke 9:35) (see F. Büchsel, *TDNT* 1:670–71).

Σύ is emph.; in the nom., it often contrasts with ἐγώ (BDAG 949d; R 677). In pred. nom. cstrs., the subj. is the pron. σύ (Wallace 43). A def. preverbal pred. nom. υἱός is often anar. (e.g., Colwell's rule; BDF §273; T 183; Wallace 256–70). Ἐγώ used in the nom. indicates emph. (BDAG 275a). Γεγέννηκα is the 1st sg. pf. act. indic. of γεννάω, "begat" (BDAG 193d). The pf. is resultative (Wallace 554), emphasizing a pres. state, confirmed by the adv. σήμερον ("today"). There are three main options regarding the timing of σήμερον in Heb 1:5:

1. the Son's resurrection
*2. the Son's exaltation/enthronement
3. the Son's parousia/second coming

Most commentators understand a ref. to the exaltation (which assumes the resurrection). This coheres with the declaration that the Son has sat down at the right hand of the Father (v. 3) and the focus on the Son's enthronement throughout the catena.

καὶ πάλιν·
or again,

The adv. πάλιν introduces the second OT citation, from 2 Sam 7:14, and links the two citations (BDAG 752d); this use of πάλιν is freq. in Hebrews. Εἶπεν is understood elliptically from the first part of the v. Note the use of a speaking vb. to introduce the OT citations.

ἐγὼ ἔσομαι αὐτῷ εἰς πατέρα, καὶ αὐτὸς ἔσται μοι εἰς υἱόν;
I will be his Father, and he will be my Son?

Parallel to the citation from Ps 2:7, both ἐγώ and αὐτός are emph. in this citation. The two prep. phrases, εἰς πατέρα and εἰς υἱόν, function as pred., reflecting Heb. influence, occurring with the fut. of εἰμί and esp. in OT citations (BDF §145; BDAG 291b). Hebrews uses "the principle of verbal analogy" (*gezera shawa*), linking υἱός in Ps 2:7 to its occurrence in 2 Sam 7:14 (Guthrie, "Hebrews" 927b). (On the chiastic structure of these 2 citations, see Lane 1:25.) The fut. tense vbs. reflect the tendency of the LXX to render the Heb. impf. as a Greek fut. indic. (T 86). The author of Hebrews understands the fulfillment of these OT prophecies to have occurred and to be divinely proclaimed at the Son's exaltation.

VERSE 6

ὅταν δὲ πάλιν εἰσαγάγῃ τὸν πρωτότοκον εἰς τὴν οἰκουμένην
Again, when he brings his firstborn into the world,

The temp. clause introduced by ὅταν (=ὅτε + ἄν , "when," "whenever") extends to οἰκουμένην. Ὅταν + aor. subjunc. usually indicates "a definite action taking place in the future but concluded before the action of the main verb" (T 112; cf. R 972), although the pres. λέγει probably indicates a contemp. event (Cockerill 104 n. 23; see discussion below). Δέ links the second pair of OT citations (the first of which is in v. 6) to the first pair of OT citations in v. 5 (BDAG 213[1]b). Εἰσαγάγῃ (3rd sg. aor. act. subjunc. of εἰσάγω, "bring into," "lead into" [BDAG 293c]) is a compound of εἰς + ἄγω; the adv. force of the prep. ("into"; BDAG 288d) is retained (Moule 87). Verbs compounded with εἰς nearly always repeat the prep. following the verb (R 559). The implied subj. is God.

The adj. πρωτότοκον (πρωτότοκος, -ον, "firstborn", BDAG 894b) functions subst. In the OT, the term indicates birth order and inheritance rights (Deut 21:17; cf. Heb 12:16) or elect status and privilege. This title is attributed to Israel (LXX Exod 4:22) and the Davidic king (LXX Ps 88:28; ET 89:27). The abs. use of this title is unique to Hebrews elsewhere in the NT, the sg. always refers to Christ (see Rom 8:29; Col 1:15, 18; Rev 1:5; BDAG 894c; W. Michaelis, *TDNT* 6:871–81; Archie T. Wright, *NIDB* 2:457–58; see esp. Larry R. Helyer, "The *Prōtotokos* Title in Hebrews," *Studia Biblica et Theologica* 6 [1976]: 3–38). The language of "entering" and "firstborn" may allude to Israel as God's firstborn entering the promised land (cf. Lane 1:27) and to the expression εἰσαγαγεῖν εἰς τὴν γῆν (e.g., Exod 3:8; Ellingworth 116–17).

A number of factors influence the timing of the action of εἰσαγάγῃ. First, πάλιν may be understood in two ways.

*1. Following its usage in v. 5, πάλιν is a connective to introduce the OT citation that follows the ὅταν clause, "and again, when he brings . . ." (ESV, NIV; NASB: "And when He again brings"; Bruce 56; Lane 1:26).

2. Πάλιν functions as an adv. modifying εἰσαγάγῃ (so NASB, CSB, NET), suggesting the second coming: "when *again* the Father led the Son in the world."

These options bear on the understanding of οἰκουμένην (οἰκουμένη, -ης, ἡ).

1. Οἰκουμένη refers to "the inhabited earth, the world" (BDAG 699c; O. Michel, *TDNT* 5.157–59), often understood in the first century as the Roman Empire (e.g., Luke 2:1). This suggests Jesus's birth as the time "when God led the firstborn into the world." Yet, although angels praised God for Jesus's birth, they did not *worship* the Son (Cockerill 104 n. 24). Moreover, Jesus was made *lower* than the angels during his incarnation (2:9).

*2. In Heb 2:5, τὴν οἰκουμένην τὴν μέλλουσιν ("the world to come") suggests a transcendent understanding of οἰκουμένη here as well (see BDAG 700a; see also 2:5), thus pointing to the Son's exaltation/enthronement (so most commentators). This fits well with the enthronement language of Psalm 2. Additionally, Hebrews uses εἰς τὸν κόσμον in Heb 10:5 in conj. with Jesus's incarnation (see also the comment on γῇ at 1:10).

λέγει
he says,

The implied speaker remains God, following from v. 5 and the implied subj. of εἰσαγάγῃ. The pres. tense underscores the author's conviction that God is still speaking the very words recorded in the OT.

καὶ προσκυνησάτωσαν αὐτῷ πάντες ἄγγελοι θεοῦ.
And let all God's angels worship him.

Προσκυνησάτωσαν is the 3rd pl. aor. act. impv. of προσκυνέω, "worship" (most EVV) or "fall down and worship" (BDAG 882c–d). The obj. of προσκυνέω takes the dat. In the NT, προσκυνέω never has a human obj. Because the OT citation is spoken by God, the referent of αὐτῷ must be the Son. The subj. of the impv. is πάντες ἄγγελοι θεοῦ. In the pred. position, πᾶς means "all (without exception)"; the omission of the art. indicates a class/group, not an individual (Z §188).

This citation appears to come from either the Song of Moses in the longer LXX form of Deut 32:43 or Ps 96:7 (ET 97:7). It may reflect a conflation of these vv., or more likely is influenced by the Song of Moses in the Odes Sol. 2:43 (Guthrie, "Hebrews" 931d–32a) or even 4QDeut (see G. Cockerill, "Hebrews 1:6: Source and Significance," *BBR* 9 [1999]: 51–64). Significantly, the OT command to worship God is now applied to the Son. The author of Hebrews may also allude to the rabbinic tradition in *Life of Adam and Eve*, where the angels worshipped Adam when God brought him into the world, paralleling the angelic worship of the exalted Son, the second Adam (Bruce 57; Guthrie, "Hebrews" 932b–33a).

VERSE 7

καὶ πρὸς μὲν τοὺς ἀγγέλους λέγει·
And about the angels he says:

Καί joins v. 6 with the OT citation in v. 7. The correl. ptcls., *μέν* and *δέ*, join this v. and the next and contrast the subservient role of angels (v. 7) with the exalted status of the Son (v. 8). *Πρός* here means "concerning" or "with reference to" (R 626; BDF §239[6]; BDAG 875a). Parallel to vv. 5–6, *λέγει* introduces the citation from Ps 104:4 (LXX 103:4). This second pair of OT citations (Deut 32:43 and Ps 104:4) stress the exalted status of the Son, whom angels worship (v. 6) and serve (v. 7). Context indicates that God is speaking.

ὁ ποιῶν τοὺς ἀγγέλους αὐτοῦ πνεύματα
He makes his angels winds,

Ποιῶν is subst. ("the one who makes"). There are two options for understanding the double acc. cstr.

1. The obj. of the ptc. is *ἀγγέλους* and the obj. complement is *πνεύματα*; "he makes winds his angels."
*2. The obj. of the ptc. is *πνεύματα* and the obj. complement is *ἀγγέλους* (so most EVV); "he makes his angels winds."

The second option is preferred because the obj. generally precedes the complement and is often art. This also suggests that *πνεύματα* functions qual. (Wallace 181–89). The par. between *πνεύματα* and *πυρὸς φλόγα* (see below) favors understanding *πνεύματα* as "winds" (*pace* Koester 193–94). The citation stresses the ephemeral nature of angels.

καὶ τοὺς λειτουργοὺς αὐτοῦ πυρὸς φλόγα,
and his servants a fiery flame,

The par. between *τοὺς ἀγγέλους* and *τοὺς λειτουργούς* (*λειτουργός, -οῦ, ὁ* "minister" [ESV, NASB, NET], "servant" [NIV, NLT; BDAG 591d]) and between *πνεύματα* and *φλόγα* (*φλόξ, -γός, ἡ*, "flame" [BDAG 1060c]) is indicated in the structural diagram above. Also par. is the double acc. cstr. in which *λειτουργούς* is the obj. of the implied ptc. *ποιῶν* and *φλόγα* is the obj. complement, which is modified by *πυρός*, a qual. gen. (= attrib., Heb. gen.; "a flame of fire" = "a fiery flame"; see BDF §167; R 498–99; T 214–15; Z §§45–46).

VERSE 8

πρὸς δὲ τὸν υἱόν·
but to the Son:

Verse 8 is linked to v. 7 by the correl. cstr. *μέν . . . δέ*. The adversative ptcl. *δέ* indicates a "contrast is to be emphasized in the second clause" (BDAG 629d). *Λέγει* is understood from v. 7. Πρός could be tr. "with ref. to" as in v. 7, although the shift from the 3rd pers. to the 2nd pers. likely indicates that the citation is spoken *to* the Son in v. 8 and not *about* the angels, as in v. 7 (Cockerill 102 n. 46). The third, and final, pair of OT citations focuses on the Son's eternality (1:8–12).

ὁ θρόνος σου ὁ θεὸς εἰς τὸν αἰῶνα τοῦ αἰῶνος,
Your throne, O God, is forever and ever,

The fifth OT citation comes from Ps 45:6–7 (LXX 44:7–8), a royal wedding psalm addressed to the bridegroom, most likely a Davidic king. In both parts of the citation in v. 8, the equative verb is omitted (see BDF §127). There are three interpretive possibilities for ὁ θεός.

1. As the subj., "God is your throne . . ."
2. As a pred. nom., "your throne is God . . ."
*3. A nom. functioning as a voc., "your throne, O God, . . ." (most EVV)

Several reasons support the third option. First, the voc. θεέ occurs only once in the NT (Matt 27:46), whereas the nom. θεός for the voc. is common, esp. with LXX citations (e.g., Heb 10:7; cf. Wallace 59; BDF §147[3]; and esp. Murray J. Harris, "The Translation and Significance of ὁ θεός in Hebrews 1:8–9," *TynBul* 36 [1985]: 138–49; Harris, "The Translation of Elohim in Psalm 45:7–8," *TynBul* 35 [1984]: 65–89). Second, the psalm addresses the Davidic king (metaphorically) as God in his capacity as God's vicegerent over Israel. Such language is clearly messianic, although it is unclear how widely the psalm was understood as such. This citation fits well with the previous citations from Psalm 2 and 2 Samuel 7, as well as the command that angels worship the Son, and serves to further ground the Christological affirmations about the Son (see Herbert W. Bateman IV, "Psalm 45:6–7 and Its Christological Contributions to Hebrews," *TJ* 22 [2001]: 3–21).

In *εἰς τὸν αἰῶνα τοῦ αἰῶνος* ("for ever and ever"; BDAG 32b), the gen. underscores the eternality already expressed by *εἰς τὸν αἰῶνα*. Harris notes that Hebrews surpasses other NT letters in stressing the Son's eternality, esp. with this expression (and par. forms). Here the expression "affirms that Christ's personal rule is eternal and implies that Christ, as ruler, is also eternal" (Harris 96). Θρόνος elsewhere in Hebrews refers to God's throne (8:1; 12:2; and prob. 4:16), making the statement here regarding the Son even more remarkable.

The author's use of this citation from Psalm 45 presents one of the most significant Christological affirmations in the epistle. Here the Son is addressed directly as "God"—not only as God's Son, but as God himself. Moreover, the author presents the psalm citation as God himself addressing the Son as God (see Murray J. Harris, *Jesus as God: The New Testament Use of* Theos *in Reference to Jesus* [Grand Rapids: Baker, 1992], esp. pp. 205–27).

καὶ ἡ ῥάβδος τῆς εὐθύτητος ῥάβδος τῆς βασιλείας σου.
and the scepter of your kingdom is a scepter of justice.

A ῥάβδος (-ου, ἡ; "a ruler's staff"; hence, "scepter" [most EVV; BDAG 902c]; see further *ISBE* 2.333; 4.206, 350) indicates authority and continues the emphasis on the Son's dominion and authority begun in the first half of the citation from Psalm 45. The gen. εὐθύτητος (εὐθύτης, -ητος, ἡ; "righteousness" [NET, NIV], "uprightness" [ESV; BDAG 406d; NT hapax]) is qual. (= attrib., Heb. gen.; "the righteous scepter"; see also BDF §167; R 498–99; T 214–15). As with the first part of this citation, an equative verb is assumed. The gen. βασιλείας is poss. (see BDF §162; R 495–96; T 207–8). The par. in this citation correlates θρόνος with βασιλεία and εὐθύτης with δικαιοσύνη (v. 9).

Although the var. αὐτοῦ has early and good support (𝔓[46] ℵ B), and represents the more difficult reading, this rdg. renders the interpretation ὁ θεός as a voc. awkward. Instead, the var. may have arisen due to confusion over πρός (see discussion above) and the nom. for voc. (Attridge 59). Important and widespread mss., as well as agreement with LXX Ps 44:7, support the rdg. σου (UBS rating {B}) (see Metzger 592–92 and the extended discussion in Murray J. Harris, *Jesus as God: The New Testament Use of* Theos *in Reference to Jesus* [Grand Rapids: Baker, 1992], 209–12).

VERSE 9

ἠγάπησας δικαιοσύνην καὶ ἐμίσησας ἀνομίαν·
You have loved righteousness and hated lawlessness;

The citation from Psalm 45 continues through this v. Ἠγάπησας is the 2nd sg. aor. act. indic. of ἀγαπάω, "love" (most EVV), "take pleasure in" (BDAG 5d). Ἐμίσησας is the 2nd sg. aor. act. indic. of μισέω, "hate" (most EVV), "detest" (BDAG 652d). Both aors. are global, viewing the action in its entirety or as a summary (BDF §332); they reflect the common LXX rendering of the Heb. The author likely understood the two aors. in ref. to Jesus's incarnation, anticipating the extended discussion of the incarnation in 2:5–18 and much of 4:14–10:18 (Cockerill 111). Δικαιοσύνη ("righteousness" [most EVV], "uprightness" [BDAG 248a; G. Schrenk *TDNT* 2:198–201]) was considered an essential trait for rulers. In 11:7, 33, righteousness is connected with faith (Ellingworth 124). The opposite of righteousness is ἀνομία (-ης, ἡ, "lawlessness").

διὰ τοῦτο ἔχρισέν σε ὁ θεὸς ὁ θεός σου ἔλαιον ἀγαλλιάσεως
this is why God, your God, has anointed you with the oil of joy

διὰ τοῦτο ("therefore"; so most EVV) is a formulaic phrase, often referring to a previous argument (Wallace 333). Ἔχρισέν is the 3rd sg. aor. act. indic. of χρίω, "anoint" (BDAG 1091d). Ἔλαιον (ἔλαιον, -ου, τό), "olive oil," was used esp. for anointing (BDAG 313b). Ἔχρισέν takes a double acc. cstr., with one acc. indicating a pers. (σε) and the other, an obj. (ἔλαιον) (see R 482–83; BDF §155[6]; Wallace 182). The gen. ἀγαλλιάσεως (ἀγαλλίασις, -εως, ἡ, "rejoicing" [NET], "joy" [NIV], "gladness" [ESV, NASB]) is a descriptive gen. ("oil of gladness"; BDAG 4c) or possibly a gen. of product, namely, "oil that produces gladness" (Wallace 107).

The purpose of the anointing is debated. In the orig. context, anointing may have been to consecrate for kingship or marriage. The focus on the Son's exaltation in Hebrews 1, however, makes consecration unlikely. Moreover, the specification of "oil of gladness" points to celebration of the Son's exaltation (so most commentators).

As with v. 8, there are several interpretive options for ὁ θεός.

1. Parallel to v. 8, ὁ θεός is a nom. for voc. (Ellingworth 124; Attridge 59–60; Koester 195). On this understanding, ὁ θεός addresses God the Son and ὁ θεός σου refers to God the Father.
*2. Ὁ θεός σου is an appos. to ὁ θεός = "God, your God" (most EVV).

The second option indicates that God the Father anoints the Son, which is consistent with the focus on the Son in the catena. (See esp. Murray J. Harris, *Jesus as God: The New Testament Use of* Theos *in Reference to Jesus* [Grand Rapids: Baker, 1992], 219–220; Harris, "The Translation and Significance of ὁ θεὸς in Hebrews 1:8–9," *TynBul* 36 [1985]: 149–51.)

παρὰ τοὺς μετόχους σου.
beyond your companions.

Παρά with the acc. indicates comp. ("in comparison to, more than"; Wallace, 378). Μετόχους is the acc. pl. masc. of μέτοχος, -ου, ὁ, "(business) partner," "companion" (BDAG 643b). In Psalm 45, this refers to David's royal companions. There are two options for the referent of μετόχους in Hebrews 1.

1. Angels (anticipating παρ' ἀγγέλους in 2:7, 9; cf. 1:4; so Ellingworth 124; cf. Lane 1:30).
*2. Believers, anticipating the "many sons" in 2:10 (Attridge 60; Bruce 61; Cockerill 111; Koester 195) and Jesus sharing (with the cognate vb., μετέχω) blood and flesh with the "children" (Heb 2:14).

The second option coheres with the use of μέτοχος elsewhere in Hebrews (3:1; 6:4; cf. 12:8). The author may have had both angels (Hebrews 1) and believers (Hebrews 2) in view (see comments on 3:1).

VERSE 10

καί· σὺ κατ' ἀρχάς, κύριε, τὴν γῆν ἐθεμελίωσας,
And: **In the beginning, Lord, you established the earth,**

Verse 10 introduces the sixth OT citation (and concludes the third pair of citations) from Psalm 102 (LXX 101):26–28, in which the psalmist contrasts his short life with the heavens and the earth; even though they will disappear, God will not. Although Psalm 102 was not considered messianic, the author of Hebrews understands the "Lord" of the psalm to refer to the Son, through whom everything was created (Heb 1:2).

The nom. *σύ* is emph. (BDF §277). Κατ' *ἀρχάς* means "in the beginning" (BDAG 138b; a "classical synonym" for *ἐν ἀρχῇ* [Ellingworth 127]). The voc., *κύριε*, is freq. in the LXX for the divine name, YHWH. In early Christian communities, the address was a "basic element of christological confessions" (Attridge 60). Here the OT address for God is applied to the Son. Ἐθεμελίωσας is the 2nd sg. aor. act. indic. of *θεμελιόω*, "lay a foundation" (NASB, ESV, NIV), "found" (NET, NRSV [BDAG 449b]). It is the "poetic equivalent" of *ποιέω* and often stresses stability (Ellingworth 127). The aor. is constative. In Hebrews, *γῆ* refers to "earth" ("in contrast to heaven," BDAG 196a), which will ultimately cease. By contrast, *οἰκουμένη* ("world") is transcendent (e.g., "world to come," 2:5) and remains eternally with the Son.

καὶ ἔργα τῶν χειρῶν σού εἰσιν οἱ οὐρανοί·
and the heavens are the works of your hands;

The subj. of a pred. nom. cstr. (*οἱ οὐρανοί*) is often art. and the pred. nom. (*ἔργα*) is usually placed before the copulative vb. (*εἰσίν*) and may be def. even though it is anar. (See the extended discussion of Colwell's rule and its subsequent clarifications in Wallace, 256–70). The pl. "heavens" reflects Heb. usage. Hebrews 4:3 also discusses God's creation work. Χειρῶν is likely a "gen. of production/producer" (see Wallace 104–106). It is used here metaphorically of divine power (cf. Ellingworth 127).

VERSE 11

αὐτοὶ ἀπολοῦνται, σὺ δὲ διαμένεις,
they will perish, but you remain.

This v. continues the citation from Psalm 102. The nom. *αὐτοί* and *σύ* are emph. (BDF §277). The referent of *αὐτοί* is the earth and heavens in v. 10. Δέ indicates contrast (BDAG 213c), namely between the created realm's impermanence and the Son's eternality. Ἀπολοῦνται is the 3rd pl. fut. mid. indic. of *ἀπόλλυμι*; in the mid., "perish" (most EVV), "be lost," "pass away," "be ruined" (BDAG 116b). The fut. is predictive. Διαμένεις is the 2nd sg. pres. act. indic. of *διαμένω*, "remain" (most EVV), "continue" (NET; BDAG 233c). The pres. is gnomic, stressing the immutability of the Son. In Hebrews, *μένω* and its compounds indicate that which remains with the Son (e.g., 10:34; 12:25–27; 13:14).

καὶ πάντες ὡς ἱμάτιον παλαιωθήσονται,
They will all wear out like clothing;

The par. between *αὐτοί* and *πάντες* suggests that the latter also refers to the earth and heavens of v. 10. Παλαιωθήσονται is the 3rd pl. fut. pass. indic. of *παλαιόω*, "make old, declare/treat as obsolete"; in the pass., "become old" (NASB), "grow old" (NET), "wear out" (ESV; oft. with the connotation of "becoming useless" [BDAG 751d]). This vb. describes the impermanent nature of the old covenant in 8:13.

The metaphorical image (signaled by ὡς, "as, like"; BDAG 1103d) of the world as a garment (ἱμάτιον, -ου, τό) that will wear out also occurs in Isa 51:6. This contrast between impermanence and permanence could suggest acquaintance with Middle Platonism, which taught that the "transcendent world is eternal, while the material creation is subject to change" (Thompson 55). Jewish eschatological thought concerning the ultimate decay of the universe, however, was likely more influential on the author's thought (cf. Attridge 61). The key here is the contrast between creation's transience and the Son's immutability and eternality: "The Son will change one order of creation for another as easily as a human being changes one cloak for another, while remaining himself unchanged" (Ellingworth 128).

VERSE 12

καὶ ὡσεὶ περιβόλαιον ἑλίξεις αὐτούς, ὡς ἱμάτιον καὶ ἀλλαγήσονται·
you will roll them up like a cloak, and they will be changed like clothing.

Parallelism indicates that ὡσεί functions synonymously with ὡς and that ἱμάτιον (also in v. 11) is some type of outer covering par. to περιβόλαιον (acc. sg. neut. of περιβόλαιον, -ου, τό, "garment" [NASB], "robe" [ESV, NET, NIV], "covering," "wrap," "cloak" [BDAG 800a]). Ἑλίξεις is the 2nd sg. fut. act. indic. of ἑλίσσω, "roll up" [BDAG 317d]. Ἀλλαγήσονται is the 3rd pl. fut. pass. indic. of ἀλλάσσω, "change" (most EVV), "alter" (BDAG 45d). This imagery also occurs in Isa 34:4. Elsewhere the heavens are likened to a tent or canopy (which could be rolled up) stretching over the earth (Ps 104:2; Isa 40:22; Koester 196).

The citation here reflects two significant alterations from the LXX. First, ἑλίξεις replaces ἀλλάξεις in the LXX, which emphasizes creation's impermanence. (Not surprisingly, a few mss. have ἀλλάξεις, which likely reflects an effort to conform to the LXX). Second, ὡς ἱμάτιον is added for par. and enhances the chiastic structure of vv. 11–12 (see Cockerill 113, for the chiastic structure of these vv.).

σὺ δὲ ὁ αὐτὸς εἶ καὶ τὰ ἔτη σου οὐκ ἐκλείψουσιν.
But you are the same, and your years will never end.

Throughout these OT citations, the nom. σύ is emph. (BDF §277). The pred. nom. is τὰ ἔτη (nom. pl. neut. of ἔτος, -ους, τό, "years"). Δέ indicates contrast (BDAG 213c), namely between the created realm's impermanence and the Son's eternality. Αὐτός functions as an identifying adj. ("same"; Wallace 349). Ἐκλείψουσιν is the 3rd pl. fut. act. indic. of ἐκλείπω, "end" (most EVV), "fail," "die out" (BDAG 306a). Often a neut. pl. noun has a sg. vb., but collective nouns may take a pl. vb. (R 403). This v. anticipates the author's statement in Heb 13:8. The fut. in this v. are predictive.

VERSE 13

πρὸς τίνα δὲ τῶν ἀγγέλων εἴρηκέν ποτε·
Now to which of the angels has he ever said:

The rep. of the rhetorical question in this v. forms an *inclusio* with v. 5. Δέ continues the contrast (BDAG 213c) between the Son and angels in vv. 5–12. The switch from the aor. (εἶπεν) in v. 5 to the pf. (εἴρηκεν) does not indicate "that the act of installation to which the citation refers took place in the past but has a continuing effect" (*pace* Attridge 61), but rather functions to indicate the summarizing function of the citation (an extensive or consummative pf.; Wallace 577).

This question introduces the seventh and final OT citation of the catena. Ps 110:1, alluded to in v. 3, is quoted here. This most freq. cited OT v. in the NT demonstrates God's vindication of Jesus and proclaims Christ's lordship (Guthrie, "Hebrews" 943d–44a). This citation culminates the author's argument from the OT regarding the Son's superiority to angels; it is possible that this v. informed the author's understanding of the previous six citations. "It was the language and symbolism of Ps 110:1 (109:1 LXX) that shaped the thought of the early Christians as they reflected on the exaltation of Jesus" (Harris 106).

κάθου ἐκ δεξιῶν μου
Sit at my right hand

Κάθου is the 2nd sg. pres. mid. impv. of κάθημαι, "sit." The subst. adj. δεξιῶν (gen. pl. neut. of δεξιός, -ά, -όν, "right") assumes either χείρ or a general ref. to the right side. Objects of prep. freq. omit the art. The use of ἐκ to indicate position is unusual, although the expression ἐκ δεξιῶν μου is stereotyped phrasing (Harris 106–7). The author's preference is ἐν δεξιᾷ (1:3; 8:1; 10:12; 12:2). Sitting on the right indicated power and honor. The pres. tense of the impv. indicates an ongoing (continuous) activity, namely, Christ's continuing position at God's right hand.

ἕως ἂν θῶ τοὺς ἐχθρούς σου ὑποπόδιον τῶν ποδῶν σου
until I make your enemies your footstool?

The conj. ἕως ("until") together with the ptcl. ἄν forms an indef. temp. clause that functions "to denote that the commencement of an event is dependent on circumstances" (BDAG 422d–423a) and anticipates the fut. subjugation of all things to the Son. Θῶ is the 1st sg. aor. act. subj. of τίθημι, "make" (most EVV), "consign" (BDAG 1004b). The obj. of the vb. is the subst. adj. τοὺς ἐχθρούς (ἐχθρός, -ά, -όν, "enemy"); ὑποπόδιον (acc. sg. neut. of ὑποπόδιον, -ου, τό, "footstool" [BDAG 1040c]) functions as an obj. complement. The gen. τῶν ποδῶν (πούς, ποδός, ὁ, "foot") indicates purpose (Wallace 100). Hebrews does not develop the second half of this citation, although the implicit subjection of the enemies (unspecified) is developed in conj. with the citation from Psalm 8 in Hebrews 2 (see the discussion of ἐχθρός by W. Foerster, *TDNT* 2:811–14).

VERSE 14

οὐχὶ πάντες εἰσὶν λειτουργικὰ πνεύματα εἰς διακονίαν ἀποστελλόμενα
Are they not all ministering spirits sent out to serve

The neg. adv. *οὐχί* is a strengthened form of *οὐ* and introduces a question that expects an affirmative answer (BDAG 742c). The noun phrase *λειτουργικά* (nom. pl. neut., *λειτουργικός, -ή, -όν*, "ministering" BDAG 591d) *πνεύματα* functions as the pred. nom., with *πάντες* as the subj. Angels are the implied referent. *Πάντες* summarizes the previous discussion about angels, and likely counters any perceived rank or hierarchy of angels (Ellingworth 132) or belief that they governed certain territories or nations (Cockerill 115). This phrasing alludes to the citation of Ps 103:4 (LXX) in v. 7. *Λειτουρέω* (BDAG 590d) and its cognates (*λειτουργός, -οῦ, ὁ* [BDAG 591d]; *λειτουργικός, -ή, -όν*) refer in nonbiblical literature to those in public service, although the word group is associated with cultic service in Hebrews. *Εἰς* indicates the purpose of *ἀποστελλόμενα* (nom. pl. neut. of the pres. pass. ptc. of *ἀποστέλλω*, "send"; the ptc. modifies *πνεύματα*). This explains why some EVV tr. this prep. phrase as an inf. ("to serve," ESV, NIV; "to render service," NASB, NLT; "to care for"). Moreover, angels are sent for a specific ministry (*διακονίαν*, acc. sg. fem. of *διακονία, -ας, ἡ* [BDAG 230b]), which is elaborated on in the following prep. phrase.

διὰ τοὺς μέλλοντας κληρονομεῖν σωτηρίαν;
those who are going to inherit salvation?

Διά in the acc. indicates cause ("for the sake of," NASB, ESV). The subst. ptc. *τοὺς μέλλοντας* (acc. pl. masc. of the pres. act. ptc. of *μέλλω*, "about to" [BDF §356]) refers to believers ("the *ones* who are about to"). *Μέλλω* is an important word in Hebrews (2:5; 6:5; 8:5; 10:1, 27; 11:8, 20; 13:14) used to describe "eschatological realities promised but not yet fully realized" (Ellingworth 133). *Κληρονομεῖν* (pres. act. inf. of *κληρονομέω*, "inherit" [BDAG 547d]) complements the ptc. Inheritance is a key theme in Hebrews (see comments on 1:2). *Κληρονομεῖν* in v. 13 forms an *inclusio* with *κληρονόμον* in v. 2 and *κεκληρονόμηκεν* in v. 4, thereby indicating the cohesion of these two opening sections.

Σωτηρίαν is not defined here or elsewhere in Hebrews. The author assumes his audience will understand what is meant and views the totality of salvation from its inception (conversion) to its final consummation (glorification). This fut. emph. is not unique to Hebrews (e.g., Rom 13:11; 1 Pet 1:5) and aligns with the exhortation to persevere throughout Hebrews. But the author also affirms his confidence in the audience's salvation in 6:9.

The Son's superiority is inferred from the fact that he effected purification for sin, whereas angels minister on behalf of those who are being saved. Verse 14 both summarizes the comp. between Son and angels (Hebrews 1) and prepares for focus on the Son's incarnation (Hebrews 2). The Son's superiority to angels leads to the *a fortiori* argument of Heb 2:1–4, which extends the discussion of salvation begun in this v.

FOR FURTHER STUDY

5. The Catena of OT Citations (1:5–14)

Allen, Leslie C. "Psalm 45:7–8 (6–7) in Old and New Testament Settings." Pages 220–42 in *Christ the Lord: Studies in Christology Presented to Donald Guthrie*. Edited by H. H. Rowden. Downers Grove, IL: InterVarsity Press, 1982.

Docherty, Susan. "The Text Form of the OT Citations in Hebrews Chapter 1 and the Implications for the Study of the Septuagint." *NTS* 55 (2009): 355–65.

Glasson, T. F. "Plurality of Divine Persons and the Quotations in Hebrews 1:6ff." *NTS* 12 (1966): 270–72.

*Jipp, Joshua W. "The Son's Entrance into the Heavenly World: The Soteriological Necessity of the Scriptural Catena in Hebrews 1.5–14." *NTS* 56 (2010): 557–75.

*Motyer, Stephen. "The Psalm Quotations of Hebrews 1: A Hermeneutic-Free Zone?" *TynBul* 50 (1999): 3–22.

*Rhee, Victor. "The Role of Chiasm for Understanding Christology in Hebrews 1:1–14."*JBL* 131 (2012): 341–62.

Schenck, Kenneth L. "A Celebration of the Enthroned Son: The Catena of Hebrews 1." *JBL* 120 (2001): 469–85.

Steyn, Gert Jacobus. "Psalm 2 in Hebrews." *Neot* 37 (2003): 262–82.

Swinson, L Timothy. "'Wind' and 'Fire' in Hebrews 1:7: A Reflection upon the Use of Psalm 104 (103)." *TJ* 28 (2007): 215–28.

Thompson, James W. "Structure and Purpose of the Catena in Heb 1:5–13." *CBQ* 38 (1976): 352–63.

Wallace, David. "The Use of Psalms in the Shaping of a Text: Psalm 2:7 and Psalm 110:1 in Hebrews 1." *ResQ* 45 (2003): 41–50.

6. The Use of the OT in Hebrews (1:5–14)

Allen, David M. *Deuteronomy and Exhortation in Hebrews: A Study in Narrative Re-presentation*. WUNT 2/238. Tübingen: Mohr Siebeck, 2008.

Attridge, Harold W. "The Psalms in Hebrews." Pages 197–212 in *The Psalms in the New Testament*. Edited by Steve Moyise and Maarten J. J. Menken. London: T & T Clark, 2004.

Barth, Marcus. "The Old Testament in Hebrews, An Essay in Biblical Hermeneutics." Pages 53–78 in *Current Issues in New Testament Interpretation: Essays in Honor of Otto A. Piper*. Edited by William Klassen and Graydon F. Snyder. New York: Harper & Brothers, 1962.

Black, Matthew. "Christological Use of the Old Testament in the New Testament." *NTS* 18 (1971): 1–14.

*Caird, George B. "The Exegetical Method of the Epistle to the Hebrews." *CJT* 5 (1959): 44–51.

Clements, Ronald E. "The Use of the Old Testament in Hebrews." *SwJT* 28 (1985): 36–45.

Cockerill, 41–57.

Docherty, Susan. *The Use of the Old Testament in Hebrews: A Case Study in Early Jewish Bible Interpretation*. Tübingen: Mohr Siebeck, 2009.

Guthrie, George H. *DLNT* 841–50.

*———. "Hebrews." Pages 919–95 in Beale and Carson.

*———. "Hebrews' Use of the Old Testament: Recent Trends in Research." *CurBR* 1/2 (2003): 271–94.

Kistemaker, Simon J. *The Psalm Citations in the Epistle to the Hebrews*. Amsterdam: Van Soest, 1961.

Lane, 1:*cxii–cxxiv*.

Leschert, Dale F. *Hermeneutical Foundations of the Epistle to the Hebrews: A Study in the Validity of the Epistle's Interpretation of Some Core Citations from the Psalms*. Lewiston, NY: Mellen, 1994.

Moyise, Steve. *The Later New Testament Writings and Scripture: The Old Testament in Acts, Hebrews, the Catholic Epistles, and Revelation*. Grand Rapids: Baker, 2012.

Rendell, R. "The Method of the Writer to the Hebrews in Using Old Testament Quotations." *EvQ* 27 (1955): 214–20.

*Steyn, Gert Jacobus. "An Overview of the Extent and Diversity of Methods Utilised by the Author of Hebrews When Using the Old Testament." *Neot* 42 (2008): 327–52.

*Witherington, 109–20.

7. Christology in Hebrews (1:5–14)

Barrett, C. K. "The Christology of Hebrews." Pages 110–27 in *Who Do You Say That I Am?: Essays on Christology*. Edited by Mark Allen Powell and David R. Bauer. Louisville, KY: Westminster John Knox, 1999.

Bauckham, Richard. "Monotheism and Christology in Hebrews 1." Pages 167–85 in *Early Jewish and Christian Monotheism*. Edited by Loren T. Stuckenbruck and Wendy E. S. North. *JSNTSup* 263. London: T & T Clark, 2004.

*Harvill, J. "Focus on Jesus (Studies in the Epistle to the Hebrews)." *ResQ* 22 (1979): 129–40.

Hughes, Philip E. "The Christology of Hebrews." *SwJT* 28 (1985): 19–27.

*Hurst, L. D. "The Christology of Hebrews 1 and 2." Pages 151–64 in *The Glory of Christ in the New Testament: Studies in Christology in Memory of George Bradford Caird*. Edited by L. D. Hurst and N. T. Wright. Oxford: Clarendon, 1987.

Hurtado, Larry W. *DLNT* 170–84.

———. *Lord Jesus Christ: Devotion to Jesus in Earliest Christianity*. Grand Rapids: Eerdmans, 2003.

Koester, 104–10.

Lane, 1:*cxxxv–cxliv*.

Lane, William L. "Detecting Divine Wisdom Christology in Hebrews 1:1–4." *NTS* 5 (1982): 150–58.

McKelvey, R. J. *Pioneer and Priest: Jesus Christ in the Epistle to the Hebrews*. Eugene, OR: Pickwick, 2013.

Osborne, Grant R. "The Christ of Hebrews and Other Religions." *JETS* 46 (2003): 249–67.

Parsons, M. C. "Son and High Priest: A Study in the Christology of Hebrews." *EvQ* 60 (1988): 195–215.

Rhee, Victor. "Christology in Hebrews 1:5–14: The Three Stages of Christ's Existence." *JETS* 59 (2016): 717–29.

Schenck, Kenneth. "Keeping His Appointment: Creation and Enthronement in Hebrews." *JSNT* 66 (1997): 91–117.

Witherington, 59–67.

———. *DLNT* 152–59.

8. Angels in Hebrews (1:5)

Charles, J. Daryl. "The Angels, Sonship and Birthright in the Letter to the Hebrews." *JETS* 33 (1990): 171–78.

Davidson, Maxwell John. *NIDB* 1:148–55.

DBI 23–25.

Kittel, G. *TDNT* 1:80–87.

Newsom, Carol A. *ABD* 1:248–53.

NIDNTTE 1:120–24.

Noll, S. F. *DLNT* 44–48.

Steyn, Gert Jacobus. "Addressing an Angelomorphic Christological Myth in Hebrews?" *HvTSt* 59 (2003): 1107–26.

Watson, Duane F. *ABD* 1:253–55.

9. The Ascension and Heavenly Session of Christ (1:13)

deSilva, D. A. *DLNT* 359–63.

Hughes, Philip E. "The Blood of Jesus and His Heavenly Priesthood in Hebrews: Part IV: The Present Work of Christ in Heaven." *BSac* 131 (1974): 26–33.

Larkin, W. J., Jr. *DLNT* 95–102.

*Saucy, Mark. "Exaltation Christology in Hebrews: What Kind of Reign?" *TJ* 14 (1993): 41–62.

Toon, Peter. *The Ascension of Our Lord*. Nashville: Nelson, 1984.

10. Psalm 110 in Hebrews (1:13)

Anderson, David R. *The King-Priest of Psalm 110 in Hebrews*. New York: Peter Lang, 2001.

*Compton, Jared M. *Psalm 110 and the Logic of Hebrews*. London: T&T Clark, 2015.

Hay, David M. *Glory at the Right Hand: Psalm 110 in Early Christianity*. Nashville: Abingdon, 1973.

Lincoln, Andrew T. "Hebrews and Biblical Theology." Pages 313–38 in *Out of Egypt: Biblical Theology and Biblical Interpretation*. Grand Rapids: Zondervan, 2004.

Loader, William R. G. "Christ at the Right Hand—Ps cx.1 in the NT." *NTS* 24 (1977–78): 119–227.

11. Salvation in Hebrews and the NT (1:14)

Barnett, Paul W. *DLNT* 1072–75.

*Colijn, Brenda B. "'Let Us Approach': Soteriology in the Epistle to the Hebrews." *JETS* 39 (1996): 571–86.

Fuhrmann, Sebastian. "Failures Forgotten: The Soteriology in Hebrews Revisited in the Light of Its Quotation of Jeremiah 38:31–34 (LXX)." *Neot* 41 (2007): 295–316.

Koester, Craig R. "God's Purposes and Christ's Saving Work according to Hebrews." Pages 361–87 in *Salvation in the New Testament: Perspectives on Soteriology*. Edited by Jan G. van der Watt. Leiden: Brill, 2005.

*Marshall, I. Howard. "Soteriology in Hebrews." Pages 253–77 in Bauckham, *Theology*.

McCruden, Kevin B. "Compassionate Soteriology in Hebrews, 1 Peter, and the Gospel of Mark." *BR* 52 (2007): 41–56.

Osborne, Grant R. "Soteriology in the Epistle to the Hebrews: Exegetical Notes on Calvinist Texts." Pages 144–66 in *Grace Unlimited.* Edited by Clark H. Pinnock. Minneapolis: Bethany Fellowship, 1975.

Stott, John. *The Cross of Christ*. Leicester: InterVarsity Press, 1986.

HOMILETICAL SUGGESTIONS

Seven OT Citations about the Son (1:5–13)

1. The first pair (Ps 2:7; 2 Sam 7:14): the Son's unique relationship to the Father (v. 5)
2. The second pair (Ps 97:7; 104:4): the positive but inferior ministry of angels (vv. 6–7)
3. The third pair (Ps 45:6–7; 102:25–27): the Son's righteous, eternal nature (vv. 8–12)
4. The climax (Ps 110:1): the Son's exaltation (v. 13)

Ten OT Truths Applied to the Son (1:5–13)

1. He is the unique Son (Ps 2:7; 2 Sam 7:14; v. 5)
2. He is worshipped (Deut 32:43; v. 6)
3. His rule is forever (Ps 45:6; v. 8)
4. His kingdom is characterized by justice (Ps 45:6; v. 8)
5. He is characterized by righteousness (Ps 45:7; v. 9)
6. He created heaven and earth (Ps 102:25–27; v. 10)
7. He controls the destiny of the universe (Ps 102:25–27; v. 12)
8. He is called "God" and "Lord" (Ps 45:6; v. 8; Ps 102:25; v. 10)
9. He is eternal (Ps 102:25–27; v. 12)
10. He is exalted by the Father (Ps 110:1; vv. 9, 13)

Clarification about Angels (1:5–14)

1. They worship the Son; they are not to be worshipped (vv. 5–7)
2. They are part of God's created order; they are not eternal (v. 7)
3. They minister on behalf of believers; they are God's servants (v. 14)

B. FIRST WARNING: HEED THE REVELATION THAT COMES THROUGH THE SON (2:1–4)

STRUCTURE

This section continues the theme of God's speaking and presents the severe consequences of not paying attention to God's final word (1:1–2). After the opening exposition concerning the Son's superiority, the author switches to exhortation. Hebrews 2:1–4 is the first of several "warning" passages in Hebrews (2:1–4; 3:7–4:13; 5:11–6:8; 10:19–39; 12:14–29). The author's rhetorical competence is seen in the continued use of alliteration (e.g., words that begin with π in v. 2). See For Further Study 12 (The Warning Passages in Hebrews).

The inf. προσέχειν completes δεῖ and forms the structure of the opening sentence and the basis for the hort. παραρυῶμεν. As with Heb 1:1–4, Heb 2:2–4 comprises one carefully constructed sentence in the Gk. (a periodic sentence; BDF §464), the anchor of which is ἐκφευξόμεθα. This rhetorical question is the apod., with the prot. (εἰ . . . μισθαποδοσίαν) introducing the first-class cond. Indentation shows the dependent nature of the prot. with regard to the apod. The substan. σωτηρίας is modified by the long rel. clause that begins with ἥτις and extends to the end of the sentence. The arrow indicates that συνεπιμαρτυροῦντος modifies ἐβεβαιώθη.

1 Διὰ τοῦτο δεῖ
περισσοτέρως
προσέχειν ἡμᾶς τοῖς ἀκουσθεῖσιν,
μήποτε παραρυῶμεν.
2 εἰ γὰρ ὁ δι᾽ ἀγγέλων λαληθεὶς λόγος ἐγένετο βέβαιος
καὶ
πᾶσα παράβασις καὶ παρακοὴ ἔλαβεν ἔνδικον μισθαποδοσίαν,
3 πῶς ἡμεῖς ἐκφευξόμεθα
τηλικαύτης ἀμελήσαντες σωτηρίας,
ἥτις ἀρχὴν λαβοῦσα λαλεῖσθαι
διὰ τοῦ κυρίου
ὑπὸ τῶν ἀκουσάντων
εἰς ἡμᾶς ἐβεβαιώθη,
4 συνεπιμαρτυροῦντος τοῦ θεοῦ
σημείοις τε καὶ τέρασιν καὶ
ποικίλαις δυνάμεσιν καὶ πνεύματος ἁγίου μερισμοῖς
κατὰ τὴν αὐτοῦ θέλησιν;

VERSE 1

Διὰ τοῦτο δεῖ περισσοτέρως προσέχειν ἡμᾶς τοῖς ἀκουσθεῖσιν,
For this reason, we must pay attention all the more to what we have heard,

The prep. phrase διὰ τοῦτο often refers to a previous argument (Wallace 333), and indicates a stronger deduction than δίο (cf. 3:7; Ellingworth 135). Here it likely refers back to the entire argument of Hebrews 1 (Ellingworth 135; Attridge 63–64). Προσέχειν (pres. act. inf. of προσέχω, "pay attention to"; BDAG 880a; H. Kuhli, *EDNT* 3:169d–170a) complements the impers. δεῖ ("it is necessary"). The subj. of the inf. (different from δεῖ) is the acc. ἡμᾶς (BDF §407); προσέχω takes a dat. obj., here ἀκουσθεῖσιν (dat. pl. neut. of aor. pass. ptc. of ἀκούω, "hear"). The neut. indicates "that which was heard," namely, the initial proclamation of the gospel. It recalls the opening emph. on God's speaking and anticipates the exhortation to hear his voice (Heb 3:7–19). The adv. περισσοτέρως is intensifying, "so much more" (BDAG 806b). It can also indicate a comp., such as "more closely than has been the case," likely anticipating the neg. example of the wilderness generation in Hebrews 3–4. Προσέχω can also indicate a ship staying on course (LSJ 1512a; cited by Koester 205; Lane 1:35) and intentionally contrasts with drifting as denoted by παραρρέω (see below). Προσέχω anticipates the rep. exhortation to "hold fast" (with the cognate κατέχω) elsewhere in Hebrews (3:6,14; 10:23 [cf. Koester 208]).

μήποτε παραρυῶμεν.
so that we will not drift away.

Μήποτε indicates neg. purpose, "oft. expressing apprehension" (BDAG 648d). It introduces the subord. clause, μήποτε παραρυῶμεν, indicating the purpose of the exhortation to "pay attention." Παραρυῶμεν is the 1st pl. aor. pass. subjunc. of παραρρέω, "drift away" (most EVV), "be washed away" (BDAG 770d; NT hapax). The vb. is used in LXX Prov 3:21, where a father exhorts his son not "to drift away" from the wisdom of the Lord.

The idea of drifting in παραρρέω may connote a nautical metaphor, perhaps suggesting "to drift away from one's course" (Lane 1:35; cf. REB). Greek writers (e.g., Herodotus and Strabo) used this vb. for the flow of a river (Attridge 64 n. 19; Koester 205). Given the tremendous importance of sea routes in the Roman Empire, it is likely that the audience would have recognized this nautical allusion. Alternatively, παραρρέω could describe "a ring slipping off a finger" (Attridge 64 n. 19; citing Plutarch). Both images underscore the author's concern that the audience is in danger of drifting away from the sound teaching that they had initially received, perhaps due to ongoing persecution and pressure to compromise.

VERSE 2

εἰ γὰρ ὁ δι' ἀγγέλων λαληθεὶς λόγος ἐγένετο βέβαιος
For if the message spoken through angels was legally binding

Γάρ explains further the necessity of paying attention. The subj. of the prot. is λόγος, which has a wide semantic range (BDAG 598d–600d; *NIDNTTE* 157–70), which is reflected in EVV ("message," ESV, NIV, NLT; "word," NASB, KJV). It refers generally to the gospel's proclamation to the audience. Λαληθείς modifying λόγος functions as a rel. clause, "the word *that was spoken*." Δι' ἀγγέλων indicates the agency of the pass. λαληθείς. The legal term, βέβαιος (nom. sg. masc. of βέβαιος, -α, -ον, "reliable, abiding, in force"; BDAG 172c; H. Schlier, *TDNT* 1:600–603), may have influenced the tr. of γίνομαι in several EVV (e.g., "proved," ESV, NASB, NKJV). This same adj. occurs in 6:19 to indicate the steadfastness of hope, which is likened to an anchor.

Εἰ introduces the prot. of a first-class cond., which "indicates the assumption of truth for the sake of argument" (Wallace 690; BDF §372). Two items are assumed true here. First, Jewish tradition maintained the presence of angels when the law was given at Sinai. Although Exodus does not record angelic mediation of the law (Exod 19–31), it was inferred based on the myriads of holy ones who accompanied the Lord on Sinai (Deut 33:2; cf. Ps 68:17). Other parts of the NT reflect this tradition (e.g., Acts 7:38, 53; Gal 3:19). See For Further Study 8 (Angels in Hebrews). The second point assumed true includes both the reliability of the law and the inevitability of punishment for infractions of it, which is elaborated in the next clause.

καὶ πᾶσα παράβασις καὶ παρακοὴ ἔλαβεν ἔνδικον μισθαποδοσίαν,
and every transgression and disobedience received a just punishment,

The first *καί* joins the first (ὁ . . . λόγος ἐγένετο βέβαιος) and second clauses (πᾶσα . . . ἔλαβεν . . . μισθαποδοσίαν) of the prot. The legal language continues with the two terms παράβασις (nom. sg. fem. of παράβασις, -εως, ἡ, "violation" [NET, NIV], "transgression" [ESV, NASB; BDAG 758d]) and παρακοή (nom. sg. fem. of παρακοή, -ῆς, ἡ, "disobedience" [most EVV]; BDAG 766d). Etymologically παρακοή means "a failure or refusal to hear" (Attridge 65), which is appropriate with the focus on paying attention and hearing in this section (cf. Cockerill 119 n. 13). The aor. ἔλαβεν is global. The rare ἔνδικον (acc. sg. fem. of ἔνδικος, -ον, "just"; BDAG 332c; occurring only here and in Rom 3:8 in BGr.) modifies μισθαποδοσίαν (acc. sg. fem. of μισθαποδοσία, -ῆς, ἡ, "recompense" [BDAG 653a; only in Hebrews in BGk.]), which may have been coined by the author. The connotation is negative: "just punishment" (NIV), "just penalty" (NASB, NET). Elsewhere in Hebrews the word is used positively (10:35; 11:26; cf.11:6), so there may be a hint of irony here (Cockerill 120; Koester 206).

VERSE 3

πῶς ἡμεῖς ἐκφευξόμεθα τηλικαύτης ἀμελήσαντες σωτηρίας,
how will we escape if we neglect such a great salvation?

Ἐκφευξόμεθα is the 1st pl. fut. mid. indic. of ἐκφεύγω, "escape" (most EVV [BDAG 312a]). The nom. ἡμεῖς is emph. (BDF §277). Once again the author includes himself in the exhortation. The correl. pron. τηλικαύτης (gen. sg. fem. of τηλικοῦτος, -αύτη, -οῦτο, "so great" [most EVV], "important," "mighty"; BDAG 1001d–1002a; BDF §64[4]) modifies the subst. σωτηρίας. The adv. ἀμελήσαντες (nom. pl. masc. of the aor. act. ptc. of ἀμελέω, "neglect" [most EVV], "ignore" [NIV], "be unconcerned"; BDAG

52c) has a cond. force, "if we neglect" (Wallace 632–33, 687; BDF §418[2]) and takes an obj. in the gen. (e.g., *σωτηρίας*). Σωτηρίας functions as a hook word that links 2:1–4 with the previous section (1:5–14). See For Further Study 11 (Salvation in Hebrews).

The apod. of the first-class cond. begun in v. 2 is actually the rhetorical question in v. 3 (introduced by the interr. ptcl. πῶς), which is part of an *a fortiori* argument, from the lesser to the greater. This also reflects the rabbinic technique known as *qal wahomer* (see Koester 209 n. 68). The Son's superiority to angels has already been demonstrated. The author now builds on this. If there were consequences (and there were) for violations of that which was mediated by angels—the law—how much greater will be the consequences for neglecting that which was mediated by the Lord himself—the gospel? This type of *a fortiori* argument is prevalent in Hebrews.

ἥτις ἀρχὴν λαβοῦσα λαλεῖσθαι διὰ τοῦ κυρίου ὑπὸ τῶν ἀκουσάντων εἰς ἡμᾶς ἐβεβαιώθη, This salvation had its beginning when it was spoken of by the Lord, and it was confirmed to us by those who heard him.

The second part of v. 3 is a single rel. clause modifying σωτηρίας, the antecedent of the indef. rel. pron. ἥτις (ὅστις, ἥτις, ὅ τι). The def. rel. pron. (ὅς) and the indef. rel. pron. (ὅστις) were no longer distinguished in Koine Gk. (BDF §293). The expression ἀρχὴν λαβοῦσα λαλεῖσθαι occurs only here in the NT, although a sim. expression is attested in HGk. (see Koester 206; Ellingworth 140–41). It is difficult to tr. (lit.: "receiving at the first that which was spoken"), with λαβοῦσα modifying the antecedent of the rel. pron. σωτηρίας (nom. case as the subj. of the rel. clause). The difficulty of this expression explains why most EVV do not tr. the ptc. λαβοῦσα. Note the awkward phrasing in Cassirer: "which took its rise by being proclaimed by the Lord himself." The subst. ἀρχήν functions equivalently to an adv. (G. Delling, *TDNT* 1:482; cf. BDAG 138a). Διὰ τοῦ κυρίου expresses intermediate agency of the pass. λαλεῖσθαι, with God implicitly understood as the subj. (cf. 1:1–2). Together the expression indicates the initial proclamation of the gospel by Jesus (e.g., Mark 1:14–15; Luke 4:18–21). The next prep. phrase, ὑπὸ τῶν ἀκουσάντων, indicates the agent of the pass. vb. ἐβεβαιώθη (3rd sg. aor. pass. indic. of βεβαιόω, "confirm" [many EVV], "attest" [ESV], "establish" [BDAG 173a]). (For intermediate and ultimate agency, see Wallace 432–34.) The legal terminology prevalent in this sentence, beginning with βέβαιος (v. 2), is continued with ἐβεβαιώθη (v. 3).

"Those who heard" may indicate eyewitnesses of Jesus's ministry or even an apostle (see Koester 206–207). Εἰς ἡμᾶς indicates ref. or advantage (e.g., "*for* us"). The distinction between those who heard the gospel message from the Lord and the audience of Hebrews supports the traditional view that both the author and recipients of the epistle were second-generation believers (*pace* Ellingworth 141). Koester rightly observes that "the preaching received by the early community was understood to continue Jesus' own preaching" (Koester 210).

VERSE 4

συνεπιμαρτυροῦντος τοῦ θεοῦ
At the same time, God also testified

The ptc. clause, *συνεπιμαρτυροῦντος τοῦ θεοῦ*, is a gen. abs. cstr. that is subord. to *ἐβεβαιώθη* in v. 3. Although logically related to the rest of the sentence, the abs. clause is not grammatically dependent on the preceding vb. as indicated by the difference in subj.—the subj. of *ἐβεβαιώθη* is the message of salvation, whereas the subj. of *συνεπιμαρτυροῦντος* (gen. sg. masc. of the pres. act. ptc. of *συνεπιμαρτυρέω*, "testify at the same time"; BDAG 969a; H. Strathmann *TDNT* 4:508–10) is *θεοῦ* (see Wallace 654–55). *Συνεπιμαρτυρέω* continues the legal terminology in this sentence and is a NT hapax. The pres. ptc. may indicate time roughly contemp. with *ἐβεβαιώθη*, although an abs. temp. value is absent from ptcs. (BDF §339).

σημείοις τε καὶ τέρασιν καὶ ποικίλαις δυνάμεσιν
by signs and wonders, various miracles,

A series of four instr. dats. follow the ptc. to indicate the means by which God attested the message of salvation. *Σημείοις* (dat. pl. neut. of *σημεῖον, -ου, τό*, "miracle"; BDAG 920b) occurs freq. in the NT. *Τέρασιν* (dat. pl. neut. of *τέρας*, "wonder," BDAG 999d), however, occurs ten times in the NT and only in combination with *σημεῖον*. The stereotyped phrase *σημείοις τε καὶ τέρασιν* occurs in the LXX in conj. with the Exodus (e.g., LXX Exod 7:3, 9; 11:9–10). The correl. conj. *τε καί* indicates a close pairing of these two entities (Wallace 672; BDF §444). The expression *σημείοις τε καὶ τέρασιν* (and vars.) also occurs with ref. to Jesus's ministry (John 4:48; Acts 2:19) and its extension by the apostles (Acts 2:43; 5:12; 14:3; 15:12). This expression suggests a par. between the miraculous signs that accompanied God's former revelation and those signs that accompanied his final revelation through the Son (cf. 1:1–2).

The adj. *ποικίλαις* (*ποικίλος, -η, -ον*; "various" [most EVV], "diversified," "manifold"; BDAG 842b–c) modifies *δυνάμεσιν* (dat. pl. fem. of *δύναμις, -εως, ἡ*, "power"; see W. Grundmann, *TDNT* 2:284–317). The second *καί* joins this third element to the first pair. The terms may have been combined for rhetorical effect (cf. Witherington 137).

καὶ πνεύματος ἁγίου μερισμοῖς κατὰ τὴν αὐτοῦ θέλησιν;
and distributions of gifts from the Holy Spirit according to his will.

Καί adds in the final dat. term *μερισμοῖς* (dat. pl. masc. of *μερισμός, -οῦ, ὁ*, "distribution" [CSB], "division"; BDAG 633a). Many EVV (e.g., ESV, NET, NIV) tr. the noun as a vb. (e.g., "distributed"). An allusion to the outpouring of the Spirit (*πνεύματος ἁγίου*) at Pentecost (Acts 2) and the subsequent distribution of spiritual gifts among the body of Christ (e.g., 1 Corinthians 12; Romans 12) seems likely. This word occurs only in Hebrews (2:4; 4:12). The gen. indicates source (so most EVV). The prep. phrase *κατὰ τὴν αὐτοῦ θέλησιν* (acc. sg. fem. of *θέλησις, -εως, ἡ*, "will"; BDAG 447c;

NT hapax) probably modifies only the final dat. μερισμοῖς, or possibly all four preceding datives. The antecedent of αὐτοῦ is either God or the Spirit; context favors the former.

The rep. of the ending -σιν (τέρασιν, δυνάμεσιν, and θέλησιν) is further indication of the author's rhetorial skill (Lane 1:35; Attridge 64 n. 25). Verse 4 underscores the reliability of the gospel by indicating that it was attested by the outpouring of the Spirit and accompanying signs, wonders, and diverse miracles and underscores the need to pay attention and hold fast.

FOR FURTHER STUDY

12. The Warning Passages in Hebrews (2:1–4)

Cowan, Christopher W. "The Warning Passages of Hebrews and the Nature of the New Covenant." Pages 189–214 in *Progressive Covenantalism: Charting a Course between Dispensational and Covenantal Theologies*. Edited by Stephen J. Wellum and Brent E. Parker. Nashville: B&H, 2016.

*Mackie, Scott D. "Early Christian Eschatological Experience in the Warnings and Exhortations of the Epistle to the Hebrews." *TynBul* 63 (2012): 93–114.

*McKnight, Scot. "The Warning Passages of Hebrews: A Formal Analysis and Theological Conclusions." *TJ* 13 (1992): 21–59.

Mugridge, Alan. "Warnings in the Epistle to the Hebrews: An Exegetical and Theological Study." *RTR* 46 (1987): 74–82.

Oberholtzer, Thomas K. "The Warning Passages in Hebrews: Parts 1–4." *BSac* 145 (1988): 83–97; 189–96; 319–28; 410–19.

*Oropeza, B. J. "The Warning Passages in Hebrews: Revised Theologies and New Methods of Interpretation." *CurBR* 10 (2011): 81–100.

Peterson, Robert A. "Apostasy in the Hebrews Warning Passages." *Presb* 34 (2008): 27–44.

Schreiner, Thomas R. *Commentary on Hebrews*. Biblical Theology for Christian Proclamation. Nashville, TN: B&H, 2015. See pages 480–91.

———. "Warning and Assurance: Run the Race to the End." Pages 89–106 in *The Perfect Saviour: Key Themes in Hebrews*. Downers Grove, IL: IVP, 2012.

Schreiner, Thomas R., and Ardel B. Caneday. *The Race Set Before Us: A Biblical Theology of Perseverance & Assurance*. Downers Grove, IL: IVP Academic, 2001. See pages 193–204.

Toussaint, Stanley D. "The Eschatology of the Warning Passages in the Book of Hebrews." *Grace Theological Journal* 3 (1982): 67–80.

Whitlark, Jason A. "The Warning against Idolatry: An Intertextual Examination of Septuagintal Warnings in Hebrews." *JSNT* 34 (2012): 382–401.

13. Pneumatology in Hebrews (2:4)

*Allen, David M. "'The Forgotten Spirit': A Pentecostal Reading of the Letter to the Hebrews?" *Journal of Pentecostal Theology* 18 (2009): 51–66.

———. "The Holy Spirit as Gift or Giver?: Retaining the Pentecostal Dimension of Hebrews 2.4." *BT* 59 (2008): 151–58.

Emmrich, Martin. "'Amtscharisma': Through the Eternal Spirit (Hebrews 9:14)." *BBR* (2002): 17–32.

———. "Pneuma in Hebrews: Prophet and Interpreter." *WTJ* 64 (2002): 55–71.

———. *Pneumatological Concepts in the Epistle to the Hebrews: Amtscharisma, Prophet, and Guide of the Eschatological Exodus*. Lanham, NY: University Press of America, 2003.

*Motyer, Stephen. "The Spirit in Hebrews: No Longer Forgotten?" Pages 213–27 in *Spirit and Christ in the New Testament and Christian Theology: Essays in Honor of Max Turner*. Edited by I. Howard Marshall, Volker Rabens, and Cornelius Bennema. Grand Rapids: Eerdmans, 2012.

HOMILETICAL SUGGESTIONS

The Message of Great Salvation (2:1–4)

1. The importance of paying attention (v. 1)
2. Anticipated by, but superior to, the law (v. 2)
3. Confirmed by witnesses (v. 3)
4. Confirmed by signs and miracles (v. 4)

How Much Greater! (2:1–3)

1. How much greater attention is needed (v. 1)
2. How much greater is the message mediated by the Son than the one mediated by angels (vv. 2–3)
3. How much greater are the consequences for neglecting the Son's message than for transgressing the law (vv. 1–3)

C. THE HUMILITY AND GLORY OF THE SON, THE PERFECT HUMAN BEING (2:5–9)

STRUCTURE

Following the focus on the Son's exaltation in Hebrews 1 and the ensuing exhortation, the focus in Heb 2:5–18 shifts to the Son's humanity and suffering and offers a significant development in the Christology of Hebrews by explaining how the "great salvation" (2:3) has been achieved. See For Further Study 41 (The Structure of Hebrews).

The use of ἀγγέλοις in the opening rhetorical question in v. 5 functions as a hook word that connects this passage with Hebrews 1. A citation from Psalm 8 extends from the second part of v. 6 to the first part of v. 8. The structure of vv. 6b–8a reflects the par. of the orig. Heb. Forms of ὑποτάσσω have been underlined for clarity. See discussion on v. 9 for the complex syntax of this verse.

5 Οὐ γὰρ ἀγγέλοις ὑπέταξεν τὴν οἰκουμένην τὴν μέλλουσαν,
περὶ ἧς λαλοῦμεν.
6 διεμαρτύρατο δέ πού τις λέγων·
τί ἐστιν ἄνθρωπος ὅτι μιμνῄσκῃ αὐτοῦ,
ἢ υἱὸς ἀνθρώπου ὅτι ἐπισκέπτῃ αὐτόν;
7 ἠλάττωσας αὐτὸν βραχύ τι παρ' ἀγγέλους,
δόξῃ καὶ τιμῇ ἐστεφάνωσας αὐτόν,
8 πάντα ὑπέταξας ὑποκάτω τῶν ποδῶν αὐτοῦ.
ἐν τῷ γὰρ ὑποτάξαι [αὐτῷ] τὰ πάντα
οὐδὲν ἀφῆκεν αὐτῷ ἀνυπότακτον.
Νῦν δὲ οὔπω ὁρῶμεν αὐτῷ τὰ πάντα ὑποτεταγμένα·
9 τὸν δὲ βραχύ τι παρ' ἀγγέλους ἠλαττωμένον
βλέπομεν
Ἰησοῦν διὰ τὸ πάθημα τοῦ θανάτου
δόξῃ καὶ τιμῇ ἐστεφανωμένον,
ὅπως χάριτι θεοῦ ὑπὲρ παντὸς γεύσηται θανάτου.

VERSE 5

Οὐ γὰρ ἀγγέλοις ὑπέταξεν τὴν οἰκουμένην τὴν μέλλουσαν,
For he has not subjected to angels the world to come

This v. recalls the previous discussion about angels, while "the world to come" anticipates Hebrews 12 and 13. Γάρ gives further grounds for paying greater attention to the message spoken by the Son. Hebrews 2:5–9 picks up the theme of subjection of all things in Ps 110:1, which is developed by ὑποτάσσω (e.g., ὑπέταξεν in v. 5; ὑπέταξας, ὑποτάξαι, and ὑποτεταγμένα in v. 8). The implied subj. of ὑπέταξεν (3rd sg. aor. act. indic. of ὑποτάσσω, "subject" [most EVV]; "subordinate"; BDAG 1042a; B.

Bergmeier, *EDNT* 3:408b) in v. 5 is presumably God, who subjects the world to the Son, whom he has exalted. The adj. ptc. μέλλουσαν (see comments on 1:14) modifies the subst. οἰκουμένην (see comments on 1:6)—"the world to come." This expression was common in rabbinic and apocalyptic writings. The rep. of the art. and the placement of the adj. ptc. are emph. (Ellingworth 402; 2nd attrib. pos.; see Wallace 306–7).

In addition to a mediatorial role, Jewish tradition maintained that angels participated in the governance of the world, perhaps based on Deut 32:8. Instead of "sons of Israel" in the MT ("people of Israel" in the CSB), the LXX (and some DSS mss.) have "sons of God," understood to refer to angels. See For Further Study 8 (Angels in Hebrews). The author's statement here follows logically from the role of angels indicated in 1:14—they cannot be ruling the world if they are ministering on behalf of those who inherit salvation. The question remains, however, to whom will the universe be subjected? The author appeals to Psalm 8 to answer this.

περὶ ἧς λαλοῦμεν
that we are talking about.

Περί in the gen. indicates ref. ("concerning"; Wallace 379). The antecedent of ἧς is οἰκουμένη. The rel. clause ἧς λαλοῦμεν is embedded within the prep. phrase: "concerning which we are speaking" (NASB); "about which we are speaking" (many EVV). The first pers. pl. λαλοῦμεν is likely "epistolary" or "editorial," rather than an indication of more than one author for Hebrews (*pace* Wallace 394–96).

VERSE 6

διεμαρτύρατο δέ πού τις λέγων
But someone somewhere has testified:

Δέ links the previous point to the citation from Psalm 8 in v. 6 (BDAG 213b; EVV). Διεμαρτύρατο (3rd sg. aor. mid. indic. of διαμαρτύρομαι, "testify" [most EVV], "bear witness"; BDAG 233b) continues the theme of God's testimony from v. 4. The adv. πού is a "marker of an undetermined position or place" ("somewhere"; BDAG 858b). This indefiniteness is furthered with the indef. pron. τις, "someone." Λέγων is redundant (or pleonastic; Wallace 649) and emphasizes that God has spoken in (and is still speaking through) this psalm. Although cumbersome, this could be understood as a ptc. of means: "testified by saying."

The author quotes LXX Ps 8:5–7 (EVV 8:4–6) nearly verbatim, although part of v. 6 is omitted (see below). In a reflection on Genesis 1 and 2, the psalm focuses on the majesty of God's creation and the wonder that dominion for this creation was entrusted to human beings, seemingly so insignificant in comp. (esp. Gen 1:26–28). Hebrews appropriates the second half of the psalm and applies it to the Son. The human author of the psalm (e.g., David) is not mentioned to underscore God's (ongoing) speaking through the psalm.

Τί ἐστιν ἄνθρωπος ὅτι μιμνῄσκῃ αὐτοῦ, ἢ υἱὸς ἀνθρώπου ὅτι ἐπισκέπτῃ αὐτόν;
What is man that you remember him, or the son of man that you care for him?

The interr. pron. τίς usually introduces an "identifying question" (e.g., "who?" "what?"), but it may also indicate a qual. question ("what sort?"), thus paralleling ποῖος (Wallace 345). The anar. ἄνθρωπος extends this qual. force (e.g., "mere mortals," TNIV; "child of Adam," NJB). Ὅτι introduces an epex. clause that further explains the question posed in the main clause. Μιμνῄσκῃ is the 2nd sg. pres. mid. indic. of μιμνῄσκομαι, "remember" (NASB), "think about" (NET, NLT), "care for" (NET), "be mindful of" (ESV, NIV), "be concerned about" (BDAG 652b) and takes a gen. obj. The antecedent for αὐτοῦ is ἄνθρωπος. The correl. disjunctive conj. ἢ ("or") introduces the second half of the citation from Ps 8:5. The structure of the LXX reflects the par. of the orig. Heb.; thus the ὅτι clause here is also epex. Ἐπισκέπτῃ is the 2nd sg. pres. mid. indic. of ἐπισκέπτομαι, "care for" (ESV, NET, NIV), "be concerned about" (NASB), "look after" (BDAG 378c). The antecedent for αὐτόν is υἱὸς ἀνθρώπου.

The expression "son of man" raises the key interpretive issue in this section. The expression could simply indicate a human being (e.g., Ezek 2:1), although "Son of Man" became an important Christological title (e.g., Matt 26:64; Mark 13:26; Luke 21:27). It is unclear, however, that the author of Hebrews intends this titular sense here. This is initially suggested by the anar. υἱὸς ἀνθρώπου and is further supported by the focus on Jesus's incarnation throughout Hebrews 2. Thus "son of man" provides a link between the orig. human being, Adam, who is alluded to in Psalm 8, and the perfect human being, Jesus, who perfectly fulfills the orig. vocation intended for humanity. Thus the dominion that was entrusted to, but forfeited by, humanity (Psalm 8) is now proleptically achieved by Jesus (Psalm 110) and will be fully achieved in the world to come. This does not deny Jesus's full divinity, as Hebrews 1 has already made clear. Although there may be a hint of the Pauline first Adam/Christ typology (e.g., Rom 5:11–21; 1 Cor 15:20–28), this is not made explicit.

VERSE 7

ἠλάττωσας αὐτὸν βραχύ τι παρ᾽ ἀγγέλους,
You made him lower than the angels for a short time;

This v. continues the citation of Psalm 8 (LXX v. 6; EVV v. 5). Ἠλάττωσας is the 2nd sg. aor. act. indic. of ἐλαττόω, "make lower" (BDAG 314a). The aor. is constative. The implied subj. is God, and the antecedent for αὐτόν continues from v. 6. The adj. βραχύ (acc. sg. neut. of βραχύς, -εῖα, -ύ) combines with the indef. pron. τι to form the adv. expression "for a short time" (BDAG 183d), although the expression could also quan. denote a lower status, which follows the orig. Heb. ("a little lower" [e.g., NIV]). The author of Hebrews exploits this overlap in mng. in v. 9, where the psalm is applied to Jesus, who was a little lower than the angels for a little while (see discussion below). Additionally, the LXX trs. rendered the Heb. *'ĕlōhîm* ("gods") with ἄγγελοι, which may have contributed to the author's reasons for citing Psalm 8 at this point in his argument. Παρά with the acc. (παρ' ἀγγέλους) indicates comp. (Wallace 378).

δόξῃ καὶ τιμῇ ἐστεφάνωσας αὐτόν,
you crowned him with glory and honor

Both dat. δόξῃ and τιμῇ are instr. (or dat. of material; Wallace 270), and appear in an emph. position (Porter, *Idioms* 295–97). Ἐστεφάνωσας is the 2nd sg. aor. act. indic. of στεφανόω, "crown" (most EVV), "honor," "reward" (BDAG 944c). The aor. is constative. In Psalm 8, the statements "you made him a little lower" and "you crowned him with glory and honor" are par. comments about the dignified status of humanity. As the author applies these statements to Jesus, however, they refer to his humiliation and subsequent exaltation and are thus opposite in mng. (Koester 216). Moreover, Jesus's temp. humiliation to the point of death (v. 9) is the basis for his exaltation and the subjection of all things (v. 8) to him.

Some important and early mss. (ℵ A C D*) include the first part of Ps 8:5 (EVV 8:6), "and you appointed him over the works of your hands," in conformity with the LXX text. The author most likely omitted this part of the v. himself, as it is difficult to explain why scribes would have omitted it. Some scribes likely added it to conform to the LXX. This part of the v., however, is included in some EVV (KJV, RV, NASB).

VERSE 8

πάντα ὑπέταξας ὑποκάτω τῶν ποδῶν αὐτοῦ.
and subjected everything under his feet.

This clause completes the citation of Psalm 8 (LXX v. 7; EVV v. 6). Paralleling the previous aor. vbs., ὑπέταξας is the 2nd sg. aor. act. indic. of ὑποτάσσω (see comments on v. 5) and is also constative. The improper prep. ὑποκάτω means "under, below" (BDAG 1038a). (Improper prep. cannot be prefixed to vbs.) The obj. of this prep. is τῶν ποδῶν (πούς, ποδός, ὁ, "foot") αὐτοῦ. The antecedent for αὐτοῦ is still ἄνθρωπος (from the first part of the citation in v. 6), although possibly it could refer to Jesus in anticipation of the author's subsequent exposition of the psalm citation. The ambiguity is likely intentional. The language echoes the earlier citation from Ps 110:1 in 1:13. The subjection of all things to humanity in Psalm 8 is understood and developed by the author in terms of the subjugation of all things to the Son in Ps 110:1. Thus the author has seen in Psalm 8 the incarnation ("little lower"), exaltation ("crowned"), and ultimate victory ("everything under his feet") of Jesus—which is even more remarkable because this psalm was not considered messianic (cf. Lane 1:44–45). Verse 5 has already indicated that this final subjugation will occur in the world to come.

ἐν τῷ γὰρ ὑποτάξαι [αὐτῷ] τὰ πάντα οὐδὲν ἀφῆκεν αὐτῷ ἀνυπότακτον.
For in **subjecting everything** to him, he left nothing that is not subject to him.

Γάρ begins the author's explanation of the psalm citation, often understood as an example of *midrash*. See For Further Study 32 (Hermeneutical Techniques in Hebrews). Ὑποτάξαι (aor. act. inf.) continues the rep. of forms of ὑποτάσσω in this v. The art. inf. ἐν τῷ . . . ὑποτάξαι functions temp. to indicate an action contemporaneous (Wallace 258; EVV) to the main vb. ἀφῆκεν (3rd sg. aor. act. indic. of ἀφίημι, "left" [most EVV]; BDAG 157a). Like the previous aor. vbs., ἀφῆκεν is constative, viewing the action as a summary. The obj. of the inf. is τὰ πάντα. The adj. οὐδέν ("nothing") functions as the obj. of ἀφῆκεν and the adj. ἀνυπότακτον (acc. sg. neut. of ἀνυπότακτος, -ον, "not made subject," "independent"; BDAG 91d) is an obj. complement. Αὐτῷ is the indir. obj. of ἀφῆκεν. The antecedent for αὐτῷ remains ambiguous, although Jesus may be intended in anticipation of v. 9.

νῦν δὲ οὔπω ὁρῶμεν αὐτῷ τὰ πάντα ὑποτεταγμένα·
As it is, we do not yet see **everything subjected** to him.

Δέ functions as an adversative (BDAG 213c). The temp. advs. (νῦν and οὔπω, "not yet"; BDAG 737b) indicate the author's recognition that present reality (ὁρῶμεν) does not align with the declaration that all things have been subjected to Jesus, the likely (although still ambiguous) antecedent of αὐτῷ (here as the obj. of the ptc. ὑποτεταγμένα). This lack of specificity would have built suspense for the orig. audience. Running through this section is the tension between subjugation as an (apparently) completed fact (Ps 8:6) and a fut. promise (Ps 110:1). Ὑποτεταγμένα (acc. pl. neut. of pf. pass. ptc.) is the final occurrence of ὑποτάσσω in this section and functions as the obj. complement to τὰ πάντα, the obj. of ὁρῶμεν. The use of τὰ πάντα may echo Heb 1:2–3.

VERSE 9

τὸν δὲ βραχύ τι παρ' ἀγγέλους ἠλαττωμένον βλέπομεν Ἰησοῦν διὰ τὸ πάθημα τοῦ θανάτου δόξῃ καὶ τιμῇ ἐστεφανωμένον,
But we do see Jesus—**made lower than the angels for a short time** . . .—**crowned with glory and honor** because he suffered death.

Δέ also functions as an adversative in this v. and begins the author's solution to the apparent problem raised in v. 8. This v. alludes back to Ps 8:4–6 by means of βραχύ τι παρ' ἀγγέλους ἠλαττωμένον (acc. sg. masc. of the pf. pass. ptc. of ἐλαττόω) and δόξῃ καὶ τιμῇ ἐστεφανωμένον (acc. sg. masc. of the pf. pass. ptc. of στεφανόω). Sandwiched between these phrases is the prep. phrase διὰ τὸ πάθημα (acc. pl. neut. of πάθημα, -ατος, τό, "suffering"; BDAG 747d; διά and acc. indicating cause) τοῦ θανάτου, which underscores the necessity of Jesus's suffering for his exaltation. The switch from the aor. (ἠλάττωσας, ἐστεφάνωσας, v. 7) to the pf. (ἠλαττωμένον, ἐστεφανωμένον) is probably rhetorically significant and draws attention to Jesus's humiliation and exaltation (e.g., "intensified," Campbell, *VA* 201). The subj. of both pass. ptcs. is God.

This deliberate interweaving of the psalm citation and the author's exposition complicates the syntax of this v. Ἰησοῦν is the obj. of the main vb. βλέπομεν. There is much semantic overlap between βλέπω and ὁράω; the alternation is likely stylistic (cf. Ellingworth 153). The ref. to seeing here is metaphorical. Both ptcs. modify and effectively bracket Ἰησοῦν, as indicated by arrows in the following diagram:

δὲ τὸν ἠλαττωμένον
↓ βραχύ τι παρ' ἀγγέλους
βλέπομεν Ἰησοῦν
↑ διὰ τὸ πάθημα τοῦ θανάτου
[τὸν] ἐστεφανωμένον,
δόξῃ καὶ τιμῇ
ὅπως χάριτι θεοῦ ὑπὲρ παντὸς γεύσηται θανάτου.

ὅπως χάριτι θεοῦ ὑπὲρ παντὸς γεύσηται θανάτου.
so that by God's grace he might taste death for everyone—

The subj. of γεύσηται (3rd sg. aor. mid. subjunc. of γεύομαι, "taste" [most EVV]; "experience" [NET], "come to know" [BDAG 195d]) is Jesus. The subj. forms a purpose clause introduced by ὅπως ("so that"; BDF §369) to indicate the reason why Jesus is crowned with glory and honor. (For more on the syntax of this v. and function of ὅπως, see James Swetnam, "The Crux at Hebrews 2,9 in Its Context," *Bib* 91 [2010]: 103–11). The metaphorical language of "tasting" does not imply anything less than experiencing death fully (so most commentators). This same expression occurs in Matt 16:28, where physical death is in view. The overall context suggests that ὑπὲρ παντός refers to people (masc.; "everyone"). Jesus's vicarious suffering and death indicated with ὑπέρ + gen. is common in the NT (e.g., Luke 22:19; John 10:11; Rom 8:32).

This clause contains one of the more significant textual issues in Hebrews. The rdg. χωρίς θεοῦ, "apart from God," is not widely attested, whereas the rdg. χάριτι θεοῦ is well supported by many early and important mss. and is rated {A} by the UBS committee. The variant most likely reflects the influence of 1 Cor 15:27, which indicates that God is excepted from the final subjugation of all things (cf. Attridge 77; Lane 1:43). (For a defense of χωρίς θεοῦ, see John Cochrane O'Neill, "Hebrews II.9" *JTS* 17 [1966]: 79–82.)

This is the first occurrence of the name "Jesus" in the epistle (cf. 3:1; 6:20; 7:22; 10:19; 12:2, 24; 13:12) as well as the first mention of his death. In Hebrews, the author uses "Jesus" to focus on the Son's humanity and incarnation. Here the author shows that the world to come is indeed subject to humanity, because it is subject to the perfect human being, Jesus. At the same time, however, Hebrews indicates that glory only follows suffering and death—exaltation and humiliation cannot be separated, as the next section makes clear.

FOR FURTHER STUDY

14. Cosmology in Hebrews (2:5)

*Adams, Edward. "The Cosmology of Hebrews." Pages 122–139 in Bauckham, *Theology.*
*Caneday, Ardel B. "The Eschatological World Already Subjected to the Son: The Οἰκουμένη of Hebrews 1:6 and the Son's Enthronement." Pages 28–39 in Bauckham, *Cloud.*
deSilva, D. A. *DLNT* 439–43.
Ellingworth, Paul. "Jesus and the Universe in Hebrews." *EvQ* 58 (1986): 337–50.
Isaacs, Marie E. *Sacred Spaces: An Approach to the Theology of the Epistle to the Hebrews. JSNTSup* 73. Sheffield: Sheffield Academic Press, 1992.
*Johnson, George. "Οἰκουμένη and κόσμος in the New Testament." *NTS* 10 (1964): 352–60.
Koester, 97–100.
Laansma, Jon. "The Cosmology of Hebrews." Pages 125–43 in *Cosmology and New Testament Theology.* Edited by Jonathan T. Pennington and Sean M. McDonough. Library of New Testament Studies 335. London: T & T Clark, 2008.
———. "Hidden Stories in Hebrews: Cosmology and Theology." Pages 9–18 in Bauckham, *Cloud.*
Painter, J. *DLNT* 250–55.
Schenck, Kenneth L. *Cosmology and Eschatology in Hebrews: The Setting of the Sacrifice.* SNTSMS 143. Cambridge: Cambridge University Press, 2007.
Stewart, Alexander E. "Cosmology, Eschatology, and Soteriology in Hebrews: A Synthetic Analysis." *BBR* 20 (2010): 545–60.

15. Psalm 8 (2:6–8)

Childs, Brevard S. "Psalm 8 in the Context of the Christian Canon." *Int* 23 (1969): 20–31.
Guthrie, George H., and Russell D. Quinn. "A Discourse Analysis of the Use of Psalm 8:4–6 in Hebrews 2:5–9." *JETS* 49 (2006): 235–46.
Wallis, Wilber B. "The Use of Psalms 8 and 110 in I Corinthians 15:25–27 and in Hebrews 1 and 2." *JETS* 15 (1972): 25–29.

16. The Son of Man in Hebrews (2:6)

*Blomberg, Craig L. "'But We See Jesus': The Relationship between the Son of Man in 2:6 and 2:9 and the Implications for English Translations." Pages 88–99 in Bauckham, *Cloud.*
France, R. T. "The Son of Man in Hebrews 2:6: A Dilemma for Bible Translators." Pages 81–96 in *New Testament Theology in Light of the Church's Mission: Essays in Honor of I. Howard Marshall.* Edited by Jon C. Laansma, Grant R. Osborne, and Ray Van Neste. Eugene, OR: Cascade, 2011.
Giles, Pauline. "Son of Man in the Epistle to the Hebrews." *ExpT* 86 (1975): 328–32.
Miller, Donald G. "Why God Became Man: Text to Sermon on Hebrews 2:5–18." *Int* 23 (1969): 408–24.

17. "By the Grace of God" or "Apart from God"? (2:9)

Elliott, J. K. "When Jesus Was Apart from God: An Examination of Hebrews 2:9." *ExpT* (1972): 339–41.

Gatiss, Lee. "Grace Tasted Death for All: Thomas Aquinas on Hebrews 2:9." *TynBul* 63 (2012): 217–36.

HOMILETICAL SUGGESTIONS

Things Are Not What They Seem (2:5–9)

1. The amazing dignity given to humanity in creation (v. 6)
2. The dominion that was originally intended for humanity (vv. 7–8a)
3. The stark contrast of present reality (v. 8)
4. The solution: Jesus the exalted one who died on behalf of all (v. 9)
5. The timing: in the world to come (v. 5)

The Humiliation and Exaltation of Jesus (2:7–9)

1. Made lower than angels by becoming incarnate (vv. 7, 9)
2. Experienced death for all (v. 9)
3. Was crowned with glory and honor (v. 9)
4. Everything will be subject to him in the world to come (v. 5)

D. THE SUFFERING, SOLIDARITY, AND VICTORY OF THE SON (2:10–16)

STRUCTURE

Ἔπρεπεν in v. 10 and the inf. τελειῶσαι comprise one verbal idea, which is indicated by the changed word order in this diagram. The arrow in v. 10 indicates that ἀρχηγόν is the obj. of τελειῶσαι. The arrows in v. 12 indicate the chiastic structure that reflects the LXX rendering of the orig. Heb. poetic par. The prep. phrase διὰ τοῦ θανάτου in v. 14 precedes καταργήσῃ, which it modifies. The spacing in v. 14 reflects the par. in the v. Both καταργήσῃ and ἀπαλλάξῃ are the finite vbs. of the ἵνα clause in v. 14. The expression τοῦτ᾽ ἔστιν is epex., further explaining the subst. ἔχοντα (indicated by the arrow). In v. 17, ὅθεν summarizes the preceding argument, beginning in v. 10.

The thesis of this passage is that it was fitting for God to lead his people to glory through the suffering of his Son, Jesus. The epistle moves from the presentation of the exalted Son (Hebrews 1) to the necessity of his incarnation and suffering to save the people of God (Hebrews 2). Verse 10 transitions from the citation of Psalm 8 in 2:5–9 to a further exposition of the psalm in light of Jesus's incarnation and suffering—suffering that uniquely qualifies him as the high priest (2:17–18). This exposition is an example of *midrash*. See For Further Study 32 (Hermeneutical Techniques in Hebrews).

10 Ἔπρεπεν γὰρ αὐτῷ *τελειῶσαι
δι᾽ ὃν τὰ πάντα καὶ
δι᾽ οὗ τὰ πάντα,
πολλοὺς υἱοὺς εἰς δόξαν
ἀγαγόντα
τὸν ἀρχηγὸν τῆς σωτηρίας αὐτῶν διὰ παθημάτων.

11 ὅ τε γὰρ ἁγιάζων καὶ
οἱ ἁγιαζόμενοι ἐξ ἑνὸς πάντες·
δι᾽ ἣν αἰτίαν οὐκ ἐπαισχύνεται
ἀδελφοὺς αὐτοὺς καλεῖν

12 λέγων·
ἀπαγγελῶ τὸ ὄνομά σου τοῖς ἀδελφοῖς μου,
ἐν μέσῳ ἐκκλησίας ὑμνήσω σε,
13 καὶ πάλιν·
ἐγὼ ἔσομαι πεποιθὼς ἐπ᾽ αὐτῷ,
καὶ πάλιν·
ἰδοὺ ἐγὼ καὶ τὰ παιδία
ἅ μοι ἔδωκεν ὁ θεός.

14 Ἐπεὶ οὖν τὰ παιδία κεκοινώνηκεν αἵματος καὶ σαρκός,
καὶ αὐτὸς παραπλησίως μετέσχεν τῶν αὐτῶν,

ἵνα διὰ τοῦ θανάτου
καταργήσῃ τὸν τὸ κράτος ἔχοντα τοῦ θανάτου,
τοῦτ᾽ ἔστιν τὸν διάβολον,

15 καὶ ἀπαλλάξῃ τούτους,

ὅσοι φόβῳ θανάτου διὰ παντὸς τοῦ ζῆν ἔνοχοι ἦσαν δουλείας.

16 οὐ γὰρ δήπου ἀγγέλων ἐπιλαμβάνεται
ἀλλὰ σπέρματος Ἀβραὰμ ἐπιλαμβάνεται.

*This verb occurs at the end of the verse in the original Greek.

VERSE 10

Ἔπρεπεν γὰρ αὐτῷ,
For . . . it was entirely appropriate that God—

Γάρ further explains why Jesus had to suffer. The impers. ἔπρεπεν (3rd sg. impf. act. indic. of πρέπω, "be fitting" [most EVV], "be seemly" [BDAG 861c]) is completed by the inf. τελειῶσαι (see below) to form one verbal action: "it was fitting to perfect." The impf. is continuative (Wallace 543). The dat. obj. αὐτῷ indicates for whom the action of perfecting was fitting (BDAG 861c). The most likely antecedent for αὐτῷ is God, possibly referring back to χάριτι θεοῦ in v. 9 or more generally understood from the logic of the passage (e.g., God perfects his Son through suffering). Greco-Roman writers often spoke of what was "fitting" for the gods to do or say, but there is no par. to the idea that suffering was fitting for God (Attridge 82; Koester 235). For a discussion of both the syntax and rhetorical significance of this cstr., see Alan C. Mitchell, "The Use of πρέπειν and Rhetorical Propriety in Hebrews 2:10," *CBQ* 54 (1992): 681–701.

δι᾽ ὃν τὰ πάντα καὶ δι᾽ οὗ τὰ πάντα,
for whom and through whom all things exist—

In this verbless clause, both δι᾽ ὃν τὰ πάντα and δι᾽ οὗ τὰ πάντα (cf. 1:2) are circumlocutions for God and are unique to Hebrews. In 1:2, the Son's agency in creation is highlighted; here the focus is on God's role. The expressions underscore the staggering truth that the Creator God would deem it fitting to use the Son's suffering to save his people (cf. v. 17).

πολλοὺς υἱοὺς εἰς δόξαν ἀγαγόντα τὸν ἀρχηγὸν τῆς σωτηρίας αὐτῶν διὰ παθημάτων τελειῶσαι.
. . . in bringing many sons and daughters to glory . . . should make the source of their salvation perfect through sufferings.

The inf. τελειῶσαι (aor. act. inf. of τελειόω, "perfect" [most EVV]; "bring to an end," "bring to its goal/completion" [BDAG 996c]) complements ἔπρεπεν, which begins this

v. The placement of τελειῶσαι at the end of the v. brackets the sentence in a rhetorically powerful way. The aor. is global. Διὰ παθημάτων (gen. pl. neut. of πάθημα, -τος, τό, "suffering") indicates means and modifies the inf. ("through suffering"; Wallace 369). The obj. of the inf. is τὸν ἀρχηγὸν τῆς σωτηρίας αὐτῶν (see discussion of ἀρχηγός below). Σωτηρίας is a descriptive gen. The ref. to σωτηρία recalls 1:14 and 2:3 and anticipates the discussion of the Son's suffering, which resulted in his being the source of eternal salvation (5:9). The antecedent of αὐτῶν is πολλούς υἱούς, which is also the obj. of ἀγαγόντα (acc. sg. masc. of the aor. act. ptc. of ἄγω, "lead" [BDAG 16c]). The aor. is global. The ptc. modifies the implied subj. of the inf., God (made explicit in many EVV), and accounts for the acc. case of the ptc. Εἰς δόξαν indicates the goal or destination (Wallace 369) to which the Son is leading, and continues the sharp contrast between suffering and glory begun in 2:9. The image of entering anticipates the discussion of entering the promised rest in Hebrews 4.

The pl. "sons" offers a deliberate contrast to the Son, who has been the focus of the epistle thus far. The term, however, should be understood inclusively (e.g., "sons and daughters"; so TNIV; cf. "brethren," NASB; "children," NRSV; so most commentators), as the inclusive term παιδία "children" in v. 14 confirms. (See D. A. Carson, *The Inclusive-Language Debate: A Plea for Realism* [Grand Rapids: Baker, 1998].)

This v. introduces the important term ἀρχηγός, which derives from ἀρχη ("first") + ηγος (from ἄγω, "lead"). The word has a wide semantic range including "originator," "founder" (BDAG 138d–139a; "source" [CSB]; "author" [NASB]). In Heb 5:9, Jesus is the "source of salvation," and in 6:20 he is the "forerunner" (πρόδρομος) who has already entered the heavenly sanctuary. This imagery suggests that ἀρχηγός indicates a "pioneer" who has gone before (so NET, NIV, NRSV; cf. "leader," NLT; "captain," KJV). In the NT, ἀρχηγός occurs only in Hebrews (2:10; 12:2) and Acts (3:15; 5:31) and only in ref. to Jesus. See For Further Study 19 (Ἀρχηγός). See also comments on ἀρχηγός at 12:2.

This v. also introduces a major theme in Hebrews, "perfection." Τελειόω (and cognates) often has cultic connotations (such as consecration for priestly service; e.g., LXX Exod 29:9; 33:35). In Hebrews, this cultic sense is developed in terms of a vocational idea of completely (or perfectly) fulfilling God's intended purpose. Thus perfection in this verse does not suggest any existing imperfection, but rather the perfect completion of God's plan to redeem his people through the suffering of his Son. See For Further Study 18 (Perfection in Hebrews).

VERSE 11

ὅ τε γὰρ ἁγιάζων καὶ οἱ ἁγιαζόμενοι
For the one who sanctifies and those who are sanctified

Τε γάρ indicates a close connection with a preceding point ("for indeed" [BDAG 189b]) and "deepens the argument of v. 10 rather than drawing a conclusion from it" (Ellingworth 163). (Τέ is encl. and has "thrown" its accent back onto ὁ). Both subst. ἁγιάζων (nom. sg. masc. of pres. act. ptc.) and ἁγιαζόμενοι (nom. pl. masc. of pres. pass. ptc.) are from ἁγιάζω ("consecrate" [REB], "make holy" [NET, NIV], "sanctify" [ESV, NASB], "dedicate" [BDAG 10a]; O. Procksch, *TDNT* 1:89–97, 111–12). The pres. is timeless or gnomic (Wallace 523). The expression ὁ ἁγιάζων occurs in the LXX to refer to God (e.g., Exod 31:13; Lev 20:8; 21:15), although here it refers to Jesus. The act. indicates that he performs the action. The second ptc. refers to the sons of v. 10; the pass. indicates that they receive the action (a divine pass.). The cultic language in v. 11 anticipates the declaration in v. 17 that Jesus is the high priest.

ἐξ ἑνὸς πάντες·
all have one Father.

A vb. is implied and supplied in many EVV, with πάντες functioning as the pred. nom. of the double subj. (ὁ ἁγιάζων καὶ οἱ ἁγιαζόμενοι). There are several options for understanding ἐξ ἑνός (from εἷς, μία, ἕν, "one"):

1. "one humanity," gen. sg. neut. referring to humanity in general, with perhaps αἷμα or σπέρματος implied (Ellingworth 164; "one stock," NEB; "the same stock," NJB);
2. "one origin," gen. sg. masc. referring to Adam (cf. Rom 5:11–21) (cf. "the same origin," NET), but Adam is not mentioned anywhere in Hebrews;
3. "one ancestor," gen. sg. masc. referring to Abraham (Ellingworth 165), or possibly the "seed of Abraham" (see James Swetnam, "Εξ ενός in Hebrews 2,11," *Bib* 88 [2007]: 517–25);

*4. "one source," gen. sg. masc. referring to God; this view fits best with the ensuing discussion of Jesus and the children, and the circumlocutions for God in v. 10 ("the same family," NIV; "one source," ESV; "one Father," NASB, NRSV; "the same father," NLT; cf. most commentators) (cf. Acts 17:26, 1 Cor 8:6, Eph 4:6).

δι' ἣν αἰτίαν οὐκ ἐπαισχύνεται ἀδελφοὺς αὐτοὺς καλεῖν
That is why Jesus is not ashamed to call them brothers and sisters,

The prep. phrase δι' ἣν αἰτίαν (acc. sg. fem. of αἰτία, "cause," "reason" [BDAG 31a]) is causal. The "antecedent" (actually a postcedent) ἣν is αἰτίαν. Ἐπαισχύνεται is the 3rd sg. pres. mid. indic. of ἐπαισχύνομαι, "be ashamed" (BDAG 357d). The pres. indicates an ongoing state (Wallace 521). The inf. καλεῖν is the complement of ἐπαισχύνεται (BDF §392; Wallace 598–99). The aor. is global. Αὐτούς is the obj. of the inf. καλεῖν, and ἀδελφούς is the obj. complement ("to call them [obj.] brothers and sisters [obj. complement]"; see discussion in Wallace 181–89).

Honor and shame were foundational aspects of Greco-Roman society, understood almost as a commodity to measure personal (or familial) worth. The audience addressed in Hebrews was facing persecution (e.g., 10:32–34) and accompanying contempt and shame, yet Jesus is not ashamed to call them siblings (cf. Mark 3:34–35). This v. could also allude to Jesus's teaching (e.g., Mark 8:38 // Luke 9:25). See For Further Study 22 (Patronage, Honor, and Shame in Hebrews).

VERSE 12

λέγων·
saying:

Λέγων pars. λέγει in 1:6 to introduce an OT citation. The pres. indicates action contemp. with the pres. ἐπαισχύνεται in v. 13. Context indicates that Jesus is speaking.

Ἀπαγγελῶ τὸ ὄνομά σου τοῖς ἀδελφοῖς μου, ἐν μέσῳ ἐκκλησίας ὑμνήσω σε
I will proclaim your name to my brothers and sisters; I will sing hymns to you in the congregation.

Ἀπαγγελῶ is the 1st sg. fut. act. indic. of ἀπαγγέλλω ("proclaim" [BDAG 95b]; "declare," NIV, NKJV; "tell," ESV). Τὸ ὄνομά σου is the obj. of the vb. (the encl. σου has "thrown" its accent back onto ὄνομα), and τοῖς ἀδελφοῖς μου is the indir. obj. In both the orig. context and here, ὄνομα refers to God's name. The prep. phrase. ἐν μέσῳ ἐκκλησίας (dat. pl. fem. of ἐκκλησία, "congregation" [ESV, NASB]; "assembly" [NET, NIV, REB, TNIV]; "assembled people" [NLT]; BDAG 303d) is a loc. adv. modifier of ὑμνήσω (1st sg. fut. act. indic. of ὑμνέω, "sing in praise to/of" [ESV, NASB, NIV], "praise" [NET, NRSV; BDAG 1027c–d]). Both vbs. are fut., reflecting the tendency of the LXX to render the Heb. impf. as Gk. fut. indic. (T 86). In the LXX, ἐκκλησία referred to the assembly of the Israelites (e.g., Deut 31:30; Judg 20:2). In the NT, this same word refers to the church (e.g., Matt 16:18; Acts 9:31).

This v. introduces the first of three OT citations to support Jesus's solidarity with those for whom he died. The first citation comes from Ps 22:22 (LXX 21:23). It is likely that the author of Hebrews understood this psalm as pointing to Jesus's own vindication ("crowned with glory and honor," v. 9) following his suffering (v. 10).

VERSE 13

καὶ πάλιν·
Again,

Πάλιν introduces the second OT citation and links it to the first citation (cf. 1:5).

Ἐγὼ ἔσομαι πεποιθὼς ἐπ' αὐτῷ,
I will trust in him.

Ἐγώ in the nom. is emph. (BDAG 275a). Πεποιθώς (nom. sg. masc. of pf. act. ptc. of πείθω, "trust in" [most EVV; BDAG 792a]), is followed by the dat. (indicating the obj. of trust), which is supplemented by ἐπί, also indicating "on the basis of" (BDAG

364d). The ptc. is periph. with ἔσομαι to form a fut. pf. cstr. ("I will have trusted in"). The fut. reflects the tendency of the LXX to render the Heb. impf. as Greek fut. indic. (T 86).

The source of this second OT citation is unclear and may reflect 2 Sam 22:3 (David's hymn of deliverance, cf. Ps 18:3), Isa 12:2, or, most likely, Isa 8:17, where Isaiah expresses confidence in God despite the impending Assyrian assault. Although the citation was likely orig. spoken by Isaiah, the speaker here is Jesus, once again indicating the author's understanding that the Word of God continues to speak, even after its initial inscripturation.

καὶ πάλιν·
And again,

Πάλιν introduces the third OT citation and links it to the first two citations.

Ἰδοὺ ἐγὼ καὶ τὰ παιδία ἅ μοι ἔδωκεν ὁ θεός.
Here I am with the children God gave me.

Ἰδού is a dem. ptcl. "that draws attention to what follows" (BDAG 468b). Although accented differently, it is the aor. mid. impv. of εἶδον, "see" ("here I am" [NET]; "here am I" [NIV]; "behold" [ESV]). Ἐγώ and τὰ παιδία form a compound subj. of an unexpressed vb. Ἅ, whose antecedent is τὰ παιδία, introduces the rel. clause that extends to θεός, which is the subj. of ἔδωκεν (3rd sg. aor. act. indic. of δίδωμι, "gave" [most EVV]; "entrust" [BDAG 242c]). The acc. ἅ functions as the obj. of ἔδωκεν and μοι is the indir. obj. The aor. is global.

This third and final OT citation is from Isa 8:18, which refers to Isaiah's own children, who, together with Isaiah, are signs to Israel of God's faithfulness. Likewise, God's children as Jesus's brothers and sisters are given to him as signs of God's faithfulness. This is the only place in the NT where believers are called Jesus's children.

VERSE 14

ἐπεὶ οὖν τὰ παιδία κεκοινώνηκεν αἵματος καὶ σαρκός,
Now since the children have flesh and blood in common,

Οὖν is an inferential conj.; together with ἐπεί it functions causally to draw conclusions from previous information and to advance the argument further (BDAG 360c). Κεκοινώνηκεν is the 3rd sg. pf. act. indic. of κοινωνέω, "share" (ESV, NASB; BDAG 552b–c); "have" (NIV). The pf. is extensive, emphasizing the pres. condition of the children (Wallace 577). The pl. neut. subj. τὰ παιδία takes a sg. vb. (BDF §133). The gen. (αἵματος and σαρκός) are required by the vb.

Although the usual order is σαρκὸς καὶ αἵματος, the inverted word order is also attested in Eph 6:12, Philo (Lane 1:52 n. *d*), and rabbinic sources (Ellingworth 171). It likely has no significance (Attridge 92). In Hebrews flesh is not associated with the sinful nature as it is in some Pauline epistles. Instead, the full expression refers to the human condition or nature (BDAG 26b; J. Behm, *TDNT* 1:172).

καὶ αὐτὸς παραπλησίως μετέσχεν τῶν αὐτῶν
Jesus also shared in these,

Καί ("also") adds an additional thought (Wallace 671). *Μετέσχεν* is the 3rd sg. aor. act. indic. of *μετέχω*, "share" (BDAG 642; "partook" [ESV, NASB]) and takes a gen. obj. The aor. is constative. *Μετέχω* and *κοινωνέω* are nearly synonymous (cf. NET, REB). The shift from the pf. *κεκοινώνηκεν* to the aor. *μετέσχεν* presents a contrast between the pres. state of the children and Jesus's incarnation viewed in its entirety (see Campbell, *VA* 166–69, 184–211). The adv. *παραπλησίως* ("similarly," "likewise," "in just the same way" [BDAG 770b]; NT hapax), together with the emph. nom. *αὐτός* (BDAG 152c), stresses that Jesus himself shares fully in the children's humanity (cf. John 1:14, Gal 4:4–5). *Αὐτῶν* functions as an identical adj. ("the same" [BDAG 153d]) and refers back to *αἵματος* and *σαρκός*.

ἵνα διὰ τοῦ θανάτου καταργήσῃ τὸν τὸ κράτος ἔχοντα τοῦ θανάτου, τοῦτ' ἔστιν τὸν διάβολον,
so that through his death he might destroy the one holding the power of death—that is, the devil—

Ἵνα followed by the subjunc. forms a purpose clause that indicates one of the goals of Jesus's incarnation, namely, to render the devil powerless. *Καταργήσῃ* is the 3rd sg. aor. act. subjunc. of *καταργέω*, "break the power" (NIV, NLT, REB); "render powerless" (NASB, TCNT); "bring to naught" (ASV, Cassirer); "set aside" (NJB); "dethrone" (Goodspeed); "make powerless, abolish" (BDAG 525). The subj. of both *καταργήσῃ* and *μετέσχεν* is Jesus. The vb. does not indicate Satan's final defeat but rather the nullification of his power to enslave through fear (*pace* "destroy" [ESV, NAB, NET], although this could reflect a proleptic understanding of the vb.). *Διὰ τοῦ θανάτου* adv. modifies *καταργήσῃ*; instr. Jesus's own death is assumed: "through his death he abolished . . ." *Ἔχοντα* is subst., with *τὸ κράτος* (*κράτος*, -*ους*, *τό*, "power" [most EVV], "rule," "sovereignty" [BDAG 565c]) as its obj. The pres. is general, indicating an ongoing state. The gen. *τοῦ θανάτου* modifies *τὸ κράτος*, as a gen. of subord. (Wallace 103). The expression *τοῦτ' ἔστιν* is characteristic in Hebrews (cf. 2:14; 7:5; 9:11; 10:20; 11:16). It is a "fixed expression," such that the neut. is used regardless of the word(s) associated with it (R 705). Here it functions epex., further explaining the subj. of *ἔχοντα*: "that is," *τὸν διάβολον* (*διάβολος*, -*ου*, *ὁ*, "slanderer" [BDAG 226d]). For an interesting suggestion regarding the repeated *t* sounds in this v., see Thomas E. Schmidt, "The Letter Tau as the Cross: Ornament and Content in Hebrews 2,14," *Bib* 76 (1995): 75–84.

VERSE 15

καὶ ἀπαλλάξῃ τούτους, ὅσοι φόβῳ θανάτου διὰ παντὸς τοῦ ζῆν ἔνοχοι ἦσαν δουλείας.
and free those who were held in slavery all their lives by the fear of death.

The subjunc. ἀπαλλάξῃ (3rd sg. aor. act. subjunc. of ἀπαλλάσσω, "free" [most EVV]; "release" [BDAG 96b–c]) continues the ἵνα clause begun in v. 14 and indicates the second purpose for Jesus's incarnation, namely, to free the children. The vb. is used in Philo to indicate manumission (*Spec. Laws* 1:77; Koester 232). Τούτους is the obj. of the vb. and points forward to ὅσοι (BDF §290 [3]). The correl. pron. ὅσοι (ὅσος, -η, -ον, "as many as" [BDAG 729b]) introduces a rel. clause that extends to the end of the v. Its antecedent is τούτους, and by extension, the children of v. 14. Ὅσοι is the subj. of ἦσαν, and ἔνοχοι (nom. pl. masc. of ἔνοχος, "subject to" [ESV, NASB], "held" [NET, NIV], "constrained," with the gen. [BDAG 338d]) is a pred. adj. Δουλείας is the gen. sg. fem. of δουλεία, "slavery, servility" (BDAG 259b).

Διά with the art. inf. τοῦ ζῆν (pres. act. inf. of ζάω, "live" [BDAG 424b–c]) indicates contemp. time (normally indicated by ἐν τῷ + inf.; see Wallace 595 n. 20; BDF §§398, 403) and is unique in the NT ("all their lives" [most EVV]; but "lifelong" [ESV]; "live each day" [CEV]). The dat. φόβῳ indicates the means by which the children have been subject to slavery. Θανάτου is an obj. gen.

The imagery continues the Exodus typology in Hebrews (see *DBI* 253–55; R. E. Watts, *NDBT* 478–87) and draws on the OT depiction of God as warrior (e.g., Isa 42:13; 49:24–26); see For Further Study 20 (The Divine Warrior Motif). Just as with the exodus, the oppressor's defeat and divine deliverance are inextricably joined.

VERSE 16

οὐ γὰρ δήπου ἀγγέλων ἐπιλαμβάνεται ἀλλὰ σπέρματος Ἀβραὰμ ἐπιλαμβάνεται.
For it is clear that he does not reach out to help angels, but to help Abraham's offspring.

The collocation οὐ γὰρ δήπου ἀγγέλων recalls οὐ γὰρ ἀγγέλοις in v. 5, suggesting an *inclusio* (cf. 1:5, 13). The adv. δήπου ("surely" [many EVV]; "it is clear" [NRSV], "of course" [BDAG 223d]; BDF §441 [3]) is a BGk. hapax and "marks an appeal to information shared by the hearers" (Lane 1:52 n. *e*). Ἐπιλαμβάνεται is the 3rd sg. pres. mid. indic. of ἐπιλαμβάνομαι, "take hold, grasp, be concerned about, with" (BDAG 374b–c; G. Delling, *TDNT* 4:9); the vb. takes a gen. obj. The exact mng. of the vb. here, however, is unclear. Some early church fathers (e.g., Chrysostom; see Hughes 115–19; Ellingworth 176–78) suggested that it meant to assume the nature of something or someone. In the LXX (Jeremiah 38 [LXX 31]:32) it means to take hold of, as in leading (e.g., its use in Heb 8:9). Many EVV tr. this vb. as "help" (e.g., ESV, NASB, NIV) or something sim. ("concern . . . for," NET; possibly "took to himself," NJB), perhaps based on a sim. usage in Sir 4:11. The vb. also means "to seize," and it is possible that the author intends this sense here, with the "fear of death" from v. 15 as the understood subj. (see Michael E. Gudorf, "Through a Classical Lens: Hebrews 2:16," *JBL* 119

[2000]: 105–8; followed by J. A. L. Lee, *A History of New Testament Lexicography* [New York: Lang, 2003], 129–36; cf. Lane 1:63). The rep. of ἐπιλαμβάνεται in this v. (untr. in most EVV) intensifies the contrast (cf. BDF §491) between angels and Abraham's seed (σπέρματος). This contrast is also indicated by ἀλλά. The ref. to angels concludes the extended focus on angels in Hebrews; hereafter they are only mentioned in passing (e.g., Heb 12:22; 13:2).

The introduction of Abraham at this point is significant. In the immediate context of Hebrews 2, it suggests that those whom Jesus is leading are the descendants of Abraham. Believers as Abraham's seed also occurs in the Pauline corpus (e.g., Rom 4:1–25; Gal 3:8–9, 29; 4:29–31). The ref. also anticipates the wilderness generation and the land promised to Abraham (Hebrews 3–4).

FOR FURTHER STUDY

18. Perfection in Hebrews (2:10)

Attridge, 83–87.

Delling, G. *TDNT* 8:81–87.

*Hoekema, Anthony A. "Perfection of Christ in Hebrews." *CTJ* 9 (1974): 31–37.

Koester, 122–25.

McCruden, Kevin B. *A Body You Have Prepared for Me: The Spirituality of the Letter to the Hebrews*. Collegeville, MN: Liturgical, 2013.

———. "Christ's Perfection in Hebrews: Divine Beneficence as an Exegetical Key to Hebrews 2:10." *BR* 47 (2002): 40–62.

———. "The Concept of Perfection in the Epistle to the Hebrews." Pages 209–29 in Mason.

*Peterson, David. *Hebrews and Perfection: An Examination of the Concept of Perfection in the 'Epistle to the Hebrews.'* SNTSMS 47. Cambridge: Cambridge University Press, 1982.

Silva, Moises. "Perfection and Eschatology in Hebrews." *WTJ* 39 (1976): 60–71.

Thomas, Gordon J. "The Perfection of Christ and the Perfecting of Believers in Hebrews." Pages 293–310 in *Holiness and Ecclesiology in the New Testament*. Edited by Kent E. Brower and Andy Johnson. Grand Rapids: Eerdmans, 2007.

Wikgren, Allen Paul. "Patterns of Perfection in the Epistle to the Hebrews." *NTS* 6 (1960): 159–67.

19. Ἀρχηγός *(2:10)*

Delling, G. *TDNT* 1:487–88.

Johnston, George. "Christ as *Archegos*." *NTS* 27 (1981): 381–85.

*Scott, J. Julius. "*Archēgos* in the Salvation History of the Epistle to the Hebrews." *JETS* 29 (1986): 47–54.

20. The Divine Warrior Motif (2:10, 14)

Aulén, Gustaf. *Christus Victor: An Historical Study of the Three Main Types of the Idea of Atonement.* Translated by A. G. Hebert. New York: Macmillan, 1969.

Aune, David E. "Heracles and Christ: Heracles Imagery in the Christology of Early Christianity." Pages 3–19 in *Greeks, Romans, and Christians: Essays in Honor of Abraham J Malherbe*. Edited by David L. Balch et al. Minneapolis: Fortress, 1990.

DBI 210–13.

Hiebert, Theodore. *ABD* 6:876–80.

Knox, Wilfred Lawrence. "The 'Divine Hero' Christology in the New Testament." *HTR* 41 (1948): 229–49.

*Longman, Tremper, III. "The Divine Warrior: The New Testament Use of an Old Testament Motif." *WTJ* 44 (1982): 290–307.

Witherington, 145–49.

21. Sanctification in Hebrews (2:11)

Geiger, Stephen. "Exegetical Brief: Hebrews 10:14—Τοὺς αγιαζομένους . . . Justification or Sanctification?" *Wisconsin Lutheran Quarterly* 103 (2006): 281–86.

Hawthorne, Gerald F. *DLNT* 485–89.

Just, Arthur A., Jr. "Entering Holiness: Christology and Eucharist in Hebrews." *CTQ* 69 (2005): 75–95.

Koester, 118–22.

McCown, Wayne G. "Holiness in Hebrews." *Wesleyan Theological Journal* 16/2 (1981): 58–78.

Procksch, O. *TDNT* 111–12.

22. Patronage, Honor, and Shame in Hebrews (2:11)

*deSilva, David A. "Despising Shame: A Cultural-Anthropological Investigation of the Epistle to the Hebrews." *JBL* 113 (1994): 439–61.

*———. *Despising Shame: Honor Discourse and Community Maintenance in the Epistle to the Hebrews. SBLDS* 152. Atlanta: Scholars, 1995.

———. *DNTB* 518–22, 766–71.

———. *The Letter to the Hebrews in Social-Scientific Perspective*. Cascade Companions 15. Eugene, OR: Cascade, 2012.

Moxnes, Halvor. "Honor and Shame." Pages 19–40 in *The Social Sciences and New Testament Interpretation*. Edited by Richard Rohrbaugh. Peabody, MA: Hendrickson, 1996.

*———. "Honor and Shame: A Reader's Guide." *BTB* 23 (1993): 167–76.

Neyrey, Jerome H. "Jesus the Broker in Hebrews: Insights from Social Sciences." Pages 145–70 in Mason.

23. The Devil (2:14–15)

Arnold, C. E. *DLNT* 1077–82.

———. *NDBT* 796–801.

Foerster, W., and G. von Rad. *TDNT* 2:72–81.

Fuller, Daniel P. *ISBE* 4:340–44.

Hamilton, Victor P. *ABD* 5:985–89.

Page, Sydney. *Power of Evil: A Biblical Theology of Satan and Demons*. Grand Rapids: Eerdmans, 1995; esp. pp. 204–7.

24. The People of God and Family Imagery in Hebrews (2:10–16)

Campbell, W. S. *DLNT* 204–19.
DBI 264–67.
Grogan, G. W. "Christ and His People: An Exegetical and Theological Study of Hebrews 2:5–18." *VE* 6 (1969): 54–71.
*———. "The Old Testament Concept of Solidarity in Hebrews." *TynBul* 49 (1998): 159–73.
Hellerman, Joseph H. *Jesus and the People of God: Reconfiguring Ethnic Identity*. Sheffield: Sheffield Phoenix, 2007.
Millar, J. G. *NDBT* 684–87.
Peeler, Amy L. B. *You Are My Son: The Family of God in the Epistle to the Hebrews*. London: T&T Clark, 2014.
Strathmann, H. *TDNT* 4:32–37, 50–57.

See For Further Study 40 (Christ's Incarnation and Humanity)

HOMILETICAL SUGGESTIONS

The Suffering, Solidarity, and Victory of the Son (2:10–16)

1. It was fitting for God to perfect the Son through suffering (v. 10)
   (a) Through whom everything was made (v. 10a)
   (b) For whom everything was made (v. 10b)
   (c) Who leads the sons and daughters to glory (v. 10c)
   (d) Who is the pioneer of their salvation (v. 10d)
2. The solidarity of the Son with humanity (vv. 11–13)
   (a) The one who sanctifies and those who are sanctified are of one source (v. 11a)
   (b) Therefore the Son is not ashamed to call them brothers and sisters (v. 11b)
   (c) Proclaiming them in the midst of the assembly (v. 12)
   (d) The children whom God has given to the Son (v. 13)
3. The victory of the Son over the devil (vv. 14–16)
   (a) The Son shares the same blood and flesh (v. 14a)
   (b) So he rendered powerless the one who enslaves by the fear of death (vv. 14b–15)
   (c) That is why he helps Abraham's descendants—and not angels (v. 16)

God's Plan to Restore Fallen Humanity (2:10–16)

1. Perfect the Son through suffering to lead the sons to glory (v. 10)
2. The Son's solidarity of sons and daughters (vv. 11–13)
3. The Son's incarnation and the nullification of the devil's power (vv. 14–16)

E. THE PERFECTED SON, THE MERCIFUL AND FAITHFUL HIGH PRIEST (2:17–18)

STRUCTURE

The author concludes with two powerful statements that draw an inference (ὅθεν) from the fittingness of Jesus's suffering. The first indic. is followed by two reasons why Jesus had to be like his brothers and sisters, namely, so he could be the fitting high priest. The second indic. presents the practical application of that priesthood.

17 ὅθεν ὤφειλεν κατὰ πάντα τοῖς ἀδελφοῖς ὁμοιωθῆναι,
ἵνα ἐλεήμων γένηται καὶ πιστὸς ἀρχιερεὺς τὰ πρὸς τὸν θεὸν
εἰς τὸ ἱλάσκεσθαι τὰς ἁμαρτίας τοῦ λαοῦ.
18 ἐν ᾧ γὰρ πέπονθεν αὐτὸς πειρασθείς,
δύναται τοῖς πειραζομένοις βοηθῆσαι.

VERSE 17

ὅθεν ὤφειλεν κατὰ πάντα τοῖς ἀδελφοῖς ὁμοιωθῆναι,
Therefore, he had to be like his brothers and sisters in every way,

The inferential conj. ὅθεν ("for which reason" [BDAG 693a]; BDF §451.6) concludes the epistle's first major section (1:5–2:18). The implied subj. of ὤφειλεν (3rd sg. impf. act. indic. of ὀφείλω, "must," "ought" [BDAG 743b–c]; see Ellingworth 180) is Jesus, the main focus of 2:10–16. Ὁμοιωθῆναι (aor. pass. inf. of ὁμοιόω, in pass., "become like" [BDAG 707b]) completes ὤφειλεν and takes a dat. (τοῖς ἀδελφοῖς). Κατὰ πάντα modifies ὁμοιωθῆναι as an acc. of respect, "in every way" (Wallace 204).

Ὤφειλεν introduces the idea of divine necessity—that the fulfillment of God's redemptive purposes necessitated that Jesus become fully like the brothers and sisters. This passage (2:10–18) counters docetic claims that Jesus only appeared to be human, by repeatedly stressing his full humanity. The focus of Hebrews 1 (the Son's divinity) and Hebrews 2 (his humanity) was later affirmed by the Council of Chalcedon in 451: "our Lord Jesus Christ . . . perfect in Godhead and also perfect in manhood; truly God and truly man."

ἵνα ἐλεήμων γένηται καὶ πιστὸς ἀρχιερεὺς τὰ πρὸς τὸν θεόν
so that he could become a merciful and faithful high priest in matters pertaining to God,

The implied subj. of γένηται remains Jesus. Γίνομαι functions as an equative vb. with ἀρχιερεύς (-έως, ὁ, "high priest" [BDAG 139a]; G. Schrenk, *TDNT* 3:265–83; see comments below) as a pred. nom., which is modified by the adjs. ἐλεήμων (nom. sg. masc. of ἐλεήμων, -ον, "merciful" [BDAG 316a]) and πιστός (-ή, -όν, "faithful"). Ἵνα indicates the result of Jesus's having been made like the brothers and sisters—namely, that he might become a merciful and faithful high priest. The expression τὰ πρὸς τὸν θεόν occurs freq. in the LXX in conj. with priestly duties (e.g., Exod 4:16, 18:19). The art. functions as a subst. ("the things"), and the prep. phrase is an acc. of respect: "the things pertaining to God" (so NASB; cf. Wallace 204; "in service to God," NIV).

εἰς τὸ ἱλάσκεσθαι τὰς ἁμαρτίας τοῦ λαοῦ.
to make atonement for the sins of the people.

Εἰς with an art. inf. indicates purpose (Wallace 590–92). Jesus is the subj. of the inf. The obj. of the inf. is τὰς ἁμαρτίας, an acc. of respect (Wallace 204). This gen. is subj. ("the people sin"). The prevalent OT expression "people of God" is significantly applied to those who now follow Jesus. The mng. of ἱλάσκεσθαι (pres. mid. inf. of ἱλάσκομαι, "to propitiate, expiate" [BDAG 474a]; F. Büschel, *TDNT* 3:314–17) is debated. There are three main options:

1. "expiation" (covering or removal of sin); this mng. aligns best with related LXX usage (although this exact expression does not occur in the LXX; see Ellingworth 188–89, and the extended discussion and bibliography in Bruce 78–79 n. 57); so NEB, NJB, RSV, Cassirer;
2. "propitiation" (satisfaction of God's wrath; atonement) (see Leon Morris, *The Apostolic Preaching of the Cross* [London: Tyndale, 1965], esp. 202–5); this view best aligns with the NT understanding of Christ's death; so ESV, NASB;
*3. both; the expression likely indicates the removal of sin (1:3; 9:13–14, 26) and satisfying divine wrath, although this language is not used in Hebrews (but cf. 4:12; 6:8; 10:30; 12:25); the focus in Hebrews, however, is on *removing impurity*, which includes both expiation and propitiation, to secure access to God (see Cockerill 151; cf. Koester 121–22); this idea is captured in "offer a sacrifice that would take away the sins," NLT; "sacrifice himself," CEV; "sacrifice of atonement," NRSV; and more generally as "atonement," NET, NIV.

The expression πιστὸς ἀρχιερεύς alludes to 1 Sam 2:35, where the Lord proclaims that he will raise up a "faithful priest," unlike Eli and (esp.) his sons. The author of Hebrews develops the theme of faithfulness (or unfaithfulness) in 3:1–4:12 and the theme of mercy in 4:15–5:10. Although the introduction of a high priest seems abrupt at this point in the epistle, it was alluded to in the exordium (Heb 1:3). This introduces the major theme of the epistle—Jesus as the perfect high priest (e.g., 3:1; 4:14–15; 5:5, 10; 6:20; 7:26, 28; 8:1, 3; 9:11; 10:21).

VERSE 18

ἐν ᾧ γὰρ πέπονθεν αὐτὸς πειρασθείς,
For since he himself has suffered when he was tempted,

The expression ἐν ᾧ functions causally (= ἐν τούτῳ ὅτι: "for the reason that" = "because" [BDAG 329d]). Together with γάρ, it introduces a dependent clause that further explains Jesus's suffering. The nom. αὐτός is emph. (BDAG 152c). Πέπονθεν is the 3rd sg. pf. act. indic. of πάσχω, "suffer" (BDAG 785a; W. Michaelis, *TDNT* 5:916–18). The pf. indicates result (Wallace 576) or adds prominence ("heighted proximity," Campbell, *VA* 201). Πειρασθείς (nom. sg. masc. of aor. pass. ptc. of πειράζω, "tempt" [BDAG 793a]; H. Seesemann, *TDNT* 6:33–36) is adv., modifying πέπονθεν either temp. ("when tempted"/"when he was tempted"; so ESV, NIV, NJB), instr. ("by being tempted"), or possibly causally ("since He Himself was tempted," NASB). A temp. understanding aligns better with the focus on Jesus's incarnation.

δύναται τοῖς πειραζομένοις βοηθῆσαι.
he is able to help those who are tempted.

Δύναται (3rd sg. pres. mid. indic. of δύναμαι, "to be able") is completed by βοηθῆσαι (aor. act. inf. of βοηθέω, "to render assistance" [BDAG 180c]; F. Büschel, *TDNT* 1:628–29). It takes a dat. obj. Πειραζομένοις (dat. pl. masc. of the pres. pass. ptc. of πειράζω) is subst.

Jesus clearly suffered temptations that were unique to his messianic calling (Bruce 88), yet he can help those who are tempted because he has been sim. tempted (cf. Cockerill 151–52).

FOR FURTHER STUDY

See For Further Study 37 (High Priest in Hebrews)

See For Further Study 42 (The Son's Suffering)

HOMILETICAL SUGGESTIONS

Our Merciful and Faithful High Priest (2:17–18)

1. It was necessary for the Son to become like the children (v. 17a)
    (a) So that he might become a merciful and faithful high priest (v. 17b)
    (b) To make atonement for sin (v. 17c)
2. He is able to help those who are tempted (v. 18b)
    (a) Because he was tempted (v. 18a)

The Personal Ministry of Our High Priest (2:17–18)

1. He is like us in every way (v. 17a)
2. He understands our temptations (v. 18a)
3. He is fully able to help (v. 18b)

III. The Son: His Faithfulness and Mercy (3:1–5:10)

A. THE APOSTLE OF OUR CONFESSION, EVEN MORE FAITHFUL THAN MOSES (3:1–6)

STRUCTURE

Jesus's merciful and faithful priesthood in Heb 2:17 sets the stage for the comp. (*synkrisis*) of Moses's and Jesus's faithfulness in Heb 3:1–6 (see Witherington 163–65). See For Further Study 2 (Ancient Rhetoric in Hebrews). Just as angels have an important, but ultimately inferior, role in God's economy with respect to the Son, the same is true for Moses. Heb 3:1–6 begins a new major section in Hebrews, but there is no consensus as to its boundary. See For Further Study 41 (The Structure of Hebrews).

The arrows indicate the chiastic structure of v. 1. A series of appos. are aligned in v. 2. The spacing in v. 4 aligns par. components. The prot. (ἐάν[περ] . . . κατάσχωμεν) of a cond. is dependent on the apod. (οὗ οἶκός ἐσμεν ἡμεῖς), as indicated by the indention in v. 6. The correl. conjs. μέν and δέ are reflected in the alignment of vv. 5 and 6.

1 Ὅθεν, ἀδελφοὶ ἅγιοι,
κλήσεως ἐπουρανίου μέτοχοι,
κατανοήσατε τὸν ἀπόστολον καὶ ἀρχιερέα τῆς ὁμολογίας ἡμῶν
Ἰησοῦν,
2 πιστὸν ὄντα τῷ ποιήσαντι αὐτὸν
ὡς καὶ Μωϋσῆς ἐν [ὅλῳ] τῷ οἴκῳ αὐτοῦ.
3 πλείονος γὰρ οὗτος δόξης παρὰ Μωϋσῆν ἠξίωται,
καθ᾽ ὅσον πλείονα τιμὴν ἔχει τοῦ οἴκου ὁ κατασκευάσας αὐτόν·
4 πᾶς γὰρ οἶκος κατασκευάζεται ὑπό τινος,
ὁ δὲ πάντα κατασκευάσας θεός.
5 καὶ Μωϋσῆς μὲν πιστὸς ἐν ὅλῳ τῷ οἴκῳ αὐτοῦ
ὡς θεράπων
εἰς μαρτύριον τῶν λαληθησομένων,

6 Χριστὸς δὲ ὡς υἱὸς
ἐπὶ τὸν οἶκον αὐτοῦ·
οὗ οἶκός ἐσμεν ἡμεῖς,
ἐάν[περ] τὴν παρρησίαν καὶ
τὸ καύχημα τῆς ἐλπίδος
κατάσχωμεν.

VERSE 1

Ὅθεν, ἀδελφοὶ ἅγιοι, κλήσεως ἐπουρανίου μέτοχοι,
Therefore, holy brothers and sisters, who share in a heavenly calling,

The conj. ὅθεν ("for which reason"; BDAG 693a; BDF §451[6]) is inferential, drawing on Heb 1:1–2:18 as the basis for considering Jesus. As with previous occurrences, ἀδελφοί should be understood inclusively, "brothers and sisters" (see discussion on 2:10). Here it functions as a hook word that links this section to the preceding one (2:10–18). The subst. is modified by ἅγιοι (ἅγιος, -α, -ον, "holy"), perhaps recalling 2:11. The nom. functions as a voc. (Wallace 56–57; BDF §147). Μέτοχοι is the nom. masc. sg. of μέτοχος, -ου, ὁ, "who share" (ESV, NIV); "partners" (NET, NLT, NRSV); "partakers" (NASB); "sharing/participating in" (BDAG 643c). Μέτοχοι is an appos. to ἀδελφοί and also functions as a voc. (Wallace 48–49). The gen. κλήσεως (κλῆσις, -εως, ἡ, "call, calling"; BDAG 549a) modifies μέτοχοι and is itself modified by ἐπουρανίος (-[ος], -ον, "heavenly"; BDAG 388b; H. Traub, *TDNT* 5:513–35). The gen. phrase is descriptive.

The important word μέτοχοι was first seen in 1:9 in the citation from Psalm 45 concerning the Son's companions. Μέτοχοι can refer to a business partner (e.g., Luke 5:7), but here it indicates that the brothers and sisters, the children (Heb 2:10–18), are actually partners with the Son and share in his heavenly vocation (cf. 3:14, 6:4; cf. 12:8). (The cognate μετέχω occurs in 2:14 in reference to Jesus sharing the blood and flesh of the children.) See Enrique Nardoni, "Partakers in Christ (Hebrews 3:14)," NTS 37 (July 1991): 456–72.

κατανοήσατε τὸν ἀπόστολον καὶ ἀρχιερέα τῆς ὁμολογίας ἡμῶν Ἰησοῦν,
consider Jesus, the apostle and high priest of our confession.

Κατανοήσατε (2nd pl. aor. act. impv. of κατανοέω, "fix your thoughts on" [NIV]; "consider" [ESV, CSB, NASB]; "think carefully about" [NLT; BDAG 522d]; "take note of" [NET]) resumes the necessity of focusing on Jesus (2:9). The obj. of the vb. is Ἰησοῦν, which is placed at the end of the clause for emph. (Cockerill 161; Ellingworth 200). The noun phrase τὸν ἀπόστολον καὶ ἀρχιερέα τῆς ὁμολογίας ἡμῶν is an appos. to Ἰησοῦν. This is the only place in the NT where Jesus is called an ἀπόστολον ("apostle" [most EVV]; but "messenger" [NLT; BDAG 122b]; "Jesus . . . who was sent forth" [Cassirer]). An apostle is sent as an "accredited representative"; although this understanding is not found in contemp. HGk., it is found in later rabbinic writings (Cockerill

159 n. 10). The author may have inferred this role for Jesus from his status as the final word that God sent (1:2), Jesus's proclaiming God's name in the congregation (2:12), and possibly his role as the ἀρχηγός (2:10). Although the title ἀπόστολος is not used for Moses in the LXX, the cognate ἀποστέλλω is used, esp. in Exodus 3. See For Further Study 25 (Jesus, Our Apostle). Although there may be some overlap between the high priest, who was viewed as God's representative, and the function of an apostle, this idea is not developed in Hebrews. The use of ἀρχιερέα (ἀρχιερεύς, -έως, ὁ, "high priest"; see comments on 2:17) functions as a hook word that links this section with its occurrence in 2:17. The single art. to modify both ἀπόστολον and ἀρχιερέα is an example of Granville Sharp's rule (see Wallace 270–90; cf. BDF §276[3]), which indicates that the apostle and high priest are the same person, namely Jesus. This cstr. also indicates "the indivisibility of the two offices" (Lane 1:76). Ὁμολογίας (ὁμολογία, -ας, ἡ, "statement of allegiance," "confession"; BDAG 709b; O. Michel, *TDNT* 5:215–16; cf. 4:14; 10:23) may reflect early creedal statements, such as "Jesus is Lord," and early apostolic teaching about Jesus (so Cockerill 161, following Koester 243), although these two titles do not appear in extant early creedal statements (Lane 1:75). The expression could indicate either a set confession ("our confession" [ESV, NASB]) or the action of confessing (so NET, NIV, NLT). See For Further Study 38 (The Confession of Christ).

The syntax of vv. 1–2 is difficult. Most EVV understand Ἰησοῦν (and its appos.) as the obj. of the impv. with the ptc. in v. 2 further modifying Ἰησοῦν, and thus tr. the ptc. clause either as a rel. clause ("who was faithful"/"who is faithful" [ESV, NEB, NET]) or as beginning a new sentence ("He was faithful" [NASB, NIV, NLT]). Some, however, understand τὸν ἀπόστολον . . . αὐτόν as a content clause: "consider that Jesus, the apostle and high priest of our confession, was faithful . . ." (NRSV; cf. Goodspeed). Although both options are possible, the lack of a conj. (e.g., ὅτι or ἵνα) after κατανοήσατε makes the second option less likely (*pace* Lane 1:71; Koester 243).

VERSE 2

πιστὸν ὄντα τῷ ποιήσαντι αὐτόν
He was faithful to the one who appointed him,

The attrib. ptc. ὄντα modifies Ἰησοῦν in v. 1. Πιστόν ("faithful") functions as a pred. adj. of the ptc.: "Jesus . . . who was faithful" (most EVV). The adj. can have an act. ("faithful") or pass. ("trustworthy") sense; probably both are intended (Cockerill 162 n. 25). Ποιήσαντι (dat. sg. masc. of aor. act. ptc. of ποιέω) is subst. and refers to God; αὐτόν is the obj. of the ptc. Although the phrase τῷ ποιήσαντι αὐτόν occurs in Isa 17:7 and Ps 149:2 ("their maker"/"its maker"), and was used to support the Arian claim that Jesus was created by God (Koester 244), the mng. "appoint" for this verb is well attested (e.g., LXX 1 Sam 12:6; Mark 3:14; Acts 2:36.; BDAG 839c; cf. Cockerill 162 n. 23; Koester 244).

ὡς καὶ Μωϋσῆς ἐν [ὅλῳ] τῷ οἴκῳ αὐτοῦ.
just as Moses was in all God's household.

The conj. ὡς ("as" [BDAG 1104b]) introduces a comp. Καί ("also") functions as a connective, adding an additional thought (Wallace 671). The prep. phrase ἐν τῷ οἴκῳ is locat. The ptc. phrase in the first part of the v. is assumed here, introducing the contrast between Ἰησοῦν and Μωϋσῆς (-έως, ὁ, "Moses") in this section. The var. rdg. is somewhat difficult. The addition of ὅλῳ is well attested, although omitted in early mss. (𝔓[13] 𝔓[46vid] B). It is likely not orig., as the UBS {C} rating suggests. It was probably added in conformity with LXX Num 12:7 or Heb 3:5.

This phrase alludes to Num 12:7, where Moses is praised for being a faithful servant in all God's house. Based on this allusion, αὐτοῦ refers to God. The previous allusion to 1 Sam 2:35 ("I will raise up a faithful priest and build him a faithful house") in 2:17 may also be in view, although there the allusion was to "faithful [high] priest" and here it is to "house." "God's house" in the OT would have been the tent of meeting, or tabernacle (e.g., Exod 23:19; 34:26; 1 Kgs 6:1; 8:20; Ps 27:4).

This is the first occurrence of Moses in Hebrews, although he was implicit in the ref. to the Sinaitic law in Heb 2:2. The author likely understood Moses as one who was sent by God, although the term "apostle" is not used of Moses in the LXX. Additionally, Moses is called a priest in Ps 99:6, so the author may have understood Moses as a type of Christ. Philo often calls Moses a high priest (e.g., *Life of Moses* 2:66–186). It is hard to overestimate the significance of Moses in the OT and Jewish tradition. He alone was able to be in God's presence (Exod 34:29–30; cf. 2 Cor 3:12–18). Later rabbinic traditions claimed that Moses was superior to angels. Extensive speculation on Moses in these traditions may also have informed the author's comp. of Moses and Jesus. Despite Moses's elevated status, however, Jesus is superior. This point can also be inferred from Deut 18:18. See For Further Study 27 (Moses in Hebrews).

VERSE 3

πλείονος γὰρ οὗτος δόξης παρὰ Μωϋσῆν ἠξίωται,
For Jesus is considered worthy of more glory than Moses,

Γάρ further develops the comp. between Moses and Jesus. The referent of the dem. pron. οὗτος is Ἰησοῦν from v. 1 (which is made explicit in many EVV). Οὗτος is the subj. of the vb. ἠξίωται (3rd sg. pf. pass. indic. of ἀξιόω, "consider worthy, deserving" [BDAG 94b]). The pf. used in conj. with Jesus is emph. ("intensified," Campbell, *VA* 201). The pass. likely reflects a divine pass. (Wallace 438 n. 103). The gen. πλείονος (πλείων, -ον, the comp. of πολύς, "more, greater" [BDAG 847a]) modifies δόξης as a gen. of comp. (Wallace 112). Παρά followed by the acc. Μωϋσῆν indicates comp. (Harris 172).

καθ᾽ ὅσον πλείονα τιμὴν ἔχει τοῦ οἴκου ὁ κατασκευάσας αὐτόν·
just as the builder has more honor than the house.

Κατά with the acc. can indicate similarity ("just as"; BDAG 513a; the form καθ' occurs before rough breathing). The subj. of ἔχει is the subst. κατασκευάσας (nom. sg. masc. of the aor. act. ptc. of κατασκευάζω, "the builder" [most EVV; BDAG 527a]). The referent of the ptc. is οὗτος, and by extension Jesus. Τοῦ οἴκου is a gen. of comp. (Wallace 111). The obj. of the vb. is τιμήν (τιμή, -ῆς, ἡ, "honor"). Τιμήν is modified by the comp. πλείονα (from πολύς, -ή, -ύ, "much" [BDAG 847d]), which is modified by the correl. pron., ὅσοι (ὅσος, -η, -ον, "as many as, as much as" [BDAG 729b])—"as much greater honor than." The antecedent for αὐτόν is οἴκῳ in v. 2. Its function here is an intensive marker—"the house itself" (BDAG 152c).

The analogy is as follows: Moses is to Jesus what a house is to its architect. The implication that Moses was worthy of glory and honor underscores Moses's esteemed position. The combination of glory and honor recalls 2:9 (cf. 1:3).

VERSE 4

πᾶς γὰρ οἶκος κατασκευάζεται ὑπό τινος,
Now every house is built by someone,

Γάρ further develops the argument and is not a parenthetical comment (*pace* ESV). Πᾶς modifies οἶκος, which is the subj. κατασκευάζεται (3rd sg. pres. pass. indic. of κατασκευάζω; see v. 3). The agent of the pass. vb. is indicated by ὑπό (Wallace 389) and the subst. indef. pron. τίνος ("someone"). The pres. is gnomic (Wallace 523–25).

ὁ δὲ πάντα κατασκευάσας θεός.
but the one who built everything is God.

The subj. is the art. subst. κατασκευάσας (nom. sg. masc. of the aor. act. ptc. of κατασκευάζω; see v. 3). Θεός functions as the pred. nom., with an equative vb. (e.g., εἰμί) understood. In pred. nom. cstr., the art. subst. is the subj. (Wallace 43). Δέ indicates contrast (BDAG 213c). This clause extends the proverbial content of the first clause in v. 4 by adding a cosmic (and possibly eschatological) development with the ref. to πάντα (cf. 1:3). Taken together, v. 3 and v. 4 imply that Jesus is God (*pace* Attridge 110; Ellingworth 206). This extension to the cosmic realm underscores Christ's glory and honor.

VERSE 5

καὶ Μωϋσῆς μὲν πιστὸς ἐν ὅλῳ τῷ οἴκῳ αὐτοῦ
Moses was faithful as a servant in all God's household,

The correl. μέν anticipates the δέ in v. 6 to indicate a contrast (BDAG 629d). Καί functions as a connective, adding an additional thought (Wallace 671). The nom. πιστός (-ή, -όν, "faithful") functions as a pred. adj. with an equative vb. (e.g., εἰμί) understood. The prep. phrase ἐν ὅλῳ τῷ οἴκῳ αὐτοῦ is repeated from the allusion to Num 12:7 in v. 2.

ὡς θεράπων εἰς μαρτύριον τῶν λαληθησομένων,
as a testimony to what would be said in the future.

The conj. ὡς ("as" [BDAG 1104b]) introduces a comp. The term θεράπων (nom. sg. masc. of θεράπων, -οντος, ὁ, "attendant," "aide," "servant," in a cultic setting [BDAG 453c; NT hapax]) is honorific, indicating Moses's elevated status as one who was intimately in God's presence (e.g., Exod 14:31; Deut 3:24). Although many EVV have "servant," "steward" may more accurately reflect the status of θεράπων (see Cockerill 167–68). The term is used for priestly service in the LXX and STL, thus strengthening a possible cultic connection here. Εἰς indicates purpose (Wallace 369) and further specifies Moses's role in terms of offering testimony (μαρτύριος, -ου, τό, "testimony" [CSB], "proof" [BDAG 619b]). Λαληθησομένων (gen. pl. neut. of fut. pass. ptc. of λαλέω, "speak," "say") is subst. Both the fut. pass. and the fut. ptc. (12x) are rare in NTGk. This is the only fut. pass. ptc. in the NT (see BDF §351[2]); thus, the unusual form was deliberately chosen by the author, likely to emphasize that what was spoken through Moses were adumbrations of truths that would later be fully revealed in Christ. The gen. indicates the content (BDF §167) of Moses's testimony, namely, things that would be spoken in a time future to Moses. This suggests a prophetic role for Moses (obscured in the NLT: "his work was an illustration of the truths God would reveal later"). The use of λαλέω continues the focus on God speaking in Hebrews. The claim that Moses was a witness to things that were spoken about Jesus further indicates his subservient role to Jesus. (See James Swetnam, "Τῶν λαληθησομένων in Hebrews 3,5," *Bib* 90 [2009]: 93–100; cf. Heb 11:23–28.)

VERSE 6

Χριστὸς δὲ ὡς υἱὸς ἐπὶ τὸν οἶκον αὐτοῦ·
But Christ was faithful as a Son over his household.

This clause is the second part of the correl. cstr. (with μέν in v. 5) and continues the contrast between the servant Moses and the Son, who is called Χριστός for the first time in Hebrews. The placement of Χριστός at the beginning of the v. is emph. (Ellingworth 208). The anar. subst. υἱός has a qual. force (Z §171; Wallace 245); see comments on 1:2. This contrast is further developed by means of ἐπί ("over" [BDAG 365d]). Whereas Moses is a servant *in* God's house, Christ is the Son *over* God's house.

The contrast of servant to son also draws on the inheritance motif that began in 1:2 with the declaration that the Son is the heir of all things. In Roman law, only a son could inherit the father's property (Koester 247). Yet belonging to an honorable household was a source of honor and often authority for a slave (Koester 253). The author's point is not to denigrate Moses, but rather to emphasize the superior role and status of Christ in comparison to the highly esteemed role and status of Moses.

οὗ οἶκός ἐσμεν ἡμεῖς
And we are that household

The antecedent of the rel. pron. οὗ is αὐτοῦ, e.g., God. The gen. indicates poss. The nom. ἡμεῖς is emph. (BDAG 275a). Οἶκος is a pred. nom. The rel. clause makes explicit the identity of God's house as the people of God. This dual understanding of οἶκος (people and structure) reflects the fact that an οἶκος was often an independent economic unit headed by a *pater familias* ("head of household"). See For Further Study 26 (God's House).

ἐάν[περ] τὴν παρρησίαν καὶ τὸ καύχημα τῆς ἐλπίδος κατάσχωμεν.
if we hold on to our confidence and the hope in which we boast.

The conj. ἐάν[περ] introduces the prot. of a general cond. (BDF §§371[1], 454[2]), also known as a third-class cond. (see Wallace 696–99). Although the shorter form, ἐάν, occurs in some important early mss. (𝔓[13] א[1] B D*), ἐάνπερ occurs in other early mss. (𝔓[46] א[2] A C D[2]). The lengthened form ἐάνπερ likely reflects the influence of 3:14. There is no significant difference between ἐάν ("if") and ἐάνπερ ("if indeed," "if only" [BDAG 268a]). The apod. is οὗ οἶκός ἐσμεν ἡμεῖς. Together with the sim. cstr. in 3:14, these cond. are debated by Reformed/Calvinists or Wesleyan/Arminians. The former group usually understands the prot. as the *evidence* of an *inference* that is indicated in the apod. The latter group often argues that the prot. is the *cause* and the apod. is the *effect* (Wallace 682–84) (see esp. the discussion of this v. and 3:14 in Herbert W. Bateman IV, ed., *Four Views on the Warning Passages in Hebrews* [Grand Rapids: Kregel, 2007]).

The hort. subjunc. κατάσχωμεν (1st pl. aor. act. subjunc. of κατέχω, "hold to, hold fast" [BDAG 533a; H. Hanse, *TDNT* 2:829–30]) recalls the impv. in v. 1 and brackets the contrast between Moses and Jesus. The pl. is inclusive (the author and the audience) and urges perseverance. The section is also framed by the use of Jesus (v. 1) and Christ (v. 6; Cockerill 167). The objs. of the vb. are παρρησίαν (παρρησία, -ας, ἡ, "courage, confidence, boldness, fearlessness" [BDAG 781d]) and καύχημα (καύχημα, -τος, τό, "boast" [BDAG 537a]). The gen. ἐλπίδος is obj., modifying καύχημα. The idea of boldness is prevalent in Hebrews (3:6; 4:16; 10:19, 35) and essentially means access to God grounded in Christ's saving work. See For Further Study 28 (Boldness/Confidence in Hebrews). Hope is another distinctive theme in Hebrews (e.g., Heb 6:18; 7:19; 10:23; 11:1). It is viewed as an obj. reality (e.g., 6:19), which is obscured in some EVV ("we . . . don't lose hope" [CEV]; "we . . . keep our hope high" [REB]).

The v. continues the emph. in Hebrews on persevering faith, introduced in Heb 2:1–4, and grounds the upcoming citation from Psalm 95 and its exposition with regard to the faithlessness of the wilderness generation. Salvation in Hebrews is understood comprehensively, both as a pres. affirmation (6:9) and a fut. consummation (1:14; cf. 12:22–24). See For Further Study 11 (Salvation in Hebrews).

FOR FURTHER STUDY

25. Jesus, Our Apostle (3:1)

Betz, Hans Dieter. *ABD* 1:309–11.
Kruse, C. G. *DLNT* 76–82.
Lane, 1:75–76.
Rengtorf, K. H. *TDNT* 1:407–24; 443–45.
Swetnam, James. "Ὁ ἀπόστολος in Hebrews 3,1." *Bib* 89 (2008): 252–62.

26. God's House (3:2)

Carter, Warren. *NIDB* 2:585–86.
Layton, Scott C. "Christ over His House (Hebrew 3:6) and Hebrew *'shr 'l-hbyt.*" *NTS* 37 (1991): 473–77.
McCartney, D. G. *DLNT* 507–11.
Michel, O. *TDNT* 5:125–28.

27. Moses in Hebrews (3:2–6)

Allison, D. C., Jr. *DLNT* 777–82.
D'Angelo, Mary Rose. *Moses in the Letter to the Hebrews. SBLDS* 42. Missoula, MT: Scholars, 1979.
Gillman, Florence Morgan. *ABD* 4:918–20.
Hay, David M. "Moses through New Testament Spectacles." *Int* 44 (1990): 240–52.
Hughes, P. E. *NDBT* 668–73.
Jeremias, J. *TDNT* 4:848–73.
*Jones, Peter Rhea. "The Figure of Moses as a Heuristic Device for Understanding the Pastoral Intent of Hebrews." *RevExp* 76 (1979): 95–107.
Lane, 1:*cxxviii*.
Lierman, John. *The New Testament Moses: Christian Perceptions of Moses and Israel in the Setting of Jewish Religion*. Tübingen: Mohr Siebeck, 2004.
MacDonald, Nathan. "By Faith Moses." Pages 274–82 in Bauckham, *Theology*.
Olson, Dennis. *NIDB* 4:151–52.
*Scott, Brett R. "Jesus' Superiority over Moses in Hebrews 3:1–6." *BSac* 155 (1998): 201–10.

28. Boldness/Confidence in Hebrews (3:6)

Hay, David. *NIDB* 1:486.
*Marrow, Stanley B. "*Parrhēsia* and the New Testament." *CBQ* (1982): 431–46.
Mitchell, Alan C. "Holding On to Confidence: *Parrēsia* in Hebrews." Pages 203–26 in *Friendship, Flattery, and Frankness of Speech: Studies on Friendship in the New Testament World*. Edited by John T. Fitzgerald. Leiden: Brill, 1996.
Schlier, H. *TDNT* 5:875–84.
Trites, Allison Albert. *NIDB* 1:716.
Vorster, Willem S. "The Meaning of *Parrēsia* in the Epistle to the Hebrews." *Ad Hebraeos: Essays on the Epistle to the Hebrews* (1971): 51–59.

HOMILETICAL SUGGESTIONS

Hold On and Consider Jesus! (3:1–6)

1. We share in his heavenly calling (v. 1a)
2. He is our apostle sent by God (v. 1b)
3. He is the one whom we confess (v. 1c)
4. He is faithful to his divine appointment (v. 2a)
5. He is worthy of greater glory than (even) Moses (v. 3)
6. He is the Son over God's house (v. 6a)
7. Therefore, we hold on to our confidence and hope! (v. 6b)

Jesus and Moses (3:2–6)

1. Both are faithful to God's call (v. 2)
2. Jesus, however, is more worthy of glory . . .
   (a) . . . as the builder is greater than the house (v. 3)
   (b) . . . as the Son is greater than the servant (vv. 5–6)

B. SECOND WARNING: LISTEN TO GOD'S VOICE WHILE IT IS STILL POSSIBLE (3:7–19)

1. The Lesson of the Wilderness Generation from Psalm 95 (3:7–11)

STRUCTURE

The passage is structured by two occurrences of διό (vv. 7 and 10). The adv. οὗ ("where") in v. 9 refers to ἐρήμῳ in v. 8 (as indicated by the arrow). The prot. of the cond. in v. 7 is indented with respect to the apod., which extends from v. 8 to v. 10a. Heb 3:7–11 is an extended quote from Ps 95:7–11 (LXX 94:7–11), followed by a midrashic exposition of the citation in 3:12–19 that draws out its contemp. application for the audience of Hebrews. Psalm 95 breaks into two parts: vv. 1–7a contain a call to worship God, based on the greatness of his creation; vv. 7b–11 warn against disobeying God, drawing on the example of the faithless wilderness generation. The liturgical use of Psalm 95 is well attested in both Jewish and Christian settings. It is likely that the audience was familiar with the entire psalm, even though only the second half is cited. Heb 3:7–4:13 presents the second "warning passage" in Hebrews. See For Further Study 12 (The Warning Passages in Hebrews).

7 Διό, καθὼς λέγει τὸ πνεῦμα τὸ ἅγιον·
σήμερον ἐὰν τῆς φωνῆς αὐτοῦ ἀκούσητε,
8 μὴ σκληρύνητε τὰς καρδίας ὑμῶν
ὡς ἐν τῷ παραπικρασμῷ
κατὰ τὴν ἡμέραν τοῦ πειρασμοῦ
→ ἐν τῇ ἐρήμῳ,
9 οὗ ἐπείρασαν οἱ πατέρες ὑμῶν ἐν δοκιμασίᾳ
καὶ εἶδον τὰ ἔργα μου
10 τεσσεράκοντα ἔτη·
διὸ προσώχθισα τῇ γενεᾷ ταύτῃ
καὶ εἶπον·
ἀεὶ πλανῶνται τῇ καρδίᾳ,
αὐτοὶ δὲ οὐκ ἔγνωσαν τὰς ὁδούς μου,
11 ὡς ὤμοσα ἐν τῇ ὀργῇ μου·
εἰ εἰσελεύσονται
εἰς τὴν κατάπαυσίν μου.

VERSE 7

Διό, καθὼς λέγει τὸ πνεῦμα τὸ ἅγιον
Therefore, as the Holy Spirit says:

Διό is an inferential conj. (BDAG 250c) that draws on both the previous exposition in 3:1–6 and the exhortation in v. 6, and points forward to the impv. in v. 8, thereby linking the citation from Psalm 95 in 3:7–11 to 3:1–6 (see BDF §451[5]). The psalm citation enables the author to contrast the positive example of Moses with the neg. example of the wilderness generation. The adv. καθώς (BDAG 493d) modifies λέγει, which introduces the citation from Ps 95:7–11. The adj. ἅγιον is attrib., modifying πνεῦμα. The subj. of the vb. is τὸ πνεῦμα τὸ ἅγιον and is the second ref. to the Spirit in Hebrews (cf. 2:4); the art. may be anaphoric (Wallace 217–20). Although pneumatology does not factor extensively in Hebrews, the ref. to the Spirit speaking coheres with the overall emphasis on God speaking throughout the epistle. Πνεῦμα as a neut. subst. does not suggest that the Spirit is impers. (cf. the grammatical gender of παιδίον, "young child," is neut. but refers to either a boy or girl). The attribution of God's Word to the Spirit, previously attributed to God (e.g., 1:5) and the Son (e.g., 2:12), suggests implicit trinitarian thought (cf. Witherington 171). See For Further Study 13 (Pneumatology in Hebrews).

Σήμερον ἐὰν τῆς φωνῆς αὐτοῦ ἀκούσητε,
Today, if you hear his voice,

'Εάν introduces the prot. of a general cond. (BDF §371[1]), or third-class cond. The conj. in this v. recalls its occurrence in 3:6. This cond. makes no assumption as to the facticity of the prot., but simply posits a hypothetical situation (see esp. Wallace 680–712). 'Εάν is usually followed by an aor. subjunc., here ἀκούσητε, which takes a gen. obj., φωνῆς ("voice"). The context implies that the antecedent of αὐτοῦ is God.

The opening adv. σήμερον ("today") originally addressed the psalmist's audience. Yet the psalm reflects back on the wilderness generation, specifically the events recorded in Exodus 17 and Numbers 14, 20. Scripture does not record the occasion on which God spoke the exact words quoted in Ps 95:7b–11, but they "effectively embody the substance of what He said again and again" (H. C. Leupold, *Exposition of the Psalms* [Grand Rapids: Baker, 1959], 678). Moreover, σήμερον "highlights the contemporary relevance of the text" for the epistle's audience (Attridge 114). Koester notes the importance of hearing and σήμερον in Deuteronomy (esp. 5:3; Koester 255). Σήμερον is important in Hebrews (cf. 3:14, 4:7–8).

VERSE 8

μὴ σκληρύνητε τὰς καρδίας ὑμῶν
do not harden your hearts

Verses 8–10a comprise the apod. of the cond. begun in 3:7. Σκληρύνητε is the 2nd pl. pres. act. subjunc. of σκληρύνω, "harden" (most EVV; BDAG 930c). Μή renders this a prohibitive subjunc. (BDF §365). Older grammars claimed that aor. prohibitions meant "do not start [an action]," whereas pres. prohibitions indicated "stop doing [an action]." This view has been soundly challenged (see Wallace 714–17 [esp. 717 n. 15]; and Kenneth L. McKay, "Aspect in Imperatival Constructions in New Testament

Greek," *NovT* [1985]: 201–26). Instead, the aor. prohibits the actions as a whole. Τὰς καρδίας (J. Behm, *TDNT* 3:611–13) ὑμῶν is the obj. of the vb.

ὡς ἐν τῷ παραπικρασμῷ
as in the rebellion,

The conj. ὡς ("as" [BDAG 1104b]) introduces the comp. between the orig. audience of the psalm (and by extension the epistle's audience) and the wilderness generation, who are implied throughout the rest of the psalm. Ἐν τῷ παραπικρασμῷ (dat. sg. masc. of παραπικρασμός, -οῦ, ὁ, "rebellion" [most EVV], "revolt" [BDAG 770a]) assumes the previous clause; e.g., "*as the wilderness generation hardened their hearts* in the rebellion." Rather than transliterate the Heb. place name Meribah (*mĕrîbâ*), the LXX trs. rendered the name in terms of what took place on the location, namely, "rebellion" (Exod 17:7; cf. Num 14:1–23; 20:2–5). This tr., however, follows the etym. of the Heb. orig., which was the name Moses gave the place due to the people's rebellion.

κατὰ τὴν ἡμέραν τοῦ πειρασμοῦ ἐν τῇ ἐρήμῳ,
on the day of testing in the wilderness,

Κατά is temp. ("on," "at," "during" [BDAG 512a]). Ἡμέρα can either indicate a specific day (BDAG 436d) or an extended season ("during the time" [BDAG 438b]). As with παραπικρασμῷ, the LXX trs. rendered the Heb. place name Massah (*massâ*) in terms of what took place at the location, namely, πειρασμοῦ (gen. sg. masc. of πειρασμός, -οῦ, ὁ, "testing" [BDAG 793c]; Exod 17:7; cf. Num 14:1–23; 20:2–5). This tr. also follows the etym. of the Heb. orig., when Moses named the location based on the people's testing. The adj. ἐν τῇ ἐρήμῳ modifying ἡμέραν is locat.

The wilderness generation's rebellion at Kadesh-Barnea "[w]as the quintessential example of disobedience" (Cockerill 174; see Lane 1:85 for extensive refs. in the OT, later Jewish writings, and the NT).

VERSE 9

οὗ ἐπείρασαν οἱ πατέρες ὑμῶν ἐν δοκιμασίᾳ
where your fathers tested me, tried me,

The adv. οὗ ("where") introduces a locat. adv. clause (Wallace 664), referring back to the place of rebellion and testing in v. 8. This v. continues the apod. begun in v. 8. The subj. of ἐπείρασαν (3rd pl. aor. act. indic. of πειράζω, "test," "try" [BDAG 793a]) is οἱ πατέρες. The gen. ὑμῶν indicates poss. Ἐν δοκιμασίᾳ (dat. sg. fem. of δοκιμασία, -ας, ἡ, "testing," "examination" [BDAG 256a; BGk. hapax]) is adv. and modifies ἐπείρασαν indicating means (or possibly temp.).

The LXX reads ἐδοκίμασαν, indicating that the fathers tested God. The author of Hebrews adapted the LXX text to support his argument (so Guthrie, "Hebrews" 954b–c; cf. Attridge 23; Ellingworth 218) by changing ἐδοκίμασαν to ἐν δοκιμασίᾳ—either to smooth out the anacoluthon of the LXX (οὗ ἐπείρασαν οἱ πατέρες ὑμῶν ἐδοκίμασαν) or (more likely) to underscore the culpability of the wilderness generation. Implicit within δοκιμασίᾳ is the idea of testing something for its genuineness ("put me to the test" [ESV, NJB]). Thus the wilderness generation ("the fathers") "tested" God "by testing" to see if God was genuine. The phrase ἐν δοκιμασίᾳ feels redundant in Eng. and is left untr. in some EVV (e.g., ESV) or tr. as an indic. "and tried me" (e.g., NET, NIV; NLT: "and tried my patience"); other EVV apparently follow the Heb. text, "tested me, tried me" (CSB). The var. rdg. ἐδοκίμασαν με, although supported by early mss., attempts to conform the text of Heb to the LXX.

καὶ εἶδον τὰ ἔργα μου
and saw my works

Καί here indicates something that is "unexpected" or "noteworthy" ("even though" [Cassirer], "and in spite of that" [BDAG 495b; a contrastive conj., Wallace 297; cf. Lane 1:82 n. *c*; Ellingworth 220]). The unexpressed subj. of εἶδον (3rd pl. aor. act. indic. of ὁράω, "see") is οἱ πατέρες. The obj. of the vb. is ἔργα, which included God's miraculous actions during the exodus and following, such as providing manna and water (e.g., Exodus 16–17). The exodus, however, also involved judgment on Egypt, so God's works also include his judgment (Num 16:1–50).

VERSE 10

τεσσεράκοντα ἔτη·
for forty years.

The cardinal τεσσεράκοντα ("forty") modifies ἔτη (ἔτος, -ους, τό, "year"). This phrase modifies εἶδον in v. 9 as an acc. of extent. This phrase marks the end of the apod. of the cond. begun in v. 7.

διὸ προσώχθισα τῇ γενεᾷ ταύτῃ
Therefore I was provoked to anger with that generation

As in v. 7, διό is a inferential conj. (BDAG 250c) that both draws on the cond. in 3:7–10a and points forward to the rest of the psalm citation in 3:10b–11. The subj. switches from the "fathers" in the previous v. to God in this v. Προσώχθισα is the 1st sg. aor. act. indic. of προσοχθίζω, "be angry" (NASB, NIV), "provoked" (ESV, NET), "incensed" (REB), "offended" (BDAG 884a; it occurs only here and in v. 17 in the NT). This vb. takes a dat. obj., τῇ γενεᾷ (γενέα, -ᾶς, ἡ, "generation" [most EVV; BDAG 192a]). The dem. ταύτῃ modifies γενεᾷ in the pred. position.

As with v. 9, the author altered the LXX text (so Attridge 115; Lane 1:88–89; Cockerill 179) by inserting διό between τεσσεράκοντα ἔτη and προσώχθισα. This has the effect of making τεσσεράκοντα ἔτη modify εἶδον, not προσώχθισα, as it does in the LXX. This alteration focuses on the forty years that the wilderness generation had to observe God's works (and faithfulness) rather than the forty years of God's anger (because of the wilderness generation's faithlessness). (Note that the author quotes this same v. in conformity with the LXX in 3:17.)

This alteration raises the question whether the author understood the forty years as a time of judgment or blessing. Although Num 14:33–34 clearly portrays the forty years as judgment, other texts focus on God's gracious provision during this time (e.g., Num 14:11, 22; Deut 2:7; Hos 2:14–15). Some suggest successive forty-year periods are in view (Attridge 115; 120 n. 95; Lane 1:89), although more probably the same period is viewed from two perspectives (cf. Ellingworth 232). The focus in Hebrews 3, however, is on judgment. An additional alteration of the LXX text is the switch of the far dem. adj. (ἐκείνῃ) to the near one (ταύτῃ). This anticipates the author's application of the psalm to his own audience in 3:12–19. The rest of the psalm citation conforms to the LXX.

καὶ εἶπον, Ἀεὶ πλανῶνται τῇ καρδίᾳ,
and said, "They always go astray in their hearts,"

The subj. of εἶπον is God, which is followed by dir. discourse. Although previous occurrences of λέγω to introduce dir. discourse have used the pres. tense (2:5, 12), the aor. in 3:10 reflects the LXX. Ἀεί is an adv. ("always" [most EVV] "continually," "constantly" [BDAG 22c]) modifying πλανῶνται (3rd pl. pres. pass. indic. of πλανάω, "go astray" [most EVV], "wander" [NET], "turn away from [NLT], "be misled" [BDAG 821d; the pass. of this vb. freq. has an act. sense]). Καρδίᾳ is a dat. of ref. (Wallace 144–46).

αὐτοὶ δὲ οὐκ ἔγνωσαν τὰς ὁδούς μου,
"and they have not known my ways."

Δέ connects closely related items (BDAG 213b), perhaps reflecting the Heb. par. The nom. of αὐτοί is emph. (BDF §277). Ἔγνωσαν (3rd pl. aor. act. indic. of γινώσκω) is modified by the neg. adv. οὐ (οὐκ before a vowel). The aor. is global. Τὰς ὁδούς μου is the obj. of the vb. God's ways indicate either how he acts (e.g., Ps 145:17) or how he expects his people to act (e.g., Ps 81:13). Here the former is intended.

VERSE 11

ὡς ὤμοσα ἐν τῇ ὀργῇ μου·
So I swore in my anger,

Ὡς is a "marker of result in connection with indication of purpose" and functions par. to ὥστε "so that" (BDAG 1105c). The subj. of ὤμοσα (1st sg. aor. act. indic. of ὀμνύω, "swear" [most EVV]; "take an oath" [BDAG 706c]) is God. The adv. prep. phrase ἐν τῇ ὀργῇ modifies the vb. temp. ("during") or *causally ("because of"). Num 14:21–22 is the likely ref. for God's oath quoted in Ps 95:11.

Εἰ εἰσελεύσονται εἰς τὴν κατάπαυσίν μου.
"They will not enter my rest."

Although εἰ often introduces an apod. of a cond., here it is a "marker of a strong or solemn assertion, without apodosis" (BDAG 278a), which reflects the LXX attempt to render the Heb. ptcl. *ʾim* ("if"). Followed by a vb., it "expresses rigorous denial" (Moule 179) or an oath (BDF §372[4], §454[5])—"they will never enter." Εἰσελεύσονται is the 3rd pl. fut. mid. indic. of εἰσέρχομαι, "enter" (most EVV [BDAG 294c]). As is common with compound vbs., the prep. is repeated after the vb. (R 559). The adv. prep. phrase is locat. The obj. of the prep. is κατάπαυσιν (κατάπαυσις, -εως, ἡ, "rest" [most EVV; BDAG 524a]).

This v. introduces the important concept of rest in Heb. The LXX trs. used κατάπαυσις to render two Heb. roots used in conj. with the idea of rest. The first root *nûaḥ* has the idea of being still or settling down and is freq. associated with God settling his people in the land (e.g., Deut 3:20), where they had security from their enemies (Josh 21:44; 1 Kgs 8:56). Rest is also associated with the dwelling place of God (Num 10:33–36; Ps 132:13–14). The second Heb. root *šābat* means "to end" or "to cease," and is freq. used with the Sabbath commandment (Exod 20:8–11; Deut 5:12–15). The author exploits both aspects of rest in his appropriation of Gen 2:2 in Hebrews 4. See For Further Study 33 (The Promised Rest and Land Typology in Hebrews). In the orig. context of Psalm 95, "my rest" suggests the land. The fact that Psalm 95, however, was written after the conquest and occupation of the land suggests that the concept of rest for the author of Hebrews extends beyond the land—a point that he will make explicit in Hebrews 4.

FOR FURTHER STUDY

29. The Text of the OT (the Septuagint) and Hebrews (3:7–11)

Bruce, F. F. "Textual Problems in the Epistle to the Hebrews." Pages 27–39 in *Scribes and Scripture: New Testament Essays in Honor of J. Harold Greenlee*. Edited by David Alan Black. Winona Lake, IN: Eisenbrauns, 1992.

Cadwallader, Alan H. "The Correction of the Text of Hebrews towards the LXX." *NovT* 34 (1992): 257–92.

Gheorghita, Radu. *The Role of the Septuagint in Hebrews*. WUNT 2/160. Tübingen: Mohr Siebeck, 2003.

McCullough, J. C. "The Old Testament Quotations in Hebrews," *NTS* 26 (1979–80): 378–79.

Thomas, Kenneth J. "The Old Testament Citations in Hebrews." *NTS* 11 (1965): 303–25.

30. Psalm 95 in Hebrews (3:7–11)

Enns, Peter. "Creation and Re-Creation: Psalm 95 and Its Interpretation in Hebrews 3:1–4:13." *WTJ* 55 (1993): 255–80.

———. "The Interpretation of Psalm 95 in Hebrews 3:1–4:13." Pages 352–63 in *Early Christian Interpretation of the Scriptures of Israel: Investigations and Proposals*. Edited by Craig A. Evans and James A. Sanders. *JSNTSup* 148. Sheffield: Sheffield Academic Press, 1997.

Healy, Mary. "Spiritual Interpretation in the Letter to the Hebrews." *Crux* 48/2 (2012): 28–36.

HOMILETICAL SUGGESTIONS

A Lesson from Psalm 95 (3:7–11)

1. The Stern Exhortation (vv. 7–8a)
2. The Negative Example (vv. 8b–9)
3. The Dire Consequences (vv. 10–11)

Hearing Today the Lessons from the Past (3:7–11)

1. Make every effort to hear God's word *today* (v. 7)
2. Do not be like those who formerly heard but . . .
   (a) . . . who hardened their hearts (v. 8a)
   (b) . . . who rebelled (v. 8b)
   (c) . . . who tested God (vv. 8c, 9a)
   (d) . . . who saw God's works and refused to believe (v. 9b)
3. Learn from the consequences of their sin
   (a) They were held accountable for refusing to believe (v. 10)
   (b) They missed out on God's promise (v. 11)

2. The Psalm Applied to the Epistle's Audience (3:12–19)

STRUCTURE

Hebrews 3:7–11 presents an extended quote from Ps 95:7–11 (LXX 94:7–11), which is followed by a midrashic exposition of the psalm citation in 3:12–19 that draws out the contemp. application for the audience of Hebrews. This section begins with two impv. (βλέπετε in v. 12 and παρακαλεῖτε in v. 13). The ἵνα clause gives the purpose for the impv. in v. 13 as indicated by the large arrow. The prot. of a cond. is dependent on the apod., as indicated by the indention in v. 14. The art. inf. in v. 15 introduces the psalm citation, which is followed by a series of rhetorical questions in vv. 16–19.

The author further interprets and develops the theme of rest in Heb 4:1–11. Taken together, 3:12–4:11 is another example of an *a fortiori* argument that argues from the lesser (if judgment for the wilderness generation resulted in their exclusion from the land) to the greater (how much worse will judgment be for this current generation if they fail to reach their destination).

12 Βλέπετε, ἀδελφοί, μήποτε ἔσται ἔν τινι ὑμῶν καρδία πονηρὰ ἀπιστίας
ἐν τῷ ἀποστῆναι ἀπὸ θεοῦ ζῶντος,
13 ἀλλὰ παρακαλεῖτε ἑαυτοὺς
καθ᾿ ἑκάστην ἡμέραν,
ἄχρις οὗ τὸ σήμερον καλεῖται,
ἵνα μὴ σκληρυνθῇ τις ἐξ ὑμῶν ἀπάτῃ τῆς ἁμαρτίας—
14 μέτοχοι γὰρ τοῦ Χριστοῦ γεγόναμεν,
ἐάνπερ τὴν ἀρχὴν τῆς ὑποστάσεως μέχρι τέλους βεβαίαν κατάσχωμεν—
15 ἐν τῷ λέγεσθαι·
σήμερον ἐὰν τῆς φωνῆς αὐτοῦ ἀκούσητε,
μὴ σκληρύνητε τὰς καρδίας ὑμῶν
ὡς ἐν τῷ παραπικρασμῷ.
16 τίνες γὰρ ἀκούσαντες παρεπίκραναν;
ἀλλ᾿ οὐ πάντες οἱ ἐξελθόντες
ἐξ Αἰγύπτου
διὰ Μωϋσέως;
17 τίσιν δὲ προσώχθισεν τεσσεράκοντα ἔτη;
οὐχὶ τοῖς ἁμαρτήσασιν,
ὧν τὰ κῶλα ἔπεσεν
ἐν τῇ ἐρήμῳ;
18 τίσιν δὲ ὤμοσεν μὴ εἰσελεύσεσθαι
εἰς τὴν κατάπαυσιν αὐτοῦ
εἰ μὴ τοῖς ἀπειθήσασιν;
19 καὶ βλέπομεν
ὅτι οὐκ ἠδυνήθησαν εἰσελθεῖν
δι᾿ ἀπιστίαν.

VERSE 12

Βλέπετε, ἀδελφοί, μήποτε ἔσται ἔν τινι ὑμῶν καρδία πονηρὰ ἀπιστίας
Watch out, brothers and sisters, so that there won't be in any of you an evil, unbelieving heart

The exposition of the psalm citation begins with the impv. βλέπετε, which begins a periodic sentence that continues through v. 15 (see comments on 1:1). The adv. μήποτε indicates negated purpose, "that not," "lest" (BDAG 648d; BDF §369[2]; "lest at any time," Moule 139). Together with the fut. indic. ἔσται (impers. here), it indicates that "the threat is real and urgent" (Attridge 116; cf. Lane 1:86). Ἔν τινι is locat. ("in anyone") and ὑμῶν is a partitive gen. (The encl. τινι has thrown its accent back onto ἐν.) The adj. πονηρά (πονηρός, -ά, -όν, "evil" [most EVV], "sinful" [NIV]; BDAG 851c; G. Harder, *TDNT* 6:554–58) modifies καρδία. Ἀπιστίας (ἀπιστία, -ας, ἡ, "unbelief"; BDAG 103c–d) is a gen. of quality (BDF §165) or ref. (Wallace 128). Καρδία πονηρὰ ἀπιστίας is the pred. nom. of ἔσται. Taken together, this difficult collocation can be woodenly tr. as follows: "Be careful, brothers and sisters, lest there be an evil, unbelieving heart in anyone among you." The author sees an analogous situation between the wilderness generation and his audience, and urges them not to follow this example.

The context makes it clear that "unbelief" is not due to honest doubt (*pace* "doubts," CEV), but rather to the hardening of one's heart due to a "refusal to believe" (Barclay) God's word (e.g., Jer 16:12, 18:12), or "an unwillingness to commit oneself to another or to respond positively to the other's words or actions" (BDAG 103c). It also entails unfaithfulness (cf. πιστός in 3:2). Ἀπιστία (occurring only in Heb 3:12, 19 in the NT) and βλέπετε form an *inclusio* with this v. and v. 19.

ἐν τῷ ἀποστῆναι ἀπὸ θεοῦ ζῶντος,
that turns away from the living God.

Ἀποστῆναι is the aor. act. inf. of ἀφίστημι ("turns away" [most EVV]; "in revolt" [Weymouth]; "fall away," "become a backslider" [BDAG 157d–158a]). Ἐν τῷ + inf. often indicates an action that is contemp. with a main vb. The use of this cstr. to indicate result is rare (Wallace 593 n. 12; BDF §404[3]; so ESV). Alternatively, the cstr. may be epex. (T 3:146–66; Ellingworth 222; cf. Koester 258; Cockerill 184 n. 40; Lane 1:82 n. *j*.; so NASB, NIV), further describing an evil, unbelieving heart. On either view, the link between a refusal to believe and falling away from the living God is clear. The alliteration with ἀπιστίας and ἀποστῆναι demonstrates the author's rhetorical competence. The adv. prep. phrase ἀπὸ θεοῦ ζῶντος (gen. sg. masc. of the pres. act. ptc. of ζάω) modifies ἀποστῆναι, indicating separation (BDF §180[2]). The phrase θεοῦ ζῶντος is used in both the OT and STL to contrast God with lifeless idols (see Koester 258–59 for extensive refs). This phrase is important in Hebrews (9:14; 10:31; 12:22; cf. 4:12). The anar. expression θεοῦ ζῶντος is qual. (Moule 114, Wallace 244), calling attention to God's character.

VERSE 13

ἀλλὰ παρακαλεῖτε ἑαυτοὺς καθ' ἑκάστην ἡμέραν,
But encourage each other daily,

Ἀλλά indicates the positive counterpart to the neg. exhortation in v. 12; rather than disbelieve, the audience is to encourage each other in the faith ("but," most EVV; "on the contrary," Cassirer). Παρακαλεῖτε is the 2nd pl. pres. act. impv. of παρακαλέω, "exhort" (ESV, NET), "encourage" (NASB, NIV), "appeal to," "urge" (BDAG 765a; O. Schmitz, *TDNT* 5:793–99). The reflex. pron. ἑαυτούς indicates a reciprocal relationship (BDAG 269a; BDF §287). The pron. is the obj. of the vb. Κατά (καθ' before rough breathing) and functions distributively: "by each day" or "daily" (cf. BDF §200[1]). The adv. prep. phrase καθ' ἑκάστην ἡμέραν modifies παρακαλεῖτε temp.

ἄχρις οὗ τὸ Σήμερον καλεῖται,
while it is still called **today**,

The prep. ἄχρις with the rel. pron. οὗ means "as long as" (BDAG 161a) and is a HGk. form of ἄχρι (BDAG 160c; see William L. Lorimer, "Roman xiii.3, Hebrews iii.13," *NTS* 12 [1966]: 390–91). Καλεῖται is the 3rd sg. pres. pass. indic. of καλέω, "call." The vb. functions impers.: "it is called . . ." (BDAG 503a). The wordplay between παρακαλεῖτε and καλεῖται is hard to render in Eng. The art. is anaphoric (Wallace 217–20), referring back to the first mention of Σήμερον in the psalm citation in v. 7 to facilitate the author's application of the psalm to his audience.

Throughout Hebrews, "today" indicates an extended but ultimately bounded time period. The exhortation here implies that there will be a fut. time when it will no longer be possible to encourage one another ("while there is still a time that can be called 'today'" [CEV]; "this *today* lasts" [NJB]; "so long as it is possible to use the word 'Today'" [Barclay]). The ref. to "today" evinces the author's conviction that the Word of God continues to speak, long after its initial inscripturation, but that at some fut. point it will no longer be possible to hear it.

ἵνα μὴ σκληρυνθῇ τις ἐξ ὑμῶν ἀπάτῃ τῆς ἁμαρτίας–
so that none of you is hardened by sin's deception.

Ἵνα introduces the purpose of daily encouragement ("so that," most EVV). Σκληρυνθῇ is the 3rd sg. aor. pass. subjunc. of σκληρύνω, "be hardened" (BDAG 930c; K. L. and M. A. Schmidt, *TDNT* 5:1030–31). The subjunc. is required by ἵνα and is neg. with μή. It may indicate permission ("allow anyone to"; BDF §314). The expression τις ἐξ ὑμῶν is sim. to ἔν τινι ὑμῶν in v. 12. The indef. pron. τις functions as the subj. of the vb. and is modified by the prep. phrase that functions sim. to a partitive gen.: "one from among you." The dat. ἀπάτῃ (dat. sg. fem. of ἀπάτη, -ης, ἡ, "deception" [NET], "deceitfulness" [ESV, NASB, NIV; BDAG 99a]) is either instr. or causal. Ἁμαρτίας is attrib. ("sinful deceit") or possibly subj. ("sin deceives"). The context indicates that the sin in view is unfaithfulness leading to apostasy.

VERSE 14

μέτοχοι γὰρ τοῦ Χριστοῦ γεγόναμεν,
For we have become participants in Christ

Γάρ further explains why the audience must avoid following the example of the wilderness generation. The subst. *μέτοχοι* (nom. pl. masc. of *μέτοχος, -ου, ὁ*) is an important word in Hebrews (see comments on 3:1). Its occurrence here links this passage to 3:1–6. The ref. to Christ sim. recalls 3:6, thereby contributing to the coherence of the overall argument. The gen. indicates association, "with Christ" (Wallace 128; Ellingworth 226–27). The pf. *γεγόναμεν* indicates intensity with heightened proximity (Campbell, *Basics* 110), although an intensive understanding (pres. state resulting from a previous action, so Wallace 574–76) is possible.

ἐάνπερ τὴν ἀρχὴν τῆς ὑποστάσεως μέχρι τέλους βεβαίαν κατάσχωμεν—
if we hold firmly until the end the reality that we had at the start.

The conj. *ἐάνπερ* introduces the prot. of a general cond. (BDF §§371[1], 454[2]), or third-class cond. (Wallace 696–99). Unlike the occurrence of *ἐάνπερ* in 3:6, there is no textual uncertainty in this v. The prot. extends through the end of the v. The apod.—the first part of v. 14—precedes the prot. There is no significant difference between the shorter form *ἐάν* ("if") and the lengthened form *ἐάνπερ* ("if indeed," "if only" [BDAG 268a]). The relationship between the prot. and the apod. could either be cause/effect or evidence/inference (see comments on 3:6).

The hort. *κατάσχωμεν* (1st pl. aor. act. subjunc. of *κατέχω*) recalls its occurrence in 3:6. The author includes himself in the exhortation. The aor. prohibits an action as a whole (Wallace 723). The obj. of the vb. is *τὴν ἀρχήν τῆς ὑποστάσεως*. The word *ὑπόστασις* (*ὑπόστασις, -εως, ἡ* [BDAG 1040d–41a;]) is one of the more difficult words in Hebrews to understand. It was used in 1:3 to indicate "essence" or "being" (see comments on 1:3). That mng. is possible here as well (Cockerill 189–90; cf. "original conviction" [NIV]; "resolve" [Attridge 118]; "steadfastness" [Cockerill 189]; "frame of mind" [BDAG 1041a]). Most EVV suggest a subjective sense of "confidence" (or "assurance" [NASB]), although extrabiblical examples of this mng. have not been found (BDAG 1041a). The art. functions like a poss. pron. ("our resolve"). *Ὑπόστασις* is used in 11:1 in conj. with the description of faith. See For Further Study 78 (*Ὑπόστασις*). The adv. prep. phrase *μέχρι* ("until") *τέλους* (*τέλος, -ους, τό* [BDAG 998c]; "to the end") is temp., modifying *κατάσχωμεν*. The adj. *βεβαίαν* (see comments on 2:2) could modify *ἀρχήν*, although the syntax of the clause argues against this. More likely it is adv. modifying *κατάσχωμεν* (BDAG 172d). The prep. phrase *μέχρι τέλους* is ambiguous and could refer to an individual's "end" (death) or eschatologically to the end of the age.

VERSE 15

ἐν τῷ λέγεσθαι·
As it is said:

It is unclear whether v. 15 concludes vv. 12–13 (NASB, TNIV; Attridge 120; Lane 1:88) or introduces vv. 16–19 (NEB; Koester 261 n. 15; Ellingworth 228). Like other vv. in Hebrews, it functions as a hinge that both concludes one section and introduces another. The art. inf. τῷ λέγεσθαι with ἐν indicates contemp. time (Wallace 595). It introduces the repeated citation from Ps 95:7, which forms the basis of the rhetorical questions in vv. 16–19. The pres. indicates ongoing action and reinforces the author's conviction that Scripture continues to speak. The voice of the inf. could be mid. ("while saying," so Attridge 119–20) or pass. ("while being said"); the pass. with Scripture (or perhaps the Spirit, from 3:7) as the understood subj. is preferred in this context.

Σήμερον ἐὰν τῆς φωνῆς αὐτοῦ ἀκούσητε,
Μὴ σκληρύνητε τὰς καρδίας ὑμῶν ὡς ἐν τῷ παραπικρασμῷ.
Today, if you hear his voice, do not harden your hearts as in the rebellion.

The citation is from Ps 95:7–8a. See comments on 3:7–8.

VERSE 16

τίνες γὰρ ἀκούσαντες παρεπίκραναν;
For who heard and rebelled?

The rhetorical questions in vv. 16–18 par. the CGk *diatribe*, used by Plato and Socrates (Koester 266), or the rhetorical technique *subjectio* (Lane 1:84). The questions assume a competent knowledge of Scripture. The first question in each pair (beginning with an interr. pron.) alludes to the psalm citation, whereas the second question presupposes Numbers 14. Specifically, in this v. the first question alludes to Ps 95:7–8 and the second to Num 14:13, 19, 22. (See the expanded list in Lane 1:88.)

Γάρ is explanatory and links the abbreviated psalm citation in v. 15 with the series of rhetorical questions (Ellingworth 228; Koester 261). The interr. pron. τίνες is used in both dir. and rhetorical questions (BDAG 1006d). Παρεπίκραναν is the 3rd pl. aor. act. indic. of παραπικραίνω ("rebelled" [most EVV]; "be disobedient, rebellious" [BDAG 770a; W. Michaelis, *TDNT* 6:125–27]), and is a cognate of παραπικρασμῷ in the psalm citation in v. 8 (cf. v. 15). The vb. describes Israel's disobedience (e.g., Deut 31:27; 32:16). The aor. is global, looking at the action as a whole. Ἀκούσαντες (nom. pl. masc. of the aor. act. ptc. of ἀκούω) either indicates a time antecedent to παρεπίκραναν ("having heard"; cf. NASB; Wallace 624–25), or more likely in light of the emph. on hearing God's Word, it is concessive ("even though they heard," NLT; "yet," ESV, REB; Wallace 634–35).

ἀλλ' οὐ πάντες οἱ ἐξελθόντες ἐξ Αἰγύπτου διὰ Μωϋσέως;
Wasn't it all who came out of Egypt under Moses?

Ἀλλά is difficult to understand and is left untr. by many EVV (but "indeed," NASB; "surely," NJB; cf. Lane 1:82 n. *s*.; see esp. Ellingworth 230–31; BDF §448[4]). Ἐξελθόντες (nom. pl. masc. of the aor. act. ptc. of ἐξέρχομαι, "lead out") is subst. and functions as the subj. of the verbless clause. The prep. phrase ἐξ Αἰγύπτου (gen. sg. of Αἴγυπτος, -ου, ἡ, "Egypt") is ablative. Διά with the gen. Μωϋσέως indicates agency. The author suggests a link between rejecting God's Word and rejecting his leaders, (e.g., Moses), a point that comes up in Hebrews 13. Πάντες likely alludes to the emph. on "all" in Num 14:1, 2, 5, 7, 10.

VERSE 17

τίσιν δὲ προσώχθισεν τεσσεράκοντα ἔτη;
With whom was God angry for forty years?

The interr. pron. τίσιν signals a rhetorical question (BDAG 1006d). Δέ connects closely related items (BDAG 213b), here the series of rhetorical questions. Although the author altered the LXX in 3:10, the citation here follows the LXX text of Ps 94:10 (see comments on 3:10).

οὐχὶ τοῖς ἁμαρτήσασιν, ὧν τὰ κῶλα ἔπεσεν ἐν τῇ ἐρήμῳ;
Wasn't it with those who sinned, whose bodies fell in the wilderness?

This question alludes to Num 14:10, 29, 32. The neg. adv. οὐχί is a strengthened form of οὐ and introduces a question that expects an affirmative answer (BDAG 742c). In Eng. this is signaled by a neg. question ("was it not" [most EVV]). Ἁμαρτήσασιν (dat. pl. masc. of the aor. act. ptc. of ἁμαρτάνω) is subst., referring to the wilderness generation. The dat. (cf. τίσιν) assumes προσώχθισεν from the first part of the v. The antecedent of ὧν is τοῖς ἁμαρτήσασιν. Ἔπεσεν is the 3rd sg. aor. act. indic. of πίπτω, "fell" (most EVV); "fall to the ground" (BDAG 815c). The subj. of the vb. is κῶλα (κῶλον, -ου, τό, "dead body," "corpse" [always pl. in BGk; BDAG 579d; NT hapax]). The use of a sg. vb. with a neut. pl. subj. is common (Wallace 399–400). Their deaths confirmed God's judgment, all the more so if their bodies were left unburied (e.g., Deut 28:26; 1 Sam 17:46; see Koester 261). Ἐν τῇ ἐρήμῳ (dat. sg. fem. of ἔρημος, -ον, here a subst.: "wilderness" [BDAG 391d]) is locat., referring generally to the places indicated in 3:8.

VERSE 18

τίσιν δὲ ὤμοσεν μὴ εἰσελεύσεσθαι εἰς τὴν κατάπαυσιν αὐτοῦ εἰ μὴ τοῖς ἀπειθήσασιν;
And to whom did he swear that they would not enter his rest, if not to those who disobeyed?

For τίσιν δέ, see v. 17. Ὤμοσεν is the 3rd sg. aor. act. indic. of ὀμνύω, "swear" (most EVV), "take an oath" [BDAG 706c]). The vb. recalls the citation of Ps 95:11 in v. 11, but is adapted from the first pers. of the psalm citation in v. 11 to the third pers. in the indir. discourse of v. 18. (See comments on 3:11.) The fut. inf. (εἰσελεύσεσθαι) is rare in the NT (occurring five times total) and reflects the fut. indic. of the dir. discourse in v. 11. The first pers. μου in v. 11 is changed to the third pers. αὐτοῦ in this v.

Unlike the two preceding sets of rhetorical questions in vv. 16–17, the "answer" to the first part of the v. is contained within the same sentence. Εἰ μή means "if not" (BDAG 276d). Ἀπειθήσασιν is the dat. pl. masc. of the aor. act. ptc. of ἀπειθέω, "disobey" (NIV) "be disobedient" (ESV, NET, NASB [BADG 99d]). The ptc. is subst. and refers to the wilderness generation. This part of the v. alludes to Num 14:30, 33, 43.

VERSE 19

καὶ βλέπομεν ὅτι οὐκ ἠδυνήθησαν εἰσελθεῖν δι' ἀπιστίαν.
So we see that they were unable to enter because of unbelief.

Καί is consecutive ("and so" [BDF §442[2]]). Both the use of βλέπομεν and ἀπιστίαν in this v. form an *inclusio* with v. 12 (see comments on v. 12), thereby bracketing the exposition (vv. 12–19) of the psalm citation (vv. 7–11). The ὅτι clause indicates the content of the vb. (Wallace 678). Ἠδυνήθησαν is the 3rd pl. aor. pass. indic. of δύναμαι ("were able") and is complemented by εἰσελθεῖν (aor. act. inf. of εἰσέρχομαι, "enter"; Wallace 598). The prep. phrase δι' ἀπιστίαν indicates cause.

The finality of this v. underscores both the magnitude of the wilderness generation's loss and the danger facing the present audience. This finality argues against drawing a distinction between temp. and eternal losses, which is not evident from the text (*pace* Thomas K. Oberholtzer, "The Warning Passages in Hebrews, Part 2: The Kingdom Rest in Hebrews 3:1–4:13," B*Sac* 146 [1989]: 67–75; Randall C. Gleason, "The Old Testament Background of Rest in Hebrews 3:7–4:11," *BSac* 157 [2000]: 281–303).

FOR FURTHER STUDY

31. The Pentateuch in Hebrews: The Exodus and the Wilderness Generation (3:7–19)

Allen, David M. "More than Just Numbers: Deuteronomic Influence in Hebrews 3:7–4:11." *TynBul* 58 (2007): 129–49.
DBI 948–51.
*Oudersluys, Richard C. "Exodus in the Letter to the Hebrews." Pages 143–51 in *Grace upon Grace: Essays in Honor of Lester J. Kuyper*. Edited by James I. Cook. Grand Rapids: Eerdmans, 1975.
Thiessen, Matthew. "Hebrews and the End of the Exodus." *NovT* 49 (2007): 353–69.

32. Hermeneutical Techniques in Hebrews (3:12–19)

Bateman, Herbert W., IV. "Second Temple Exegetical Practices: Extrabiblical Examples of Exegesis Compared with Those in the Book of Hebrews." *SwJT* 53 (2010): 26–54.

*France, R. T. "The Writer of Hebrews as a Biblical Expositor." *TynBul* 47 (1996): 245–76.

*Lincoln, 69–81.

Moffitt, David M. "The Interpretation of Scripture in the Epistle to the Hebrews." Pages 77–97 in Mason.

Osborne, G. R. *DLNT* 471–84.

Thompson, James W. "The Hermeneutics of the Epistle to the Hebrews." *ResQ* 38 (1996): 229–37.

———. "The New Is Better: A Neglected Aspect of the Hermeneutics of Hebrews." *CBQ* 73 (2011): 547–61.

*Wenkel, David H. "Gezerah Shawah as Analogy in the Epistle to the Hebrews." *BTB* 37 (2007): 62–68.

HOMILETICAL SUGGESTIONS

A Lesson from the Wilderness Generation (3:7–19)

1. The Text: Psalm 95:7–11 (vv. 7–11)
2. The Exhortation: Do Not Harden Your Heart as They Did (vv. 12–15)
3. The Example: The Dangers of Refusing to Believe (vv. 16–19)

We're in This Together (3:12–15)

1. Look out for one another—refusing to believe leads away from the living God (v. 12)
2. Encourage one another—while there is still time to warn of sin's deception (v. 13)
3. Hold firm to the truth that we first learned (v. 14)

C. THE SABBATH REST OF GOD THAT REMAINS (4:1–11)

STRUCTURE

Following the extended citation of Psalm 95 in Heb 3:7–11, the midrashic exposition in 3:12–19 focuses on the wilderness generation with implicit connection to the pres. audience. In 4:1–11, the text shifts to dir. application to the pres. audience (e.g., the hort. subjunc. in vv. 1, 11 and the first pers. pl. in v. 3). There is debate concerning whether v. 11 ends a previous section (so most EVV) or begins a new one (CEV, RSV). It is included with vv. 1–10 here on the basis of various *inclusios*, such as the use of the hort. subjunc. in v. 1 and v. 11 (see comments below) and the fact that v. 11 ends the discussion of the wilderness generation. Subsections are indicated by the phrase εἰσελθεῖν/εἰσελεύσονται εἰς τὴν κατάπαυσιν αὐτοῦ (v. 1 and v. 5; v. 6 and v. 11). A prot. is dependent with respect to the apod., as indicated in the indentation in the structural analysis (vv. 7, 8). The spacing in v. 10 reflects the par. within this v.

1 φοβηθῶμεν οὖν,
μήποτε καταλειπομένης ἐπαγγελίας
εἰσελθεῖν εἰς τὴν κατάπαυσιν αὐτοῦ
δοκῇ τις ἐξ ὑμῶν
ὑστερηκέναι.
2 καὶ γάρ ἐσμεν εὐηγγελισμένοι
καθάπερ κἀκεῖνοι·
ἀλλ᾽ οὐκ ὠφέλησεν ὁ λόγος τῆς ἀκοῆς ἐκείνους
μὴ συγκεκερασμένους
τῇ πίστει
τοῖς ἀκούσασιν.
3 Εἰσερχόμεθα γὰρ εἰς [τὴν] κατάπαυσιν οἱ πιστεύσαντες,
καθὼς εἴρηκεν·
ὡς ὤμοσα ἐν τῇ ὀργῇ μου·
εἰ εἰσελεύσονται εἰς τὴν κατάπαυσίν μου,
καίτοι τῶν ἔργων ἀπὸ καταβολῆς κόσμου γενηθέντων.
4 εἴρηκεν γάρ που περὶ τῆς ἑβδόμης οὕτως·
καὶ κατέπαυσεν ὁ θεὸς
ἐν τῇ ἡμέρᾳ τῇ ἑβδόμῃ
ἀπὸ πάντων τῶν ἔργων αὐτοῦ,
5 καὶ ἐν τούτῳ πάλιν·
εἰ εἰσελεύσονται εἰς τὴν κατάπαυσίν μου.
6 ἐπεὶ οὖν ἀπολείπεται τινὰς εἰσελθεῖν
εἰς αὐτήν,
καὶ οἱ πρότερον εὐαγγελισθέντες οὐκ εἰσῆλθον
δι᾽ ἀπείθειαν,
7 πάλιν τινὰ ὁρίζει ἡμέραν, σήμερον,

ἐν Δαυὶδ
λέγων
μετὰ τοσοῦτον χρόνον,
καθὼς προείρηται·
σήμερον ἐὰν τῆς φωνῆς αὐτοῦ ἀκούσητε,
μὴ σκληρύνητε τὰς καρδίας ὑμῶν.
8 εἰ γὰρ αὐτοὺς Ἰησοῦς κατέπαυσεν,
οὐκ ἂν περὶ ἄλλης ἐλάλει μετὰ ταῦτα ἡμέρας.
9 ἄρα ἀπολείπεται σαββατισμὸς τῷ λαῷ τοῦ θεοῦ.
10 ὁ γὰρ εἰσελθὼν εἰς τὴν κατάπαυσιν αὐτοῦ
καὶ αὐτὸς κατέπαυσεν ἀπὸ τῶν ἔργων αὐτοῦ
ὥσπερ ἀπὸ τῶν ἰδίων
ὁ θεός.
11 Σπουδάσωμεν οὖν εἰσελθεῖν
εἰς ἐκείνην τὴν κατάπαυσιν,
ἵνα μὴ ἐν τῷ αὐτῷ τις ὑποδείγματι πέσῃ τῆς ἀπειθείας.

VERSE 1

Φοβηθῶμεν οὖν, μήποτε καταλειπομένης ἐπαγγελίας εἰσελθεῖν εἰς τὴν κατάπαυσιν αὐτοῦ
Therefore, since the promise to enter his rest remains, let us beware

The postpos. *οὖν* draws an inference from the exposition in 3:12–19 ("so, therefore, consequently"; BDAG 736c; an intensive force with commands) and begins the application to the pres. audience. *Φοβηθῶμεν* is the 1st pl. aor. pass. subjunc. of *φοβέω*, "be afraid, become frightened" (BDAG 1061c; the vb. is always pass. in BGk, BDAG 1060d). The hort. subjunc. can urge action that contrasts with previous action and may thus be ingressive ("let us begin to fear"; BDF §337[1]), following the neg. example of the wilderness generation (3:12–17; cf. 3:7–11). Notice that the author includes himself in the exhortation. The collocation *φοβηθῶμεν . . . μήποτε* functions sim. to *βλέπετε . . . μήποτε* in 3:12, although *φοβέω* is "stronger" (Ellingworth 238). "Fear" in view of God's judgment is an important theme in Hebrews (e.g., 10:27, 31; 12:29), which is obscured in some EVV ("take care," NRSV; "be wary," NET; "let us be careful," NIV; but captured well by Cassirer, "stand in anxious dread"). See For Further Study 96 (The Fear/Judgment of God). *Μήποτε* is the lengthened form of the neg. adv. *μή* and "is an expression of apprehension" (BDF §370[1]). It is usually followed by an aor. subjunc., so the pres. subjunc. *δοκῇ* is unusual (see comments below).

Καταλειπομένης is a gen. sg. fem. of the pres. pass. ptc. of *καταλείπω*, "remains" (NASB); "still stands" (ESV, NIV); "be left over . . . *specif. in the sense be incomplete, unfinished, open*" (BDAG 521a). The ptc. is temp. ("while") or causal ("since" [CSB, NIV]). *Καταλειπομένης* introduces a gen. abs. cstr., in which the subj. of the gen. clause (*ἐπαγγελίας*) differs from the subj. of the main vb. (*φοβηθῶμεν*) (see comments on 2:4). The inf. *εἰσελθεῖν* complements *καταλειπομένης* (see BDF §393[6]) or (less likely) is epex., further defining the ptc. *Εἰς τὴν κατάπαυσιν αὐτοῦ* adv. modifies εἰσελθεῖν and recalls the citation from Ps 95:11 (see comments on 3:11). Verbs compounded with εἰς nearly always repeat the prep. as seen here (R 559). This is the first occurrence of ἐπαγγελία in Hebrews, which introduces another important theme in Hebrews that centers on the promises to Abraham (6:12–17 [see comments there]; 7:6; 11:9–17) and the new covenant promises (8:6; 9:15). The cognate vb. stresses God's faithfulness (10:23, 36; cf. 11:33, 39; 12:26). See For Further Study 45 (Promise in Hebrews).

δοκῇ τις ἐξ ὑμῶν ὑστερηκέναι.
that none of you be found to have fallen short.

Δοκῇ is the 3rd sg. pres. act. subjunc. of *δοκέω*, "seem" (BDAG 255a). The subjunc. often occurs following vbs. of fearing (*φοβηθῶμεν*) to indicate a warning or caution (Wallace 477). It is modified by *μήποτε* ("lest anyone might seem"). The indef. pron. *τις* is the subj. of *δοκῇ* and is modified by *ἐξ ὑμῶν*, as a partitive gen.: "one from among you" (cf. 3:13). The vb. has either an obj. sense ("be found," NIV, REB) or a subj. sense ("seem," ESV, NASB, NET; "think," NJB). *Ὑστερηκέναι* is the pf. act. inf. of *ὑστερέω*, "fallen short" (NIV), "miss," "fail to reach" (BDAG 1043c); it complements *δοκῇ*. The pf. indicates intensity with heightened proximity (Campbell, *Basics* 110; cf. Cockerill 202).

The author's use of "today" already suggests that a promise remains for his audience, but the wilderness generation's failure could have led the pres. audience to conclude that the promise of entering God's rest was abrogated. Thus the exhortation of 4:1 infers from the exposition of 3:12–19 that this is not the case. Although the wilderness generation failed to enter God's rest, the promise still remains, so the pres. audience must not fail to enter that rest. Whereas God's oath in Ps 95:11 had been the basis of a warning (3:12–17), in this passage it will become the basis for a promise, as the subsequent argumentation will demonstrate.

VERSE 2

καὶ γάρ ἐσμεν εὐηγγελισμένοι καθάπερ κἀκεῖνοι·
For we also have received the good news just as they did.

Καὶ γάρ together mean "for even" (BDF §452[3]) and link the preceding section more closely with what follows (Attridge 126; Ellingworth 240). *Ἐσμέν* is the 1st pl. pres. act. indic. of *εἰμί*. *Εὐηγγελισμένοι* is the nom. pl. masc. of the pf. pass. ptc. of *εὐαγγελίζω*; with the pass., "have good news announced to one" (BDAG 402c; G. Friedrich, *TDNT* 2:717–21; "received the gospel" [NJB]; "the gospel was preached to us" [NKJV]). The pf. periph. cstr. *ἐσμεν εὐηγγελισμένοι* is semantically equivalent to a pf. indic. (Wallace 647–48), although it may indicate emph. The 1st pl. is inclusive (the author and the audience; cf. 2:3–4). The conj. *καθάπερ*, "just as" (BDAG 488c), is often used with ellipsis; here *εὐαγγελίζω* is assumed. The conj. further indicates the analogous situation between the wilderness generation and the pres. audience. The form κἀκεῖνοι derives from καί + ἐκεῖνος ("and those ones"; BDAG 500a). Its unstated antecedent is the wilderness generation from 3:12–19. Εὐαγγελίζω could refer to the "good news" of salvation (e.g., the gospel; cf. 2:3) or the good report of Caleb and Joshua (Num 14:26–30), or even more generally the "good news" of the exodus (cf. Exod 19:3–6). The overlap in mng. is intentional and emphasizes the analogous situation between the wilderness generation and the present audience.

ἀλλ' οὐκ ὠφέλησεν ὁ λόγος τῆς ἀκοῆς ἐκείνους
But the message they heard did not benefit them,

Ἀλλά indicates a "strong alternative" (BDAG 45c), which contrasts the terrifying choice and fate of the wilderness generation with the desired choice and fate that the author is urging for his audience. Ὠφέλησεν is the 3rd sg. aor. act. indic. of ὠφελέω, "profit" (NASB), "benefit" (ESV; BDAG 1107d; cf. "no value" [NIV]). The aor. is global. Ἀκοῆς is the gen. sg. fem. of ἀκοή, -ῆς, ἡ, "message" (most EVV [BDAG 36c]). Ἀκοή is a cognate of ἀκούω ("what was heard"). The gen. is either obj. (NJB) or descriptive, functioning par. to a rel. clause (Moule 175; most EVV). The dem. pron. ἐκείνους is the obj. of the vb. Like κἀκεῖνοι, its antecedent is the wilderness generation discussed in 3:12–19.

μὴ συγκεκερασμένους τῇ πίστει τοῖς ἀκούσασιν.
since they were not united with those who heard it in faith.

Συγκεκερασμένους is an acc. pl. masc. of the pf. mid. ptc. of συγκεράννυμι, "unite" (most EVV), "blend" (BDAG 951d–952a). The ptc. is attrib., agreeing with ἐκείνους. The mid. voice focuses on the agent rather than the action (Wallace 415). The dat. τῇ πίστει follows the prep. σύν prefixed in συγκεράννυμι (see BDF §202) and modifies τοῖς ἀκούσασιν (*pace* ESV). The art. ptc. ἀκούσασιν is subst. The vb. can mean "hear" or "obey," although there is little difference between "hearing with faith" or "obeying with faith"—the emph. is on faith. The ptc. likely refers to Caleb and Joshua. The somewhat difficult syntax may be rendered as follows: "but the word that was heard did not benefit those ones [the wilderness generation], the ones who were not united with the ones who heard/obeyed [Joshua and Caleb] with faith." Alternatively, the author could mean that the wilderness generation was not united with the faith of the pres. audience (cf. Heb 11:40; so Attridge 126).

The rdg. συγκεκερασμένους is attested by early and widespread mss. and has a {B} UBS rating by the UBS committee. The var. rdg. συγκεκερασμένος (attested by fewer mss., but ℵ) indicates that the word "heard" had not benefited the wilderness generation because *the word* had not been united with those who *heard* it *in faith*. Although some EVV (NASB, NIV, REB) adopt this rdg., it should be rejected on both external and internal grounds (*pace* Lane 1:93 n. *h*.). Not only does the pl. better explain the orig. of the sg. (agreeing with ὠφέλησεν), the pl. rdg. coheres with an implicit emph. on unity, indicated by exhortations that there not be anyone from among the audience with an unbelieving heart (e.g., 3:12, 13; 4:1) and the ref. to being "participants" with Christ (3:14).

VERSE 3

εἰσερχόμεθα γὰρ εἰς [τὴν] κατάπαυσιν οἱ πιστεύσαντες,
For we who have believed enter the rest,

Γάρ gives a further reason why the example of the wilderness generation must not be followed, specifically that the pres. audience *is in the process of entering* the promised rest. There is debate concerning whether the pres. εἰσερχόμεθα indicates pres. time (Lane 1:99) or is futuristic (Ellingworth 246; Koester 270; "soon to be admitted," Weymouth), pointing to either an individual's death or the eschaton. Best is perhaps an ongoing, progressive idea (Attridge 126; Cockerill 205). Εἰσέρχομαι is also used of Christ, who has gone before as a forerunner into the inner sanctuary (Heb 6:19, 20), which could indicate that an inaugurated process (begun but not realized) is intended here as well (cf. 2:10). For some, this process has suggested a "pilgrimage" motif in Heb (although the Gnostic view presupposed by Ernst Käsemann, *The Wandering People of God: An Investigation of the Letter to the Hebrews* [ET: Minneapolis: Augsburg, 1984] has been widely refuted). See For Further Study 79 (The Pilgrimage Motif in Hebrews).

Εἰς [τὴν] κατάπαυσιν recalls the earlier citation from Ps 95:11 (see comments on 3:11; a few early mss. omit the art., but it is attested by other early and widespread mss.; the square brackets reflect the UBS {C} rating). The obj. of a prep. is freq. anar. (Wallace 247). Πιστεύσαντες is the nom. pl. masc. of the aor. act. ptc. of πιστεύω. The pres. of πιστεύω is not used in Hebrews (Wallace 621 n. 22), so the aor. is not significant. The subst. ptc. functions as the equivalent of a rel. clause: "we who have believed" (cf. BDF §412[5]; most EVV; NLT adds a distinction between "only we who believe" and "the others" that is unsupported by the Gk. [cf. CEV]; nor is it causal: "because we have faith" in REB).

Until this point in Hebrews, "rest" has presupposed the rest associated with entering the land. But the statement, "we who believe are entering the rest" raises the question of what is meant by rest here. Attridge understands rest in Hebrews to be "a complex symbol for the whole soteriological process," which is never clearly defined in Hebrews (Attridge 128). Many attempts to define the concept of rest in Hebrews attempt to discern the conceptual background of the author. See For Further Study 61 (Conceptual Backgrounds of Hebrews). Two main options are possible based on the overall context of Hebrews. See For Further Study 33 (The Promised Rest and Land Typology in Hebrews).

*1. A *place*, where entering the land pars. entering glory or the heavenly realm, the unshakable kingdom (12:22–29), and the city to come (11:10, 13–16; 13:14). There are some pars. in apocalyptic literature (*4 Ezra* 8:52; Rev 14:1, 13; Koester 268). This view is more future oriented.

2. A *condition*, where entering the land pars. access to God (in worship), and which is anticipated by the Sabbath. This view is both pres. and fut. oriented and coheres with the emph. in Hebrews on access to God's presence and the

"Sabbath rest" of 4:9, although the focus of Hebrews 3–4 seems to be slightly more on rest as a place.

καθὼς εἴρηκεν
in keeping with what he has said,

The adv. *καθώς* introduces a quotation (BDAG 493d). The switch from the pres. *λέγει* (3:12; cf. 3:15) to the pf. *εἴρηκεν* is likely extensive, emphasizing what was spoken (cf. Wallace 577). The subj. of the vb. is either God, or more specifically, the Spirit (3:7).

Ὡς ὤμοσα ἐν τῇ ὀργῇ μου,
Εἰ εἰσελεύσονται εἰς τὴν κατάπαυσίν μου
So I swore in my anger,
"They will not enter my rest,"

The citation from LXX Ps 94:11 is repeated in this v. See comments on 3:11.

καίτοι τῶν ἔργων ἀπὸ καταβολῆς κόσμου γενηθέντων
even though his works have been finished since the foundation of the world.

The conj. *καίτοι* means "and yet" (concessive) when followed by a gen. abs. (BDAG 494; BDF §425[1]). *Γενηθέντων* is the gen. pl. neut. of aor. pass. ptc. of *γίνομαι*, which has a wide semantic range. Most EVV indicate some sense of completion ("have been finished," NIV; "were accomplished," NET), which coheres with the context of the passage. The aor. is global. The subj. of the ptc. is *τῶν ἔργων* (Wallace 654–55), with the art. functioning equivalent to a poss. pron. (Wallace 215). *Καταβολῆς* is the gen. sg. fem. of *καταβολή, -ῆς, ἡ*, "foundation" (BDAG 515a). *Ἀπὸ καταβολῆς κόσμου* is temp., modifying *γενηθέντων* (Moule 73). The exact nature of God's works is not delineated.

VERSE 4

εἴρηκεν γάρ που περὶ τῆς ἑβδόμης οὕτως
For somewhere he has spoken about the seventh day in this way:

Γάρ further explains the nature of the promised rest. As in v. 3, the switch from *λέγει* (3:12; cf. 3:15) to *εἴρηκεν* is likely extensive, emphasizing what was spoken (cf. Wallace 577). The fem. adj. *ἑβδόμης* (gen. sg. fem. of *ἑβδόμος, -η, -ον*, "seventh" [BDAG 269d]) assumes *ἡμέρα*, which is freq. elided (Wallace 294 n. 4). The prep. *περί* modifies *εἴρηκεν* adv., indicating ref. ("with reference to," "concerning"). The subj. of *εἴρηκεν* is ambiguous; EVV are split between "he" (e.g., God or the Spirit; cf. 3:7) or "Scripture." The locat. adv. *πού*, "somewhere" (BDAG 858b), adds to the ambiguity of the citation. The adv. *οὕτως* means "in this way" (CSB), "as follows" (BDAG 742b) and introduces the following citation. This rhetorical technique is attested in Philo and rabbinic authors and may serve to focus on God's speaking rather than the exact place that records his words. (See comments on 2:6.)

Καὶ κατέπαυσεν ὁ θεὸς ἐν τῇ ἡμέρᾳ τῇ ἑβδόμῃ ἀπὸ πάντων τῶν ἔργων αὐτοῦ,
And on the seventh day God rested from all his works.

Κατέπαυσεν is the 3rd sg. aor. act. indic. of καταπαύω, "rest" (most EVV); "*cease some activity*" (BDAG 524a), and is intrans. It is clear that the author had Gen 2:2 in mind. The adj. ἑβδόμῃ modifies ἡμέρᾳ, which was elided in v. 3. The rep. of the art. and the placement of the adj. are emph. (Ellingworth 402; 2nd attrib. pos.; see Wallace 306–7). Ἔργων is here explicitly understood as "his works" (αὐτοῦ) and is further modified by πάντων. Ἐν modifies the vb. temp.: "on the seventh day." The adv. prep. phrase ἀπὸ πάντων τῶν ἔργων modifies the vb. and indicates separation (BDAG 105a). (The works in view are limited to God's creation works. Ps 95:9 indicates that God's sustaining, preserving work was evident to the wilderness generation; cf. John 5:17).

The author has either adapted the citation from LXX Gen 2:2 or was following a different textual tradition, which is also attested in Philo. The citation of Gen 2:2 may seem random, but the link is lexical: κατάπαυσιν in LXX Ps 94:11 suggests the cognate κατέπαυσεν in Gen 2:2. (This lexical connection is less apparent in the Heb. text, which uses two different words for "rest" in Gen 2:2 and Ps 95:11.) This rabbinic technique, called *gezera shawa*, is "an exegetical argument in which a term in one verse of scripture is interpreted according to its use in another" (Attridge 129; cf. Lane 1:95). The connection to God's creation rest is already suggested by "my rest" in Psalm 95, where God's rest could not be fully and ultimately understood as the land. Thus "my rest" understood as "God's rest" would naturally lead to Genesis, where God's rest is discussed. Moreover, this connection is also suggested by the first part of Psalm 95, which praises God for creation. Some have suggested that Gen 2:2 and Psalm 95 were linked in synagogue liturgy, although it is possible that the author himself connected these two texts, which are quoted only in Hebrews in the NT.

The point that the author is making, however, also draws on the rabbinic idea of drawing inferences from what is *not* stated in a scriptural text. Whereas the end of each of the first six days of creation is explicitly noted (Gen 1:5, 8, 13, 19, 23, 31), there is no corresponding statement about the seventh day. This led to the widespread idea that the seventh day was ongoing (cf. Attridge 129). Thus, if God rested on the seventh day, and the seventh day has not ended, then God's rest must also be ongoing. Moreover, if God's rest existed long before the wilderness generation failed to enter the land, their failure did not exhaust the promise of entering God's rest. See For Further Study 32 (Hermeneutical Techniques in Hebrews).

VERSE 5

καὶ ἐν τούτῳ πάλιν·
Again, in that passage he says,

As in 2:13, καὶ πάλιν, introduces the psalm citation and links it to Gen 2:2. The prep. phrase likely means "in this place" and refers generally to the previous discussion of the psalm citation (Ellingworth 249; cf. Lane 1:93 n. *o*.).

Εἰ εἰσελεύσονται εἰς τὴν κατάπαυσίν μου
They will never enter my rest.

The citation is from LXX Ps 94:11. (See comments on Heb 3:11.)

VERSE 6

ἐπεὶ οὖν ἀπολείπεται τινὰς εἰσελθεῖν εἰς αὐτήν,
Therefore, since it remains for some to enter it,

Οὖν is an infer. conj. that draws conclusions from previous information; ἐπεί is causal (BDAG 360c; BDF §456[3]; "since, then"). Ἀπολείπεται is the 3rd sg. pres. pass. indic. of ἀπολείπω. The pass. vb. is impers. ("it remains" [most EVV; BDAG 115c; cf. "is left" [NET, NIV]). Εἰσελθεῖν is a complementary inf. (Wallace 599), with the indef. pron. τινάς as the acc. subj. of the inf. Εἰς αὐτήν adv. modifies εἰσελθεῖν locat.; the antecedent of αὐτήν is κατάπαυσιν in v. 5.

καὶ οἱ πρότερον εὐαγγελισθέντες οὐκ εἰσῆλθον δι' ἀπείθειαν,
and those who formerly received the good news did not enter because of disobedience,

The adv. πρότερον ("formerly" [most EVV]; "earlier," "beforehand," "previously" [BDAG 888d; BDF §62]) modifies the ptc. Εὐαγγελισθέντες is the nom. pl. masc. of the aor. pass. ptc. of εὐαγγελίζω (see comments on v. 2). The subst. ptc. refers back to the wilderness generation, which was implied in v. 2. Εἰσῆλθον is the 3rd pl. aor. act. indic. of εἰσέρχομαι, "enter." The aor. is global, looking at the action as a whole. The prep. phrase δι' ἀπείθειαν modifies εἰσῆλθον, indicating cause. Ἀπείθειαν is the acc. sg. fem. of ἀπείθεια, -ης, ἡ, "disobedience" (most EVV) "disbelief" (BDAG 99c). The cognate ἀπειθέω occurs in 3:18.

By restating that the wilderness generation did not enter the land because of their disbelief, the author stresses that this was not because the rest was unavailable. The first part of the v. draws on the conclusion just established, namely, that God's rest has been available from the beginning of the world; it is not temporally bounded. Therefore it remains possible for *some* still to enter that rest.

VERSE 7

πάλιν τινὰ ὁρίζει ἡμέραν, Σήμερον, ἐν Δαυὶδ λέγων μετὰ τοσοῦτον χρόνον,
he again specifies a certain day—**today.** He specified this speaking through David after such a long time:

As in v. 5, πάλιν introduces a psalm citation, here the one-word citation from Ps 95:7. Ὁρίζει is the 3rd sg. pres. act. indic. of ὁρίζω, "ordains" (NET), "appoints" (ESV), "fixes" (NASB), "set" (NIV), "determine," (BDAG 723a). The subj. is either God (made explicit in NET, NIV), the Spirit (cf. 3:7), or more generally, Scripture. The indef. pron. τινά modifies ἡμέραν—"a certain day." The adv. prep. phrase ἐν Δαυίδ modifies ὁρίζει either to indicate instr./agency ("through David") or locat. ("in David," e.g., the Psalter; BDF §219[1]). Λέγων is pleonastic or redundant (Wallace 649) with the vbs. ὁρίζει and προείρηται, which already introduce the dir. discourse. Μετά with the acc. means "after." The correl. adj. τοσοῦτον (τοσοῦτος, -αύτη, -οῦτον, "so long"; BDAG 1012b) modifies the subst. χρόνον. Μετὰ τοσοῦτον χρόνον adv. modifies λέγων temp. ("after so long a time" [e.g., after the wilderness generation's failure]).

καθὼς προείρηται, Σήμερον ἐὰν τῆς φωνῆς αὐτοῦ ἀκούσητε, μὴ σκληρύνητε τὰς καρδίας ὑμῶν.
Today, if you hear his voice, do not harden your hearts.

As in v. 3, καθώς introduces a quotation. Προείρηται is the 3rd sg. pf. pass. indic. of προεῖπον, "the words already quoted" (ESV), "just as has been said before" (NASB; cf. BDAG 868b); the vb. is defective (see BDAG 867d). The rest of the citation is from Ps 95:7. (See comments on 3:7.) The CSB does not tr. καθὼς προείρηται; other tr. include "as in the passage already quoted" (NIV) and "as in the words quoted before" (NET).

The MT does not ascribe Davidic authorship to Psalm 95, although the LXX does. Jewish tradition also linked this psalm to David (Ellingworth 217). It is possible that the ref. is more general, indicating the Psalter as a whole (Bruce 75). Although the role of the human OT author is generally overlooked in Hebrews, Davidic ascription of the psalm is essential to the author's argument. The fact that David wrote so long after the failure of the wilderness generation establishes that the promise of entering God's *rest* remained after entry into the *land*. The author's appeal to this psalm would have been invalid if entry into the land under Joshua had completely fulfilled the promise of rest. But this was not the case, as the author will make explicit in v. 8.

VERSE 8

εἰ γὰρ αὐτοὺς Ἰησοῦς κατέπαυσεν,
For if Joshua had given them rest,

Γάρ further explains why Scripture talks of "another day." Εἰ with an aug. tense in the prot., together with ἄν in the apod., identifies "an unreal case" (BDF §360[4]), or second-class cond. (see Wallace 694–96). The prot. presents a cond. understood to be false, which is signaled by a past-tense vb. in Eng. ("if he had given them rest . . ."). Κατέπαυσεν is the 3rd sg. aor. act. indic. of καταπαύω (see comments on v. 4). The subj. of the vb. is Ἰησοῦς, which could refer to either Joshua or Jesus (see below), although the context indicates Joshua (so most EVV; except KJV). The obj. of the vb. is αὐτούς, the antecedent of which is οἱ πρότερον εὐαγγελισθέντες in v. 7 (e.g., the wilderness generation).

οὐκ ἂν περὶ ἄλλης ἐλάλει μετὰ ταῦτα ἡμέρας.
God would not have spoken later about another day.

The neg. ptcl. οὐκ modifies ἐλάλει. As is common in Hebrews, a speaking vb. indicates the ongoing "voice" of Scripture. The impf. is required by the cond. The subj. is

God (so NIV; or possibly the Spirit; cf. 3:7). Ἄλλης is the gen. sg. fem. of ἄλλος, -η, -ον, "another" (BDAG 47a) and modifies ἡμέρας. The prep. phrase μετὰ ταῦτα refers generally to the events of the conquest ("after these things").

The use of Ἰησοῦς in this v. suggests that Joshua is a possible type of Jesus the ἀρχηγός. The author did not exploit this connection even though he was likely aware of it (so Attridge 130; Ellingworth 253; cf. Bruce 109). Despite the idealized language of Josh 21:44 and 22:4 concerning rest (cf. Deut 3:20; 12:9–10; 25:19), it is evident that Joshua did not fully effect the promised rest. Thus the rest *in the land* is clearly not the rest of Psalm 95, which is the point that the author wants to establish by introducing Joshua into the argument. Specifically, if Psalm 95 speaks of rest after the conquest and during the time of David (when the land was nearly fully occupied), then there must yet exist a rest that surpasses the rest associated with the land. The earlier association with God's own (protological) rest suggests that the promised rest is also eschatological.

VERSE 9

ἄρα ἀπολείπεται σαββατισμὸς τῷ λαῷ τοῦ θεοῦ.
Therefore, a Sabbath rest remains for God's people.

The inferential conj. ἄρα indicates result (BDAG 127c). Ἀπολείπεται is the 3rd sg. pres. pass. indic. of ἀπολείπω; in the pass. "remain" (BDAG 115c; see comments on v. 6). This v. is formally par. to v. 6, and further specifies the promised rest. The subj. of the vb. is σαββατισμός. The ref. to λαῷ recalls its earlier occurrence in 2:17 and suggests continuity with the OT designation for the people of God and the pres. audience.

Hebrews 4:9 is the earliest attested occurrence of σαββατισμός ("Sabbath rest") in extant sources. The author likely coined the word, perhaps based on the cognate σαββατίζω, which the LXX uses to render the Heb. *šābat* (e.g., Exod 16:30). Σαββατισμός is not a synonym of κατάπαυσις, but instead indicates the way God's people participate in God's own rest. It implies worship and anticipates the worship in the heavenly Zion (12:22–24). There is a range of opinions concerning this word's mng. (see E. Lohse, *TDNT* 7:34–35; Attridge 131; Herold Weiss, "*Sabbatismos* in the Epistle to the Hebrews," *CBQ* 58 [1966]: 674–89). The par. in this passage between entering the land and entering God's rest indicates that rest is closely linked with experiencing God's presence.

VERSE 10

ὁ γὰρ εἰσελθὼν εἰς τὴν κατάπαυσιν αὐτοῦ
For the person who has entered his rest

Γάρ further explains the Sabbath rest. The referent of the subst. ptc. εἰσελθών is ambiguous (see below). Εἰς τὴν κατάπαυσιν αὐτοῦ adv. modifies εἰσελθών and recalls the citation from Ps 95:11 (see comments on 3:11).

καὶ αὐτὸς κατέπαυσεν ἀπὸ τῶν ἔργων αὐτοῦ
has rested from his own works,

Καί functions as an adv. ("also"; BDAG 495d). Κατέπαυσεν is the 3rd sg. aor. act. indic. of καταπαύω (see comments on 4:4). Αὐτός is emph. in the nom. (BDAG 152c). The prep. phrase ἀπὸ τῶν ἔργων αὐτοῦ recalls the earlier citation from Gen 2:2 in Heb 4:4, although the adj. πάντων is omitted.

There are several options for the referents of the subst. ptc. and the pers. prons. in this v. (See the summary in Ellingworth 254–57; Cockerill 211–12.)

1. Ὁ εἰσελθών refers to Christ, par. the sim. use of the aor. εἰσέρχομαι with Christ elsewhere (6:20; 9:12, 24); thus, the pers. prons. also refer to Christ. On this view, the aor. indic. is global and would refer back to God's works of preservation (3:9) and creation (4:4).
*2. Ὁ εἰσελθών refers to a believer; the first αὐτοῦ would then refer to God, whereas the second and third would refer to the believer. The aor. may be proleptic/futuristic (Wallace 563–64) or gnomic (Campbell, *Basics* 88). In this view, it is unclear what the "works" constitute, but ἔργων is not further qualified, so a sense of "works righteousness" is not supported by the text (see the summary in Koester 273). A fut. orientation could suggest understanding "works" in terms of remaining faithful or perseverance.

ὥσπερ ἀπὸ τῶν ἰδίων ὁ θεός.
just as God did from his.

The conj. ὥσπερ connects this verbless clause with the previous clause (BDAG 1107a). Θεός is the subj. of the elliptically understood κατέπαυσεν. The adj. ἰδίων assumes ἔργων. This clause alludes to Gen 2:2.

VERSE 11

Σπουδάσωμεν οὖν εἰσελθεῖν εἰς ἐκείνην τὴν κατάπαυσιν,
Let us then make every effort to enter that rest,

Οὖν draws conclusions from previous information. Σπουδάσωμεν is the 1st pl. aor. act. subjunc. of σπουδάζω, "make every effort" (most EVV), "be zealous, eager" (BDAG 939b–c; G. Harder, *TDNT* 7:565–67). Together with v. 10, this v. suggests that the effort (e.g., "work" in v. 10) is perseverance. The par. imagery of entering the land and entering the promised rest also supports this understanding. The aor. is probably ingressive. The 1st pl. is inclusive. The hort. subjunc. in this v. forms an *inclusio* with the one in v. 1. Εἰσελθεῖν complements the subjunc. Εἰς ἐκείνην τὴν κατάπαυσιν is locat. The dem. ἐκείνην likely refers back to σαββατισμός in v. 9, distinguishing it from the previous discussion of κατάπαυσις.

ἵνα μή ἐν τῷ αὐτῷ τις ὑποδείγματι πέσῃ τῆς ἀπειθείας.
so that no one will fall into the same pattern of disobedience.

Ἵνα introduces a purpose clause, with the neg. πέσῃ, "so that someone might not fall away." Πέσῃ is the 3rd sg. aor. act. subjunc. of πίπτω, "fall" (most EVV: "*with a transcendent or moral sense*"; "perhaps w. ref. to the final judgment" [BDAG 815d]; cf. "perish" [TNIV]). Its use here recalls 3:17 and the sim. idea in v. 12: ἐν τῷ ἀποστῆναι ἀπὸ θεοῦ ζῶντος. The subj. is the indef. pron. τις, which recalls its sim. usage in v. 1. Ὑποδείγματι (dat. sg. neut. of ὑπόδειγμα, -ατος, τό, "example" [NASB, NIV, REB], "pattern" [NET; BDAG 1037a]) is modified by αὐτῷ, which functions as an "identifying adj." (Wallace 349; BDAG 153d)—"the same example," referring back to the wilderness generation. The gen. ἀπειθείας is descriptive, further modifying ὑποδείγματι. Ἀπειθείας is used only here and in v. 6, thereby forming an *inclusio*. Ἐν τῷ αὐτῷ . . . ὑποδείγματι is either instr. (so most EVV) or locat. ("into," CSB). On the unusual word order of this clause, see BDF §473(1); Moule 168.

FOR FURTHER STUDY

33. The Promised Rest and Land Typology in Hebrews (4:1–11)

Attridge, 126–28.
———. "'Let Us Strive to Enter That Rest'—The Logic of Hebrews 4:1–11." *HTR* 73 (1980): 279–88.
*Brand, John. "Sabbath-Rest, Worship, and the Epistle to the Hebrews: Celebrating the Rule of Yahweh." *Didaskalia* 1/2 (1990): 3–13.
Burge, Gary M. *NIDB* 3:570–75.
DBI 647–48.
*deSilva, David A. "Entering God's Rest: Eschatology and Socio-Rhetorical Strategy on Hebrews." *TJ* 21 (2000): 25–43.
Janzen, W. *ABD* 4:143–54.
Kaiser, Walter C., Jr. "The Promise Theme and the Theology of Rest." *BSac* 130 (1973): 135–50.
*Laansma, Jon. *'I Will Give You Rest': The Rest Motif in the New Testament with Special Reference to Mt 11 and Heb 3–4*. WUNT 2/98. Tübingen: Mohr Siebeck, 1997.
Lincoln, A. T. "Sabbath, Rest, and Eschatology in the New Testament." Pages 197–220 in *From Sabbath to Lord's Day: A Biblical, Historical, and Theological Investigation*. Edited by D. A. Carson. Grand Rapids: Zondervan, 1982.
Millar, J. G. *NDBT* 623–27.
Moore, Nicholas J. "Jesus as 'the One Who Entered His Rest': The Christological Reading of Hebrews 4:10." *JSNT* 36 (2014): 383–400.
von Rad, Gerhard. "There Remains Still a Rest for the People of God: An Investigation of a Biblical Conception." Pages 94–102 in *The Problem of the Hexateuch and Other Essays*. New York: McGraw-Hill, 1966.
Witherington, 180–82.
Yeo, Khiok-Khng. "The Meaning and Usage of the Theology of 'Rest' (καταπαυσις and σαββατισμος) in Hebrews 3:7–4:13." *AsJT* 5 (1991): 2–33.

34. Typology and Interpretation (4:1–11)

Alsup, John E. *ABD* 6:682–85.

Baker, David L. *Two Testaments, One Bible: A Study of the Theological Relationship between the Old and New Testaments*. 3rd ed. Downers Grove, IL: InterVarsity Press, 2010.

Davidson, Richard M. *Typology in Scripture: A Study of Hermeneutical Typos Structures*. Berrien Springs, MI: Andrews University Press, 1981.

Goppelt, Leonhard. *TDNT* 8:246–59.

*———. *Typos: The Typological Interpretation of the Old Testament in the New*. Translated by Donald H. Madvig. 1939. Repr., Eugene, OR: Wipf and Stock, 2001. See pages 161–78.

Harris, Dana M. "Typological Trajectories in the Epistle to the Hebrews." Pages 280-92 in *Interpreting the Old Testament Theologically: Essays in Honor of Willem A. VanGemeren*. Edited by Andrew T. Abernathy. Grand Rapids: Zondervan, 2018.

Martin, Oren R. *Bound for the Promised Land: The Land Promise in God's Redemptive Plan*. NSBT 34. Downers Grove, IL: Apollos, 2015.

*Ribbens, Benjamin J. "Typology of Types: Typology in Dialogue." *JTI* 5 (2011): 81–95.

Seitz, C. R. *Figured Out: Typology and Providence in Christian Scripture*. Louisville, KY: Westminster John Knox, 2001.

Smith, Jerome. A. *A Priest For Ever: A Study of Typology and Eschatology in Hebrews*. London: Sheed and Ward, 1969.

35. Joshua Typology (4:8)

Ounsworth, Richard. *Joshua Typology in the New Testament*. WUNT 2/328. Tubingen: Mohr Siebeck, 2012.

Whitfield, Bryan J. *Joshua Traditions and the Argument of Hebrews 3 and 4*. BZNW 194. Berlin: Walter de Gruyter, 2013.

———. "Pioneer and Perfecter: Joshua Traditions and the Christology of Hebrews." Pages 80–87 in Bauckham, *Cloud*.

*———. "The Three Joshuas of Hebrews 3 and 4." *PRSt* 37 (2010): 21–35.

HOMILETICAL SUGGESTIONS

Three Conclusions to Draw . . . (4:1–11)

1. Therefore, let us fear missing out on the promised rest (vv. 1–5)
2. Therefore, there remains a Sabbath rest (vv. 6–10)
3. Therefore, let us be diligent to enter that rest (v. 11)

Lessons from Scripture (4:1–11)

1. The Promise of Rest from the Oath of Ps 95:11 (vv. 1–3)
   (a) The promise still remains (v. 1)
   (b) The lesson from those who previously heard the good news (v. 2)
   (c) The present reality of entering God's rest (v. 3)
2. The Nature of God's Rest from Gen 2:2 (vv. 4–6)
   (a) It extends back to creation (v. 4)

   (b) It can thus still be entered (vv. 5–6)

3. The Urgency of "Today" from Ps 95:7 (vv. 7–11)
   (a) God promised another day to enter his rest (v. 7)
   (b) Not the day when Joshua conquered the land (v. 8)
   (c) But the promise of a different "Sabbath rest" (v. 9)
   (d) A rest that comes from Christ's complete work (v. 10)
   (e) THEREFORE, we must enter that rest! (v. 11)

D. THE PENETRATING NATURE OF GOD'S WORD (4:12–13)

STRUCTURE

These vv. function as a conclusion for the previous section on hearing God's voice. The subj. ὁ λόγος in v. 12 is modified by five preds., which is reflected in the spacing in the structural diagram. The spacing in v. 13 reflects the par. within that v.

12 Ζῶν γὰρ ὁ λόγος τοῦ θεοῦ
καὶ ἐνεργὴς
καὶ τομώτερος
ὑπὲρ πᾶσαν μάχαιραν δίστομον
καὶ διϊκνούμενος
ἄχρι μερισμοῦ ψυχῆς καὶ πνεύματος,
ἁρμῶν τε καὶ μυελῶν,
καὶ κριτικὸς ἐνθυμήσεων καὶ ἐννοιῶν καρδίας·
13 καὶ οὐκ ἔστιν κτίσις ἀφανὴς ἐνώπιον αὐτοῦ,
πάντα δὲ γυμνὰ καὶ
τετραχηλισμένα τοῖς ὀφθαλμοῖς αὐτοῦ,
πρὸς ὃν ἡμῖν ὁ λόγος.

VERSE 12

Ζῶν γὰρ ὁ λόγος τοῦ θεοῦ καὶ ἐνεργής
For the word of God is living and effective

In pred. nom. cstrs., the subj. is art. (ὁ λόγος; Wallace 43). An equative vb. (such as εἰμί) is implied (Wallace 40). Ζῶν is the nom. sg. masc. of the pres. act. ptc. of ζάω ("living" [most EVV]; "offer life" [BDAG 426b]). The ptc. is pred. (Wallace 618). Θεοῦ is poss., modifying λόγος. Ἐνεργής is the nom. sg. masc. of ἐνεργής, -ές, ἡ ("active" [most EVV], "effective," "powerful" [BDAG 335d]). It functions as a second pred., further defining ὁ λόγος.

καὶ τομώτερος ὑπὲρ πᾶσαν μάχαιραν δίστομον
and sharper than any double-edged sword,

Καί adds the third pred. adj. τομώτερος (nom. sg. masc.), which is the comp. form of the adj. τομός, -ή, -όν, "sharp" (BDAG 1010d; BGk hapax). The prep. ὑπέρ indicates the obj. compared ("more than"; Harris 209). Πᾶς modifies μάχαιραν (μάχαιρα, -ας, ἡ), but with the sense of "any." Μάχαιρα most likely refers to the smaller dagger carried by Roman soldiers, although the ref. here is metaphorical (BDAG 622a; W. Michaelis, *TDNT* 4:524–27; Koester 274; cf. Isa 49:2). The "double-edged" ῥομφαία of Revelation (1:16; 2:12; 19:15, 21) refers to a longer, broader sword, although the distinction between μάχαιρα and ῥομφαία was fading (see Attridge 135 n. 30; Ellingworth 262). An allusion to Num 14:43–45 may be intended, when those who sought to enter the land, despite God's prohibition, were driven back by the sword of the Amalekites and Canaanites (Lane 1:102–103; Koester 280). The adj. *δίστομον* (acc. sg. fem. of *δίστομος, -ον*, "double-edged" [most EVV; BDAG 252]) modifies *μάχαιραν*. Both *τομώτερος* and *δίστομον* share the same root (*τομος*-; Koester 274).

Although *ὁ λόγος τοῦ θεοῦ* could ref. generally to Scripture, the placement of v. 12 immediately following the extended exposition on Psalm 95 suggests that this psalm (specifically vv. 7–11) is the primary referent (so most commentators). *Γάρ* would therefore give a further reason to be diligent to listen to God's "voice" *today*. Neither this context nor the overall context of Hebrews suggests a Christological understanding of *λόγος* (as in John 1:1, Rev 19:13). Rather, the focus is on the Word of God, spoken in the past (e.g., Gen 2:2; Ps 95:7–11), which still speaks "today" (cf. Isa 55:11; 1 Pet 1:23). See For Further Study 36 (*Ὁ Λόγος τοῦ Θεοῦ*).

καὶ διϊκνούμενος ἄχρι μερισμοῦ ψυχῆς καὶ πνεύματος, ἁρμῶν τε καὶ μυελῶν,
penetrating as far as the separation of soul and spirit, joints and marrow.

The fourth pred. adj. is the attrib. ptc. *διϊκνούμενος* (nom. sg. masc. of the pres. mid. ptc. of *διϊκνέομαι*, "pierce" [NASB, NET], "penetrate" [NIV; BDAG 245d; BGk hapax]). The prep. *ἄχρι* indicates "as far as" (BDAG 161a) and takes a gen. obj., *μερισμοῦ* (gen. sg. masc. of *μερισμός, οῦ, ὁ*, "division," "separation"; BDAG 633a; cf. "dividing" [NIV]). This word occurs in the NT only here and in 2:4 regarding the distribution of the gifts of the Spirit. The gen. is used after *μερισμός*. *Ψυχῆς* and *πνεύματος* concern the psychological aspects of a human, with no significant distinction between the two. The second pair of terms focuses on physiology. *Ἁρμῶν* is the gen. pl. masc. of *ἁρμός, -οῦ, ὁ*, "joint" (BDAG 132c; BGk hapax). *Μυελῶν* is the gen. pl. masc. of *μυελός, -οῦ, ὁ*, "marrow" (BDAG 660b; NT hapax). The focus here is on the effect of God's word (cf. Koester 274), not anatomy. (See Ellingworth 263 for further discussion of these terms.) The paired conjs. *τε καί* indicate a close relationship between the two nouns they join (BDAG 993c).

καὶ κριτικὸς ἐνθυμήσεων καὶ ἐννοιῶν καρδίας·
It is able to judge the thoughts and intentions of the heart.

The fifth and final pred. is the adj. *κριτικός, -ή, -όν*, "discerning" (ESV), "(is able to) judge/judges" (NASB, NIV; BDAG 570c; BGk hapax), which is followed by a gen. obj. The heart, more than the mind, is understood to be the locus of one's will (cf. 3:12). *Ἐνθυμήσεων* is the gen. pl. fem. of *ἐνθύμησις, -εως, ἡ*, "thoughts" (ESV, NASB), "desires" (NET), "idea" (BDAG 336d). *Ἐννοιῶν* is the gen. pl. fem. of *ἔννοια, -ας, ἡ*, "thoughts (NET), "intentions" (ESV, NASB), "attitudes" (NIV), "knowledge," insight" (BDAG 337d; the word occurs only here and 1 Pet 4:1). Both gens. are modified by *καρδίας*.

VERSE 13

καὶ οὐκ ἔστιν κτίσις ἀφανὴς ἐνώπιον αὐτοῦ,
No creature is hidden from him,

The vb. is impers. ἐνώπιον ("there is"). Κτίσις is the nom. sg. fem. of κτίσις, -εως, ἡ, "creature" (most EVV; BDAG 573a). The adj. ἀφανής (nom. sg. fem. of ἀφανής, -ές, "hidden" [most EVV]; "invisible" [BDAG 154d]; alpha-privative + φανός, "visible") modifies κτίσις. The prep. ἐνώπιον ("before") takes the gen. αὐτοῦ, the antecedent of which is God (v. 12).

πάντα δὲ γυμνὰ καὶ τετραχηλισμένα τοῖς ὀφθαλμοῖς αὐτοῦ,
but all things are naked and exposed to the eyes

Δέ after a neg. means "rather" (BDAG 213c). This clause assumes ἐστίν. Πάντα functions subst.: "everything" (NIV, NLT); "creature" (ESV, NASB). Γυμνά is the nom. pl. neut. of γυμνός, -ή, -όν, "naked" (ESV, NET), "open" (NASB), "uncovered" (NIV), "bare" (BDAG 208c) and functions as a pred. of πάντα. Τετραχηλισμένα is the nom. pl. neut. of the pf. pass. ptc. of τραχηλίζω, "exposed" (ESV, NET), "laid bare" (NASB; BDAG 1014). The pf. pass. ptc. is the functional equivalent of an adj. (cf. Moule 104). The image may be of a wrestling hold or a sacrificial animal with its head tilted back (Attridge 136; Ellingworth 265), yet the latter is convincingly challenged by John Muddiman ("Wrestling with Hebrews: A Note on *tetrachelismena* at Hebrews 4:13," in *Understanding, Studying and Reading: New Testament Essays in Honour of John Ashton*, 165–73 [Sheffield: Sheffield Academic, 1998]). The dat. τοῖς ὀφθαλμοῖς αὐτοῦ functions par. to ἐνώπιον αὐτοῦ. Similar statements about being laid bare before God occur in 1 Sam 16:7; Ps 139:7–10; 1 En. 9:5, and Philo (see Attridge 133–36).

πρὸς ὃν ἡμῖν ὁ λόγος.
of him to whom we must give an account.

The antecedent of the rel. pron. is θεοῦ in v. 12. Whereas λόγος in v. 12 referred to God's word, here the word is attested in the commercial realm concerning accounting (e.g., "account" [CSB]). The author likely intends a pun: "God's word (*logos*) demands a human account (*logos*)" (Koester 275; cf. BDF §239[5]). The dat. is either ref. or instr.

FOR FURTHER STUDY

36. Ὁ Λόγος τοῦ Θεοῦ *(4:12)*

Kittel, G. *TDNT* 100–19.
Rainbow, P. A. *DLNT* 665–67.
Smillie, Gene R. "'Ὁ ΛΟΓΟΣ ΤΟΥ ΘΕΟΥ' in Hebrews 4:12–13." *NovT* 46 (2004): 338–59.
———. "'The Other Λογος" at the End of Heb. 4:13." *NovT* 47 (2005): 19–25.
Swetnam, James. "Jesus as Logos in Heb 4:12–13." *Bib* 62 (1981): 214–24.
Trompf, Garry W. "Conception of God in Hebrews 4:12–13." *ST* 25 (1971): 123–32.

HOMILETICAL SUGGESTIONS

God's Word (4:12–13)

1. Characteristics of God's Word (v. 12)
   (a) Alive (v. 12a)
   (b) Powerful (v. 12b)
2. Effects of God's Word (v. 12)
   (a) Sharply penetrating (v. 12c)
   (b) Perfectly discerning (v. 12d)
3. Power of God's Word (v. 13)
   (a) None can escape it (v. 13a)
   (b) All must give an account (v. 13b)

E. JESUS THE SON, THE GREAT HIGH PRIEST (4:14–16)

STRUCTURE

Heb 4:14–16 is a key section that concludes the exhortation of 3:1–4:13. This brief passage is anchored with two hort. subjunc. (v. 14 and v. 16). The structure of ἵνα λάβωμεν ἔλεος καὶ χάριν εὕρωμεν is chiastic (see spacing in v. 16). The author's brief mention of Jesus's high priesthood in 2:17–18 is resumed in this passage, which also introduces the central section of Hebrews, focusing on Jesus's high priesthood (5:1–10:18). Significant pars. between 4:14–16 and 10:19–25 form a major *inclusio* in Hebrews (see Witherington 192).

14 Ἔχοντες οὖν ἀρχιερέα μέγαν
διεληλυθότα τοὺς οὐρανούς,
Ἰησοῦν τὸν υἱὸν τοῦ θεοῦ,
κρατῶμεν τῆς ὁμολογίας.
15 οὐ γὰρ ἔχομεν ἀρχιερέα
μὴ δυνάμενον
συμπαθῆσαι ταῖς ἀσθενείαις ἡμῶν,
πεπειρασμένον δὲ
κατὰ πάντα
καθ' ὁμοιότητα
χωρὶς ἁμαρτίας.
16 προσερχώμεθα οὖν
μετὰ παρρησίας
τῷ θρόνῳ τῆς χάριτος,
ἵνα λάβωμεν ἔλεος καὶ
χάριν
εὕρωμεν
εἰς εὔκαιρον βοήθειαν.

VERSE 14

Ἔχοντες οὖν ἀρχιερέα μέγαν διεληλυθότα τοὺς οὐρανούς, Ἰησοῦν τὸν υἱὸν τοῦ θεοῦ, Therefore, since we have a great high priest who has passed through the heavens—Jesus the Son of God—

Οὖν draws an inference from 4:12–13 ("so," "therefore," "consequently"; BDAG 736c). Ἔχοντες introduces an adv. ptc. clause that modifies κρατῶμεν causally (so most EVV). The pres. indicates time contemp. with the main vb. The designation of Jesus as ἀρχιερέα (here acc. sg. masc.) has already been established (see comments on 2:17). Ἀρχιερέα is the obj. of the ptc. The collocation ἀρχιερέα μέγαν is unique in the NT, but occurs in 1 Macc 13:42, and Philo, *On Dreams* 1.214, 219; 2.183 (Koester 282). Here the designation emphasizes the uniqueness of Jesus's high priesthood. The phrase Ἰησοῦν τὸν υἱὸν τοῦ θεοῦ is appos. to ἀρχιερέα. Within this phrase, τὸν υἱὸν τοῦ θεοῦ is an appos. to Ἰησοῦν. Διεληλυθότα is the acc. sg. masc. of pf. act. ptc. of διέρχομαι, "to pass through" (most EVV; BDAG 244b). The pf. is resultative (Wallace 574). The ptc. attrib. modifies ἀρχιερέα. Τοὺς οὐρανούς is the obj. of the ptc. The pl. "heavens" reflects Heb. usage. The imagery recalls the focus on Jesus's exaltation in Hebrews 1. The passage through the heavens refers to Jesus's entrance into the true tabernacle (cf. 6:19–20; 8:1–2; 9:11, 24; 10:20).

κρατῶμεν τῆς ὁμολογίας.
let us hold fast to our confession.

Κρατῶμεν is the 1st pl. pres. act. subjunc. of κρατέω, "to hold fast (many EVV); "to adhere strongly to" (BDAG 565a; followed by gen.). The hort. subjunc. recalls the hort. subjunc. in 4:1 and 4:11. The pres. is ingressive or progressive (Wallace 721). Ὁμολογίας is the gen. sg. fem. ὁμολογία, "confession" (BDAG 709a) and is the obj. of the subjunc. The art. functions as a pers. pron., "our confession." This recalls an earlier, sim. exhortation (see comments on 3:1). The collocation Ἰησοῦν τὸν υἱὸν τοῦ θεοῦ may reflect an early hymn (Lane 1:104). This exhortation to faithfulness flows naturally from the previous example of the wilderness generation's unfaithfulness.

VERSE 15

οὐ γὰρ ἔχομεν ἀρχιερέα μὴ δυνάμενον συμπαθῆσαι ταῖς ἀσθενείαις ἡμῶν,
For we do not have a high priest who is unable to sympathize with our weaknesses,

Γάρ gives further support for the exhortation in v. 14 and indicates that Jesus's passing through the heavens does not imply distance from the audience. Ἔχομεν is progressive. Δυνάμενον (acc. sg. masc. of the pres. mid. ptc. of δύναμαι) is attrib, modifying ἀρχιερέα. Double negs. are not uncommon in Gk., but most EVV tr. the neg. ptc. as "unable." Συμπαθῆσαι is the aor. act. inf. of συμπαθέω, "sympathize with" (BDAG 958b–c; W. Michaelis, *TDNT* 5:935–36; used only in Hebrews). The inf. complements δυνάμενον. Ἀσθενείαις (dat. pl. fem. of ἀσθένεια, -ας, ἡ, "weaknesses" [BDAG 142c]) is an associative dat. ("with"; R 530). The mng. here is more existential—Jesus has truly shared in our weaknesses (Lane 1:108 n. *c*.). The high priest was not expected to sympathize with the people's weaknesses (see esp. Koester 283).

πεπειρασμένον δὲ κατὰ πάντα καθ' ὁμοιότητα χωρὶς ἁμαρτίας.
but one who has been tempted in every way as we are, yet without sin.

Δέ after a neg. means "rather" (BDAG 213c). Πεπειρασμένον is the acc. sg. masc. of the pf. pass. ptc. of πειράζω, "tempted" (most EVV); "put to the test" (BDAG 793a). The pf. may indicate intensity. The ptc. πεπειρασμένον is attrib., modifying ἀρχιερέα, par. to δυνάμενον. Πειράζω, δύναμαι, and ἀρχιερέα were sim. linked in 2:17–18. Πεπειρασμένον is further modified by three prep. phrases, alliteratively beginning with a *k* sound (Koester 283). The first κατά means "with respect to" (BDAG 513b–c) "all things" (πάντα). Ὁμοιότητα is the acc. sg. fem. of ὁμοιότης, -ητος, ἡ, "in every way" (many EVV); "similarly" (BDAG 707a). The second κατά (καθ' before rough breathing) indicates "in a similar manner" (BDAG 513b), referring to sim. of the temptation. The prep. is less likely causal ("because of his likeness to us" [NEB]). The phrasing here recalls 2:17 (Ellingworth 269). Χωρίς ("without") takes a gen. obj. (ἁμαρτίας). The idea is that, although Jesus was truly tempted, his temptation did not result in sin (see Harris 263–65; see also comments on 2:18). See For Further Study 39 (Christ's Sinlessness).

VERSE 16

προσερχώμεθα οὖν μετὰ παρρησίας τῷ θρόνῳ τῆς χάριτος,
Therefore, let us approach the throne of grace with boldness,

Οὖν draws an inference from the argument thus far ("so," "therefore," "consequently" [BDAG 736c]; "with commands and invitations, an intensive force"). Προσερχώμεθα is the 1st pl. pres. mid. subjunc. of προσέρχομαι, "approach" (most EVV; BDAG 878b–c). The hort. subjunc. here and in v. 14 bracket this section (*inclusio*). Προσερχώμεθα is used in Hebrews to describe worshippers approaching God (cf. 7:25; 10:1, 22; 11:6; 12:18, 22); this use is freq. in the LXX (e.g., Exod 16:9; 34:32; Lev 9:5; Ellingworth 269; see esp. John M. Scholer, *Proleptic Priests: Priesthood in the Epistle to the Hebrews* [Sheffield: JSOT Press, 1991], 95–149). The vb. is often used in worship contexts and is nearly synonymous with ἐγγίζω (Cockerill 335; Lane 1:189). Προσέρχομαι is followed by the dat. (BDAG 878b); here θρόνῳ. The pres. indicates ongoing action. Μετὰ παρρησίας adv. modifies προσερχώμεθα, indicating manner. See comments on 3:6. The focus on confidence here counters the fear evoked in 4:12–13. The dat. τῷ θρόνῳ is locat., modifying προσερχώμεθα. (See comments on 1:8; see also Koester 284–85.) The gen. (χάριτος) is descriptive or qual.

ἵνα λάβωμεν ἔλεος καὶ χάριν εὕρωμεν εἰς εὔκαιρον βοήθειαν.
so that we may receive mercy and find grace to help us in time of need.

Ἵνα with the subjunc. (λάβωμεν) introduces purpose. The obj. of the vb. is ἔλεος, the nom. sg. neut. of ἔλεος, -ους, τό, "mercy" (BDAG 316c). The noun recalls the use of the cognate ἐλεήμων in 2:17. Εὕρωμεν is the 1st pl. aor. act. subjunc. of εὑρίσκω, "find." The obj. of the vb. is χάριν. Εἰς often indicates purpose, or even result (BDAG 290c). Its obj. is βοήθειαν, the acc. sg. fem. of βοήθεια, -ας, ἡ, "assistance," "help" (BDAG 180b; cf. βοηθέω in 2:18), which is modified by εὔκαιρον, the acc. sg. fem. of εὔκαιρος, -ον, "well timed, suitable" (BDAG 407a; "help in time of need" [e.g., ESV]). The noun βοήθειαν is tr. as an inf. in many EVV (e.g., ESV, NIV). The adj. εὔκαιρον adv. modifies εὕρωμεν temp. This v. is another example of the author's proficient use of alliteration: προσερχώμεθα . . . παρρησίας . . . εὕρωμεν . . . εὔκαιρον (Attridge 141).

FOR FURTHER STUDY

37. High Priest in Hebrews (4:14–16)

Attridge, 97–103; 146–47.
Brasser, H. W. *DNTB* 824–27.
*Culpepper, Robert H. "The High Priesthood and Sacrifice of Christ in the Epistle to the Hebrews." *TTE* 32 (1985): 46–62.
Demarest, Bruce A. *A History of Interpretation of Hebrews 7:1–10 from the Reformation to the Present.* Tübingen: Mohr Siebeck, 1976.
deSilva, David A. "The Invention and Argumentative Function of Priestly Discourse in the Epistle to the Hebrews." *BBR* 16 (2006): 295–323.
Ellingworth, 183–88.
———. *NDBT* 698–701.
Galloway, Lewis F. "Hebrews 4:14–5:10." *Int* 57 (2003): 294–96.
Gray, Patrick. "Brotherly Love and the High Priest Christology of Hebrews." *JBL* 122 (2003): 335–51.
Hurst, L. D. *DLNT* 963–97.
Isaacs, Marie E. "Priesthood and the Epistle to the Hebrews." *HeyJ* 38 (1997): 51–62.
*MacLeod, David J. "The Present Work of Christ in Hebrews." *BSac* 148 (1991): 184–200.
Mason, Eric F. *'You Are a Priest Forever': Second Temple Jewish Messianism and the Priestly Christology of the Epistle to the Hebrews.* Leiden: Brill, 2008.
Rehm, Merlin D. *ABD* 4:297–310.
Schaefer, James R. "The Relationship between Priestly and Servant Messianism in the Epistle to the Hebrews." *CBQ* 30 (1968): 359–85.
Schrenk, G. *TDNT* 265–83.
Songer, Harold S. "A Superior Priesthood: Hebrews 4:14–7:27." *RevExp* 82 (1985): 345–59.
Vanhoye, Albert. *Old Testament Priests and the New Testament Priest according to the New Testament.* Petersham, MA: St Bede's, 1986.
Vos, Geerhardus. "The Priesthood of Christ in Hebrews." Pages 126–60 in *Redemptive History and Biblical Interpretation: The Shorter Writings of Geerhardus Vos.* Edited by Richard B. Gaffin. Phillipsburg, NJ: Presbyterian and Reformed, 1980.
Witherington, 227–30.

38. The Confession of Christ (4:14)

Mackie, Scott D. "Confession of the Son of God in Hebrews." *NTS* 53 (2007): 114–29.
Michel, O. *TDNT* 5:215–17.
Neufeld, V. H. Pages 133–35 in *The Earliest Christian Confessions.* Leiden: Brill, 1963.

39. Christ's Sinlessness (4:15)

Stewart, Roy A. "The Sinless High-Priest." *NTS* 14 (1967): 126–35.
Williamson, Ronald. "Hebrews 4:15 and the Sinlessness of Jesus." *ExpT* 86 (1974): 4–8.

HOMILETICAL SUGGESTIONS

Jesus, Our Great High Priest (4:14–16)

1. The Marvel of Our Great High Priest (vv. 14–16)
   (a) He is not just a high priest, but a great high priest! (v. 14a)
   (b) He is the Son of God who has passed through the heavens (v. 14b)
   (c) He is able to sympathize because he has also been tempted (v. 15a)
   (d) He is completely without sin (v. 15b)
   (e) He will give mercy and grace because we need it (v. 16b)
2. The Only Appropriate Response (vv. 14, 16)
   (a) Hold on to our confession of faith (v. 14c)
   (b) Approach the throne with boldness (v. 16a)

F. THE SON'S SUFFERING AS QUALIFICATIONS FOR HIS MERCIFUL PRIESTHOOD (5:1–10)

STRUCTURE

The resumed discussion of Jesus as the great high priest in Heb 4:14–16 is further developed in 5:1–10, which also resumes the focus on Jesus as the exalted, enthroned Son. This section follows a chiastic structure, with v. 1 and v. 10 forming a thematic *inclusio* concerning the divine appointment of high priest. This thematic chiasm is diagrammed by Lane (1:111; cf. Cockerill 229–32) as follows:

A the function of the high priest (5:1)
B the person of the high priest (5:2–3)
C the appointment of the high priest (5:4)
C´ the appointment of Jesus as great high priest (5:5–6)
B´ the person of Jesus as great high priest (5:7–8)
A´ the function of Jesus as great high priest (5:9–10)

The structural diagram below does not reflect this chiasm, but rather reflects that vv. 1–3 and vv. 7–10 each constitute one carefully constructed sentence in the Gk. (a periodic sentence; BDF §464), bracketing the psalm citations in vv. 5–6. The first periodic sentence is anchored by the indics. καθίσταται and ὀφείλει; the second one, by ἔμαθεν and ἐγένετο.

This section begins the next major section of Heb (5:1–10:18), which focuses on the Son as high priest (5:1–7:28) and his once-and-for-all offering in heaven (8:1–10:18). Additionally, 4:14–16 and 10:19–25 form a major *inclusio* that brackets the main argument of Hebrews. See For Further Study 41 (The Structure of Hebrews).

1 Πᾶς γὰρ ἀρχιερεὺς ↓ ἐξ ἀνθρώπων
↓ λαμβανόμενος
ὑπὲρ ἀνθρώπων
καθίσταται τὰ πρὸς τὸν θεόν,
ἵνα προσφέρῃ δῶρά τε καὶ θυσίας
ὑπὲρ ἁμαρτιῶν,
2 μετριοπαθεῖν δυνάμενος τοῖς ἀγνοοῦσιν καὶ πλανωμένοις,
ἐπεὶ καὶ αὐτὸς περίκειται ἀσθένειαν
3 καὶ δι' αὐτὴν
ὀφείλει, καθὼς περὶ τοῦ λαοῦ,
οὕτως καὶ περὶ αὐτοῦ
προσφέρειν
περὶ ἁμαρτιῶν.

4 καὶ οὐχ ἑαυτῷ τις λαμβάνει τὴν τιμήν
ἀλλὰ καλούμενος
ὑπὸ τοῦ θεοῦ
καθώσπερ καὶ Ἀαρών.
5 Οὕτως καὶ ὁ Χριστὸς οὐχ ἑαυτὸν ἐδόξασεν γενηθῆναι ἀρχιερέα
ἀλλ' ὁ λαλήσας πρὸς αὐτόν,
Υἱός μου εἶ σύ,
ἐγὼ σήμερον γεγέννηκά σε·
6 καθὼς καὶ ἐν ἑτέρῳ λέγει,
Σὺ ἱερεὺς εἰς τὸν αἰῶνα
κατὰ τὴν τάξιν Μελχισέδεκ,
7 ὃς ἐν ταῖς ἡμέραις τῆς σαρκὸς αὐτοῦ
δεήσεις τε καὶ ἱκετηρίας
πρὸς τὸν δυνάμενον σῴζειν αὐτὸν
ἐκ θανάτου
μετὰ κραυγῆς ἰσχυρᾶς καὶ δακρύων
προσενέγκας
καὶ εἰσακουσθεὶς
ἀπὸ τῆς εὐλαβείας,
8 καίπερ ὢν υἱός,
ἔμαθεν
ἀφ' ὧν ἔπαθεν τὴν ὑπακοήν,
9 καὶ τελειωθεὶς
ἐγένετο
πᾶσιν τοῖς ὑπακούουσιν αὐτῷ
αἴτιος σωτηρίας αἰωνίου,

10 προσαγορευθεὶς
ὑπὸ τοῦ θεοῦ
ἀρχιερεὺς
κατὰ τὴν τάξιν Μελχισέδεκ.

VERSE 1

Πᾶς γὰρ ἀρχιερεὺς ἐξ ἀνθρώπων λαμβανόμενος ὑπὲρ ἀνθρώπων καθίσταται τὰ πρὸς τὸν θεόν,
For every high priest taken from among men is appointed in matters pertaining to God for the people,

Γάρ extends the discussion of Jesus, the high priest, in vv. 14–16 by presenting a high priest's qualifications. Πᾶς modifies ἀρχιερεύς (see comments on 2:17), which is the subj. of the ptc. λαμβανόμενος. The prep. phrase ἐξ ἀνθρώπων adv. modifies λαμβανόμενος as a partitive gen. ("from among mortals" [NRSV]). The ptc. clause alludes to Num 8:2, 6 (cf. Exod 28:1). The circum. ptc. agrees with the indic. καθίσταται and is tr. as an indic. by some EVV (NET, NIV, NJB, REB; *pace* Cockerill 232 n. 12, who takes the ptc. as attrib.). Ὑπέρ means "in behalf of," "for one's benefit" (R 630). Λαμβάνω frames vv. 1–4, with the pass. ptc. in v. 1 and the act. indic. in v. 4. Καθίσταται is the 3rd sg. pres. pass. indic. of καθίστημι, "appoint" (most EVV), "authorize" (BDAG 492c–d). Both the pass. ptc. and the pass. indic. are divine pass., as v. 4 makes explicit. The pres. for both vbs. is gnomic (Wallace 523–24) or "general description" (Ellingworth 271). The cstr. τὰ πρὸς τὸν θεόν ("things pertaining to God" [NASB]) is an "adv. acc." modifying the intrans. vb. καθίσταται (R 486). See comments on 2:17.

ἵνα προσφέρῃ δῶρά τε καὶ θυσίας ὑπὲρ ἁμαρτιῶν,
to offer both gifts and sacrifices for sins.

Ἵνα with the subjunc. introduces a purpose clause. Προσφέρῃ is the 3rd sg. pres. act. subjunc. of προσφέρω, "offer" (most EVV), "bring," "present" (BDAG 886 b–c; K. Weiss, *TDNT* 9:65–68). The vb. occurs more freq. in Hebrews (nineteen times) than elsewhere in the NT and is from "the sacrificial vocabulary of the LXX" (Lane 1:108 n. *i*). Δῶρά is the acc. pl. neut. of δῶρον, -ου, τό, "gift, present" (BDAG 267c; F. Büschel, *TDNT* 2:166–67). Θυσίας is the acc. pl. fem. of θυσία, -ας, ἡ, "sacrifice, offering" (BDAG 462d; J. Behm, *TDNT* 3:180–90); the noun occurs twenty-one times in Hebrews, and only seven times elsewhere in the NT. Both terms are used only in the pl. in Hebrews; δῶρον only occurs in conj. with θυσία. The τε καί cstr. may distinguish the terms (e.g., "*both* gifts *and* sacrifices for sins"; Lane 1:108 n. *j*), although many EVV (e.g., ESV, NIV, NJB; cf. BDAG 993c) do not make this distinction. There is debate, however, if (or how) the author distinguished the terms (see Ellingworth 274–75). The fixed expression δῶρά τε καὶ θυσίας may refer generally to all offerings and sacrifices, or more specifically to the Day of Atonement. The prep. phrase ὑπὲρ ἁμαρτιῶν adv. modifies προσφέρῃ.

VERSE 2

μετριοπαθεῖν δυνάμενος τοῖς ἀγνοοῦσιν καὶ πλανωμένοις,
He is able to deal gently with those who are ignorant and are going astray,

Μετριοπαθεῖν is the pres. act. inf. of μετριοπαθέω, "deal gently" (most EVV: cf. "deal compassionately" [NET], "moderate one's feelings" [BDAG 643d; W. Michaelis, *TDNT* 5:938; BGk. hapax]). It complements the ptc. δυνάμενος and is followed by the dat. (R 541). The pres. for both vbs. is gnomic (Wallace 523–24) or "general description" (Ellingworth 275). The adv. circum. ptc. modifies προσφέρῃ (v. 1), although most EVV begin a new sentence here. Μετριοπαθέω and συμπαθέω (4:15) are closely related, but not synonymous. Μετριοπαθέω concerns controlling emotion, esp. anger (Ellingworth 275; Lane 1:116–17). "The ordinary high priest controls his anger; Christ actively sympathizes" (Attridge 144). Ἀγνοοῦσιν is the dat. pl. masc. of the pres. act. ptc. of ἀγνοέω, "lapse," "do wrong," "sin unintentionally" (BDAG 13b); the ptc. is tr. as "ignorant" in most EVV. Πλανωμένοις is the dat. pl. masc. of the pres. mid. ptc. of πλανάω, "go astray," "be deluded" (BDAG 822a). This ptc. is also tr. as an adj. by many EVV: "misguided" (NASB), "wayward" (ESV), "erring" (NET). The two subst. ptcs. share the same art., indicating that they refer to the same entity. This is related to but not a clear example of Granville Sharp's rule (see Wallace 270–90). The two ptcs. may form a hendiadys (BDF §442[16]; Z §184): "go astray through ignorance." The expression alludes to Num 15:22–31 (cf. Lev 4:2; see esp. Ellingworth 276). Πλανάω in Deuteronomy refers to apostasy (Ellingworth 276).

ἐπεὶ καὶ αὐτὸς περίκειται ἀσθένειαν
since he is also clothed with weakness.

The subord. conj. ἐπεί gives a reason for the preceding ptc. clause ("because," "since," "for" [BDAG 360c]), namely, the high priest's own weakness. There are no pars. for this idea in contemp. Jewish sources; Philo suggested that the high priest's humanity was suspended on the Day of Atonement (Lane 1:116). Καί functions as an adv. ("also" [BDAG 495d]). Αὐτός is emph. in the nom. (BDAG 152c; Wallace 322). Περίκειται is the 3rd sg. pres. mid. indic. of περίκειμαι, "*wear someth., have someth. on*" (BDAG 801d–802a; R 485; "clothed with weakness" [CSB]). Many EVV, however, do not capture this metaphor (e.g., ESV, NIV). Here it "suggests a burden" (Ellingworth 277). Ἀσθένειαν is the acc. sg. fem. of ἀσθένεια, -ας, ἡ, "weakness" (BDAG 142b; cf. 4:15; 7:28). A contrast to the focus in Jewish sources on the special vestments the high priest wore may be intended here (cf. Koester 286–87; Cockerill 234–35).

VERSE 3

καὶ δι' αὐτὴν ὀφείλει καθὼς περὶ τοῦ λαοῦ οὕτως καὶ περὶ αὐτοῦ προσφέρειν περὶ ἁμαρτιῶν.
Because of this, he must make an offering for his own sins as well as for the people.

The first καί is a connective (R 1181), linking the final clause to the rest of the sentence that begins in v. 1. Δία with the acc. indicates cause (BDAG 225c). The antecedent of αὐτήν is ἀσθένειαν in v. 2. Ὀφείλει is the 3rd sg. pres. act. indic. from ὀφείλω, "be obligated" (BDAG 743b–c; with inf. following). The pres. is gnomic (Wallace

523–24). The adv. καθώς indicates a comp., "just as" (BDAG 493c). Περί with the gen. means "about," "concerning" (Harris 180). The use of λαοῦ recalls its earlier occurrences in 2:17 and 4:9, although the focus here is on the OT context. Περὶ τοῦ λαοῦ adv. modifies προσφέρειν, which is understood elliptically.

Οὕτως ("in this manner," "thus," "so" [BDAG 741d]) is a correl. with καθώς. The second καί functions as an adv. ("also" [BDAG 495d]). Περὶ αὐτοῦ par. the preceding περὶ τοῦ λαοῦ, indicating that the high priest (the antecedent of αὐτοῦ) must offer sacrifices for himself. The pers. pron. functions refl. Προσφέρειν is the pres. act. inf. of προσφέρω (see comments on v. 1). The prep. phrase περὶ ἁμαρτιῶν adv. modifies προσφέρειν, indicating ref. or respect. In the NT, the preps. περί and ὑπέρ can be used interchangeably (cf. ὑπὲρ ἁμαρτιῶν in v. 1; see BDF §229[1]; Z 96; Moule 63; Harris 180, 210; cf. E. H. Riesenfeld, *TDNT* 6:55; 8:512). This v. alludes to Lev 16:6, 17. This is developed further in Heb 7:27 and 9:7.

VERSE 4

καὶ οὐχ ἑαυτῷ τις λαμβάνει τὴν τιμήν
No one takes this honor on himself;

Καί adds a new point to the argument (BDAG 494c). Λαμβάνει forms an *inclusio* with the pass. ptc. in v. 1. The adv. οὐ negates the vb. (οὐχ occurs before rough breathing). The indef. pron. τις is the subj. of the vb.; τιμήν is the obj. of the vb. Josephus uses this noun for the "office" of high priest (*Ant.* 3.188–89; cf. Exod 28:1; Num 3:10; 18:1; Ellingworth 280; Lane 1:117; cf. BDAG 1005d). Ἑαυτῷ may be a dat. of advantage ("for himself") or "may simply emphasize the subject as agent" (Ellingworth 280). The pres. tense of the vb. and the ptc. are gnomic (Wallace 523–24) or "general description" (Cockerill 237 n. 42).

ἀλλὰ καλούμενος ὑπὸ τοῦ θεοῦ καθώσπερ καὶ Ἀαρών.
instead, a person is called by God, just as Aaron was.

Ἀλλά indicates a contrast to what precedes (BDAG 44c). Λαμβάνει and τὴν τιμήν are understood elliptically. Καλούμενος is the nom. sg. masc. of the pres. pass. ptc. of καλέω, "call" (most EVV); "call to an office" (BDAG 503c–d). Ὑπὸ τοῦ θεοῦ indicates the (ultimate) agent of the pass. (Wallace 433). The ptc. adv. modifies λαμβάνει for means. Καθώσπερ is an alternate form of καθώς, "just as" (BDAG 494a; BGk. hapax). The second καί functions as an adv. ("also" [BDAG 495d]). The ref. to Aaron (Ἀαρών, ὁ; indecl.) alludes to Exod 28:1 and Num 16:40. Καλούμενος is understood elliptically in the second part of the clause. The points made concerning the Aaronic high priest are developed and applied to Jesus in chiastic order in vv. 5–10. The similarities and contrasts between the Aaronic priesthood and Jesus's are the focus of Hebrews 7–10.

VERSE 5

Οὕτως καὶ ὁ Χριστὸς οὐχ ἑαυτὸν ἐδόξασεν γενηθῆναι ἀρχιερέα
In the same way, Christ did not exalt himself to become a high priest,

The adv. οὕτως ("in this way" [BDAG 742b]) introduces vv. 5–10, which outline similarities between the Aaronic priesthood and Jesus's. Καί functions as an adv. ("also" [BDAG 495d]); cf. v. 4. The art. with Χριστός is possibly anaphoric, referring back to 3:6. Ἐδόξασεν is the 3rd sg. aor. act. indic. of δοξάζω, "exalt" (ESV), "glorify" (NASB, NET; BDAG 258d); cf. 1:3; 2:7, 9; 3:3. Although glory and honor are closely related (cf. 2:9), Hebrews "reserves the term 'glory' for Jesus" and uses τιμή for Moses (3:3) and Aaron (5:4; Koester 287). The refl. pron. ἑαυτόν is the obj. of the vb. The inf. γενηθῆναι (aor. mid. inf. of γίνομαι) is epex. (further defining ἐδόξασεν; Moule 127) or possibly purpose (R 1089). Ἀρχιερέα (see comments on 2:17) is the obj. of the inf.

ἀλλ' ὁ λαλήσας πρὸς αὐτόν, Υἱός μου εἶ σύ, ἐγὼ σήμερον γεγέννηκά σε·
but God who said to him, **You are my Son; today I have become your Father,**

Ἀλλά continues the contrast begun in v. 4. Although the aspect of subst. ptcs. is usually diminished, the aor. ptc. λαλήσας likely reflects antecedent time (Campbell, *Basics* 94). The referent of the ptc. is God (made explicit in many EVV), "referred to indirectly for rhetorical and/or reverential reasons" (Ellingworth 282). The ref. to God speaking also recalls 1:1–2. The v. recalls the sim. use of πρός in 1:8 (see comments there). The rest of the v. is a citation from Ps 2:7 (see comments on 1:5).

This v. indicates that just as Aaron did not take the honor of the high priesthood on himself, neither did Jesus. The appeal to Ps 2:7 confirms Jesus's divine appointment to the office. The title ὁ Χριστός also indicates this appointment (Lane 1:118).

VERSE 6

καθὼς καὶ ἐν ἑτέρῳ λέγει,
also says in another place,

The adv. καθώς indicates a comp., "just as" (BDAG 493c), here comparing the citation of Ps 2:7 in v. 5 with the citation from Ps 110:4 in this v., which further supports Jesus's divine appointment as high priest and links it to his eternal Sonship. The overall context of Hebrews indicates that Jesus fully entered into his high priesthood at his exaltation (see esp. Attridge 146–47; Cockerill 238–39). Καί functions as an adv. ("also" [BDAG 495d]); cf. v. 5. The prep. phrase ἐν ἑτέρῳ adv. modifies λέγει locat., with τόπῳ understood (e.g., "another place" [most EVV; BDAG 339d; cf. Ellingworth 283). For the use of λέγει to introduce scripture, see comments on 3:7. God is the implied subj. of the vb.

Σὺ ἱερεὺς εἰς τὸν αἰῶνα κατὰ τὴν τάξιν Μελχισέδεκ,
You are a priest forever according to the order of Melchizedek.

The citation is from Ps 110:4. Although Ps 110:1 is cited or alluded to more often than any other OT v. in the NT, Heb is the only NT writing to cite v. 4. Ἱερεύς is the nom. sg. masc. from ἱερεύς, -έως, ὁ, "priest" (BDAG 469d; A. Sand, *EDNT* 2:174b–175a; G. Schrenk, *TDNT* 3:260–65). Σύ is emph. (BDAG 949d; R 677). In pred. nom. cstrs., the subj. is the pron. (σύ) with ἱερεύς functioning as the pred. nom. (cf. Wallace 43). The adv. prep. phrase εἰς τὸν αἰῶνα ("forever" [most EVV], "eternally," "in perpetuity" [BDAG 32b]) modifies an assumed equative vb. (εἶ) temp. This prep. phrase has already been used in conj. with the nature of the Son (1:8, 12) and is now associated with the Son's priesthood (cf. 6:20; 7:16–17, 24–25). See the extended discussion in Harris 94–96. Κατά functions as "*a marker of norm of similarity or homogeneity*, according to, in accordance with, in conformity with, according to" (BDAG 512c–d; cf. BDAG 989b). Τάξιν is the acc. sg. fem. of τάξις, -εως, ἡ, "order" or "nature" ("rank," Moffatt). The noun can mean "succession" (so NEB: "in the succession of Melchizedek"), but the idea of succession does not apply with Melchizedek (and indeed is contrary to the argument that the author will develop). Instead the term indicates "kind" or "nature" ("according to the nature of" [BDAG 989b]). The prep. κατά can indicate "equality"; e.g., "just as" (BDAG 513a). The prep. phrase κατὰ τὴν τάξιν Μελχισέδεκ adj. modifies ἱερεύς. Μελχισέδεκ (gen. sg. masc.) is transliterated from the Heb. and is indecl. The descriptive gen. is inferred from the context.

The citation of Ps 110:4 alludes to Gen 14:17–20, which is developed in Hebrews 7 (see comments on 7:1–3). This psalm citation factors significantly in Hebrews (e.g., 5:10; 6:20; 7:17, 21).

VERSE 7

ὃς ἐν ταῖς ἡμέραις τῆς σαρκὸς αὐτοῦ
During his earthly life,

The rel. pron. introduces the author's extended exposition of Jesus's suffering. Although a rel. clause is syntactically subord., rel. clauses "introduced by ὅς . . . are always in Hebrews major statements about the passion and exaltation of Christ (1:2; 12:2), esp. as high priest (as here and in 7:27; 8:1; cf. 7:16; 9:14)" (Ellingworth 286). The antecedent of the rel. pron. is ὁ Χριστός in v. 5. The prep. phrase ἐν ταῖς ἡμέραις temp. modifies προσενέγκας in the next clause. The gen. σαρκός is attrib.: "his fleshly days," e.g., his incarnation (cf. 2:14). Αὐτοῦ is poss., the antecedent of which is Jesus.

δεήσεις τε καὶ ἱκετηρίας πρὸς τὸν δυνάμενον σῴζειν αὐτὸν ἐκ θανάτου μετὰ κραυγῆς ἰσχυρᾶς καὶ δακρύων προσενέγκας
he offered prayers and appeals with loud cries and tears to the one who was able to save him from death,

Δεήσεις is the acc. pl. fem. of δέησις (-εως, ἡ), "prayer" (BDAG 213d). Ἱκετηρίας is the acc. pl. fem. of ἱκετηρία (-ας, ἡ), "supplication" (BDAG 473b; F. Büschel, *TDNT* 3:296–97; NT hapax). The correls. τε καί indicate a close connection between the two terms (BDAG 993c), but are simply tr. as "and" in most EVV. This expression occurs only here in the NT, but is attested in Greco-Roman literature and Philo (Attridge 149–50). The subst. ptc. *δυνάμενον* refers to God, the one to whom Jesus's prayers and supplications are directed. *Πρὸς τὸν δυνάμενον* adv. modifies *προσενέγκας*, indicating purpose. *Σῴζειν* is the pres. act. inf. of *σῴζω*, "save" (BDAG 982c), here from physical death. The inf. complements *δυνάμενον*. *Αὐτόν* is the obj. of the inf.; the pron.'s antecedent is Jesus. *Ἐκ θανάτου* adv. (gen. of separation) modifies *σῴζειν*. *Προσενέγκας* is the nom. sg. masc. of the aor. act. ptc. of *προσφέρω* (see comments on v. 1). The aor. is global. The ptc. recalls the subjunc. in v. 1 and contrasts the offering of the Levitical high priest with Jesus's own sacrificial offering (cf. Lane 1:119), although the priestly focus is not developed here. *Κραυγῆς* is the gen. sg. fem. of *κραυγή, -ῆς, ἡ*, "loud cry" (BDAG 565d), which is amplified by the adj. *ἰσχυρᾶς* (*ἰσχυρός, -ά, -όν*, "loud" [most EVV], "violent," "mighty" [BDAG 483d–484a]). *Δακρύων* is the gen. pl. neut. of *δάκρυον, -ου, τό*, "tear" (BDAG 211b). *Μετὰ κραυγῆς ἰσχυρᾶς καὶ δακρύων* adv. modifies *προσενέγκας* for manner. The ptc. is circum., dependent on the fin. vb. *ἔμαθεν* in 5:8.

καὶ εἰσακουσθεὶς ἀπὸ τῆς εὐλαβείας,
and he was heard because of his reverence.

Καί adds a new point to the argument (BDAG 494c). *Εἰσακουσθείς* is the nom. sg. masc. of the aor. pass. ptc. of *εἰσακούω*, "hear" (BDAG 293d). The pass. is a divine pass. The ptc. is circum., dependent on the finite vb. *ἔμαθεν* in 5:8. The prep. phrase adv. modifies the ptc. (see below). There are several interrelated interpretive decisions in this clause. The first involves the mng. *εὐλαβείας* (gen. sg. fem. of *εὐλάβεια, -ας, ἡ*; BDAG 407c; R. Bultmann, *TDNT* 2:751–54):

1. "fear" (of death or God);
*2. "awe" (as in reverence or piety; "godly fear").

The first option would suggest that *ἀπό* retains its common mng. of "separation" and modifies *σῴζειν* (e.g., "to save from death"). The second option suggests that *ἀπό* functions causally (attested, although rare; see R 580; BDF §210[1]; cf. BDF §211; BDAG 106c) and modifies *εἰσακουσθείς*: "heard because of his reverence or piety." The second option is preferred because elsewhere Hebrews uses *φόβος* to indicate "fear" (e.g., 2:15) and *εὐλάβεια* to indicate "awe" (12:28; cf. 11:7; "reverent submission," NIV, NRSV; "devotion," NET; "piety," NASB). The noun and vb. are used only in Hebrews, but the cognate adj. occurs in Luke with the sense of "reverence" (see Bruce 129 n. 61). Moreover, the second option better fits the syntax of this v. (See the extended discussion in Harris 65–66.) The idea is thus that Jesus was "saved" in his resurrection: "Jesus was not kept from the experience of death, but death had no lasting dominion over him" (Lane 1:120).

The precise correl. of this v. to events in Jesus's earthly life is debated. The imagery could refer to the gospel traditions of Gethsemane (Matt 26:36–46; Mark 14:32–42; Luke 22:40–46) and/or the cross (Matt 27:46–50). The pars. are not exact, however, and others have suggested the background of the "righteous sufferer" in Psalm 116 (cf. Psalm 22 [e.g., Guthrie, "Hebrews" 962b]).

VERSE 8

καίπερ ὢν υἱός, ἔμαθεν ἀφ' ὧν ἔπαθεν τὴν ὑπακοήν,
Although he was the Son, he learned obedience from what he suffered.

The conj. *καίπερ* indicates concession ("although" [BDAG 497c]) and is only used with ptcs. (BDF §425[1]); *ὢν* is thus concessive [Wallace 635; M 102]; "son though he was," REB) and dependent on *ἔμαθεν*. *Ἔμαθεν* is the 3rd sg. aor. act. indic. of *μανθάνω*, "learn" (BDAG 615c; "less through instruction than through experience"; K. H. Rengstorf, *TDNT* 4:390–412). The obj. of *ἔμαθεν* is *ὑπακοήν* (acc. sg. fem. of *ὑπακοή, -ῆς, ἡ*, "obedience" [BDAG 1028c]). *Ἔπαθεν* is the 3rd sg. aor. act. indic. of *πάσχω*, "suffer" (most EVV), "endure," "undergo" (BDAG 785d; W. Michaelis, *TDNT* 5:904–19). The rel. clause *ὧν ἔπαθεν* ("that which he suffered") is embedded in the prep. phrase (*ἀφ'* before rough breathing; for the syntax of this cstr., see Wallace 480). The antecedent of the rel. pron. *ὧν* (gen. pl. neut.) is implied (e.g., "those things"; "*ἀπὸ τούτων ἅ*" [R 720]). The prep. phrase *ἀφ' ὧν ἔπαθεν* adv. modifies *ἔμαθεν* for means: "he learned through that which he suffered."

Learning obedience through suffering entails practicing obedience (Koester 290), which is a key part of the author's argument of how the exalted Son became the great high priest who can sympathize with those who turn to him. The wordplay between *ἔμαθεν* and *ἔπαθεν* was "very widespread, and probably originates in popular speech" (Ellingworth 291; cf. BDF §488[2]) and evinces more of the author's rhetorical acumen. It might be roughly equivalent to the Eng. expression "No pain no gain." See also Lane 1:121.

VERSE 9

καὶ τελειωθεὶς ἐγένετο πᾶσιν τοῖς ὑπακούουσιν αὐτῷ αἴτιος σωτηρίας αἰωνίου,
After he was perfected, he became the source of eternal salvation for all who obey him,

Καί adds a new point to the argument (BDAG 494c). *Τελειωθείς* is the nom. sg. masc. of the aor. pass. ptc. of *τελειόω*, "perfected" (most EVV); cf. "qualified" (NLT); "bring to its goal/completion" (BDAG 996c). See For Further Study 18 (Perfection in Hebrews). The use of *σωτηρία* here recalls its use in 2:10 and anticipates 9:28 (see Ellingworth 293–94). The aor. indicates either antecedent time in relation to *ἐγένετο* ("having been perfected") or is causal ("because he was perfected"). The pass. is a divine pass. The aor. *ἐγένετο* is ingressive. Note the contrast between "being" (*ὤν*) a Son and "becoming" (*ἐγένετο*) a high priest (cf. Ellingworth 294). *Αἴτιος* is the nom. sg. masc. of *αἴτιος, -ία, -ον*, "source, cause" (BDAG 31b; the adj. occurs only as a subst. in BGk.). Here it functions as a pred. nom. of the equative *ἐγένετο*. *Σωτηρίας* modifes *αἴτιος* as an obj. gen.; it is modified by *αἰωνίος, -ον*, "eternal" (cf. 9:12; Isa 45:17).

Ὑπακούουσιν (dat. pl. masc. of the pres. act. ptc. of ὑπακούω, "obey" [most EVV], "follow" [BDAG 1028d]) is subst. It is followed by a dat. obj. αὐτῷ, the antecedent of which is the Son (v. 8). The ptc. is modified by πᾶσιν ("all"). The dat. πᾶσιν τοῖς ὑπακούουσιν is a dat. of advantage (BDF §188).

The use of αἰωνίος introduces a series of benefits made possible by the Son, namely eternal salvation (5:9), eternal redemption (9:12), eternal inheritance (9:15), and an eternal covenant (13:20 [Bruce 132]).

VERSE 10

προσαγορευθεὶς ὑπὸ τοῦ θεοῦ ἀρχιερεὺς κατὰ τὴν τάξιν Μελχισέδεκ.
and he was declared by God a high priest according to the order of Melchizedek.

Προσαγορευθείς is the nom. sg. masc. of the aor. pass. ptc. of προσαγορεύω, "designate" (most EVV [BDAG 875d]). The idea here is par. to v. 1 and v. 4 (Koester 291). Προσαγορεύω pars. the semantically related καλέω in v. 4 (Cockerill 250). A pred. acc. can become nom. (ἀρχιερεύς) with pass. vbs. (R 485). Note the switch from ἱερεύς in the psalm citation to ἀρχιερεύς in this v. (Ellingworth 296). Ὑπὸ τοῦ θεοῦ indicates agency of the pass. ptc. The adj. prep. phrase κατὰ τὴν τάξιν Μελχισέδεκ modifies ἀρχιερεύς, indicating conformity to a norm, "according to" (BDAG 512c). For τάξις and Μελχισέδεκ, see comments on v. 6.

FOR FURTHER STUDY

40. Christ's Incarnation and Humanity (5:1–10)

*Campbell, John C. "In a Son: The Doctrine of Incarnation in the Epistle to the Hebrews." *Int* 10 (1956): 24–38.
*Dukes, Jimmy W. "The Humanity of Jesus in Hebrews." *TTE* 32 (1985): 38–45.
*Marshall, I. Howard. *NDBT* 576–81.
McCormack, Bruce L. "'With Loud Cries and Tears': The Humanity of the Son in the Epistle to the Hebrews." Pages 37–68 in Bauckham, *Theology*.
Melbourne, Bertram L. "An Examination of the Historical-Jesus Motif in the Epistle to the Hebrews." *AUSS* 26 (1988): 281–97.
Peeler, Amy. "With Tears and Joy: The Emotions of Christ in Hebrews." *Koinonia* 20 (2008): 12–26.
Williamson, Ronald. "The Incarnation of the Logos in Hebrews." *ExpT* 95 (1983): 4–8.

41. The Structure of Hebrews (5:1–10)

Black, David Alan. "The Problem of the Literary Structure of Hebrews: An Evaluation and a Proposal." *GTJ* 7 (1986): 163–77.
*Decker, Rodney J. "The Intentional Structure of Hebrews." *Journal of Ministry and Theology* 4 (2000): 80–105.
Ellingworth, 50–59.
*Guthrie, 54–57.

Guthrie, George H. *The Structure of Hebrews: A Text-Linguistic Analysis*. Grand Rapids: Baker, 1994.

Heath, David M. "The Problem of Peak in Hebrews." *Neot* 48 (2014): 405–16.

Heil, John Paul. *Hebrews: Chiastic Structures and Audience Response*. *CBQ* Monograph Series 46. Washington, DC: Catholic Biblical Association of America, 2010.

*Joslin, Barry Clyde. "Can Hebrews Be Structured?: An Assessment of Eight Approaches." *CurBR* 6 (2007): 99–129.

Landgraf, Paul David. "The Structure of Hebrews: A Word of Exhortation in Light of the Day of Atonement." Pages 19–28 in Bauckham, *Cloud*.

*Lane, 1: *lxxxiv–ciii*.

———. *DLNT* 449–56.

Lincoln, 23–33.

Lindars, Barnabas. "The Rhetorical Structure of Hebrews." *NTS* 35 (1989): 382–406.

*MacLeod, David J. "The Literary Structure of the Book of Hebrews." *BSac* (1989): 185–97.

Martin, Michael W., and Jason A Whitlark. "The Encomiastic Topics of Syncrisis as the Key to the Structure and Argument of Hebrews." *NTS* 57 (2011): 415–39.

Rice, George E. "The Chiastic Structure of the Central Section of the Epistle to the Hebrews." *AUSS* 19 (1981): 243–47.

*Stanley, Steve. "The Structure of Hebrews from Three Perspectives." *TynBul* 45/2 (1994): 245–71.

Swetnam, James. "Form and Content in Hebrews 1–6." *Bib* 53 (1972): 368–85.

———. "Form and Content in Hebrews 7–13." *Bib* 55 (1974): 333–48.

Vanhoye, A. *Structure and Message of the Epistle to the Hebrews*. Rome: Pontifical Biblical Institute, 1989.

Westfall, Cynthia Long. *A Discourse Analysis of the Letter to the Hebrews: The Relationship between Form and Meaning*. London: Continuum, 2006.

42. The Son's Suffering (5:7–8)

Attridge, Harold W. "Heard Because of His Reverence (Heb 5:7)." *JBL* 98 (1979): 90–93.

DeYoung, Kevin. "Divine Impassibility and the Passion of Christ in the Book of Hebrews." *WTJ* 68 (2006): 41–50.

Lightfoot, Neil R. "The Saving of the Savior: Hebrews 5:7ff." *ResQ* 16 (1973): 166–73.

Omark, Reuben E. "The Saving of the Savior: Exegesis and Christology in Hebrews 5:7–10." *Int* 12 (1958): 39–51.

Richardson, Christopher. "The Passion: Reconsidering Hebrews 5:7–8." Pages 51–67 in Bauckham, *Cloud*.

Swetnam, James. "The Crux at Hebrews 5, 7–8." *Bib* 81 (2000): 347–61.

Young, Norman H. "Suffering: A Key to the Epistle to the Hebrews." *ABR* 51 (2003): 47–59.

HOMILETICAL SUGGESTIONS

Our Perfected High Priest (5:1–10)

1. The divine appointment of OT high priests (vv. 1–4)
2. The divine appointment of Christ (vv. 5–6)

3. The unique qualification process and outcome of Christ's high priesthood (vv. 7–10)

The Aaronic High Priest and the High Priest in the Order of Melchizedek (5:1–10)

(adapted from Lane 1:111)

1. The selection and call of the Aaronic high priest (v. 1)
2. The sacrifice offered by the Aaronic high priest (v. 1)
3. The weakness of the Aaronic high priest (vv. 2–3)
4. The appointment of the Aaronic high priest (v. 4)
5. The appointment of Christ, the high priest in the order of Melchizedek (vv. 5–6)
6. The suffering of Christ, the high priest (vv. 7–8)
7. The sacrificial provision of Christ, the high priest (v. 9)
8. The new office of Christ, the high priest (v. 10)

IV. Perseverance in the Promises (5:11–6:20)

A. PRELUDE: IT'S TIME TO GROW UP AND MOVE ON TO MATURITY (5:11–6:3)

STRUCTURE

The author abruptly breaks off from discussion of the Melchizedekian priesthood to exhort the audience about the necessity of persevering. This section introduces a new major subsection in Hebrews that demonstrates more of the author's rhetorical skill. Cockerill (252) notes the movement from shame (5:11–6:3) to warning (6:4–8), and finally to consolation (6:9–12) and confidence (6:13–20). In 5:11–6:3, the author hopes the audience will respond: "No! We are not lazy! No! We are not babies!" For the rhetorical effect of such exhortation in a shame/honor culture, see deSilva 210–14; Witherington 203–5.

The first part of the section (5:11–14) begins with a verbless clause and is followed by two indic., which are followed by another verbless clause and an indic. Three acc. are associated with the inf. in v. 12; the subj. of the inf. *τινά* is indented under the inf. The obj. and its complement are aligned par. The pred. in v. 14, *τελείων*, is further modified by the subst. ptc. *τῶν ἐχόντων*, which is aligned par. The second part of the section is anchored with the hort. subjunc. in 6:1. The obj. of *καταβαλλόμενοι* is *θεμέλιον*, which is modified by six gen. (aligned in the outline).

11 Περὶ οὗ
πολὺς ἡμῖν ὁ λόγος
καὶ
δυσερμήνευτος λέγειν,
ἐπεὶ νωθροὶ γεγόνατε ταῖς ἀκοαῖς.
12 καὶ γὰρ ὀφείλοντες εἶναι διδάσκαλοι
διὰ τὸν χρόνον,
πάλιν χρείαν ἔχετε τοῦ διδάσκειν ὑμᾶς
τινὰ

τὰ στοιχεῖα
τῆς ἀρχῆς τῶν λογίων τοῦ θεοῦ
καὶ γεγόνατε χρείαν ἔχοντες γάλακτος
[καὶ] οὐ στερεᾶς τροφῆς.

13 πᾶς γὰρ ὁ μετέχων γάλακτος ἄπειρος λόγου δικαιοσύνης,
νήπιος γάρ ἐστιν·
14 τελείων δέ ἐστιν ἡ στερεὰ τροφή,
τῶν διὰ τὴν ἕξιν
τὰ αἰσθητήρια
γεγυμνασμένα
ἐχόντων
πρὸς διάκρισιν καλοῦ τε καὶ κακοῦ.
6:1 Διὸ ἀφέντες τὸν τῆς ἀρχῆς τοῦ Χριστοῦ λόγον
ἐπὶ τὴν τελειότητα
φερώμεθα,
μὴ πάλιν θεμέλιον καταβαλλόμενοι
μετανοίας ἀπὸ νεκρῶν ἔργων
καὶ πίστεως ἐπὶ θεόν,
2 βαπτισμῶν διδαχῆς
ἐπιθέσεώς τε χειρῶν,
ἀναστάσεώς τε νεκρῶν
καὶ κρίματος αἰωνίου.
3 καὶ τοῦτο ποιήσομεν,
ἐάνπερ ἐπιτρέπῃ ὁ θεός.

VERSE 11

Περὶ οὗ πολὺς ἡμῖν ὁ λόγος καὶ δυσερμήνευτος λέγειν,
We have a great deal to say about this, and it is difficult to explain,

Περί with the gen. means "about," "concerning" (Harris 180). The antecedent of οὗ is the preceding discussion of the Melchizedekian priesthood ("this" [most EVV]; so Cockerill 254), rather than either Melchizedek (so NEB, REB) or Christ. Πολύς ("many") modifies ὁ λόγος. Ἡμῖν is possibly an "epistolary" pl. (cf. 2:5; Wallace 396); the dat. indicates poss. This unusual expression may reflect CGk (BDF §393[6]). Most EVV tr. it as "we have much to say" (e.g., ESV, NASB, NIV), thereby obscuring the ref. to λόγος (Cockerill 255). The adj. δυσερμήνευτος (BGk. hapax) is the nom. sg. masc. of δυσερμήνευτος, -ον, "hard to explain" (BDAG 265a), modifying λόγος. Λέγειν complements δυσερμήνευτος (R 1076).

ἐπεὶ νωθροὶ γεγόνατε ταῖς ἀκοαῖς.
since you have become too lazy to understand.

The conj. ἐπεί indicates cause or reason (BDAG 360c). The pf. γεγόνατε is intensive (Campbell, *VA* 201). Νωθροί is the nom. pl. masc. of νωθρός, -ά, -όν, "lazy," "sluggish" (BDAG 683c) and functions as a pred. adj. Its occurrence in this v. and 6:12 forms an *inclusio* around the third "warning" passage in Hebrews. These are the only two NT occurrences of this adj. (For the rhetorical effect of this *inclusio*, see Owen Nease, "Sound Familiar?: Paronomasia in Hebrews," *TJ* 33 (2012): 77–94.) The subst. ἀκοαῖς (dat. pl. fem. of ἀκοή, -ῆς, ἡ) can indicate either "hearing" or "ear" (BDAG 36b–c; H. Preisker, *TDNT* 4:1126) and is a dat. of respect: "lazy with respect to hearing"; "sluggish in hearing" (NET), "slow to learn," or even, "you no longer try to understand" (TNIV). See For Further Study 12 (The Warning Passages in Hebrews).

VERSE 12

καὶ γὰρ ὀφείλοντες εἶναι διδάσκαλοι διὰ τὸν χρόνον,
Although by this time you ought to be teachers,

Καί in the collocation καὶ γάρ has virtually lost its force (BDF §452[3]). Ὀφείλοντες is the nom. pl. masc. of the pres. act. ptc. of ὀφείλω, "be obligated" (BDAG 743b–c; with inf. foll.). Εἶναι is the complement of the ptc., which is dependent on ἔχετε and indicates concession: "even though you ought to be teachers." The subst. διδάσκαλοι (nom. pl. masc. of διδάσκαλος, -ου, ὁ, "teacher") is a pred. nom. In Hebrews the term does not denote a particular office, but rather the responsibility of mature believers (cf. Ellingworth 302). Διὰ τὸν χρόνον modifies ὀφείλοντες εἶναι casually ("because enough time has passed," or simply, "by this time" [most EVV; cf. Ellingworth 302]).

πάλιν χρείαν ἔχετε τοῦ διδάσκειν ὑμᾶς τινὰ τὰ στοιχεῖα τῆς ἀρχῆς τῶν λογίων τοῦ θεοῦ
you need someone to teach you the basic principles of God's revelation again.

Πάλιν indicates that the audience had already received instruction (cf. Cockerill 256). Χρείαν is the acc. sg. fem. of χρεία, -ᾶς, ἡ, "need" (BDAG 1088c) and is the dir. obj. of ἔχετε, although many EVV tr. the noun as a vb. (e.g., "you need" [CSB]). The inf. τοῦ διδάσκειν indicates purpose, following the verbal idea implicit in χρείαν (BDF §400[1]; the art. inf. in this cstr. occurs only here in the NT). Usually, when an inf. has two acc., the first acc. is the subj. of the inf. and the second acc. is its obj. In this example, however, context indicates that τινά is the subj. of the inf. and ὑμᾶς is its obj. (Wallace 194, 196). The third acc. is στοιχεῖα (acc. pl. neut. of στοιχεῖον, -ου, τό, "elementary truths" [NIV]; "basic principles" [ESV]; "ABC of God's oracles" [REB]; "elements, fundamental principles" [BDAG 946b]); it is the obj. complement of ὑμᾶς (BDF §155[1]; acc. of "person" and "thing," R 482). See For Further Study 43 (Στοιχεῖα and Elemental Teachings). Ἀρχῆς is a gen. of quality and may recall the initial proclamation of the gospel (e.g., 2:3; Koester 302). Λογίων is the gen. pl. neut. of λόγιον, -ου, τό; this noun is "always in the pl., and always with ref. to God's revelation" (*NIDNTTE* 3:157); "oracles of God" (ESV, KJV); "God's word" (NIV, NLT). The expression τῶν λογίων τοῦ θεοῦ commonly refers to (the OT) Scripture (e.g., Acts

7:38). Biblical instruction in the basic truths of the faith and in God's Word was part of early church catechism.

καὶ γεγόνατε χρείαν ἔχοντες γάλακτος [καὶ] οὐ στερεᾶς τροφῆς.
You need milk, not solid food.

The use of *γίνομαι* in a pf. periph. cstr. (*γεγόνατε . . . ἔχοντες*) is unusual (R 903); it denotes "the beginning of a state or condition" (BDF §354). The pf. pars. its usage in v. 11. *Χρείαν* is the obj. of the ptc. *Γάλακτος* is the gen. neut. sg. of *γάλα, γάλακτος, τό,* "milk" (BDAG 186c). The gen. is required by *χρεία*. Although the external evidence is inconclusive, *καί* is omitted in early and widespread mss. and is probably not original. *Στερεᾶς* (gen. sg. fem. of *στερεός, -ά, -όν,* "solid" [BDAG 943b]) modifies *τροφῆς* (gen. sg. fem. of *τροφή, -ῆς, ἡ,* "nourishment," "food" [BDAG 1017c]). The imagery of milk and solid food to discuss spiritual maturity (or here, spiritual regression) also occurs in 1 Cor 3:1–4; the imagery in 1 Pet 2:2, however, is positive—that of longing for God's work as a baby longs for milk. Food imagery was common to indicate educational/maturity levels in Greco-Roman writings (Attridge 158–60; M. J. Wilkins, *DLNT* 736–38).

VERSE 13

πᾶς γὰρ ὁ μετέχων γάλακτος ἄπειρος λόγου δικαιοσύνης, νήπιος γάρ ἐστιν·
Now everyone who lives on milk is inexperienced with the message about righteousness, because he is an infant.

Γάρ offers further implications of the audience's spiritual status. *Πᾶς* modifies *ὁ μετέχων* (nom. sg. masc. of the pres. act. ptc. of *μετέχω*, EVV "to partake of something in common" [BDAG 642d; followed by gen.]). The ptc. is subst. The cognate *μέτοχος* occurs in 1:9; 3:1; 3:14 (see comments on 3:1). A form of an equative vb. is implied (R 395). The adj. *ἄπειρος* (nom. sg. masc. of *ἄπειρος, -ον,* "not accustomed to" (NASB), "inexperienced" (NET), "not acquainted with" (NIV [BDAG 100c; NT hapax]) functions as a pred. adj. and is freq. followed by the gen. (*λόγου*), here indicating ref. (Wallace 128). The subj. of *ἐστίν* is elliptically understood to be *ὁ μετέχων*. *Νήπιος* is the nom. sg. masc. of *νήπιος, -ου, ὁ,* "infant" (NASB, NET, NIV), "child" (ESV [BDAG 671b]). It functions as a pred. nom. Similar to the ref. to milk, the imagery indicates the audience's spiritual immaturity (cf. 1 Cor 3:1).

The options for *λόγου δικαιοσύνης* are wide-ranging. Following Lane (1:137–38), there are several main options (see also Ellingworth 306–7).

1. The gen. *δικαιοσύνης* indicates "definition" or "quality"—"right speech," which is not possible for infants (G. Schrenk, *TDNT* 2:199–200; cf. BDF §165).
2. Drawing on the ethical vocabulary in this section (see Thompson, *Philosophy* 35–37), the expression could mean "correct reasoning" (see discussion in Koester 302).
3. The expression pars. "solid food" and indicates maturity.

4. The gen. indicates ref.—"the teaching about righteousness," ostensibly, the content of the Christian faith; e.g., "the teaching about righteousness" (NIV); "the word of righteousness" (ESV).
*5. The word refers to teaching about Christ's high priesthood and the perseverance that it makes possible (so Cockerill 258–59). This view draws on but is more specific than option 4 and fits the overall context of Hebrews better.
6. A technical use indicating martyrdom that draws on later par., esp. Polycarp (Lane 1:137–38); it is unclear, however, that this technical use was intended by the author (see discussion on 12:1).

VERSE 14

τελείων δέ ἐστιν ἡ στερεὰ τροφή,
But solid food is for the mature—

Δέ connects closely related items (BDAG 213b). The subj. of *ἐστίν* is *ἡ στερεὰ τροφή* (see comments on v. 12). The adj. *τελείων* (*τέλειος, -α, -ον*) is subst. ("mature" [BDAG 995d]). The gen. functions as a pred. adj. (BDF 89, 4[A]; R 497).

τῶν διὰ τὴν ἕξιν τὰ αἰσθητήρια γεγυμνασμένα ἐχόντων πρὸς διάκρισιν καλοῦ τε καὶ κακοῦ.
for those whose senses have been trained to distinguish between good and evil.

The ptc. *ἐχόντων* is subst. (*τῶν . . . ἐχόντων*). The obj. of the ptc. is *αἰσθητήρια* (acc. pl. neut. of *αἰσθητήρια, -ου, τό*, "powers of discernment" [ESV], "senses" [NASB], "perceptions" [NET], "faculty" [BDAG 29b–c; NT hapax]; "'organs" of spiritual perception [Ellingworth 309]; "ethical discernment" [Attridge 161]), which is modified by *γεγυμνασμένα* (acc. pl. neut. of the pf. pass. ptc. of *γυμνάζω*, "train," "undergo discipline" [BDAG 208b]) and functions equivalently to a rel. clause ("which has been trained" [R 789]). The adv. prep. *διὰ τὴν ἕξιν* modifies *γεγυμνασμένα* causally. *Ἕξιν* is the acc. sg. fem. of *ἕξις, -εως, ἡ*, "maturity" (BDAG 350b; BGk. hapax). Although many EVV and older lexica (e.g., BAGD 1979) gloss *ἕξις* as "habit," "exercise," or "practice," the word indicates a "mature state or condition." (See John A. L. Lee, "Hebrews 5:14 and ἝΞΙΣ: A History of Misunderstanding," *NovT* 39 [1997]: 151–76; cf. Mark C. Kiley, "A Note on Hebrews 5:15," *CBQ* 42 [1980]: 501–3; followed by Cockerill 259.)

Διάκρισιν is the acc. sg. fem. of *διάκρισις, -εως, ἡ*, "distinguishing," "differentiation" (BDAG 231d); the noun is tr. as an inf. in many EVV ("to distinguish" [NASB, NIV], "to discern" [ESV, NET]). The gen. *καλοῦ* and *κακοῦ* are ablatival (R 514). The correls. *τε καί* indicate a close connection between the two terms (BDAG 993c). The adv. prep. *πρὸς διάκρισιν καλοῦ τε καὶ κακοῦ* modifies *γεγυμνασμένα* for result (cf. Harris 189). The expression may allude to Num 14:23.

The series of analogies in 5:11–14 were well known in Greco-Roman writings and may be listed as follows (cf. Attridge 162): infants // immature Christians; milk // basic

Christian doctrine; adults // mature Christians; solid food // harder instruction (the author's teaching on the Melchizedekian priesthood). Lane (1:137), however, notes the importance of recognizing the irony in this section. The author is not suggesting a progression from milk to solid food, but rather is calling attention to the seriousness of the audience's failure to pay attention (cf. 2:1–4; 3:7–19; 4:12–13). The irony is evident when the author resumes discussion of Melchizedek in 7:1–10.

VERSE 1

Διὸ ἀφέντες τὸν τῆς ἀρχῆς τοῦ Χριστοῦ λόγον ἐπὶ τὴν τελειότητα φερώμεθα,
Therefore, let us leave the elementary teaching about Christ and go on to maturity,

Διό is an inferential conj. (BDAG 250c) that links the rebuke/exhortation in 5:11–14 to the exhortation in 6:1–3 (see BDF §451[5]). Ἀφέντες is the nom. pl. masc. of the aor. act. ptc. of ἀφίημι, "leave (behind) to go on to someth. else" (BDAG 156d; R. Bultmann, *TDNT* 1:510–12). The ptc. is circum. This does not indicate rejecting something as much as moving forward. Ἀφέντες may have been a rhetorical device in Gk. literature to signal a transition to a new topic (Koester 303). The obj. of ἀφέντες is λόγον, modified by τῆς ἀρχῆς, which is further modified by τοῦ Χριστοῦ. There are several interrelated issues regarding this cstr.:

1. Λόγος likely indicates "message" (Attridge 155; Cockerill 254) or "teaching" (BDAG 599d; Lane 1:130).
2. The gen. τῆς ἀρχῆς indicates the "initial" (cf. BDAG 137d; Attridge 155) or "beginning" (BDAG 138c) element in a sequence or series; cf. "preliminary" (Bruce 137); "elementary" (Lane 1:130; Cockerill 254); "the first lessons" (GNT).
3. The gen. τοῦ Χριστοῦ is obj. ("the teaching about Christ"; so most EVV) rather than subj. ("Christ's teaching"; *pace* Attridge 162).

Another difficulty, however, is that the items listed in vv. 1–2 are not distinctively Christian (vs. Jewish). This may reflect the author's understanding that the ultimate significance of Jewish (OT) practices and beliefs, with which his audience was familiar and to which they may have been tempted to return, is now understood Christologically. Regardless, the author's point is to grow beyond initial, foundational (Christian) teaching to deeper spiritual maturity.

Φερώμεθα is the 1st pl. pres. pass. subjunc. of φέρω; it is used fig. to indicate "spiritual direction"—"let us move on to . . ." (BDAG 1052a); the subjunc. is hort. The voice may be *mid. (permissive) or pass. (BDAG 1051d; a divine pass.; e.g., Lane 1:131 n. *k*). The pl. is likely authorial. The ptc. is dependent on φερώμεθα and indicates a contemp. action that picks up the hort. force of the subjunc. ("let us . . . go on to" [CSB]; Lane 1:131 n. *i*.). Τελειότητα is the acc. sg. fem. of τελειότης, -ητος, ἡ, "maturity" (most EVV), "perfection," "completeness" (BDAG 996b); the word occurs only here and in Col 3:14. It denotes a result more than a process (Lane 1:131–32 n. *l*.). The adv. prep. phrase ἐπὶ τὴν τελειότητα modifies φερώμεθα to indicate purpose or goal (BDAG 366a).

μὴ πάλιν θεμέλιον καταβαλλόμενοι μετανοίας ἀπὸ νεκρῶν ἔργων καὶ πίστεως ἐπὶ θεόν,
not laying again a foundation of repentance from dead works, faith in God,

As with 5:12, πάλιν indicates that the audience had already laid the initial foundation of their faith (cf. Cockerill 256). The neg. adv. μή modifies καταβαλλόμενοι, which is the nom. pl. masc. of the pres. mid. ptc. of καταβάλλω, "found," "lay a foundation" (BDAG 514c). Parallel to ἀφέντες, καταβαλλόμενοι is dependent on φερώμεθα and indicates a contemp. action. The ptc. may also pick up the hort. force of the subjunc. ("let us not again lay a foundation"), but more likely is instr. (indicating how the audience is to move forward). The obj. of the ptc. is θεμέλιον, which is the acc. sg. masc. from θεμέλιος, -ου, ὁ, "foundation" (BDAG 449a). It is modified by μετανοίας, which is the gen. sg. fem. of μετανοία, -ας, ἡ, "repentance" (most EVV), "turning about," "conversion" (BDAG 640d; Behm, *TDNT* 4:989–1006). The gen. is appos. or definition (R 498).

The prep. phrase ἀπὸ νεκρῶν ἔργων adj. modifies μετανοίας, indicating separation. The subst. ἔργων is modified by the adj. νεκρῶν (gen. pl. neut.). The expression νεκρῶν ἔργων is debated—it seems to indicate sinful deeds generally (so Bruce 139; cf. Attridge 164; see esp. Koester 304–305). Πίστεως further modifies θεμέλιον as a gen. of appos. or definition (R 498). The prep. phrase ἐπὶ θεόν modifies πίστεως. The use of ἐπί here may "derive from the notion of turning away from former objects of devotion . . . it usually refers to the initial act of conversion" (Harris 235). Repentance is a key OT concept, and was preached by John the Baptist, Jesus, and the apostles (see Scripture refs. in Attridge 164).

VERSE 2

βαπτισμῶν διδαχῆς
teaching about ritual washings,

Βαπτισμῶν is the gen. pl. masc. of βαπτισμός, -οῦ, ὁ, "washings" (ESV, NASB), "baptisms" (NET), "cleansing rites" (NIV), "cleansing" (BDAG 165d; A. Oepke, *TDNT* 1:545). The cognate βάπτισμα (-ατος, τό) denotes the result of an action (BDF §109[2]); the sg. is used in conj. with Christian baptism (e.g., Eph 4:5). Βαπτισμός occurs in the pl. in Mark 7:4 and Heb 9:10 to indicate ceremonial washings, whereas the sg. in Col 2:12 indicates Christian baptism. Here the word likely denotes ceremonial washings (so Lane 1:132 n. *o*; *pace* BDAG 165d; Koester 305). Διδαχῆς is the gen. sg. fem. of διδαχή, -ῆς, ἡ, "teaching" (BDAG 241c). Although usually gen. modifiers follow the word they modify, they occasionally precede, as is the case here. The gen. βαπτισμῶν is obj. (R 501) or indicates ref.: "teaching with ref. to baptisms" (BDF §§ 168[2], 474[4]).

The rdg. διδαχῆς has strong external evidence, including several important codices (e.g., ℵ A C D; UBS rating {A}). Although the external evidence for the rdg. διδαχήν ($\mathfrak{P}^{46}$ B) is not as extensive, it is "early and weighty" (Lane 1:132 n. *n*). Internal evidence is not decisive. The gen. could reflect assimilation of an orig. acc. to the surrounding gen. Alternatively, the acc. could be "a stylistic improvement introduced in order to avoid so many genitives" (Metzger 596). Overall, however, the acc. makes better sense as the second dir. obj. of *καταβαλλόμενοι*, par. to θεμέλιον (cf. Lane 1:132 n. *n*; Bruce 137 n. 3; Attridge 155 n. 10). This then would indicate two groupings of the six elements in vv. 1–2: first, a foundation of repentance and faith; second, teaching about washings, laying on of hands, resurrection from the dead, and eternal judgment (cf. Koester 310; Attridge 155; Bruce 139). If the var. rdg. is rejected, there are likely three groupings of two elements (e.g., inward events: *μετανοία* and *πίστις*; outward acts: *βαπτισμοί* and *ἐπίθεσις*; the future: *ἀναστάσις* and *κρίμα*; see Ellingworth 313), with the six gen. all modifying θεμέλιον as gen. of content or ref.

ἐπιθέσεώς τε χειρῶν,
laying on of hands,

Ἐπιθέσεως is the gen. sg. fem. of ἐπίθεσις, -εως, ἡ, "laying on" (BDAG 371d). The noun requires the gen. (e.g., χειρῶν). The correl. ptcls. *τε καί* (*καί* occurring at the end of the v.) indicate a par. connection between two or more terms (BDF §444[4]). The ptcl. τε joins the second part of the initial instruction, namely, laying on of hands, which was a common practice in the early church, esp. in association with the Holy Spirit (e.g., Acts 8:17–18; see Attridge 165 n. 125–27; Bruce 143; Ellingworth 316).

ἀναστάσεώς τε νεκρῶν
the resurrection of the dead,

Ἀναστάσεως is the gen. sg. fem. of ἀναστάσις, -εως, ἡ, "resurrection" (BDAD 71d). The subst. adj. νεκρῶν is masc., referring to people. The gen. is ablative. The ptcl. τε adds the third topic of instruction. Resurrection of the dead is adumbrated in the OT (e.g., Isa 26:19; Dan 12:2; cf. Heb 11:35) and implied in Exod 3:6 (see Mark 12:26–27).

καὶ κρίματος αἰωνίου.
and eternal judgment.

Καί closes off the list of topics about which the audience had received instruction. Κρίματος is the gen. sg. neut. from κρίμα, -ματος, τό, "judgment" (BDAG 567a). The adj. αἰωνίος modifies the subst. Eternal judgment anticipates its mention in 9:27–28 and 10:26–30; it recalls OT teaching (e.g., Gen 18:25) and pars. other NT teaching (e.g., Matt 25:31–46; Rev 20:11–15). See also comments on αἰωνίος on 5:9.

VERSE 3

καὶ τοῦτο ποιήσομεν, ἐάνπερ ἐπιτρέπῃ ὁ θεός.
And we will do this if God permits.

Καί is a connective (R 1181) linking the final clause to the sentence that begins in v. 1. The pl. ποιήσομεν is likely inclusive, although the tone is probably ironic (e.g., "let's grow up" [CEV]). The dem. τοῦτο likely refers conceptually to moving on to maturity or perfection (Wallace 335). The collocation καὶ τοῦτο ποιήσομεν comprises the apod. of a cond. The conj. ἐάνπερ introduces the prot. of a general cond. (BDF §§371[1], 454[2]; a third-class cond.; see Wallace 696–99). Ἐπιτρέπῃ is the 3rd sg. pres. act. subjunc. of ἐπιτρέπω, "permit" (most EVV), "allow" (BDAG 385a).

The exhortation to move on to spiritual maturity precedes one of the most difficult passages in the NT. It is important, therefore, to underscore the pastoral concern and care in 5:11–6:3. The author assumes that the audience has been grounded in Christian basics and is accountable for their immaturity. The strong warning (6:4–8) is followed by the author's assurances about the audience (6:9–12) and the eventual resumption of the difficult teaching about Melchizedek (7:1–10).

FOR FURTHER STUDY

43. Στοιχεια and Elemental Teachings (5:12; 6:1–3)

Adams, J. Clifford. "Exegesis of Hebrews 6:1f." *NTS* 13 (1967): 378–85.
Delling, G. *TDNT* 7:670–87.
NIDNTTE 4:379.
Peterson, David. "Situation of the 'Hebrews' (5:11–6:12)." *RTR* 35 (1976): 14–21.
Wainwright, G. *DLNT* 112–25.

HOMILETICAL SUGGESTIONS

Spiritual Growth and Spiritual Maturity Are Expected of All Believers—It's Time to Grow Up! (5:11–6:3)

1. Spiritual laziness prevents maturing believers from . . . (vv. 11–14)
   (a) . . . learning deeper spiritual truths (v. 11)
   (b) . . . teaching others (v. 12a)
   (c) . . . moving beyond the ABCs (v. 12b)
   (d) . . . moving on to solid food (vv. 12c–14)
2. Spiritual growth and spiritual maturity build on elementary truths (vv. 1–2)
   (a) Foundational truths (v. 1)
   Repentance from dead works (v. 1b)
   Faith in God (v. 1c)
   (b) Basic teaching (v. 2)
   Ceremonial washings (v. 2a)
   Laying on of hands (v. 2b)
   Resurrection (v. 2c)
   Eternal judgment (v. 2d)
3. Spiritual growth and spiritual maturity press on (v. 3)

B. THIRD WARNING: THERE IS ONLY ONE WAY TO BE RENEWED (6:4–8)

STRUCTURE

Verses 4–6 comprise one sentence that begins with the pred. adj. *ἀδύνατον* (whose complement is *ἀνακαινίζειν* in v. 6). A series of five art. (subst.) ptcs. occurs between the pred. adj. and inf., which is followed by two anar. (causal) ptcs. The next sentence (v. 7) is anchored on the finite vb. *μεταλαμβάνει*, which is elliptically understood in v. 8. This section is the third "warning" passage in Hebrews, and is often a key passage for Wesleyan/Arminian and Reformed/Calvinist debates. See For Further Study 12 (The Warning Passages in Hebrews). Significant also is the shift from the first pers. pl. in 5:11–6:3 to the third pers. pl. in this section, which suggests that the author is not describing the audience's pres. experience; indeed the strong warning seeks to prevent such apostasy. See discussion in Wallace 393. See also the syntactic chart in Guthrie, *Hebrews* 217.

4 Ἀδύνατον γὰρ τοὺς ἅπαξ φωτισθέντας,
γευσαμένους τε τῆς δωρεᾶς τῆς ἐπουρανίου
καὶ μετόχους γενηθέντας πνεύματος ἁγίου
5 καὶ . . . γευσαμένους
καλὸν θεοῦ ῥῆμα
δυνάμεις τε μέλλοντος αἰῶνος
6 καὶ παραπεσόντας,
πάλιν ἀνακαινίζειν
εἰς μετάνοιαν,
ἀνασταυροῦντας ἑαυτοῖς τὸν υἱὸν τοῦ θεοῦ
καὶ παραδειγματίζοντας.
7 γῆ γὰρ ἡ πιοῦσα τὸν ἐπ' αὐτῆς ἐρχόμενον πολλάκις ὑετὸν
καὶ τίκτουσα βοτάνην εὔθετον ἐκείνοις
δι' οὓς καὶ γεωργεῖται,
μεταλαμβάνει εὐλογίας ἀπὸ τοῦ θεοῦ·
8 ἐκφέρουσα δὲ ἀκάνθας καὶ τριβόλους,
ἀδόκιμος καὶ κατάρας ἐγγύς,
ἧς τὸ τέλος εἰς καῦσιν.

VERSE 4

Ἀδύνατον γὰρ τοὺς ἅπαξ φωτισθέντας,
For it is impossible . . . those who were once enlightened,

Γάρ is causal, giving a further reason why the audience must press on to maturity. *Ἀδύνατον* is the nom. sg. neut. of *ἀδύνατος, -ον* (BDAG 22a). The adj. is pred. with an implied form of *εἰμί* and an impers. subj. ("it is impossible" [most EVV]). The position of the adj. is emph. (Lane 1:141). The complement of the pred. adj. is the inf.

ἀνακαινίζειν in v. 6. Φωτισθέντας is the acc. pl. masc. of the aor. pass. ptc. of φωτίζω, "enlighten" (most EVV); "seen the light" (CEV); "to make known in reference to the inner life or transcendent matters" (BDAG 1074a). The ptc. is subst., with humans as the understood subj. and presumably God as the agent. The adv. ἅπαξ "once" (most EVV) "once and for all" (BDAG 97b) can be understood as quan. (one point in time) or qual. ("once and for all"; cf. Koester 313).

There are several related syntactic issues in vv. 4–6. First, many agree that the art. governs φωτισθέντας and likely each of the following four ptcs. in vv. 4–6 (so Cockerill 268), which is supported by the fact that the ptcs. are all aor. (*pace* Attridge 167, who sees the first four ptcs. comprising three ptc. clauses and takes the fifth ptc. with the two additional ptcs. in v. 6). Although this is not tech. an example of Granville Sharp's rule, the art. likely indicates that each of the ptcs. applies to the same group (see the discussion in Wallace 278–86). Thus the five ptcs. together describe those for whom restoration (ἀνακαινίζειν) is impossible, by offering different aspects of the same experience of salvation (Lane 1:141). Second, the placement of the adv. ἅπαξ after the art. and before the first ptc. probably indicates that it also modifies all five ptcs. rather than only the first ptc. (*pace* Ellingworth 319). The significance of these two points becomes clearer in the discussion of the fifth ptc.

The use of φωτίζω may allude to the pillar of fire that led the Israelites through the wilderness (Neh 9:12, 19; Guthrie, "Hebrews" 962c). The OT freq. associates light with God (e.g., Ps 27:1) and movement toward God and his Word (e.g., Ps 119:130), whereas darkness indicates sin and death (Prov 2:13; 4:19). Additionally, light was a common metaphor for conversion among early Christians (e.g., John 1:9; see Lane 1:141).

Discussion of items that are "impossible" also occurs in 6:18 (for God to lie), 10:4 (for the blood of bulls/goats to cleanse the conscience), and 11:6 (to please God without faith; Koester 312). The implied subj. in vv. 4–6 is most likely God (e.g., "it is impossible for God . . ."), although it could indicate human agency. See comments on v. 6. See esp. Koester 319–20; Ellingworth 319.

γευσαμένους τε τῆς δωρεᾶς τῆς ἐπουρανίου
who tasted the heavenly gift,

Γευσαμένους is the acc. pl. masc. of the aor. mid. ptc. of γεύομαι, "taste" (most EVV); "to experience something cognitively or emotionally" (BDAG 195d). The usage of γεύομαι in 2:9 (Christ tasting death) suggests a complete, not partial, experience here. Δωρεᾶς is the gen. sg. fem. of δωρεά, -ᾶς, ἡ, "gift" (BDAG 266c). The gen. is partitive (BDG §163[3]). The adj. ἐπουρανίου (ἐπουράνιος, -ον, "heavenly": BDAG 388b; cf. 3:1) is attrib. (second attrib. pos.; see Wallace 307). The expression may allude to the heavenly gift of manna (Exod 16:15; Neh 9:15) (Guthrie, "Hebrews" 962c); a ref. to the Eucharist is possible but not likely (cf. Ellingworth 320). The explicit ref. to the Holy Spirit in the next clause argues against understanding the gift of the Spirit in this clause. The correl. conj. τε καί indicates the pairing of two or more related entities (Wallace 672; BDF §444).

καὶ μετόχους γενηθέντας πνεύματος ἁγίου
who shared in the Holy Spirit,

Καί joins the third ptc. to the list begun with *τε* in the previous clause. *Γενηθέντας* is the acc. pl. masc. of the aor. pass. ptc. of *γίνομαι*. The ptc. is subst. The subst. *μετόχους* (acc. pl. masc. of *μέτοχος, -ου, ὁ*, "sharing/participating in" [BDAG 643c]) expands on the earlier use of this word in Heb 3:1, 14; see comments on 3:1. Here it functions as the pred. of the ptc. The gen. *πνεύματος* is partitive. The adj. *ἁγίου* is attrib.

VERSE 5

καὶ καλὸν γευσαμένους θεοῦ ῥῆμα δυνάμεις τε μέλλοντος αἰῶνος
who tasted God's good word and the powers of the coming age,

Καί joins the fourth ptc. to the list begun with *τε* in v. 4. *Γευσαμένους* is the acc. pl. masc. of the aor. mid. ptc. of *γεύομαι* and functions par. to its usage in v. 4. The adj. *κάλος* (*-η, -ον*) is either attrib. modifying *ῥῆμα* ("tasting the good word"; par. with *δυνάμεις*), or more prob. a pred. that functions as the obj. of the ptc. ("tasting that the word is good"; Moule 36; Lane 1:133 n. *u*; see also Wallace 310 n. 47). In Hebrews, *λόγος* and *ῥῆμα* are used interchangeably (Cockerill 270 n. 12; Attridge 170; Ellingworth 321). *Μέλλοντος* is the gen. sg. masc. of the pres. act. ptc. of *μέλλω*, "coming" (most EVV; see comments on 1:14). The second *τε* is used to join a single item, which here is the sec. obj. (*δυνάμεις*) of the ptc. (BDF §443[2]). Both *ῥῆμα* and *δυνάμεις* echo the exodus (e.g., Exod 4:28–30). Numerous OT citations depict the Word of God as "food" (e.g., Ps 34:9; Amos 8:11).

VERSE 6

καὶ παραπεσόντας, πάλιν ἀνακαινίζειν εἰς μετάνοιαν,
and who have fallen away . . . [it is impossible (v. 4)] to renew to repentance

Καί joins the fifth ptc. to the list begun with *τε*. *Παραπεσόντας* is the acc. pl. masc. of the aor. act. ptc. of *παραπίπτω*, "fall away" (most EVV), "commit apostasy" (NET; BDAG 770a; Michaelis, *TDNT* 6:171; NT hapax). A sim. image occurs in 3:12. *Ἀνακαινίζειν* is the pres. act. inf. of *ἀνακαινίζω*, "restore," "renew" (BDAG 64d; NT hapax). The adv. prep. phrase *εἰς μετάνοιαν* modifies the inf., indicating purpose or even result (Moule 70; Harris 90). The adv. *πάλιν* modifies the inf.

This ptc. is the *crux interpretum* for debates concerning soteriology in Hebrews. There is a long tradition (e.g., KJV, Moffatt, RSV, Barclay, NIV) of taking the ptc. as adv., with cond. force ("and if they fall away"; Lane 1:133 n. *v*), or less freq. concessive ("even though"; Ellingworth 323). This ptc. is the fifth (and final) in a series of aor. ptcs.; if this ptc. is construed as adv., then it is unclear why the preceding three ptcs. should not also be thus construed (e.g., that the art. in v. 4 governs only the first ptc.; cf. Wallace 633). The bracketing of the ptcs. between the pred. adj. in v. 4 and its complement in v. 6 strongly suggests that the ptcs. be treated as a group, which is also supported by the fact that all five ptcs. are global/constative aor. (cf. Cockerill 268; see esp. John A. Sproule, "Parapesontas in Hebrews 6:6" *GTJ* 2 [1981]: 327–32). Thus this ptc. indicates a progression that follows the first four ptcs. ("and then have fallen away" [ESV]). The force of the author's argument is amplified by the increasing length of the first four ptcs., which sharply contrasts with the unmodified fifth ptc. (see Ellingworth 322). See For Further Study 44 (The Warning Passage in Hebrews 6).

ἀνασταυροῦντας ἑαυτοῖς τὸν υἱὸν τοῦ θεοῦ καὶ παραδειγματίζοντας.
This is because, to their own harm, they are recrucifying the Son of God and holding him up to contempt.

Ἀνασταυροῦντας is the acc. pl. masc. of the pres. act. ptc. of ἀνασταυρόω, "crucify," "crucify again" (Schneider, *TDNT* 7:583–84; NT hapax). The vb. could simply indicate "crucify" (Attridge 171; Ellingworth 324; Koester 315), although the prefix suggests "crucify again" (fig. mng.; BDAG 72c; so Cockerill 274). The refl. ἑαυτοῖς is a dat. of disadvantage (*incommodi*; Wallace 144; R 539), "to their own detriment." Παραδειγματίζοντας is the acc. pl. masc. of the pres. act. ptc. of παραδειγματίζω, "subjecting . . . to public disgrace" (NIV), "holding . . . up to contempt" (ESV, NET), "put . . . to open shame" (NASB), "to disgrace someone publicly" (BDAG 761c; NT hapax). The ptc. alludes to Jesus's public disgrace on the cross (Matt 27:27–44; Mark 15:16–32; Luke 23:35–39). "The word . . . was used for public punishments that made an example out of the victim" (Koester 315). This is the only dir. ref. to crucifixion in Hebrews (but cf. Heb 12:2; 13:12).

Both ptcs. are pres. in contrast with the preceding aor. ptcs. The pres. could indicate "a continuous and obdurate stance toward Christ" (Attridge 172). Additionally, both ptcs. are adv., with two further options.

*1. Both are causal, indicating why it is impossible for the individuals described in vv. 4–6 to be renewed (so most EVV and commentators; e.g., Attridge 171; Cockerill 274; Koester 315).
2. Both ptcs. are temp., indicating contemp. time ("it is impossible . . . while they are crucifying again"; so J. K. Elliott, "Is Post-Baptismal Sin Forgivable?" *BT* 28 [1977]: 330–32). This view is dismissed as tautologous by many (but cf. Bruce 149; Koester 315).

VERSE 7

γῆ γὰρ ἡ πιοῦσα τὸν ἐπ' αὐτῆς ἐρχόμενον πολλάκις ὑετόν
For the ground that drinks the rain that often falls on it

Γάρ gives further reasons for the impossibility of renewal because of the reality of future judgment. The art. functions equivalently to a rel. pron. Πιοῦσα is the nom. sg. fem. of the aor. act. ptc. of πίνω, "drink" (BDAG 814c). The adj. ptc. modifies γῆ. Ὑετόν is the acc. sg. masc. of ὑετός, -οῦ, ὁ, "rain" (BDAG 1024b), which is modified by τόν and ἐρχόμενον, with the embedded prep. phrase ἐπ' αὐτῆς (BDF §443[5c]). 'Επί is spatial (R 603). The antecedent of αὐτῆς is γῆ. The ptc. is further modified by the adv. πολλάκις, "many times," "often," "frequently" (BDAG 846b). The statement may allude to Deut 11:11 or Isa 55:10.

καὶ τίκτουσα βοτάνην εὔθετον ἐκείνοις δι' οὓς καὶ γεωργεῖται,
and that produces vegetation useful to those for whom it is cultivated

Γῆ is assumed from the first part of this v. Τίκτουσα is the nom. sg. fem. of the pres. act. ptc. of τίκτω, "brings forth" (NASB), "yields" (NET), "produces" (NIV; BDAG 1004c). The ptc. par. πιοῦσα is the second modifier of γῆ. Βοτάνην is the acc. sg. fem. of βοτάνη, -ης, ἡ, "herb," "plant" (BDAG 181c; here "crop" [ESV, NIV], "vegetation" [NET]), and is the obj. of the ptc. This subst. is modified by the adj. εὔθετον, which is the acc. sg. fem. of εὔθετος, -ον, "useful" (most EVV: BDAG 405c). The dem. pron. ἐκείνοις functions as a pers. pron. (Wallace 352); it is subst., with human beings understood. The dat. indicates interest (R 708). Γεωργεῖται is the 3rd sg. pres. pass. indic. of γεωργέω, "cultivate" (BDAG 195d; BGk. hapax). The implied subj. is γῆ. The prep. phrase δι' οὓς adv. modifies γεωργεῖται, indicating cause. Καί is adjunctive, "also" (BDF §442).

μεταλαμβάνει εὐλογίας ἀπὸ τοῦ θεοῦ·
receives a blessing from God.

Μεταλαμβάνει is the 3rd sg. pres. act. indic. of μεταλαμβάνω, "receive" (most EVV), "have a share in" (BDAG 639b). Parallel to γεωργεῖται, the implied subj. is γῆ. The vb. is followed by εὐλογίας, the gen. sg. fem. of εὐλογία, -ας, ἡ, "blessing" (most EVV: BDAG 409a). The adv. prep. phrase ἀπὸ τοῦ θεοῦ modifies μεταλαμβάνει, indicating ultimate agency (Wallace 433). Agricultural metaphors in conj. with blessings or curses are freq. in the OT (e.g., Isa 5:1–7; Ezek 19:10–14), esp. in conj. with covenantal blessings and curses (e.g., Deut 11:26–28) and divine judgment (Deut 32:35; cf. Lane 1:143).

VERSE 8

ἐκφέρουσα δὲ ἀκάνθας καὶ τριβόλους, ἀδόκιμος καὶ κατάρας ἐγγύς,
But if it produces thorns and thistles, it is worthless and about to be cursed,

The subj. γῆ is elliptical from v. 7. Δέ indicates a general contrast (BDF §442), namely, the land that does not receive blessing, the converse of v. 7. 'Εκφέρουσα is the nom. sg. fem. of the pres. act. ptc. of ἐκφέρω, "bears" (ESV), "produces" (NET, NIV; BDAG 312a) and functions par. to τίκτουσα. Ἀκάνθας is the acc. pl. fem. of ἄκανθα, -ης, ἡ, "thorn-plant" (BDAG 34d). Τριβόλους is the acc. pl. masc. of τρίβολος, -ου, ὁ, "thistle" (BDAG 1015c) and is modified by ἀδόκιμος (nom. sg. masc. of ἀδόκιμος, -ον, "useless" (NET), "worthless" [ESV, NASB, NIV; BDAG 21c]). Both subst. function as the obj. of the ptc. This v. alludes to Gen 3:17; cf. ἐπικατάρατος in LXX Gen 3:14

and ἀκάνθας καὶ τριβόλους in LXX Gen 3:17–18; Lane 1:143). It may also allude to the judgment on Sodom and Gomorrah (Genesis 19).

Κατάρας is the gen. sg. fem. of κατάρα, -ας, ἡ, "curse," "imprecation" (BDAG 525b); the gen. is due to the adv. ἐγγύς, which means temp. "close" (BDAG 271b–c). The syntax of καὶ κατάρας ἐγγύς is difficult, with a form of εἰμί implied; "close to being cursed" (NASB); "on the verge of being cursed" (NRSV).

ἧς τὸ τέλος εἰς καῦσιν
and at the end will be burned.

The antecedent of ἧς is the implied γῆ at the beginning of v. 8. Τέλος is the subj. of the rel. clause. A form of εἰμί is likely implied in this verbless clause. Εἰς indicates purpose. Καῦσιν is the acc. sg. masc. of καῦσις, -εως, ἡ, "burning" (BDAG 536a). The use of τέλος furthers the image of imminent judgment in the preceding clause.

FOR FURTHER STUDY

44. The Warning Passage in Hebrews 6 (6:4–8)

Compton, R. Bruce. "Persevering and Falling Away: A Reexamination of Hebrews 6:4–6." *Detroit Baptist Seminary Journal* 1 (1996): 135–67.

Davis, Casey Wayne. "Hebrews 6:4–6 from an Oral Critical Perspective." *JETS* 51 (2008): 753–67.

*Decker, Rodney J. "The Warning of Hebrews 6." *Journal of Ministry and Theology* 5/2 (2001): 26–48.

deSilva, David A. "Hebrews 6:4–8: A Socio-Rhetorical Investigation (Parts 1–2)." *TynBul* 50 (1999): 33–57; 225–35.

Emmrich, Martin. "Hebrews 6:4–6—Again!: (A Pneumatological Inquiry)." *WTJ* 65 (2003): 83–95.

Gleason, Randall C. "The Old Testament Background of the Warning in Hebrews 6:4–8." *BSac* 155 (1998): 62–91.

Grudem, Wayne A. "Perseverance of the Saints: A Case Study from Hebrews 6:4–6 and the Other Warning Passages in Hebrews." Pages 133–182 in *Still Sovereign: Contemporary Perspectives on Election, Foreknowledge, and Grace*. Edited by Thomas R. Schreiner and Bruce A. Ware. Grand Rapids: Baker, 2000.

Hughes, Philip E. "Hebrews 6:4–6 and the Peril of Apostasy." *WTJ* 35 (1973): 137–55.

Mathewson, Dave. "Reading Heb 6:4–6 in Light of the Old Testament." *WTJ* 61 (1999): 209–25.

Nongbri, Brent. "A Touch of Condemnation in a Word of Exhortation: Apocalyptic Language and Graeco-Roman Rhetoric in Hebrews 6:4–12." *NovT* 45 (2003): 265–79.

Verbrugge, Verlyn D. "Towards a New Interpretation of Hebrews 6:4–6." *CTJ* 15 (1980): 61–73.

Witherington, 215–18.

See For Further Study 69 (Apostasy in Hebrews)

HOMILETICAL SUGGESTIONS

The Impossibility of Renewal (6:4–8)

1. The Description of Those at Risk (vv. 4–6)
   - (a) Once enlightened (v. 4a)
   - (b) Tasted the heavenly gift (v. 4b)
   - (c) Shared in the Holy Spirit (v. 4c)
   - (d) Tasted the goodness of the Word of God and eschatological power (v. 5)
   - (e) Fallen away (v. 6a)
2. The Impossibility of Repentance (v. 6)
   - (a) Because they are denying the Son's crucifixion (v. 6a)
   - (b) Because they are publicly repudiating the Son (v. 6b)
3. An Analogy from the Land (vv. 7–8)
   - (a) Abundant growth is a sign of blessing (v. 7)
   - (b) Worthless weeds will be cursed and burned (v. 8)

C. THE CONVICTION OF BETTER THINGS (6:9–12)

STRUCTURE

Following the stern warning of 6:4–8, the author strongly affirms his deep conviction concerning the audience's current spiritual condition. Notice the return to the first pers., following the third pers. of the previous section. This section centers around the two indic. in v. 9 and v. 11. The first is followed by a reason for the author's confidence; the second is followed by a purpose clause supporting the impv. force of the indic. The use of νωθροί in v. 12 forms an *inclusio* with its occurrence in 5:11.

9 Πεπείσμεθα δὲ περὶ ὑμῶν, ἀγαπητοί, τὰ κρείσσονα καὶ ἐχόμενα σωτηρίας,
εἰ καὶ οὕτως λαλοῦμεν.
10 οὐ γὰρ ἄδικος ὁ θεὸς
ἐπιλαθέσθαι τοῦ ἔργου ὑμῶν
καὶ τῆς ἀγάπης
ἧς ἐνεδείξασθε
εἰς τὸ ὄνομα αὐτοῦ,
διακονήσαντες τοῖς ἁγίοις
καὶ διακονοῦντες.
11 ἐπιθυμοῦμεν δὲ
ἕκαστον ὑμῶν τὴν αὐτὴν ἐνδείκνυσθαι σπουδὴν
πρὸς τὴν πληροφορίαν τῆς ἐλπίδος
ἄχρι τέλους,
12 ἵνα μὴ νωθροὶ γένησθε,
μιμηταὶ δὲ τῶν
↓ διὰ πίστεως καὶ μακροθυμίας
κληρονομούντων τὰς ἐπαγγελίας.

VERSE 9

Πεπείσμεθα δὲ περὶ ὑμῶν, ἀγαπητοί, τὰ κρείσσονα καὶ ἐχόμενα σωτηρίας, in your case we are confident of things . . . dearly loved friends, . . . that are better and that pertain to salvation.

Δέ indicates a general contrast (BDF §442), namely, between the stern warning and the author's present conviction concerning the audience; the contrast is also signaled by the return to the 1st pl. Πεπείσμεθα is the 1st pl. pf. pass. indic. of πείθω; the pass. indicates "be confident of" (NRSV), "feel sure of" (ESV), "be convinced" (NASB, NET, NIV), "be certain" (BDAG 792b). Although the pl. could be "epistolary," Wallace (396) suggests the intriguing possibility that Hebrews is written by two people since the author rarely uses the 1st sg. (but cf. 13:19, 22–23, which makes this proposal less likely). Elsewhere the pl. is inclusive, indicating that the author includes himself in exhortations. The pf. is likely extensive, and thus emph. The adv. prep. phrase περὶ ὑμῶν modifies πεπείσμεθα, indicating ref. (cf. Harris 179). Although the expression ἀγαπητοί is relatively common in the NT (esp. in Pauline epistles), it only occurs here in Hebrews (Ellingworth 329).

The syntax of the next phrase is complicated. The comp. κρείσσονα is the acc. pl. neut. of κρείττων, "better" (BDAG 566b) and functions here as a subst., "better things." It likely recalls the land that is blessed and perhaps blessing in general. This continues the key theme of "better" in Hebrews (see comments on 1:4). Ἐχόμενα is the acc. pl. neut. of the pres. mid. ptc. of ἔχω; here the pl. subst. ptc. indicates "things that belong to salvation" (BDAG 422d; cf. Attridge 174 n. 98). The gen. σωτηρίας is likely epex., explaining the better things (Wallace 98–99; W. Foerster, *TDNT* 7:996). The expression καὶ ἐχόμενα σωτηρίας is epex. to τὰ κρείσσονα (Lane 1:133 n. *bb*). The entire collocation τὰ κρείσσονα καὶ ἐχόμενα σωτηρίας functions as the obj. of πεπείσμεθα (for obj. with pass. vbs., see BDF §159[1]).

εἰ καὶ οὕτως λαλοῦμεν.
Even though we are speaking this way,

Εἰ καί indicates concession ("even if," "even though" [most EVV]; Moule 167). Λαλοῦμεν is modified by the adv. οὕτως, "thusly," which refers back to the stern warning of 6:4–8. The sudden change of tone and expression of confidence reflects a rhetorical device intended to persuade (Attridge 174; Koester 316).

VERSE 10

οὐ γὰρ ἄδικος ὁ θεὸς ἐπιλαθέσθαι τοῦ ἔργου ὑμῶν καὶ τῆς ἀγάπης
For God is not unjust; he will not forget your work and the love

Γάρ is causal, giving further reason for the author's confidence. A form of εἰμί is likely implied. Ἄδικος (-ον, "unjust" [BDAG 21a]) functions as a pred. adj. with ἐστίν implied. The negated alpha privative (ἄδικος) is an example of litotes (Attridge 174 n. 100). The assertion that God is just is freq. in the OT (see Koester 316). Ἐπιλαθέσθαι is an aor. mid. inf. from ἐπιλανθάνομαι, "forget" (most EVV), "overlook" (ESV), "neglect," "care nothing about" (BDAG 374d). "The infinitive *without* ὥστε (also without any expressed subject in the acc.) is used . . . to express result" (BDF §391; e.g., "God is not unjust with the result that he forgets"). Alternatively, the inf. may be epex. (Ellingworth 330). This anticipates the discussion of God's faithfulness in 6:13–20. The vb. is followed by the gen (cf. R 508).

ἧς ἐνεδείξασθε εἰς τὸ ὄνομα αὐτοῦ,
you demonstrated for his name

The antecedent of ἧς is ἀγάπης. The case of the rel. pron. has been attracted to the case of the antecedent. Ἐνεδείξασθε is the 2nd pl. aor. mid. indic. from ἐνδείκνυμι, "show" (NASB, ESV, NIV), "demonstrate" (NET; BDAG 331d). Εἰς τὸ ὄνομα αὐτοῦ adv. modifies ἐνεδείξασθε, indicating ref. This prep. phrase is unusual (Ellingworth 331). Here it indicates acting for the sake of God's name and honor (Koester 317).

διακονήσαντες τοῖς ἁγίοις καὶ διακονοῦντες.
by serving the saints—and by continuing to serve them.

Διακονήσαντες is the nom. pl. masc. of the aor. act. ptc. of διακονέω, "help" (NIV), "serve" (ESV, NET; BDAG 229d; H. Beyer, *TDNT* 2:81–87); διακονοῦντες is the nom. pl. masc. of the pres. act. ptc. from the same vb. As in the rest of the NT, the subst. use of ἅγιος freq. refers to believers (BDAG 11c). Both ptcs. modify ἐνεδείξασθε instr. The aor. and pres. emphasize the audience's service, as a whole (aor.), and in the pres. time; the ptcs. indicate relative time to the finite vb. (BDF §339). These actions are elaborated in 10:32–34.

VERSE 11

ἐπιθυμοῦμεν δὲ ἕκαστον ὑμῶν τὴν αὐτὴν ἐνδείκνυσθαι σπουδήν
Now we desire each of you to demonstrate the same diligence

Δέ indicates a general contrast between the audience's previous service and the exhortation to continue in perseverance (cf. BDF §447). Ἐπιθυμοῦμεν is the 1st pl. pres. act. indic. from ἐπιθυμέω, "desire" (ESV, NASB), "long for" (BDAG 372a; F. Büchsel, *TDNT* 3:168–71; cf. "passionately want" [NET]). The pl. is likely epistolary. The vb. followed by the acc. and inf. is "unusual" (Ellingworth 332). Ἕκαστον (acc. sg. masc. from ἕκαστος, -η, -ον, "each/each one") is subst. and the "subj." of the inf. The gen. ὑμῶν is partitive; "each one from among you all." Ἐνδείκνυσθαι is the pres. mid. inf. from ἐνδείκνυμι, "show" (NIV), "demonstrate" (NET; BDAG 331d). The inf. is the complement of ἐπιθυμοῦμεν (BDF §392). Σπουδήν is the acc. sg. fem. from σπουδή, -ῆς, ἡ, "eagerness" (NET), "earnestness" (ESV), "diligence" (NASB, NIV), "willingness," "zeal" (BDAG 939d–940a). Αὐτήν functions as an identical adj. (Wallace 349–50). Τὴν αὐτὴν . . . σπουδήν is the obj. of the inf.

πρὸς τὴν πληροφορίαν τῆς ἐλπίδος ἄχρι τέλους,
for the full assurance of your hope until the end,

Πληροφορίαν is the acc. sg. fem. of πληροφορία, -ας, ἡ, "full assurance" (ESV, NASB), "certainty" (BDAG 827d; G. Delling, *TDNT* 6:310–11; Ellingworth 332). The gen. ἐλπίδος is descriptive. The prep. phrase πρὸς τὴν πληροφορίαν τῆς ἐλπίδος either adj. modifies σπουδήν ("diligence for the fulfillment of hope") or *adv. modifies the inf. for purpose ("to demonstrate the fullness of your hope" [see Cockerill 282 n. 11]). The adv. prep. phrase ἄχρι τέλους (gen. sg. neut. from τέλος, -ους, τό) temp. modifies ἐνδείκνυσθαι.

VERSE 12

ἵνα μὴ νωθροὶ γένησθε,
so that you won't become lazy

Ἵνα with the subjunc. introduces a purpose clause. The aor. γένησθε may be ingressive (Cockerill 283 n. 12). Νωθροί is the nom. pl. masc. from νωθρός, -ά, -όν, "lazy" (NIV), "sluggish" (ESV, NASB, NET; BDAG 683c) and functions as a pred. adj. Its occurrence in this v. and 5:11 forms an *inclusio* around the third "warning" passage in Hebrews. The neg. expression here contrasts with 5:11 to indicate the author's confidence for the audience should they heed his warnings.

μιμηταὶ δὲ τῶν διὰ πίστεως καὶ μακροθυμίας κληρονομούντων τὰς ἐπαγγελίας.
but will be imitators of those who inherit the promises through faith and perseverance.

Δέ following μή is adversative and indicates a strong contrast (Lane 1:133 n. *gg*; BDF §447[1]). Μιμηταί is the nom. pl. masc. from μιμητής, -οῦ, ὁ, "imitator" (BDAG 652a; W. Michaelis, *TDNT* 4:666–74; Ellingworth 333). Γένησθε is assumed. Imitation of those who have gone before introduces a major theme in Hebrews, esp. Hebrews 11 (Attridge 176). The supreme example to be imitated is Abraham, who is introduced in 6:13, although the pl. also anticipates Hebrews 11. These inheritors are the counterexample to the wilderness generation. Κληρονομούντων is the gen. pl. masc. of the pres. act. ptc. of κληρονομέω, "inherit" (BDAG 547d). The ptc. is subst. (τῶν κληρονομούντων). Ἐπαγγελίας is the acc. pl. fem. from ἐπαγγελία, -ας, ἡ, "promise" (BDAG 356a). The important theme of promise was introduced in 4:1. The pl. is the obj. of the ptc. Μακροθυμίας is the gen. sg. fem. from μακροθυμία, -ας, ἡ, "patience" (ESV, NIV), "endurance" (NLT), "perseverance" (NET), "steadfastness" (BDAG 612d; J. Horst, *TDNT* 4:386). Δία with the gen. is instr., "through." The adv. prep. διὰ πίστεως καὶ μακροθυμίας modifies the ptc. Πίστεως καὶ μακροθυμίας is a hendiadys: "faithful perseverance" or "persevering faith" (Attridge 176). Ellingworth (330) notes the early Christian tradition of linking faith, hope, and love.

HOMILETICAL SUGGESTIONS

Assurances in the Midst of Tough Love (6:9–12)

1. Assurances about salvation (vv. 9–10)
   (a) Pastoral care undergirds strong warnings (v. 9)
   (b) God does not forget what believers do for his name (v. 10)
2. Pastoral desires for those who are dearly loved (vv. 11–12)
   (a) That they remain diligent in the certainty of their hope (v. 11)
   (b) That they not become lazy (v. 12a)
   (c) That they imitate those who inherit God's promises through faith and perseverance (v. 12b)

D. THE UNCHANGEABLE NATURE OF GOD'S PURPOSES (6:13–20)

STRUCTURE

The shift from exhortation (6:9–12) to exposition (6:13–20) signals a new section (Lane 1:148). As is common in Hebrews, a number of hook words provide a transition from one section to the next and provide cohesion: e.g., *ἐπαγγελία* in v. 12 and *ἐπαγγειλάμενος* in v. 13, and *μακροθυμίας* in v. 12 and *μακροθυμήσας* in v. 15. Similarly, *κατὰ τὴν τάξιν* Μελχισέδεκ recalls its use in 5:10 and anticipates 7:17 (Ellingworth 334). This section discusses God's promises to Abraham, which prepares for the resumed discussion about Melchizedek in Hebrews 7 (begun in Hebrews 5, but which was interrupted by the warning of 5:11–6:8).

The subj. of vv. 13–14 is θεός, as indicated by the placement of θεός below. The ptc. λέγων is redundant to ὤμοσεν. (The main vbs. of this section are slightly indented under their subjs. below.) The citation from Gen 22:17 is indented. The (unexpressed) subj. of v. 15 is Abraham (οὕτως). Verse 16 presents a truism, the par. parts of which are aligned. In v. 17, the inf. ἐπιδεῖξαι complements βουλόμενος. The indir. obj. and obj. of the inf. are indented beneath it. The ἵνα clause modifies ἐμεσίτευσεν. The complement of ἀδύνατον (ψεύσασθαι) is aligned accordingly. Κρατῆσαι is the complement of παράκλησιν. The rel. clause in v. 19 is indented under its antecedent, with the three modifiers of ἐλπίδος aligned underneath. The placement of Ἰησοῦς indicates that it is an appos. to πρόδρομος. The adj. γενόμενος further modifies Ἰησοῦς. and is modified by two prep. phrases (indicated by small arrows).

13 Τῷ γὰρ Ἀβραὰμ ἐπαγγειλάμενος
ὁ θεός
↓ἐπεὶ κατ᾽ οὐδενὸς εἶχεν μείζονος ὀμόσαι,
ὤμοσεν καθ᾽ ἑαυτοῦ
14 λέγων·
εἰ μὴν εὐλογῶν εὐλογήσω σε
καὶ πληθύνων πληθυνῶ σε·
15 καὶ οὕτως
μακροθυμήσας
ἐπέτυχεν τῆς ἐπαγγελίας.
16 ἄνθρωποι γὰρ
↓κατὰ τοῦ μείζονος
ὀμνύουσιν,
καὶ πάσης αὐτοῖς ἀντιλογίας πέρας εἰς βεβαίωσιν ὁ ὅρκος·
17 ἐν ᾧ
περισσότερον βουλόμενος
ὁ θεὸς ἐπιδεῖξαι
τοῖς κληρονόμοις τῆς ἐπαγγελίας
τὸ ἀμετάθετον τῆς βουλῆς αὐτοῦ
ἐμεσίτευσεν ὅρκῳ,

18 ἵνα διὰ δύο πραγμάτων ἀμεταθέτων,
ἐν οἷς ἀδύνατον
ψεύσασθαι [τὸν] θεόν,
ἰσχυρὰν παράκλησιν ἔχωμεν οἱ καταφυγόντες
κρατῆσαι τῆς προκειμένης ἐλπίδος·
19 ἣν ὡς ἄγκυραν ἔχομεν τῆς ψυχῆς
ἀσφαλῆ τε
καὶ βεβαίαν
καὶ εἰσερχομένην
εἰς τὸ ἐσώτερον
τοῦ καταπετάσματος,
20 ὅπου πρόδρομος ὑπὲρ ἡμῶν εἰσῆλθεν
Ἰησοῦς,
κατὰ τὴν τάξιν Μελχισέδεκ
ἀρχιερεὺς γενόμενος
εἰς τὸν αἰῶνα.

VERSE 13

Τῷ γὰρ Ἀβραὰμ ἐπαγγειλάμενος ὁ θεός,
For when God made a promise to Abraham,

Γάρ offers further clarification (BDAG 189d) of the promise mentioned in v. 12, which now focuses on Abraham (Ellingworth 335–36). Ἀβραάμ is indecl.; the dat. (indicated by the art.) is the indir. obj. of ἐπαγγειλάμενος, which is the nom. sg. masc. of the aor. mid. ptc. (agreeing with θεός) of ἐπαγγέλλομαι, "make a promise" (most EVV), "promise" (BDAG 356b). The ptc. is temp. ("when"; so most EVV).

Abraham was briefly introduced in 2:16. Throughout Hebrews (and elsewhere in the Bible), Abraham is the supreme example of persevering faith, which is intensified in Hebrews by the implicit contrast between his faithfulness and the wilderness generation's faithlessness. Moreover, previous use of inheritance language in Hebrews (e.g., 1:2, 4, 14) anticipates the explicit focus on the Abrahamic promises in this section, which anticipates discussion of Melchizedek in Hebrews 7.

ἐπεὶ κατ' οὐδενὸς εἶχεν μείζονος ὀμόσαι, ὤμοσεν καθ' ἑαυτοῦ
since he had no one greater to swear by, he swore by himself:

The conj. ἐπεί introduces a causal clause (BDAG 360c), indicating the reason that God swore (ὤμοσεν) by himself. Κατά + gen. indicates the pers. or obj. by which one swears (Wallace 205 n. 96; R 475, 607; Ellingworth 336), here indicated by the subst. adj. οὐδενός (gen. sg. masc. of οὐδείς, οὐδεμία, οὐδέν, "no one"). The adj. could be neut. ("no one"), but the par. with καθ' ἑαυτοῦ argues against this (Attridge 179 n. 14). (Κατά elides before a vowel or diphthong [κατ'] and rough breathing [καθ'].) The comp. μείζονος (from μέγας, μεγάλη, μέγα, "greater" [BDAG 624c]) agrees with οὐδενός. Εἶχεν is the 3rd sg. impf. act. indic. of ἔχω. Ὀμόσαι is the aor. act. inf. of ὀμνύω, "swear" (most EVV), "take an oath" (BDAG 705d–706a). The inf. complements the vb. ("since he had no one greater to swear by" / "since he could swear by no one greater" [CSB, NET]). The implied subj. is God. Ὤμοσεν is the 3rd sg. aor. act. indic. of ὀμνύω. The aor. is constative.

The *a fortiori* (lesser to greater) argument assumes the widespread practice of swearing by one greater than oneself (e.g., a god or a king) in the ancient world (Koester 326; Witherington 222–24). In the OT, people often swore by God (e.g., Gen 14:22; Deut 6:13). If such an oath undertaken by a human could not be annulled, how much more certain would be God's oath confirming his promise to Abraham? Indeed, it is staggering that God would add an oath to his (already certain) promise. The refl. ἑαυτοῦ indicates that God could only swear by himself (e.g., Isa 45:23; Jer 22:5). The allusion here is to God's oath to Abraham in Gen 22:16 and possibly also the oath of Ps 110:4 in conj. with the priest in the order of Melchizedek (cf. 6:20).

VERSE 14

λέγων

Λέγων (not tr. by CSB) pars. λέγει in 1:6 to introduce an OT citation, here Gen 22:17. The pres. indicates action contemp. with the aor. ὤμοσεν in v. 13. Context indicates that God is speaking.

εἰ μὴν εὐλογῶν εὐλογήσω σε καὶ πληθύνων πληθυνῶ σε·
I will indeed bless you, and I will greatly multiply you.

The collocation εἰ μήν is asseverative or corroborative, reflecting the LXX tr. of the Heb. (R 1004); "surely," "certainly" (BDAG 279b; cf. BDF §441[1]; NT hapax). Εὐλογήσω is the 1st sg. fut. act. indic. of εὐλογέω, "bless" (BDAG 408b; H. W. Beyer, *TDNT* 2:761–63); the cognate εὐλογῶν is the nom. sg. masc. of the pres. act. ptc. (agreeing with εὐλογήσω). The acc. σε is the obj. of εὐλογήσω. Πληθυνῶ is the 1st sg. fut. act. indic. of πληθύνω, "multiply" (most EVV; BDAG 826a; G. Delling, *TDNT* 6:281); the cognate πληθύνων is the nom. sg. masc. of the pres. act. ptc. (agreeing with πληθυνῶ). Both futs. are predictive (Wallace 568). The fut., with its cognate ptc., reflects the LXX tr. of the Heb. inf. abs. (BDF §422; Z §60–61, 369). The acc. σε is the obj. of πληθυνῶ. The author changes the LXX text of Gen 22:17 from πληθυνῶ τὸ σπέρμα σου to πληθυνῶ σε, thereby shifting the focus to Abraham. Genesis 22 records Abraham's obedience to God's command to sacrifice Issac, which represented perhaps the most serious threat to God's promises to Abraham. After God's faithful provision of the ram, he further indicated the certainty of his promises to Abraham by confirming them with an oath.

VERSE 15

καὶ οὕτως μακροθυμήσας ἐπέτυχεν τῆς ἐπαγγελίας.
And so, after waiting patiently, Abraham obtained the promise.

The adv. οὕτως ("thus" [BDAG 741d]) modifies ἐπέτυχεν, drawing an inference from vv. 13–15 (Ellingworth 338). Μακροθυμήσας is the nom. sg. masc. of the aor. act. ptc. of μακροθυμέω, "have patience," "wait" (BDAG 612c). The aor. ptc. could be causal ("because" [NJB]), temp. ("after" [NEB, NIV]), instr. ("by" [NET]), or *circum. ("having patiently waited" [ESV, NASB]). Ἐπέτυχεν is the 3rd sg. aor. act. indic. of ἐπιτυγχάνω, "obtain" (BDAG 385c). The vb. is followed by the gen. ἐπαγγελίας (ἐπαγγελία, -ας, ἡ, "promise"; BDAG 356a). Abraham is the implied subj. for the ptc. and vb.

The statement that Abraham obtained the promise appears to contradict Heb 11:13. There are two main interpretive options for v. 15.

1. The author believes that Abraham received a confirmation of the promise but not its actual fulfillment ("Abraham inherited the promise" [NET]; "obtained the promise" [ESV, NASB]). Yet force of the vb. and the context of Hebrews argue against this (Ellingworth 338–39; Cockerill 285).
*2. The author believes that Abraham received [part of] the promise with the birth of Isaac ("Abraham received what was promised" [NIV]; "he received what God had promised" [NLT]; "fulfillment of the promise" [NJB]).

The second option coheres better with the overall argument of Hebrews. The author distinguishes between the promise of descendants (fulfilled) and of land (unfulfilled). Hebrews 6 focuses on Abraham's perseverance after the promise of descendants was first articulated in Genesis 12 (when Abraham was about seventy-five) and until its final fulfillment in Genesis 21 (when Abraham was around one hundred). This focus on the promise of descendants is confirmed by the author's citation from Gen 22:17a, which omits the land promise (Gen 22:17b–18). See also the discussion at 11:8–16.

VERSE 16

ἄνθρωποι γὰρ κατὰ τοῦ μείζονος ὀμνύουσιν,
For people swear by something greater than themselves,

Γάρ is causal, introducing a proverbial statement to support the point made in v. 13. Ἄνθρωποι is best understood generically ("people" [ESV, NET, NLT]; "human beings" [NRSV]). Ὀμνύουσιν is the 3rd pl. pres. act. indic. of ὀμνύω, "swear" (BDAG 705d–706a), agreeing with ἄνθρωποι. The prep. phrase κατὰ τοῦ μείζονος par. the sim. expression in v. 13 with vbs. of swearing (R 607). (For a detailed comp. of human and divine oaths in this passage, see Ellingworth 339; see Lane 1:149 for discussion of the legal terms in this passage.)

καὶ πάσης αὐτοῖς ἀντιλογίας πέρας εἰς βεβαίωσιν ὁ ὅρκος·
and for them a confirming oath ends every dispute.

The clause is verbless. The subj. is the art. ὅρκος (nom. sg. masc. of ὅρκος, -ου, ὁ, "oath" [BDAG 723d]), which is modified adj. by εἰς βεβαίωσιν (acc. sg. fem. of βεβαίωσις, -εως, ἡ, "confirmation," "validation" [BDAG 173b]; A. Fuchs, *EDNT* 1:210–11). Εἰς βεβαίωσιν indicates purpose; it is sometimes tr. as a finite vb. ("the oath confirms" [NIV], "the oath serves as a confirmation" [NET], "an oath given as confirmation" [NRSV]). The pred. nom. is πέρας (nom. sg. neut. of πέρας, -ατος, τό, "end" [NET, NIV], "conclusion" [BDAG 797b]), which is modified by ἀντιλογίας (gen. sg. fem. of ἀντιλογία, -ας, ἡ, "argument" [NIV], "contradiction," "dispute" [ESV, NET]) (BDAG 89d), which is further modified by the adj. πάσης. Αὐτοῖς is dat. of association ("among them"). Many EVV do not tr. the pers. pron. The entire clause may allude to Exod 22:10.

VERSE 17

ἐν ᾧ περισσότερον βουλόμενος ὁ θεὸς ἐπιδεῖξαι τοῖς κληρονόμοις τῆς ἐπαγγελίας τὸ ἀμετάθετον τῆς βουλῆς αὐτοῦ
Because God wanted to show his unchangeable purpose even more clearly to the heirs of the promise,

The expression ἐν ᾧ functions causally (ἐν ᾧ = ἐν τούτῳ ὅτι: "for the reason that" = "because"; BDAG 329d; BDF §219[2]). Alternatively, the rel. pron. could refer generally to the preceding argument (Attridge 180) or to ὅρκος (Cockerill 287 n. 8). Βουλόμενος is the nom. sg. masc. of the pres. mid. ptc. of βουλόμαι, "want" (NET, NIV), "desire" (ESV, NASB), "intend," "plan," "will" (BDAG 182c); agreeing with θεός. The ptc. is likely causal ("because" [NIV], "since" [REB]; Cockerill 187) rather than temp. ("when" [CEV, ESV]). Ἐπιδεῖξαι is the aor. act. inf. of ἐπιδείκνυμι, "demonstrate," "show" (BDAG 370b; "to give proof," Lane 1:149). Περισσότερον (πετισσότερος, -τέρα, -ον; comp. of περισσός, "greater," "more," "even more") (BDAG 806a; BDF §60[1]) is emphatic or elative and modifies the inf. ("to demonstrate more clearly" [NET]), although it could modify the ptc. ("desiring even more" [NASB]). The inf. complements the ptc. (cf. BDAG 182d). The dat. pl. κληρονόμοις (κληρονόμος, -ου, ὁ; "heir", BDAG 548b) is the ind. obj. of the inf. Ἐπαγγελίας modifies the ptc., as a descriptive gen. The obj. of the inf. is ἀμετάθετον, which is the acc. neut. sg. of ἀμετάθετος, -ον, "unalterable," "unchangeable" (BDAG 53b); here the neut. is functioning subst. (cf. BDF §263[2]). Βουλῆς is the gen. sg. fem. of βουλή, -ῆς, ἡ, "(divine) will" (BDAG 182a). The poss. gen. βουλῆς modifies ἀμετάθετον (e.g., "the unchangeable character of his purpose" [ESV]). The entire clause (ἐν ᾧ . . . τῆς βουλῆς αὐτοῦ) is dependent on ἐμεσίτευσεν.

ἐμεσίτευσεν ὅρκῳ,
he guaranteed it with an oath,

Ἐμεσίτευσεν is the 3rd sg. aor. act. indic. of μεσιτεύω, "confirm" (NIV), "guarantee" (ESV; BDAG 634b; NT hapax). The implied subj. is God. The dat. ὅρκῳ (ὅρκος, -ου, ὁ, "oath") is instr.

The immutability of God's will was affirmed in secular and Jewish writings as well as in the OT (e.g., Num 23:19). The distinction between the promise of descendants and land again underlies the argument. The affirmation of the unchangeability of God's will was necessary not only for Abraham (who apart from the birth of Isaac did not see these promises fulfilled; see comments on 11:8–16), but also for subsequent generations of heirs. The overall context of assurance and exhortation indicates that the author believes that he and his audience are included among the heirs.

VERSE 18

ἵνα διὰ δύο πραγμάτων ἀμεταθέτων,
so that through two unchangeable things,

Ἵνα introduces a purpose clause, the main vb. of which is ἔχωμεν ("in order that we might have"). Πραγμάτων is the gen. pl. neut. of πρᾶγμα, -ατος, τό, "thing" (BDAG 858d–859a). The numeral δύο modifies πραγμάτων, which is further modified by the adj. ἀμεταθέτων (see comments on v. 17). The prep. διά is instr. (Harris 70–71). Most commentators agree that the two things refer to God's promise and his oath. The two "things" may also function as the two legally required witnesses (Deut 17:6; so Ellingworth 335; Koester 328). (See David R. Worley, "Fleeing to Two Immutable Things, God's Oath-Taking and Oath-Witnessing: The Use of Litigant Oath in Hebrews 6:12–20," *ResQ* 36 [1994]: 223–36.) God's oath is clearly stated in Gen 22:17, but the author may have also had Ps 110:4 in mind, anticipating the upcoming discussion about a priest in the order of Melchizedek.

ἐν οἷς ἀδύνατον ψεύσασθαι [τὸν] θεόν,
in which it is impossible for God to lie,

The antecedent of οἷς is πραγμάτων. Ἐν is instr. ("by which"). Ἀδύνατον is the nom. sg. neut. of ἀδύνατος, -ον, "impossible." The adj. is pred. with an implied form of εἰμί and an impers. subj. ("it is impossible"). Its use here recalls 6:4. Ψεύσασθαι is the aor. mid. inf. of ψεύδομαι, "lie" (BDAG 1096d). The inf. is the complement of ἀδύνατον. The "subj." of the inf. is θεόν (Wallace 192–95). Some important mss. ($\mathfrak{P}^{46}$ א* A C P 33 1739) include the art. [τόν], although most mss. omit it. The force of the anar. subst. may be that "it is impossible for one who is God to lie" (see Lane 1:148 n. *i*). The assumption that God could not lie was a common assertion (e.g., Num 23:19, 1 Sam 15:29).

ἰσχυρὰν παράκλησιν ἔχωμεν οἱ καταφυγόντες κρατῆσαι τῆς προκειμένης ἐλπίδος·
we who have fled for refuge might have strong encouragement to seize the hope set before us.

The obj. of ἔχωμεν is παράκλησιν (acc. sg. fem. of παράκλησις, -εως, ἡ, "encouragement" [most EVV; BDAG 766a; O. Schmitz, *TDNT* 5:793–99]). It is modified by ἰσχυράν (ἰσχυρός, -ά, -όν, "strong" [BADG 483d]). Καταφυγόντες is the nom. pl. masc. of the aor. act. ptc. of καταφεύγω, "take refuge" (BDAG 529b). The vb. is used in the LXX in conj. with those fleeing to cities of refuge (e.g., Deut 4:42; Lane 1:153). The ptc. is an appos. (R 778) that functions par. to a rel. clause ("we who flee"; BDF §412[5]). The aor. may be ingressive, although aspect is diminished with subst. ptcs. Κρατῆσαι is the aor. act. inf. of κρατέω, "take hold" (NASB, NIV), "hold fast" (ESV, NET), "seize" (CSB), "to adhere strongly to" (BDAG 565b); the vb. is followed by the gen. The aor. inf. is ingressive (Z §250). This imagery also recalls the OT, where individuals could grab hold of the horns of the altar to seek sanctuary (Koester 328). The obj. of the inf. is ἐλπίδος. Προκειμένης is the gen. sg. fem. of the pres. mid. ptc. of πρόκειμαι, "lie before," "be present" (BDAG 871b). The ptc. is attr., modifying ἐλπίδος (first attr. pos., Wallace 618). Hope in Hebrews has an "objective content" (Lane 1:153) and is depicted as entering the heavenly sanctuary (vv. 19–20). A tension between pres. and fut. realities "lies at the heart of the situation which the writer addresses" (Ellingworth 344; cf. Cockerill 289 n. 17).

VERSE 19

ἣν ὡς ἄγκυραν ἔχομεν τῆς ψυχῆς ἀσφαλῆ τε καὶ βεβαίαν
We have this hope as an anchor for the soul, firm and secure.

The antecent of ἥν is ἐλπίδος. The rel. pron. functions as the obj. of ἔχομεν in the rel. clause. Ἄγκυραν is the acc. sg. fem. of ἄγκυρα, -ας, ἡ, "anchor" (BDAG 12a). The comp. marker ὡς indicates "the perspective from which a . . . thing [ἐλπίς] . . . is viewed [e.g., ἄγκυρα]" (BDAG 1105a). The anchor metaphor occurs only here in the Bible, although it is freq. in nonbiblical sources (e.g., Plato, Philo; see Ellingworth 346; Koester 329) as a metaphor for stability. (For a possible early Christian interpretation of anchor imagery, see Charles A. Kennedy, "Early Christians and the Anchor," *Biblical Archaeologist* 38 [1975]: 115–24.) The gen. ψυχῆς indicates the purpose of ἄγκυραν ("for our souls"; see Wallace 100–101). Ἀσφαλῆ is the acc. sg. fem. of ἀσφαλής, -ές, "certain," "safe," "secure" (BDAG 147b). Βεβαίαν ("reliable"; cf. 2:2) recalls the use of βεβαίωσις in v. 16. The correl. τε καί indicates a close association between ἀσφαλῆ and βεβαίαν and is often tr. simply as "and" ("firm and secure" [NIV], "sure and steadfast" [ESV, NET]; cf. BDAG 993c). The separation of the two adjs. from the subst. they modify (ἄγκυραν) is emph. (R 417–18).

καὶ εἰσερχομένην εἰς τὸ ἐσώτερον τοῦ καταπετάσματος,
It enters the inner sanctuary behind the curtain.

Εἰσερχομένην is the acc. sg. fem. of the pres. mid. ptc. of εἰσέρχομαι, "enter." Εἰς is spatial ("into"). The rep. of the prep. after a compound vb. is common in the NT, esp. with εἰς (R 559). The adj. ἐσώτερον, -α, -ον ("inside") functions par. to a prep.

("behind") here (BDAG 398c). Καταπετάσματος is the gen. sg. neut. of καταπέτασμα, -οτος, τό, "curtain" (most EVV; BDAG 524b; cf. "veil" [NASB]). The expression τὸ ἐσώτερον τοῦ καταπετάσματος refers to the holy of holies in the LXX, which was located behind the inner curtain in the tabernacle (Exod 26:33; Lev 16:2, 12, 15; Cockerill 291 n. 22). Only the high priest could enter behind this curtain, and only on the Day of Atonement (Lev 16:2). The imagery here depicts the heavenly sanctuary (BDAG 524b). In Hebrews, καταπέτασμα "is viewed primarily as a means of access to God" (Ellingworth 347).

There is debate over how to align the three acc. (ἀσφαλῆ, βεβαίαν, εἰσερχομένην) in v. 19, although understanding all three as modifiers of ἄγκυραν makes the best sense of the syntax and imagery—hope is like an anchor that is safe, secure, and enters into the ultimate place of security. The imagery here is an anchor secured to the immovable throne of God (cf. Bruce 155).

VERSE 20

ὅπου πρόδρομος ὑπὲρ ἡμῶν εἰσῆλθεν Ἰησοῦς,
Jesus has entered there on our behalf as a forerunner,

The ptcl. ὅπου indicates place ("where" [BDAG 717b]). Πρόδρομος is the nom. sg. masc. of πρόδρομος, -ον, pertaining "to being a precursor, going (lit. running) *before, going ahead*" (BDAG 867d; Ellingworth 348; Bauernfeind, *TDNT* 8:235; NT hapax; "forerunner" [most EVV]); the pl. is used of military scouts in secular sources (Lane 1:154). Here it is an appos. of Ἰησοῦς, which is placed at the end of the clause for emph. (Cockerill 292–93). Εἰσῆλθεν is the aor. act. indic. of εἰσέρχομαι, "enter." Ὑπὲρ ἡμῶν adv. modifies the vb. ("entered on our behalf").

Conceptually, πρόδρομος parallels ἀρχηγός in 2:10 (cf. 12:2), presenting Jesus as the one who goes before to the place to which he is leading the sons and daughters. The author distinguishes between hope, which is almost personified and is currently entering (εἰσερχομένην) the heavenly sanctuary and Jesus who has already entered (εἰσῆλθεν) it.

κατὰ τὴν τάξιν Μελχισέδεκ ἀρχιερεὺς γενόμενος εἰς τὸν αἰῶνα.
because he has become a high priest forever according to the order of Melchizedek.

Κατὰ τὴν τάξιν Μελχισέδεκ modifies the ptc. γενόμενος; its placement at the beginning of the clause is emph. (Ellingworth 349). (See comments on 5:6.) Γενόμενος adj. agrees with Ἰησοῦς. The aor. is consummative (Wallace 559–61), "having become." The cstr. pars. an equative vb., with ἀρχιερεύς (see comments on 2:17) functioning as the pred. nom. The adv. prep. phrase εἰς τὸν αἰῶνα ("eternally, in perpetuity"; BDAG 32b) modifies the ptc. temp. (see Harris 94–96). Εἰς τὸν αἰῶνα alludes to Ps 110:4. Its placement at the end of the sentence is emph. (Cockerill 292–93). (See comments on 5:6.) This allusion prepares for the extended discussion of Melchizedek in Hebrews 7. Psalm 110:4 citation is significant in Hebrews (e.g., 5:6, 10; 6:20; 7:17, 21).

FOR FURTHER STUDY

45. Promise in Hebrews (6:13–20)

Ellingworth, 238–39.

Gordon, Robert P. "Better Promises: Two Passages in Hebrews against the Background of the Old Testament Cultus." Pages 434–49 in *Templum Amicitiae: Essays on the Second Temple Presented to Ernst Bammel*. Edited by William Horbury. Sheffield: JSOT Press, 1991.

Guthrie, G. H. *DLNT* 967–70.

Koester, 110–12.

McComiskey, Thomas Edward. *The Covenants of Promise: A Theology of the Old Testament Covenants*. Grand Rapids: Baker, 1985.

46. The Tabernacle Veil (6:19–20)

Davidson, Richard M. "Christ's Entry 'within the Veil' in Hebrews 6:19–20: The Old Testament Background." *AUSS* 39 (2001): 175–90.

———. "Inauguration or Day of Atonement?: A Response to Norman Young's 'Old Testament Background to Hebrews 6:19–20 Revisited.'" *AUSS* 40 (2002): 69–88.

Gurtner, Daniel M. "LXX Syntax and the Identity of the NT Veil." *NovT* 47 (2005): 344–53.

Meyers, Carol. *ABD* 6:785–86.

Rice, George E. "Hebrews 6:19: Analysis of Some Assumptions concerning *kata-petasma*." *AUSS* 25 (1987): 65–71.

Schneider, C. *TDNT* 3:628–30.

Young, Norman H. "The Day of Dedication or the Day of Atonement?: The Old Testament Background to Hebrews 6:19–20 Revisited." *AUSS* 40 (2002): 61–68.

———. "'Where Jesus Has Gone as a Forerunner on Our Behalf' (Hebrews 6:20)." *AUSS* 39 (2001): 165–73.

See For Further Study 68 (The Veil of the Heavenly Sanctuary)

47. Jewish Mysticism (6:19–20)

Barnard, Jody A. *The Mysticism of Hebrews: Exploring the Role of Jewish Apocalyptic Mysticism in the Epistle to the Hebrews*. WUNT 2/331. Tübingen: Mohr Siebeck, 2012.

Mackie, Scott D. "Ancient Jewish Mystical Motifs in Hebrews' Theology of Access and Entry Exhortations." *NTS* 58 (2012): 88–104.

*———. "Heavenly Sanctuary Mysticism in the Epistle to the Hebrews." *JTS* 62 (2011): 77–117.

HOMILETICAL SUGGESTIONS

The Nature of God's Promises (6:13–20)

1. God's Specific Promise to Abraham (vv. 13–14)
   - (a) Innumerable descendants for Abraham (v 14)
   - (b) Sworn with God himself as guarantor (v. 13)

(c) Received by Abraham after patiently waiting (v. 15)

2. God's Promise Compared with Human Promises (vv. 13, 16–18)
   (a) It is customary to guarantee a promise with an oath sworn to someone of superior rank (v. 16)
   (b) But there is none of superior rank to God . . . (v. 13)
   (c) . . . so God adds an oath to his promise (v. 17b)
   (d) To assure Abraham's descendants of the unchangeableness of God's purpose (v. 17a)
   (e) Thus two things (God's promise and his oath) affirm the reliability of God's promise (v. 18a)
3. God's Promise as the Basis of Our Present Encouragement (v. 18)
   (a) God cannot lie (v. 18b)
   (b) The hope of his promise is a refuge for those who flee to God (v. 18c)
4. The Certain Hope of God's Promise Is Our Anchor (vv. 19–20)
   (a) This anchor grounds our souls (v. 19a)
   (b) It tethers us to the heavenly sanctuary (v. 19b)
   (c) where Jesus is already as the one who has gone before us (v. 20)

God's Promises: Our Hope (6:13–20)

1. Our Example: Abraham, Who Patiently Endured (vv. 14, 15)
2. Our Guarantor: God Himself (vv. 13, 16)
3. Our Assurance: God's Oath Added to His Promise (vv. 17–18)
4. Our Hope: The Anchor that Tethers Us to Jesus (vv. 19–20)

V. The Son: The Superior High Priest (7:1–10:18)

A. THE NEW ORDER OF PRIESTHOOD (7:1–28)

1. Melchizedek and the Order of His Priesthood (7:1–10)

STRUCTURE

Several factors confirm that Heb 7:1–28 is a major section within Hebrews, such as *inclusio*, hook words, refs. to the Son in v. 3 and v. 28, and the concentration of "distinctive terms" (Lane 1:178–79). Additionally, 7:1–10 interprets Gen 14:17–20, and "7:11–28 directs attention to the significance of each phrase in Ps 110:4" (Lane 1:180). Hebrews 7 subdivides into three subsections: vv. 1–10, vv. 11–19 and vv. 20–28.

Heb 7:1–10 further divides into vv. 1–3 (explaining who Melchizedek is following the ref. to Ps 110:4 in Heb 6:20) and vv. 4–10 (the superiority of the Melchizedekian priesthood to the Levitical one; note the use of μὲν . . . δέ in vv. 5–6 and v. 8). Verses 1–3 are one sentence in Greek (anchored by μένει), providing another example of a periodic sentence (see comments on 1:1). Suggestions that the author drew from a preexisting hymn for these vv. are not convincing (Lane 1:160; Koester 349–50; Ellingworth 351–54). The passage is an example of "homiletical midrash," in which an OT passage (Gen 14:17–20) is explained and applied to a contemp. situation (Lane 1:158). Additionally, the author applies the principle of *gezera shava,* in which Ps 110:4 is understood in light of Gen 14:17–20 (see comments on 4:4; cf. Koester 338, 346–47). Repetition of συναντάω in vv. 1 and 10 forms an *inclusio* that brackets the passage. For chiastic elements in the passage, see Lane 1:160. The arrow indicates that "the people" and the Levitical priests' "brothers" are par.

Genesis 14:1–17 records that four eastern kings defeated the kingdoms of Sodom, Gomorrah, Adam, Zeboiim, and Bela, capturing Lot and his family in the process. Abraham and his men fought back and defeated these eastern kings. The passage of concern to Hebrews (Gen 14:17–20) picks up after these events.

1 Οὗτος γὰρ ὁ Μελχισέδεκ
βασιλεὺς Σαλήμ,
ἱερεὺς τοῦ θεοῦ τοῦ ὑψίστου,
ὁ συναντήσας Ἀβραὰμ ὑποστρέφοντι ἀπὸ τῆς κοπῆς τῶν βασιλέων
καὶ εὐλογήσας αὐτόν,
2 ᾧ καὶ δεκάτην ἀπὸ πάντων ἐμέρισεν Ἀβραάμ,
πρῶτον μὲν ἑρμηνευόμενος βασιλεὺς δικαιοσύνης
ἔπειτα δὲ καὶ βασιλεὺς Σαλήμ,
ὅ ἐστιν βασιλεὺς εἰρήνης,
3 ἀπάτωρ
ἀμήτωρ
ἀγενεαλόγητος,
μήτε ἀρχὴν ἡμερῶν μήτε ζωῆς τέλος ἔχων,
ἀφωμοιωμένος δὲ τῷ υἱῷ τοῦ θεοῦ,
μένει ἱερεὺς εἰς τὸ διηνεκές.
4 Θεωρεῖτε δὲ πηλίκος οὗτος,
ᾧ [καὶ] δεκάτην Ἀβραὰμ ἔδωκεν ἐκ τῶν ἀκροθινίων
ὁ πατριάρχης.
5 καὶ οἱ μὲν ἐκ τῶν υἱῶν Λευὶ τὴν ἱερατείαν λαμβάνοντες ἐντολὴν ἔχουσιν
ἀποδεκατοῦν τὸν λαὸν
κατὰ τὸν νόμον,
τοῦτ᾽ ἔστιν τοὺς ἀδελφοὺς αὐτῶν,
καίπερ ἐξεληλυθότας ἐκ τῆς ὀσφύος Ἀβραάμ·
6 ὁ δὲ μὴ γενεαλογούμενος ἐξ αὐτῶν δεδεκάτωκεν Ἀβραὰμ
καὶ τὸν ἔχοντα τὰς ἐπαγγελίας
εὐλόγηκεν.
7 χωρὶς δὲ πάσης ἀντιλογίας τὸ ἔλαττον ὑπὸ τοῦ κρείττονος εὐλογεῖται.
8 καὶ ὧδε μὲν δεκάτας ἀποθνῄσκοντες ἄνθρωποι λαμβάνουσιν,
ἐκεῖ δὲ μαρτυρούμενος ὅτι ζῇ.
9 καὶ ὡς ἔπος εἰπεῖν,
δι᾽ Ἀβραὰμ
καὶ Λευὶ ὁ δεκάτας λαμβάνων δεδεκάτωται·
10 ἔτι γὰρ ἐν τῇ ὀσφύϊ τοῦ πατρὸς ἦν
ὅτε συνήντησεν αὐτῷ
Μελχισέδεκ.

VERSE 1

Οὗτος γὰρ ὁ Μελχισέδεκ, βασιλεὺς Σαλήμ, ἱερεὺς τοῦ θεοῦ τοῦ ὑψίστου,
For this Melchizedek, king of Salem, priest of God Most High,

The dem. adj. οὗτος in the pred. pos. modifies ὁ Μελχισέδεκ ("this Melchizedek"); it functions anaphorically (R 697; T 44–45), pointing to 6:20, and resumes the topic "that is difficult to explain," which was cut off after 5:10. Γάρ is explanatory, picking up from 6:20 (cf. Ellingworth 354; Cockerill 296). Βασιλεύς is an appos. of Μελχισέδεκ. Like Μελχισέδεκ, Σαλήμ is transliterated from the Heb. and is indecl. Its function as a descriptive gen. is inferred from the context. Ἱερεύς (-έως, ὁ, "priest"; see comments on 5:6) functions as another appos. to Μελχισέδεκ. The gen. θεοῦ is poss., which is further modified by ὑψίστου (ὕψίστος, -η, -ον, "most high" [most EVV]; the highest in status" [BDAG 1045b; Wallace 302 n. 22]). The rep. of the art. and the placement of the adj. are emph. (Ellingworth 402; 2nd attrib. pos.; see Wallace 306–7).

There was much speculation about Melchizedek in Jewish apocalyptic (e.g., 11QMelch), rabbinic, and gnostic writings, as well as in Philo, where he is sometimes depicted as a messianic or angelic figure (see esp. Lane 1:160–63). The author, however, stays close to the biblical text, drawing out inferences from what is said or *not* said. In Genesis 14, Melchizedek is presented as the king of Salem and a priest of God Most High (v. 18). Salem was likely what became Jerusalem under David (i.e., the King's Valley in Gen 14:17 later became Jerusalem [2 Sam 18:18]; Koester 341). Genesis 14:18 represents the first occurrence of a priest in the OT. The origin of the designation "God Most High" is unclear, but Abraham's words (Gen 14:22) confirm that this is the God of Abraham (cf. Exod 18:1; Koester 341). What is key is that Melchizedek combines the offices of king and priest and reveals the existence of a non-Levitical priesthood.

ὁ συναντήσας Ἀβραὰμ ὑποστρέφοντι ἀπὸ τῆς κοπῆς τῶν βασιλέων καὶ εὐλογήσας αὐτόν,
met Abraham and blessed him as he returned from defeating the kings,

The subst. *συναντήσας* (nom. sg. masc. of the aor. act. ptc. of *συναντάω*, "meet" [BDAG 965b]) functions as a rel. clause ("who met"). The vb. is followed by the dat. Although indecl., Ἀβραάμ is dat., as confirmed by ὑποστρέφοντι (dat. sg. masc. of the pres. act. ptc. of ὑποστρέφω, "return") that modifies Ἀβραάμ. Κοπῆς is the gen. sg. fem. of *κοπή*, -ῆς, ἡ, "defeat" (most EVV), "slaughter" (ESV; BDAG 558c; NT hapax). The ref. is to Gen 14:17. Ἀπὸ τῆς κοπῆς modifies the ptc. adv. indicating separation. The gen. *τῶν βασιλέων* is obj. Εὐλογήσας is the nom. sg. masc. of the aor. act. ptc. of εὐλογέω, "bless." Αὐτόν is the obj. of this ptc. As an example of Granville Sharp's rule (Wallace 271–75), the single art. (ὁ) indicates that both subst. ptcs. (*συναντήσας* and εὐλογήσας) refer to the same individual, Melchizedek. The fact that Melchizedek blessed Abraham indicates his superiority, which the author will make explicit later. Blessing also identifies Melchizedek as a priest. The author does not mention that Melchizedek brought bread and wine to Abraham, most probably because these details were not relevant to his argument (Attridge 188; Ellingworth 355; Cockerill 296–97).

VERSE 2

ᾧ καὶ δεκάτην ἀπὸ πάντων ἐμέρισεν Ἀβραάμ,
and Abraham gave him a tenth of everything.

The antecdent of ᾧ is Melchizedek. Καί adds an additional narrative element (Runge 24–25). Ἐμέρισεν is the 3rd sg. aor. act. indic. of μερίζω, "gave" (NIV), "apportioned" (ESV, NASB, NET; BDAG 632a). The subj. of the vb. is Ἀβραάμ; the obj. is δεκάτην (acc. sg. fem. of δέκατος, -η, -ον, "tenth"); the subst. use of this adj., ἡ δεκάτη, specifically indicates "a tithe" (BDAG 216d; A. J. Hess, *EDNT* 1:284d–285a). The adj. is modified by the partitive ἀπὸ πάντων, where πάντων is understood as the spoils from the kings whom Abraham defeated. Whereas the LXX does not identify the subj. of ἐμέρισεν, the author of Hebrews adds Ἀβραάμ. Ὧ functions as the indir. obj. of the vb.

πρῶτον μὲν ἑρμηνευόμενος βασιλεὺς δικαιοσύνης ἔπειτα δὲ καὶ βασιλεὺς Σαλήμ, ὅ ἐστιν βασιλεὺς εἰρήνης,
First, his name means king of righteousness, then also, king of Salem, meaning king of peace.

Etymology was a common rabbinic technique to understand names, including Melchizedek (e.g., Philo and Josephus; Lane 1:164; Witherington 237). Speculation about Melchizedek was extensive, with human and angelic interpretations, as well as preincarnate manifestations of Christ (see esp. Bruce 159–60 n. 20; Koester 339–40; Cockerill 298–300; 303 n. 31). The author of Hebrews, however, again stays close to the biblical text. The correls. πρῶτον μέν . . . ἔπειτα ("then," BDAG 361b) δέ "are designations of enumeration which separate one thought from another in a series" (Lane 1:158). The ptc. is elliptically understood following ἔπειτα δέ (Ellingworth 357). Ἑρμηνευόμενος is the nom. sg. masc. of the pres. pass. ptc. of ἑρμηνεύω, "means" (NET, NIV), "by translation of" (ESV, NASB), "translate" (BDAG 393a). The ptc. agrees with Μελχισέδεκ, the subj. of v. 1. The first (πρῶτον) interpretation, βασιλεὺς δικαιοσύνης ("king of righteousness"), flows directly from the orig. Heb. (*melek*, "king" + *ṣedeq*, "righteousness"; cf. "king of justice" [NLT]). The title βασιλεὺς Σαλήμ is interpreted as βασιλεὺς εἰρήνης, also following the orig. Heb. closely (*melek*, "king" + *šālôm*, "peace"). Both δικαιοσύνης and εἰρήνης are attributive gens. (Wallace 88). Righteousness and peace are essential characteristics of God. Although there could be messianic connections, the author does not treat Melchizedek as more than a historical figure (*pace* Attridge 189–92; for more on the messianic implications, see Cockerill 297 n. 8). The expression ὅ ἐστιν indicates an explanation, regardless of the case of the antecedent (BDAG 727a; "that is to say" [BDF §132(2)]). The rel. pron. is nom., indicating its function as the subj. of the rel. clause.

VERSE 3

ἀπάτωρ ἀμήτωρ ἀγενεαλόγητος,
Without father, mother, or genealogy,

Each of these terms is formed with a prefixed alpha privitive that offers rhetorical alliteration (cf. Ellingworth 357). Both ἀπάτωρ (nom. sg. masc. of ἀπάτωρ, -ορος, ὁ, "without a father" [BDAG 99b]; G. Schrenk, *TDNT* 5:1019–21) and ἀμήτωρ (nom. sg.

fem. of ἀμήτωρ, -ορος, ὁ, "without a mother" [BDAG 54a]) are BGk. hapax, although Philo (*Drunkenness* 61) uses ἀμήτωρ with Sarah because Genesis does not record her mother's name. The Syriac Peshitta captures the sense of these terms: "his father and mother are not listed in genealogies" (Bruce 159 n. 19; cf. "there is no record of his . . . ancestors" [GNT, NLT]). The adj. ἀγενεαλόγητος (-η, -ον, "without genealogy" [BDAG 9c]; F. Büchsel, *TDNT* 1:665) appears to have been coined by the author (Koester 343) and does not occur elsewhere except in later ref. to this v. Although some suggest these terms indicate a supernatural birth or heavenly orig. for Melchizedek, most commentators agree that such an interpretation does not fit the argument of Hebrews (see esp. Koester 342–43). Instead, Melchizedek provides an example of a priest apart from Levitical genealogy. This view aligns with understanding τάξις (Ps 110:4) as "kind" or "nature"—see comments on 5:6.

μήτε ἀρχὴν ἡμερῶν μήτε ζωῆς τέλος ἔχων,
having neither beginning of days nor end of life,

Ἔχων agrees with Melchizedek and is modified by two dir. objs.: ἀρχὴν ἡμερῶν and ζωῆς τέλος. Ἔχων is circum. and modifies μένει. The acc. subst. ἀρχήν and τέλος form a merism—"beginning and end," whereas the gen. modifiers ἡμερῶν and ζωῆς are virtually synonymous and offer stylistic variation (cf. Ellingworth 358). Both gens. are descriptive. The correl. μήτε . . . μήτε negate the two obj. phrases ("neither beginning . . . nor end").

ἀφωμοιωμένος δὲ τῷ υἱῷ τοῦ θεοῦ, μένει ἱερεὺς εἰς τὸ διηνεκές.
but resembling the Son of God, he remains a priest forever.

Ἀφωμοιωμένος (nom. sg. masc. of the pf. pass. ptc. of ἀφομοιόω, with pass: "be like," "resemble" [BDAG 158b]; J. Schneider, *TDNT* 5:198; most EVV) is circum. and modifies μένει. It is likely a divine pass. (Lane 1:166). The vb. is followed by the dat. (cf. BDAG 707b). Δέ introduces a new element that transitions from the five neg. descriptors to two positive ones (Ellingworth 359). The use of μένω as an equative vb., with Melchizedek as the understood subj. and ἱερεύς (see comments on 5:6) as the pred. nom., is unusual (Wallace 40 n. 11). In Hebrews, μένω (see F. Hauck, *TDNT* 4:574–76) is usually associated with the Son (e.g., 10:34; 12:25–27; 13:14) and often has an eschatological sense (e.g., what remains in Hebrews includes Christ the high priest like Melchizedek [7:3]; the better possession of the faithful [10:34]; the city to come [13:14]). Εἰς τὸ διηνεκές (acc. sg. neut. of διηνεκής, -ές, "without interruption," "for all time" [BDAG 245c]) occurs only in Hebrews in the NT (7:3; 10:1, 12, 14).

Ἀφωμοιωμένος is the key for understanding the author's appeal to Melchizedek, who is not understood to be divine or messianic, but rather providentially was made to resemble Christ in various ways. "Jesus is not portrayed after the pattern of Melchizedek, but Melchizedek is 'made conformable to the Son of God'" (Bruce 160). More importantly, Hebrews focuses on the priesthood, not the person, of Melchizedek. The author draws several profound inferences from what is *not* stated in the Genesis account of Melchizedek. (Argumentation based on the principle that "even the silence of Scripture is charged with significance" occurs in rabbinic and Alexandrian exegesis [Lane 1:159; cf. Ellingworth 358].) Specifically, Melchizedek is without a (Levitical) genealogy; he appears in the narrative without beginning or end; and his priesthood appears to be ongoing. Thus he is a *type* of Christ, who alone is truly without beginning or end. Moreover, the terms ἀπάτωρ, ἀμήτωρ, and ἀγενεαλόγητος could not be applied to Christ (Cockerill 301–2). Claims that εἰς τὸ διηνεκές distinguishes the perpetual nature of Melchizedek's priesthood from Christ's eternal one (εἰς τὸν αἰῶνα; based on Ps 110:4) miss the fact that these two phrases are compared, not contrasted (Ellingworth 359; cf. Cockerill 300 n. 19).

VERSE 4

Θεωρεῖτε δὲ πηλίκος οὗτος,
Now consider how great this man was:

Having explained the person and priesthood of Melchizedek, the author now draws out the contemp. implications of Gen 14:17–20 in vv. 4–10. Δέ is thus transitional (Ellingworth 360). Θεωρεῖτε is the 2nd pl. pres. act. impv. of θεωρέω (M. Völkel, *EDNT* 146d–47c). The majority of commentators and EVV take the vb. as an impv.; although the indic. is possible ("you see" [GNT]), it does not fit the context as well. The interr. pron. πηλίκος (-η, -ον, "pert. to extraordinary importance, *how great*" [BDAG 811c]) is used as "a term of exclamation" (T 50), although some sense of an indir. question (R 292, 741) may also be present. The dem. pron. οὗτος refers to Melchizedek.

ᾧ [καὶ] δεκάτην Ἀβραὰμ ἔδωκεν ἐκ τῶν ἀκροθινίων ὁ πατριάρχης.
even Abraham the patriarch gave a tenth of the plunder to him.

The rel. clause repeats much of v. 2 as the author draws out implications for his argument. The antecedent of ᾧ remains Melchizedek. The mss.'s support for the omission ($\mathfrak{P}^{46}$ B D* 6 1739 1881) or inclusion (ℵ A C D^2, other codices and minuscules) of καί is not conclusive. If orig., its function would be ascensive ("even" [BDF §442(12)]). It may have been added in conformity with v. 2 (Ellingworth 361). In v. 2, the author switched to ἐμέρισεν from the LXX's ἔδωκεν, which is retained in v. 4. The subj. remains Ἀβραάμ. Whereas δεκάτην is modified by ἀπὸ πάντων in v. 2, here it is modified by ἐκ τῶν ἀκροθινίων (gen. pl. neut. of ἀκροθίνιον, -ου, τό, "plunder" [NET, NIV], "spoils" [BDAG 40a; BGk. hapax]), again in conformity with the LXX. For δεκάτην, see comments on v. 2. The placement of the appos. (R 399) ὁ πατριάρχης ("patriarch" [BDAG 788c]) is emph. (R 418; Cockerill 307) and draws "attention to the staggering fact that the patriarch Abraham, one of the greatest figures in the OT, gave a tenth of the spoils to Melchizedek" (Lane 1:158 n. *g*; cf. T 107).

VERSE 5

καὶ οἱ μὲν ἐκ τῶν υἱῶν Λευὶ τὴν ἱερατείαν λαμβάνοντες ἐντολὴν ἔχουσιν ἀποδεκατοῦν τὸν λαὸν κατὰ τὸν νόμον,
The sons of Levi who receive the priestly office have a command according to the law to collect a tenth from the people—

Verses 5–6 develop the content of v. 2a. The *μέν* (v. 5) . . . *δέ* (v. 6) cstr. signals a contrast. The arts. (*οἱ* and *ὁ*) function as pers. pron. (Wallace 212–13). *Καί* is explicative of v. 4 (Ellingworth 362). The subst. ptc. *λαμβάνοντες* is the subj. of *ἔχουσιν*. The obj. of the ptc. is *ἱερατείαν* (acc. sg. fem. of *ἱερατεία, -ας, ἡ*, "priestly office"/"priest's office" [ESV, NASB, NET], "service" [BDAG 469b]; G. Schrenk, *TDNT* 3:251; cf. "who become priests" [NIV]). The prep. phrase *ἐκ τῶν υἱῶν Λευί* is likely derivative (e.g., "those who descended" [Cassirer; NLT; Cockerill 308 n. 56; cf. Ellingworth 362]), rather than partitive ("those of the descendants of Levi" [NET; Attridge 195 n. 121; cf. BDF §164(1)]); or simply, "the descendants of Levi" (NIV, REB). The difference between the two is not significant. *Λευί* (indecl.; "Levi" [BDAG 592d]) modifies *υἱῶν* as a gen. of relationship ("the sons of Levi"; Wallace 83). The stipulations for Levitical priests concerning tithes are outlined in Num 18:1, 21–32 (see Attridge 195; cf. Ellingworth 362). *Ἐντολήν* is the obj. of *ἔχουσιν*. *Ἀποδεκατοῦν* (pres. act. inf. of *ἀποδεκατόω*, "to collect a tithe" [BDAG 109a]) is the complement of *ἐντολήν* (R 1076), with *τὸν λαόν* as its obj. The pres. indicates "general description" (Cockerill 309 n. 59). The prep. phrase *κατὰ τὸν νόμον* modifies *ἐντολήν*, distinguishing a command (*ἐντολή*) from the overall Mosaic law (Lane 1:168; Cockerill 309). This is the first of fourteen occurrences of *νόμος* in Hebrews.

τοῦτ' ἔστιν τοὺς ἀδελφοὺς αὐτῶν, καίπερ ἐξεληλυθότας ἐκ τῆς ὀσφύος Ἀβραάμ·
that is, from their brothers and sisters—though they have also descended from Abraham.

The expression *τοῦτ' ἔστιν* (see comments on 2:14) further elaborates *τὸν λαόν*, here understood as the Levites' brothers (*τοὺς ἀδελφοὺς αὐτῶν*). The conj. *καίπερ*, "although" (BDAG 497c), only occurs with ptcs. in the NT (R 1154). The adj. *ἐξεληλυθότας* (acc. pl. masc. of pf. act. ptc. of *ἐξέρχομαι*, "come out"; here "descend" [most EVV]) modifies *ἀδελφούς*. The ptc. is concessive (R 1129). *Ὀσφύος* is the gen. sg. fem. of *ὀσφῦς, -υος, ἡ*, "loins" (BDAG 730d; H. Seesemann, *TDNT* 5:496–97). The prep. phrase *ἐκ τῆς ὀσφύος Ἀβραάμ* adv. modifies the ptc. The gen. is partitive (BDF §164[1]). The language recalls LXX Gen 15:4. The argument is that if Melchizedek is greater than Abraham (evinced by Abraham paying tithes to him), and if the Levites are Abraham's descendants, then Melchizedek must also be greater than the Levites. The implication then follows that the priesthood that derives from Melchizedek must also be greater than the priesthood that derives from the Levites (descended from Abraham).

VERSE 6

ὁ δὲ μὴ γενεαλογούμενος ἐξ αὐτῶν δεδεκάτωκεν Ἀβραὰμ καὶ τὸν ἔχοντα τὰς ἐπαγγελίας εὐλόγηκεν.
But one without this lineage collected a tenth from Abraham and blessed the one who had the promises.

The art. ὁ refers anaphorically to Melchizedek (v. 1). Γενεαλογούμενος is the nom. sg. masc. of the pres. pass. ptc. of γενεαλογέω, "trace . . . genealogy" (NASB), "trace . . . descent" (NIV; BDAG 192b; NT hapax). The neg. μή ptcl. modifies the subst. ptc., which elaborates on ἀγενεαλόγητος from v. 3. Ἐξ αὐτῶν is partitive ("from them") and modifies the ptc. Melchizedek is the implied subj. of δεδεκάτωκεν (3rd sg. pf. act. indic. of δεκατόω, "collect a tenth" [NIV], "collect a tithe" [NET], "receive tithes" [ESV; BDAG 217a]). This compound vb. is less emph. than ἀποδεκατόω in v. 5 (Ellingworth 365) and occurs only here and in v. 9 in BGk. Although Ἀβραάμ is indecl., its gen. (ablative) function is inferred from the context. The subj. of εὐλόγηκεν (3rd sg. pf. act. indic. of εὐλογέω, "bless") remains Melchizedek, with the subst. ptc. ἔχοντα functioning as the obj. Melchizedek's blessing Abraham revealed his priestly status and superiority (cf. Bruce 162). The mention of ἐπαγγελίας (acc. pl. fem.; functioning as the obj. of the ptc.) recalls the important theme of the Abrahamic promises introduced in Heb 6:9–20. A contrast between promise and law is likely intended (Lane 1:169).

The pfs. used in this v. and v. 9 (cf. vv. 11, 16, 20, 23) are sometimes referred to as "perfects of allegory" (Moule 14–15; cf. Wallace 582) or "narrative perfects" (T 70); with "reference to an OT event [the perfect] can mean that this event still retains its (exemplary) meaning" (BDF §342[5]).

VERSE 7

χωρὶς δὲ πάσης ἀντιλογίας τὸ ἔλαττον ὑπὸ τοῦ κρείττονος εὐλογεῖται.
Without a doubt, the inferior is blessed by the superior.

The expression χωρὶς δὲ πάσης ἀντιλογίας (gen. sg. fem. of ἀντιλογία, -ας, ἡ) is idiomatic ("without question" [NLT], "beyond dispute"/"without any dispute" [ESV, NASB], "without doubt" [NIV; cf. BDAG 89d]). Δέ introduces a "new point" in the argument (Ellingworth 366). Ἔλαττον functions as the comp. of μικρός (ἔλασσων, -ον, "inferior" [BDAG 313d; BDF §61(1)]); the Attic form (with τ) is used in Hebrews (see BDF §34[1]). Κρείττονος is the gen. sg. neut. of κρείττων, "greater" (see comments on 1:4). The neut. art. indicates a generic (or categorical) use of the art. to present a generic principle (Wallace 227–30). Alternatively, the neut. "is used also of persons if the emphasis is on quality" (Z §141). The agent of the pass. εὐλογεῖται (3rd sg. pres. pass. indic. of εὐλογέω, "bless") is indicated by ὑπὸ τοῦ κρείττονος. The pres. is gnomic. In an honor/shame culture, the lesser would normally bless the greater, but the author stresses the reversal of this general principle in the case of Melchizedek and Abraham.

VERSE 8

καὶ ὧδε μὲν δεκάτας ἀποθνῄσκοντες ἄνθρωποι λαμβάνουσιν, ἐκεῖ δὲ μαρτυρούμενος ὅτι ζῇ.
In the one case, men who will die receive a tenth, but in the other case, Scripture testifies that he lives.

Καί introduces new information, namely the focus on "life" (Ellingworth 367). The expression ὧδε μέν . . . ἐκεῖ δέ indicates a comp. between the Levites and Melchizedek (an "emphatically marked opposition" [Attridge 196]). The adv. ὧδε is often spatial ("here"), but in this v. it is metaphorical, as is the adv. ἐκεῖ ("there")—"in this case . . . in that case" [NASB]; "in the one case . . . in the other" [ESV, NET, NIV]). Although ἄνθρωποι is generic, context points to the Levites as the ones who receive (λαμβάνουσιν) tithes (δεκάτας, acc. pl. fem.; see v. 2). Ἀποθνῄσκοντες (nom. pl. masc. of the pres. act. ptc. of ἀποθνῄσκω) modifies ἄνθρωποι adj. ("people who die" [Moule 104]; "dying human beings" [Cockerill 311]; "mortal men" [NASB, NET], "people who die" [NIV]).

The final part of the v. is elliptical, with Melchizedek implied (Attridge 196 n. 138). Μαρτυρούμενος is the nom. sg. masc. of the pres. pass. ptc. of μαρτυρέω, "being attested" (BDAG 618c; cf. BDF §312 [1]). The pass. is divine. The vb. in Hebrews "always refers to the witness of Scripture" (Ellingworth 368). The Scripture here is Gen 14:17–20, "interpreted with the assistance of" Ps 110:4 (Cockerill 311). The "declarative" ὅτι is freq. in the NT, esp. with vbs. of declaring or testifying (R 1034–35). Ζῇ is the 3rd sg. pres. act. indic. of ζάω, "live." The sense is that "Scripture testifies that he lives" (CSB). The author infers this from v. 3 (μήτε ζωῆς τέλος ἔχων). Μαρτυρούμενος is key: the author claims that the narrative declares Melchizedek to be without "end of days," whereas the Levites clearly died. Again, the comp. is between the Levitical priesthood and Christ's; thus, the author is not claiming that Melchizedek was eternal.

VERSE 9

καὶ ὡς ἔπος εἰπεῖν, δι' Ἀβραὰμ καὶ Λευὶ ὁ δεκάτας λαμβάνων δεδεκάτωται·
And in a sense Levi himself, who receives a tenth, has paid a tenth through Abraham,

Ἔπος is the nom. sg. neut. of ἔπος, -ους, τό, "word" (BDAG 388a). Εἰπεῖν is an inf. abs. (R 1093; Wallace 608–9). This literary use of ὡς (BDF §391a) occurs only here in the NT (Bruce 161 n. 25; Attridge 197). The classical expression ὡς ἔπος εἰπεῖν is idiomatic: "one might even say" (ESV, NIV), "so to speak" (NASB), "it could be said" (NET), "one might almost say" (BDAG 388a). It could be emph. (cf. BDAG 388a). The prep. phrase δι' Ἀβραάμ (gen.) is instr. ("through Abraham"; the final α of the prep. elides before a vowel; BDF §17). The second καί is ascensive ("even"). The subj. of δεδεκάτωται (3rd sg. pf. pass. indic. of δεκατόω; see v. 6) is Levi. (For the use of the pf. tense, see comments on v. 6.) The art. ptc. λαμβάνων modifies Λευί as an appos.

(cf. Z §371). The obj. of the ptc. is δεκάτας ("tithes"); the pl. form of the adj. is more general than the sg. one (Ellingworth 367) (see comments on v. 2).

VERSE 10

ἔτι γὰρ ἐν τῇ ὀσφύϊ τοῦ πατρὸς ἦν ὅτε συνήντησεν αὐτῷ Μελχισέδεκ.
for he was still within his ancestor when Melchizedek met him.

Γάρ is explanatory for the claim in v. 9. The adv. ἔτι ("yet," "still") modifies ἦν. The implied subj. of ἦν is Λευί. Ὀσφύϊ is the dat. sg. fem. of ὀσφῦς, -υος, ἡ, "the loins" (see comments on v. 5). Ἐν τῇ ὀσφύϊ τοῦ πατρός locat. modifies ἦν. The ptcl. ὅτε ("when" [BDAG 731b]) introduces a temp. clause. Συνήντησεν is the 3rd sg. aor. act. indic. of συναντάω, "meet" [BDAG 965b]); the vb. is followed by the dat. The subj. of the vb. is Μελχισέδεκ. The antecedent of αὐτῷ is Abraham. Although one could dismiss this v. as "a playful exegesis of the Genesis story" (Attridge 187), the claim that Levi actually paid tithes to Melchizedek emphasizes the author's main claim that the priesthood associated with Melchizedek is superior to the Levitical one, which prepares for the discussion of the Son's superior priesthood.

FOR FURTHER STUDY

48. Melchizedek (7:1–10)

Allison, D. C., Jr. *DLNT* 729–31.
Astour, Michael C. *ABD* 4:684–86.
Attridge, 192–95.
*Bird, Chad L. "Typological Interpretation within the Old Testament: Melchizedekian Typology." *Concordia Journal* 26 (2000): 36–52.
Brooke, George J. *ABD* 4:687–88.
*Cockerill, Gareth Lee. "Melchizedek or 'King of Righteousness.'" *EQ* 63 (1991): 305–12.
*———. "Melchizedek without Speculation: Hebrews 7:1–25 and Genesis 14:17–24. Pages 128–44 in Bauckham, *Cloud.*
Crocker, Lacy K. "A Holy Nation." *RTR* 72 (2013): 185–201.
Delcor, M. "Melchizedek from Genesis to the Qumran Texts and the Epistle to the Hebrews." *JSJ* 2 (1971): 115–35.
*Demarest, Bruce A. "Hebrews 7:3, A *Crux Interpretum* Historically Considered." *EQ* 49 (1977): 141–62.
Ellingworth, Paul. "'Like the Son of God': Form and Content in Hebrews 7:1–10." *Bib* 64 (1983): 255–62.
Evans, C. A. *DNTB* 693–95.
Fitzmyer, Joseph A. "Further Light on Melchizedek from Qumran Cave 11." *JBL* 86 (1967): 25–41.
*———. "'Now This Melchizedek' (Heb 7:1)." *CBQ* 25 (1963): 305–21.
Granerød, Gard. "Melchizedek in Hebrews 7." *Bib* 90 (2009): 188–202.

Lefler, Nathan. "The Melchizedek Traditions in the Letter to the Hebrews: Reading through the Eyes of an Inspired Jewish-Christian Author." *Pro Ecclesia* 16 (2007): 73–89.

Longenecker, Richard N. "The Melchizedek Argument of Hebrews: A Study in the Development and Circumstantial Expression of New Testament Thought." Pages 161–85 in *Unity and Diversity in New Testament Theology: Essays in Honor of George E Ladd*. Edited by Robert A. Guelich. Grand Rapids: Eerdmans, 1978.

Mason, Eric F. "Hebrews 7:3 and the Relationship between Melchizedek and Jesus." *BR* 50 (2005): 41–62.

*Pearson, Birger A. "Melchizedek in Early Judaism, Christianity, and Gnosticism." Pages 176–202 in *Biblical Figures outside the Bible*. Edited by Michael E. Stone and Theodore A Bergen. Harrisburg, PA: Trinity Press International, 1998.

Peterson, D. G. *NDBT* 658–60.

Seid, Timothy W. "Synkrisis in Hebrews 7: The Rhetorical Structure and Strategy." Pages 322–47 in *Rhetorical Interpretation of Scripture: Essays from the 1996 Malibu Conference*. Sheffield: Sheffield Academic, 1999.

Tait, Michael. "The Search for Valid Orders: The Melchizedek Christology in Hebrews." *Churchman* 124 (2010): 127–42.

Thompson, James W. "Conceptual Background and Purpose of the Midrash in Hebrews 7." *NovT* 19 (1977): 209–23.

HOMILETICAL SUGGESTIONS

Focus on Melchizedek (7:1–10)

1. Reviewing the Scriptural Record about Melchizedek (vv. 1–2)
   (a) King of Salem, priest of God Most High (v. 1a)
   (b) Met and blessed by Abraham after the defeat of the eastern kings (v. 1b)
   (c) Received a tithe from Abraham (v. 2a)
2. Explanation of His Name (vv. 2–3)
   (a) Melchizedek means "king of righteousness" (v. 2b)
   (b) King of Salem means "king of peace" (v. 2c)
3. What Is Not Said about Melchizedek (vv. 2–3)
   (a) No genealogy (v. 3a)
   (b) No record of his birth or death (v. 3b)
   (c) Significance: he was providentially made to anticipate the Son of God (v. 3c)
4. There Is Someone Greater than the Patriarch Abraham!
   (a) Abraham paid tithes to Melchizedek (v. 4)
      (1) The law specifies that tithes be paid to Levites (v. 5a)
      (2) Although even Levites are Abraham's descendants (v. 5b)
   (b) Thus Abraham paid tithes to a non-Levite (which underscores Melchizedek's superior status (vv. 6–7)
   (c) The Levites who received tithes died, but there is no record of Melchizedek's death (v. 8)

(d) As Abraham's descendants, the Levites also "paid" tithes to Melchizedek (vv. 9–10)

There Is Someone Greater than Abraham (and the Levites)! (7:1–10)

1. The Scriptural Record of Melchizedek the King-Priest (vv. 1–3)
2. The Significance of This Record (vv. 4–10)
   (a) Abraham's tithe revealed Melchizedek's superiority (v. 4)
   (b) The law prescribes tithes be paid to Levites (even though they are also Abraham's descendants) (v. 5)
   (c) But Abraham paid tithes to Melchizedek and was blessed by him (vv. 6–7)
   (d) There is one who receives tithes (Melchizedek) who does not die (as the Levites do) (v. 8)
   (e) Because Levites are Abraham's descendants, in some sense, they also paid tithes to Melchizedek (vv. 9–10)

2. The Aaronic and Melchizedekian Priesthoods Contrasted (7:11–19)

STRUCTURE

Hebrews 7:1–10 is foundational for the argument in Heb 7:11–28, which expands on the two key points that were established in that passage: (1) Melchizedek is greater than Abraham (hence his priesthood is greater than the Levitical one), and (2) the Melchizedekian priesthood is eternal. Hebrews 7:11–28 divides into two subsections (vv. 11–19 and vv. 20–28). The focus of vv. 11–19 is on the inferiority of the Levitical priesthood, whereas the focus of vv. 20–28 is on the superiority of the Melchizedekian one. An *inclusio* formed by τελείωσις (v. 11) and ἐτελείωσεν (v. 19) and another one with νομοθετέω (v.11) and νόμος (v. 19) confirms the boundary of the section (Lane 1:178). As noted (see comments on the structure of 7:1–10), each phrase in Ps 110:4 is interpreted in vv. 11–19 (Lane 1:180). That the author's interest is in the priesthood rather than the person of Melchizedek is confirmed by the fact that Genesis 14 is not referenced again (cf. Lane 1:180).

The section opens with a cond. (v. 11), the prot. of which is dependent on the apod., as indicated by indentation. Parallel elements in this v. are aligned. The dependent ptc. in v. 12 is indented accordingly. Parallel elements in v. 14 are also aligned accordingly. Verses 14, 15, and 17 each introduce further reasons for the superiority of the Melchizedekian priesthood.

11 Εἰ μὲν οὖν τελείωσις διὰ τῆς Λευιτικῆς ἱερωσύνης ἦν,
↑ὁ λαὸς γὰρ ἐπ' αὐτῆς νενομοθέτηται,
τίς ἔτι χρεία κατὰ τὴν τάξιν Μελχισέδεκ ἕτερον ἀνίστασθαι ἱερέα
καὶ οὐ κατὰ τὴν τάξιν Ἀαρὼν λέγεσθαι;
12 ↓μετατιθεμένης γὰρ τῆς ἱερωσύνης
ἐξ ἀνάγκης καὶ νόμου μετάθεσις γίνεται.
13 ἐφ' ὃν γὰρ λέγεται ταῦτα, φυλῆς ἑτέρας μετέσχηκεν,
ἀφ' ἧς οὐδεὶς προσέσχηκεν τῷ θυσιαστηρίῳ·
14 πρόδηλον γὰρ
ὅτι ἐξ Ἰούδα ἀνατέταλκεν ὁ κύριος ἡμῶν,
εἰς ἣν φυλὴν περὶ ἱερέων οὐδὲν Μωϋσῆς ἐλάλησεν.
15 καὶ περισσότερον ἔτι κατάδηλόν ἐστιν,
εἰ κατὰ τὴν ὁμοιότητα Μελχισέδεκ ἀνίσταται ἱερεὺς ἕτερος,
16 ὃς οὐ κατὰ νόμον ἐντολῆς σαρκίνης γέγονεν
ἀλλὰ κατὰ δύναμιν ζωῆς ἀκαταλύτου.
17 μαρτυρεῖται γὰρ
ὅτι σὺ ἱερεὺς εἰς τὸν αἰῶνα κατὰ τὴν τάξιν Μελχισέδεκ.
18 ἀθέτησις μὲν γὰρ γίνεται προαγούσης ἐντολῆς
διὰ τὸ αὐτῆς ἀσθενὲς καὶ ἀνωφελές—
19 οὐδὲν γὰρ ἐτελείωσεν ὁ νόμος—
ἐπεισαγωγὴ δὲ κρείττονος ἐλπίδος
δι' ἧς ἐγγίζομεν τῷ θεῷ.

VERSE 11

Εἰ μὲν οὖν τελείωσις διὰ τῆς Λευιτικῆς ἱερωσύνης ἦν,
Now if perfection came through the Levitical priesthood

Μὲν οὖν often summarizes one section and transitions to the next (BDF §451[1]), although here it may function as a rhetorical device for emph. (Ellingworth 371) and to draw an inference (Moule 163; Lane 1:180; "now if" [BDAG 630c]). The cstr. εἰ . . . ἦν indicates the prot. of an "unreal (contrary-to-fact)" (BDF §360[4]) or second-class cond. (see comments on 4:8). The prot. introduces the rhetorical question in the apod.: "Now if perfection were attainable through the Levitical priesthood, what further need would arise . . . ?" Τελείωσις (-εως, ἡ, "perfection" [BDAG 997a]) only occurs here in Hebrews, although the cognate τελειόω occurs in 2:10 and 5:9 in ref. to the Son (see comments on 2:10 and For Further Study 18 [Perfection in Hebrews]). The concept of perfection is now applied to the people of God (Lane 1:180), which "point[s] to the establishment of right relationship with God through the cleansing of the conscience and the consummation of this relationship in everlasting glory, rest, and celebration in God's heavenly city" (Koester 353). It is thus an eschatological concept (Lane 1:181). Λευιτικός (-ή, -όν, "Levitical" [BDAG 593a; BGk. hapax]) only occurs in the LXX on the title page of Leviticus, from which the author of Heb may have drawn (cf. Lane 1:181). It is also possible that the author coined the term himself (Cockerill 314 n. 3). The prep. phrase διὰ τῆς Λευιτικῆς is instr. Ἱερωσύνης is the gen. sg. fem. of ἱερωσύνη, -ης, ἡ, "priestly office," "priesthood" (BDAG 471d; G. Schrenk, *TDNT* 3:247–48).

ὁ λαὸς γὰρ ἐπ' αὐτῆς νενομοθέτηται,
(for on the basis of it the people received the law),

Γάρ adds an explanatory, even parenthetical (BDF §465), comment. Νενομοθέτηται is the 3rd sg. pf. pass. indic. of νομοθετέω, "given" (NIV), "received" (ESV, NET), "legislate" (BDAG 676c; W. Gutbrod, *TDNT* 4:1090), with the pass. indicating "to be regulated by the law" (Lane 1:174 n. *b*). (For the function of the pf. tense, see comments on 7:6.) The antecedent of αὐτῆς could be ἱερωσύνης or τελείωσις, but the former is the better option, based on both proximity as well as the overall context (Ellingworth 372; Lane 1:174). There are several options for translating ἐπί (see Lane 1:174 n. *b*; Koester 353):

1. "about," functioning par. to περί (cf. "concerning," Lane 1:173; Koester 353);
*2. "on the basis of" (CSB, NASB, NJB; BDF §234[8]; Attridge 200, Cockerill 316 n. 14, Ellingworth 372), even though this mng. would accord better with the dat. (Koester 353);
3. "through" (ESV); "under" (KJV).

τίς ἔτι χρεία κατὰ τὴν τάξιν Μελχισέδεκ ἕτερον ἀνίστασθαι ἱερέα καὶ οὐ κατὰ τὴν τάξιν Ἀαρὼν λέγεσθαι;
what further need was there for another priest to appear, said to be according to the order of Melchizedek and not according to the order of Aaron?

The interr. *τίς* modifies *χρεία* (nom. sg. fem. of *χρεία, -ας, ἡ*, "need"). The adv. *ἔτι* likely modifies *χρεία* (e.g., "further need") rather than *ἀνίστασθαι* (e.g., "yet arise"). The entire clause constitutes the apod., which is a rhetorical question (signaled by the interr.; cf. Attridge 200). The adj. *ἕτερον* (*ἕτερος, -α, -ον*, "different" [R 748]) modifies *ἱερέα* (acc. sg. masc. of *ἱερεύς, -έως, ὁ*, "priest"), which is in turn modified by the prep. phrase *κατὰ τὴν τάξιν Μελχισέδεκ* (see comments on 5:6). The distinction between *ἕτερος* ("different") and *ἄλλος* ("another"; many EVV) is maintained in Hebrews (see R 748; Bruce 165 n. 45). *Ἀνίστασθαι* is the pres. mid. inf. of *ἀνίστημι*, which here means to "come" (NIV), "appear" (CSB), "arise" (ESV, NET; BDAG 83d); the vb. has "messianic associations" (Ellingworth 373). *Λέγεσθαι* indicates "to be designated" (Lane 1:174 n. *c*). Both *ἀνίστασθαι* and *λέγεσθαι* complete the verbal idea implicit in *χρεία*—"what need would there be . . . to arise . . ." *Κατὰ τὴν τάξιν Ἀαρών* was likely derived by the author to par. *κατὰ τὴν τάξιν Μελχισέδεκ* (Lane 1:174 n. *d*) and sim. indicates "in accordance with" (BDAG 513a). There is debate whether the neg. ptcl. *οὐ* modifies *λέγεσθαι* (most EVV; Cockerill 316 n. 12) or *κατὰ τὴν τάξιν Ἀαρών* (GNB, NET, NIV; BDF §429). The second option is slightly preferred since *μή* would normally be used to negate an inf. (Ellingworth 372), although it is difficult to render in Eng. Some EVV draw out the contrast with "instead of" (NLT, REB), sometimes leaving both the neg. ptcl. and the final inf. untr.

The promise of a priesthood of a different order indicated in Ps 110:4 implies that the Levitical order was ultimately ineffective, even while it was still functioning. Additionally, one could not argue that the Aaronic priesthood superseded the Melchizedekian one because the promise of Ps 110:4 was given *after* the Aaronic order was well established (Bruce 165). Moreover, a new priesthood would require a new priest. The argumentation here confirms the traditional view that the epistle's recipients were primarily Jewish believers who may have been tempted to retreat to the old order.

VERSE 12

μετατιθεμένης γὰρ τῆς ἱερωσύνης ἐξ ἀνάγκης καὶ νόμου μετάθεσις γίνεται.
For when there is a change of the priesthood, there must be a change of law as well.

Γάρ links this v. to the parenthetical clause in v. 11 (Ellingworth 374). *Μετατιθεμένης* is the gen. sg. fem. of the pres. pass. ptc. of *μετατίθημι*, "change" (most EVV; BDAG 642b; C. Maurer, *TDNT* 8:161). For *ἱερωσύνης*, see v. 11. *Μετατιθεμένης τῆς ἱερωσύνης* is a gen. abs. cstr. in which the subj. of the gen. clause (*ἱερωσύνης*) is not the same as the main clause (*γίνεται*). *Γίνεται* functions as an impers., equative vb. ("there is necessity"). Its extensive use in Hebrews 7 is a "general term to cover the event of the institution of Christ's priesthood" (Ellingworth 375). It is either circum. ("whenever the priesthood is altered"; most EVV; Lane 1:174 n. *e*) or cond. ("if the priesthood is changed," NLT; "if the priesthood is altered"; R 1022–23, 1129; Wallace 633; Attridge 200–201 n. 34). Either option is possible. Ἐξ ἀνάγκης (gen. sg. fem. of ἀνάγκη, -ης, ἡ, "necessity" [BDAG 61a]) adv. modifies γίνεται ("necessarily" [ESV]; tr. "must" in many EVV). Μετάθεσις is the nom. sg. fem. of μετάθεσις, -εως, ἡ, "change" (most EVV); "transformation" (BDAG 639a; C. Maurer, *TDNT* 8:161). Change here implies also abrogation (Bruce 164 n. 38). Καί is adjunctive, "also" (Wallace 671). The gen. νόμου is of ref. ("a change with ref. to the law" [Wallace 127–28]).

The argument here is remarkable. Many would have assumed the Levitical law was permanent (e.g., Num 18:19; 25:13) and that the priesthood depended on the law, but the author argues the opposite: if the priesthood changes, then the law must also change. Thus the law was temp. bound until Christ's advent. Paul draws a sim. conclusion (but for different reasons) in Gal 3:24.

VERSE 13

ἐφ' ὃν γὰρ λέγεται ταῦτα, φυλῆς ἑτέρας μετέσχηκεν, ἀφ' ἧς οὐδεὶς προσέσχηκεν τῷ θυσιαστηρίῳ·
For the one these things are spoken about belonged to a different tribe. No one from it has served at the altar.

Γάρ again functions as a connective. The antecedent for the rel. pron. ὅν is an unstated "the one" (R 721 [ἐφ' ὅν = οὗτος ἐφ' ὅν]), but ἕτερον (ἱερέα) in v. 11 is implied. Ἐπί elides before rough breathing (ἐφ'). The adv. prep. phrase ἐφ' ὅν modifies λέγεται, with ταῦτα functioning as its subj. ("these things are spoken about this one"). The antecedent of ταῦτα is likely the entire previous discussion, but esp. the discussion of Ps 110:4 (cf. "to whom that prophecy refers" [Weymouth]). The entire rel. clause (ἐφ' ὅν . . . λέγεται ταῦτα) functions as the subj. of μετέσχηκεν (3rd sg. pf. act. indic. of μετέχω, "share" [BDAG 642c]; many EVV have "belong") and takes a gen. obj. The vb. is never used for physical descent; here it may recall its use in 2:14 (the only other occurrence in Hebrews) in conj. with Jesus's incarnation (Ellingworth 375; Cockerill 318 n. 28). The subst. φυλῆς (-ῆς, ἡ, "tribe" [BDAG 1069a) is modified by the adj. ἑτέρας (ἕτερος, -α, -ον, "different" [R 748]).

The antecedent for the rel. pron. ἧς is φυλῆς. (Ἀπό elides before rough breathing [ἀφ']). The adj. οὐδείς (οὐδείς, οὐδεμία, οὐδέν) functions as the subj. of προσέσχηκεν, which is the 3rd sg. pf. act. indic. of προσέχω, "serve at the altar" (ESV, NIV), "officiate at the altar" (NASB, NET; BDAG 880b). The pf. here may be emph. (Cockerill 318). This vb. is not used elsewhere in conj. with serving at the altar and may have been chosen for "euphony" with μετέχω (Cockerill 318 n. 26; see below). The vb. is followed by the dat., here θυσιαστηρίῳ (dat. sg. neut. of θυσιαστήριον, -ου, τό, "altar" [BDAG 463b; J. Behm, *TDNT* 3:180–90]). Serving at the altar was an essential duty of priests (e.g., Num 18:5).

Lane notes the paronomasia (a wordplay based on sounds) that the author achieves with ἐφ' ὅν and ἀφ' ἧς, and μετέσχηκεν and προσέσχηκεν. This "characteristic concern for phonetic effectiveness" makes the numerous var. rdgs. for this v. unlikely (Lane 1:174–75 n. *g*; cf. R 580). (For the function of the pf. tense, see comments on 7:6.)

Although this v. could refer to Melchizedek, it more likely anticipates the discussion about Jesus, whose tribe is known (Judah) and from which no one served at the altar (so Attridge 201; Cockerill 318–19; Koester 354). Thus Jesus is the understood antecedent of the implied dem. pron. οὗτος (Ellingworth 375). The overlap with Melchizedek is probably intentional.

VERSE 14

πρόδηλον γὰρ ὅτι ἐξ Ἰούδα ἀνατέταλκεν ὁ κύριος ἡμῶν,
Now it is evident that our Lord came from Judah,

Γάρ adds the final element in the argument to this point. Πρόδηλον is the nom. sg. neut. of πρόδηλος, -ον, "clear" (NET, NIV), "evident" (ESV, NASB), "known" (BDAG 867b). The prefix indicates an intensive force ("perfectly clear"; Lane 1:175 n. *h*). Ὅτι may be adv., "because," offering a supporting reason for v. 13, or *may introduce the content of v. 14. The adv. prep. phrase ἐξ Ἰούδα modifies ἀνατέταλκεν; its placement is emph. (Lane 1:182). The subj. of the vb. (ἀνατέταλκεν) is ὁ κύριος ἡμῶν (the gen. is poss.). The phrase may allude to an early confession (Lane 1:182–83; cf. Heb 13:20).

Ἀνατέταλκεν is the 3rd sg. pf. act. indic. of ἀνατέλλω and could mean "to be a descendent" (so ESV, NASB, NET, NIV; BDAG 73d; H. Schlier, *TDNT* 1:351–53), although it is not used elsewhere with this mng. In the LXX, it refers to the sprouting of a messianic branch (Isa 11:1) or the rising of a star (Num 24:17; Jer 23:5); both passages were considered messianic in STL. This may explain the author's usage here (Lane 1:182) and accounts for some EVV (e.g., "sprung" [RV, REB]; see the extended discussion in Cockerill 319–21). That Jesus belonged to the line of Judah is recorded in the birth narratives (Matt 1:2–3; 2:6) and often understood in terms of Davidic descent widely assumed in early Christian teaching (e.g., Acts 2:29–36). Here the focus is not on physical descent but rather "a different tribe" from the Levites.

εἰς ἣν φυλὴν περὶ ἱερέων οὐδὲν Μωϋσῆς ἐλάλησεν.
and Moses said nothing about that tribe concerning priests.

The "antecedent" of the rel. pron. ἥν is φυλήν, which is embedded into the rel. clause (R 719; Wallace 340). Although εἰς ἥν φυλήν functions par. to ἐξ Ἰούδα, εἰς indicates "with ref. to" (BDAG 291a; but see R 719). The subj. of ἐλάλησεν is Μωϋσῆς (-έως, ὁ, "Moses"). The obj. of the vb. is οὐδέν ("nothing"). The prep. phrase περὶ ἱερέων (gen. pl. masc. of ἱερεύς, -έως, ὁ, "priest") modifies οὐδέν, indicating "concerning."

VERSE 15

καὶ περισσότερον ἔτι κατάδηλόν ἐστιν,
And this becomes clearer

Καί may be ascensive and introduces new information ("what is more" [Ellingworth 377]). Περισσότερον (πετισσότερος, -τέρα, -ον; comp. of περισσός, "greater," "more," "even more" [BDAG 806a; BDF §60[1, 3]) is elative and modifies the pred. nom. κατάδηλον (nom. sg. neut. κατάδηλος, "very clear," "quite plain" (BDAG 516c; with περισσότερον, "it is clearer still"; "a double comp." [R 663]). The adv. ἔτι modifies κατάδηλος and heightens the comp. (T 29). The subj. of ἐστίν is unclear, although it may be generally understood as the argument for Jesus's superiority (Ellingworth 377). Some EVV supply an implied subj. (e.g., "what we have said," NIV). The expression intensifies the language and extends the argument of v. 14 (Lane 1:183).

εἰ κατὰ τὴν ὁμοιότητα Μελχισέδεκ ἀνίσταται ἱερεὺς ἕτερος,
if another priest like Melchizedek appears,

Εἰ with an unaugmented tense (ἀνίσταται) introduces the prot. of a first-class conditional sentence, which "indicates the assumption of truth for the sake of argument" (Wallace 690; BDF §372[1a]). The use of ἀνίσταται (3rd sg. pres. mid. indic.) pars. its usage in v. 11 (see comments there). The subj. of the vb. is ἱερεύς, which is modified by ἕτερον (ἕτερος, -α, -ον, "different"); some EVV render the adj. as "new" (e.g., REB). The position of ἱερεὺς ἕτερος is emph. (Ellingworth 378). Κατά indicates "in accordance with" (BDAG 513a). Ὁμοιότητα is the acc. sg. fem. of ὁμοιότης, -ητος, ἡ, "likeness" (ESV, NASB), "resembling" (NRSV), "similarly" (BDAG 707a; J. Schneider, *TDNT* 5:189–90). Although the substitution of ὁμοιότητα for τάξις may be "stylistic" (Ellingworth 378), more likely it is intentional (cf. Cockerill 322 n. 40), indicating that τάξις does not mean succession, but rather "order" or "nature" (see comments on 5:6). Moreover, it affirms that the author's interest is in the typological connection between the Melchizedekian priesthood and the one associated with Christ rather than in Melchizedek as an angelic or divine figure (cf. Koester 355; see comments on 7:3). Whereas vv. 11–14 focused on the limitations of the Levitical order, vv. 15–19 focus on the positive implications of Ps 110:4.

VERSE 16

ὃς οὐ κατὰ νόμον ἐντολῆς σαρκίνης γέγονεν ἀλλὰ κατὰ δύναμιν ζωῆς ἀκαταλύτου.
who did not become a priest based on a legal regulation about physical descent but based on the power of an indestructible life.

The antecedent of ὅς is ἱερεύς in v. 15, which is also the implied pred. nom. of γέγονεν ("the one who has become a priest"). (For the function of the pf. tense of γίνομαι, see comments on 7:6). Κατά indicates "in accordance with" (BDAG 513a), "by virtue of" (Moule 59), or even "because of" (Ellingworth 378). The anar. obj. of the prep., νόμος, may be qual. (Cockerill 322), although the obj. of a prep. is often anar. (Wallace 247). Σαρκίνης (gen. sg. fem. of σάρκινος, -η, -ον) relates to "the physical realm," or more simply, "human" (BDAG 914c; cf. E. Schweizer, *TDNT* 7:141–43; BDF §113[2]). The term also implies "earthly" or "temporary," as the EVV reveal ("a Law regulating only earthly matters" [TCNT], "a system of earth-bound rules" [NEB], "any temporary Law" [Weymouth]). An allusion to physical genealogies may also be intended ("a legal requirement concerning physical descent" [NRSV]; Lane 1:175 n. *k*). The term "hints" that the Mosaic law is "concerned only with external and physical matters" (Attridge 202). Unlike σαρκικός, -ή, -όν (notice accents), which could imply "fleshly," this term need not imply "sinful nature" (e.g., KJV ["carnal commandment"]), but rather "fleshy" (BDAG 914a). The var. rdgs., however, suggest that a tight distinction between the two terms was not maintained (BDAG 914a). Σαρκίνης modifies ἐντολῆς, which in turn modifies νόμον as a partitive gen. The distinction between a command (ἐντολή) and the law (νόμος) continues from v. 5 (Cockerill 309; Lane 1:168). The obj. of the second κατά is δύναμιν. The adj. ἀκαταλύτου (gen. sg. fem. of ἀκατάλυτος, -ον, "indestructible" [most EVV], "endless" [KJV; BDAG, 35b; F. Büchsel, *TDNT* 4: 338–39; BGk. hapax]) modifies ζωῆς, drawing an inference from the interpretation of Melchizedek in v. 3 and Ps 110:4. Both its position and its rarity render ἀκαταλύτου emph. (Ellingworth 379).

The two prep. phrases comprise the apod. of the cond. begun in v. 15 and present a strong contrast (confirmed by ἀλλά). The neg. ptcl. οὐ modifies κατὰ τὸν νόμον ἐντολῆς σαρκίνης, paralleling v. 11. The prep. phrase in this v. makes explicit the limitation of the Aaronic order suggested in v. 11, namely, that it depends on a human ordinance concerning physical genealogies. Similarly the second prep. phrase in this v. recalls κατὰ τὴν τάξιν Μελχισέδεκ in v. 11 and makes explicit the power of the Melchizedekian order, namely, that it depends on an "indestructible" or "endless" life. The ref. may have Jesus's resurrection in view (Koester 355), which is also suggested by εἰς τὸν αἰῶνα in v. 17. It is more likely, however, that death could not destroy the Son's "indestructible life" ("a life beyond the reach of death" [TCNT], "a life that cannot be destroyed" [NAB]; Cockerill 323–24; Lane 1:184). Although this v. draws on inferences based on Melchizedek, it lays the foundation for the author's conclusion about Jesus in v. 22.

VERSE 17

μαρτυρεῖται γὰρ ὅτι σὺ ἱερεὺς εἰς τὸν αἰῶνα κατὰ τὴν τάξιν Μελχισέδεκ.
For it has been testified:
You are a priest forever according to the order of Melchizedek.

Γάρ offers scriptural support for the "indestructible life" mentioned in v. 16. Μαρτυρεῖται is the 3rd sg. pres. pass. indic. of μαρτυρέω, "is declared" (NIV), "is attested" (NASB; BDAG 618c); the vb. indicates a divine pass. (see comments on 7:8). Ὅτι introduces the citation from Ps 110:4, which is understood as a "witness" (or even prophecy) of Christ's priesthood (cf. "he is attested by the prophecy" [NJB]). (For discussion of the citation from Ps 110:4, see comments on 5:6.)

VERSE 18

ἀθέτησις μὲν γὰρ γίνεται προαγούσης ἐντολῆς διὰ τὸ αὐτῆς ἀσθενὲς καὶ ἀνωφελές—
So the previous command is annulled because it was weak and unprofitable

The correl. *μὲν . . . δέ* cstr. begins in this v. and concludes in the second half of v. 19. *Γάρ* explains why the regulation is annulled. *Γίνομαι* is used extensively in Hebrews 7 as a "general term" (see comments on v. 12). The subj. of *γίνεται* is *ἀθέτησις* (-εως, ἡ, "annulment" [BDAG 24c]; NT hapax); "a stronger word than *μετάθεσις*" (Bruce 168 n. 56). This is reflected in several EVV (e.g., "disannulling" [KJV], "abolition" [TCNT], "abrogation" [NRSV; Koester 355], "cancellation" [Barclay], "repealed" [REB]), but is not reflected in others (e.g., "a setting aside" [NASB], "is replaced by" [NJB]). *Ἀθέτησις* is modified by *ἐντολῆς* as an obj. gen. (Wallace 113–16). *Προαγούσης* is the gen. sg. fem. of the pres. act. ptc. of *προάγω*, "go before" ("preceding" [BDF §308]). The ptc. is adj., agreeing with *ἐντολῆς*.

Διά + acc. is causal. *Ἀσθενές* is the acc. sg. neut. of *ἀσθενής, -ές, τό*, "inefficient" (TCNT), "impotent" (NEB), "weak," "feeble," "ineffectual" (BDAG 143a). *Ἀνωφελές* is the acc. sg. of *ἀνωφελής, -ές*, "useless" (BDAG 92d–93a). Both adjs. are functioning subst. and are modified by the single art. *τό* (cf. BDF §263[2]; T 14; Z §140). This is not an example of Granville Sharp's rule because the subst. are impers., although they are "overlapping" (Wallace 287). The antecedent of *αὐτῆς* is *ἐντολή*; the gen. indicates poss.

The implication is that Christ's priesthood resulted in the annulment of the former regulation because it revealed its weakness, namely, dependence on mortal humans (Cockerill 326). Moreover, it was useless because it could not effect lasting cleansing. The juxtaposition *εἰς τὸν αἰῶνα* (v. 17) and *ἀθέτησις* in this v. further contrasts the two priesthoods. Alliteration in this v. (*ἀθέτησις, αὐτῆς, ἀσθενές, ἀνωφελές*) again reveals the author's rhetorical competency.

VERSE 19

οὐδὲν γὰρ ἐτελείωσεν ὁ νόμος—ἐπεισαγωγὴ δὲ κρείττονος ἐλπίδος δι' ἧς ἐγγίζομεν τῷ θεῷ.
(for the law perfected nothing), but a better hope is introduced, through which we draw near to God.

Γάρ introduces a parenthetical comment (most EVV) that links this v. to vv. 15–17 (Ellingworth 380). *Ἐτελείωσεν* is the 3rd sg. aor. act. indic. of *τελειόω*, "bring to an end; bring to its goal/completion" (BDAG 996c); "perfect" (most EVV); see comments on 2:10. The aor. is consummative (Wallace 559). The subj. of the vb. is *νόμος*; the obj. is *οὐδέν* (acc. sg. neut. of *οὐδείς, οὐδεμία, οὐδέν*).

Ἐπεισαγωγή (-ῆς, ἡ, "is introduced" [most EVV]; "bringing in" [KJV, NASB]; "introduction" BDAG 361a; BGk. hapax; "establishing" [Cockerill 325 n. 58]) is the pred. of this verbless clause. Κρείττονος is the gen. sg. fem. of κρείττων "better" (see comments on 1:4). The comp. modifies ἐλπίδος, which modifies ἐπεισαγωγή as a subj. gen. The verbless clause following the parenthetical aside assumes the annulment of the former regulation, which introduces a better hope (cf. Koester 356). Likely γίνεται is implied (Ellingworth 382). The contrast between ἀθέτησις and ἐπεισαγωγή is stressed by the placement of each word at the beginning of its respective clause (Lane 1:185).

Ἐγγίζομεν is the 1st pl. pres. act. indic. of ἐγγίζω "draw near" (most EVV), "come near," "approach" (BDAG 270c; H. Preisker, *TDNT* 2:329). The antecedent of ἧς is ἐλπίς. The prep. δι' (elided before a vowel) is instr.—the means by which we draw near to θεῷ (the dat. indicates the indir. obj.). The art. τῷ may be an example of "par excellence" (Wallace 223 n. 35). In the LXX, ἐγγίζομεν τῷ θεῷ occurs with priests (Exod 19:22; Lev 21:21) and other worshippers (e.g., LXX Ps 144:18; 148:14; Lane 1:186; cf. Cockerill 327; Koester 356), although ἐγγίζω does not have the same cultic associations as προσέρχομαι (e.g., 4:16 [Ellingworth 382]).

This v. prepares for the upcoming discussion of the new covenant and Jesus's fully (and finally) efficacious sacrifice that enables perfection of worshippers, namely, the cleansing of their consciences. The better hope is thus the access to God, which was not possible under the Levitical order. The author's point is that the regulations of the law were temp. and ineffectual in light of the eternal and efficacious work of Christ. (For more on the numerous contrasts in this passage, see Cockerill 323–26.)

FOR FURTHER STUDY

49. Mosaic Law (7:11–28)

Attridge, 204–5.
Gutbrod, W. *TDNT* 4:1059–85.
Koester, 114–15.
*Joslin, Barry C. *Hebrews, Christ, and the Law: The Theology of the Mosaic Law in Hebrews 7:1–10:18*. Colorado Springs: Paternoster, 2008.
———. "Hebrews 7–10 and the Transformation of the Law." Pages 100–117 in Bauckham, *Cloud*.
Moo, Douglas J. "The Law of Christ as the Fulfillment of the Law of Moses: A Modified Lutheran View." Pages 319–76 in *Law, the Gospel, and the Modern Christian: Five Views*. Edited by Wayne G. Strickland. Grand Rapids: Zondervan, 1993.
Sanders, E. P. *ABD* 4:254–65.
Schmitt, Mary. "Restructuring Views on Law in Hebrews 7:12." *JBL* 128 (2009): 189–201.
Schreiner, T. R. *DLNT* 644–49.

HOMILETICAL SUGGESTIONS

The Implications of the Melchizedekian Priesthood (7:11–19)

1. The Limitations of the Levitical Priesthood (v. 11)

    (a) It was not able to achieve perfection (v. 11a)
    (b) If it had, there would not be another priesthood (v. 11b)
2. A New Priesthood Means a New Law (v. 12)
3. A New Priesthood Not Based on Genealogy (vv. 13–17)
    (a) The tribe of Judah did not serve at the earthly altar (vv. 13, 14a)
    (b) The Lord is of the tribe of Judah (v. 14a)
    (c) There is a different priest in the order of Melchizedek (v. 15)
    (d) Not based on genealogy but an indestructible life (v. 16)
    (e) Confirmed in Ps 110:4 (v. 17)
4. Summary (vv. 18–19)
    (a) The old law was annulled because it was ineffective (v. 18)
    (b) The old law could not achieve perfection (v. 19a)
    (c) The ineffectiveness of the old law points to something better (v. 19b)

The Hope of Drawing Near to God (7:11–19)

1. This Was Not Possible under the Old Priestly Order (vv. 11a, 19a)
2. But There Is Another Priestly Order! (v. 11b)
3. This Changes Everything! (vv. 12–19)
    (a) New Priesthood = new rules (vv. 12a, 18)
    (b) Not geneaology but indestructible life (vv. 12b–17)
4. A New Priesthood Makes Access to God Possible (v. 19b)

3. The Superiority of the New Priesthood (7:20–28)

STRUCTURE

The argument begun in Heb 7:1–10 concerning Christ's priesthood is first developed concerning its superiority to the law (vv. 11–19) and then concerning its eternality (vv. 20–28). The boundaries of this final section are established by an *inclusio* formed with ὁρκωμοσία in vv. 20 and 28. The section divides into three subsections: (1) the divine oath associated with the better priesthood and covenant (vv. 20–22, one sentence in the Gk.); (2) the permanence of Christ's priesthood (vv. 23–25); (3) the sufficiency of Christ's priesthood (vv. 26–28). This final subsection provides the foundation for the ensuing discussion in 8:1–10:18 (cf. "the main point" in 8:1). Verses 23 and 24 are chiastic, as reflected in the outline. The emph. on perfection (τετελειωμένον) in v. 28 summarizes the argument thus far and forms an *inclusio* with v. 11 (τελείωσις). The οἱ μὲν . . . ὁ δέ cstr. in this passage (vv. 20 and 21, 23 and 24) further contrasts the Levitical priests and Jesus.

20 Καὶ καθ' ὅσον οὐ χωρὶς ὁρκωμοσίας·
οἱ μὲν γὰρ χωρὶς ὁρκωμοσίας εἰσὶν ἱερεῖς γεγονότες,
21 ὁ δὲ μετὰ ὁρκωμοσίας
διὰ τοῦ λέγοντος πρὸς αὐτόν·
ὤμοσεν κύριος
καὶ οὐ μεταμεληθήσεται·
σὺ ἱερεὺς εἰς τὸν αἰῶνα.
22 κατὰ τοσοῦτο [καὶ] κρείττονος διαθήκης γέγονεν ἔγγυος Ἰησοῦς.
23 Καὶ οἱ μὲν πλείονές εἰσιν γεγονότες ἱερεῖς
διὰ τὸ θανάτῳ κωλύεσθαι παραμένειν·
24 ὁ δὲ διὰ τὸ μένειν αὐτὸν εἰς τὸν αἰῶνα
ἀπαράβατον ἔχει τὴν ἱερωσύνην·
25 ὅθεν καὶ σῴζειν εἰς τὸ παντελὲς δύναται τοὺς προσερχομένους δι' αὐτοῦ τῷ θεῷ,
πάντοτε ζῶν
εἰς τὸ ἐντυγχάνειν ὑπὲρ αὐτῶν.
26 Τοιοῦτος γὰρ ἡμῖν καὶ ἔπρεπεν ἀρχιερεύς,
ὅσιος
ἄκακος
ἀμίαντος,
κεχωρισμένος ἀπὸ τῶν ἁμαρτωλῶν
καὶ ὑψηλότερος τῶν οὐρανῶν γενόμενος,
27 ὃς οὐκ ἔχει καθ' ἡμέραν ἀνάγκην,
ὥσπερ οἱ ἀρχιερεῖς,
πρότερον ὑπὲρ τῶν ἰδίων ἁμαρτιῶν θυσίας ἀναφέρειν
ἔπειτα τῶν τοῦ λαοῦ·
τοῦτο γὰρ ἐποίησεν ἐφάπαξ
ἑαυτὸν ἀνενέγκας.

28 ὁ νόμος γὰρ ἀνθρώπους καθίστησιν ἀρχιερεῖς
ἔχοντας ἀσθένειαν,
ὁ λόγος δὲ τῆς ὁρκωμοσίας τῆς μετὰ τὸν νόμον υἱὸν
εἰς τὸν αἰῶνα τετελειωμένον.

VERSE 20

Καὶ καθ' ὅσον οὐ χωρὶς ὁρκωμοσίας·
None of this happened without an oath.

Καί adds a new development in the argument (cf. Ellingworth 383). Καθ' ὅσον is causal ("since" [NET], left untr. by most EVV; R 733, 963). Καθ' occurs before rough breathing. The correl. prons. in the phrases καθ' ὅσον (v. 20) . . . κατά τοσοῦτο (v. 22) connect the oath with the "guarantor" of the better covenant (R 710). The correl. phrases also imply a connection between the oath and the guarantor (Lane 1:186; cf. Ellingworth 383). Χωρίς means "without" (most EVV). The double neg. οὐ χωρίς is an example of litotes (Ellingworth 383). The prep. takes a gen. obj. Ὁρκωμοσίας is the gen. sg. fem. of ὁρκωμοσία, -ας, ἡ, "oath" (most EVV); "oath taking" (BDAG 723d; J. Schneider, *TDNT* 5:463–64). In the NT, this word only occurs in Hebrews (twice in this v., 7:21, 28). This term is more "solemn" than ὅρκος, used in 6:16 (Cockerill 329). The anar. ὁρκωμοσίας is indef. ("an oath").

There is debate whether ἱερεῖς γεγονότες should be understood in this verbless clause (e.g., "this new system" [NLT]) or whether the clause should be read back into v. 19 (NRSV); "and it was not without an oath that this better hope was introduced" (see Lane 1:175 n. *p*). Many EVV are unclear on this point.

οἱ μὲν γὰρ χωρὶς ὁρκωμοσίας εἰσὶν ἱερεῖς γεγονότες,
For others became priests without an oath,

Γάρ introduces an explanatory parenthesis in vv. 20b–21 (KJV, NASB, RV; R 435). The correl. μὲν . . . δέ cstr. continues the contrast between the old order (this v.) and the new (v. 21). The art. (οἱ and ὁ) function as pers. pron.; οἱ refers to the Levitical priests (BDF §250; Wallace 212–130). The cstr. may also have a (far) "demonstrative force" (T 36; cf. R 695), as seen in some EVV ("formerly" [ESV]; cf. "others" [many EVV]). Γεγονότες forms a periph. cstr. with εἰσίν. There is no syntactic difference between periph. and the simple finite (γεγόνασιν; cf. v. 16). This may reflect the author's "elegant" style (Bruce 170 n. 62; cf. Attridge 208 n. 25). (See comments on 7:6 for the pf. tense of γίνομαι in Hebrews 7.) Ἱερεῖς (nom. pl. masc.; see comments on 5:6) is a pred. nom. The adv. prep. phrase χωρὶς ὁρκωμοσίας modifies εἰσὶν . . . γεγονότες instr.

VERSE 21

ὁ δὲ μετὰ ὁρκωμοσίας διὰ τοῦ λέγοντος πρὸς αὐτόν·
but he became a priest with an oath made by the one who said to him:

The art. ὁ functions as a pers. pron., referring to Jesus (cf. BDF §250). The periph. cstr. (ἐστὶν γεγονότες) is elliptically understood from the previous v. Μετά + gen. means "with." (For ὁρκωμοσία, see 7:20.) The adv. prep. phrase διὰ τοῦ λέγοντος indicates agency (e.g., God [cf. 5:5; Z §112; Bruce 170 n. 63]), modifying the elliptical periph. cstr. Πρὸς αὐτόν modifies the ptc., indicating ref. Διὰ τοῦ λέγοντος πρὸς αὐτόν introduces the following citation from Ps 110:4 and continues the motif of God speaking in Hebrews.

ὤμοσεν κύριος καὶ οὐ μεταμεληθήσεται· σὺ ἱερεὺς εἰς τὸν αἰῶνα.
The Lord has sworn and will not change his mind, "You are a priest forever."

The subj. of ὤμοσεν (3rd sg. aor. act. indic. of ὀμνύω, "swear"; BDAG 706c) is κύριος (here understood as God). The neg. ptcl. οὐ modifies μεταμεληθήσεται (3rd sg. fut. pass. indic. of μεταμέλλομαι, "change one's mind" [most EVV; BDAG 639c; see Koester 363]). The pass. form is better understood as a mid. in function (R 334), which focuses on the "actor" rather than the "action" (Wallace 414). Καί connects the two finite vbs. (For the citation from Ps 110:4, see comments on 5:6.) The prep. phrase κατὰ τὴν τάξιν Μελχισέδεκ appears in some mss. (e.g., ℵ² A D Ψ Maj.). The UBS committee felt it more likely that scribes would have added the phrase rather than omit it (Metzger 597); the text is rated {A}. The omission may have intended to shift focus from Melchizedek to Christ (Ellingworth 382).

The ref. to an oath recalls the previous discussion of God's oath in conj. with the Abrahamic promises (6:13–20). Just as the mention of the oath there underscored the utter reliability of God's promises, so also here the oath confirms the superiority and eternality of the priesthood based on Christ's indestructible life and the covenant of which it is part. The oath also contrasts with the "regulation" (ἐντολή) associated with the Levitical priesthood.

VERSE 22

κατὰ τοσοῦτο [καὶ] κρείττονος διαθήκης γέγονεν ἔγγυος Ἰησοῦς.
Because of this oath, Jesus has also become the guarantee of a better covenant.

Τοσοῦτο (τοσοῦτος, -αύτη, -οῦτον) is a correl. adj. (with καθ᾽ ὅσον in v. 20), although κατὰ τοσοῦτο is also causal (R 965). Καί is omitted in early and important mss. but appears in ℵ* B C* 33. If original, it is ascensive (BDF §442[12]; "also" [NASB, NRSV]; cf. "even Jesus" [Cockerill 313]), although it is untr. by many EVV. The subj. of the clause is Ἰησοῦς. The placement of Ἰησοῦς at the end of the sentence begun in v. 20 is emph. (Bruce 171). The name Ἰησοῦς is less freq. in Hebrews (2:9; 3:1; 4:8, 14; 6:20; 10:10, 19; 12:2, 24; 13:8, 12, 20, 21), which may also add emph. (Ellingworth 385). Γέγονεν functions as an equative vb. The pf. is likely emph. (e.g., "intensified," Campbell, *VA* 201).

Ἔγγυος (-ου, ὁ) has a wide semantic range: "surety" (Barclay, Moffatt, RSV), "guarantor" (ESV, NEB, NIV, TNIV), "guarantee" (NASB, NET); cf. "Jesus . . .guarantees"

(NLT); "under good security" (BDAG 271a; H. Preisker, *TDNT* 2:329; BGk. hapax). Κρείττονος is the gen. sg. fem. of κρείττων ("better"; see comments on 1:4). The comp. modifies ἔγγυος. Ἔγγυος is a legal term that can refer to a person "who offers his own life as the guarantor of another person," or to post bond or collateral (cf. Sir 29:15–17; Koester 363–64; Lane 1:188). It is not normally used in conj. with a covenant, although it fits this context (Attridge 208)—Jesus is the guarantor of God's promises (Attridge 208; Cockerill 330–31). (For the difference between ἔγγυος and μεσίτης, see comments on Heb 8:6.)

Διαθήκης is the gen. sg. fem. of διαθήκη, -ης, ἡ, "covenant" (BDAG 228c). This is the first occurrence in Hebrews of διαθήκη, which will be the focus of subsequent passages in Hebrews 8–10. More than half (seventeen) of the NT occurrences of διαθήκη (thirty) occur in Hebrews. In secular sources it is a legal term for a last will or testament, although the LXX translators used it to render *bĕrît* ("covenant"). (See comments on 8:7; 9:17.) See For Further Study 60 (Διαθήκη).

VERSE 23

Καὶ οἱ μὲν πλείονές εἰσιν γεγονότες ἱερεῖς διὰ τὸ θανάτῳ κωλύεσθαι παραμένειν·
Now many have become Levitical priests, since they are prevented by death from remaining in office.

Καί is continuative ("now" [NIV]; cf. BDF §441[2]). The correl. μὲν . . . δέ cstr. continues the contrast between the old (this v.) and the new (v. 24). The art. οἱ functions as a pers. pron. referring to the Levitical priests (BDF §250; Wallace 212–30). The cstr. may also have a "demonstrative force" (T 36; cf. R 695; "former priests" [ESV], "those priests" [NIV]). Εἰσιν γεγονότες is periph. (see comments on v. 20). It is unlikely that the pf. implies that priests were still functioning in the temple at the time of the epistle's composition (Koester 364; see comments on 7:6 for the pf. tense of γίνομαι in Hebrews 7; see also For Further Study 54 (The Date of Hebrews). Πλείονες is the nom. pl. masc. of πλείων, πλεῖον; comp. of πολύς. Although the form is a comp. it is used here as a pos. ("many" [most EVV]). The contrast between the many and the one recalls the opening vv. of Hebrews (see comments on 1:1–2). Πλείονες could modify ἱερεῖς (e.g., "many . . . priests" [NLT]) or, more likely, functions as a pred. nom. with the periph. cstr. functioning as an equative vb. ("those priests have been many" [cf. NET, NIV; Bruce 171]).

Κωλύεσθαι is the pres. mid. inf. of κωλύω, "prevent" (most EVV), "hinder," "forbid" (BDAG 580a). Διὰ τί + inf. is causal (Wallace 597); its subj. (Levitical priests) is inferred from context. The dat. θανάτῳ is instr. Παραμένειν is the pres. act. inf. of παραμένω, "remain in office" (most EVV; BDAG 769a; F. Hauck, *TDNT* 4:577–78.); this mng. is confirmed by nonbiblical sources (Lane 1:175 n. *t*, 188; Ellingworth 390). The second inf. completes the mng. of the first ("hindered from remaining" [cf. R 1085]).

According to Josephus (*Ant.* 20.227), there were eighty-three high priests from the beginning of the Aaronic priesthood to the destruction of the temple in AD 70. Thus the multiplicity of priests was diachronic, with each priest having to be replaced after his death (Attridge 209; Koester 364). The NEB captures this well: "those other priests are appointed in numerous succession." This limitation of the Levitical priesthood was already noted in 7:8.

VERSE 24

ὁ δὲ διὰ τὸ μένειν αὐτὸν εἰς τὸν αἰῶνα ἀπαράβατον ἔχει τὴν ἱερωσύνην·
But because he remains forever, he holds his priesthood permanently.

Ὁ functions par. to a pers. pron., referring to Jesus (cf. BDF §250; Wallace 212). Ὁ δέ indicates the completion of the contrast begun in v. 23. The use of μένω recalls 7:3, where it describes the perpetual nature of Melchizedek's priesthood. This continues the important use of μένω in Hebrews (see comments on 7:3). Lane notes that the vb. is often used of God in the LXX (Lane 1:188), which may also explain the author's choice of παραμένω in ref. to the Levitical priests in v. 23. The pres. is durative and the abs. use of the vb. suggests Christ's eternality (cf. Attridge 209). The vb., however, need not have any Platonic implications (*pace* Attridge 209–10). The art. inf. διὰ τό + inf. is causal (Wallace 597; BDF §404[3]). The antecedent of αὐτόν is Jesus; the pron. is the "subj." of the inf. (BDF §410), although the pron. is "superfluous" (R 1039) because the subj. of the inf. is the same as the subj. of the finite vb. on which it depends. Thus the pron. may be emph. ("Jesus himself"). Εἰς τὸν αἰῶνα ("forever" [most EVV]) recalls Ps 110:4 (see comments on 5:6). The subj. of ἔχει is Jesus. The pres. is also durative. The adj. ἀπαράβατον is the acc. sg. masc. or neut. of ἀπαράβατος, -ον, "permanent," "unchangeable" (BDAG 97b; J. Schneider, *TDNT* 5:742–43). An act. understanding ("does not pass on" [GNT]; "untransferable" [Bruce 171]) is not attested in extant literature (Lane 1:175–76 n. *u*; Ellingworth 390). Christ's priesthood is "not passed on; it is, as part of the eternal realm, absolute" (Attridge 210). The ending -ον could be the masc. form of the two-ending adj., which would be used to modify ἱερωσύνην ("priesthood" [most EVV; BDAG 471d; see 7:11]), which functions as a pred. (T 186) or even parallels a rel. clause ("he has the priesthood that is permanent"). The latter would offer additional (subtle) contrast with the impermanent Levitical priesthood (R 656; Moule 109). Alternatively, the ending may be acc. sg. neut. and function as an adv., "permanently" (many EVV). The placement of ἀπαράβατον is also emph. (Cockerill 334 n. 93). The art. could indicate that Jesus's priesthood is unique (cf. Wallace 223–24), although it not tr. by most EVV. A poss. sense of the article is also possible (ESV, NET).

VERSE 25

ὅθεν καὶ σῴζειν εἰς τὸ παντελὲς δύναται τοὺς προσερχομένους δι' αὐτοῦ τῷ θεῷ,
Therefore, he is able to save completely those who come to God through him,

The conj. ὅθεν ("for which reason"; BDAG 693a; BDF §451[6]) draws an inference from vv. 23–24. Καί is ascensive ("also" [BDF §442(12)]), although it is left untr. in most EVV. Ὅθεν καί "suggests a corollary" (Ellingworth 391). The subj. of δύναται remains Jesus. Σῴζειν is the pres. act. inf. of σῴζω, "save/preserve from eternal death" (BDAG 982d). The inf. completes δύναται. Προσερχομένους is the acc. pl. masc. of the pres. mid. ptc. of προσέρχομαι, "come to" (NET, NIV), "draw near" (ESV), "approach." The ptc. is subst. The art. τῷ indicates "one of a kind" (BDF §254). The pres. tense of all three vb. forms underscores the ongoing, continuous action. The adv. prep. phrase δι' αὐτοῦ indicates agency. The antecedent of αὐτοῦ is Jesus.

Παντελές is the acc. sg. neut. of παντελής, -ές "completely, forever, for all time" (BDAG 754d; G. Delling, *TDNT* 8:66–67). This adj. only occurs here and in Luke 13:11 in the NT. There are two interpretive options for the adv. prep. phrase εἰς τὸ παντελές.

*1. qual., "completely" or "absolutely" (so most EVV, but "to the uttermost" [ESV]; Moule 165; Cockerill 334 n. 100; Koester 365; Lane 1:174);
2. temp., "perpetually," "for all time" (NRSV), "forever" (CEV, NASB).

The first option could supplement εἰς τὸν αἰῶνα (v. 24) by adding in a qual. understanding rather than simply par. εἰς τὸν αἰῶνα. It is likely that both options are intended (Ellingworth 391; Koester 365; Lane 1:176; but see Cockerill 335). Moule notes that "perpetually" ("for good and all"; cf. "once and forever" [NLT]) might best render both εἰς τὸ παντελές and εἰς τὸ διηνεκές (7:3), although the two expressions are not interchangeable (Moule 165). The subsequent discussion of Jesus's fully efficacious sacrifice will make clear that the author understands the salvation effected by Jesus to be complete and unlimited in any way.

πάντοτε ζῶν εἰς τὸ ἐντυγχάνειν ὑπὲρ αὐτῶν.
since he always lives to intercede for them.

Ζῶν is the nom. sg. masc. of the pres. act. ptc. of ζάω. The ptc. is causal (BDF §418[1]; most EVV) or possibly modal (BDF §418[5]), adv. modifying σῴζειν. Hebrews uses ζάω in ref. to God (Heb 3:12; 9:14; 10:31; 12:22; cf. 4:12; 10:20 [Cockerill 336]). It also recalls various aspects of the author's argument in Hebrews 7 (e.g., vv. 3, 6, 15). The adv. πάντοτε ("always") modifies ζῶν. Ἐντυγχάνειν is the pres. act. inf. of ἐντυγχάνω, "intercede" or "make intercession" (most EVV; but "plead" [GNT, REB]; "approach, appeal" [BDAG 341d]; H. Balz, *EDNT* 1:461b–462a). When this vb. is followed by ὑπέρ + the gen. (αὐτῶν) and the one approached is God, it often means "pray" (Lane 1:190; see esp. Koester 366). In the OT, intercession was mainly the function of priests (Attridge 211). The art. inf. εἰς τό + inf. indicates purpose (Wallace 591; BDF §404[3]). The antecedent of αὐτῶν is τοὺς προσερχομένους. Ὑπέρ indicates "on behalf of," "for the benefit of" (Harris 209). The two infs. (σῴζειν and ἐντυγχάνειν) show the scope of Jesus's ministry (Lane 1:189). Jesus's intercessory work is also presented in Luke 22:32; John 17; and Rom 8:34 (also with ἐντυγχάνω). For the history of interpretation of this v., see Attridge 211–12.

VERSE 26

Τοιοῦτος γὰρ ἡμῖν καὶ ἔπρεπεν ἀρχιερεύς,
For this is the kind of high priest we need:

Verses 26–28 comprise one sentence in the Greek (a periodic sentence; BDF §464; see comments on 1:1). Γάρ "loosely" connects this final sentence to the previous discussion (Attridge 212). Καί is adjunctive ("precisely" [R 1181]; "also" [BDF §442(12)]); it functions to emphasize ἔπρεπεν (Lane 176 n. *w*; Cockerill 339 n. 4). The correl. adj. τοιοῦτος (-αῦτη, -οῦτον, "such"; "demon. of quality" [R 710]) modifies ἀρχιερεύς and pairs with ὅς in v. 27. Ἡμῖν is a dat. of adv. It also signals the application of the preceding discussion to the audience. Ἔπρεπεν (3rd sg. impf. act. indic. of πρέπω, "be fitting" [see comments on 2:10]) is usually impers., but here τοιοῦτος ἀρχιερεύς may be understood as the subj. (R 1086; T 147). The impf. is continuative (Wallace 543). The use of ἔπρεπεν recalls its use in 2:10 concerning the fittingness of suffering for Christ's perfection (see comments on 2:10). The use of ἱερεύς throughout most of Hebrews 7 reflects the author's exposition of Ps 110:4. The switch from ἱερεύς of Psalm 110 to ἀρχιερεύς resumes an important theme in Hebrews (see comments on 2:17).

ὅσιος ἄκακος ἀμίαντος, κεχωρισμένος ἀπὸ τῶν ἁμαρτωλῶν καὶ ὑψηλότερος τῶν οὐρανῶν γενόμενος,
holy, innocent, undefiled, separated from sinners, and exalted above the heavens.

The fittingness of Jesus as high priest is now elaborated with a list of relatively rare adj. and attrib. ptc., all of which modify ἀρχιερεύς. The uncommon adj. ὅσιος (-α, -ον, "holy" [BDAG 728b]; F. Hauck, *TDNT* 5:489–92) is closely related to the more common ἅγιος. It is used in ref. to Christ in Acts 2:27 and 13:35, both times in the citation of Ps 16:10. In the LXX, the word applies both to God and to individuals and has the basic sense of "loyal to covenant obligations" (Bruce 176 n. 84; cf. "covenant keeping" [Cockerill 339]). The term may recall the Son's obedience to the Father in 5:7–8 (Lane 1:191), but the actual word only occurs here in Hebrews. Ἄκακος (-ον, "innocent, guileless" [BDAG 32d; W. Grundmann, *TDNT* 3:482]) indicates "untouched by evil" (Cockerill 340). Ἀμίαντος (-ον) has a moral sense: "undefiled," "pure" (BDAG 54a; cf. F. Hauck, *TDNT* 4:647); "unstained" (ESV, NLT). Both adj. are formed with an alpha privative, indicating that there is nothing blameworthy or defiled in Christ, the high priest. All three terms have to do with cultic and priestly purity in the LXX (Lane 1:191) and thus underscore Jesus's abs. qualifications for his priesthood (Cockerill 340–41).

Κεχωρισμένος is the nom. sg. masc. of the pf. pass. ptc. of χωρίζω, "divide," "separate" (BDAG 1095a). The prep. phrase ἀπὸ τῶν ἁμαρτωλῶν is a gen. of separation (Wallace 108; "ablative" [R 667]). Here again is a contrast with the Levitical high priest who was ceremonially "set apart" from other sinful humans so that he could perform his priestly duties. Christ, however, is not made ceremonially clean, but is completely separate from sinners by virtue of his sinlessness, despite taking on humanity's sin (cf. 4:15). This separation is emphasized in the final clause of the v. This vb. followed by ἀπό implies a locat. sense (Cockerill 341). Thus the sense here is that the exaltation removed Jesus from the realm of sinful humanity (cf. Lane 1:176 n. *x*, 191) and indicates his "final triumph over sin" (Cockerill 341), and those who opposed him (12:3; Attridge 213). Such separation, however, does not entail distance, but rather opens the way for "those who draw near to God" (Cockerill 341). Hence a qual. separation is implied if κεχωρισμένος ἀπὸ τῶν ἁμαρτωλῶν is read with ἀμίαντος (cf. Barclay), whereas a locat. one is implied if the ptc. clause is taken with the clause that follows. Perhaps both are in view (Koester 367).

Ὑψηλότερος is the comp. of ὕψιστος, -η, -ον, "highest" (BDAG 1045a); τῶν οὐρανῶν is a gen. of comp. (Wallace 111). This expression recalls 1:3. The image contrasts the entrance of the Levitical high priest into the earthly holy of holies with Christ, who has passed through the heavens (4:14) and is now in the highest heaven on God's throne. This will be developed in 8:1–6 and 9:11–28. Numerous rhetorical elements (see esp. Attridge 212), such as alliteration, have suggested to some that this v. may reflect an early Christian hymn (Bruce 175 n. 81), although this cannot be proved (Cockerill 338 n. 2).

VERSE 27

ὃς οὐκ ἔχει καθ' ἡμέραν ἀνάγκην, ὥσπερ οἱ ἀρχιερεῖς,
He doesn't need to offer sacrifices every day, as high priests do—

The antecedent of ὅς is ἀρχιερεύς. Here it functions as a correl. with τοιοῦτος (R 710). The obj. of ἔχει is ἀνάγκην (see 7:12). Κατά is distributive ("every day" [Harris 155]); καθ' occurs before rough breathing. The comp. ptcl. ὥσπερ ("as") makes explicit the comp. between Jesus's priesthood and that of the Levitical high priests (οἱ ἀρχιερεῖς). The art. likely has dem. force (see comments on v. 23).

The prep. phrase καθ' ἡμέραν presents an interpretive problem. The daily offering of (regular) priests (e.g., Lev 6:19–21) was not the double offering of the high priest on the Day of Atonement for both his sins and the people's sins (Leviticus 16). Some have suggested that the author had literary, not experiential, knowledge of the sacrificial system (Attridge 214), and that he was drawing from Philo (*Spec. Leg.* 3.131), who "suggests that the high priest offered sacrifices daily," although his discussion on the point is not exact (Attridge 214). Yet the author is aware of the difference between the daily offerings of ordinary priests (10:11) and the Day of Atonement sacrifices offered by the high priest (9:7, 25; 10:1, 3; cf. Attridge 213). It is possible that καθ' ἡμέραν is emphasizing that the Day of Atonement sacrifices needed to be offered repeatedly (Cockerill 343), although this interpretation feels strained (cf. Attridge 214). The most plausible option, however, is that the author intentionally conflated the Day of Atonement sacrifices and other sacrifices (Koester 367–68; cf. Attridge 213; Ellingworth 395). Similarly, the author may have generalized the Day of Atonement sacrifice (see Lane 1:193–94; Ellingworth 395). Finally, his placement of the prep. phrase emphasizes that Christ had no need for these daily offerings (Cockerill 343).

πρότερον ὑπὲρ τῶν ἰδίων ἁμαρτιῶν θυσίας ἀναφέρειν ἔπειτα τῶν τοῦ λαοῦ·
first for their own sins, then for those of the people.

Πρότερον (see comments on 4:6) indicates the "first of two acts" ("first" [most EVV]) and is paired with ἔπειτα ("then"; BDAG 361b; BDF §62). Ἀναφέρειν is the pres. act. inf. of ἀναφέρω, "offer up" (BDAG 75d; Weiss, *TDNT* 9:60–61; simply "offer" in most EVV). Ἀναφέρειν complements the verbal idea inherent in ἀνάγκην (ἀνάγκη, -ης, ἡ, "need to offer"). This vb. also occurs in 9:28 and 13:15, although προσφέρω is more common in Hebrews. The difference between the two vbs. is slight (cf. Attridge 213 n. 102). The pres. is continuous, indicating the rep. of the offering (and contrasts with the following aor. ptc). The obj. of ἀναφέρειν is θυσίας (acc. pl. fem. of θυσία, -ας, ἡ, "offering," "sacrifice"; see comments on 5:1).

The double offering of the Day of Atonement is elaborated, where the high priest had to offer for his own sins (τῶν ἰδίων, functions par. to a poss. pron. [T 191; cf. R 691]) as well as those of the people (τοῦ λαοῦ). The second art. τῶν elliptically assumes ἁμαρτιῶν. The high priest's offering was a calf, whereas the offering for the people was a goat (Lev 16:6, 11, 15).

τοῦτο γὰρ ἐποίησεν ἐφάπαξ ἑαυτὸν ἀνενέγκας.
He did this once for all time when he offered himself.

Γάρ explains why Jesus did not have to offer daily sacrifices. The antecedent for τοῦτο is unclear, although most commentators agree that it refers to the last phrase, ἔπειτα τῶν τοῦ λαου, and not the offering of sacrifices for himself, which would contradict the argument so far (cf. Attridge 214; Bruce 175; Cockerill 343; Ellingworth 394; Lane 1:176 n. *aa*). This is reflected in some EVV ("their sins" [NIV]), although it is ambiguous in others. Moreover, the placement of θυσίας ἀναφέρειν indicates a separation between the two sacrifices (Cockerill 343 n. 27). The adv. ἐφάπαξ, "once for all," "once and never again" (BDAG 417d; H. Balz, *EDNT* 2:91–92; G. Stählin, *TDNT* 1:381–84; cf. 9:12, 10:10), contrasts with καθ' ἡμέραν, indicating the fully efficacious nature of Christ's offering. (See also James W. Thompson, "Ephapax: The One and the Many in Hebrews." *NTS* 53 [2007]: 566–81.) This adv. indicates "the quantitative sense of singularity and the qualitative sense of completeness" (Koester 368; cf. Lane 1:193).

Ἀνενέγκας is the nom. sg. masc. of the aor. act. ptc. of ἀναφέρω. The aor. is global, and contrasts with the pres. indic. used with the Levitical high priests. The ptc. is instr. The obj. of the ptc. is ἑαυτόν, whose antecedent is Jesus. Jesus offering himself may allude to Isa 53:10 and Mark 10:45. The cleansing, or atonement, effected by Jesus has already been presented in 1:3 and 2:17. This is the first time in the epistle that Jesus's sacrifice of himself is made explicit. This theme will now be developed in Hebrews 8–10.

VERSE 28

ὁ νόμος γὰρ ἀνθρώπους καθίστησιν ἀρχιερεῖς ἔχοντας ἀσθένειαν,
For the law appoints as high priests men who are weak,

Γάρ adds the final explanation concerning the superiority of Jesus's priesthood and offering. Καθίστησιν is the 3rd sg. pres. act. indic. of καθίστμι, "appoint" (most EVV), "authorize" (BDAG 492c–d; A. Oepke, *TDNT* 3:444–47). The act. with this vb. is unique to Hebrews (R 315). The vb. is followed by a double (pred.) acc. (R 480) in which the first acc. (ἀνθρώπους) is the obj. of the vb. and the second (ἀρχιερεῖς) is the pred. The anar. ἀνθρώπους is qual. (R 794). Ἀσθένειαν is the acc. sg. fem. of ἀσθένεια, -ας, ἡ, "weakness" (BDAG 142b; cf. 4:15; 5:2). Ἔχοντας (agreeing with ἀρχιερεῖς) functions par. to a rel. clause ("who are weak"). The weakness is both sin and death (Koester 368). An implied μέν sets up for the constrast that is explicit with δέ in the second part of the v.

ὁ λόγος δὲ τῆς ὁρκωμοσίας τῆς μετὰ τὸν νόμον υἱὸν εἰς τὸν αἰῶνα τετελειωμένον.
but the promise of the oath, which came after the law, appoints a Son, who has been perfected forever.

Λόγος refers to God's word (understood as his promise), as is made clear with the poss. gen. modifier ὁρκωμοσίας (gen. sg. fem. of ὁρκωμοσία, -ας, ἡ, "oath" [BDAG 723d]), which recalls its previous use in v. 20 and the previous discussion in Hebrews 6. The rep. of ὁρκωμοσία in v. 20 and this v. forms an *inclusio*. Μετὰ τὸν νόμον modifies ὁρκωμοσίας, which is indicated by the repetition of the art. τῆς. This second attrib. pos. (Wallace 306–07; cf. T 185) functions par. to a rel. clause ("the oath, which was given after the law"). The anar. υἱόν is qual. (R 794; cf. 1:4) and is the subj. of καθίστησιν, which is elliptically understood from the previous clause. Τετελειωμένον is the acc. sg. masc. of the pf. pass. ptc. of τελειόω, "perfected," so most EVV; see comments on 2:10). The placement of the ptc. is emph. (R 418). The pf. is rhetorically significant and draws attention to Jesus's humiliation and exaltation (e.g., "intensified," Campbell, *VA* 201; "absolutely efficacious" [Bruce 179]; "permanent and absolute" [Attridge 215; see esp. Ellingworth 396–97]). Εἰς τὸν αἰῶνα adv. modifies the ptc. (see comments on 5:6).

Numerous contrasts are summarized here: ὁ νόμος and ὁ λόγος τῆς ὁρκωμοσίας; ἄνθρωποι and υἱός; and ἔχοντας ἀσθένειαν and τετελειωμένον (Lane 1:194). The presentation of Jesus as the perfect high priest has been building throughout the epistle (2:17–18; 4:14–16; 5:1–10). The culmination of this presentation in Heb 7:26–28 lays the foundation for the arguments of Hebrews 8–10.

HOMILETICAL SUGGESTIONS

The Superiority of the New Priesthood (7:20–28)

1. It Is Based on God's Oath (vv. 20–22, 28)

   (a) Unlike the Levitical order (v. 20)
   (b) Based on the oath in Ps 110:4 (v. 21)
   (c) The oath guarantees a better covenant (v. 22)
   (d) The oath appoints the Son, perfected forever (v. 28)
2. It Is Eternal (vv. 23–24)
   (a) Levitical priests could not remain permanently in office because they died (v. 23)
   (b) But our great high priest remains forever (v. 24)
3. It Is Fully Efficacious (v. 25)
   (a) Our high priest saves completely (v. 25a)
   (b) Our high priest intercedes for us (v. 25b)
4. It Meets Our Needs (vv. 26–27)
   (a) Our high priest is completely holy (vv. 26, 27a)
   (b) Our high priest offers the once-for-all-time sacrifice (v. 27b)

What We Truly Need (7:20–28)

1. A Guarantee Based on God's Oath (vv. 20–22)
2. A Permanent Priest (vv. 23–24)
3. Complete Salvation (v. 25a)
4. Continual Intercession (v. 25b)
5. A Priest Who Is Undefiled by Sin (vv. 26–27a)
6. A Priest Who Offers a Once-for-All Offering (v. 27b)
7. The Perfect Son! (v. 28)

B. THE NEW COVENANT (8:1–13)

1. The Superior Ministry of Jesus (8:1–6)

STRUCTURE

The focus on Jesus as the "fitting" high priest in Hebrews 7 now shifts to Jesus as the mediator of a new covenant, which is introduced in Heb 8:1–6, and developed in Heb 8:7–13 (with the extensive quotation of Jer 31:31–34) and Heb 9:1–28 (which is chiastically structured; see Ellingworth 397). Hebrews 8–10 unpacks the significance of Christ's self–sacrifice in terms of sanctuary, covenant, and sacrifice—"a symphony in three movements": 8:1–13; 9:1–22; 9:23–10:18, each of which begins with sanctuary, focuses on sacrifice, and ends with covenant (see G. L. Cockerill, "Structure and Interpretation in Hebrews 8:1–10:18: A Symphony in Three Movements," *BBR* 11 [2001]: 179–201; cf. Harold W. Attridge, "The Uses of Antithesis in Hebrews 8–10," *HTR* 79 [1986]: 1–9). See For Further Study 41 (The Structure of Hebrews).

Hebrews 8:1–6 continues the numerous contrasts between the Levitical high priests and Christ, but the focus is more on Christ (see esp. Ellingworth 398). This passage is structured around the opening two verses (which comprise one sentence) that both summarizes the argument so far, and introduces the discussion on the heavenly sanctuary. Verse 3 makes a generalizing comment about priests, paralleled by a statement of continuity regarding Christ's priesthood. The cond. in v. 4, however, outlines discontinuity, which is developed by means of a dependent ptc., a rel. clause, and a comp. clause in vv. 4b–6.

1 Κεφάλαιον δὲ ἐπὶ τοῖς λεγομένοις,
τοιοῦτον ἔχομεν ἀρχιερέα,
ὃς ἐκάθισεν
ἐν δεξιᾷ τοῦ θρόνου τῆς μεγαλωσύνης
ἐν τοῖς οὐρανοῖς,
2 τῶν ἁγίων λειτουργὸς καὶ τῆς σκηνῆς τῆς ἀληθινῆς,
ἣν ἔπηξεν ὁ κύριος,
οὐκ ἄνθρωπος.
3 Πᾶς γὰρ ἀρχιερεὺς εἰς τὸ προσφέρειν δῶρά τε καὶ θυσίας καθίσταται·
ὅθεν ἀναγκαῖον ἔχειν τι καὶ τοῦτον
ὃ προσενέγκῃ.
4 εἰ μὲν οὖν ἦν ἐπὶ γῆς,
οὐδ᾽ ἂν ἦν ἱερεύς,
ὄντων τῶν προσφερόντων κατὰ νόμον τὰ δῶρα·
5 οἵτινες ὑποδείγματι καὶ σκιᾷ λατρεύουσιν τῶν ἐπουρανίων,
καθὼς κεχρημάτισται Μωϋσῆς
μέλλων ἐπιτελεῖν τὴν σκηνήν·
ὅρα γάρ φησιν, ποιήσεις πάντα

κατὰ τὸν τύπον
τὸν δειχθέντα
σοι
ἐν τῷ ὄρει·

6 νυν[ὶ] δὲ διαφορωτέρας τέτυχεν λειτουργίας,
ὅσῳ καὶ κρείττονός ἐστιν διαθήκης μεσίτης,
ἥτις ἐπὶ κρείττοσιν ἐπαγγελίαις νενομοθέτηται.

VERSE 1

Κεφάλαιον δὲ ἐπὶ τοῖς λεγομένοις,
Now the main point of what is being said is this:

Κεφάλαιον is the nom. sg. neut. of κεφάλαιον, -ου, τό, "point" (ESV), "main point" (NASB, NET, NIV; BDAG 541c). The term can denote *(1) the "main point" in an argument (G. Schneider, *EDNT* 2:284b); (2) a "summary" of main points ("the sum" [Moffatt]; or (3) the "crowning affirmation" (summarized from Lane 1:200 n. *a*). Λεγομένοις is subst. (e.g., "what we are saying" [most EVV, understanding κεφάλαιον as retrospective]). Ἐπί with the dat. could indicate "in addition to" (BDAG 365b; R 605; BDF §235[3]) or "about," "concerning" (Ellingworth 400). Hebrews 8:1 draws on previous points about Christ's priesthood and sacrifice (although not an exhaustive summary) and lays the foundation for discussion of covenant and sanctuary (cf. Attridge 217; Cockerill 349). Thus κεφάλαιον as "main point" is preferred (cf. Cockerill 349; Ellingworth 400; Koester 374–75; most EVV). Δέ is thus resumptive (Ellingworth 400).

τοιοῦτον ἔχομεν ἀρχιερέα,
We have this kind of high priest,

The correl. adj. τοιοῦτον (τοιοῦτος, -αῦτη, -οῦτον, "such"; "demon. of quality" [R 710]) modifies ἀρχιερέα (acc. sg. masc. of ἀρχιερεύς, -εως, ὁ, "high priest" [BDAG 139a]) and pairs with ὅς in the next clause. The expression τοιοῦτον . . . ἀρχιερέα recalls τοιοῦτος . . . ἀρχιερεύς in 7:27 (a "catchword" [Attridge 217 n. 10]). Ἀρχιερέα is the dir. obj. of ἔχομεν.

ὃς ἐκάθισεν ἐν δεξιᾷ τοῦ θρόνου τῆς μεγαλωσύνης ἐν τοῖς οὐρανοῖς,
who sat down at the right hand of the throne of the Majesty in the heavens,

The antecedent of ὅς is ἀρχιερεύς. Here it is a correl. with τοιοῦτος (R 710). The rest of the v. is the rel. clause, which recalls the nearly identical wording in 1:3 (see comments there; cf. 4:16; 12:2). Although μεγαλωσύνης could be taken as an attrib. gen., "majestic throne," this would miss the par. with 1:3, where the adj. is clearly a circumlocution for the divine name ("the Majesty"; Lane 1:200 n. *c*; see also Harris 106–7). To the expression in 1:3, τοῦ θρόνου is added here (cf. 4:16). This gen. is descriptive. The idea of a heavenly throne is also "a periphrasis for God, and at the same time, a standard feature of the heavenly temple" (Attridge 217). This addition anticipates the ensuing discussion of the tabernacle. Also differing from 1:3 is the substitution of ἐν τοῖς οὐρανοῖς for ἐν ὑψηλοῖς, which may reflect the ref. to the heavens in 7:26. The dat. is locat. The expression also anticipates 12:2. All three vv. (1:3; 8:1; 12:2) allude to Ps 110:1. There may also be an allusion to Zech 6:13 and the prophecy of the high priest Joshua sitting on the temple's throne (Lane 1:206).

VERSE 2

τῶν ἁγίων λειτουργὸς καὶ τῆς σκηνῆς τῆς ἀληθινῆς,
a minister of the sanctuary and the true tabernacle

Λειτουργός is the nom. sg. masc. of λειτουργός, -οῦ, ὁ, "priest," ([BDAG 591d–592a]; cf. 1:7). The term is freq. used of priests in the LXX (Attridge 217; cf. H. Strathmann, *TDNT* 4:229–31). The vb. and its cognates (e.g., 1:14; 8:6; 9:21; 10:11) have a range of mngs. (see Ellingworth 400–401). Here it is an appos. to ἀρχιερέα in v. 1. The difference between ἀρχιερεύς and λειτουργός is debated. Λειτουργός may focus more on activity, whereas ἀρχιερεύς focuses on status (Lane 1:205). Most EVV tr. λειτουργός as "minister," although some render the noun as a vb. ("serves" [CEV, NIV]). Λειτουργός marks the beginning of an *inclusio* with λειτουργίας in v. 6. The anar. λειτουργός is qual. (Cockerill 352 n. 9). The subst. pl. ἁγίων refers to the OT sanctuary, likely in its entirety (Lane 1:205), although some argue that the pl. refers only to the holy of holies (Attridge 217–18). It clearly refers to the entire sanctuary elsewhere in Hebrews (9:2, 3, 12, 24, 25; 10:19; 13:22). Like the pl. οἱ οὐρανοί (1:10; 7:26; 8:1), οἱ ἅγιοι reflects a Heb. idiom (an "idiomatic plural" [R 408; cf. T 27]). Σκηνῆς is the gen. sg. fem. of σκηνή, -ῆς, ἡ, "tent," "tabernacle" (BDAG 928b). This Gk. word is used in the LXX to tr. the Heb. words for "tent" or "dwelling," and specifically the tabernacle built by the Israelites in the wilderness. The art. τῆς (σκηνῆς) indicates something that is "well-known" (Wallace 225; cf. Ellingworth 401). Ἀληθινῆς is the gen. sg. fem. of ἀληθινός, -ή, -όν, "true" (ESV, NASB, NET, NIV), "real" (CEV, REB), "genuine," "authentic" (BDAG 43d). The adj. modifies σκηνή. The rep. of the art. and the placement of the adj. are emph. (Ellingworth 402; 2nd attrib. pos.; see Wallace 306–7). The gen. ἁγίων and σκηνῆς are both descriptive.

Reference to a "true sanctuary" (most EVV) has suggested to some par. with Philo, who distinguishes between the earthly as that which is understood by the senses (phenomenal), and the heavenly as that which "was accessible only to the mind" (noumenal; cf. Cockerill 353; see esp. the extensive discussion about ancient views of the universe as God's temple). Yet in Hebrews the distinction is between provisional and temporary (earthly) and true and eternal (heavenly). As with much of Hebrews, there is a typological relationship between the old (earthly) order and the new (heavenly) order (cf. Lane 1:206). Moreover, Hebrews does not present a heavenly/true/immaterial vs. earthly/shadow/material dualism as found in Platonic writers (e.g., Philo). The key distinction is between that which remains, which is with the Son (often indicated by means of μένω), and that which does not remain (i.e., "shaken" in Hebrews 12), which is not with the Son. See For Further Study 62 (Platonism, Philo, and Hebrews).

There are three main interpretive options for the relationship between τῶν ἁγίων and τῆς σκηνῆς τῆς ἀληθινῆς:

*1. Καί is epex. (BDF §442[9]; Ellingworth 402); τῆς σκηνῆς τῆς ἀληθινῆς further explains τῶν ἁγίων ("that is," GNT; Koester 375–76). This view is supported by the sg. rel. pron. in the next clause, which views the two entities as one (cf. Koester 376; Lane 1:200 n. *e*; *pace* Attridge 218). Cockerill notes that the effectiveness of the terms "depends both on their diverse connotations and their common referent" (Cockerill 357). The omission of καί in some EVV suggests an epex. understanding (e.g., ESV, NIV).
2. Τῶν ἁγίων and τῆς σκηνῆς τῆς ἀληθινῆς form a hendiadys, in which the two entities are very closely related, but one entity depends on the other (BDF §441[16]).
3. Τῶν ἁγίων and τῆς σκηνῆς τῆς ἀληθινῆς are distinguished as indicated by "and" (most EVV); the Greek terms refer to the holy of holies and the outer tent respectively, a distinction made in Hebrews 9 (so Attridge 218; see the extensive refutation of this view in Cockerill 354–57).

The focus on the tabernacle and not the temple in Hebrews is consistent with the author's focus on the *historical events* of the wilderness generation rather than those of the Davidic monarchy. Christological points, however, are clearly drawn from Davidic pss. and prophecies (e.g., 1:5).

ἣν ἔπηξεν ὁ κύριος, οὐκ ἄνθρωπος.
that was set up by the Lord and not man.

The antecedent of ἥν is either τῆς σκηνῆς τῆς ἀληθινῆς alone or, more likely, τῶν ἁγίων understood as τῆς σκηνῆς τῆς ἀληθινῆς. The rest of the v. comprises the rel. clause. Ἔπηξεν is the 3rd sg. aor. act. indic. of πήγνυμι "set up" (most EVV), "pitched" (NASB), "build" (BDAG 811a; NT hapax). The only other occurrence of πήγνυμι in BGk. is LXX Num 24:6 (σκηναί, ἃς ἔπηξεν κύριος ["tents (of Jacob), which the Lord pitched"]), to which this v. likely alludes (Ellingworth 402; cf. Lane 1:205; see also LXX Josh 18:1). Ὁ κύριος here likely refers to God (cf. Ellingworth 402), based on the allusion to Num 24:6. Both ἥν and ἔπηξεν are elliptically understood with οὐκ ἄνθρωπος ("which a human did not build"), which clearly contrasts with a divinely built tent. This v. contrasts with the tent erected by Moses in v. 5.

VERSE 3

Πᾶς γὰρ ἀρχιερεὺς εἰς τὸ προσφέρειν δῶρά τε καὶ θυσίας καθίσταται·
For every high priest is appointed to offer gifts and sacrifices;

This v. explicitly pars. Heb 5:1. Γάρ introduces a general principle "on which the 'unreal' cond. of vv. 4–5" and the contrast in v. 6 are based (Ellingworth 403). Πᾶς modifies ἀρχιερεύς (-έως, ὁ, "high priest" [BDAG 139a]), which is the subj. of καθίσταται

(3rd sg. pres. pass. indic. of καθίστημι, "appoint" [most EVV; BDAG 492d]). The pass. is a divine pass. Προσφέρειν is the pres. act. inf. of προσφέρω, "offer" (see comments on 5:1). Εἰς τό + inf. indicates purpose (Wallace 591; BDF §404[3]). The pres. for both the inf. and the indic. is gnomic (Wallace 523–24) or "general description" (Ellingworth 271). (For δῶρά τε καὶ θυσίας, see comments on 5:1.)

ὅθεν ἀναγκαῖον ἔχειν τι καὶ τοῦτον ὃ προσενέγκῃ.
therefore, it was necessary for this priest also to have something to offer.

The inferential conj. ὅθεν ("for which reason"; BDAG 693a; BDF §451[6]) draws a logical deduction from the general principle presented in the first part of the v. (Attridge 218; cf. Ellingworth 403). Ἀναγκαῖον is the nom. sg. neut. of ἀναγκαῖος, -α, -ον, "necessary" (BDAG 60d). This word recalls the closely related term in ἀνάγκη (cf. 7:12, 27). A form of εἰμί is understood. The inf. ἔχειν indicates purpose. The dem. pron. τοῦτον refers to Christ (made explicit in the CEV; cf. "this high priest" [NASB]), possibly adding emph. (Wallace 326–27). The indef. pron. refers to that which Christ offers ("something" [most EVV]), which has been explicitly stated in 7:27 and will be again in 9:14. The indef. pron. builds suspense for the subsequent revelation that what Christ offers is himself (9:14). The focus here is on the heavenly sanctuary and the covenant (cf. Ellingworth 404; Lane 1:206). When an inf. has two acc. subst. associated with it, the first often indicates its "subj.," and the second, its obj. In this case, however, the subj. and obj. must be inferred from the context. Since the focus here is on a contrast between the Levitical high priest and Christ, τοῦτον is the subj. and τι is the obj. (cf. 5:12; Wallace 196). Προσενέγκῃ is the 3rd sg. aor. act. subjunc. of προσφέρω, "offer." The subjunc. indicates purpose (R 989; "to offer" [most EVV]). This vb. is freq. in Hebrews (see comments on 5:1). It comprises the rel. clause in this v.

The author heightens the contrast between the Levitical priests and Christ by using the pres. (προσφέρειν) with the former (indicating the rep.—hence incomplete—nature of their work) and the aor. (προσενέγκῃ) with Christ (indicating the complete nature of his work; cf. Cockerill 358; Koester 377). (See comments on 7:27.)

VERSE 4

εἰ μὲν οὖν ἦν ἐπὶ γῆς, οὐδ᾽ ἂν ἦν ἱερεύς,
Now if he were on earth, he wouldn't be a priest,

Εἰ with an aug. tense in the prot. (ἦν), together with ἄν in the apod., identifies "an unreal case (contrary-to-fact)" cond. (BDF §360[4]; or second-class cond. [see Wallace 694–96]). The prot. presents a statement understood to be false. The same cstr. appears in v. 7; cf. 4:8, 7:11. Μὲν οὖν usually indicates a summary and transition (BDF §451[1]), although here it is resumptive (Attridge 219; "now if" [BDAG 630c]). The implied subj. of both occurrences of ἦν is Christ. The prep. phrase ἐπὶ γῆς is locat.; "earth" contrasts with "heavenly" in v. 5. Ἱερεῖς (-έως, ὁ, "priest") is a pred. nom. The neg. conj. οὐδ᾽ (οὐ + δέ, which elides before a vowel [ἄν]) implies more than "not"

(Ellingworth 405) as is reflected in EVV ("even" [NEB, NLT], "at all" [many EVV; Cockerill 359]).

ὄντων τῶν προσφερόντων κατὰ νόμον τὰ δῶρα·
since there are those offering the gifts prescribed by the law.

The rest of the v. comprises a gen. abs. cstr. where the subj. of the gen. ptc. (understood as the Levitical priests; e.g., "there are priests" [most EVV]) is not the same as the main clause (understood as Christ). The ptc. ὄντων is causal (Ellingworth 405). Προσφερόντων is the gen. pl. masc. of the pres. act. ptc. of προσφέρω, "offer" (see comments at 5:1). The ptc. is subst. Again the pres. tense is associated with the Levitical priests, underscoring the rep., or "frequentative" (Lane 1:201 n. *h*), nature of their work. The pres. tense, however, does not indicate "pres. time" in the sense that the temple was still operational when the epistle was written (cf. Attridge 219 n. 36; Ellingworth 405). Κατὰ νόμον adv. modifies the ptc. (see comments on 7:16). Τὰ δῶρα is the obj. of the ptc. (see comments on v. 3). The art. τά is anaphoric, referring back to v. 3.

VERSE 5

οἵτινες ὑποδείγματι καὶ σκιᾷ λατρεύουσιν τῶν ἐπουρανίων,
These serve as a copy and shadow of the heavenly things,

The indef. rel. pron. οἵτινες "signals a development" (Ellingworth 406). Its antecedent is inferred from the context to be the Levitical priests, who are the implied subj. of λατρεύουσιν (3rd pl. pres. act. indic. of λατρεύω, "serve" [BDAG 587c]). The vb. is "often used for [priestly] service at a sanctuary" (Koester 377; cf. H. Strathmann, *TDNT* 4:58–65) and is never used with Christ in Hebrews (Cockerill 359 n. 6). Note again the pres. tense associated with the Levitical priests. Ὑποδείγματι (dat. sg. neut. of ὑπόδειγμα, -ατος, τό, "example," "model" [NJB], "pattern" [BDAG 1037a]) was used in 4:11 in the warning not to follow the "example" of the wilderness generation. Here (and in 9:23) it indicates a "pattern" to follow, rather than a "copy" of something (Cockerill 359–60; *pace* many EVV; but cf. "sketch" [NET, NRSV]). See For Further Study 51 (Ὑπόδειγμα).

Σκιᾷ is the dat. sg. fem. of σκιά, ᾶς, ἡ, "shadow" (BDAG 930a; S. Schulz, *TDNT* 7:394–400). Both dat. are locat. The two terms could be understood as a hendiadys ("shadowy symbol" [REB], "shadowy copy" [Barclay; Attridge 219]), distinct terms (most EVV), or less likely as synonyms (Ellingworth 406). Cockerill notes that a hendiadys obscures "the positive function of these terms" as pointers to Christ (Cockerill 359 n. 7; 360). Σκηνή (or τὰ ἅγια) is elliptically understood from v. 2 and is modified by ἐπουρανίων (gen. pl. neut. of ἐπουράνιος, -ον, "heavenly" [BDAG 388b]) as a descriptive gen. Its omission puts the emph. on the heavenly nature of the sanctuary (Cockerill 359).

As with ἀληθινός, ὑπόδειγμα and σκιά are often understood as evidence of the author's Platonic (mediated through Philo) conceptual background. Although the author uses some of the language of Philo, he does not share the same worldview (cf. Bruce 184). As Lane correctly notes, "The distinction between 'earthly' and 'heavenly' in 8:1–5 is eschatological rather than philosophical" (Lane 1:208). Additionally, the author's understanding of Exod 25:40 differs significantly from Philo's (see esp. Cockerill 361–62).

καθὼς κεχρημάτισται Μωϋσῆς μέλλων ἐπιτελεῖν τὴν σκηνήν·
as Moses was warned when he was about to complete the tabernacle.

Καθώς introduces an indir. quotation (BDAG 493d; cf. Heb 3:7). Κεχρημάτισται is the 3rd sg. pf. pass. indic. of χρηματίζω (with pass. "was warned" [NASB, NET, NIV], "received a warning" [BDAG 1089b]; B. Reicke, *TDNT* 9:480–82; "was instructed" [ESV]). The pass. is more freq. in the NT, with "the sense of being given a divine revelation, instruction, or warning" (Ellingworth 407). Here it could also be understood as a divine pass. (Lane 1:201 n. *j*; cf. T 70). The pf. tense is a "narrative perfect" (see comment on 7:6). The subj. of κεχρημάτισται is Μωϋσῆς (-έως, ὁ, "Moses"; see comments on 3:2). The ptc. μέλλων (see comments on 1:14) adv. modifies the vb. temp. ("when he was about to"). Ἐπιτελεῖν is the pres. act. inf. of ἐπιτελέω, "complete" (NET), "accomplish" (BDAG 383d; R. Mahoney, *EDNT* 2:42a–c). Several EVV tr. according to the context: "erect the tent" (ESV, NRSV). The pres. is conative (Wallace 534). The inf. is complementary (or supplementary) to the ptc. and "denotes an intended action" (Lane 1:201 n. *k*). Σκηνήν (acc. sg. fem. of σκηνή) is the obj. of the inf.

ὅρα γάρ φησιν, ποιήσεις πάντα κατὰ τὸν τύπον τὸν δειχθέντα σοι ἐν τῷ ὄρει·
For God said, **Be careful that you make everything according to the pattern that was shown to you on the mountain.**

Φησίν is the 3rd sg. pres. act. indic. of φημί, "say." The unexpressed subj. is God (R 392). Γάρ φησίν functions as a parenthesis (BDF §465[2]) to introduce the OT citation of Exod 25:40. Ὅρα is the 2nd sg. pres. act. impv. of ὁράω, here: "be careful" (CSB). The fut. (ποιήσεις) pars. the impv. and functions as a volative (R 874). Πάντα is the obj. of ποιήσεις. Κατά indicates "in accordance with" (BDAG 513a). The adv. prep. phrase modifies ποιήσεις. Τύπον is the acc. sg. masc. of τύπος, -ου, ὁ, "an archetype serving as a model," "design" (NET, NJB) "pattern" (ESV, NASB, NIV, REB; BDAG 1020b; L. Goppelt, *TDNT* 8:246–59). Δειχθέντα is the acc. sg. masc. of the aor. pass. ptc. of δείκνυμι, "point out," "show," "make known" (BDAG 214d). The ptc. adj. modifies τύπον and functions par. to a rel. clause ("which was shown"). The dat. σοι is the indir. obj. of the ptc. The prep. phrase ἐν τῷ ὄρει (ὄρος, -ους, τό, "mountain") is locat.

There is much debate whether Exod 25:40 (cf. Num 8:4) indicates that Moses saw a model or a blueprint of the heavenly tabernacle, or the heavenly sanctuary itself. This explains the range of EVV for both ὑπόδειγμα and τύπος. The citation follows the LXX closely. The likely addition of πάντα by the author to the citation (perhaps due to its inclusion in Exod 25:9 or 25:39) may suggest that everything in the earthly copy derives from the heavenly model (Attridge 220) or that the author intended to use every detail of the earthly sanctuary to demonstrate Christ's superiority (Cockerill 360–61). The second alteration from the LXX is from the pf. ptc. δεδειγμένον to the aor. ptc. δειχθέντα, likely to indicate that the author views the command given to Moses as a whole. In Exodus, the fact that the earthly tabernacle was to be a copy of the heavenly one would have been understood positively; in Hebrews, however, this reveals the inferiority and impermanence of the earthly sanctuary (Ellingworth 408).

VERSE 6

νυν[ὶ] δὲ διαφορωτέρας τέτυχεν λειτουργίας,
But Jesus has now obtained a superior ministry,

Νυν δέ (or the intensified form νυνὶ δέ) is "logical rather than temporal" (Lane 1:201 n. *n*; *pace* Cockerill 362) and "introduces a declaration set in opposition to the contrary-to-fact condition . . . in v. 4" (Lane 1:208). Moreover, δέ contrasts with μέν in v. 4 (Cockerill 362 n. 20). Τέτυχεν is the 3rd sg. pf. act. indic. of τυγχάνω, "obtain" (most EVV), "receive" (NIV), "attain," "gain," "find" (BDAG 1019b–c). The expected form of the vb. would be τέτυχηκεν, but this vb. takes a Hellenistic (Ionic) pf. with a gen. obj. (BDF §101; cf. R 801, T 232). The vb. is rare and "almost always indicates something good" (Ellingworth 409). Λειτουργίας is the gen. sg. fem. of λειτουργία, -ας, ἡ, "service" (BDAG 591b–c). Διαφορωτέρας (gen. sg. fem.) is the comp. of the adj. διάφορος (-ον; "superior" [NET, NIV], "more excellent" [ESV, NASB], "outstanding" [BDAG 240a]; cf. Heb 1:4) and modifies λειτουργίας. Attridge aptly notes that this clause summarizes the previous five vv. (Attridge 220).

ὅσῳ καὶ κρείττονός ἐστιν διαθήκης μεσίτης,
and to that degree he is the mediator of a better covenant,

The dat. of the correl. adj. ὅσῳ (ὅσος, -η, -ον; [by] "as much as" [BDAG 729c]) is instr. and joins Christ's ministry (λειτουργία) with the covenant (διαθήκη) as "a supporting clause" (Cockerill 363 n. 23). Καί is adjunctive, "also" (NASB; BDF §442[12]), although it is omitted in some EVV (e.g., ESV). Μεσίτης is the nom. sg. masc. of μεσίτης, -ου, ὁ, "mediator" (most EVV), "arbitrator" (BDAG 634b). It is a pred. nom. with Christ as the implied subj. of ἐστίν, which is made explicit in many EVV ("Christ" [ESV]; "Jesus" [CSB, NET, NIV]). The omission, however, rhetorically builds suspense until Christ is named in 9:14 (cf. Lane 1:201 n. *o*). Διαθήκης is the gen. sg. fem. of διαθήκη, -ης, ἡ, "covenant" (see comments on 7:22; 8:7; and 9:17). Κρείττονος is the gen. sg. fem. of κρείττων (see comments on 1:4). This clause links Christ's priestly ministry with the (new) covenant, which will be the focus of the rest of Hebrews 8 and much of Hebrews 9.

The phasing here recalls 7:22 (see comments there), where ἔγγυος instead of μεσίτης was used. The primary function of an ἔγγυος is as a guarantor, whereas a μεσίτης adds mediation to the function of a guarantor (see Koester 387–88). The mediator *par excellence* in the OT was Moses, who mediated the covenant between God and the people (cf. Attridge 221). An allusion to Moses here would point typologically to the superior mediator, Christ (cf. Cockerill 363). Μεσίτης "occurs in Hebrews only in ref. to the second covenant," which is perhaps more important for understanding the word than nonbiblical par. (Ellingworth 410). The strength of this covenant, however, is that it is not dependent on two parties (e.g., God and humans)—a point that the author will draw out in the next section. (For more on the difference between ἔγγυος and μεσίτης, see Ellingworth 388–89; Cockerill 330 n. 79.) See For Further Study 52 (Mediator).

ἥτις ἐπὶ κρείττοσιν ἐπαγγελίαις νενομοθέτηται.
which has been established on better promises.

The antecedent of the indef. rel. pron. ἥτις is διαθήκη. The indef. rel. pron. has a causal sense (Z §215; R 728). The def. rel. pron. (ὅς) and the indef. rel. pron. (ὅστις) were no longer distinguished in the NT (BDF §293). The rest of the v. comprises a rel. clause. Νενομοθέτηται is the 3rd sg. pf. pass. indic. of νομοθετέω, "legislate" (BDAG 676c; cf. Heb 7:11). The pf. tense adds emph. (e.g., "intensified," Campbell, *VA* 201). Ἐπαγγελίαις is the dat. pl. fem. of ἐπαγγελία, -ας, ἡ, "promises." Κρείττοσιν is the dat. pl. fem. of κρείττων (see comments on 1:4) and modifies ἐπαγγελίαις. Ἐπί indicates "on the basis of" (BDF §235[2]).

Mention of promises recalls the discussion of the Abrahamic promises in Heb 6:13–20, which were the bases of the Sinaitic covenant. The author suggests another typological connection here with mention of better promises on which the covenant of which Christ is the mediator is legislated. These better promises will be developed in the extended quotation from Jer 31:31–34, which is the focus of the rest of Hebrews 8.

FOR FURTHER STUDY

50. Heavenly Sanctuary/Tabernacle (8:1–5)

Attridge, 222–24.
Chilton, B. *DLNT* 1159–66.
Church, Philip A. F. "'The True Tent Which the Lord Has Pitched': Balaam's Oracles in Second Temple Judaism and in Hebrews." Pages 145–57 in Bauckham, *Cloud.*
Cody, Aelred. *Heavenly Sanctuary and Liturgy in the Epistle to the Hebrews: The Achievement of Salvation in the Epistle's Perspectives.* St. Meinrad, IN: Grail, 1960.
Davies, G. N. *DLNT* 1154–56.
DBI 837–40; 849–51.
Friedman, Richard Elliott. *ABD* 6:292–300.
Janzen, Waldemar. *NIDB* 5:447–58.
Koester, Craig R. *The Dwelling of God: The Tabernacle in the Old Testament, Intertestamental Jewish Literature, and the New Testament*. Washington, DC: Catholic Biblical Association of America, 1989.
MacRae, George W. "Heavenly Temple and Eschatology in the Letter to the Hebrews." *Semeia* 12 (1978): 179–99.

Motyer, Stephen. "The Temple in Hebrews: Is It There?" Pages 177–89 in *Heaven on Earth*. Edited by T. Desmond Alexander and Simon Gathercole. Carlisle, Cumbria, UK: Paternoster, 2004.

51. Ὑπόδειγμα (8:5)

Lee, Edwin Kenneth. "Words Denoting 'Pattern' in the New Testament." *NTS* 8 (1962): 166–73.

Schlier, H. *TDNT* 2:32–33.

*Steyn, Gert Jacobus. "'On Earth as It Is in Heaven . . . ': The Heavenly Sanctuary Motif in Hebrews 8:5 and Its Textual Connection with the 'Shadowy Copy' [υποδείγματι καὶ σκια] of LXX Exodus 25:40." *HvTSt* 67 (2011): 1–6.

52. Mediator (8:6)

Nash, Ronald H. "Notion of Mediator in Alexandrian Judaism and the Epistle to the Hebrews." *WTJ* 40 (1977): 89–115.

Oepke, A. *TDNT* 4:598–624.

Schenck, Kenneth. *NIDB* 4:8–15.

Wallace, R. S. *ISBE* 3:299–305.

HOMILETICAL SUGGESTIONS

The Superiority of Our High Priest (8:1–6)

1. Seated at the Right Hand of God (v. 1a)
2. Minister of the Heavenly Sanctuary (v. 1b–2)
   (a) The true sanctuary (v. 2a)
   (b) Established by God, not humans (v. 2b)
3. Has an Offering . . . (vv. 3–5)
   (a) Appropriate for the heavenly sanctuary (v. 3)
   (b) Unacceptable for the earthly sanctuary (v. 4)
      (1) This sanctuary was only a shadowy copy of the heavenly sanctuary (v. 5a)
      (2) Even if it was constructed carefully according to divine revelation (v. 5b)
4. Has a Superior Ministry (v. 6)
   (a) The mediator of a better covenant (v. 6a)
   (b) A better covenant based on better promises (v. 6b)

2. The Superior Covenant (8:7–13)

STRUCTURE

The extended citation from Jer 31:31–34 (LXX 38:31–34) unpacks the nature of the "better promises" (v. 6), the foremost of which is the promise that God will remember the people's sins no more (v. 12). The complete exposition of these promises is delayed until 10:15–18 (Cockerill 364). The section opens with a cond., the prot. of which is indented with respect to the apod. The first λέγει introduces the citation from Jer 31; the second and third occurrences (λέγει κύριος) structure the actual citation. Following the syntax of the Heb., par. clauses are aligned. The section concludes with a summarized statement concerning the first covenant.

7 Εἰ γὰρ ἡ πρώτη ἐκείνη ἦν ἄμεμπτος,
οὐκ ἂν δευτέρας ἐζητεῖτο τόπος.
8 μεμφόμενος γὰρ αὐτοὺς
λέγει·
ἰδοὺ ἡμέραι ἔρχονται,
λέγει κύριος,
καὶ συντελέσω ἐπὶ τὸν οἶκον Ἰσραὴλ καὶ
ἐπὶ τὸν οἶκον Ἰούδα
διαθήκην καινήν,
9 οὐ κατὰ τὴν διαθήκην,
ἣν ἐποίησα τοῖς πατράσιν αὐτῶν
ἐν ἡμέρᾳ ἐπιλαβομένου μου
τῆς χειρὸς αὐτῶν
ἐξαγαγεῖν αὐτοὺς ἐκ γῆς Αἰγύπτου,
ὅτι αὐτοὶ οὐκ ἐνέμειναν ἐν τῇ διαθήκῃ μου,
κἀγὼ ἠμέλησα αὐτῶν,
λέγει κύριος·
10 ὅτι αὕτη ἡ διαθήκη,
ἣν διαθήσομαι τῷ οἴκῳ Ἰσραὴλ
μετὰ τὰς ἡμέρας ἐκείνας, λέγει κύριος·
διδοὺς νόμους μου εἰς τὴν διάνοιαν αὐτῶν
καὶ ἐπὶ καρδίας αὐτῶν ἐπιγράψω αὐτούς,
καὶ ἔσομαι αὐτοῖς εἰς θεόν,
καὶ αὐτοὶ ἔσονταί μοι εἰς λαόν·
11 καὶ οὐ μὴ διδάξωσιν ἕκαστος τὸν πολίτην αὐτοῦ
καὶ ἕκαστος τὸν ἀδελφὸν αὐτοῦ λέγων·
γνῶθι τὸν κύριον,
ὅτι πάντες εἰδήσουσίν με ἀπὸ μικροῦ ἕως μεγάλου
αὐτῶν,
12 ὅτι ἵλεως ἔσομαι ταῖς ἀδικίαις αὐτῶν
καὶ τῶν ἁμαρτιῶν αὐτῶν οὐ μὴ μνησθῶ ἔτι.

13 ἐν τῷ λέγειν καινὴν
πεπαλαίωκεν τὴν πρώτην·
τὸ δὲ παλαιούμενον καὶ γηράσκον ἐγγὺς ἀφανισμοῦ.

VERSE 7

Εἰ γὰρ ἡ πρώτη ἐκείνη ἦν ἄμεμπτος,
For if that first covenant had been faultless,

Both γάρ and ἐκείνη (with διαθήκη as its antecedent) indicate a new section and link this section back to the previous one (Ellingworth 411). Εἰ with an aug. tense in the prot. (ἦν), together with the presence of ἄν in the apod. identifies "an unreal case (contrary-to-fact)" cond. (See comments on 4:8.) The art. ἡ refers to διαθήκη ("covenant"), which is understood from v. 6 and is modified by πρώτη ("first") and by the dem. pron. ἐκείνη ("that first covenant"). The use of the superl. for comp. is common in the NT (Wallace 303). Here the sense is "former." The use of πρώτη in v. 7 forms an *inclusio* with its use in v. 13. The position of ἐκείνη is "ambiguous" due to the ellipsis of διαθήκη (R 708). Ἄμεμπτος is the nom. sg. fem. of ἄμεμπτος, -ον, "faultless" (most EVV), "blameless" (BDAG 52d). The noun is formed with an alpha privative (cf. 7:3, 26). It functions here as a pred. adj. The cognate ἀμελέω is used in Heb 2:3. Recall the sim. statements about the law in Heb 7:11, 18 (Cockerill 366).

Although the LXX uses διαθήκη in conj. with several OT covenants (e.g., Abrahamic and Davidic), Hebrews uses διαθήκη only in conj. with the Sinaitic, or "first," covenant and the "new" covenant of Jeremiah 31. This reveals a distinction that the author draws between the "promissory" nature of the Abrahamic (e.g., ἐπαγγελία in conjunction with Abraham, esp. in Hebrews 6) and Davidic covenants (inferred from the author's use of Psalm 2 and 2 Sam 7:14 in Hebrews 1).

οὐκ ἂν δευτέρας ἐζητεῖτο τόπος.
there would have been no occasion for a second one.

Ἐζητεῖτο is the 3rd sg. impf. pass. indic. of ζητέω, "seek." The neg. ptcl. modifies the vb. Τόπος normally indicates a location, but it is used here metaphorically in keeping with Hellenistic usage (Attridge 226). The word could mean "opportunity" (e.g., 12:17 [cf. Koester 385]), "occasion" (ESV, NASB, REB; Cockerill 363; Ellingworth 412), or "need" (CEV, NLT, NRSV). The most likely subj. of the vb. is God (a divine pass.), which would suggest the following: "If the first covenant had not been defective, God would not have sought an occasion to establish a second" (Ellingworth 412), although most EVV do not make the subj. explicit. The gen. δευτέρας (δεύτερος, -α, -ον, "second" [most EVV], "another" [NIV]) indicates purpose (BDF §166). As with πρώτη, διαθήκη is assumed.

The logic of the v. flows from the ref. to a "new" covenant in Jeremiah 31, which indicates some limitation with the former ("old") one. Hebrews is the only part of the NT that talks about an "old" and a "new" covenant together (cf. Luke 22:20; 1 Cor

11:25; 2 Cor 3:6). This is the same logic regarding the priesthood: if Ps 110:4 speaks of a different priesthood, then there must have been some deficiency with the former priesthood (Cockerill 364). Although "covenant" is also associated with Noah, Abraham, and David, the author of Hebrews differentiates between the "promises" made to Abraham and the Sinaitic and new "covenants" (cf. Koester 384).

VERSE 8

μεμφόμενος γὰρ αὐτοὺς λέγει·
But finding fault with his people, he says:

Γάρ continues the argument begun in v. 7. *Μεμφόμενος* is the nom. sg. masc. of the pres. mid. ptc. of *μέμφομαι*, "to find fault with" (most EVV), "blame" (BDAG 629c; W. Grundmann, *TDNT* 4:571–74; cognate of *ἄμεμπτος* in v. 7 [Cockerill 365]). The ptc. is causal. God is the implied subj. of *λέγει* (made explicit in most EVV). The pres. tense likely reflects the emph. in Hebrews on the abiding nature of God speaking (see comments on 1:2). This also accounts for the pres. tense of the ptc., although most EVV tr. both with past tenses. The textual evidence for the var. rdg. *αὐτοῖς* (as the indir. obj. of *λέγει*) and the text *αὐτούς* (as the obj. of the ptc.) is fairly evenly divided. The author's style, however, favors *αὐτούς* since there are no other examples of *λέγω* with a dat. obj. in Hebrews (Koester 385; *pace* Lane 1:202 n. *s*; cf. Metzger 597). The UBS committee gives *αὐτούς* a {B} rating. For a defense of *αὐτοῖς*, see Johannes L. P. Wolmarans, "The Text and Translation of Hebrews 8:8," *ZNW* 75 (1984): 139–44.

ἰδοὺ ἡμέραι ἔρχονται, λέγει κύριος,
See, the days are coming, says the Lord,

Ἰδού is a dem. ptcl. "that draws attention to what follows" (BDAG 468b). Although accented differently, it is the aor. mid. impv. of *εἶδον*, "see" ("behold" [ESV, NASB], "look" [NET, NJB]; left untr. NIV, NLT, NRSV, REB). The subj. of *ἔρχονται* (3rd pl. pres. mid. indic.) is *ἡμέραι* ("days"). This eschatological ref. recalls the expression *ἐπ' ἐσχάτου τῶν ἡμερῶν τούτων* in Heb 1:2. *Κύριος* here refers to God.

καὶ συντελέσω ἐπὶ τὸν οἶκον Ἰσραὴλ καὶ ἐπὶ τὸν οἶκον Ἰούδα διαθήκην καινήν,
when I will make a new covenant with the house of Israel and with the house of Judah—

Καί is temp., "when" (BDF §442[4]; Z §455*δ*). *Συντελέσω* is the 1st sg. fut. act. indic. of *συντελέω*, "make" (most EVV), "establish" (ESV), "complete" (NET), "accomplish" (BDAG 975b; G. Delling, *TDNT* 8:62–64). Many EVV tr. the vb. as "make," which misses the connection with the cognate *τελειόω* (see below); but cf. "conclude" [REB], "complete" [NET]. The fut. is predictive. The *συν-* prefix is reflected in most EVV ("a covenant *with*"), leaving *ἐπί* essentially untr. *Διαθήκην* ("covenant") is the obj. of *συντελέσω* and is modified by *καινήν*. Its placement is emph. *Οἶκον* ("house") refers to the dynasties or people (CEV, GNT, NLT) of Israel and Judah. *Ἰσραήλ* ("Israel") is indecl. Here it functions par. to Ἰούδα (gen. sg. masc. of Ἰούδας, -α, ὁ, "Judah") as a gen. of poss. (the unusual gen. form for Ἰούδας is Doric [R 255]).

Heb 8:8–12 quotes Jer 31:31–34 (LXX Jer 38:31–34) and agrees generally with the LXX, although συντελέσω substitutes for διατίθεμαι. There is debate concerning whether this reflects a different version of the LXX, a stylistic variation on the part of the author, or a deliberate choice, perhaps alluding to the "perfection" achieved by Christ, the mediator of the new covenant (i.e., συντελέω [Attridge 227; Cockerill 368 n. 18; Koester 386]). Arguing in favor of the author altering the text is the retention of διατίθεμαι in v. 10. This is the only place in the NT that quotes Jeremiah 31. (For discussion of other minor var. rdgs., see esp. Ellingworth 415–17.)

VERSE 9

οὐ κατὰ τὴν διαθήκην,
not like the covenant

Κατά indicates "in accordance with" (BDAG 513a; "it will not be like" [NIV]). The vb. συντελέσω (or διατίθεμαι) is elliptically understood to indicate that the new covenant will not be implemented as the former one was.

ἣν ἐποίησα τοῖς πατράσιν αὐτῶν ἐν ἡμέρᾳ ἐπιλαβομένου μου τῆς χειρὸς αὐτῶν
that I made with their ancestors on the day I took them by the hand

The antecedent of ἥν is διαθήκη. The author has apparently substituted ἐποίησα for the LXX διεθέμην (1st sg. aor. mid. indic. of διατίθημι; see v. 10), perhaps recalling the use of ποιέω in Heb 1:2, although its association with the *former* covenant (as a less specific term than διατίθημι) likely contrasts with the possible allusion to "perfection" via συντελέω associated with the new covenant (cf. Cockerill 369; *pace* Attridge 227; see discussion above). Τοῖς πατράσιν (cf. 1:1) is the indir. obj. of the vb. The dat. indicates association ("with"). The pers. pron. αὐτῶν is poss. Ἐν ἡμέρᾳ is temp. and modifies ἐπιλαβομένου. Obj. of prep. are often anar., although not indef. ("the day" [most EVV]). Hebrews substitutes ἐποίησα for διεθέμην in the LXX. As with v. 8, this could be intentional (so Attridge 227) or could reflect a different LXX version (Koester 385).

Ἐπιλαβομένου is the gen. sg. masc. of the aor. mid. ptc. of ἐπιλαμβάνομαι "take by the hand" (most EVV), "grasp" (BDAG 374b; cf. Heb 2:16). The vb. takes a gen. obj., here τῆς χειρός αὐτῶν. A gen. abs. cstr. normally has a subj. that is different from the subj. of the main vb. on which it depends. Here, however, the subj. of the gen. abs. (ἐπιλαβομένου μου) and the vb. (ἐποίησα) are the same. This may reflect the underlying Heb. (R 514). The ptc. here has a "circumstantial temporal" sense (R 1123–24). Moreover, the gen. abs. depends on ἐν ἡμέρᾳ ("on which day I took" [BDF §432(5)]). Thus the gen. μου indicates the "subj." of the ptc.

ἐξαγαγεῖν αὐτοὺς ἐκ γῆς Αἰγύπτου,
to lead them out of the land of Egypt.

Ἐξαγαγεῖν is the aor. act. inf. of ἐξάγω, "lead out" (most EVV), "bring . . . out" (ESV; BDAG 343d). The inf. indicates purpose ("to lead them out"); the subj. is the same as the implied subj. of ἐποίησα (God). The obj. of the inf. is αὐτούς, referring back to Israel and Judah. Αἰγύπτου is the gen. sg. fem. of Αἴγυπτος, -ου, ὁ, "Egypt." The gen. is descriptive, modifying γῆς. Place names, esp. Αἴγυπτος, are often anar. (BDF §261[7]). The prep. phrase ἐκ γῆς Αἰγύπτου is ablatival.

ὅτι αὐτοὶ οὐκ ἐνέμειναν ἐν τῇ διαθήκῃ μου,
. . . because they did not continue in my covenant.

Ὅτι is causal, giving the reason why God will complete a new covenant with his people, namely, because they did not keep his former one. The antecedent of αὐτοί is again Israel and Judah. The use of the pers. pron. in the nom. is emph. ("they themselves," although not reflected in most EVV). Ἐνέμειναν is the 3rd pl. aor. act. indic. of ἐμμένω, "persevere in," "stand by" (BDAG 322d). The vb. is followed by the dat. (διαθήκῃ). The rep. of the prep. ἐν (after the compound vb. ἐνέμειναν) may emphasize the locat. sense (R 559–60). Μου is poss. Perseverance in Hebrews is often associated with μένω; here faithlessness is indicated by the neg. cognate ἐμμένω ("did not continue" [ESV, NET], "did not remain faithful" [NIV]). This part of the citation recalls the earlier focus on the faithlessness of the wilderness generation.

κἀγὼ ἠμέλησα αὐτῶν, λέγει κύριος·
. . . I showed no concern for them, says the Lord,

Κἀγώ ("and I") likely reflects the underlying Heb. *wav* consecutive of the LXX tr. Ἠμέλησα is the 1st sg. aor. act. indic. of ἀμελέω, "neglect, be unconcerned" (BDAG 52c; cf. 2:3). The vb. has a pejorative sense here, as indicated in many EVV (e.g., "I grew weary of" [NAB 1970], "I . . . abandoned them" [NJB], "I turned my back on them" [NLT], "I turned away from them" [NIV]; "I paid no attention to them" [Koester 386]). Again, κύριος refers to God, who is speaking (λέγει) in the Jeremiah citation.

VERSE 10

ὅτι αὕτη ἡ διαθήκη, ἣν διαθήσομαι τῷ οἴκῳ Ἰσραὴλ μετὰ τὰς ἡμέρας ἐκείνας, λέγει κύριος·
For this is the covenant that I will make with the house of Israel after those days, says the Lord:

Ὅτι "loosely" connects v. 10 with the previous vv. (BDAG 732c) by expanding on the "new covenant" that God will accomplish in v. 8. It is left untr. by some EVV. The near dem. pron. αὕτη (οὗτος, αὕτη, τοῦτο, "this") in the pred. modifies διαθήκη, but more specifically refers to the "new covenant" in v. 8. The antecedent of the rel. pron. ἥν is also the διαθήκη of v. 8. Διαθήσομαι is the 1st sg. fut. mid. indic. of διατίθημι, "make" (most EVV), "establish" (ESV), "decree," "ordain" (BDAG 238b–c; J. Behm, *TDNT* 2:104–06); the vb. is a cognate of διαθήκη (Wallace 169) and is followed by the dat. (οἴκῳ). Ἰσραήλ ("Israel") is indecl., but functions as a gen. of poss. The fut. is predictive. Μετά + the acc. indicates "after." The far dem. pron. ἐκείνας (ἐκεῖνος, -η, -ο, "those") in pred. modifies ἡμέρας. Again, κύριος refers to God, who is speaking (λέγει) in the Jeremiah citation.

διδοὺς νόμους μου εἰς τὴν διάνοιαν αὐτῶν καὶ ἐπὶ καρδίας αὐτῶν ἐπιγράψω αὐτούς,
I will put my laws into their minds and write them on their hearts.

The ptc. διδούς adv. modifies ἐπιγράψω instr. The syntax of the ptc. and vb. may reflect the Heb. (e.g., Heb. inf. abs. [Attridge 228 n. 36; Moule 180]). Νόμους is the obj. of the ptc. Μου is poss. Διάνοιαν is the acc. sg. fem. of διάνοια, ας, ἡ, "mind" (BDAG 234b). Εἰς τὴν διάνοιαν αὐτῶν modifies διδούς locat. The antecedent of αὐτῶν is Israel and Judah; the gen. is poss. Καί is coordinate. Ἐπιγράψω is the 1st sg. fut. act. indic. of ἐπιγράφω, "write in" (fig.; BDAG 370a). Ἐπὶ καρδίας αὐτῶν modifies ἐπιγράψω locat.

The promise here goes beyond memorization of God's laws or even an interiorization of them. Instead it points to one of the focal points of Hebrews 9 and 10—the cleansing of the very conscience of the worshipper (cf. Attridge 227).

καὶ ἔσομαι αὐτοῖς εἰς θεόν, καὶ αὐτοὶ ἔσονταί μοι εἰς λαόν·
I will be their God, and they will be my people.

Both καίs are coordinating. The antecedent of both αὐτοῖς and αὐτοί is Israel and Judah. The nom. of αὐτοί is emph. ("they themselves"). Both αὐτοῖς and μοι are dat. of advantage. The two prep. phrases, εἰς θεόν and εἰς λαόν, function as preds., reflecting Semitic influence, occurring with the fut. of εἰμί and esp. in OT citations (BDF §145; BDAG 291b; Wallace 47). This promise is the essence of God's covenantal relationship with his people (see the extensive biblical refs. in Koester 387).

VERSE 11

καὶ οὐ μὴ διδάξωσιν ἕκαστος τὸν πολίτην αὐτοῦ καὶ ἕκαστος τὸν ἀδελφὸν αὐτοῦ
And each person will not teach his fellow citizen, and each his brother or sister,

Διδάξωσιν is the 3rd pl. aor. act. subjunc. of διδάσκω, "teach." The subjunc. with the strong negation οὐ μή "is the most definite form of negation regarding the future" (BDF §365). Ἕκαστος is the subj. of the vb. The rep. likely reflects the underlying Heb. (R 746). Πολίτην is the acc. sg. masc. of πολίτης, -ου, ὁ, "fellow citizen" (BDAG 846b; H. Strathmann, *TDNT* 6:534–35). The var. rdg. πλησίος ("neighbor[s]," or "neighbour") is less well attested, although it is adopted in some EVV (ESV, NIV, NJB, NLT). The idea of "neighbor" however, is closely related to that of "fellow citizen" (NASB, REB) since it would be part of a commonwealth. The subst. is left untr. in EVV (e.g., CEV, NRSV). Also supporting the use of πολίτης is the cognate πολίς, used of the city of God in Hebrews (i.e., 11:9–20; 13–16; 12:23; 13:14 [Koester 387]). The UBS committee gives πολίτην an {A} rating.

λέγων· γνῶθι τὸν κύριον,
saying, "Know the Lord,"

Λέγων (agreeing with ἕκαστος) introduces the quotation, γνῶθι τὸν κύριον. Γνῶθι is the 2nd sg. aor. act. impv. of γινώσκω, "know." Here "know" encompasses both relationship and obedience (cf. Koester 387). Κύριον is the obj. of the impv.

ὅτι πάντες εἰδήσουσίν με ἀπὸ μικροῦ ἕως μεγάλου αὐτῶν,
because they will all know me, from the least to the greatest of them.

Ὅτι is causal, indicating the reason why God's people will no longer need to teach each other. Πάντες is subst. ("all people"). Εἰδήσουσιν is the 3rd pl. fut. act. indic. of οἶδα, "know" (R 361; the form could also be understood as a fut. pf. [R 906]). The fut. is predictive. The obj. of the vb. is με. Both μικροῦ (gen. sg. masc. of μικρός, -ά, -όν, "small," "little") and μεγάλου (gen. sg. masc. of μέγας, μεγάλη, μέγα, "large," "great") are pos. that are used as superlatives (e.g., smallest and largest). The prep. ἕως ("to") takes the gen. The gen. αὐτῶν is partitive ("among them"). The expression ἀπὸ μικροῦ ἕως μεγάλου is a merism—a rhetorical device in which two end points indicate totality.

VERSE 12

ὅτι ἵλεως ἔσομαι ταῖς ἀδικίαις αὐτῶν καὶ τῶν ἁμαρτιῶν αὐτῶν οὐ μὴ μνησθῶ ἔτι.
For I will forgive their wrongdoing, and I will never again remember their sins.

Ὅτι is causal, adding further support to the reason given in v. 11. Ἵλεως (nom. sg. masc. of ἵλεως, -ων, "merciful" [ESV, NASB, NET; BDAG 474c]) is a pred. nom. Several EVV tr. the collocation as a vb.: "I will be merciful" (ESV, NET); "I will forgive" (NIV). In BGk. the adj. is only used of God. It is followed by the dat. ταῖς ἀδικίαις (ἀδικία, -ης, ἡ, "wickedness" [NIV, NLT], "iniquities" [ESV, NASB], "wrongdoing" [BDAG 20c]). Αὐτῶν in both instances is poss. Καί is coordinating. Μνησθῶ is the 1st sg. aor. pass. subjunc. of μιμνῄσκομαι, "remember" (BDAG 652b; cf. 2:6) and takes a gen. obj., ἁμαρτιῶν. The adv. ἔτι with οὐ means "no longer." Remembering means "not holding past sins against people" (Koester 388) because they have been completely forgiven. This promise anticipates the sacrifice that cleanses the conscience and thus fulfills this promise.

VERSE 13

ἐν τῷ λέγειν καινὴν πεπαλαίωκεν τὴν πρώτην·
By saying **a new covenant**, he has declared that the first is obsolete.

This v. offers a "concluding comment" on the scriptural citation (cf. 1:4; 10:18, 39 [Attridge 228 n. 40]). Ἐν τῷ + the inf. (λέγειν) indicates time contemp. with the main vb. (BDF §404[3]; e.g., NASB, NET, NLT) or is instr. (cf. Wallace 598; Ellingworth 318; e.g., "by saying" or "by calling" [NIV, REB]). Καινήν (καινός, -ή, -όν, "new") is the obj. of the inf., with διαθήκη understood ("while speaking about the new covenant"). Πεπαλαίωκεν is the 3rd sg. pf. act. indic. of παλαιόω, "make obsolete" (ESV, NET, NIV, NLT), "declare obsolete" (BDAG 751d; H. Seesemann, *TDNT* 5:720). The pf. is consummative (R 895). The implied subj. is God, the one speaking in the prophecy in Jeremiah. As with 8:6, the pf. tense adds emphasis (e.g., "intensified," Campbell, *VA* 201). In v. 7 πρώτη is contrasted with δευτέρα, but here it contrasts with καινή (Attridge 227 n. 19; see comments on 8:7).

τὸ δὲ παλαιούμενον καὶ γηράσκον ἐγγὺς ἀφανισμοῦ.
"And what is obsolete and growing old is about to pass away."

Δέ indicates a "transition from the specific to the general" (Ellingworth 418). Παλαιούμενον is the nom. sg. neut. of the pres. pass. ptc. of παλαιόω (see above). Γηράσκον is the nom. sg. neut. of the pres. act. ptc. of γηράσκω, "aging" (NET), "outdated" (NIV), "grow old" (ESV, NASB; BDAG 196d; cf. "out of date" [CEV, NLT]). Both ptcs. are subst. and both are neut., referring to a general concept ("that which is . . ."), which here refers to the former covenant. A form of εἰμί is implied. Ἀφανισμοῦ is the gen. sg. masc. of ἀφανισμός, -οῦ, ὁ, "disappearance" (H. Balz, *EDNT* 1:180c); "destruction" (BDAG 155a). The noun is the obj. of the prep. ἐγγύς "near." The cstr. ἐγγύς ἀφανισμοῦ functions as the pred. nom. ("is not far from extinction" [Barclay], "is close to disappearing" [NAB], "is ready to vanish away" [ESV], "is about to disappear" [NET]).

Most contemp. Jewish writings maintained the everlasting nature of the Sinaitic covenant (e.g., Sir 17:12; see Koester 388 for additional refs.), although there may be some evidence that the Qumran community understood the new to replace the old (Ellingworth 418). Even so, the author's claim was likely shocking. Yet, as with the rest of Hebrews, the author is only drawing inferences from what is said in Jeremiah (cf. Bruce 195). "As soon as God promised a 'new' covenant, the Old was 'near passing away'" (Cockerill 370). This logic prepares for Hebrews 9, which focuses more fully on the "typological function" of the old order (Cockerill 370).

FOR FURTHER STUDY

53. New Covenant in Hebrews (8:7–13)

Ellingworth, 385–89.

Gräbe, Peter. "The New Covenant and Christian Identity in Hebrews." Pages 119–27 in Bauckham, *Cloud*.

Kaiser, W. C. "The Old Promise and the New Covenant: Jeremiah 31:31–34." *JETS* 15 (1972): 11–23.

Kent, Homer A., Jr. "The New Covenant and the Church." *GTJ* 6 (1985): 289–98.

*Lehne, Susanne. *The New Covenant in Hebrews. Journal of the Society for New Testament*: Supplement Series 44. Sheffield: JSOT Press, 1990.

Lundbom, Jack. *ABD* 4:1088–94.

Morrison, Michael D. *Who Needs a New Covenant?: Rhetorical Function of the Covenant Motif in the Argument of Hebrews*. Eugene, OR: Pickwick, 2008.
Newman, C. C. *DLNT* 245–50.
Omanson, R. L. "A Superior Covenant: Hebrews 8:1–10:18." *RevExp* 82 (1985): 361–73.
Peterson, David G. "The Prophecy of the New Covenant in the Argument of Hebrews." *RTR* 38 (1979): 74–81.
Vos, Geerhardus. "Hebrews, the Epistle of the Diatheke." *Princeton Theological Review* 13 (1915): 587–632; 14 (1916): 1–61.

HOMILETICAL SUGGESTIONS

The New Covenant (8:7–13)

1. The Need for a New Covenant Due to the Limitations of the First Covenant (v. 7)
   (a) Prophesied about through Jeremiah (v. 8)
   (b) Not based on the compliance of the people (v. 9)
2. The Promises of the New Covenant
   (a) An internalization of God's law (v. 10a)
   (b) A covenantal bond between God and his people (v. 10b)
   (c) A democratization of teachers of the Lord's ways (v. 11)
   (d) Complete forgiveness of sins (v. 12)
3. The New Covenant Reveals the Obsolescence of the Old Covenant (v. 13)

C. THE NEW SANCTUARY AND SACRIFICE (9:1–10:18)

1. The Limitations of the Old Order (9:1–10)

STRUCTURE

The description of the outer and inner chambers of the earthly tabernacle is structured around the rep. of σκηνή in v. 2 (ἡ πρώτη) and v. 3 ("the second" by implication). The abrupt end to this description is signaled by περὶ ὧν οὐκ ἔστιν νῦν λέγειν κατὰ μέρος, after which the author focuses on the regulations for worship. Verse 6 specifies duties of the regular priests (οἱ ἱερεῖς), while v. 7 focuses on the high priest (ὁ ἀρχιερεύς). Verse 8a begins with a declarative clause, which introduces the Spirit's revelation of the true significance of the old cultic order, outlined in vv. 8b–10. The rel. clauses, ἥτις and καθ' ἥν, both refer to ἡ πρώτη σκηνή.

1 Εἶχε μὲν οὖν [καὶ] ἡ πρώτη δικαιώματα λατρείας τό τε ἅγιον κοσμικόν.
2 σκηνὴ γὰρ κατεσκευάσθη
ἡ πρώτη
ἐν ᾗ ἥ τε λυχνία καὶ ἡ τράπεζα καὶ ἡ πρόθεσις τῶν ἄρτων,
ἥτις λέγεται Ἅγια·
3 μετὰ δὲ τὸ δεύτερον καταπέτασμα
σκηνὴ
ἡ λεγομένη Ἅγια Ἁγίων,
4 χρυσοῦν ἔχουσα θυμιατήριον
καὶ τὴν κιβωτὸν τῆς διαθήκης
περικεκαλυμμένην πάντοθεν χρυσίῳ,
ἐν ᾗ στάμνος χρυσῆ
ἔχουσα τὸ μάννα
καὶ ἡ ῥάβδος Ἀαρὼν ἡ βλαστήσασα
καὶ αἱ πλάκες τῆς διαθήκης,
5 ὑπεράνω δὲ αὐτῆς Χερουβὶν δόξης
κατασκιάζοντα τὸ ἱλαστήριον·
περὶ ὧν οὐκ ἔστιν νῦν λέγειν κατὰ μέρος.

6 Τούτων δὲ οὕτως κατεσκευασμένων
εἰς μὲν τὴν πρώτην σκηνὴν
διὰ παντὸς
εἰσίασιν οἱ ἱερεῖς
τὰς λατρείας ἐπιτελοῦντες,
7 εἰς δὲ τὴν δευτέραν
ἅπαξ τοῦ ἐνιαυτοῦ
μόνος ὁ ἀρχιερεύς,
οὐ χωρὶς αἵματος
ὃ προσφέρει

ὑπὲρ ἑαυτοῦ καὶ τῶν τοῦ λαοῦ ἀγνοημάτων,
8 τοῦτο δηλοῦντος τοῦ πνεύματος τοῦ ἁγίου
μήπω πεφανερῶσθαι τὴν τῶν ἁγίων ὁδὸν
ἔτι τῆς πρώτης σκηνῆς ἐχούσης στάσιν,
9 ἥτις παραβολὴ
εἰς τὸν καιρὸν τὸν ἐνεστηκότα,
καθʼ ἣν δῶρά τε καὶ θυσίαι προσφέρονται
μὴ δυνάμεναι κατὰ συνείδησιν τελειῶσαι
τὸν λατρεύοντα,
10 μόνον ἐπὶ βρώμασιν καὶ πόμασιν καὶ διαφόροις
βαπτισμοῖς,
δικαιώματα σαρκὸς
μέχρι καιροῦ διορθώσεως ἐπικείμενα.

VERSE 1

Εἶχε μὲν οὖν [καὶ] ἡ πρώτη δικαιώματα λατρείας τό τε ἅγιον κοσμικόν.
Now the first covenant also had regulations for ministry and an earthly sanctuary.

Μὲν οὖν indicates a transition to a new aspect of the first covenant (BDF §451[1]); thus it is also continuative (BDAG 630c). Μέν in Heb 9:1 correlates with δέ in 9:11, such that the first covenant (9:1–10) is contrasted with the new one (Cockerill 372 n. 5; Koester 393), although the distance between the correl. may argue against this (Ellingworth 420). The impf. εἶχε indicates the incomplete nature of the old order (e.g., imperfective aspect) as well as provides the background ("offline information"; Campbell, *Basics* 40–45) for the ensuing discussion in vv. 6–10 (cf. Ellingworth 420). If original, καί would have an ascensive ("also") force and would (wrongly) imply that the new covenant also had regulations for worship in an earthly tabernacle (cf. Attridge 230 n. 1; Lane 2:214). Although the mss. evidence is evenly divided, the UBS committee rates the inclusion of καί {C}. It is translated in many EVV as "also" (e.g., NIV, NJB; cf. "even" [ESV, NASB]).

The art. ἡ refers to διαθήκη ("covenant"), which is understood from Hebrews 8 and is modified by πρώτη. (See comments on 8:7.) Ἡ πρώτη [διαθήκη] is the subj. of εἶχε. Δικαιώματα is the acc. pl. neut. of δικαίωμα, -ατος, τό, "regulation" (ESV, NET, NIV), "ordinances" (REB), "requirement," "commandment" (BDAG 249d; K. Kertelge, *EDNT* 1:334d–335d). Λατρείας is the gen. sg. fem. of λατρεία, -ας, ἡ, "worship" (most EVV), "ministry" (CSB), "service" (REB; BDAG 587b: H. Strathmann, *TDNT* 4:65). The gen. indicates ref. ("regulations for worship"). These regulations are elaborated in vv. 6–10. The expression δικαιώματα λατρείας forms an *inclusio* with δικαιώματα σαρκός in v. 10 (Lane 2:217).

The postpos., encl. τέ shows close relationship between the regulations and the sanctuary (BDF §443[2]). The art. τό indicates something that is well known (Ellingworth 421). The adj. ἅγιον functions subst., referring to the "sanctuary" as a whole, although the sg. is not used elsewhere in Hebrews with this mng. (Ellingworth 421). Κοσμικόν is the acc. sg. neut. of *κοσμικός, -ή, -όν*, "earthly" (BDAG 560d; H. Sasse, *TDNT* 3:897–98), indicating the opposite of heavenly (Lane 2:214–15 n. *c*). The adj. *κοσμικόν* is in the pred. pos., which parallels the function of a rel. clause ("the sanctuary, which . . . was a terrestrial one" [Z §187]). The expression recalls 8:5 and is pejorative (Attridge 232; Lane 2:219). The regulations for worship and the earthly tabernacle are discussed in reverse order, beginning with the tabernacle (vv. 2–5) and then the regulations (vv. 6–10).

VERSE 2

σκηνὴ γὰρ κατεσκευάσθη ἡ πρώτη ἐν ᾗ ἥ τε λυχνία καὶ ἡ τράπεζα καὶ ἡ πρόθεσις τῶν ἄρτων,
For a tabernacle was set up, and in the first room . . . were the lampstand, the table, and the presentation loaves.

Γάρ indicates a specific statement following the general one in v. 1 (Ellingworth 422). *Κατεσκευάσθη* is the 3rd sg. aor. pass. indic. of *κατασκευάζω*, "prepare" (ESV, NASB, NET), "set up" (NIV), "furnish," "equip" (BDAG 527a; H. Balz, *EDNT* 2:268c). The aor. is global. The subj. of the vb. is *σκηνή* (see comments on 8:2). Although in v. 1 *ἡ πρώτη* referred to the first (temp.) covenant, here it refers to the first (outer/spatial) section of the tent (*σκηνή*). The lack of punctuation (asyndeton) between the initial clause (*σκηνὴ γὰρ κατεσκευάσθη*) and *ἡ πρώτη* accounts for the addition of "and" in some EVV (e.g., CSB) or the beginning of a new sentence in others (e.g., NIV, NLT). The use of "first" and "second" to refer to the outer and inner chambers, respectively, of the tabernacle "is not attested elsewhere," although an inexact par. occurs in Josephus (Lane 2:219; cf. W. Michaelis, *TDNT* 7:375–77).

The antecedent of *ᾗ* is the elliptically understood *σκηνή*. *Ἐν* is locat. *Ἦ* is the impf. act. indic. of *εἰμί*. *Τε* introduces a list of coordinate items (BDAG 993d) found in the outer court: the *λυχνία* (*-ας, ἡ*, "lampstand" [BDAG 606b–c]; Heb. *mĕnôrâ* in LXX); the *τράπεζα* (*-ης, ἡ*, "table" [BDAG 1013b]); and the *πρόθεσις* (*-εως, ἡ*, "presentation" [BDAG 869c; C. Maurer, *TDNT* 8:164–68]), which is modified by the descriptive gen. *τῶν ἄρτων*. The exact phrase *ἡ πρόθεσις τῶν ἄρτων* does not occur in the Exodus account (but cf. 2 Chr 13:11; Attridge 233 n. 37; Ellingworth 423). Together *ἡ τράπεζα καὶ ἡ πρόθεσις τῶν ἄρτων* could form a hendiadys (e.g., "the table of presentation" [cf. Bruce 198–99; Lane 2:215 n. *e*]), although two separate items are likely intended (e.g., "the table with its consecrated bread" [NIV]; sim. most EVV).

Exodus 25–31 and 34–40 describe the design and construction of the earthly tabernacle. Specifically, Exod 25:31–40 describes the lampstand, or menorah. The table and the presentation loaves are described in Exod 25:23–30 and Lev 24:5–9. The altar of incense, also apparently in the outer room, is not mentioned (cf. Exod 30:1–10). (See comments on v. 4.)

ἥτις λέγεται Ἅγια·
which is called the holy place,

The antecedent of the indef. rel. pron. ἥτις is ἡ πρώτη [σκηνή], which is called (λέγεται; the pres. is gnomic) "the holy place." In Koine, the distinction between the rel. pron. and the indef. rel. pron. was fading, as the interchange between the two here attests (T 47). The anar. Ἅγια (nom. pl. neut.) to indicate the outer chamber only (not the entire tabernacle) occurs only here in Hebrews (cf. 8:2; 9:8, 12, 24, 25; 10:19; 13:11; Attridge 233 n. 46; Lane 2:215 n. *g*). The uniqueness of this cstr. accounts for the var. rdgs.

VERSE 3

μετὰ δὲ τὸ δεύτερον Καταπέτασμα σκηνὴ ἡ λεγομένη Ἅγια Ἁγίων,
Behind the second curtain was a tent called the most holy place.

Δέ adds additional information (Ellingworth 424). Καταπέτασμα is the acc. sg. neut. of καταπέτασμα, -ατος, τό, "curtain" (see comments on 6:9) and is modified by δεύτερον (δεύτερος, -α, -ον, "second"). This is apparently the only place in the NT where μετά has a spatial ("behind," "beyond"), not temp. ("after"), sense (R 612); although BDF §226 suggests "after the [second] curtain . . ." The descriptions move from the "first" ("outer") to the "second" ("inner") section of the sanctuary. The second curtain was made of embroidered linen (Exod 26:31–33), behind which was the holy of holies. The first curtain, through which one entered the outer compartment of the tabernacle, was also made of linen (Exod 26:36–37).

A vb. is implied (e.g., ἦν), par. to v. 2 (so most EVV). Λεγομένη is subst. and functions par. to ἥτις λέγεται in v. 2. The difference is stylistic (Ellingworth 424). The art. parallels a rel. pron. ("which is called"; cf. Wallace 215). The designation Ἅγια Ἁγίων reflects the cognate gen. in Heb. to indicate the superl. ("the most holy place"; Koester 394; Lane 2:220; cf. Wallace 298). The anar. cstr. is unusual, which explains the addition of the art. in the var. rdgs.

VERSE 4

χρυσοῦν ἔχουσα θυμιατήριον καὶ τὴν κιβωτὸν τῆς διαθήκης περικεκαλυμμένην πάντοθεν χρυσίῳ,
It had the gold altar of incense and the ark of the covenant, covered with gold on all sides,

The adj. ptc. ἔχουσα (modifying σκηνή) functions par. to a rel. pron. (e.g., "which had"). Χρυσοῦν (χρυσοῦς, -ῆ, -οῦν, "golden") modifies θυμιατήριον (acc. sg. neut. of θυμιατήριον, -ου, τό, "incense altar" [BDAG 461c; G. Schneider, *EDNT* 2:159c]; BGk. hapax). Κιβωτόν is the acc. sg. fem. of κιβωτός, -ου, ἡ, "ark" (most EVV; BDAG 544b; G. Schneider, *EDNT* 2:292c–293a). The gen. διαθήκης ("covenant") is descriptive. Περικεκαλυμμένην is the acc. sg. fem. of the pf. pass. ptc. of περικαλύπτω, "cover" (BDAG 801d). The adv. πάντοθεν ("on all sides," "entirely" [BDAG 755a]) modifies the ptc. Χρυσίῳ (dat. sg. neut. of χρυσίον, -ου, τό, "gold"). (See Exod 25:10–15 [cf. 37:1–5].) Note the bracketing of the clause with χρυσοῦν at the beginning and χρυσίῳ at the end (Cockerill 375).

The exact meaning of θυμιατήριον is debated. It could indicate the incense altar (or sim. so most EVV) or the incense shovel ("censer" [KJV, RV]). The LXX uses this word to refer to the censer (e.g., Ezek 8:11; 2 Chr 26:17), but a censer is not included in the Exodus description of the tabernacle. Moreover, the LXX does not use this word to refer to the incense altar, although other Jewish lit. does (see Attridge 234; Koester 395). If, however, the incense altar is intended (as is likely), another problem occurs because the Exodus account does not clearly locate this altar in the inner chamber (Exod 30:1–10; cf. 40:18–29); the wording "in front of the curtain" (v. 6) is ambiguous. In Solomon's temple, the altar was inside the inner chamber (1 Kgs 6:20). This apparent discrepancy accounts for the var. rdgs. (Metzger 598). (See esp. Attridge 236–38; cf. Cockerill 375–77; Ellingworth 425–27; Koester 401–5; Harold S. Camacho, "The Altar of Incense in Hebrews 9:3–4," *AUSS* 24 [1986]: 5–12.)

ἐν ᾗ στάμνος χρυσῆ ἔχουσα τὸ μάννα καὶ ἡ ῥάβδος Ἀαρὼν ἡ βλαστήσασα καὶ αἱ πλάκες τῆς διαθήκης,
in which was a gold jar containing the manna, Aaron's staff that budded, and the tablets of the covenant.

The antecedent of ᾗ is the elliptically understood σκηνή. Ἐν is locat. A vb. is implied (e.g., ἦν). Ἔχουσα here means "contains" (so most EVV). Στάμνος is the nom. sg. fem. of στάμνος, -ου, ἡ, "jar" (BDAG 940b; BGk. hapax); the -ος ending with the fem. is an Attic form (R 253). Στάμνος is modified by χρυσῆ (χρυσοῦς, -ῆ, -οῦν, "golden"). Μάννα is the nom. sg. neut.; the word is transliterated from the Heb. and is indecl. Ῥάβδος is the nom. sg. fem (-ου, ἡ, "staff"). Ἀαρών is indecl.; its gen. function (poss.) is inferred from the context. Βλαστήσασα is the nom. sg. fem. of the aor. act. ptc. of βλαστάνω, "bud" (ESV, NASB, NET, NIV), "sprout" (CEV, NLT; BDAG 177d). The rep. of the art. and the placement of the adj. are emph. (Ellingworth 402; 2nd attrib. pos.; see Wallace 306–7). Πλάκες is the nom. pl. fem. of πλάξ, πλακός, ἡ, "tablet" (BDAG 822d). The gen. διαθήκης ("covenant") is descriptive. The καί́s are connective.

The description in Hebrews offers details that are unattested in the OT. The jar containing the manna (Exod 16:33) is not described as golden, although it is so described in LXX Exod 16:33. Additionally, the Exodus account does not specify that the jar and Aaron's staff were in the ark but rather before the Lord's presence (the manna; Exod 16:32–34) and before the ark (Aaron's staff; Num 17:10–11). The author may have been following a rabbinic tradition that located these items within the ark (Lane 2:221).

VERSE 5

ὑπεράνω δὲ αὐτῆς Χερουβὶν δόξης κατασκιάζοντα τὸ ἱλαστήριον·
The cherubim of glory were above the ark overshadowing the mercy seat.

Δέ adds the final item in the tabernacle description. The compound prep. ὑπεράνω (ὑπέρ + ἀνῶ) retains the original sense of ὑπέρ as "above something or someone, without actual contact"; the compound is a NT hapax (Harris 207; R 629; BDF §245; R 517). The antecedent of αὐτῆς is στάμνος. A form of εἰμί is implied (e.g., ἦν), the subj. of which is Χερουβίν ("cherubim" [most EVV], "winged creature" [BDAG 1084a]; E. Lohse, *TDNT* 9:438–39). Χερουβίν is transliterated from the Heb. (neut., indecl.). Τῆς δόξης is a descriptive gen. ("cherubim of glory" [so most EVV]; cf. Wallace 79–81) rather than an attrib. one ("the glorious winged creatures" [*pace* NJB]). The cherubim are described in Exod 25:18–22 (cf. 37:7–9).

Κατασκιάζοντα is the nom. pl. neut. of the pres. act. ptc. of κατασκιάζω, "overshadow" (most EVV; BDAG 527b; BGk. hapax). The ptc. adj. modifies Χερουβίν. Ἱλαστήριον is the acc. sg. neut. of ἱλαστήριον, -ου, τό, "place of expiation" (NAB) or "place of propitiation" (REB; BDAG 474b; R 154), or "mercy seat" [most EVV; BDAG 474c]). This is "the earthly counterpart of the '[heavenly] throne of grace'" (Bruce 204). The "mercy seat" refers to the lid of the ark (Exod 25:22; Num 7:89), in front of which the high priest was to sprinkle blood on the Day of Atonement (Lev 16:14; Koester 396). The placement of τὸ ἱλαστήριον is emph. and anticipates the focus on the Day of Atonement in vv. 6–10 (Attridge 238). (See Felix H. Cortez, "From the Holy to the Most Holy Place: The Period of Hebrews 9:6–10 and the Day of Atonement as a Metaphor of Transition," *JBL* 125 [2006]: 527–547; David P. Wright, *ABD* 2:72–76.)

περὶ ὧν οὐκ ἔστιν νῦν λέγειν κατὰ μέρος.
It is not possible to speak about these things in detail right now.

Περί with the gen. indicates "about," or "concerning." The antecedent of ὧν is the preceding description of the earthly tabernacle ("concerning these things"). The cstr. οὐκ ἔστιν here means "not possible" (CSB). Λέγειν complements ὧν (Wallace 598–99). Νῦν "implies 'at this stage in the argument'" (Ellingworth 431). Κατὰ μέρος means "in detail" (Moule 60) and adv. modifies the inf. (R 550). This expression signals both an abrupt end to the description of the tabernacle as well a shift to a new topic, which is taken up in vv. 6–10 (Lane 2:217, 221). Unlike Philo and Josephus, the author does not find allegorical significance in the contents or arrangement of the tabernacle (see Koester 401–02).

VERSE 6

Τούτων δὲ οὕτως κατεσκευασμένων εἰς μὲν τὴν πρώτην σκηνὴν
With these things prepared like this . . . the first room

Δέ indicates a transition in the argument (Ellingworth 433). The antecedent of τούτων is the description of the earthly tabernacle ("these things"; cf. ὧν in v. 5). Κατεσκευασμένων is the gen. pl. neut. of the pf. pass. ptc. of κατασκευάζω (see v. 2); the use of this vb. in v. 2 and v. 6 forms an *inclusio*. The pf. is intensive (Wallace 574; Campbell, *VA* 201). The gen. abs. (see comments on 2:4) summarizes vv. 1–5 and shifts the focus to regulations for worship in vv. 6–10, which comprise one sentence in the Gk. (a periodic sentence [BDF §464]). The subj. of the vb. is τούτων. The adv. οὕτως ("in this way") modifies the ptc. The postpos. correl. μέν in v. 6 is matched by δέ in v. 7; note the par. prep. phrases: εἰς μὲν . . . εἰς δέ; εἰς is spatial. The obj. of the prep. is σκηνή (see v. 2), which is modified by πρώτη (see v. 1). Ἡ σκηνὴ πρώτη refers to the outer chamber of the tabernacle.

διὰ παντὸς εἰσίασιν οἱ ἱερεῖς τὰς λατρείας ἐπιτελοῦντες,
the priests enter . . . repeatedly, performing their ministry.

Εἰσίασιν is the 3rd pl. pres. act. indic. of εἴσειμι, "enter" (most EVV). This vb. is rare in the NT, but was used of the high priest in the LXX. The author uses εἰσέρχομαι in conj. with Christ (Cockerill 379 n. 39) rather than εἴσειμι. The subj. of the vb. is ἱερεῖς ("priests"). Ἐπιτελοῦντες is the nom. pl. masc. of the pres. act. ptc. of ἐπιτελέω, "complete," "perform" (BDAG 383c–d). The ptc. indicates purpose ("to carry on their ministry" [NIV]) or is circum. ("as they perform their duties" [NET]). Λατρείας (see v. 1) is the obj. of the ptc. Διὰ παντός means "regularly" (ESV, NIV, NLT), "continually" (NASB, NET), "always," "constantly," and adv. modifies the ptc. It underscores the rep. of the priestly service (cf. Attridge 238; Cockerill 379) and intentionally contrasts with ἅπαξ τοῦ ἐνιαυτοῦ in the next v. The LXX uses διὰ παντός in conj. with the priests' daily duties (Koester 396). As before, the author uses the pres. tense with the Levitical priests (see comments on 8:3), which stresses the iterative nature of the priestly work (Cockerill 379). The (regular) priests' service included daily trimming the lamps and offerings, and weekly replacing the loaves, all of which took place in the outer ("first") chamber (Exod 27:20–21; 29:38–43; Lev 24:8–9).

VERSE 7

εἰς δὲ τὴν δευτέραν ἅπαξ τοῦ ἐνιαυτοῦ μόνος ὁ ἀρχιερεύς,
But the high priest alone enters the second room,

Δέ continues the description of the priestly service and correlates with μέν in v. 6. Ἐνιαυτοῦ is the gen. sg. masc. of ἐνιαυτός, -οῦ, ὁ, "year." The adv. prep. (R 637) ἅπαξ, "once" (BDAG 97b) is temp. (R 769; Exod 30:10; Lev 16:34). The gen. indicates the time within which an event occurs (BDF §186[2]). The art. has a distributive sense (BDF §252)—"once every year." Although the high priest entered the inner chamber twice on the Day of Atonement, entrance was limited to that one day (see Leviticus 16). The adj. μόνος occurs in the pred. pos., modifying ὁ ἀρχιερεύς (R 776), offering another contrast with the regular priests (see esp. Ellingworth 432; see comments on 2:17).

οὐ χωρὶς αἵματος ὃ προσφέρει ὑπὲρ ἑαυτοῦ καὶ τῶν τοῦ λαοῦ ἀγνοημάτων,
and he does that only once a year, and never without blood, which he offers for himself and for the sins the people had committed in ignorance.

Χωρίς ("without") takes a gen. obj. (αἵματος). The cstr. is an example of litotes (a double neg. indicating a strong pos. [Ellingworth 434]), which emphasizes the importance of the blood offering (Attridge 239). The antecedent of ὅ is αἵματος. Ὁ ἀρχιερεύς is the subj. of προσφέρει ("offer"; see comments on 5:1). The pres. is customary or habitual (Wallace 521). The rest of this v. recalls 5:2–3, where nearly identical phrasing occurs (see comments there; cf. 7:27). The switch from περί in 5:2–3 to ὑπέρ in this v. is apparently stylistic (Ellingworth 436). Whereas the vbs. ῥαίνω ("sprinkle") and ἐπιτίθημι ("apply") are freq. in the LXX, the author makes a "striking" and unprecedented change to προσφέρω, which is subsequently used of Christ's sacrificial death, thereby suggesting a "typological parallel between the high point of the atonement ritual under the old covenant and the self-offering of Christ on the cross" (Lane 2:223; cf. Cockerill 380 n. 42).

Ὑπέρ with the gen. means "on behalf of" (Harris 209). The first obj. of the prep. is the refl. pron. ἑαυτοῦ, referring to the high priest. The second obj. is λαοῦ, which is modified by ἀγνοημάτων (gen. pl. neut. of ἀγνόημα, -ατος, τό "[sin committed] in ignorance"; most EVV; cf. ἀγνοέω in 5:2; BDAG 13b; cf. "inadvertent" REB; "unintentional" [ESV; BDAG 13b]). This v. alludes to Lev 4:2, 13, 22, 27; Num 15:27–29, although the Day of Atonement sacrifices were not limited to sins of ignorance. This discrepancy is debated: the author may have considered ἀγνόημα and ἁμαρτία as nearly synonymous (cf. Koester 397; but see Ellingworth 435), drawn on Jewish tradition (Attridge 239), or *deliberately conflated aspects of the old order to underscore its limitations (cf. Cockerill 380 n. 43; Ellingworth 436).

The offering for the high priest was a bull (Lev 16:2, 3); a goat was offered for the people (Lev 16:6–17). The author does not mention the required scapegoat in Leviticus 16. The focus here is on the limited access to the holy of holies (only one person; only once a year), the limited effect of the offering (repeated every year), and the limited nature of the high priest (who had to offer for his own sins and could not enter the holy of holies without sacrificial blood; cf. Bruce 208). The ref. to blood anticipates the focus on Christ's blood in the rest of Hebrews 9.

VERSE 8

τοῦτο δηλοῦντος τοῦ πνεύματος τοῦ ἁγίου,
The Holy Spirit was making it clear

Δηλοῦντος is the gen. sg. neut. of the pres. act. ptc. of δηλόω, "show" (NIV), "make clear" (NET), "indicate" (ESV), "signify" (NASB), "explain," "clarify" (BDAG 222d). The subj. of the ptc. is τοῦ πνεύματος τοῦ ἁγίου. The author uses a gen. abs. cstr. (see comments on 2:4) to introduce the indir. discourse in the rest of the v. Attridge notes the connection between the Holy Spirit, Scripture, and contemporary significance ("today") that is also present in 3:7 (Attridge 240; Koester 397). Thus the Spirit reveals limitations that were inherent in the OT itself (Cockerill 381 n. 45). The pres. likely indicates the ongoing relevance of the Spirit's explanation. Τοῦτο (acc. sg. neut.)

is the obj. of the ptc. It "points forward" to the inf. clause in the next part of the v. (*pace* Ellingworth 437).

μήπω πεφανερῶσθαι τὴν τῶν ἁγίων ὁδὸν ἔτι τῆς πρώτης σκηνῆς ἐχούσης στάσιν,
that the way into the most holy place had not yet been disclosed while the first tabernacle was still standing.

Πεφανερῶσθαι is the pf. pass. inf. of φανερόω, "reveal," "disclose" (NASB, NIV), "appear" (NET). The pf. is likely emph. (e.g., "intensified," Campbell, *VA* 201). The adv. μήπω ("not yet") modifies the inf. and implies "a contrast of time," thus anticipating Christ's sacrifice in v. 11 (Ellingworth 437). The "subj." of the inf. (see R 1039–40) is ὁδόν, which is modified by τῶν ἁγίων as a gen. of "direction" (BDF §166). The referent of ἁγίων is clearly the heavenly sanctuary (Cockerill 381). The ptc. ἐχούσης modifies σκηνῆς ("tent"; see v. 2), which is also modified by πρώτης ("first"; see v. 1).

Στάσιν is the acc. sg. fem. of στάσις, -ατος, τό, "existence," "occurrence" (BDAG 940c; G. Delling, *TDNT* 7:568–71). It is the obj. of the ptc. The adv. ἔτι ("still," "yet") modifies the ptc. The entire inf. clause (μήπω . . . στάσιν) is in appos. to τοῦτο as the content of the Holy Spirit's disclosure (R 700). The precise meaning of ἐχούσης is debated. "Having its existence" or "still standing" (most EVV) could suggest the mere physical existence of the tabernacle (with no indication of whether the Herodian temple was still standing when Hebrews was written). Alternatively, and more likely, given the author's concern with the significance of the tabernacle, the meaning is something like retaining "its normative status" (Attridge 240; cf. Bruce 206 n. 48; Lane 2:216 n. *t*), which was lost when Christ passed through the heavenlies to the heavenly sanctuary (Bruce 206 n. 48; cf. Koester 397). There are two main options for understanding the referent of ἡ πρώτη σκηνή, either as the outer chamber of the tabernacle or as the tabernacle as a whole (see discussion on v. 10).

VERSE 9

ἥτις παραβολὴ εἰς τὸν καιρὸν τὸν ἐνεστηκότα,
This is a symbol for the present time,

The antecedent of ἥτις is ἡ πρώτη σκηνή, i.e., the outer chamber (Attridge 241; Lane 2:224) and not the tabernacle as a whole (*pace* Bruce 195 n. 60; Ellingworth 439). This coheres with the focus on the outer chamber in the previous v. Παραβολή (BDAG 759b; C. Haufe, *EDNT* 3:15d) can indicate a "parable," although the meaning "symbol" fits the context better (so most EVV). It is "a rhetorical figure of speech involving a comparison" (Ellingworth 440; cf. "illustration" [NIV, NLT]; the parentheses in the ESV obscure this). (See Steve Stanley, "Hebrews 9:6–10: The 'Parable' of the Tabernacle," *NovT 37* [1995]: 385–99.) Εἰς indicates "an extension in time," "to," "until" (BDAG 289d). Ἐνεστηκότα is the acc. sg. masc. of the pf. act. ptc. of ἐνίστημι, "be now," "happen now" (BDAG 337b). The ptc. modifies καιρόν ("present time" [most EVV]; *pace* "the time then present" [KJV, NET]; see discussion on v. 10).

καθ' ἣν δῶρά τε καὶ θυσίαι προσφέρονται μὴ δυνάμεναι κατὰ συνείδησιν τελειῶσαι τὸν λατρεύοντα,
during which gifts and sacrifices are offered that cannot perfect the worshiper's conscience.

Καθ' ἥν means "in accordance with which" (Moule 59; καθ' appears before rough breathing). There are two options for the antecedent of the indef. rel. pron. Either ἥν (together with ἥτις) refers to τῆς πρώτης σκηνῆς in v. 8 (Cockerill 393; Lane 2:223–24) or παραβολή (Bruce 206 n. 49; Attridge 242). The first option coheres better with the argument, although the difference between the options is not significant (Koester 398). On both views, the "first tent" is a symbol that reveals the most significant limitation of the old order, which was its inability to "perfect" the worshiper's conscience. (On the overlap with the indef. rel. pron. and rel. pron., see comments on v. 2.)

Προσφέρονται is the 3rd pl. pres. pass. indic. of προσφέρω, "offer" (see comments on 5:1). The expression δῶρά τε καὶ θυσίαι is the subj. of the vb. (see comments on 5:2), with the Levitical priests understood as the agents of the pass. vb. Δυνάμεναι is the nom. pl. fem. of the pres. mid. ptc. of δύναμαι, here with "the strong sense of 'have the power to'" (Ellingworth 442). The adj. ptc. modifies both δῶρά and θυσίαι. Τελειῶσαι (aor. act. inf. of τελειόω, "perfect," so most EVV; see comments on 2:10) complements the ptc. δυνάμεναι. The aor. is global. The obj. of the inf. is the subst. λατρεύοντα (acc. sg. masc. of the pres. act. ptc. of λατρεύω, "serve" [BDAG 587c]). This term includes both the high priest and priests, but it likely extends more broadly to worshippers (cf. Attridge 242; Ellingworth 441; Koester 399). Κατά indicates "with ref. to" (BDAG 513b–c). Its obj. is συνείδησιν (συνείδησις, -εως, ἡ, "moral consciousness," "conscience" [BDAG 976d–968a). This word is rare in the LXX, but was more common in contemp. Hellenistic literature. It indicates both the faculty for and the awareness of sin, morality, and ultimately holiness; it is used esp. in Pauline epistles (Attridge 242; cf. Ellingworth 442; Lane 2:240–41). See For Further Study 55 (Conscience in the NT).

The concept of perfection in Hebrews is significant (see comments on 2:10). In the context of worship, perfection focuses on the worshipper and access to God, which cannot be realized until the conscience is fully cleansed—something that was not possible in the old order (cf. Lane 2:224). See For Further Study 18 (Perfection in Hebrews).

VERSE 10

μόνον ἐπὶ βρώμασιν καὶ πόμασιν καὶ διαφόροις βαπτισμοῖς,
They are physical regulations and only deal with food, drink, and various washings

This v. introduces a parenthetical aside (R 413), in which a vb. implied (e.g., "they are" [most EVV]). The placement of μόνον is emph. (Cockerill 385). This clause is in appos. to δικαιώματα σαρκός. 'Επί may mean "on the basis of" (BDF §235[2]), although that meaning would be unclear. More likely it is something like "a matter of"

(NIV), "deals with" (ESV, NLT; cf. BDAG 365b). The regulations under the old order were not able to perfect the conscience but only concerned externals, such as dietary and purification rituals (cf. Cockerill 385 nos. 65–66). Βρώμασιν is the dat. pl. neut. of βρῶμα, -ατος, τό, "food" (BDAG 184b). Πόμασιν is the dat. pl. neut. of πόμα, -ατος, τό, "drink" (BDAG 850c). Here the adj. διαφόροις (dat. pl. masc. of διάφορος, -ον) means "various" or "diverse" (unlike the comp. form used in 1:4 and 8:6). It modifies βαπτισμοῖς (dat. pl. masc. of βαπτισμός, -οῦ, ὁ), which refers to ceremonial washing (ablutions), not baptisms (see comments on 6:2).

δικαιώματα σαρκὸς μέχρι καιροῦ διορθώσεως ἐπικείμενα.
physical regulations . . . imposed until the time of the new order.

The rep. of δικαιώματα (nom. pl. neut.) from v. 1 (see comments there) forms an *inclusio*. The gen. σαρκός indicates ref., and contrasts with συνείδησις in v. 9. The meaning is thus "for the body" ([ESV, NASB], "physical" [NLT], or "external" [NET, NIV]). The expression δικαιώματα σαρκός summarizes δῶρά τε καὶ θυσίαι in v. 9 (cf. R 413). The prep. μέχρι ("until") is followed by the gen. (καιροῦ). Διορθώσεως is the gen. sg. fem. of διόρθωσις, -εως, ἡ, "reformation" (ESV, NASB), "new order" (most EVV); BDAG 251b; H. Preisker, *TDNT* 5:450; BGk. hapax). The gen. is descriptive, modifying καιροῦ. This expression is unique in BGk. Nonbiblical sources use the word in conj. with legal reforms, building reconstruction, or account rectification (Attridge 243; Ellingworth 444; see discussion below). Ἐπικείμενα is the nom. pl. neut. of the pres. pass. ptc. of ἐπίκειμαι, "be imposed" (ESV, NASB, NET; BDAG 373d; cf. "applying" [NIV], "were in effect" [NLT]). The pass is a divine pass. The ptc. modifies δικαιώματα.

Whereas the previous discussion focused on the Day of Atonement (esp. Leviticus 16), this v. focuses on other priestly regulations. The terms used in Hebrews are not used in the LXX, but Leviticus 11 and Numbers 15 may be generally in view. The logic is that if the Day of Atonement is not effective, then certainly other (lesser) regulations are not either (Ellingworth 442–43).

There are two main options for understanding ἡ πρώτη σκηνή, παραβολή, εἰς τὸν καιρὸν τὸν ἐνεστηκότα, and μέχρι καιροῦ διορθώσεως ἐπικείμενα.

*1. Ἡ πρώτη σκηνή refers to the outer chamber of the tabernacle in vv. 8–10, just as it does in 9:2 (Lane 2:216 n. *s*). The "symbol" of v. 8 is that the outer chamber symbolizes the entire earthly cultic system, and the inner chamber (the holy of holies) symbolizes the heavenly sanctuary (cf. Ellingworth 437). The inner chamber represents complete access to God, which was extremely limited and incomplete under the old covenant, with priestly activity largely restricted to the outer chamber (Attridge 241). As long as the outer chamber and former covenant are "in force," access to the inner chamber (the heavenly sanctuary) is barred (Lane 2:224; cf. Attridge 240, Koester 397). The outer chamber points toward the pres. time, when Christ has come, which explicitly reveals the limitations of the old order (Attridge 241). On this view, the pres. time and "the time of correction" are either synonymous (Attridge 241) or (better) overlapping (Koester 398), sim. to the overlap between the pres. time and the "age to come" (Attridge 241–42; Ellingworth 441; Koester 398; but see Cockerill 384 n. 60).

2. Ἡ πρώτη σκηνή refers to the earthly tabernacle as a whole in vv. 8–10. On this view, the Spirit shows that as long as the cultic system associated with the first covenant is operational, then access to the heavenly sanctuary is not possible. This would move from a spatial understanding to a temp. one, beginning with the first (Mosaic) tabernacle as a whole (and perhaps by extension, subsequent temples, culminating with Herod's temple; Bruce 208; *pace* Ellingworth 438–39). The way to the true (heavenly) holy of holies cannot be revealed as long as the earthly tabernacle is still operational (i.e., still standing). The pres. age thus aligns with the old order and contrasts with "the time of reformation." The limitation of this view, however, is the "first tent" as the earthly sanctuary implies that it precedes the "second," heavenly one, after which the earthly was patterned, which clearly cannot be the case (Cockerill 382). This discussion has been understood variously whether Hebrews was composed before or after the destruction of the temple in AD 70.

FOR FURTHER STUDY

54. The Date of Hebrews (9:1–10)

Cockerill, 34–41.
Ellingworth, 29–33.
Lane, 1:*lx–lxvi.*
*Porter, Stanley E. "The Date of the Composition of Hebrews and Use of the Present Tense-Form." Pages 295–313 in *Crossing the Boundaries: Essays in Biblical Interpretation in Honour of Michael D Goulder*. Edited by Michael D. Goulder. Leiden: Brill, 1994.
*Walker, Peter. "Jerusalem in Hebrews 13:9–14 and the Dating of the Epistle." *TynBul* 45 (1994): 39–71.

55. Conscience in the NT (9:9)

Kugler, Robert. *NIDB* 1:717–27.
Lüdemann, G., *EDNT* 3:301b–303a.
Maurer, C. *TDNT* 7:898–919.
McCarthney, D. G. *DLNT* 241–43.
Pierce, Claude Anthony. *Conscience in the New Testament: A Study of Syneidēsis in the New Testament in the Light of Its Sources*. Naperville, IL: Allenson, 1955.
*Selby, G. S. "The Meaning and Function of *Syneidesis* in Hebrews 9 and 10." *ResQ* 28 (1985–86): 145–54.
Wall, Robert W. *ABD* 1:1128–30.

HOMILETICAL SUGGESTIONS

The Earthly Tabernacle (9:1–10)

1. Had Its Own Regulations for Ministry (v. 1)
2. Had a Specific Setup (vv. 2–3)
   (a) In the first room (the holy place): lampstand, table, loaves of presentation (v. 2)
   (b) In the second room (the holy of holies): golden altar, golden ark (v. 3)
      (1) Inside the ark: golden manna jar, Aaron's staff, covenant tablets (v. 4)
      (2) Over the ark: the cherubim of glory (v. 5)
3. The Ministers of the Earthly Tabernacle (vv. 6–7)
   (a) The (regular) priests minister in the first (outer) room (v. 6)
   (b) Only the high priest ministers in the second (inner) room (v. 7)
      (1) Only once a year (v. 7a)
      (2) Offering blood for himself and the people (v. 7b)
4. The Significance of the Earthly Tabernacle (vv. 8–10)
   (a) Its presence was not the ultimate reality (v. 8)
   (b) Its presence was a symbol for present realities (v. 9)
   (c) Its ministry only pertained to physical regulations (v. 10)

2. The Eternal Redemption of the Son (9:11–14)

STRUCTURE

The chiastic structure in vv. 11–12 is noted by many (Lane 2:237; Ellingworth 451; Koester 407). Clauses A/A′ state positively how Christ approached the heavenly sanctuary; clauses B/B′ contrast this approach with the heavenly sanctuary (cf. Lane 2:237):

A διὰ τῆς μείζονος καὶ τελειοτέρας σκηνῆς
B οὐ χειροποιήτου, τοῦτ ' ἔστιν οὐ ταύτης τῆς κτίσεως,
B′ οὐδὲ δι ' αἵματος τράγων καὶ μόσχων
A′ διὰ δὲ τοῦ ἰδίου αἵματος (v. 11b–12a)

Syntactically, the sentence in vv. 11–12 begins with the subj. (Χριστὸς) in v. 11 of the vb. in v. 12. (εἰσῆλθεν). The statements preceding the vb. begin the contrast between what animal blood could accomplish and what the superior blood of Christ actually accomplished. The cond. in v. 13. introduces an *a fortiori* argument that extends through v. 14.

11 Χριστὸς δὲ
παραγενόμενος ἀρχιερεὺς τῶν γενομένων ἀγαθῶν
διὰ τῆς μείζονος καὶ τελειοτέρας σκηνῆς
οὐ χειροποιήτου,
τοῦτ' ἔστιν οὐ ταύτης τῆς κτίσεως,
12 οὐδὲ δι' αἵματος τράγων καὶ μόσχων
διὰ δὲ τοῦ ἰδίου αἵματος
εἰσῆλθεν ἐφάπαξ
εἰς τὰ ἅγια
αἰωνίαν λύτρωσιν εὑράμενος.
13 εἰ γὰρ τὸ αἷμα τράγων καὶ ταύρων καὶ σποδὸς δαμάλεως
ῥαντίζουσα
τοὺς κεκοινωμένους ἁγιάζει
πρὸς τὴν τῆς σαρκὸς καθαρότητα,
14 πόσῳ μᾶλλον τὸ αἷμα τοῦ Χριστοῦ,
ὃς διὰ πνεύματος αἰωνίου ἑαυτὸν προσήνεγκεν ἄμωμον τῷ θεῷ,
καθαριεῖ τὴν συνείδησιν ἡμῶν
ἀπὸ νεκρῶν ἔργων
εἰς τὸ λατρεύειν θεῷ ζῶντι.

VERSE 11

Χριστὸς δὲ παραγενόμενος ἀρχιερεὺς τῶν γενομένων ἀγαθῶν
But Christ has appeared as a high priest of the good things that have come.

Δέ likely correlates with *μέν* in Heb 9:1 (Lane 2:229 n. *a*), indicating the contrast between the earthly sanctuary (vv. 1–10) and the heavenly one (vv. 11–22); "but" in most EVV. It highlights the "sharp contrast" between what the old order could not do, but which Christ has done, and signals the shift in focus to sacrifice (Cockerill 387). The initial position of Χριστός (beginning both a sentence and section) is unique in Hebrews—"the effect is strongly emphatic" (Ellingworth 448). Moreover, the juxtaposition of *μέχρι καιροῦ διορθώσεως* in v. 10 and Χριστός in v. 11 indicates that the "time of correction" has arrived in Christ (cf. Lane 2:236).

Παραγενόμενος is the nom. sg. masc. of the aor. mid. ptc. of *παραγίνομαι*, "came" [NIV]; "appeared" [ESV; cf. BDAG 760d; H. Balz, *EDNT* 3:17b]). The vb. suggests "an official public appearance" (Ellingworth 449; cf. "Christ has made his appearance" [Cassirer]). The ptc. temp. modifies *εἰσῆλθεν* in v. 12 (e.g., "when Christ came" [NIV]). Alternatively, the ptc. could be coordinate to the main vb., functioning par. to a finite vb. (Cockerill 389; cf. "attendant circumstance ptc." [Wallace 640–44]). This is indicated in many EVV (e.g., CEV, NET, NLT) by translating the ptc. as a finite vb. This word recalls the cognate *γενόμενος*, used in conj. with the Son "becoming" high priest (6:20; 7:26; cf. 1:4; Attridge 245 n. 8). Ἀρχιερεύς is the complement of the ptc. and an appos. of Χριστὸς. (For *ἀρχιερεύς*, see comments on 2:17.)

The ptc. *γενομένων* adj. modifies *ἀγαθῶν* (gen. pl. neut.). The aor. is inceptive (Lane 2:229 n. *b*). The "good things" are associated with the new covenant. The use of *μέλλω* earlier in Heb (1:14; 2:5; 6:5) and its use in 10:1 (and 13:14) likely explain the var. rdg. of *μελλόντων* (supported by important mss.; adopted by the KJV, NJB, NASB, NET) as an attempt to conform to these vv. (Metzger 598; Lane 2:229 n. *b*). Yet the focus here is on what has already begun with Christ (Lane 2:236). Moreover, *γενομένων* has earlier and more widespread witnesses (e.g., 𝔓[46] B D* 1739; Metzger 598; so most EVV; e.g., "good things that are now already here" [NIV]).

διὰ τῆς μείζονος καὶ τελειοτέρας σκηνῆς οὐ χειροποιήτου,
In the greater and more perfect tabernacle not made with hands

Διά occurs three times in vv. 11–12. The occurrences in v. 12 are instr. That meaning in this v. is less likely (*pace* Koester 408–9), where a spatial understanding ("through") fits well with the image of Jesus passing through the heavens (4:14; cf. 6:20) and contrasts with the high priest passing through the tabernacle's second curtain (albeit in a very limited way; cf. Attridge 245–46; Ellingworth 450–51; Lane 2:237–38). (On the same prep. having different meanings in the same sentence, see Harris 41–43.) Understanding *διά* as instr. in this v. often requires that the "greater and more perfect tabernacle" be understood metaphorically, perhaps as the incarnate body of Christ, his resurrected body, or even the church (for more options and the long history of interpretation of this v., see Attridge 246–47; Koester 409; Lane 2:236–37).

The subst. *σκηνῆς* (see comments on 8:2) is modified by the comp. *μείζονος* (from *μέγας, μεγάλη, μέγα*, "greater" [BDAG 624c]) and *τελειοτέρας* (from *τέλειος, -α, -ον*, "perfect"; BDAG 995c). The use of *μείζονος* pars. the prevalent use of *κρείττων* in Hebrews (see comments on 1:4). The use of *τελειοτέρας* contributes to the emph. in

Hebrews on "perfection" (see comments on 2:10). Σκηνῆς is further modified by the negated adj. χειροποιήτου (χειροποιήτος, -ον, "made by human hands" [BDAG 1083c]; E. Lohse, *TDNT* 9:436–37). This same negated adj. occurs in Mark 14:58 and Acts 7:48; 17:24 (cf. John 2:19–22), with the same meaning, and will occur again in 9:24. The unnegated form is "always pejorative" in BGk., and is often used to describe idols (Ellingworth 451). This v. contrasts with the earthly tabernacle in 9:1, but develops the idea introduced in 8:2.

This v. touches on the question of cosmology in Hebrews. Debated is whether the author understands levels or divisions of the heavens as analogous to the sections of the earthly tabernacle or *if he understands the greater and more perfect tabernacle to refer to the heavenly sanctuary as a whole (see esp. Ellingworth 446–48). See also For Further Study 14 (Cosmology in Hebrews).

τοῦτ' ἔστιν οὐ ταύτης τῆς κτίσεως,
(that is, not of this creation),

The expression τοῦτ' ἔστιν (see comments on 2:14) is epex., further explaining the tabernacle not made with human hands. The dem. ταύτης modifies κτίσεως (gen. sg. fem. of κτίσις, -εως, ἡ, "creation" [most EVV]; "creature" [BDAG 573a]) in pred. pos. The transience of creation has already been established in Heb 1:10–12 (cf. 12:27).

VERSE 12

οὐδὲ δι' αἵματος τράγων καὶ μόσχων διὰ δὲ τοῦ ἰδίου αἵματος
. . . not by the blood of goats and calves, but by his own blood,

The neg. conj. οὐδέ (οὐ + δέ) continues the contrast between Christ and the Levitical high priest (Ellingworth 405). Τράγων is the gen. pl. masc. of τράγος, -ου, ὁ, "he-goat" (BDAG 1013a). Μόσχων is the gen. pl. masc. of μόσχος, -ου, ὁ, "calf, young bull" (BDAG 660a). Both gen. are descriptive, modifying αἵματος. The pls. are generalizing (Bruce 213 n. 9). Δέ makes explicit the contrast between animal blood and Christ's own (ἰδίου) blood. Once again, the author alludes to the Day of Atonement sacrifices in Leviticus 16. *Sacrificial* blood could cleanse (perhaps because life is in the blood [e.g., Lev 17:11]; cf. Cockerill 393; Ellingworth 454), whereas blood "lost through violent death or menstruation" defiled (Koester 415). Although the high priest took actual animal blood into the holy of holies, the author is not suggesting that Christ carried his own blood into the heavenly tabernacle (so most commentators, many of whom note NJB's misleading translation "taking with him . . . his own blood"). Instead, both occurrences of διά (δι' before a vowel) are instr. (see esp. Harris 119–20). Thus Jesus's blood shed on the cross is the means by which he has entered the heavenly tabernacle (so most commentators). Less likely, the blood could refer to the *life* that Christ offers in the heavenly sanctuary. It is possible that the author intends an element of both since Christ's blood cannot be separated from his life, all of which was offered on the cross (cf. Ellingworth 456). What is key is that Christ's perfect atonement depends on his own blood, and not that of animals. Only Christ's blood signifies a *substitutionary* death (see v. 28). See For Further Study 57 (Blood in Hebrews).

εἰσῆλθεν ἐφάπαξ εἰς τὰ ἅγια αἰωνίαν λύτρωσιν εὑράμενος.
he entered the most holy place once for all time, . . . having obtained eternal redemption.

The subj. of εἰσῆλθεν is Christ. The adv. ἐφάπαξ, "once for all," recalls 7:27 (see comments there), where it contrasted the sg. offering of Christ with the high priests' repeated offerings. Here it contrasts Christ's definitive entrance into the heavenly sanctuary with the high priests' restricted entrance into the holy of holies. Εἰς is spatial. Unlike 9:2, τὰ ἅγια here refers to the sanctuary as a whole ("the most holy place" [most EVV]). (See A. P. Salom, "*Ta hagia* in the Epistle to the Hebrews," *AUSS* 5 [1967]: 59–70.) Εὑράμενος is the nom. sg. masc. of the aor. mid. ptc. of εὑρίσκω, "obtaining" [or sim.; many EVV]). The mid. is an "indirect mid.," in which the subj. acts for himself or herself ("he himself" [NET]; R 809; Wallace 421). Here the vb. has a "strong meaning": "secured" (e.g., NET; Ellingworth 452). The obj. of the ptc. is λύτρωσιν (λύτρωσις, -εως, ἡ, "redemption" [most EVV], but also "ransoming," "release" [BDAG 606b]), which is modified by the adj. αἰωνίος, -ον, "eternal" (cf. 5:9). This word appears only here and in Luke 1:68 and 2:38, perhaps due to LXX influence (*NIDNTTE* 3:185); the more common form is ἀπολύτρωσις. Λύτρωσις indicates both "deliverance from bondage" and "forgiveness of sin" (Koester 408; cf. Attridge 249; Cockerill 395–96), although the concept of ransom is not stated explicitly (*NIDNTTE* 3:185).

Εὑράμενος is temp. and modifies εἰσῆλθεν . The precise temp. relationship, however, is debated.

*1. The ptc. indicates antecedent action. This is the most common temp. function for an aor. ptc., whether it precedes or follows the finite vb.: "having obtained" (most EVV; cf. Moule 100 n. 1). This view coheres well with Christ's atoning work as the basis for his exaltation to God's right hand in 1:3 (Cockerill 395). If the ptc. is understood as causal, it would align with antecedent action.
2. The ptc. indicates coincident action. This is freq. for an aor. ptc., whether it precedes or follows the finite vb.: "he entered . . . and secured our redemption" (NLT; cf. GNB, NEB, NJB; so Attridge 248–49; Ellingworth 453).
3. The ptc. indicates subsequent action: "thus obtaining" (NRSV; cf. Lane 2:230 n. *f*; but he also accepts coincident). Some challenge this function for an aor. ptc. (R 861–63).

VERSE 13

εἰ γὰρ τὸ αἷμα τράγων καὶ ταύρων καὶ σποδὸς δαμάλεως
For if the blood of goats and bulls and the ashes of a young cow,

Εἰ with an unaugmented tense (ἁγιάζει) introduces the prot. of a first-class cond., which "indicates the assumption of truth for the sake of argument" (Wallace, 690; BDF §372[1a]). Γάρ presents the grounds for vv. 11–12 (Ellingworth 454). (For τράγων, see

v. 12.) Ταύρων is the gen. pl. masc. of ταῦρος, -ου, ὁ, "bull" (BDAG 991d). Both gen. are descriptive, modifying αἷμα, which is the subj. of the prot. Σποδός is the nom. sg. fem. of σποδός, -ου, ἡ, "ashes" (BDAG 939a). Δαμάλεως is the gen. sg. fem. of δάμαλις, -εως, ἡ, "heifer, young cow" (BDAG 211d). The gen. is also descriptive. The term σποδὸς δαμάλεως alludes to Num 19:9–21.

ῥαντίζουσα τοὺς κεκοινωμένους ἁγιάζει πρὸς τὴν τῆς σαρκὸς καθαρότητα,
sprinkling those who are defiled, sanctify for the purification of the flesh,

Ῥαντίζουσα is the nom. sg. fem. of the pres. act. ptc. of ῥαντίζω, "sprinkle" (BDAG 903c; H. Balz, EDNT 3:207d–208b). Although the fem. ptc. directly modifies σποδός (circum.), the action of sprinkling is likely also connected with the blood (Ellingworth 455). Κεκοινωμένους is the acc. pl. masc. of the pf. pass. ptc. of κοινόω, "defiled" (most EVV; BDAG 552b), "ceremonially unclean" (NIV). The ptc. is subst. and is the obj. of the vb. ἁγιάζει (3rd sg. pres. act. indic. of ἁγιάζω, "sanctify" [see comments on 2:11]). Although the subst. ptc. could be the obj. of the ptc. ῥαντίζουσα, blood was not usually sprinkled on people (*pace* most EVV; but "sanctifies those who have been defiled" [NRSV]). Moreover, the absence of an obj. for ἁγιάζει would be syntactically awkward. The subj. of the sg. vb. ἁγιάζει includes both the blood and the ashes (Ellingworth 455). Πρός indicates purpose (Harris 189). The obj. of the prep. is καθαρότητα (acc. sg. fem. of καθαρότης, -ητος, ἡ, "purity" [BDAG 490a; H. Thyen, *EDNT* 2:220d; NT hapax]). There is a range of translations for the prep. phrase: "purification of the flesh" (ESV); "outwardly clean" (NIV); "provided ritual purity" (NET); "considered clean" (CEV).

The ashes of a heifer were not a part of the Day of Atonement, but rather a different purification ritual (Num 19:1–21). The ref. to bulls in v. 13 also deviates from the requisite calf for the Day of Atonement. Thus there is debate whether the author has conflated purification rituals, sin offerings, and Day of Atonement sacrifices because they collectively reveal the external inefficacy of the old order (so Cockerill 396; Lane 2:239; cf. Attridge 249), or whether he drew on rabbinic tradition that indicated that the high priest was to be sprinkled with these ashes for the seven days leading up to the Day of Atonement (Bruce 215–16).

VERSE 14

πόσῳ μᾶλλον τὸ αἷμα τοῦ Χριστοῦ,
how much more will the blood of Christ,

Μᾶλλον is the comp. of the rare adv. μάλα, "very, exceedingly" (BDAG 613d). The pron. πόσῳ together with μᾶλλον indicates an exclamation (most EVV; BDAG 855d; Ellingworth 456) or a rhetorical question (KJV, NASB). This is another (perhaps the most powerful) example of an *a fortiori* argument, which is prevalent in Hebrews (see comments on 2:3). The gen. Χριστοῦ is poss.

ὃς διὰ πνεύματος αἰωνίου ἑαυτὸν προσήνεγκεν ἄμωμον τῷ θεῷ,
who through the eternal Spirit offered himself without blemish to God,

The antecedent of ὅς is Χριστός. The rel. pron. may have a causal force, perhaps reflecting CGk. (Lane 2:230 n. *j*). The adj. *αἰωνίου* ("eternal") modifies *πνεύματος* and recalls its use in v. 12. The refl. pron. *ἑαυτόν* makes clear that the blood that Christ offered should be understood as "metonymy [for] the sacrifice as a whole" (Attridge 250).

The referent of "eternal spirit" is debated:

*1. The Holy Spirit (implied by "Spirit" in most EVV; cf. "eternal spirit which was his" [Cassirer]). The expression may be understood as periph. (cf. "Majesty" in 1:3 and 8:1 [Lane 2:230 n. *k*; cf. Ellingworth 457; Koester 410–11]). There could also be an allusion to the Spirit on the Servant in Isaiah (Bruce 217–18). The use of *αἰωνίου* may have been intended to link the Spirit's work to the "eternal redemption" (v. 12) and "eternal inheritance" (v. 15; so Ellingworth 457). The unusual expression (rated {A} by the UBS committee) accounts for the var. rdgs., where scribes "corrected" the v. to the more expected *ἁγίου* (Metzger 598–99). The anar. may emphasize "the 'eternal' quality of the Spirit" (Cockerill 398). See the extended discussion in Cockerill 397–400.
2. Christ's divine nature (for advocates of this position and evaluation, see Cockerill 398).
3. The "spiritual quality" of Christ's willing sacrifice; the expression indicates "that portion of his being that was truly himself" (Attridge 251); "an eternal and spiritual sacrifice" (CEV, NEB); cf. "the spirit of the eternal" (Moffatt).

Προσήνεγκεν is the 3rd sg. aor. act. indic. of *προσφέρω*, "offer" (see comments on 5:1). *Ἄμωμον* (acc. sg. masc. of *ἄμωμος, -ον*, "unblemished" [NIV], "blameless" [BDAG 56a]) alludes to Num 6:14; 19:2, which specifies that sacrificial animals must be without blemish. "The sinless high priest . . . was also the spotless victim" (Lane 2:240). Ellingworth suggests that it is the power of the Spirit that enabled Christ to be both high priest and sacrifice simultaneously (Ellingworth 457).

καθαριεῖ τὴν συνείδησιν ἡμῶν ἀπὸ νεκρῶν ἔργων εἰς τὸ λατρεύειν θεῷ ζῶντι.
cleanse our consciences from dead works so that we can serve the living God?

Καθαριεῖ is the 3rd sg. fut. act. indic. of *καθαρίζω*, "cleanse" (NASB, NIV), "purify" (ESV, NET, NLT; BDAG 488d–489a; H. Thyen, *EDNT* 2:220d). The unusual fut. form is Attic (R 355). The fut. could be gnomic (BDG §349[1]). Its obj. is *συνείδησιν* ("conscience"; see comments on 9:9), which deliberately contrasts *σάρξ* in v. 13 (Ellingworth 458). The textual evidence is divided between *ἡμῶν* ("our" [most EVV]) and *ὑμῶν* ("your" [KJV, NASB, RSV]). The first pers. coheres better with the prevalent use of the first pers. pl. in Hebrews (cf. Metzger 599). *Ἀπό* indicates separation (BDF §180). The adj. *νεκρῶν* modifies *ἔργων*. "Dead works" likely parallels its usage in 6:1, where it refers to sinful deeds generally ("deadness of our former ways" [REB]; "acts that lead to death" [NIV]; "sins that defile the conscience" [Attridge 252]). Λατρεύειν is the pres. act. inf. of λατρεύω, "serve" (most EVV; see comments on 8:5). Εἰς τό + inf. indicates purpose (Wallace 591; BDF §404[3]). The dat. following λατρεύω indicates the one who is served (BDAG 587c), here θεῷ, who is further described as ζῶντι, "living" (dat. sg. masc. of the pres. act. ptc. of ζάω). The idea of the "living God" is prevalent in Hebrews; cf. 3:12 and 10:31.

FOR FURTHER STUDY

56. Atonement (9:11–14)

Green, Joel B. *NIDB* 1:344–48.
Hughes, Philip E. "The Blood of Jesus and His Heavenly Priesthood in Hebrews: Part II: The High-Priestly Sacrifice of Christ." *BSac* 130 (1973): 195–212.
*Joslin, Barry Clyde. "Christ Bore the Sins of Many: Substitution and the Atonement in Hebrews." *SBJT* 11 (2007): 74–103.
Kibbe, Michael. "Is It Finished? When Did It Start? Hebrews, Priesthood, and Atonement in Biblical, Systematic, and Historical Perspective." *JTS* 65 (2014): 25–61.
*Kistemaker, Simon J. "The Atonement in Hebrews: 'A Merciful and Faithful High Priest.'" Pages 163–75 in *The Glory of the Atonement: Biblical, Theological, and Practical Perspectives. Essays in Honor of Roger Nicole*. Edited by Charles E. Hill and Frank A. James III. Downers Grove, IL: InterVarsity Press, 2004.
Long, Thomas G. "Bold in the Presence of God: Atonement in Hebrews." *Int* 52 (1998): 53–69.
McRay, John. "Atonement and Apocalyptic in the Book of Hebrews." *ResQ* 23 (1980): 1–9.
Moffitt, David M. *Atonement and the Logic of Resurrection in the Epistle to the Hebrews*. Leiden: Brill, 2011.
*Motyer, Stephen. "The Atonement in Hebrews." Pages 136–49 in *Atonement Debate: Papers from the London Symposium on the Theology of Atonement*. Edited by Derek Tidball, David Hilborn, and Justin Thacker. Grand Rapids: Zondervan, 2008.
Smalley, Stephen S. "The Atonement in the Epistle to the Hebrews." *TynBul* 7–8 (1961): 28–35.
Tuckett, C. M. *ABD* 1:518–22.
Yarbrough, R. W. *NDBT* 388–92.

57. Blood in Hebrews (9:11–14)

Behm, J. *TDNT* 1:172–77.
Graystone, K. "Salvation Proclaimed: III. Hebrews 9:11–14." *ExpT* 93 (1982): 164–68.
Hughes, Philip E. "The Blood of Jesus and His Heavenly Priesthood in Hebrews: Part I: The Significance of the Blood of Jesus." *BSac* 130 (1973): 99–109.
Kuma, Hermann V. A. *The Centrality of Aima (Blood) in the Theology of the Epistle to the Hebrews: An Exegetical and Philological Study*. Lewiston, NY: Mellen, 2012.
Morris, Leon. "The Biblical Use of the Term 'Blood.'" *JTS* 3 (1952): 216–27.
Renz, T. *NDBT* 402–04.

58. The Greater and More Perfect Tabernacle (9:11–12)

Hughes, Philip E. "The Blood of Jesus and His Heavenly Priesthood in Hebrews: Part I: The Significance of the Blood of Jesus." *BSac* 130 (1973): 305–14.

Kubo, Sakae. "Hebrews 9:11–12: Christ's Body, Heavenly Region, or . . . ?" Pages 97–109 in *Scribes and Scripture: New Testament Essays in Honor of J. Harold Greenlee*. Edited by David Alan Black. Winona Lake, IN: Eisenbrauns, 1992.

Swetnam, James. "Greater and More Perfect Tent: A Contribution to the Discussion of Hebrews 9:11." *Bib* 47 (1966): 91–106.

Thompson, James W. "Hebrews 9 and Hellenistic Concepts of Sacrifice." *JBL* 8 (1979): 567–78.

Young, Norman H. "The Gospel according to Hebrews 9." *NTS* 27 (1981): 198–210.

HOMILETICAL SUGGESTIONS

Christ's Superior Offering (9:11–14)

1. The Superior Anticipated High Priest (v. 11a)
2. The Superior Heavenly Tabernacle (v. 11b)
3. The Superior Offering
   (a) His very own blood offered willingly through the eternal Spirit (vv. 12a, 14a)
   (b) Not sacrificed animal blood (v. 13a)
4. The Superior Outcome
   (a) Eternal redemption and cleansed consciences vs. limited purification of the flesh (vv. 12b, 13b, 14b)
   (b) Service for the living God (v. 14c)

3. The Mediator of the New Covenant (9:15–22)

STRUCTURE

Verse 15 serves both to summarize vv. 11–14 and to introduce the discussion on the necessity of Christ's death. The gen. abs. (*θανάτου . . . παραβάσεων*) in v. 15 is inserted into the *ὅπως* clause (which ends with *κληρονομίας*), which is reflected by the indentation and the arrow below. (The embedded prep. phrase *ἐπὶ τῇ πρώτῃ διαθήκῃ* has been indented under the word that it modifies.) Both v. 16 and v. 18 give further reasons for why Jesus had to die, as indicated by *γάρ* and *ὅθεν* in the structural analysis. Verse 19 begins with a gen. abs. (*λαληθείσης . . . λαῷ*), which is followed by the adv. ptc. *λαβών*, both of which are subordinate to *ἐρράντισεν*. Ellingworth describes vv. 19–21 as a "triptych," in which v. 20 is the "central panel," and vv. 19 and 21 "elaborate details" (Ellingworth 467). Verse 22 concludes the section with a general principle.

15 Καὶ διὰ τοῦτο διαθήκης καινῆς μεσίτης ἐστίν,
ὅπως
θανάτου γενομένου
εἰς ἀπολύτρωσιν τῶν . . . παραβάσεων
ἐπὶ τῇ πρώτῃ διαθήκῃ
τὴν ἐπαγγελίαν λάβωσιν οἱ κεκλημένοι
τῆς αἰωνίου κληρονομίας.
16 Ὅπου γὰρ διαθήκη,
θάνατον ἀνάγκη φέρεσθαι τοῦ διαθεμένου·
17 διαθήκη γὰρ ἐπὶ νεκροῖς βεβαία,
ἐπεὶ μήποτε ἰσχύει
ὅτε ζῇ ὁ διαθέμενος.
18 ὅθεν οὐδὲ ἡ πρώτη χωρὶς αἵματος ἐγκεκαίνισται·
19 λαληθείσης γὰρ πάσης ἐντολῆς
κατὰ τὸν νόμον
ὑπὸ Μωϋσέως
παντὶ τῷ λαῷ,
λαβὼν τὸ αἷμα τῶν μόσχων [καὶ τῶν τράγων]
μετὰ ὕδατος καὶ ἐρίου κοκκίνου καὶ ὑσσώπου
αὐτό τε τὸ βιβλίον καὶ πάντα τὸν λαὸν ἐρράντισεν
20 λέγων·
τοῦτο τὸ αἷμα τῆς διαθήκης
ἧς ἐνετείλατο πρὸς ὑμᾶς ὁ θεός.
21 καὶ τὴν σκηνὴν δὲ καὶ πάντα τὰ σκεύη τῆς λειτουργίας τῷ αἵματι ὁμοίως
ἐρράντισεν.
22 καὶ σχεδὸν ἐν αἵματι πάντα καθαρίζεται
κατὰ τὸν νόμον
καὶ χωρὶς αἱματεκχυσίας οὐ γίνεται ἄφεσις.

VERSE 15

Καὶ διὰ τοῦτο διαθήκης καινῆς μεσίτης ἐστίν,
Therefore, he is the mediator of a new covenant,

Καί links this section (vv. 15–22) with the previous one (vv. 11–14), although it is left untr. in many EVV. As in 2:1, διὰ τοῦτο ("therefore"; "for this reason," [most EVV]) here refers to a previous argument (vv. 11–14) and indicates a strong inference to be drawn from these vv.: *because* Christ has entered the heavenly sanctuary by means of his own blood; *therefore*, he is the mediator of the new covenant (v. 15). The rest of this section (vv. 16–22) further explains this primary claim (cf. Lane 2:234). The unusual combination of καὶ διὰ τοῦτο occurs only here in Hebrews, and rarely in the GNT (Ellingworth 459). Christ is the implied subj. of ἐστίν. Μεσίτης is the pred. nom. (see comments on 8:6) and is modified by the obj. gen. διαθήκης, which is modified by the adj. καινῆς (see comments on 8:8).

ὅπως θανάτου γενομένου εἰς ἀπολύτρωσιν τῶν ἐπὶ τῇ πρώτῃ διαθήκῃ παραβάσεων
. . . because a death has taken place for redemption from the transgressions committed under the first covenant.

The syntax of the rest of this v. is complex (note the reversed order of the Greek clauses in many EVV; but cf. NASB, NJB). Ὅπως ("so that" [BDAG 718b; BDF §369]) introduces the purpose for which Christ became the mediator of the new covenant; the clause is anchored with the subjunc. λάβωσιν (see below). As with 1:14, reception of the promised inheritance is both a pres. reality and a fut. promise for believers (see Ellingworth 461).

Θανάτου γενομένου forms a gen. abs. cstr. (see comments on 2:4) in which the subj. of the gen. abs. (θανάτου [as reflected in the ESV and NASB]) is not the same as the subj. of the finite vb. λάβωσιν (οἱ κεκλημένοι). Most EVV translate the gen. abs. with a finite vb. The gen. abs. ends with παραβάσεων and is embedded in the ὅπως clause. The ptc. is causal ("because" [most EVV]), and both summarizes vv. 11–14 and anticipates vv. 15–16—see discussion on v. 17. The death in view in this v. is Christ's (made explicit in CEV, NIV, NLT). The curses stipulated for violations of the Sinaitic covenant included exile and death (Deut 30:15–20). Thus Christ's death fulfilled the self-maledictory curses associated with the Sinaitic covenant and terminated that covenant (see Lane 2:241–42)—see discussion on 9:17. This v. links two key aspects of Christ's death: it both fulfills the requirements of the (broken) first covenant and is the sacrifice that inaugurates the new covenant.

Ἀπολύτρωσιν is the acc. sg. fem. of ἀπολύτρωσις, -εως, ἡ, "ransom" (NIV); "redemption" (NASB; BDAG 117c). Εἰς ἀπολύτρωσιν . . . indicates purpose (Harris 88–89; "that redeems" [ESV]; "to set [them] free" [NET, NLT]; "to rescue" [CEV]). The use of the more common ἀπολύτρωσις recalls and parallels the earlier use of the cognate λύτρωσις in 9:12 (*NIDNTTE* 3:186; see comments there). Παραβάσεων (gen. pl. fem. of παράβασις, -εως, ἡ, "sins" [NIV, NLT]; "violations" [NET]; "transgressions" [ESV,

NASB; cf. BDAG 758d]) is a gen. of separation ("from" [most EVV]; cf. Ellingworth 461) and less likely an obj. gen. (R 501). Ἐπί may indicate circumstance (Harris 138)—locat. in an expression of time (R 604; "under" [most EVV]; "at the time of" [Z 673–74]) or "on the basis of" (BDF §235[2]; Koester 417). The adj. πρώτῃ modifies διαθήκῃ (see comments on 8:7).

τὴν ἐπαγγελίαν λάβωσιν οἱ κεκλημένοι τῆς αἰωνίου κληρονομίας.
. . . so that those who are called might receive the promise of the eternal inheritance,

Λάβωσιν is the 3rd pl. aor. act. subjunc. of λαμβάνω. The subj. of the vb. is the subst. ptc. κεκλημένοι ("those who are called" [most EVV]). The pass. is a divine pass. The cstr. οἱ κεκλημένοι is paralleled only in Matt 22:8 and Rev 19:9 (but cf. Matt 22:3, 4); the concept, however, recalls 3:1 (see comments there). The pf. may be intensive (e.g., "intensified," Campbell, *VA* 201). The obj. of the vb. is ἐπαγγελίαν, which recalls the focus on the Abrahamic promises in Hebrews 6 (see comments on 6:13). (This connection is missed in the CEV: "guarantee of God's eternal blessings".) Ἐπαγγελίαν is modified by κληρονομίας (κληρονομία, -ας, ἡ, "inheritance" [BDAG 548a]), which is itself modified by the adj. αἰωνίου (cf. Lane 2:231 n. *o*). The gen. is either epex. (specifying the content of the promise [Ellingworth 461; cf. Wallace 95–99; BDF §167]) or more likely obj. ("the eternal inheritance God has promised" [NLT]; cf. "the promised eternal inheritance"—translating ἐπαγγελία as an adj. [ESV, NIV]), although this is left unspecified in many EVV ("promise of the eternal inheritance" [NASB, NEB]). Syntactically, the gen. phrase τῆς αἰωνίου κληρονομίας cannot be construed with the subst. ptc. οἱ κεκλημένοι ("those who are called to an eternal inheritance" [*pace* NJB]). The use of αἰωνίος recalls its previous use in 5:9 (eternal salvation) and 9:12 (eternal redemption), and anticipates 13:20 (eternal covenant). The suspension of the gen. modifier to the end of the clause may be emph. (Ellingworth 462). The content of the "eternal" inheritance is not stated directly, but is progressively revealed in Hebrews as "salvation" (1:14), entering God's rest (4:1), the Abrahamic promise (6:17), and ultimately as worship in the heavenly Zion (12:22–24). See For Further Study 4 (Inheritance in Hebrews).

VERSE 16

Ὅπου γὰρ διαθήκη, θάνατον ἀνάγκη φέρεσθαι τοῦ διαθεμένου·
Where a will exists, the death of the one who made it must be established.

Γάρ likely indicates another reason (in addition to vv. 11–14) why Jesus had to die to become the mediator of the new covenant. Many, however, understand the γάρ clause to further explain reception of the eternal inheritance (see discussion on v. 17). The spatial particle ὅπου ("where") is metaphorical here ("in the case of" [NIV]; R 969). The meaning of διαθήκη in this v. and v. 17 is much debated (see discussion on 9:17). Ἀνάγκη is the nom. sg. fem. of ἀνάγκη, -ης, ἡ, "constraint as inherent in the nature of things" (BDAG 61a). The subst. is pred. with an implied vb. and an impers. subj. ("it is necessary" [NIV, NLT]), although many EVV make "death" the subj. (e.g., CSB). Φέρεσθαι is the pres. pass. inf. of φέρω. Many claim that φέρω here "probably has a technical legal sense of 'to be reported' or 'registered' and thus officially recognized" (Attridge 256; cf. "to prove" [NIV]; "be established" [ESV]; "to demonstrate the reality of something or establish" [BDAG 1052b], but see comments on 9:17). The inf. complements ἀνάγκη. Θάνατον is the obj. of the inf. Διαθεμένου is the gen. sg. masc. of the aor. mid. ptc. of διατίθημι, "decree," "arrange," "make a will" (BDAG 238b–c). The ptc. is subst. (see comments on 9:17). The gen. is subj. ("the one making a will dies").

VERSE 17

διαθήκη γὰρ ἐπὶ νεκροῖς βεβαία,
For a will is valid only when people die,

For διαθήκη, see comments below. Νεκροῖς is the dat. pl. masc. of νεκρός, -ά, -όν, "dead"; the gender must be determined from the context (see comments below). Ἐπί with the dat. means "on the basis of" (Harris 138; cf. "in the presence of" [R 604]). Βεβαία is the nom. sg. fem. (modifying διαθήκη) of βέβαιος, -α, -ον, "valid" (NASB), "take effect" (ESV, NET), "in force" (NIV; BDAG 172c; cf. Heb 2:2). Context determines that the adj., although anar., is pred. ("a covenant is in force" [see discussion on pred. in Wallace 311–12]).

ἐπεὶ μήποτε ἰσχύει ὅτε ζῇ ὁ διαθέμενος.
since it is never in effect while the one who made it is living.

The subord. conj. ἐπεί is causal ("because," "since," "for" [BDAG 360c]), explaining the preceding clause, namely the validity of a διαθήκη. Elsewhere in Hebrews μήποτε introduces a neg. purpose clause ("lest not" [2:1; 3:12; 4:1]). Here, however, it means "never" (e.g., NIV; BDAG 648c; Lane 2:232 n. *u*), following Attic use of ἐπεί with the indic. in causal clauses (R 1159). BDF §428(5), however, claims that ἐπεὶ μήποτε plus the indic. is "clearly interrogative." This may explain the var. rdg. μη τοτε ℵ* D* (although changed to ποτε by later scribes in each case [Metzger 599]), which would change the statement to a question, but which is only adopted by the RSV.

Ἰσχύει is the 3rd sg. pres. act. indic. of ἰσχύω, "to be valid," "[to be] in force" (NASB; NIV; BDAG 484d; "takes effect" [ESV]). The pres. is gnomic. The use of ὅτε ("while" [most EVV]) with the pres. is rare (R 971); this ptcl. introduces a dependent temp. clause, here indicating "a period of time coextensive with another" (BDAG 731c; see discussion below). Ζῇ is the 3rd sg. pres. act. indic. of ζάω. The subj. of the vb. is the subst. ptc. ὁ διαθέμενος (nom. sg. masc. of the aor. mid. ptc. of διατίθημι; see discussion below).

Several interrelated issues emerge in Heb 9:16–17 that affect the understanding of διαθήκη, ὁ διαθέμενος, and ἐπὶ νεκροῖς. There is consensus that διαθήκη should be understood as "covenant" in Heb 7:20–9:15. Most EVV (except NASB) and many commentators (except Lane and Cockerill), however, argue that διαθήκη refers to a "will" or "testament" in Heb 9:16–17, and consequently ὁ διαθέμενος refers to the one who made the will (e.g., the testator [most EVV]). (Some try unsuccessfully to combine both [e.g., Cassirer, REB].) Many note the freq. use of διαθήκη in Greco-Roman legal writings to designate a "last will and testament" (e.g., J. Behm, *TDNT* 2:124). Despite the fact that switching from "covenant" (7:22–9:15) to "will" (9:16–17) and back to "covenant" (implied in 9:18) is readily acknowledged to be awkward, many claim that the use of κληρονομία in Heb 9:15 necessitates this shift in meaning (cf. Attridge 254; Koester 417) as does the ref. to Christ's death in v. 15 (Ellingworth 460). Attridge suggests that the author engages in a wordplay here (254–56; cf. Ellingworth 462; Barclay). On this view, the γάρ clause in v. 16 explains why Jesus's death was necessary for reception of the eternal inheritance (vs. mediating the new covenant).

Understanding διαθήκη in Heb 9:16–17 as "will," however, presents significant interpretive difficulties. For example, it is often assumed that the death of the testator was required to effect a will. On this view, however, it is unclear why the death of the sg. διαθέμενος in v. 17 is specified by the pl. νεκροῖς. It is unlikely that νεκροῖς is simply a "stylistic variant" (*pace* Ellingworth 464; cf. Attridge 256). The attempt to resolve this difficulty by claiming that νεκροῖς means something like "with reference to dead people" is also not convincing (*pace* Bruce 212 n. 102). Moreover, wills were not necessarily effected on the basis of a death, but rather when they were notarized (John J. Hughes, "Hebrews IX 15ff. and Galatians III 15ff.: A Study in Covenant Practice and Procedure," *NovT* [1979]: 44, 60–61; followed by Lane 2:229–32; 242–43). Additionally, the distribution of an inheritance before death was fairly widespread (Hughes, "Hebrews IX," 62). Heb 9:16, however, speaks of the *necessity* of a death. Furthermore, applying the concept of "will" to Hebrews is problematic because it implies that Christ is the testator whose death makes the will effective, but this does not cohere with the depiction of the Son as the *heir*, which in turn implies that God the Father is the testator. Since clearly God the Father does not die, many simply assume that the Son takes on the role of testator, dies, and thereby effects the "will" (Attridge 254; Ellingworth 95; Koester 418). Yet, as Scott W. Hahn ("Covenant, Cult, and the Curse-of-Death: Διαθήκη in Heb 9:15–22," in *Hebrews: Contemporary Methods—New Insights*, ed. Gabriella Gelardini, BIS 75 [Leiden: Brill, 2005], 70) correctly notes, Christ "does not die in order to *leave* an inheritance to the Church, but rather to *enter* the inheritance himself (Heb 1:3–4; 2:9; 9:11–12; 10:12–13), which he then shares with his 'brothers' (Heb 2:10–3:6)" (italics orig.).

These difficulties, however, are resolved when διαθήκη is understood as "covenant" throughout Heb 9:15–18. Hughes shows that Heb 9:16–17 explains why Jesus had to die to become the mediator of the new covenant (v. 15; see structural analysis above with γάρ and ὅθεν), not that his death was necessary to obtain the eternal inheritance (Hughes, "Hebrews IX," 33–34; cf. Lane 2:242). Furthermore, Hahn proposes that Heb 9:16–17 refers specifically to the *broken* Sinaitic covenant, not covenants in general. Thus these verses explain that Jesus had to die because the covenant had been broken and not as a general principal for inaugurating covenants (Cockerill 405–6).

On this view ὁ διαθέμενος means something like "covenant-maker" (Cockerill 406). The death specified in v. 17 involves the animals (hence the pl. νεκροῖς), sacrificed in association with the Sinaitic covenant, who represented those who offered them (e.g., Exod 24:3–8), possibly in terms of a self-maledictory curse (Lane 2:242–43). Furthermore, φέρω is freq. used in cultic contexts and infrequently in legal writings (Hughes, "Hebrews IX," 65). Thus this view accords well with understanding φέρεσθαι as "to be brought forth" or "be borne" (see esp. Hughes, "Hebrews IX," 42–43; Cockerill 406), and avoids claiming that φέρω means "establish" here without clear pars. elsewhere (Scott W. Hahn, "A Broken Covenant and the Curse of Death: A Study of Hebrews 9:15–22," *CBQ* 66 [2004]: 419). The διαθέμενος would then be the nation Israel as a whole, led by Moses. These representative animal deaths anticipated Jesus's own death as the substitute for those who broke the Sinaitic covenant. Thus a possible translation might be: "For where there is a [broken] covenant, the death of the covenant-maker must be borne"—this death is thus borne by Jesus, possibly anticipating the allusion to Isa 53:12 in Heb 9:28 (see Cockerill 406–407). Hughes concludes, "Christ's death . . . is seen both as the sacrifice which consummated the old covenant order and as that which inaugurated the new" ("Hebrews IX," 47–48). Understanding διαθήκη as "will" in Heb 9:16–17 obscures these important connections. Moreover, the function of covenant concerns the forgiveness of sin, whereas the function of will concerns the reception of the promised inheritance. Only the new *covenant* effects forgiveness and thus the reception of the promise, that is, the eternal inheritance. As Cockerill concludes, "the translation 'will' fits very poorly with the larger context and conceptual world of Hebrews" (Cockerill 405).

VERSE 18

ὅθεν οὐδὲ ἡ πρώτη χωρὶς αἵματος ἐγκεκαίνισται·
That is why even the first covenant was inaugurated with blood.

The conj. ὅθεν ("for which reason"; BDAG 693a; BDF §451[6]) draws an inference from vv. 16–17 about the necessity of Christ's death (see discussion on v. 17). The art. ἡ refers to διαθήκη ("covenant"), which is understood elliptically from Hebrews 8 and is modified by πρώτη (see comments on 8:7). Χωρίς ("without") takes a gen. obj. (αἵματος). The cstr. οὐδέ (οὐ + δέ) . . . χωρὶς αἵματος is an example of litotes (a double neg. indicating a strong pos. [Ellingworth 434]), which emphasizes the importance of the blood offering (Attridge 239). The expression recalls 9:7. The author here makes explicit the par. between the necessity of Christ's blood for the new covenant (vv. 15–17) and the (representative) sacrificial blood associated with the first covenant (v. 18).

Ἐγκεκαίνισται is the 3rd sg. pf. pass. indic. of ἐγκαινίζω, "to ratify" (RSV); "inaugurate" (ESV, NASB, NET; BDAG 272d); "put into effect" (NIV, NLT). (For the pf. tense, see comments on 7:6.) This rare word (in the NT, only here and Heb 10:20; both in conj. with covenant inauguration) was not used in conj. with covenants in the LXX, but rather "for putting the altar (Num 7:10) and temple (1 Kgs 8:63) into service" (Koester 418; cf. "dedicated" [ASV, KJV, RV]). The vb. can also mean "consecrate" (J.

Behm, *TDNT* 3:453–54). Thus, the author might have used this vb. to show the close connection between the covenant and the sanctuary (Koester 418). See the extended discussion in Ellingworth 466.

VERSE 19

λαληθείσης γὰρ πάσης ἐντολῆς κατὰ τὸν νόμον ὑπὸ Μωϋσέως παντὶ τῷ λαῷ,
For when every command had been proclaimed by Moses to all the people according to the law,

Γάρ offers support for v. 18 (Ellingworth 467). Λαληθείσης is the gen. sg. fem. of aor. pass. ptc. of λαλέω. The ptc. introduces a temp. ("when" [most EVV]; "after" [NJB, NLT]) gen. abs. (R 1131; see comments on 2:4) cstr. that ends with λαῷ. The ptc. is translated as a finite vb. in most EVV. The subj. of the gen. abs. is ἐντολῆς, which is modified by πάσης. Ὑπὸ Μωϋσέως adv. modifies the pass. ptc. for agency. Moses is the understood subj. of the following ptc. (λαβών) and finite vb. (ἐρράντισεν). The dat. λαῷ is the indir. obj. of the ptc., which is further modified by παντί. Κατὰ τὸν νόμον likely pars. its usage in Heb 7:5 and modifies ἐντολῆς ("the ordinances according to the law" [Cockerill 403]; cf. ESV, NIV) rather than λαληθείσης (NASB, NRSV); the prep. phrase distinguishes individual commands (ἐντολαί) from the overall Mosaic law.

λαβὼν τὸ αἷμα τῶν μόσχων [καὶ τῶν τράγων] μετὰ ὕδατος καὶ ἐρίου κοκκίνου καὶ ὑσσώπου
he took the blood of calves and goats, along with water, scarlet wool, and hyssop,

Λαβών is the nom. sg. masc. of the aor. act. ptc. of λαμβάνω. The ptc. clause modifies ἐρράντισεν (see below), indicating instr. or possibly attendant circumstances (see Wallace 640–44). The subj. of the ptc. is Moses (understood from the first part of the v.). Many EVV translate the ptc. as a finite vb. ("he took"). The obj. of the ptc. is αἷμα. The ref. to calves and bulls recalls the sim. cstr. in 9:12 (see comments there). The var. rdg. is either an accidental omission (due to homoeoteleuton [e.g., τῶν μόσχων]) or more likely due to scribal attempts to conform this v. to 9:12; the UBS rates it {C} but includes the text in brackets to indicate the uncertainty (Metzger 599). Μετά ("with" followed by the gen.) has three objs.: ὕδατος ("water"), ἐρίου (gen. sg. neut. of ἔριον, -ου, τό, "wool" [BDAG 392c]), and ὑσσώπου (gen. sg. fem. of ὕσσωπος, -ου, ἡ, "hyssop" [BDAG 1043c]). Ἐρίου is further modified by κοκκίνου (gen. sg. neut. of κόκκινος, -η, -ον, "red," "scarlet" [BDAG 554c]). The prep. phrase adv. modifies ἐρράντισεν (see below) indicating instr.

αὐτό τε τὸ βιβλίον καὶ πάντα τὸν λαὸν ἐρράντισεν
and sprinkled the scroll itself and all the people,

The postpos. ptcl. τέ "indicates a somewhat closer unity than does καί" (R 1178; e.g., "*both* the book itself and all the people" [NASB]). Αὐτό functions as an "adjectival intensive" (R 686) modifying βιβλίον (-ου, τό, "book," "scroll"—"the book itself"

[ESV, NASB, NET]; "the scroll itself" [NRSV]). Both *αὐτό τὸ βιβλίον* and *πάντα τὸν λαόν* are the obj. of the vb. ἐρράντισεν, which is the 3rd sg. aor. act. indic. of ῥαντίζω, "sprinkle" (BDAG 903c).

This v. alludes to Exod 24:3–8, but there are several important variations in its appropriation in Hebrews. The Exodus account describes the sprinkling of blood on the altar and the people, whereas the author of Hebrews mentions the book (of the law) instead of the altar. Some suggest that the book was within the altar (cf. Lane 2:244; Cockerill 408), or that the law (the book) and the sacrifices (on the altar) were "inseparable" for the author of Hebrews (Koester 419). Exodus 24 does not mention goats, water, wool, or hyssop. Thus the addition of the prep. phrase (μετὰ . . . ὑσσώπου) appears to conflate Exodus 24 with other purification rites (so Lane 2:244; Ellingworth 468; Koester 419), such as for lepers (e.g., Lev 14:1–8), mold (Lev 14:48–53), or contact with a corpse (Num 19:1–22). The author may have intended to show that "the whole covenant is included in its inauguration" (Cockerill 408).

VERSE 20

λέγων·
saying,

Λέγων parallels λέγει in 1:6 to introduce an OT citation, although here the speaker is Moses, not God. The pres. indicates action contemp. with the aor. ἐράντισεν in v. 19.

τοῦτο τὸ αἷμα τῆς διαθήκης ἧς ἐνετείλατο πρὸς ὑμᾶς ὁ θεός.
This is the blood of the covenant that God has ordained for you.

The dem. τοῦτο in this verbless clause functions as a "forward pointing device" that draws attention to τὸ αἷμα τῆς διαθήκης (see Runge 63–68). The gen. διαθήκης is descriptive. The antecedent of ἧς is διαθήκης. As the obj. of ἐνετείλατο, the rel. pron. should be acc., but it has been attracted to the gen. of the antecedent (R 716; BDF §294). Ἐνετείλατο is the 3rd sg. aor. mid. indic. of ἐντέλλω, "command" (many EVV; BDAG 339c), "ordain" (NRSV), "enjoined upon" (NAB, NEB, Cassirer). The subj. of the vb. is θεός, and its placement is emph. (Cockerill 408–9). Πρὸς ὑμᾶς adv. modifies ἐνετείλατο, indicating "with ref. to" (BDF §239[6]).

This v. is a citation of Exod 24:8. The author, however, has altered the LXX text as follows: τοῦτο replaces ἰδού, ἐνετείλατο replaces διέθετο, and θεός replaces κύριος. There is debate whether the author's alterations (esp. τοῦτο) were influenced by Jesus's institution of the Lord's Supper (Matt 26:28; Mark 14:24; cf. Luke 22:20; 1 Cor 11:25). Yet many note the absence of refs. to the Lord's Supper in Hebrews (e.g., Attridge 258; Bruce 219 n. 109; Koester 419). It is more likely that the author altered the text to clarify his argument (e.g., διατίθημι is not used in Hebrews in conj. with the old covenant, and κύριος has been associated elsewhere with Christ, so θεός would avoid possible confusion here [so Attridge 257–58; Ellingworth 469–70; Lane 2:245]). Moreover, ἐνετείλατο continues Hebrews's focus on "perfection" by use of a τελ- cognate (cf.

Cockerill 408 n. 31). The switch from κύριος to θεός also argues against an allusion to the Lord's Supper (Koester 419). The citation facilitates the par. that the author draws between the first and new covenants, namely that both were established by sacrificial blood (Ellingworth 470).

VERSE 21

καὶ τὴν σκηνὴν δὲ καὶ πάντα τὰ σκεύη τῆς λειτουργίας τῷ αἵματι ὁμοίως ἐρράντισεν.
In the same way, he sprinkled the tabernacle and all the articles of worship with blood.

The first καί and δέ resume "the list begun in v. 19, and interrupted by the quotation in v. 20." Σκεύη is the acc. pl. neut. of σκεῦος, -ους, τό, "vessels" (ESV, NASB, REB; BDAG 927d); "utensils" (NET). Πάντα is likely generalizing (e.g., "everything used in its ceremonies" [NIV]). (For a list of the liturgical items, see Koester 419.) Both σκηνήν ("tent"; see comments on 8:2) and τὰ σκεύη are the obj. of ἐρράντισεν (see v. 19), and are joined by the second καί. Λειτουργίας is the gen. sg. fem. of λειτουργία, -ας, ἡ, "service" (BDAG 591b–c). This noun was used in association with Jesus's superior ministry (Heb 8:6). The gen. indicates purpose (BDF §166). Αἵματι is instr. The adv. ὁμοίως ("likewise") draws a par. between the sprinkling in v. 19 and in this v.

The sprinkling of the tabernacle and liturgical items is not indicated in Exod 24:3–8 (before the tabernacle's cstr. [Exodus 35–40]). The author may have drawn on Jewish tradition (e.g., Josephus, *Ant.* 3.206), in which the tabernacle is anointed both with oil (Exod 40:9; Lev 8:11) and blood (Exod 29:10–21; Lev 8:15; so Lane 2:244; Koester 420). Alternatively, the author may have assimilated details from Aaron's ordination (Lev 8:15) or the Day of Atonement (Lev 16:15–19 [cf. Koester 420]).

VERSE 22

καὶ σχεδὸν ἐν αἵματι πάντα καθαρίζεται κατὰ τὸν νόμον
According to the law almost everything is purified with blood,

Καί adds a new element in the discussion; "indeed" [ESV, NET], "in fact" [NIV, NLT]), although untr. in some EVV. The adv. σχεδόν means "almost" (most EVV; BDAG 981b) or "nearly" (NIV, NLT) and modifies πάντα ("everything," "all things"; *pace* NASB ["one may almost say"], which translates the adj. as an adv.). Σχεδόν acknowledges that, in addition to blood, water (Lev 16:26, 28; 22:6) and fire (Num 31:21–24) also purified (Koester 420). Καθαρίζεται is the 3rd sg. pres. pass. indic. of καθαρίζω, "cleanse" (NASB, NIV), "purify" (ESV, NET; BDAG 488d–489a). The pres. is gnomic. The adv. prep. phrase ἐν αἵματι modifies καθαρίζεται indicating impers. means (Wallace 434–35). Κατὰ τὸν νόμον modifies καθαρίζεται, indicating "conformity with" (Harris 152).

καὶ χωρὶς αἱματεκχυσίας οὐ γίνεται ἄφεσις.
and without the shedding of blood there is no forgiveness.

Αἱματεκχυσίας is the gen. sg. fem. of αἱματεκχυσία, -ας, ἡ, "the shedding of blood" (most EVV) or "pouring out of blood" (BDAG 27b; J. Behm, *TDNT* 1:176–77; BGk. hapax). The author may have coined this term himself (from αἷμα and ἐκχύννω ["pour out"]; cf. Lane 2:232 n. *bb*; Koester 420). Since the actual shedding of blood was not expiatory, but rather its manipulation by the high priest, the word here seems to mean "pouring out" or "offering" of the blood (Koester 420; see Timothy C. G. Thornton, "The Meaning of αἱματεκχυσία in Heb 9:22," *JTS* 15 [1964]: 63–65.). Χωρίς ("without") takes a gen. obj. (αἱματεκχυσίας). Γίνεται functions both impers. and as an equative ("there is" [most EVV]). Ἄφεσις (-εως, ἡ, "forgiveness" [most EVV]; but "remission" [ASV, NJB], "release" [Cockerill]) functions as a pred. nom. Although a few EVV tr. ἄφεσις as "forgiveness of sins" (ESV; cf. Moffatt), ἁμαρτία does not occur in this v.

There is debate whether the second clause refers only to the first covenant or to both covenants. If limited to the first, then the author may be drawing on a Jewish maxim (perhaps derived from Lev 17:11; cf. Attridge 259). Lane, however, argues that here "ἄφεσις signals a definitive putting away of defilement or a decisive purgation" (Lane 2:232–33, 247). Cockerill understands ἄφεσις as "release"—both from the consequences of breaking the first covenant and in terms of cleansing, which is only possible through Christ's blood (Cockerill 410–11).

FOR FURTHER STUDY

59. Covenants in the Bible (9:15–22)

Beckwith, Roger T. "The Unity and Diversity of God's Covenants." *TynBul* 38 (1987): 93–118.

Fensham, F. C. "The Covenant as Giving Expression to the Relationship between Old and New Testament." *TynBul* 22 (1971): 82–94.

Fischer, John. "Covenant, Fulfillment and Judaism in Hebrews." *Evangelical Review of Theology* 13 (1989): 175–87.

Fisher, Jeffrey. "The Covenant-Idea as the Heart of Hebrews and Biblical Theology: An Original Contribution of Old Princeton in the Teaching of Geerhardus Vos." *CTJ* 48 (2013): 270–89.

Gentry, Peter John, and Stephen J. Wellum. *Kingdom through Covenant: A Biblical-Theological Understanding of the Covenants*. Wheaton: Crossway, 2012.

Goldengay, John. *NIDB* 1:767–78.

Haber, Susan. "From Priestly Torah to Christ Cultus: The Re-Vision of Covenant and Cult in Hebrews." *JSNT* 28 (2005): 105–24.

Hahn, Scott. "Covenant in the Old and New Testaments: Some Recent Research (1994–2004)." *CurBR* 3 (2005): 263–92.

Hays, Richard B. "'Here We Have No Lasting City': New Covenantalism in Hebrews." Pages 151–73 in Bauckham, *Theology*.

Koester, 112–14.

*Mendenhall, G. E., and Gary A. Herion. *ABD* 1:1179–1202.

Robertson, O. Palmer. *The Christ of the Covenants*. Grand Rapids: Baker, 1980.

Williamson, P. R. *NDBT* 419–29.

60. Διαθήκη *(9:16)*

*Behm, J. *TDNT* 2:124–34.

Campbell, K. M. "Covenant or Testament? Heb 9:16, 17 Reconsidered." *EQ 44* (1972): 197–211.

Lincoln, Lucy. "Translating Hebrews 9:15–22 in Its Hebraic Context." *JOTT* 12 (1999): 1–29.

Murray, Scott R. "The Concept of διαθήκη in the Letter to the Hebrews." *CTQ* 66 (2002): 41–60.

Pretorius, E A. "Diathēkē in the Epistle to the Hebrews." *Ad Hebraeos: Essays on the Epistle to the Hebrews* (1971): 37–50.

Swetnam, James. "Suggested Interpretation of Hebrews 9:15–18." *CBQ* 27 (1965): 373–90.

Wiid, J. S. "The Testamental Significance of Διαθήκη in Hebrews 9:15–22." *Neot* 26 (1992): 149–56.

HOMILETICAL SUGGESTIONS

The Mediator of the New Covenant (9:15–22)

1. Christ has become the mediator of the new covenant (v. 15) by his shed blood (vv. 11–14)
   (a) His death has redeemed transgressions committed under the first covenant (v. 15a)
   (b) His death makes possible reception of the eternal inheritance (v. 15b)
      (1) Because death was necessary for those who broke the first covenant (v. 16)
      (2) The death of the covenant maker has been borne (by Jesus) (v. 17)
   (c) His death inaugurated the new covenant (implied)—just as blood inaugurated the first covenant (vv. 18–21)
2. General principle: shed blood purifies and effects forgiveness (v. 22)

4. The Perfect Sacrifice (9:23–28)

STRUCTURE

Οὖν in v. 23 signals a new section, which draws on the necessary link between blood and cleansing. The μὲν . . . δέ cstr. signals a contrast between the two clauses in v. 23 as reflected in their par. alignment above. Verses 24–26 outline two contrasts: first, between the earthly and heavenly sanctuaries, and second, between the priestly offerings (Lane 2:248). In vv. 24–25, οὐ γάρ, ἀλλά, and οὐδ᾽ ἵνα each explicate Jesus's entry into heaven. Another contrast is signaled by δέ in v. 26. The rep. of ἅπαξ binds together vv. 26–28. There are many pars. (especially the contrast of the one and the many) between this section and 9:11–14 (Attridge 260). Although most commentators treat 9:23–28 as one unit, Cockerill offers compelling reasons for viewing 9:23–10:4 as a unit (Cockerill 419–20).

23 Ἀνάγκη οὖν τὰ μὲν ὑποδείγματα τῶν ἐν τοῖς οὐρανοῖς τούτοις καθαρίζεσθαι,
αὐτὰ δὲ τὰ ἐπουράνια κρείττοσιν θυσίαις παρὰ ταύτας.
24 οὐ γὰρ . . . Χριστός . . . εἰσῆλθεν . . . εἰς χειροποίητα . . . ἅγια,
ἀντίτυπα τῶν ἀληθινῶν,
ἀλλ᾽ εἰς αὐτὸν τὸν οὐρανόν,
νῦν ἐμφανισθῆναι τῷ προσώπῳ τοῦ θεοῦ ὑπὲρ ἡμῶν·
25 οὐδ᾽ ἵνα πολλάκις προσφέρῃ ἑαυτόν,
ὥσπερ ὁ ἀρχιερεὺς εἰσέρχεται
εἰς τὰ ἅγια
κατ᾽ ἐνιαυτὸν
ἐν αἵματι ἀλλοτρίῳ,
26 ἐπεὶ ἔδει αὐτὸν πολλάκις παθεῖν
ἀπὸ καταβολῆς κόσμου·
νυνὶ δὲ . . . ἅπαξ
ἐπὶ συντελείᾳ τῶν αἰώνων
εἰς ἀθέτησιν [τῆς] ἁμαρτίας
διὰ τῆς θυσίας αὐτοῦ
. . . πεφανέρωται.
27 καὶ καθ᾽ ὅσον ἀπόκειται τοῖς ἀνθρώποις ἅπαξ ἀποθανεῖν,
μετὰ δὲ τοῦτο κρίσις,
28 οὕτως καὶ ὁ Χριστὸς...
ἅπαξ προσενεχθεὶς
εἰς τὸ πολλῶν ἀνενεγκεῖν ἁμαρτίας
ἐκ δευτέρου
χωρὶς ἁμαρτίας
... ὀφθήσεται τοῖς αὐτὸν ἀπεκδεχομένοις
εἰς σωτηρίαν.

VERSE 23

Ἀνάγκη οὖν τὰ μὲν ὑποδείγματα τῶν ἐν τοῖς οὐρανοῖς τούτοις καθαρίζεσθαι,
Therefore, it was necessary for the copies of the things in the heavens to be purified with these sacrifices,

Οὖν draws on and presupposes the emph. on blood in vv. 18–22, and more specifically from the principle expressed in v. 22 (Attridge 260; Ellingworth 475). The μὲν . . . δέ cstr. contrasts the earthly and the heavenly sanctuaries, recalling Heb 8:1–5. As with 9:16, ἀνάγκη emphasizes the logical necessity of Christ's sacrificial death (see comments there; cf. 7:12, 27). The subst. ἀνάγκη is pred. with an implied vb. and an impers. subj. The timing of the cleansing of the heavenly sanctuary is debated: either the author aligns it with Jesus's entry into heaven *("it was necessary" [ESV, NASB, NIV]) or presents it as an ongoing reality ("it is necessary"). The position of ἀνάγκη is emph. (Ellingworth 474). Καθαρίζεσθαι is the pres. pass. inf. of καθαρίζω, "cleanse" (NASB, REB); "purify" (most EVV); "be made holy" (CEV); BDAG 488d–489a. The pass. is divine. Καθαρίζεσθαι complements the pred. ἀνάγκη. The use of this vb. recalls its use in 9:14, 22 and anticipates 10:2. Although v. 23 begins a new section, καθαρίζω functions as a hook word that joins this section to the previous one.

Ὑποδείγματα is the nom. pl. neut. of ὑπόδειγμα, -ατος, τό, "copies" [many EVV]; "sketches" (NET, NRSV); "symbols" (REB); "example," "model," "pattern" (BDAG 1037a; cf. 8:5; see comments there). As with 8:5, this word indicates the typological (and thus impermanent) function of the earthly tabernacle (cf. Cockerill 415). Τῶν functions subst. ("the things" [most EVV]) and is thus gen. pl. neut. The prep. phrase ἐν τοῖς οὐρανοῖς modifies the art. locat. (For the pl. of οὐρανός, see comments on 1:10, 11.) Cosmology in Hebrews is complex, but in general the author tends to associate the pl. οὐρανοί with the created order that will pass away (e.g., 1:11) and through which Jesus has passed (e.g., 4:14), whereas the sg. οὐρανός aligns with the dwelling place of God (e.g., 9:24; cf. Ellingworth 476–77). The dem. τούτοις functions as a pron., with its antecedent understood generally as the former sacrifices and regulations (e.g., 9:1–10; "ceremonies" [CEV]; "rites" [ESV, NAB]; Cockerill 415) or (less likely) the tabernacle and its objects (e.g., 9:19–21; made explicit in NLT; so Ellingworth 477; Lane 2:247). Attridge suggests that the ref. is "disparaging" (Attridge 261). The dat. is of means ("by these things").

αὐτὰ δὲ τὰ ἐπουράνια κρείττοσιν θυσίαις παρὰ ταύτας.
but the heavenly things themselves to be purified with better sacrifices than these.

Ἐπουράνια is the acc. pl. neut. of ἐπουράνιος, -ον, "heavenly" (so most EVV; BDAG 388b; cf. ἐπουρανίων in 8:5). This neut. adj. is subst. and is modified by αὐτά, which functions as an "intensive marker" (BDAG 152c; R 686; Wallace 349)—"the heavenly things *themselves*." Καθαρίζεσθαι is understood elliptically from the previous clause. Κρείττοσιν is the dat. pl. fem. of κρείττων (see comments on 1:4) and modifies θυσίαις (dat. pl. fem. of θυσία, -ας, ἡ, "offering," "sacrifice"). The antecedent of the dem. pron.

is θυσίαις. The pl. may be generalizing (Bruce 228 n. 150), with no suggestion that the author envisioned multiple sacrifices. Alternatively, the pl. may be due to the influence of the pl. τούτοις (Lane 2:247), or for the sake of the analogous "general principle" that the author is drawing (Attridge 261). Παρά followed by the acc. indicates comparison (Wallace 297 n. 10).

The expression *αὐτὰ τὰ ἐπουράνια* has suggested a Platonic conceptual background to some (e.g., Attridge 261 n. 13). As is the case elsewhere in Hebrews, however, sim. terminology does not necessitate a conceptual overlap, much less dependence. The distinction is not between heavenly and ideal *versus* earthly and phenomenal, but rather between heavenly and the perfection achieved by Jesus *versus* earthly and the transitory nature of the old priestly order. Moreover, the distinction is less spatial (heavenly–earthly) than temp. (old covenant–new covenant).

The cleansing of the heavenly sanctuary has been variously understood. (For an extensive survey, see David J. MacLeod, "The Cleansing of the True Tabernacle," *BSac* 152 [1995]: 60–71). Some combination of options 1 and 2 most coheres with the overall argumentation of Hebrews.

1. The author is making an analogy, presented first in terms of general principles drawn from the earthly sanctuary, which is then applied to the heavenly sanctuary for the sake of the argument; the point-by-point analogy accounts for the pl. θυσίαις and the pl. τὰ ἐπουράνια (cf. Cockerill 416).
2. The author develops an analogy between the earthly means (sacrifices) to cleanse the earthly high priest so that he could enter the earthly sanctuary without defiling it, and the spiritual/heavenly means (Jesus's sacrifice) to cleanse the conscience of believers to enable them to enter the heavenly sanctuary without defiling it. Thus just as defilement created a barrier that had to be cleansed (temp.) before the high priest could enter the presence of God in the earthly sanctuary, so also sin created a barrier that prevented humans from entering God's presence in the heavenly realm. Christ's sacrificial death has removed this barrier, so that believers, whose consciences are now cleansed, are able to enter God's presence (Bruce 229; Cockerill 417). The cleansing is both obj. (removing the barrier of sin) and subj. (cleansing individual consciences [Cockerill 417]).
3. The cleansing of the heavenly (transcendent) concerns the interiority of a human being understood along Platonic lines, and thus Christ's sacrifice fulfills the interiorization of the new covenant (Attridge 260). This view (e.g., Attridge 262), however, does not cohere with the spatial imagery of the passage.
4. There is such a close correl. between the earthly and the heavenly that the pollution from the earthly (e.g., the fall) has also affected the heavenly (Lane 2:247); this nuance, however, is not clear from the overall context of Hebrews. A variant is that "[s]ince sin affects all creation, Christ's work extends to all creation" (Koester 421).

5. The cleansing was necessary because of Satan's presence in heaven (Luke 10:18; John 12:31; Rev 12:7–9); this view, however, is foreign to the argumentation of Hebrews (see Attridge 261–62 n. 17; Bruce 228–29 n. 152; Ellingworth 477)
6. Καθαρίζεται here is less about purification than about consecration; both covenants were inaugurated and consecrated with blood (cf. Ellingworth 477); consecration, however, still suggests some element of cleansing (Cockerill 417 n. 17).

Another question that arises is how to understand the timing of the two clauses in this v., which must be inferred from the context. It is likely that both clauses are past-referring, with the first (Ἀνάγκη . . . καθαρίζεσθαι) referring to the inauguration of the first covenant and the second (αὐτὰ . . . ταύτας) to the inauguration of the new covenant. It is also possible to understand the first clause as past-referring and the second indicating the ongoing effects of the new order (see Ellingworth 475–76). Most EVV, however, do not make a clear distinction between the two clauses.

VERSE 24

οὐ γὰρ εἰς χειροποίητα εἰσῆλθεν ἅγια Χριστός,
For Christ did not enter a sanctuary made with hands

Γάρ offers support for v. 23 and presents the first of two contrasts that the author draws between the old priestly order and Christ, regarding entrance to the sanctuary. Here the focus is on the differences between the two sanctuaries. Χριστός is the subj. of εἰσῆλθεν and its position is emph. (Ellingworth 480). The aor. is global. Ἅγια refers to the sanctuary as a whole (most EVV, but "holy places" [ESV]), which is modified by χειροποίητα (acc. pl. neut. of χειροποιήτος, -ον, "made with [human, NIV] hands" [ESV, NLT, NASB]; see comments on 9:11). The prep. phrase εἰς χειροποίητα . . . ἅγια adv. modifies εἰσῆλθεν spatially. Its unusual placement is emph. (Ellingworth 479). Verbs compounded with εἰς nearly always repeat the prep. (R 559).

ἀντίτυπα τῶν ἀληθινῶν,
(only a model of the true one)

Ἀντίτυπα (acc. pl. neut. of ἀντίτυπος, -ον) occurs only here and in 1 Pet 3:21 in the Gk. NT. The word could indicate a "copy" (most EVV; cf. "model" [NJB], "representation" [NET], "pattern" [ASV], "symbol" [NEB]). Alternatively, the word could indicate a *prefiguration (e.g., "a pointer" [REB]; "type" [Moffatt]; "foreshadowed" [TCNT], which is its meaning in 1 Pet 3:21; cf. BDAG 91a; see also L. Goppelt, *TDNT* 8:248–49). The contrast between the two sanctuaries is less spatial (e.g., heavenly vs. earthly) than qual. (e.g., partial/anticipatory vs. perfect/final [cf. Cockerill 417–18 n. 18]). Again, a Platonic conceptual background does not cohere with the author's line of reasoning. Ἀληθινῶν is the gen. pl. neut. of ἀληθινός, -ή, -όν, "true" (most EVV); "real" (NJB); "genuine," "authentic," (BDAG 43d). The adj. modifies ἀντίτυπα. The verbless ἀντίτυπα τῶν ἀληθινῶν is an appos. of χειροποίητα . . . ἅγια, functioning epex. (as indicated by parentheses in the CSB). This par. likely explains the pl. in this phrase, which, like ἅγια, refers to the sanctuary as a whole and not its individual parts (cf. Ellingworth 480). The ultimate significance of the earthly tabernacle was as a model or type of the (true) heavenly sanctuary (cf. Lane 2:248).

Ἀλλ' εἰς αὐτὸν τὸν οὐρανόν,
but into heaven itself,

Ἀλλ' (elided before a vowel) indicates a strong contrast (Wallace 671). Εἰσῆλθεν is elliptically understood from the previous clause. Εἰς αὐτὸν τὸν οὐρανόν par. εἰς χειροποίητα . . . ἅγια in the previous v. As in v. 23, αὐτόν functions as an "intensive marker" (BDAG 152c; Wallace 349) modifying οὐρανόν—"heaven *itself*" (most EVV). This intensification is aug. by the sg. οὐρανόν, which is pl. elsewhere (see comments on 1:10–11; 9:23). The sg. aligns with God's dwelling place, which is why it is the *true* sanctuary (Cockerill 418). Τὰ ἐπουράνια (v. 23) and οὐρανός (v. 24) function as hook words to bind these vv. together (Cockerill 414).

νῦν ἐμφανισθῆναι τῷ προσώπῳ τοῦ θεοῦ ὑπὲρ ἡμῶν·
so that he might now appear in the presence of God for us.

Ἐμφανισθῆναι is the aor. pass. inf. of ἐμφανίζω, "appear" (most EVV; "make visible" [BDAG 325d]; A. Sand, *EDNT* 1:447b–c). The inf. indicates the purpose for which Christ has entered heaven ("so that" [CSB], although not indicated in many EVV) and is subord. to an implied εἰσῆλθεν. This vb. can be used to indicate the supernatural manifestation of a deity, although it is also used in official contexts, such as appearing before a magistrate (Attridge 263; Ellingworth 480). Here it refers to the "divine acceptance and favor" experienced by Jesus appearing before God (Cockerill 418). This is the first of three refs. to "appearing" in this passage (Harris 264).

The temp. adv. νῦν modifies the inf., underscoring the contemp. significance of Jesus's appearance in heaven (Attridge 263). Νῦν is not restricted to the pres. moment, but includes the time begun with and continuing from Jesus's initial appearance in heaven. Προσώπῳ is used here as an idiom for God's presence (most EVV; but "before the very face of God" [Cassirer]). In the LXX, the expression is associated with prayer and seeking God's favor (Koester 422). Ὑπὲρ ἡμῶν adv. modifies ἐμφανισθῆναι indicating advantage (cf. 6:20), thereby underscoring the contemp. significance of Christ's work and perhaps recalling Christ's intercessory work in 7:25 (cf. Attridge 263), as well as 4:14 and 6:19–20.

VERSE 25

οὐδ' ἵνα πολλάκις προσφέρῃ ἑαυτόν,
He did not do this to offer himself many times,

Verses 25–26 present the second contrast between the old and new orders, now focusing on the sacrifices. Whereas the earthly high priest presented sacrificed animal offerings repeatedly (both daily and the yearly Day of Atonement), Jesus presented his very self—once and for all. Ἵνα followed by the subjunc. (προσφέρῃ) indicates a dependent purpose clause, which modifies the understood εἰσῆλθεν from v. 24, which is in turn negated by οὐδ (= οὐ + δέ, which elides before a vowel or rough breathing [R 207])—"he did not [enter] . . . to offer . . ." (cf. CSB; Ellingworth 478). Thus v. 24 states positively why Christ entered heaven, whereas v. 25 restates this negatively (Ellingworth 481). Προσφέρῃ is the 3rd sg. pres. act. subjunc. of προσφέρω, "offer" (see comments on 5:1). The refl. pron. ἑαυτόν refers to Christ. Πολλάκις ("again and again" [NIV, NRSV], "repeatedly" [ESV]; "often" [NASB], "frequently" [BDAG 846]) modifies προσφέρῃ.

ὥσπερ ὁ ἀρχιερεὺς εἰσέρχεται εἰς τὰ ἅγια κατ' ἐνιαυτὸν ἐν αἵματι ἀλλοτρίῳ,
as the high priest enters the sanctuary yearly with the blood of another.

The conj. ὥσπερ ("just as," "as") introduces a comp. clause that compares Jesus's entry into the heavenly sanctuary with that of the high priest's into the earthly sanctuary. Ἀρχιερεύς (-έως, ὁ, "high priest" [BDAG 139a]) resumes an important theme in Hebrews (see comments on 2:17). Εἰς τὰ ἅγια adv. modifies εἰσέρχεται locat. Verbs compounded with εἰς nearly always repeat the prep. (R 559). As with v. 24, τὰ ἅγια indicates the entire sanctuary. The pres. εἰσέρχεται is gnomic or "timeless" (Ellingworth 482). Note the par. between v. 24 and v. 25. Ἐνιαυτόν is the acc. sg. masc. of ἐνιαυτός, -οῦ, ὁ, "year" (BDAG 337d). Κατ' ἐνιαυτόν is distrib. (Harris 155–56); "each year" [CEV]; "every year" [ESV, NIV]). The translation "year after year" (NET, NLT, REB; Cockerill 420 n. 2) underscores esp. well the rep. nature of the Levitical sacrificial order. The prep. phrase modifies εἰσέρχεται temp.

Ἀλλοτρίῳ is the dat. sg. neut. of ἀλλότριος, -α, -ον, "not his own" (most EVV). The adj. could carry the implication of "strange"(BDAG 47c), "alien" (F. Büchsel, *TDNT* 1:265) or "unclean" (Cockerill 421; see his extensive discussion). The implication of animal blood is made explicit in the CEV and NLT. The adj. modifies αἵματι. The prep. phrase ἐν αἵματι modifies εἰσέρχεται indicating "accompanying circumstance" (R 589; "associative dative" [BDF §198(2)]; cf. Harris 36). Less likely, the prep. is instr. ("by the blood of another"). As with Hebrews 5 and 7, the author alludes to the Day of Atonement (Lev 16). The ref. to ἐν αἵματι ἀλλοτρίῳ recalls the extended discussion in 9:11–14, but here the contrast focuses on the repeated nature of the Levitical offerings vs. Christ's singular offering (ἑαυτόν; cf. the use of ἅπαξ in vv. 26–28). This v. anticipates the sim. point in 10:1–4.

VERSE 26

ἐπεὶ ἔδει αὐτὸν πολλάκις παθεῖν ἀπὸ καταβολῆς κόσμου·
Otherwise, he would have had to suffer many times since the foundation of the world.

This clause concludes the second contrast begun in v. 25. The subord. conj. ἐπεί is causal. The impers. vb. ἔδει (3rd sg. impf. act. indic. of δεῖ, "it is necessary" [BDAG 214a; R 1085]) occurs only here in Hebrews. This expression is an implied contrary-to-fact (second-class) cond. in which only the apod. appears (R 887, 920, 963; Ellingworth 482); the prot. must be inferred (i.e., "if repeated sacrifices had been necessary" [Cockerill 422 n. 11]; cf. "if he had offered himself every year" [CEV]). The impf. without ἄν can be used of "something which is or was actually necessary . . . but which does not or did not take place" (BDF §358[1]). Thus in this context ἐπεί is best translated "otherwise" (most EVV [cf. BDAG 360c]). The antecedent of αὐτόν is Christ, which is the "subj." of the inf. (Wallace 195), but is translated as the subj. of the main clause in many EVV (e.g., CSB). Παθεῖν (aor. act. inf. of πάσχω "to suffer" [BDAG 785b]) complements ἔδει. The adv. πολλάκις (see comments on v. 25; most EVV translate this Gk. word the same way in both vv.) modifies the inf., par. its use with the subjunc. in v. 25. Καταβολῆς is the gen. sg. fem. of καταβολή, -ῆς, ἡ, "foundation" (BDAG 515a). The adv. prep. ἀπὸ καταβολῆς κόσμου is temp. (Moule 73), modifying παθεῖν. The ref. to the "foundations of the world" implicitly affirms Jesus's eternality by indicating that if he had to suffer repeatedly, then this rep. would have to extend back to the eternal past. The expression ἀπὸ καταβολῆς κόσμου may hint at the "universal scope of Christ's work" (Ellingworth 484), perhaps affirming the need for "atonement since primeval times" (Koester 422). It also stresses the faulty logic of the analogy (cf. Attridge 264).

This clause continues the contrast between the Levitical high priest and Jesus. Like the high priest, Jesus also entered the sanctuary with an offering. Unlike that priest's offering of animal blood, however, the blood of Jesus's offering was his very own. Moreover, if Jesus had been like earthly high priests, then (since he offered himself) he would have had to suffer repeatedly. Since Jesus's suffering entailed dying on the cross (cf. 5:8), this would be clearly impossible since (as v. 27 makes explicit) humans can only die once.

νυνὶ δὲ ἅπαξ ἐπὶ συντελείᾳ τῶν αἰώνων εἰς ἀθέτησιν [τῆς] ἁμαρτίας διὰ τῆς θυσίας αὐτοῦ πεφανέρωται.
But now he has appeared one time, at the end of the ages, for the removal of sin by the sacrifice of himself.

Νυνί is an emph. form of νῦν (BDAG 682a). Together with δέ it presents a strong contrast, both logically and temp. (Koester 422; *pace* Lane 1:201). Δέ usually follows the temp. adv. νυνί in the NT (Ellingworth 408). The adv. ἅπαξ (most EVV, "once" [BDAG 97b]) is temp. (R 769; cf. 9:6) and par. the use of ἐφάπαξ in 9:12 (cf. Bruce 231 n. 159). Note the rep. use of νῦν/νυνί and ἅπαξ, which contrasts with πολλάκις in vv. 24–26 (cf. v. 28) as a means of underscoring the rep. work of the earthly high priest vs. Christ's complete and final work (cf. Attridge 264; see also 7:27). Πεφανέρωται is the 3rd sg. pf. pass. indic. of φανερόω; with the pass. "appear" (ESV, NET, NIV), "been manifested" (NASB). The pf. is likely emph. (e.g., "intensified," Campbell, *VA* 201). The time referent is Christ's incarnation, whereas his appearing "a second time" in v.

28 refers to his second coming. This is the second of three refs. to "appearing" in this passage (Harris, *Prepositions* 264).

Συντελείᾳ is the dat. sg. fem. of συντέλεια, -ας, ἡ, "end" (ESV), "consummation" (NASB, NET), "culmination" (NIV, TNIV), "climax of history" (REB), "completion," "close" (BDAG 974d). This word continues the repeated use of the τελ- word group in Hebrews (e.g., 8:8 and 9:20) that is associated with the perfection achieved by Christ. The prep. phrase ἐπὶ συντελείᾳ τῶν αἰώνων adv. modifies πεφανέρωται temp. (R 604; cf. Moule 50). The expression is common in Jewish apocalyptic writings and, in var. forms, occurs elsewhere in the NT (cf. Matt 28:20; 1 Cor 10:11; G. Delling, *TDNT* 8:64–66; Bruce 231 nos. 161–63; Cockerill 422 n. 15). The expression also recalls "these last days" (Heb 1:2) and reveals Christ's death as the "decisive eschatological event" (Attridge 264).

Ἀθέτησιν is the acc. sg. fem. of ἀθέτησις, -εως, ἡ, "annulment" (BDAG 24d). The word continues the use of legal language in Heb (Lane 2:249). Many EVV, however, translate this noun as a vb. (e.g., "abolish" [REB]; "remove" [NLT, NRSV]; "put away" [ESV, NASB, NET]; "do away with" [NIV]; see comments on 7:18). The gen. ἁμαρτίας indicates separation (ablatival). The sg. ἁμαρτίας (cf. the pl. in v. 28) may indicate the "human condition" (Koester 422), or the "source of pollution and separation from God" (Cockerill 423). The mss. evidence for the inclusion of the art. is not decisive; it may have been omitted due to assimilation to 10:2 (Ellingworth 485). The prep. phrase εἰς ἀθέτησιν [τῆς] ἁμαρτίας adv. modifies πεφανέρωται, indicating purpose. Διά plus the gen. indicates instr. The antecedent of αὐτοῦ is Christ. The gen. is either *verbal ("the sacrifice of himself" [ESV, NIV]) or poss. ("his sacrifice" [NAB, NET]).

The collocation of ἀθέτησιν and ἁμαρτίας occurs only here in BGk. (Ellingworth 482). The use of ἀθέτησις in 7:18 may suggest a connection between the two vv.—namely that because Christ's work has abolished sin, it has also "abolished the old priestly system that could not deal with sin" (Cockerill 423).

The ref. to the "foundation of the world" suggests that Christ's work has effected the removal of sin not only beginning with his atoning death but also before that, extending back to the beginning of time. The author will restate this truth in terms of the "perfection" of OT saints that was achieved by Christ (e.g., Heb 11:39–40 [Cockerill 423 n. 18]).

VERSE 27

καὶ καθ' ὅσον ἀπόκειται τοῖς ἀνθρώποις ἅπαξ ἀποθανεῖν, μετὰ δὲ τοῦτο κρίσις,
And just as it is appointed for people to die once—and after this, judgment—

Καί joins the discussion of the sg. nature of Christ's death (vv. 25–26) to an analogy from human experience (vv. 27–28). Just as (mere) human beings die *once*, so also Jesus has died *once*—but with very different consequences (cf. Lane 2:249). The claim that people die once was commonly affirmed, although it was less commonly linked with the concept of judgment after death (Cockerill 425; see esp. Koester 422–23). The cstr. καθ' ὅσον (v. 27) . . . οὕτως (v. 28) indicates a comp. ("[just] as . . . so"

[BDAG 513a]) and correlates "the validity of Christ's work" to "the human situation" (Cockerill 425 n. 29). (Καθ' occurs before rough breathing). Ἀπόκειται is the 3rd sg. pres. mid. indic. of ἀπόκειμαι, "destined" (NIV, NLT; cf. BDAG 113a); "appointed" (most EVV). The dat. ἀνθρώποις is generic (cf. Ellingworth 486). Ἀποθανεῖν is the pres. act. inf. of ἀποθνήσκω, "die." The inf. complements ἀπόκειται. The adv. ἅπαξ ("once") modifies the inf. Τοῦτο refers generally back to the preceding clause as a whole (Wallace 333–34). Μετὰ τοῦτο adv. modifies the ellipsis of the copula in the second clause temp. The use of κρίσις may recall Heb 6:2. The reality of final judgment is developed in Heb 12:25–29.

VERSE 28

οὕτως καὶ ὁ Χριστὸς ἅπαξ προσενεχθεὶς εἰς τὸ πολλῶν ἀνενεγκεῖν ἁμαρτίας
so also Christ, having been offered once to bear the sins of many,

Οὕτως καί introduces the final elements of the comp. begun in v. 27. This v. also anticipates the extended discussion of Christ's sacrifice in Hebrews 10. Προσενεχθείς is the nom. sg. masc. of the aor. pass. ptc. of προσφέρω, "offered"; cf. "sacrificed" [NIV] (see comments on 5:1). The ptc. is temp. ("having been" [ESV, NASB]; "after" [NET]), but is left unspecified in many EVV. The agent of the pass. vb. is God, although Hebrews makes it clear that Jesus's death was willingly undertaken (v. 25; cf. 5:7 and 10:7–10; cf. Cockerill 426 n. 33). The adv. ἅπαξ modifies προσενεχθείς. Ἀνενεγκεῖν is the aor. act. inf. of ἀναφέρω, "bear" (most EVV; cf. BDAG 75b–c). Εἰς with an art. inf. indicates purpose (Wallace 590–92). Ἁμαρτίας (acc. pl.), the obj. of the inf., is a gen. of ref. ("with respect to" [Wallace 127–28]). The entire ptc. clause modifies ὀφθήσεται temp. (see below).

The wording of this v. alludes to LXX Isa 53:12: καὶ αὐτος ἁμαρτίας πολλῶν ἀνήνεγκεν (Cockerill 426 n. 34; Ellingworth 486–87). The vicarious nature of Christ's sacrifice is evinced in the salvation that he brings, which is inextricably associated with Jesus leading his people to the place where he already sits exalted at God's right hand.

ἐκ δευτέρου χωρὶς ἁμαρτίας ὀφθήσεται τοῖς αὐτὸν ἀπεκδεχομένοις εἰς σωτηρίαν.
will appear a second time, not to bear sin, but to bring salvation to those who are waiting for him.

The anchor of this main clause is ὀφθήσεται (3rd sg. fut. pass. indic. of ὁράω); in the pass., "appear" (most EVV; BDAG 719d; but "manifest" [NJB]; "come again" [NLT]). The fut. is ingressive (R 871). The same vb. is associated elsewhere with Christ's second coming (e.g., Matt 24:30; 26:64 and par. [Attridge 266]). The vb. is modified temp. by the prep. phrase ἐκ δευτέρου. This is one of the clearest NT statements about Christ's second coming (cf. Ellingworth 487). The use of a dependent ptc. clause in the first part of this v. to discuss Christ's definitive, sacrificial offering and the use of a finite vb. to depict Christ's second coming puts the emph. on the latter and thus continues the theme of believers' coming salvation (cf. 1:14), and anticipates the discussion of the heavenly Zion in Hebrews 12 (cf. Cockerill 426). This is the final of three refs. to "appearing" in this passage (Harris 264).

Χωρίς ("without") takes a gen. obj. (ἁμαρτίας). In Heb 4:15, χωρὶς ἁμαρτίας referred to Jesus's sinlessness. In this v., the phrase indicates "not with the purpose of atoning for sin" (Lane 2:233 n. *pp*; cf. BDAG 1095d; Ellingworth 487; Koester 423; "without reference to sin" [NASB]). Many EVV translate the prep. phrase as a negated purpose inf.: "not to bear sin" (NET, NIV); "not to deal with sin" (ESV, NLT). Thus, the purpose of Jesus's second coming concerns the final salvation effected by his atoning sacrifice through which he dealt decisively with "the annulment of sin" (Harris 264; see his extended discussion of χωρίς on pp. 263–65). Moreover, his second coming is "the ultimate proof that his sacrifice was 'once for all'" (Cockerill 426).

Ἀπεκδεχομένοις is the dat. pl. masc. of the pres. mid. ptc. of ἀπεκδέχομαι. The double compound (ἀπό + ἐκ + δέχομαι) likely has an "intensive force" (*NIDNTTE* 133), thus "eagerly await" (most EVV; BDAG 100c), which is not captured by "waiting for" (NIV). The ptc. is subst. Αὐτόν is the obj. of the ptc.; its antecedent is Christ. Εἰς σωτηρίαν indicates purpose and result, with its final placement being emph. (Ellingworth 488). It modifies ὀφθήσεται (e.g., CSB; cf. Heb 1:14; Harris 264), rather than ἀπεκδεχομένοις (e.g., "appear . . . to those who are waiting for him to obtain their salvation" [Cassirer]). The imagery here may recall the Israelites, who waited expectantly for the reappearance of the high priest on the Day of Atonement, which affirmed that his offering had been accepted (Bruce 232; Cockerill 427; Koester 423; Lane 2:250; *pace* Attridge 266 n. 72). Thus the image here is both priestly and apocalyptic (Koester 423).

HOMILETICAL SUGGESTIONS

The Perfect Sacrifice that Brings Salvation (9:23–28)

1. An Analogy: Animal Sacrifices Cleansed the Earthly Tabernacle, Thus Better Sacrifice(s) Cleanse the Heavenly Tabernacle (v. 23)
2. Christ Alone Has Entered the True, Heavenly Sanctuary in God's Presence (v. 24)
3. His Appearance in Heaven and His Sacrifice Has Removed Sin (v. 26b)
   (a) He does not enter repeatedly with animal blood (v. 25)
   (b) If that were true, he would have to suffer death multiple times (v. 26a)
   (c) But humans only die one time and then face judgment (v. 27)
4. His Death Bore Sin; His Return Will Bring Salvation (v. 28)

5. Shadow and Reality, Sacrifice and Obedience (10:1–10)

STRUCTURE

The final arguments concerning the superiority of Christ's (obj.) sacrifice are summed up in 10:1–18, with a view to their subj. relevance for the audience (cf. Lane 2:258). Specifically, 10:1–4 recaps the "shadowy" ineffectiveness of the old sacrificial order (cf. 9:1–10), and 10:5–10, Christ's willing sacrifice of his own body (cf. 9:11–14). The author concludes the central argument of Hebrews in 10:11–18 with discussion of Christ's sacrifice as the inauguration of a new covenant (cf. 9:15–22).

The anchor for v. 1 is *δύναται . . . τελειῶσαι* with *ὁ νόμος* as the subj. The rep. of the sacrifices of the Levitical system is stressed by the alignment of *κατ' ἐνιαυτόν* and *εἰς τὸ διηνεκές*. The unreal cond. in v. 2 is strongly contrasted (*ἀλλά*) by the reality of the former sacrificial system in v. 3, which then is followed by the general principle in v. 4. Verses 5–7 comprise a citation from Psalm 40, which is then explicated in v. 8 (*ἀνώτερον λέγων ὅτι*) and v. 9 (*τότε εἴρηκεν*), followed by a concise summary in v. 9b. The psalm citation underscores Christ's obedience to God's will, which is the basis for believer's sanctification (v. 10) as indicated by the arrow below.

1 Σκιὰν γὰρ ἔχων ὁ νόμος
τῶν μελλόντων ἀγαθῶν,
οὐκ αὐτὴν τὴν εἰκόνα τῶν πραγμάτων,
↓κατ' ἐνιαυτὸν
ταῖς αὐταῖς θυσίαις
ἃς προσφέρουσιν εἰς τὸ διηνεκὲς
οὐδέποτε δύναται τοὺς προσερχομένους τελειῶσαι·
2 ἐπεὶ οὐκ ἂν ἐπαύσαντο προσφερόμεναι
διὰ τὸ μηδεμίαν ἔχειν ἔτι συνείδησιν ἁμαρτιῶν τοὺς λατρεύοντας
ἅπαξ κεκαθαρισμένους;
3 ἀλλ' . . . ἐν αὐταῖς
. . . ἀνάμνησις ἁμαρτιῶν
κατ' ἐνιαυτόν·
4 ἀδύνατον γὰρ αἷμα ταύρων καὶ τράγων ἀφαιρεῖν ἁμαρτίας.
5 Διὸ εἰσερχόμενος εἰς τὸν κόσμον
λέγει·
θυσίαν καὶ προσφορὰν οὐκ ἠθέλησας,
σῶμα δὲ κατηρτίσω μοι·
6 ὁλοκαυτώματα καὶ περὶ ἁμαρτίας οὐκ εὐδόκησας.
7 τότε εἶπον·
ἰδοὺ ἥκω . . . τοῦ ποιῆσαι ὁ θεὸς τὸ θέλημά σου.
ἐν κεφαλίδι βιβλίου γέγραπται περὶ ἐμοῦ,
8 ἀνώτερον λέγων ὅτι
θυσίας καὶ προσφορὰς καὶ ὁλοκαυτώματα καὶ περὶ ἁμαρτίας
οὐκ ἠθέλησας οὐδὲ εὐδόκησας,

αἵτινες κατὰ νόμον προσφέρονται,
9 τότε εἴρηκεν·
ἰδοὺ ἥκω τοῦ ποιῆσαι τὸ θέλημά σου.
ἀναιρεῖ τὸ πρῶτον
ἵνα τὸ δεύτερον στήσῃ,
10 ἐν ᾧ θελήματι ἡγιασμένοι ἐσμὲν
διὰ τῆς προσφορᾶς τοῦ σώματος Ἰησοῦ Χριστοῦ ἐφάπαξ.

VERSE 1

Σκιὰν γὰρ ἔχων ὁ νόμος τῶν μελλόντων ἀγαθῶν,
Since the law has only a shadow of the good things to come,

Γάρ (untr. in many EVV) links the previous discussion of Christ's entrance into the heavenly sanctuary (9:23–28) to the "good things to come," of which the law was only a shadow (cf. Ellingworth 492). Many EVV tr. ἔχων as a finite vb. ("has" [ESV, NASB]; "possesses" [NET]; "contains" [REB]; "is" [e.g., NIV]). The ptc. adv. modifies δύναται. Νόμος is the subj. of the ptc. ἔχων. Σκιάν is the acc. sg. fem. of σκία, -ᾶς, ἡ, "shadow" (most EVV; but "reflection" [NJB]; see comments on 8:5). Its initial position is emph. (Lane 2:254 n. *a*). It is the obj. of ἔχων. Μελλόντων (see comments on 1:14) modifies the subst. adj. ἀγαθῶν (gen. pl. neut.), "good things to come" (most EVV). The gen. is subj. (e.g., the good things "create" the shadow) or possibly partitive. The entire clause adv. modifies δύναται (see below). In 8:5, σκία applied to the Levitical priests and their sanctuary service. The former order as a shadow of the reality in Christ is "fundamental to the pastor's interpretation of the OT" (Cockerill 428).

οὐκ αὐτὴν τὴν εἰκόνα τῶν πραγμάτων,
and not the reality itself of those things,

Many EVV supply a conj. ("and" [NASB]; "but" [NET]; "instead of" [ESV]) between the first clause and this one, although a dash (e.g., NIV) is sometimes used to capture the lack of punctuation (asyndeton) in the Gk. Εἰκόνα (acc. sg. fem. of εἰκών, -όνος, ἡ) has a wide semantic range, including denoting images on coins or statues (Koester 430; cf. BDAG 282b; G. Kittel, *TDNT* 2:392–97). Εἰκών can be understood as an exact representation of something; "very form" (NASB), "true form" (ESV). It is the obj. of ἔχων. Αὐτήν functions as an "intensive marker" (BDAG 152c; R 686; Wallace 349) modifying εἰκόνα (e.g., "the reality itself" [NET]; cf. 9:23). Πραγμάτων is the gen. pl. neut. of πρᾶγμα, -ατος, τό, "thing" (BDAG 859a), likely par. to τῶν μελλόντων ἀγαθῶν (Ellingworth 492). Thus "it denotes reality itself" (Lane 2:254 n. *c*). The overlap between εἰκών and πρᾶγμα explains the conflation of the two terms (e.g., "the realities themselves" [NIV]) or the omission of πραγμάτων (e.g., NET).

The distinction between σκία and εἰκών is debated. In earlier Platonic writings, the two terms were synonymous (H. Kuhli, *EDNT* 390a; Cockerill 428; Ellingworth 490; Koester 431). The logic of Heb 10:1, however, suggests a distinction (Metzger 600; cf.

Bruce 234 n. 1). Σκία points forward eschatologically (as "a dim preview" [NLT; cf. Lane 2:259); thus τῶν μελλόντων ἀγαθῶν points beyond the law to the reality (εἰκών) in Christ (Cockerill 429; Koester 431). This contrast is indicated in some EVV, which add "only a shadow" (e.g., NASB). As with previous "shadow/reality" or "earthly/heavenly" language in Hebrews, the distinction is qual. or temp., not phenomenal vs. noumenal. "[T]he good things" are future with respect to the law, although the audience has begun to experience this new reality (9:11; cf. 6:5). Even so, the final realization of these good things awaits Christ's return and the "world to come" (2:5 [cf. Attridge 269; Cockerill 429]).

κατ' ἐνιαυτὸν ταῖς αὐταῖς θυσίαις
. . . by the same sacrifices . . . year after year.

For κατ' ἐνιαυτόν, see discussion on 9:25. The prep. phrase modifies προσφέρουσιν (see below) and forms an *inclusio* with κατ' ἐνιαυτόν in v. 3 (Ellingworth 493). Αὐταῖς functions as an identifying adj. ("same"; Wallace 349), modifying θυσίαις (see comments on 5:1). The dat. is instr., modifying προσφέρουσιν (see below). Many EVV tr. the final clause of this v. before κατ' ἐνιαυτὸν ταῖς αὐταῖς θυσίαις and ἃς προσφέρουσιν εἰς τὸ διηνεκές (e.g., NAB) or insert the prep. phrase and rel. clause into the final clause following English syntax (e.g., ESV, NET, NIV).

ἃς προσφέρουσιν εἰς τὸ διηνεκές
. . . they continually offer . . .

The antecedent of ἅς is θυσίαις. Προσφέρουσιν is the 3rd pl. pres. act. indic. of προσφέρω, "offer" (see comments on 5:1). The pres. is gnomic. The implied subj. of the vb. is the Levitical high priests, drawing on 9:1–10 (e.g., "they" [NASB]). Some, however, view the vb. as impers. with a pass. sense (a "general or rhetorical plural" [R 392]; Lane 2:255 n. *f*; cf. Ellingworth 493; "repeated endlessly" [NIV]). (For εἰς τὸ διηνεκές, see comments on 7:3.) This adv. prep. phrase ("continually" [most EVV]) likely modifies προσφέρουσιν temp., although in some EVV it modifies τελειῶσαι (e.g., "it can never bring the worshippers to perfection for all time" [NEB]). This prep. phrase, however, usually follows the vb. it modifies (e.g., 7:3; 10:12, 14; Lane 2:255 n. *g*; cf. Ellingworth 492).

οὐδέποτε δύναται τοὺς προσερχομένους τελειῶσαι·
it can never perfect the worshipers . . .

Οὐδέποτε is a strengthened form of οὐ ("never" [most EVV; BDAG 735d]). Since it usually precedes the vb. it modifies, the position here is not emph. (Ellingworth 493). "For this reason" (NIV) must be inferred from the context. Προσερχομένους is the acc. pl. masc. of the pres. mid. ptc. of προσέρχομαι, "approach" (see comments on 4:16); here it refers to "those who come to worship" (NAB), or "worshippers" (NJB). The ptc. is subst. and is the dir. obj. of τελειῶσαι. The var. rdg. δύνανται (for δύναται) has strong ms. support and likely reflects assimilation to προσφέρουσιν, yet the sg. is likely original with νόμος the understood subj. of the sg. (cf. Metzger 600; see esp. Ellingworth 491–92). Τελειῶσαι (aor. act. inf. of τελειόω; "perfect" [most EVV]; see comments on 2:10 and 9:9) is the complement of δύναται.

This v. summarizes much of the previous argument, but expands it from the ineffectiveness of the old sacrificial system itself to its application to worshippers. The background for vv. 1–3 continues to be the Day of Atonement.

VERSE 2

ἐπεὶ οὐκ ἂν ἐπαύσαντο προσφερόμεναι
Otherwise, wouldn't they have stopped being offered,

Ἐπεί is causal. Similar to its usage in 9:26 (see comments there), the prot. of a contrary-to-fact (second-class) cond. is implied (i.e., "if the sacrifices had perfected worshippers"), with only the apod. stated explicitly (R 963; cf. Lane 2:255 n. *h*). Thus, ἐπεί is best tr. "otherwise" (most EVV; "if it could" [NIV 1983, REB]; cf. BDF §360(2)]). The particle οὐ (οὐκ before a vowel) introduces an interr. expecting an affirmative answer, which from the context is best understood as a rhetorical question (cf. R 1175; Ellingworth 494; Koester 431). This is reflected in most EVV (e.g., "would they not have . . .?" ; *pace* GNB, NJB, NLT). Ἐπαύσαντο is the 3rd pl. aor. mid. indic. of παύω, "stopped" (NIV, NLT), "cease" (ESV, NASB, NET; cf. BDAG 790a–b). The mid. voice often draws attention to the actor vs. the action (cf. Wallace 419); when παύω is in the mid., it is almost always followed by a ptc. (R 1102; cf. Ellingworth 494). Προσφερόμεναι is the nom. pl. fem. of the pres. pass. ptc. of προσφέρω, "offered" (most EVV; see 5:1). The ptc. complements ἐπαύσαντο (Wallace 646).

διὰ τὸ μηδεμίαν ἔχειν ἔτι συνείδησιν ἁμαρτιῶν
. . . would no longer have any consciousness of sins? . . .

The cstr. διὰ τό plus an inf. (ἔχειν) is causal ("since" [most EVV]; Wallace 596–97), modifying ἐπαύσαντο προσφερόμεναι. The adv. ἔτι ("no longer" [most EVV]) modifies the inf. The implied subj. of the inf. is τοὺς λατρεύοντας. The neg. adj. μηδεμίαν (μηδείς, μηδεμία, μηδέν) modifies συνείδησιν (συνείδησις, -εως, ἡ, "consciousness" [see comments on 9:9]), which is the obj. of ἔχειν. The gen. ἁμαρτιῶν is obj. (e.g., "consciousness of sins" [many EVV]; "sense of sin" [REB]).

τοὺς λατρεύοντας ἅπαξ κεκαθαρισμένους;
. . . since the worshipers, purified once and for all . . .

Λατρεύοντας is the acc. pl. masc. of the pres. act. ptc. of λατρεύω, "worshipers" (most EVV; BDAG 587c; see comments on 8:5). The term parallels τοὺς προσερχομένους in v. 1 (cf. Ellingworth 495). The subst. ptc. is the "subj." of the inf. ἔχειν. Κεκαθαρισμένους is the acc. pl. masc. of the pf. pass. ptc. of καθαρίζω, "cleanse" (ESV, NASB, NIV) or "purify" (NET, NLT; BDAG 488d–489a; H. Thyen, *EDNT* 2:220d). The anar. ptc. is pred. (R 778, Wallace 618), making an assertion about τοὺς λατρεύοντας (e.g., "have been purified" [NET]). This is a common function of the pf. pass. ptc. (Wallace 618). The pf. tense may be emph. (cf. Lane 2:255 n. *i*; Cockerill 430). The adv. ἅπαξ (modifying κεκαθαρισμένους) can be both quan. (one point in time, "once") and qual. ("once and for all" [most EVV]; cf. BDAG 97b; Koester 313). The author has held the ptc. until the end for emph. (Cockerill 430), although this syntax is awkward in English. Thus most EVV switch this clause to before διὰ τὸ . . . ἁμαρτιῶν and indicate this causal cstr. with "since," which is placed before the "subj." of the cstr., namely, "the worshipers" (e.g., CSB).

Some see evidence in this v. for the ongoing existence of the Jerusalem temple and hence evidence that Hebrews was written before AD 70 (e.g., Bruce 236). The author's point, however, is a logical one about the inadequacies of the law, not a temp. one concerning whether the cultic system was still operational. Thus, even if the temple were standing, the author's point would remain unchanged. See For Further Study 54 (The Date of Hebrews).

VERSE 3

ἀλλ' ἐν αὐταῖς ἀνάμνησις ἁμαρτιῶν κατ' ἐνιαυτόν·
But in the sacrifices there is a reminder of sins year after year.

Ἀλλά contrasts the implied contrary-to-fact cond. in v. 2 with the "real situation" in v. 3 (e.g., "but" [most EVV]; "but in fact" [NJB; BDF §448]; "otherwise" [BDF §360(2)]). An impers. use of εἰμί is implied in this verbless clause. Ἀνάμνησις is the nom. sg. fem. of ἀνάμνησις, -εως, ἡ, "reminder" (most EVV), "remembrance" (ASV, NAB; BDAG 68b; H. Patsch, *EDNT* 1:85d). The verbal noun is rendered as a vb. in some EVV ("brought to mind" [REB]; "are recalled" [NJB]). The word is the pred. nom. of an implied copulative vb. Parallel to v. 2, ἁμαρτιῶν is obj. The antecedent of αὐταῖς is θυσίαις, which is made explicit in many EVV. Ἐν αὐταῖς is either instr. (NAB, REB; Ellingworth 495) or *locat. in a metaphorical sense ("in" [most EVV]), although some EVV render the dat. as the subj. of the clause (e.g., NIV, NLT). (For κατ' ἐνιαυτόν, see discussion on 9:25.) Here the prep. phrase adj. modifies ἀνάμνησις.

Ἀνάμνησις likely contrasts with the promise of God "not remembering" sin in the citation of Jeremiah 31 in Heb 8:12, which is repeated in 10:17 (cf. Attridge 272; Ellingworth 497). The comment is pejorative: all that the old sacrificial system accomplished was the remembrance of sin. There is likely an allusion to the Day of Atonement, but the author emphasizes the consciousness of sin that permeated that day (see esp. Lane 2:261) and probably also the "annual cycle of sacrifices climaxing with the Day of Atonement" (Cockerill 431).

VERSE 4

ἀδύνατον γὰρ αἷμα ταύρων καὶ τράγων ἀφαιρεῖν ἁμαρτίας.
For it is impossible for the blood of bulls and goats to take away sins.

This v. recaps the argument in Heb 9:13, 23 and functions as the conclusion of vv. 1–3. The allusion to the Day of Atonement continues. The cstr. here parallels Heb 6:4. Γάρ is causal ("for" [most EVV]). Ἀδύνατον is the nom. sg. neut. of ἀδύνατος, -ον (BDAG 22a). The adj. is pred. with an implied vb. and an impers. subj. ("it is impossible" [most EVV]). The position of the adj. is emph. (cf. Lane 1:141). The complement of the pred. adj. is ἀφαιρεῖν (pres. act. inf. of ἀφαιρέω, "take away" [most EVV], "do away with," "remove" [BDAG 154b]). Although in the NT ἀφαιρέω has the sense of taking away sins only in Rom 11:27 (citing Isa 27:9), this mng. occurs in the LXX (e.g., Exod 34:7, 9 [Ellingworth 498; Koester 432]). The subj. of the inf. is αἷμα, which is modified by ταύρων and τράγων (see comments on 9:12–13). The order here (ταύρων and τράγων) follows the LXX. The obj. of the inf. is ἁμαρτίας (acc. pl. fem.).

VERSE 5

Διὸ εἰσερχόμενος εἰς τὸν κόσμον
Therefore, as he was coming into the world,

Διό is an inferential conj. ("therefore" [most EVV; BDAG 250c]; "so" [NET]; "consequently" [ESV]) that both draws on the summary in 10:1–4 and points to the ensuing argument (cf. Ellingworth 499). The implied subj. of εἰσερχόμενος is Christ (drawing on 9:28 and anticipating v. 10), which is made explicit in some EVV (e.g., ESV, NIV, NLT). The ptc. is temp., modifying λέγει, indicating contemp. time. Εἰς τὸν κόσμον adv. modifies εἰσερχόμενος locat. The phrase recalls Heb 1:6 (εἰς τὴν οἰκουμένην). Whereas οἰκουμένη in 1:6 indicates the "world to come," κόσμος specifies the created world and refers to Jesus's incarnation. The expression likely par. ἰδοὺ ἥκω in the psalm citation in v. 7 (Lane 2:262). What was true of David is typologically fulfilled in Christ (cf. Cockerill 434).

λέγει·
he said:

Christ (mentioned in 9:28) is the implied speaker of the vb. The use of λέγει/λέγων to introduce OT citations is common in Hebrews and evinces the author's conviction that God is still speaking the very words recorded in the OT. The pres. is thus timeless. What makes this occurrence remarkable is that the psalmist's words are presented as Jesus's own rather than as spoken by the Father about the Son, as in Hebrews 1. This par. Heb 2:12–13, where the words of David (Ps 22) and Isaiah are attributed to Jesus (cf. Ellingworth 499).

θυσίαν καὶ προσφορὰν οὐκ ἠθέλησας,
You did not desire sacrifice and offering,

Θυσίαν ("sacrifice" [most EVV]) here likely refers in a general way to animal sacrifice (Attridge 274; Koester 433; see comments on 5:1). Προσφοράν is the acc. sg. fem. of προσφορά, -ᾶς, ἡ, "offering" (most EVV; BDAG 887a), which is used in the LXX for the meal offering ("cereal offering" [NJB]; Attridge 274; Koester 433). Ἠθέλησας is the 2nd sg. aor. act. indic. of θέλω, "desire" (most EVV).

σῶμα δὲ κατηρτίσω μοι·
but you prepared a body for me.

Κατηρτίσω is the 2nd sg. aor. mid. indic. καταρτίζω, "prepare" (most EVV); with the mid., "prepare something for someone" (BDAG 526c). Σῶμα is the obj. of κατηρτίσω. Μοί is a dat. of advantage.

The citation of Ps 40:6–8 continues until v. 7. Psalm 40 (LXX 39) is ascribed to David. There are several minor variations between the author's citation and the LXX, which he likely made to enhance his argument (see discussion in Cockerill 435–7; Lane 2:262–63). The most important textual issue, however, concerns differences between the LXX and the MT. The MT reads, "ears you have opened/pierced for me," whereas some of the most important LXX mss. (e.g., ℵ A B) read, "a body you prepared for me." Some suggest that the change represents a scribal error. Original mss. were written uppercase without word divisions. Thus a scribe may have misread ΗΘΕΛΗΣΑΣΩΤΙΑ ("you desired . . . an ear") for ΗΘΕΛΗΣΑΣ (Σ)ΩΜΑ ("you desired . . . a body"), where the final sigma of the vb. was read twice and TI misread for M (see Ellingworth 500; Koester 433). More likely, however, the LXX translators themselves employed synecdoche (a part [ear] is read for the whole [body]), since the orig. Heb. may not have been understood as a ref. to willing obedience to LXX readers (cf. Attridge 274; Cockerill 436; Koester 433; Lane 2:255 n. *m*). Thus in the psalmist's claim that God had prepared a body for him, the author of Hebrews saw a clear prophecy of Jesus's incarnation, obedience, and sacrificial offering of his body (cf. Lane 2:262). This understanding of Psalm 40 appears to have been unique to the author.

VERSE 6

ὁλοκαυτώματα καὶ περὶ ἁμαρτίας οὐκ εὐδόκησας.
You did not delight in whole burnt offerings and sin offerings.

Ὁλοκαυτώματα is the acc. pl. neut. of ὁλοκαύτωμα, -ατος, τό, "whole burnt offering" [NASB, NET], "burnt offerings" (ESV, NIV), "holocaust" (NAB; cf. BDAG 703d), referring to an offering for cleansing and expiation of sin that was entirely consumed by fire (Koester 433; cf. "animals sacrifices burned whole on the altar" [Barclay]). Περὶ ἁμαρτίας is used in the LXX as "a technical expression" for sin offerings (Moule, *Idiom-Book*, 63; see Harris 182–83; so most EVV). Εὐδόκησας is the 2nd sg. aor. act. indic. of εὐδοκέω, "please" (NIV), "delight in" (NET), "desire" (ESV, NRSV), "take pleasure" (NASB), "like," "approve" (BDAG 404c). The trans. usage of εὐδοκέω occurs in the LXX (R 474).

VERSE 7

τότε εἶπον·
Then I said,

The psalm citation continues through the end of this v. Although previous occurrences of λέγω to introduce citations have used the pres. tense (e.g., v. 5), the aor. here reflects the LXX. The subj. of εἶπον remains Jesus.

ἰδοὺ ἥκω, ἐν κεφαλίδι βιβλίου γέγραπται περὶ ἐμοῦ, τοῦ ποιῆσαι ὁ θεὸς τὸ θέλημά σου.
"See—it is written about me in the scroll—I have come to do your will, O God."

Ἰδού is a dem. ptcl. "that draws attention to what follows" (BDAG 468b). Although accented differently, it is the aor. mid. impv. of εἶδον, "behold" (ESV, NASB); "here I am" (NET, NIV, NJB). Ἥκω is the 1st sg. pres. act. indic., "have come" (BDAG 435c). The complement of ἥκω is ποιῆσαι, which indicates purpose (R 1088). The phrase τὸ θέλημά σου is the obj. of the inf. Ὁ θεός is a nom. functioning as a voc. Elsewhere in the NT, γέγραπται introduces Scripture citations ("it is written"). Here the "citation" is actually indir. discourse within the psalm. Per the author's focus on God's word still *speaking*, this is the only occurrence of γράφω in Hebrews.

Κεφαλίδι is the dat. sg. fem. of κεφαλίς, -ίδος, ἡ; technically this word refers to the knob on the top of a scroll (Ellingworth 502; BDAG 542c; G. Schneider, *EDNT* 2:287a; NT hapax). Βιβλίου (βιβλίον, -ου, τό) may be a "gen. of definition," e.g., "in the scroll which is in book form" (Bruce 242 n. 44; Lane 2:255 n. *o*; cf. "the scroll of the book" [ESV, NASB, NET]). More likely, however, the entire phrase simply refers to the scroll (so most EVV; Attridge 275; Cockerill 438–39 n. 28; Ellingworth 502). Ἐν κεφαλίδι βιβλίου modifies γέγραπται locat. Περὶ ἐμοῦ adv. modifies γέγραπται, indicating ref. In the context of Hebrews, περὶ ἐμοῦ refers to Christ. The clause ἐν κεφαλίδι βιβλίου γέγραπται περὶ ἐμοῦ is best understood as a parenthetical statement (e.g., NASB, NET, NIV; cf. Lane 2:254). The "scroll" in the psalm is probably the Pentateuch (e.g., "book of the Law" [GNT]), although the author of Hebrews may have had the entire OT in view (Cockerill 438).

VERSE 8

ἀνώτερον λέγων ὅτι
After he says above,

Ἀνώτερον is the acc. sg. neut. of ἀνώτερος (comp. of ἄνω=ἀνώτερον εἶναί τινος), "after" (NASB), "first" (NIV, NLT), "above" (ESV, NET; cf. BDAG 92d). Here the adj. functions as an adv. modifying λέγων. Ἀνώτερον λέγων modifies εἴρηκεν (v. 9; see below), indicating antecedent time. The ptc. used in connection with εἴρηκεν puts emph. on the latter (Ellingworth 503). Ὅτι introduces the psalm citation (ὅτι *recitativum*; BDF §397[5]), which the author now applies to his audience.

θυσίας καὶ προσφορὰς καὶ ὁλοκαυτώματα καὶ περὶ ἁμαρτίας
. . . in sacrifices and offerings, whole burnt offerings and sin offerings . . .

See comments on 10:5–6.

In the citation from Psalm 40, the author of Hebrews has concatenated the four terms (and pluralized the first two), suggesting that he was not concerned about individual distinctions between the terms but rather viewed them as representing the whole sacrificial system, perhaps as a merism (cf. Bruce 240–41; Cockerill 438; Ellingworth 502). The rhetorical effect "underscores the inadequacy of all these offerings" (Koester 434). See also comments below.

οὐκ ἠθέλησας οὐδὲ εὐδόκησας,
. . . You did not desire or delight . . .

See comments on 10:5–6.

The author combines the two vbs. of the psalm citation for rhetorical effect (see comments below). Significantly, the pos. points the author has derived from the psalm citation are not repeated, furthering his neg. assessment of the former sacrificial system (Ellingworth 504).

αἵτινες κατὰ νόμον προσφέρονται,
(which are offered according to the law),

The antecedents of the indef. rel. pron. are the four sacrifices of Psalm 40. Προσφέρονται is the 3rd pl. pres. pass. indic. of *προσφέρω* (see comments on 5:1). The subj. of the pass. is likely the Levitical high priests. For *κατὰ νόμον*, see comments on 7:16. The prep. phrase adv. modifies *προσφέρονται*. Although the clause could be viewed as parenthetical (e.g., CSB), it is an important reaffirmation of the earlier discussion of the law as a shadow. A concessive force for the indef. rel. pron. ("although the law required them to be made" [REB; cf. NLT]) is inconsistent with its function par. to a rel. pron. in Hebrews (e.g., 2:3; 10:11, 35; "which are offered according to the law" [NASB, NET; cf. Lane 2:255–56 n. *q*]).

Although the law prescribed sacrifices (which were pleasing to the Lord [e.g., Lev 1:9; 2:2; Num 15:3]), such offerings were never intended to substitute for sincere obedience from a transformed heart. This is an important OT theme (e.g., 1 Sam 15:22; Ps 51:16–17).

VERSE 9

τότε εἴρηκεν·
he then says,

The expression *τότε εἴρηκεν* recalls *τότε εἶπον* from the psalm citation. The pf. (*εἴρηκεν*) summarizes the author's exposition so far (an extensive or consummative pf.; Wallace 577). The pf. is also likely rhetorically emph. to underscore Jesus's obedience in offering up himself (cf. Cockerill 440). It is unclear if the expression is to be understood as part of psalm citation or *as part of the author's exposition of the citation (cf. Ellingworth 504; *pace* Cockerill 440 n. 39).

ἰδοὺ ἥκω τοῦ ποιῆσαι τὸ θέλημά σου.
See, I have come to do your will.

See comments on v. 7.

As in v. 8, the author paraphrases the psalm citation in rhetorically significant ways. He changes the indir. discourse to a dir. statement, now on the lips of Jesus. By excluding the introductory formula (γέγραπται) and the voc., the art. gen. inf. expressing purpose is emph.

ἀναιρεῖ τὸ πρῶτον ἵνα τὸ δεύτερον στήσῃ,
He takes away the first to establish the second.

In v. 4., ἀφαιρέω was used in conj. with taking away sin (see comments there), whereas here ἀναιρεῖ (3rd sg. pres. act. indic.) "denotes 'to suppress, to abolish, to annul'"—a sense attested in HGk (Lane 2:256 n. *r*). The vb. indicated the "annulment of laws . . . and wills" (Koester 434). It could also mean "kill," "destroy" (BDAG 64b). Thus the author makes his strongest statement about the old (or "first") sacrificial order: "Christ by his sacrifice 'abolishes' or 'destroys' it" (Ellingworth 504; cf. Cockerill 440–41). Many EVV do not capture this (e.g., "takes away" [NASB]; "sets aside" [NIV], but "abolish" [NJB, NRSV], "annul" [NEB]). Τὸ πρῶτον likely refers generally to the entire Levitical system. It is the obj. of ἀναιρεῖ. (The superl. πρῶτον is used for the comp., cf. 8:7.) By contrast, the "second" (δεύτερος, -α, -ον) refers to the new order established by Christ's obedient sacrifice (cf. Cockerill 441). It is the obj. of στήσῃ (3rd sg. aor. act. subjunc. of ἵστημι). In the LXX, ἵστημι is used in conj. with God establishing covenants (e.g., Gen 6:1; 17:7; Exod 6:4 [Koester 434]; Lane 2:256 n. *t*; "establish" [most EVV]). The ἵνα clause modifies ἀναιρεῖ, indicating purpose.

In highly compressed language, the author summarizes the essence of his argument: because of Christ's incarnation and self-sacrifice, the old order has been abolished or annulled, which establishes the new (second) order inaugurated by his resurrection and entrance into heaven. This v. recalls 8:13, in which the old and new covenants are sim. contrasted. The pres. vbs. are thus timeless.

VERSE 10

ἐν ᾧ θελήματι
By this will,

Although this v. is not part of the psalm citation, θέλημα, προσφορά, and σῶμα draw on the psalm (cf. Ellingworth 505). The antecedent of ᾧ is τὸ θέλημα in v. 9. Here the rel. pron. has been incorporated into the rel. clause (R 719). The cstr. links Christ doing God's will (from the psalm citation) to the application of this to the author's contemp.

context. The cstr. adv. modifies ἡγιασμένοι ἐσμέν instr. ("by" [most EVV]). It is also possible that the instr. ἐν ᾧ also has a causal force ("because of that will" [GNB]; BDF §118; Harris 36; Lane 2:256 n. *u*).

ἡγιασμένοι ἐσμὲν διὰ τῆς προσφορᾶς τοῦ σώματος Ἰησοῦ Χριστοῦ ἐφάπαξ.
we have been sanctified through the offering of the body of Jesus Christ once for all time.

Ἡγιασμένοι is the nom. pl. masc. of the pf. pass. ptc. of ἁγιάζω ("sanctify" [ESV, NASB]; "been made holy" [NET, NIV, NLT]; "consecrate" [REB], "purify" [GNB], "dedicate" [BDAG 10a]). The ptc. recalls the usage of ἁγιάζω in 2:11 and anticipates 10:14. The close connection between sanctification/holiness (ἁγιάζω) and cleansing (καθαρίζω) was seen in 9:13, although impf. and anticipatory of Christ's full sanctification (Cockerill 443 n. 47). The pf. may be emph. (cf. Campbell, *VA* 201). It forms a periph. cstr. with ἐσμέν. There is no syntactic difference between periph. and the simple finite. The pl. is inclusive (i.e., both the author and the audience [Wallace 396]). The prep. phrase διὰ τῆς προσφορᾶς ("sacrifice" [NIV]) modifies the periph. cstr. instr. Τοῦ σώματος is an obj. gen. Ἰησοῦ Χριστοῦ is either in appos. to σώματος or is a gen. of poss. There is debate whether ἐφάπαξ modifies ἡγιασμένοι ἐσμέν or the verbal noun προσφορᾶς. Given the focus of Hebrews on Jesus's fully efficacious offering (e.g., 7:27; 9:12), the latter is probably likely (Koester 435; Lane 2:256 n. *v*). Conversely, the focus on the application of Christ's obedience to the audience and the tendency for the adv. to modify a vb. would support the former (Cockerill 445 n. 53). The placement of the emph. form of the adv. (cf. ἅπαξ) is also emph. (Bruce 243; Cockerill 445 n. 52; Ellingworth 505). The entire prep. phrase indicates how Jesus fulfilled God's will (v. 9 [Cockerill 443]).

The compound name Ἰησοῦ Χριστοῦ occurs only here in Hebrews. In general, the name Jesus pertains to his humanity, whereas Christ pertains to his exaltation in Hebrews. Here, with the efficacy of Jesus's death for removing the barrier for believers to enter God's presence so clearly established, the compound name probably indicates the close linking of the heavenly and earthly because of Christ's sacrifice (Attridge 277).

FOR FURTHER STUDY

61. Conceptual Backgrounds for Hebrews (10:1–10)

Anderson, Hugh. "The Jewish Antecedents of the Christology of Hebrews." Pages 512–35 in *The Messiah: Developments in Earliest Judaism and Christianity*. Edited by James H. Charlesworth. Minneapolis: Fortress, 1992.

Cockerill, 24–34.

Fairhurst, Alan M. "Hellenistic Influence in the Epistle to the Hebrews." *TynBul* 7–8 (1961): 17–27.

Hurst, L. D. *The Epistle to the Hebrews: Its Background of Thought*. SNTSMS 65. Cambridge: Cambridge University Press, 1990.

Isaacs, Marie E. "Hebrews." Pages 145–59 in *Early Christian Thought in Its Jewish Context*. Edited by John Barclay and John Sweet. New York: Cambridge, 1996.
Lane, 1:*ciii–cxii*.
*Lincoln, 40–51.
Thompson, James W. *The Beginnings of Christian Philosophy: The Epistle to the Hebrews*. *CBQ* Monograph Series 13. Washington, DC: Catholic Biblical Association of America, 1982.
Williamson, Ronald. "Background of the Epistle to the Hebrews." *ExpT* 87 (1976): 232–37.

62. Platonism, Philo, and Hebrews (10:1–10)

Borgen, Peder. *ABD* 5:333–42.
Carlston, Charles E. "The Vocabulary of Perfection in Philo and Hebrews." Pages 133–60 in *Unity and Diversity in New Testament Theology: Essays in Honor of George E. Ladd*. Edited by Robert A. Guelich. Grand Rapids: Eerdmans, 1978.
Dillon, J. M. *DNTB* 804–7.
Hay, David M. "Philo of Alexandria." Pages 356–79 in *Justification and Variegated Nomism*. Vol. 1. The Complexities of Second Temple Judaism. Edited by D. A. Carson, Peter T. O'Brien, and Mark A. Seifrid. Grand Rapids: Baker, 2001.
*Hurst, L. D. "Eschatology and 'Platonism' in the Epistle to the Hebrews." Pages 41–75 in *Society of Biblical Literature Seminar Papers* 23. Edited by Kent Harold Richards. Chico, CA: Scholars, 1984.
———. "How 'Platonic' Are Heb. viii.5 and ix.23f?" *JTS* 34 (1983): 156–68.
Runia, D. T. *Philo in Early Christian Literature*. Assen, Netherlands: van Gorcum, 1993.
Sowers, Sidney G. *The Hermeneutics of Philo and Hebrews: A Comparison of the Interpretation of the Old Testament in Philo Judaeus and the Epistle to the Hebrews*. Richmond: Knox, 1965.
Sterling, G. E. *DNTB* 789–93.
Svendsen, Stefan Nordgaard. *Allegory Transformed: The Appropriation of Philonic Hermeneutics in the Letter to the Hebrews*. Tübingen: Mohr Siebeck, 2009.
Thompson, James W. "What Has Middle Platonism to Do with Hebrews?" Pages 31–52 in Mason.
Thurston, Robert W. "Philo and the Epistle to the Hebrews." *EQ* 58 (1986): 133–43.
Williamson, Ronald. *Philo and the Epistle to the Hebrews*. Leiden: Brill, 1970.
———. "Platonism and Hebrews." *SJT* 16 (1963): 415–24.

63. Qumran, the DSS, and Hebrews (10:1–10)

Attridge, Harold W. "How the Scrolls Impacted Scholarship on Hebrews." Pages 203–30 in *The Scrolls and Christian Origins*. Edited by James H. Charlesworth. Vol. 3 of *The Bible and the Dead Sea Scrolls: The Princeton Symposium on the Dead Sea Scrolls*. Waco, TX: Baylor University Press, 2006.
Brooke, George J. *NIDB* 2:52–63.
Bruce, F. F. "Recent Contributions to the Understanding of Hebrews." *ExpT* 80 (1969): 260–64.
Collins, John J. *ABD* 2:85–101.
Fensham, F. C. "Hebrews and Qumrân." *Neot* 5 (1971): 9–21.

Mason, Eric F. "Cosmology, Messianism, and Melchizedek: Apocalyptic Jewish Tradition and Hebrews." Pages 53–76 in Mason.

*———. "Hebrews and the Dead Sea Scrolls: Some Points of Comparison." *PRSt* 37 (2010): 457–79.

64. "Shadow and Reality" (10:1)

Bruce, F. F. "A Shadow of Good Things to Come (Heb 10:1)." Pages 77–94 in *The Time Is Fulfilled: Five Aspects of the Fulfillment of the Old Testament in the New*. Grand Rapids: Eerdmans, 1978.

Shultz, S. *TDNT* 7:394–98.

Stylianopoulos, Theodore G. "Shadow and Reality: Reflections on Hebrews 10:1–18." *Greek Orthodox Theological Review* 17 (1972): 215–30.

65. The Use of Psalm 40 in Hebrews (10:1–10)

Compton, Jared M. "The Origin of σωμα in Heb 10:5: Another Look at a Recent Proposal." *TJ* 32 (2011): 19–29.

Jobes, Karen H. "The Function of Paronomasia in Hebrews 10:5–7." *TJ* 13 (1992): 181–91.

———. "Rhetorical Achievement in the Hebrews 10 'Misquote' of Psalm 40." *Bib* 72 (1991): 387–96.

Kaiser, Walter C., Jr. "The Abolition of the Old Order and the Establishment of the New: A Study of Psalm 40:6–8 and Hebrews 10:5–10." Pages 19–37 in *Tradition and Testament: Essays in Honor of Charles Lee Feinberg*. Edited by John S. Feinberg and Paul D. Feinberg. Chicago: Moody, 1981.

Van der Bergh, Ronald H. "A Textual Comparison of Hebrews 10:5b–7 and LXX Psalm 39:7–9." *Neot* 42 (2008): 353–82.

HOMILETICAL SUGGESTIONS

Sacrifice and Obedience (10:1–10)

1. The Law's Shadowy Incompleteness
   - (a) The Law is a shadow of the reality of God's final intentions (v. 1a)
   - (b) Repeated sacrifices cannot achieve perfection (v. 1b)
   - (c) If they had, they would no longer be offered (v. 2)
   - (d) Instead, the sacrifices are a yearly reminder of sin (v. 3)
   - (e) PRINCIPLE: Animal blood cannot remove sin (v. 4)
2. The Son's Perfection
   - (a) Instead of animal sacrifices, a human body is needed (v. 5)
   - (b) God does not delight in rep. offerings, but instead wants those who do his will (vv. 6–8)
   - (c) The Son has accomplished God's will (v. 9)
   - (d) Consequently, the offering of Christ's body has achieved sanctification (v. 10)

6. The Finality of Christ's Sacrifice and Priesthood (10:11–18)

STRUCTURE

A series of indics. in this section continues the contrast between the Levitical priesthood and Christ's. The indic. in v. 11 is modified by two adv. ptcs. and a rel. clause. Similarly the independent indic. in v. 12 is modified by two adv. ptcs. The pf. in v. 14 indicates a summarizing conclusion, which is anchored in the citation from Jeremiah 31, introduced in v. 15. The par. of the orig. Heb. is reflected in the alignment of vv. 16–17. A second summarizing statement occurs in v. 18.

11 Καὶ πᾶς μὲν ἱερεὺς ἕστηκεν καθ' ἡμέραν
λειτουργῶν
καὶ τὰς αὐτὰς πολλάκις προσφέρων θυσίας,
αἵτινες οὐδέποτε δύνανται περιελεῖν ἁμαρτίας,
12 οὗτος δὲ μίαν ὑπὲρ ἁμαρτιῶν προσενέγκας θυσίαν εἰς τὸ διηνεκὲς
ἐκάθισεν ἐν δεξιᾷ τοῦ θεοῦ,
13 τὸ λοιπὸν ἐκδεχόμενος
ἕως τεθῶσιν οἱ ἐχθροὶ αὐτοῦ ὑποπόδιον τῶν ποδῶν αὐτοῦ.
14 μιᾷ γὰρ προσφορᾷ τετελείωκεν εἰς τὸ διηνεκὲς τοὺς ἁγιαζομένους.
15 Μαρτυρεῖ δὲ ἡμῖν καὶ τὸ πνεῦμα τὸ ἅγιον·
μετὰ γὰρ τὸ εἰρηκέναι,
16 Αὕτη ἡ διαθήκη ἣν διαθήσομαι πρὸς αὐτοὺς μετὰ τὰς ἡμέρας ἐκείνας,
λέγει κύριος·
διδοὺς νόμους μου ἐπὶ καρδίας αὐτῶν
καὶ ἐπὶ τὴν διάνοιαν αὐτῶν ἐπιγράψω αὐτούς,
17 καὶ τῶν ἁμαρτιῶν αὐτῶν καὶ τῶν ἀνομιῶν αὐτῶν
οὐ μὴ μνησθήσομαι ἔτι.
18 ὅπου δὲ ἄφεσις τούτων, οὐκέτι προσφορὰ περὶ ἁμαρτίας.

VERSE 11

Καὶ πᾶς μὲν ἱερεὺς ἕστηκεν καθ' ἡμέραν λειτουργῶν
Every priest stands day after day ministering

Καί links this section (vv. 11–18) with the previous one (vv. 1–10), although it is left untr. in many EVV (but retained in ESV, NASB, NET). It adds a new element to the argument (Ellingworth 507). The μὲν . . . δέ cstr. signals a contrast between the Levitical priests (v. 11) and Christ (v. 12). For ἱερεύς ("priest"), see comments on 5:6. The var. rdg. ἀρχιερεύς ("high priest") is less well attested and likely reflects a correction to 5:1 or 8:3 (Metzger 600). Ἱερεύς may have been chosen with a view to the upcoming allusion to Ps 110:1 (Ellingworth 507). Πᾶς modifies ἱερεύς, making a general statement about Levitical priests as a group and not one in particular (cf. Ellingworth 507), thus shifting the focus from the high priest (Cockerill 447).

Ἱερεύς is the subj. of ἕστηκεν (3rd sg. pf. act. indic. of ἵστημι). The pf. has pres. mng. (BDF §97 [1]). More important is the impf. aspect, indicating the ongoing (but incomplete) nature of the priests' work. Standing was the required posture for priestly service (e.g., Deut 10:8; see Koester 434). Καθ' ἡμέραν is distributive ("every day" [Harris 155]); καθ' occurs before rough breathing. The prep. phrase modifies ἕστηκεν temp. Λειτουργῶν is the nom. sg. masc. of the pres. act. ptc. of λειτουργέω, "performs . . . religious duties" (NIV); "serving" (NET); "ministering" (NASB); "render service" (BDAG 591a; H. Balz, *EDNT* 2:348b–c). It is a circum. ptc. modifying ἕστηκεν. Once again, the author is broadening the scope of the previous argument from the Day of Atonement to the priestly ministry in general (Cockerill 447).

καὶ τὰς αὐτὰς πολλάκις προσφέρων θυσίας,
and offering the same sacrifices time after time,

Καί joins this aspect of the priests' work with the previous clause. Προσφέρων is the nom. sg. masc. of the pres. act. ptc. of προσφέρω, "offer." It is also a circum. ptc. modifying ἕστηκεν. The ptc. is modified by πολλάκις, "again and again" (NET, NIV, NLT); "repeatedly" (ESV); "time after time" (NASB); "often," "frequently" (BDAG 846b). The alliteration in this v. (πολλάκις προσφέρων) recalls sim. alliteration (e.g., 1:1), which also critiqued "the multiplicity of sacrifices" (Attridge 279). Θυσίας is the obj. of the ptc. (see comments on 5:1 and 7:27). The attrib. pos. αὐτάς functions as an "identifying adj." (Wallace 349–50; R 687), modifying θυσίας ("the same sacrifices"). Note also the impf. (ongoing) aspect of the two pres. ptcs.

αἵτινες οὐδέποτε δύνανται περιελεῖν ἁμαρτίας,
which can never take away sins.

Οὐδέποτε is a strengthened form of οὐ ("never" [most EVV; BDAG 735d]; cf. "completely unable" [10:1, NET]). Since it usually precedes the vb. (e.g., δύνανται), the position here is not emph. (Ellingworth 493). Περιελεῖν is the aor. act. inf. of περιαιρέω, "take away" (most EVV); "remove" (NEB; BDAG 799b; cf. ἀφαιρεῖν in 10:4). The compounded περί is "perfective" (i.e., "to take away altogether" [R 617]); cf. Ellingworth 508–9. The inf. complements δύναται.

The pars. between v. 1 and v. 11 are striking: κατ' ἐνιαυτόν (v. 1) and καθ' ἡμέραν (v. 11); αὐταῖς θυσίαις (v. 1) and αὐτὰς . . . θυσίας (v. 11); οὐδέποτε δύναται . . . τελειῶσαι (v. 1) and οὐδέποτε δύνανται περιελεῖν (v. 11; Lane 2:266). In this way, the author contrasts the law, the Day of Atonement (v. 1–4), and the daily priestly offering (v. 11) with Christ's fully efficacious work in one summarizing v.

VERSE 12

οὗτος δὲ μίαν ὑπὲρ ἁμαρτιῶν προσενέγκας θυσίαν εἰς τὸ διηνεκές
But this man, after offering one sacrifice for sins forever,

Δέ introduces the contrast to v. 11. The sg. dem. pron. contrasts the multiplicity implied in πᾶς ἱερεύς. The ref. is clearly to Christ (cf. 3:3), which is made explicit in some EVV (CEV, ESV, REB; cf. "our High Priest" [NLT]). The one sacrifice (μίαν θυσίαν) that he offered contrasts with the multiple offerings of the priests. Προσενέγκας is the nom. sg. masc. of the aor. act. ptc. of προσφέρω, "offer." The pf. aspect (cf. "global" [Wallace 557–58]) of the aor. contrasts with the ongoing, impf. aspect of the pres. λειτουργῶν and προσφέρων in v. 11. The ptc. is either instr. (e.g., "by offering" [Cockerill 450]), *temp. ("having offered" [NASB, REB], "when" [ESV, NET, NIV]), or causal ("because"). There is also an implied contrast between the inability of the former sacrifices to take away sin and Christ's offering for sins (ὑπὲρ ἁμαρτιῶν). Finally, εἰς τὸ διηνεκές (see comments on 7:3) contrasts with both καθ' ἡμέραν and πολλάκις in v. 11. There is debate whether εἰς τὸ διηνεκές modifies προσενέγκας or ἐκάθισεν. This prep. phrase usually follows the vb. it modifies, which would suggest προσενέγκας (cf. 10:1; ESV, NASB, NET, NIV; Bruce 244 n. 57). The author, however, appears to be contrasting the priests standing "daily" (v. 1) and Christ seated forever in this v. (Cockerill 449), in which case the prep. phrase would modify ἐκάθισεν (NAB, NJB; cf. Attridge 280; Ellingworth 509–10). Cockerill notes the irony of using the same phrase (εἰς τὸ διηνεκές) to stress both the ineffectiveness of the repeated sacrifices ("continually") of the old order (v. 1) and the complete efficacy of Christ's offering in this v. (Cockerill 449).

ἐκάθισεν ἐν δεξιᾷ τοῦ θεοῦ,
sat down at the right hand of God.

The comp. is completed with the contrast between the priests who stand, thus indicating that their work is not finished, and *this* one who has sat down, indicating the finality of his work (see the side-by-side comp. of vv. 11–12 in Ellingworth 506). This clause recalls the nearly identical wording in 1:3 (see comments there; cf. 8:1; 12:2), although the periph. τῆς μεγαλωσύνης ἐν ὑψηλοῖς in 1:3 is replaced with τοῦ θεοῦ. The resumed attention to Psalm 110 is fitting as the author draws his main argument to a conclusion. In both Hebrews 1 and Hebrews 10, the allusion to Ps 110:1 focuses on Christ's exaltation following a statement concerning the efficacy of his atoning sacrifice. This imagery may also intend to suggest royal status, as one sitting on a throne (cf. Ellingworth 507).

VERSE 13

τὸ λοιπὸν ἐκδεχόμενος ἕως τεθῶσιν οἱ ἐχθροὶ αὐτοῦ ὑποπόδιον τῶν ποδῶν αὐτοῦ.
He is now waiting until his enemies are made his footstool.

This v. continues the allusion to Ps 110:1. Ἐκδεχόμενος is the nom. sg. masc. of the pres. mid. ptc. of ἐκδέχομαι, "wait" (most EVV; "expect" [BDAG 300c]). The vb. suggests eager expectation par. to its usage in 11:10 and possibly par. to ἀπεκδέχομαι in 9:28 (Ellingworth 510). Τὸ λοιπόν is a fixed expression with the art. adj. functioning as an adv. ("from that time" [ESV], "since that time" [NIV]; "finally," "henceforth" [Moule 34], "by now" [BDF §451(6)]; cf. R 487). Ἕως introduces a dependent temp. clause. The subj. of this dependent clause is the subst. adj. ἐχθροί ("enemies"). Τεθῶσιν is the 3rd pl. aor. pass. subjunc. of τίθημι, "are made" (most EVV), "to be made" (NIV). (For ὑποπόδιον τῶν ποδῶν, see comments on 1:13.) In 1:13, both ἐχθροί and ὑποπόδιον were in the acc., with ἐχθροί as the obj. and ὑποπόδιον the obj. complement. Here the obj. ἐχθρούς of 1:3 has become the subj. ἐχθροί of the causative pass. τεθῶσιν ("are made"), and the obj. complement ὑποπόδιον remains in the acc. As with 1:13, the "enemies" are not further specified. Both occurrences of αὐτοῦ indicate poss.

Elsewhere the author has only cited the first part of Ps 110:1, whereas here he alludes to the rest of the v. There is debate as to the significance. Most likely this ref. indicates that all that remains following Christ's exaltation is the final subjugation of all things to him (2:8) and the final judgment (12:25–29 [Cockerill 450; cf. Attridge 280]). It may also be that the author anticipates the upcoming exhortation to his audience and thus offers a subtle warning lest they should end up as Christ's enemies (Bruce 246).

VERSE 14

μιᾷ γὰρ προσφορᾷ
For by one offering

Γάρ ("for" [most EVV]) draws on vv. 12–13 to indicate the contemp. significance of Christ's "one sacrifice," understood to refer to his death, as the means by which believers are sanctified. The dat. μιᾷ προσφορᾷ is instr. ("by" [most EVV]).

τετελείωκεν εἰς τὸ διηνεκὲς τοὺς ἁγιαζομένους.
he has perfected forever those who are sanctified.

Τετελείωκεν is the 3rd sg. pf. act. indic. of τελειόω; "has perfected" (most EVV); "has made perfect" (NIV). The use of τελειόω continues an important theme in Hebrews (see comments on 2:10). The pf. indicates "consummative effect" (R 895). The prep. phrase εἰς τὸ διηνεκές (see comments on 7:3) modifies the finite vb. temp. Ἁγιαζομένους is the acc. pl. masc. of the pres. pass. ptc. of ἁγιάζω ("sanctified" [many EVV]; "being made holy" [NIV, NLT]; "consecrated" [NAB, REB]; "purified" [GNT]; cf. BDAG 10a). The use of ἁγιαζομένους here recalls 2:10–11. The pres. tense could be timeless (Bruce 247; Lane 2:268) or "descriptive" (R 891), but more likely ongoing ("durative" [R 1111; cf. Cockerill 452; Ellingworth 511]). The last option coheres best with the focus on perseverance in Hebrews. The subst. ptc. is the obj. of the finite vb.

VERSE 15

Μαρτυρεῖ δὲ ἡμῖν καὶ τὸ πνεῦμα τὸ ἅγιον·
The Holy Spirit also testifies to us about this.

Δέ continues the line of reasoning begun in v. 14. Μαρτυρεῖ is the 3rd sg. pres. act. indic. of μαρτυρέω, "testify" (NAB, NASB, NIV, NRSV), "bear witness" (ESV), "attest" (NJB), "witness" (NET; BDAG 618c), whose subj. is τὸ πνεῦμα τὸ ἅγιον. Καί is ascensive ("also" [most EVV]). Ἡμῖν is a dat. of advantage and indicates the application of the Scripture citation to the audience (Ellingworth 512). Some EVV understand this clause to be a single sentence (e.g., NIV). This statement affirms the "divine authority" of the "Spirit-inspired Scripture" on which the promise in Jeremiah rests (Cockerill 454).

μετὰ γὰρ τὸ εἰρηκέναι,
For after he says:

Γάρ links the specific words spoken by the Spirit (v. 16) with the general statement at the beginning of this v. (cf. Ellingworth 513). Μετά with the art. inf. is temp. ("after" [most EVV]); this is the only place in the NT with pf. for this cstr. (Wallace 594). The pf. (εἰρηκέναι) here parallels εἴρηκεν in v. 9. and may also be emph. (cf. Cockerill 440). The implied subj. of the inf. is the Holy Spirit. The connection between the Spirit speaking as a means of introducing Scripture recalls the sim. cstr. in 3:7 to introduce Psalm 95. This continues the important theme of Scripture's ongoing witness to God's (ongoing) speaking (cf. Lane 2:268). This v. also indicates the important link between Psalm 110 (Christ's exaltation and subjugation of all his enemies) and Jeremiah 31 (the promise that God will remember sin no more).

VERSE 16

αὕτη ἡ διαθήκη ἣν διαθήσομαι πρὸς αὐτοὺς μετὰ τὰς ἡμέρας ἐκείνας,
This is the covenant I will make with them after those days,

The citation of Jer 31:33 varies slightly from its citation in Heb 8:10. The author has replaced τῷ οἴκῳ Ἰσραήλ with πρὸς αὐτούς, possibly to indicate the "more universal scope" of the new covenant (Attridge 281; cf. Koester 435), although it is not clear whether that was necessarily to accommodate any Gentiles present (*pace* Ellingworth 513). Most likely it indicates the author's understanding of the continuity of God's people to whom his word was, and is, addressed (cf. Cockerill 456). See comments for 8:10.

λέγει κύριος·
the Lord says,

See comments for 8:10.

διδοὺς νόμους μου ἐπὶ καρδίας αὐτῶν καὶ ἐπὶ τὴν διάνοιαν αὐτῶν ἐπιγράψω αὐτούς,
I will put my laws on their hearts and write them on their minds,

The continuation of the citation of Jer 31:33 again varies slightly from its citation in Heb 8:10. The author switches διδοὺς νόμους μου εἰς τὴν διάνοιαν αὐτῶν to διδοὺς νόμους μου <u>ἐπὶ καρδίας αὐτῶν</u> (the change is underlined). He then switches ἐπὶ καρδίας αὐτῶν ἐπιγράψω αὐτούς to <u>ἐπὶ τὴν διάνοιαν αὐτῶν</u> ἐπιγράψω αὐτούς (the change is underlined). Multiple reasons are offered for this. Perhaps the most plausible is that the change (including the switch from εἰς to ἐπί) emphasizes the heart, which was representative of the whole person (cf. 3:12–19; Cockerill 457–58). Less likely is the idea that the more common term (καρδία) occurred to the author first (*pace* Ellingworth 513).

VERSE 17

καὶ τῶν ἁμαρτιῶν αὐτῶν καὶ τῶν ἀνομιῶν αὐτῶν οὐ μὴ μνησθήσομαι ἔτι.
and **I will never again remember their sins and their lawless acts.**

The lack of punctuation between the citation of Jer 31:33 and Jer 31:34 has led some EVV to add some introductory formula par. to τότε εἴρηκεν in the citation of Psalm 40 in Heb 10:9 ("then he adds" [ESV, NIV], "then he says" [NET, NLT]). By arranging these vv. as the author has, the emphasis is now on God's remembering sin no more (cf. Ellingworth 512).

The citation from Jer 31:34 varies slightly from its citation in 8:12. To the LXX clause καὶ τῶν ἁμαρτιῶν αὐτῶν οὐ μὴ μνησθῶ ἔτι the author has added καὶ τῶν ἀνομιῶν αὐτῶν, possibly as a paraphrase of ἵλεως ἔσομαι ταῖς ἀδικίαις αὐτῶν in the LXX (Ellingworth 514), which emphasizes the "totality of God's remission" (Cockerill 458). Ἀνομιῶν is the gen. pl. fem. of ἀνομία, -ας, ἡ, "lawless acts" (NIV), "lawless deeds" (ESV, NASB, NET; BDAG 84c). He has also switched μνησθῶ (1st sg. fut. pass. subjunc.) to μνησθήσομαι (1st sg. fut. pass. indic.), perhaps as a "more vivid and emph." form (Attridge 281; cf. Cockerill 458). (See also comments for 8:12.) The author has summarized the promises of the new covenant by re-citing the first and last promises enumerated in the full citation of Jer 31:33–34 in Hebrews 8, without denying the intervening promises (Cockerill 456).

The first citation of Jeremiah 31 in Hebrews 8 established that Scripture itself had prophesied about the Mosaic covenant's limitations and eventual end. Following the author's exposition of Christ's sacrifice as the penalty paid for the broken Mosaic covenant and inauguration the new covenant, the citation of Jeremiah 31 again here at the conclusion of the author's main argument makes explicit that Christ is the means by which Jeremiah's prophecy is fulfilled. The internalization of God's laws and the complete forgiveness of sins with the resultant cleansed conscience promised in Jeremiah 31 has now been achieved by Christ's efficacious sacrifice and eternal exaltation. The focus in this section is thus on the application of the author's main argument to his audience (cf. Cockerill 453–54; Lane 2:268).

VERSE 18

ὅπου δὲ ἄφεσις τούτων,
Now where there is forgiveness of these,

Δέ adds the final summary of the argument ("now" [CSB]). Although ὅπου ("where") is gen. loc. (cf. 6:20), here it is understood logically and possibly causally (BFD §456[3]; Cockerill 459 n. 19). Ἄφεσις (-εως, ἡ, "forgiveness" [most EVV]; "remission" [ASV, KJV]) functions as a pred. nom. (ἐστίν is understood [e.g., "there is"]). Some EVV tr. the noun as a vb. (e.g., "have been forgiven" [NIV, NJB, NLT]). Although a few EVV tr. ἄφεσις as "forgiveness of [sins]" (ESV), ἁμαρτία does not occur in this v., as was the case in 9:22. The antecedent of the dem. pron. is either ἁμαρτιῶν or both ἁμαρτιῶν and ἀνομιῶν from v. 17.

οὐκέτι προσφορὰ περὶ ἁμαρτίας.
there is no longer an offering for sin.

The adv. οὐκέτι (οὐ[κ] + ἔτι ["no longer"; BDAG 736a]) modifies an understood equative vb. Προσφορά is the nom. sg. fem. of προσφορά, -ας, ἡ, "offering" (most EVV; BDAG 887a; cf. "sacrifice" [NIV]). In the LXX citation, περὶ ἁμαρτίας was "a technical expression" for sin offerings (see comments on 10:6). Here it may have the same sense, elliptically understood as ἡ προσφορά ἡ περὶ ἁμαρτίας, although it is not tr. as "sin offerings" in most EVV (see discussion in Harris 182; cf. Z 96).

As with 8:13 and 9:22, the author offers a summarizing statement following his exposition of Scripture. In this remarkable summary, this final clause is probably intended to be understood in several ways at the same time. First, there is no longer any Levitical offering for sin available because that system is no more. Second—and in anticipation of the upcoming warning passage in 10:19–31—the author wants his audience to understand that, apart from Christ's offering, no other offering for sin exists (e.g., 10:26–31). Finally, "the cessation of sacrifice implies purification . . . as well as forgiveness" (Cockerill 459).

FOR FURTHER STUDY

66. Sacrifice in Hebrews (10:11–18)

Anderson, Gary A. *ABD* 5:870–86.
Barnett, P. W. *DLNT* 1069–75.
Beckwith, Roger T. *NDBT* 754–62.
———. "The Death of Christ as a Sacrifice in the Teaching of Paul and Hebrews." Pages 130–35 in *Sacrifice in the Bible*. Edited by Roger T. Beckwith and Martin J. Selman. Grand Rapids: Baker; Carlisle, UK: Paternoster, 1995.
Dunnill, John. *Covenant and Sacrifice in the Letter to the Hebrews*. Society for New Testament Studies Monograph Series 75. Cambridge: Cambridge University Press, 1993.
Eberhart, Christian. "Characteristics of Sacrificial Metaphors in Hebrews." Pages 37–64 in *Hebrews: Contemporary Methods—New Insights*. Edited by Gabriella Gelardini. Biblical Interpretation Series 75. Leiden: Brill, 2005.
Hooker, Morna D. "Christ, the 'End' of the Cult." Pages 189–212 in Bauckham, *Theology*.
Klauck, Hans-Josef. *ABD* 5:886–91.
Marchant, G. J. C. "Sacrifice in the Epistle to the Hebrews." *EQ* 20 (1948): 196–210.
*Nelson, Richard D. "'He Offered Himself': Sacrifice in Hebrews." *Int* 57 (2003): 251–65.

Reid, D. G. *DNTB* 1036–1050.
Seifrid, M. A. *DLNT* 267–87.
Stott, Wilfrid. "Conception of 'Offering' in the Epistle to the Hebrews." *NTS* 9 (1962): 62–67.
Swetnam, James. "Sacrifice and Revelation in the Epistle to the Hebrews: Observations and Surmises on Hebrews 9:26." *CBQ* 30 (1968): 227–34.
Williamson, Ronald. "Eucharist and the Epistle to the Hebrews." *NTS* 21 (1975): 300–312.

HOMILETICAL SUGGESTIONS

The Fully Efficacious Sacrifice (10:11–18)

1. Daily Sacrifices Can Never Remove Sin (v. 11)
   (a) These priests stand because their work is not finished (v. 11a)
   (b) They offer the same sacrifice over and over (v. 11b)
2. Only Christ's Onetime Sacrifice Can Remove Sin (vv. 12–14)
   (a) He sits because his work is finished (v. 12)
   (b) He awaits only the final subjugation of all remaining enemies (v. 13)
   (c) Indeed this one sacrifice has achieved sanctification and perfection (v. 14)
3. This One Sacrifice Fulfills the Promised New Covenant (vv. 15–17)
   (a) The Spirit testifies to the truth of this (v. 15)
   (b) God's laws are now internalized (v. 16)
   (c) Sins are completely forgotten (v. 17)
4. PRINCIPLE: Offerings Are No Longer Necessary When Sins Are Forgiven (v. 18)

VI. Perseverance and Faith (10:19–12:29)

A. PRESENT EXHORTATIONS BASED ON CHRIST'S ETERNAL REDEMPTION (10:19–39)

1. Approaching God's Throne and Meeting Together (10:19–25)

STRUCTURE

There are numerous pars. between 4:14–16 and 10:19–25 (see esp. Cockerill 464–65). Additionally there is a par. between the preliminary exhortation of 5:11–6:20 and the concluding exhortation of 10:19–39 (Lane 2:279–80; Ellingworth 515). This section (vv. 19–25) comprises one periodic sentence in the Gk. (Attridge 283; Lane 2:282), centered around the three hort. subjunc. (προσερχώμεθα, κατέχωμεν, κατανοῶμεν), which are modified by five dependent ptcs. (vv. 19, 22, 25). This rhetorical technique "summarizes" a section (Koester 447).

19 Ἔχοντες οὖν, ἀδελφοί,
παρρησίαν
εἰς τὴν εἴσοδον τῶν ἁγίων
ἐν τῷ αἵματι Ἰησοῦ,
20 ἣν ἐνεκαίνισεν ἡμῖν ὁδὸν πρόσφατον καὶ ζῶσαν
διὰ τοῦ καταπετάσματος,
τοῦτ᾽ ἔστιν τῆς σαρκὸς αὐτοῦ,
21 καὶ ἱερέα μέγαν ἐπὶ τὸν οἶκον τοῦ θεοῦ,
22 προσερχώμεθα
μετὰ ἀληθινῆς καρδίας
ἐν πληροφορίᾳ πίστεως
ῥεραντισμένοι τὰς καρδίας
ἀπὸ συνειδήσεως πονηρᾶς
καὶ λελουσμένοι τὸ σῶμα ὕδατι καθαρῷ·
23 κατέχωμεν τὴν ὁμολογίαν τῆς ἐλπίδος ἀκλινῆ,
πιστὸς γὰρ ὁ ἐπαγγειλάμενος,

24 καὶ κατανοῶμεν ἀλλήλους
εἰς παροξυσμὸν ἀγάπης καὶ καλῶν ἔργων,
25 μὴ ἐγκαταλείποντες τὴν ἐπισυναγωγὴν ἑαυτῶν,
καθὼς ἔθος τισίν,
ἀλλὰ παρακαλοῦντες,
καὶ τοσούτῳ μᾶλλον ὅσῳ βλέπετε ἐγγίζουσαν τὴν ἡμέραν.

VERSE 19

Ἔχοντες οὖν, ἀδελφοί, παρρησίαν εἰς τὴν εἴσοδον τῶν ἁγίων ἐν τῷ αἵματι Ἰησοῦ,
Therefore, brothers and sisters, since we have boldness to enter the sanctuary through the blood of Jesus—

Οὖν introduces a conclusion ("therefore" [most EVV]) from the preceding argument, most likely extending back to Heb 8:1, although possibly 5:1 (Cockerill 465) or even 4:14 (Ellingworth 517). Specifically, vv. 19–20 summarize 8:1–10:18, and v. 21 recalls 7:1–28 (Attridge 284). Οὖν also transitions to an extended paraenesis. Ἀδελφοί functions as a voc. and as a discourse marker, signaling "a major turn in the argument" (Ellingworth 517; cf. Lane 2:279). The term reminds the audience of their unity in Christ and prepares for the exhortation in vv. 19–39 (Lane 2:279; cf. Ellingworth 517). As with 3:1 and 3:12 (cf. 2:11–15), ἀδελφοί is inclusive (*pace* ESV, NASB, NIV). The familial connotation is missed with "my friends" (NEB, NRSV). (See comments on 3:1.) Ἔχοντες is the nom. pl. masc. of the pres. act. ptc. of ἔχω. The ptc. is causal ("since" [most EVV]; cf. Lane 2:274 n. *a*; Ellingworth 517). The first obj. of the ptc. is παρρησίαν (acc. sg. fem. of παρρησία, -ας, ἡ). Παρρησία forms an *inclusio* with its use in v. 35. The mng. of παρρησία is wide-ranging: "boldness" (ASV); "confidence" (ESV, NASB, NET, NIV); cf. BDAG 781d. The mng. here is mainly objective, as indicated by the modifier ἐν τῷ αἵματι Ἰησοῦ, and reflected well in some EVV: "the right to enter" (JB; cf. "the right of free access to God" [Lane 2:283]), "free access" (Weymouth, Goodspeed); cf. "authorization" (Cockerill 466); Harris 195. A subjective sense (e.g., "confidence") flows from this objective reality (Lane 2:274 n. *b*); "confidence of entrance" (NAB).

This v. recalls the sim. phrase in 9:8—τὴν τῶν ἁγίων ὁδόν. Εἴσοδον is the acc. sg. fem. of εἴσοδος, -ου, ἡ, "entrance" (BDAG 294d), "entry or access" (W. Michaelis, *TDNT* 5:106). The noun occurs freq. with εἰς (Lane 2:274 n. *c*) and can refer to entrance or the action of entering (cf. Attridge 284; Ellingworth 517; Koester 442). The par. with ὁδόν (v. 20) suggests the former (Attridge 284; Cockerill 466); see discussion below. The gen. τῶν ἁγίων is an obj. gen. (BDF §163) and (par. to 9:8) refers to the heavenly sanctuary (e.g., most EVV). Εἰς τὴν εἴσοδον τῶν ἁγίων modifies παρρησίαν, indicating purpose. Thus many EVV tr. the noun as an inf. (e.g., "to enter"; but "confidence . . . in entering" [NJB]). Ἐν τῷ αἵματι Ἰησοῦ modifies εἴσοδος, παρρησίαν, or more likely both (e.g., "boldness to enter"). The phrase is instr. ("by," "through" [Harris 119–20]; so most EVV). Some EVV (e.g., CEV, NAB, REB) tr. the obj. of the prep. (Christ) as the subj. of the clause. The gen. Ἰησοῦ is poss. The explicit ref. to Jesus underscores his humanity and sacrificial offering of his own body ("through the sacrificial death of Jesus" [Barclay]; cf. Lane 2:283). The ref. also anticipates the ref. to Jesus's flesh in v. 20 (Cockerill 467).

VERSE 20

ἣν ἐνεκαίνισεν ἡμῖν ὁδὸν πρόσφατον καὶ ζῶσαν διὰ τοῦ καταπετάσματος,
he has inaugurated for us a new and living way through the curtain

The antecedent of ἥν is εἴσοδον. Ἐνεκαίνισεν is the 3rd sg. aor. act. indic. of ἐγκαινίζω. The vb. has a wide range of mngs.: "opened" (most EVV), "inaugurated" (NASB), "dedicate" (ASV), "consecrate" (KJV), "ratify" (BDAG 272d); cf. "to make a way which was not there before" (J. Behm, *TDNT* 3:454). (See comments on 9:18.) Here the word suggests a par. between Moses inaugurating the earthly sanctuary and Christ opening the way to the heavenly sanctuary (Cockerill 467). The vb. is a cognate of καινός, perhaps with an intended allusion to the new covenant in 8:8, 13; 9:15 (Koester 443). Ἡμῖν is a dat. of advantage (BDF §188).

Ὁδόν (ὁδός, -οῦ, ἡ, acc. sg. fem., "way" [most EVV]) is epex. to εἰσόδός. The rel. pron. functions as the obj. of ἐνεκαίνισεν and ὁδόν as the obj. complement. Both words are likely "a spatial metaphor" for "access to God's presence" (Ellingworth 518) and develop the "journey" motif prevalent in Hebrews (2:10, 4:3, 10; 6:19; 9:12, 24; 10:1–5; 11:13–14 [Attridge 284]). The noun is modified by πρόσφατον (acc. sg. fem. of πρόσφατος, -ον, "new" [most EVV]), "fresh" (Moffatt, NET), "recent" (BDAG 886a; C. Maurer, *TDNT* 6:766–67; NT hapax). The adj. is both temp. and qual. (Lane 2:283), indicating something unprecedented (Koester 443). Ὁδόν is further modified by ζῶσαν (acc. sg. fem. of the pres. act. ptc. of ζάω), "living" (most EVV). The image is of a way that leads to life (e.g., CEV; cf. Lane 2:283; Ellingworth 519; Koester 443). The use of ζάω is prevalent in Hebrews (3:12; 4:12; 7:25; 9:14; 10:31; 12:22).

Καταπετάσματος is the gen. sg. neut. of καταπέτασμα, -οτος, τό, "veil" (Moffatt, NASB), "curtain" (most EVV); cf. BDAG 524b. Its usage here recalls both Heb 6:19 and Heb 9:3, which refer to the "second" or inner curtain through which one entered the holy of holies. Its mng. here is debated (see discussion below). Διὰ τοῦ καταπετάσματος modifies ὁδόν (Lane 2:284). Taking this prep. phrase with ἐνεκαίνισεν is a less natural way of understanding the syntax. An allusion to the ripping of the temple's curtain (e.g., Matt 27:51, Mark 15:38 [so Bruce 251]) is not obvious (*pace* Barclay).

τοῦτ' ἔστιν τῆς σαρκὸς αὐτοῦ,
(that is, through his flesh)—

The expression τοῦτ' ἔστιν is fixed (neut. sg., "that is") regardless of its antecedent (see comments on 2:14). The gen. τῆς σαρκὸς αὐτοῦ is instr., with διά understood elliptically from the previous clause (made explicit in many EVV ["through" or "by"]). Σάρξ refers to Jesus's body (GNB, JB, NIV; *pace* "physical nature" [Goodspeed]), which he offered up on the cross (cf. 2:14; 5:7 [Koester 444; Lane 2:284]). The word does not carry a neg. connotation here.

There are three options for understanding τοῦτ' ἔστιν τῆς σαρκὸς αὐτοῦ, of which the second and possibly the third are preferred.

1. The clause modifies ὁδὸν πρόσφατον καὶ ζῶσαν; e.g., "the way of his flesh" (NEB, REB; see discussion in Lane 2:275 n. *j*). Although possible, this is not a natural reading of the Gk. (cf. Bruce 251; cf. Attridge 286; Cockerill 469; Koester 443).
*2. The clause modifies διὰ τοῦ καταπετάσματος, epex. (as an appos.), which parallels the usage of τοῦτ' ἔστιν elsewhere in Hebrews (Attridge 286; Koester 443; cf. Ellingworth 519). This is reflected in most EVV. This is also the most natural reading of the Gk. (Bruce 252). Additionally, διὰ τοῦ καταπετάσματος is understood locat. and [διὰ] τῆς σαρκὸς αὐτοῦ is understood instr., par. ἐν τῷ αἵματι Ἰησοῦ in v. 19 (Lane 2:275 n. j; Cockerill 470; Ellingworth 521; Koester 444). On this view, the veil is no longer a barrier (Cockerill 468–70; Ellingworth 520; cf. Attridge 285), but rather an entrance, by virtue of Jesus's death and resurrection.
3. The clause modifies the entire previous clause (cf. Ellingworth 519–521). This view depends on recognizing numerous par. between vv. 19 and 20 (see Lane 2:275 n. *j*), with v. 19 focusing on Christians and v. 20 focusing on Christ (Lane 2:284).

VERSE 21

καὶ ἱερέα μέγαν ἐπὶ τὸν οἶκον τοῦ θεοῦ,
and since we have a great high priest over the house of God,

Καί adds the second obj. (ἱερέα) of the ptc. ἔχοντες in v. 19, which is repeated in most EVV. This wording (ἔχοντες οὖν . . . ἱερέα μέγαν) parallels 4:14 (ἔχοντες οὖν ἀρχιερέα μέγαν [Lane 2:285]). Ἱερέα is the acc. sg. masc. of ἱερεύς (see comments on 5:6), and is modified by μέγαν. "High priest" rather than "priest" (following the Gk.; most EVV) appears in several EVV (e.g., NLT). Ἐπὶ τὸν οἶκον τοῦ θεοῦ recalls the sim. phrase in Heb 3:6 (see comments there). The gen. θεοῦ indicates poss. As with 3:6, οἶκος refers to the people of God, not the heavenly sanctuary (*pace* NJB, BDAG 699a). The concept of Christ as the Son over the house of God is now developed in terms of Christ as the ἱερέα μέγαν. The expression ἱερέα μέγαν occurs in the LXX (e.g., Lev 21:10; Num 35:25; see Ellingworth 521–22).

VERSE 22

προσερχώμεθα μετὰ ἀληθινῆς καρδίας ἐν πληροφορίᾳ πίστεως
let us draw near with a true heart in full assurance of faith,

Προσερχώμεθα is the 1st pl. pres. mid. subjunc. of the προσέρχομαι, "draw near" (many EVV), "make our approach" (REB) (see comments on Heb 4:16). The par. with 4:16 (cf. 7:25; 11:6) clarifies that God is the one approached. The first pers. pl. is inclusive (Wallace 396). The pres. is progressive (Campbell, *Basics* 63). Although a few early mss. (e.g., $\mathfrak{P}^{46}$) read the indic. for the subjunc., the context confirms the subjunc. (most EVV). This hort. subjunc. is the first of three in Heb 10:19–25. Whereas ἀληθινῆς (gen. sg. fem. of ἀληθινός, -ή, -όν) indicated "real" in contrast with "shadow" in 8:2 and 9:24, here the adj. means "true" (ESV), "sincere" (NASB, NET, NIV); it modifies καρδίας. Μετά with the gen. means "with." Πληροφορίᾳ is the dat. sg. fem. of πληροφορία, -ας, ἡ, "full assurance" (ESV, NASB, NIV), "absolute trust" (NAB), "unfaltering faith" (Weymouth), "certainty" (BDAG 827d; cf. 6:11). The gen. πίστεως is likely obj. (Ellingworth 525; unspecified in most EVV; but cf. "assurance that faith brings" [NET]).

ῥεραντισμένοι τὰς καρδίας ἀπὸ συνειδήσεως πονηρᾶς
with our hearts sprinkled clean from an evil conscience

Ῥεραντισμένοι is the nom. pl. masc. of the pf. pass. ptc. of ῥαντίζω, "sprinkled clean" (most EVV), "sprinkled to cleanse" (NIV), "purified" (see comments on 9:13). The pf. tense is intensive (Wallace 574; cf. Campbell, *VA* 201). The ptc. could possibly be a permissive mid. (Cockerill 473). The imagery here likely recalls Moses in Heb 9:18–22 (Lane 2:287) or alludes to Aaron's consecration (e.g., Exod 29:4; Lev 8:12, 30; 16:4). Καρδίας is the obj. of the ptc. The acc. obj. can be retained with a pass. vb. in BGk. (R 485; BDF §159[3]), although the acc. καρδίας is tr. as a subj. in many EVV (e.g., NIV). The art. indicates poss. (Wallace 215–16). The ptc. is either causal ("because" [NET]) or *circum. ("with" [ESV]; "having" [NASB, NIV]), modifying προσερχώμεθα. An impv. force is less likely (e.g., "let's keep our hearts pure" [CEV]). Ἀπό indicates separation (BDF §211). Συνειδήσεως is the gen. sg. fem. of συνείδησις, -εως, ἡ, "conscience" (most EVV; see comments on 9:9), which is modified by πονηρᾶς (πονηρός, -ά, -όν, "evil" [ESV, NASB, NET], "guilty" [NIV]). The expression συνειδήσεως πονηρᾶς recalls the sim. one (καρδία πονηρά) in 3:12.

καὶ λελουσμένοι τὸ σῶμα ὕδατι καθαρῷ·
and our bodies washed in pure water.

Λελουσμένοι is the nom. pl. masc. of the pf. pass. ptc. of λούω, "washed" (most EVV). The pf. is intensive (Wallace 574; cf. Campbell, *VA* 201). The ptc. could possibly be a permissive mid. (Cockerill 473; BDAG 603d). Καί indicates that λελουσμένοι functions par. to ῥεραντισμένοι (most EVV). The obj. of the ptc. is σῶμα, which par. καρδίας and is correctly understood as pl. (most EVV). The art. indicates poss. (Wallace 215–16). Καθαρῷ is the dat. sg. neut. of καθαρός, -ά, -όν, "pure" (most EVV). The adj. modifies ὕδατι. There are several OT rituals to which ὕδατι καθαρῷ may allude, including purification rituals (e.g., Num 5:17) and the prophecy of Ezek 36:25–26. A ref. to Christian baptism, however, also seems likely (so most commentators), although baptism as the author's "primary referent" is rightly challenged by Cockerill (475).

The distinction between "inwardly" (ῥεραντισμένοι) and "outwardly" (λελουσμένοι) in the REB is artificial.

VERSE 23

κατέχωμεν τὴν ὁμολογίαν τῆς ἐλπίδος ἀκλινῆ,
Let us hold on to the confession of our hope without wavering,

Κατέχωμεν is the 1st pl. pres. act. subjunc. of κατέχω, "hold to" (NET, NIV); "hold fast" (ESV, NASB; cf. BDAG 533a). The hort. subjunc. recalls the use of κατέχω in Hebrews 3 (vv. 6, 14) and is the second hort. subjunc. in 10:19–25. Similar exhortations occur in 4:14 and 6:18 with κρατέω; see comments there. The pres. is progressive (Campbell, *Basics* 63). Ὁμολογίαν is the acc. sg. fem of ὁμολογία, -ας, ἡ, "confession" (most EVV) (see comments on 3:1). Ὁμολογίαν is the obj. of κατέχωμεν and is modified by the obj. gen. ἐλπίδος (e.g., "the hope that we confess" [NET], "the hope we profess" [NIV]; cf. Lane 2:276 n. *q*). Less likely, the gen. is appos. (BDF §167)—"the content of the confession and of the hope are the same" (Ellingworth 525). A sim. obj. understanding of hope is evident in 6:18 (Lane 2:288). In NT Gk., if the head noun (ὁμολογίαν) is art., then the gen. modifier is usually also art. ("Apollonius's Canon," Wallace 240). Ἀκλινῆ is the acc. sg. fem. of ἀκλινής, -ές, which is nearly synonymous with βέβαιος (cf. 2:2; 3:14; 6:19; 9:17 [Attridge 289; Ellingworth 525–6]). The acc. adj. functions as an adv. ("without wavering" [most EVV; BDAG 36a; NT hapax]; cf. "unwaveringly" [NET], "unswervingly" [NIV]). Less likely, the adj. modifies ὁμολογίαν as a pred. ("hold the confession firm" [Cockerill 477]).

πιστὸς γὰρ ὁ ἐπαγγειλάμενος,
since he who promised is faithful.

Γάρ introduces the grounds for the exhortation in the first part of the v. Ἐπαγγειλάμενος is the nom. sg. masc. of the aor. mid. ptc. of ἐπαγγέλλομαι, "promised" (most EVV). The ptc. is subst. and the subj. of the verbless clause. Πιστός ("faithful" [most EVV]; cf. "trustworthy" [NAB, NET]) is a pred. adj. In pred. statements the subj. is usually art. and the pred. precedes the subj. (Wallace 307). The clause may reflect an early confession (cf. Lane 2:289). The one who promises in Hebrews is God (6:13). This recalls the focus on God's promises in 6:13–17. Similar statements about Christ's faithfulness were expressed in 2:17 and 3:2 (Attridge 289 n. 71; Ellingworth 526).

VERSE 24

καὶ κατανοῶμεν ἀλλήλους εἰς παροξυσμὸν ἀγάπης καὶ καλῶν ἔργων,
And let us watch out for one another to provoke love and good works,

Κατανοῶμεν is the 1st pl. pres. act. subjunc. of κατανοέω ("consider" [ESV, NASB, NIV]; "think of" [NLT]; "take thought of" [NET]; "be concerned about" [BDAG 522d]). The pres. is progressive (Campbell, *Basics* 63). This is the third hort. subjunc.

in this passage. Παροξυσμόν is the acc. sg. masc. of *παροξυσμός*, -ου, ὁ. The word often has neg. connotations (e.g., "provoking" [BDAG 780b]; "irritation," H. Seesemann, *TDNT* 5:857; cf. Lane 2:276 n. *s*). The context, however, suggests something positive or perhaps ironic (e.g., "provoke not to anger but good deeds" [cf. Cockerill 478]). Εἰς indicates purpose. As with v. 19, the prep. phrase is tr. as an inf. in many EVV (e.g., "to stir up" [ESV], "to spur on" [NET, NIV], "to provoke" [CSB]; "to stimulate" [NASB]).

The reciprocal pron. *ἀλλήλους* ("one another" [most EVV]) underscores the importance of community and is the obj. of the vb. Many EVV tr. the implicit verbal idea in *παροξυσμόν* as the vb. (e.g., "how we may spur one another on" [NIV]). Both *ἀγάπης* and *ἔργων* are obj. gen. modifying *παροξυσμόν*. In many EVV, they are tr. as the obj. of *παροξυσμόν*, rendered as an inf. Καλῶν modifies *ἔργων*. The cstr. *καλῶν ἔργων* does not occur elsewhere in BGk. (Ellingworth 527). Ἀγάπης *καὶ καλῶν ἔργων* could form a hendiadys (e.g., "loving good deeds," "good deeds of love" [cf. Cockerill 478]). These contrast with "dead works" in 9:14 (Cockerill 478–88).

The ref. to love completes a triad common in early Christian writings (Lane 2:289): faith (v. 22), hope (v. 23), and love (v. 24). The focus here shifts "from the vertical to the horizontal dimension of Christian living" (Ellingworth 526).

VERSE 25

μὴ ἐγκαταλείποντες τὴν ἐπισυναγωγὴν ἑαυτῶν,
not neglecting to gather together,

Ἐγκαταλείποντες is the nom. pl. masc. of the pres. act. ptc. of *ἐγκαταλείπω*, "abandoning" (NET), "forsaking" (NASB), "deserting" (BDAG 273c–d); "wrongful abandonment" (Attridge 290). The ptc. is negated by *μή* and further modifies the hort. subjunc. in v. 24, indicating means (implicit in most EVV) or continuing the impv. force of the hort. subjunc. in v. 24 ("not giving" [NIV]).The pres. tense may be customary or habitual (Wallace 521–22).

Ἐπισυναγωγήν is the acc. sg. fem. of *ἐπισυναγωγή*, -ῆς, ἡ. The word indicates either the action of gathering or the gathered group (BDAG 382d; Attridge 290; Cockerill 480). The former is reflected by translating *ἐπισυναγωγήν* as an inf. (e.g., ESV). The latter is reflected with a noun (e.g., "meeting" [NIV]). The word is rare, although it is closely related to *συναγωγή*, which is not used in Hebrews. (Ellingworth 528). The prefix may have "local connotations" (e.g., a local house church [Koester 446]). Cognates of this word are used elsewhere (Matt 23:37; Mark 13:27; 2 Thess 2:1) for the gathering of God's people at the final judgment (Cockerill 480; see Schrage, *TDNT* 7:842–43). Ἑαυτῶν is a refl. pron. Although it is third pers., it is not unusual for it to be used in a first pers. context (Z §209; here it parallels *ἀλλήλους* [BDF §287]). The gen. is either poss. ("our . . . meetings" [NET]; BDF §284[2]) or obj. ("meeting together" [NIV, NLT]; Cockerill 480).

καθὼς ἔθος τισίν,
as some are in the habit of doing,

Καθώς ("as" [BDAG 493c]) indicates a comp. between the audience and some other group or house church. The reason why these individuals are withdrawing is not specified, but persecution is possible (e.g., 10:32–34), as is weariness or discouragement (perhaps over waiting for Christ's return [Bruce 259; Cockerill 479]). See For Further Study 73 (Persecution in the First Century). Ἔθος is the nom. sg. neut. of ἔθος, -ους, τό, "habit" (most EVV; cf. BDAG 277a). The dat. indef. pron. (τισίν) could indicate poss. ("the habit of some" [ESV, NASB]) or ref. ("the habit" in reference to "some" [NIV; Lane 2:276 n. *v*]).

ἀλλὰ παρακαλοῦντες,
but encouraging each other,

Ἀλλά ("but" [most EVV]) contrasts what the audience should not do (neglect) with what they are to do (encourage). Παρακαλοῦντες is the nom. pl. masc. of the pres. act. ptc. of παρακαλέω, "encourage" (most EVV; but "admonishing" [Moffatt]). The ptc. par. μὴ ἐγκαταλείποντες and modifies the hort. subjunc. in v. 24, indicating means (e.g., implicit in many EVV) or continuing the impv. force of the hort. subjunc. in v. 24. (e.g., "encouraging" [NIV]). Ἑαυτῶν is supplied in most EVV.

καὶ τοσούτῳ μᾶλλον ὅσῳ βλέπετε ἐγγίζουσαν τὴν ἡμέραν.
and all the more as you see the day approaching.

The dat. of the correl. adj. τοσοῦτος (-αύτη, -οῦτον; "so great, so large, so much" [BDAG 1012c]) indicates the "degree of difference" in a comp. (R 532; Wallace 166–67). The cstr. τοσούτῳ μᾶλλον ὅσῳ (ὅσος, -η, -ον; [by] "as much as" [BDAG 729c]) means "all the more as" (most EVV; cf. "even more so because" [NET]). Βλέπετε is the 2nd. pl. pres. act. indic. of βλέπω. The obj. of the vb. is ἡμέραν, which is modified by ἐγγίζουσαν (acc. sg. fem. of the pres. act. ptc. of ἐγγίζω "approaching" [NIV, NRSV]; "drawing near" [ESV, NASB, NET]). The "day" is eschatological, referring to Christ's return and future judgment (cf. Harris 264; see esp. Cockerill 481; Koester 446). This is made explicit in some EVV (e.g., "the day of his return" [NLT]).

FOR FURTHER STUDY

67. The New and Living Way (10:19–25)

Dahl, Nils Alstrup. "A New and Living Way: The Approach to God according to Heb 10:19–25." *Int* 5 (1951): 401–12.

Leithart, Peter J. "Womb of the World: Baptism and the Priesthood of the New Covenant in Hebrews 10.19–22." *JSNT* 78 (2000): 49–65.

68. The Veil of the Heavenly Sanctuary (10:20)

Jennings, Mark A. "The Veil and the High Priestly Robes of the Incarnation: Understanding the Context of Heb 10:20." *PRSt* 37 (2010): 85–97.

*Moffitt, David M. "Unveiling Jesus' Flesh: A Fresh Assessment of the Relationship between the Veil and Jesus' Flesh in Hebrews 10:20." *PRSt* 37 (2010): 71–84.

Young, Norman H. "*Tout' estin tēs sarkos autou* (Heb 10:20): Apposition, Dependent or Explicative?" *NTS* 20 (1973): 100–104.

See For Further Study 46 (The Tabernacle Veil)

HOMILETICAL SUGGESTIONS

Three Imperatives for All Believers (10:19–25)

1. Let Us Draw Near with Sincere Hearts (vv. 19–22)
   (a) As brothers and sisters (v. 19a)
   (b) Christ's blood gives us boldness to enter the sanctuary (v. 19b)
   (c) He has opened a new and living way into the sanctuary (v. 20)
   (d) We have a high priest in God's house (v. 21)
   (e) We have cleansed consciences and washed bodies (v. 22b)
2. Let Us Hold On to Our Confession of Faith (v. 23)
   (a) Without wavering (v. 23a)
   (b) Because the One who promised is faithful (v. 23b)
3. Let Us Meet Together (vv. 24–15)
   (a) Spurring each other on in love and good works (v. 24a)
   (b) Not neglecting each other (v. 25a)
   (c) But encouraging each other while we can (v. 25b)

2. Fourth Warning: The Reality of God's Judgment (10:26–31)

STRUCTURE

This passage presents the fourth (of five) warning passages in Hebrews. There are numerous par. between 6:4–8 and 10:26–31 (see esp. the outline in Lane 2:291). In contrast to the previous series of hort. subjunc., this passage is anchored with a series of indic. verbs (vv. 26, 28, 29, 30) and two verbless clauses (vv. 27, 31).

26 Ἑκουσίως γὰρ ἁμαρτανόντων ἡμῶν
μετὰ τὸ λαβεῖν τὴν ἐπίγνωσιν τῆς ἀληθείας,
οὐκέτι περὶ ἁμαρτιῶν ἀπολείπεται θυσία,
27 φοβερὰ δέ τις ἐκδοχὴ κρίσεως
καὶ πυρὸς ζῆλος ἐσθίειν μέλλοντος τοὺς ὑπεναντίους.
28 ἀθετήσας τις νόμον Μωϋσέως
χωρὶς οἰκτιρμῶν
ἐπὶ δυσὶν ἢ τρισὶν μάρτυσιν
ἀποθνῄσκει·
29 πόσῳ δοκεῖτε χείρονος ἀξιωθήσεται τιμωρίας
ὁ τὸν υἱὸν τοῦ θεοῦ καταπατήσας
καὶ τὸ αἷμα τῆς διαθήκης κοινὸν ἡγησάμενος,
ἐν ᾧ ἡγιάσθη,
καὶ τὸ πνεῦμα τῆς χάριτος ἐνυβρίσας;
30 οἴδαμεν γὰρ τὸν εἰπόντα·
ἐμοὶ ἐκδίκησις,
ἐγὼ ἀνταποδώσω.
καὶ πάλιν·
κρινεῖ κύριος τὸν λαὸν αὐτοῦ.
31 φοβερὸν τὸ ἐμπεσεῖν
εἰς χεῖρας θεοῦ ζῶντος.

VERSE 26

Ἑκουσίως γὰρ ἁμαρτανόντων ἡμῶν
For if we deliberately go on sinning

Γάρ links the previous exhortations (10:19–25) with the shocking outcome for those who forsake Christ. (The NLT inexplicably begins the v. with "Dear friends.") Ἁμαρτανόντων is the gen. pl. masc. of the pres. act. ptc. of ἁμαρτάνω ("sinning" [most EVV]). The ptc. clause is a gen. abs. cstr., subord. to ἀπολείπεται (see below). The ptc. has cond. force ("if" [most EVV]; Wallace 632–33) and is durative (e.g., "go on sinning" [ESV, NASB], "keep on sinning" [NET, NIV], "persist in sin" [NRSV; Koester 451; Lane 2:292], "continuing rejection of Christ" [Attridge 292; cf. Ellingworth 532]). The "subj." of the gen. abs. is ἡμῶν ("we"). As is freq. in Hebrews, the author includes himself in the warning. The adv. ἑκουσίως ("deliberately" [ESV, NET, NIV], "willfully" [NASB, NRSV], "intentionally" [BDAG 307b]) modifies the ptc. Its position is emph. (Lane 2:277 n. *y*; Ellingworth 531). The adv. connotes "a conscious expression of an attitude that displays contempt for God" (Lane 2:292).

μετὰ τὸ λαβεῖν τὴν ἐπίγνωσιν τῆς ἀληθείας,
after receiving the knowledge of the truth,

The art. inf. (λαβεῖν) preceded by μετά is temp. ("after" [most EVV]; R 612; Wallace 595). The idiomatic Gk. is tr. as either a ptc. (e.g., ESV, NASB, NET) or a finite vb. (e.g., NIV, NLT). Ἐπίγνωσιν (acc. sg. fem. of ἐπίγνωσις, -εως, ἡ ["knowledge," most EVV]) is the obj. of the inf. There does not appear to be any difference between ἐπίγνωσις and γνῶσις (Attridge 292–93). The gen. ἀληθείας is obj. The expression τὴν ἐπίγνωσιν τῆς ἀληθείας (cf. 1 Tim 2:4; 2 Tim 2:25; 3:7; Titus 1:1) may reflect an early Christian formula (Ellingworth 532; Lane 2:292), perhaps indicating conversion (Attridge 292; Koester 451; cf. Ellingworth 532; but challenged by Cockerill 485). Note the par. to Heb 6:4–5. In BGk., if the head noun (ἐπίγνωσιν) is art., then the gen. modifier is also art. ("Apollonius' Canon," Wallace 239–40).

οὐκέτι περὶ ἁμαρτιῶν ἀπολείπεται θυσία,
there no longer remains a sacrifice for sins,

Ἀπολείπεται is the 3rd sg. pres. pass. indic. of ἀπολείπω, "remains" (most EVV; BDAG 115c). The pass. verb. is impers. (e.g., "there . . . remains" [ESV, NASB]). The adv. οὐκέτι (οὐ[κ] + ἔτι [BDAG 736a]) modifies ἀπολείπεται (see comments on 2:4). The implication is that there is no other sacrifice, apart from Christ's, that can be offered for sins (e.g., "no sacrifice . . . is left" [NIV]; "no further sacrifice" [NET; Ellingworth 533]). Θυσία functions as a pred. nom. (see comments on 5:1 and 7:27). Both its position at the end of this clause and οὐκέτι at the beginning are emph. (Cockerill 485; Ellingworth 533). The use of περί par. ὑπέρ ("for" in most EVV [BDF §229(1)]; cf. Harris 182–83, 210).

This v. (esp. ἑκουσίως) may allude to the distinction in the OT (and secular sources) between deliberate (high-handed) and inadvertent sins (e.g., Num 15:22–31 [Harris 197; Attridge 292; Koester 451]), although the vocabulary used in Hebrews does not correl. directly with Num 15 (see Cockerill 483–84). As was true in Hebrews 6, if Christ's fully efficacious sacrifice for sins (the pl. is "comprehensive" [Cockerill 485]) is rejected, there is nowhere else to seek forgiveness—all that remains is judgment.

VERSE 27

φοβερὰ δέ τις ἐκδοχὴ κρίσεως καὶ πυρὸς ζῆλος
but a terrifying expectation of judgment and the fury of a fire

Δέ introduces the contrast to the final clause of v. 26. Ἀπολείπεται is understood elliptically from v. 26 (made explicit in NJB). Ἐκδοχή (-ῆς, ἡ, "expectation" [most EVV], "prospect" [NAB, NRSV; Cockerill 486]; BDAG 301c; NT hapax) is modified by φοβερά (nom. sg. fem. of φοβερός, -ά, -όν, "fearful" [ESV, NET, NIV], "frightful" [BDAG 1060d]). The indef. pron. τις "intensifies" φοβερά (R 743; BDF §301[1]) and adds "rhetorical emph." (BAGD 1008d). This is reflected in some EVV (e.g., "only" [NIV]) and implied in others (e.g., "terrifying" [NASB]). Κρίσεως (gen. sg. fem. of κρίσις, -εως, ἡ, "judgment") modifies ἐκδοχή as an obj. gen. The use of κρίσις may recall the cognate κρίμα in Heb 6:2. The reality of final judgment is developed in Heb 12:25–29. Ζῆλος (-ου, ὁ, "zeal" [BDAG 427a]) is modified by πυρός as a descriptive gen. ("blazing indignation" [Goodspeed], "fiery wrath" [NJB]) or possibly a gen. of appos. ("zeal that is fire" [Cockerill 486; cf. Ellingworth 535; BDF §167]); this is somewhat obscured with "raging fire" (NIV, NLT) or is ambiguous (e.g., "fury of fire" [many EVV]). Like θυσία, ἐκδοχή and ζῆλος function as pred. nom. of ἀπολείπεται. Καί may be epex., further explaining κρίσεως.

ἐσθίειν μέλλοντος τοὺς ὑπεναντίους.
about to consume the adversaries.

Μέλλοντος is the gen. sg. neut. of the pres. act. ptc. of μέλλω, "about to" (BDF §356). The inf. ἐσθίειν complements the ptc. and together are the "virtual equivalent" of the fut. (e.g., "will" [many EVV; Ellingworth 535]). An intensified understanding of ἐσθίω is clear from the context (e.g., "consume" [most EVV]; "devour" [NJB]). This imagery is common in apocalyptic literature (Ellingworth 535). Ὑπεναντίους is the acc. pl. masc. of ὑπεναντίος, -α, -ον, "opposed, contrary, hostile" (BDAG 1030b). The art. adj. functions as a subst. ("adversaries" [ESV, NASB], "enemies" [NIV]); some EVV further specify "God's enemies" (NET, REB), "his enemies" (NLT), or "enemies of God" (NIV). There is a likely allusion to Isa 26:11 (cf. Zeph 1:18).

VERSE 28

ἀθετήσας τις νόμον Μωϋσέως
Anyone who disregarded the law of Moses

Ἀθετήσας is the nom. sg. masc. of the aor. act. ptc. of ἀθετέω, "disregards" (NJB), "rejected" (NET, NIV), "set aside" (ESV, NASB), "treat . . . as if it did not exist" (Barclay); cf. BDAG 24c; M. Limbeck, *EDNT* 1:35b–d; Ellingworth 536). The vb. suggests "rejection of the Law as a whole" by blasphemy or idolatry (Attridge 294) and confirms that the sin in view is apostasy. The circum. ptc. modifies ἀποθνήσκει (see below). The aor. is global or possibly gnomic (Wallace 557, 562). The indef. pron. τις ("anyone") is the subj. of the ptc. It indicates comprehensiveness (e.g., "no exceptions" [Cockerill 487]). Νόμον is the obj. of the ptc., which is modified by Μωϋσέως, indicating poss.

χωρὶς οἰκτιρμῶν
. . . without mercy,

Οἰκτιρμῶν is the gen. pl. masc. of οἰκτιρμός, -οῦ, ὁ, "mercy" (most EVV), "pity" (NAB, NEB). The pl. reflects "Hebraic usage" (BDF §142) and is not distinguished from the sg. (BDAG 700c). The prep. phrase alludes to Deut 13:8, which declares that those who reject the law of Moses must die without mercy.

ἐπὶ δυσὶν ἢ τρισὶν μάρτυσιν ἀποθνῄσκει·
based on the testimony of two or three witnesses . . . died

Ἐπί with the dat. means "on the basis of" (BDF §235[2]) or "in the presence of" (R 604); "based on" or "on" (most EVV). Μάρτυσιν is the dat. pl. masc. of μάρτυς, μάρτυρος, ὁ, "witness" (most EVV; BDAG 619c). The implicit understanding of "testimony" is made explicit in many EVV. The word refers to a witness in a legal context; the idea of a "martyr" (one who dies for one's faith) postdates the composition of Hebrews. Μάρτυσιν is modified by the cardinals δυσίν and τρισίν. Ἤ is a correl. disjunctive conj. ("or"). The prep. phrase modifies ἀποθνῄσκει, which is the 3rd sg. pres. act. indic. of ἀποθνῄσκω. The pres. is iterative (Cockerill 487) or perhaps timeless (Ellingworth 536). This v. refers to Deut 17:6, which prescribes the death penalty for idolatry on the basis of two or more witnesses (cf. Deut 19:15–21). The argument is an *a fortiori* one, arguing from the lesser (v. 28, death for rejecting Mosaic law) to the greater (v. 29, final judgment for rejecting Christ). Note the par. with Heb 2:1–4.

VERSE 29

πόσῳ δοκεῖτε χείρονος ἀξιωθήσεται τιμωρίας
How much worse punishment do you think one will deserve

The pron. πόσῳ could indicate a rhetorical question (many EVV; Ellingworth 538; Koester 452), or possibly an exclamation (NJB, NLT), that introduces the "greater" part of the *a fortiori* argument. Τιμωρίας is the gen. sg. fem. of τιμωρία, -ας, ἡ, "punishment" (BDAG 1006c–d; NT hapax). Χείρονος (χείρων, -ον, comp. of κακός [BDAG 1083d]) is a gen. of comp., modifying τιμωρίας ("how much worse punishment" [ESV, NRSV]; "much greater punishment" [NET]; "more severe a punishment" [BDAG 1006c–d]). Δοκεῖτε is the 2nd pl. pres. act. indic. of δοκέω. The vb. forms a rhetorical parenthetical aside (BDF §465[2]; Attridge 294)—"do you think" (most EVV)—although it is tr. as an impv. in some EVV (NLT, REB). The second pers. "involves directly the addressees and invites them to draw the appropriate conclusion" (Attridge 294). Ἀξιωθήσεται is the 3rd sg. fut. pass. indic. of ἀξιόω, "deserve" (most EVV; BDAG 94b). The pass. is divine and possibly eschatological (Ellingworth 539). The vb. is followed by a gen. obj. (τιμωρίας [R 511]). The subj. is understood to be the individual (or group) described with the following three subst. aor. ptc. (e.g., "the one who . . . is worthy of much worse punishment").

ὁ τὸν υἱὸν τοῦ θεοῦ καταπατήσας καὶ τὸ αἷμα τῆς διαθήκης κοινὸν ἡγησάμενος,
who has trampled on the Son of God, who has regarded as profane the blood of the covenant

Καταπατήσας is the nom. sg. masc. of the aor. act. ptc. of καταπατέω, "trample underfoot" (ESV, NASB, NIV), "dishonor" (CEV), "spurn" (NRSV), "treat with distain"

(BDAG 523d; H. Seesemann, *TDNT* 5:943–45). The vb. is used elsewhere of physical trampling (e.g., Matt 5:13), but never "with God or Christ as object" (Ellingworth 540). The vb. is understood metaphorically here (Attridge 294). The image is of "utter contempt" (Cockerill 489 n. 32; cf. NET). Whereas the Son's enemies will be subjugated under his feet, here the apostate tramples the Son under foot (Cockerill 489; Koester 452–53). The ptc. is subst. and is the implicit subj. of ἀξιωθήσεται. Ὁ functions par. to a rel. pron., introducing this ptc. clause. The obj. of the ptc. is τὸν υἱὸν τοῦ θεοῦ. This latter expression may reflect an early Christian confession (Lane 2:294); its position is emph. (Ellingworth 540). Καί joins the two ptc. in this clause.

Ἡγησάμενος is the nom. sg. masc. of the aor. mid. ptc. of ἡγέομαι, "regard" (NASB) "treat as" (NIV), "consider" (BDAG 434b). This ptc. is also governed by ὁ, indicating that the same individual (or group) is in view (Granville Sharp's rule). The obj. of ἡγησάμενος is αἷμα, which is modified by διαθήκης as a descriptive gen. The expression alludes to Exod 24:8 (cf. Heb 9:20), now understood as Christ's blood, which inaugurated the new covenant. Κοινόν (acc. sg. neut. of κοινός, -ή, -όν) is the obj. complement (i.e., "double" acc. [BDF §157(3)]) of ἡγησάμενος. Although the word can mean "common" (NLT) or "ordinary" (BDAG 552a), the juxtaposition with ἡγιάσθη (see below) indicates that it means "profane" (Cockerill 489; cf. Ellingworth 540; Koester 453), "unholy" (NIV), or "unclean" (NASB). Some EVV tr. κοινὸν ἡγησάμενος as one vb. ("profanes/d" [ESV, NET, REB]).

ἐν ᾧ ἡγιάσθη,
by which he was sanctified,

The antecedent of ᾧ is αἷμα. Ἡγιάσθη is the 3rd sg. aor. pass. indic. of ἁγιάζω, "sanctify" (most EVV), "make . . . holy" (NET, NLT), "consecrate" (REB; BDAG 10a). The subj. of the vb. is the "one" who has trampled and profaned in the previous clause. The vb. is a divine pass. (Ellingworth 541). The prep. phrase ἐν ᾧ is instr., modifying ἡγιάσθη.

καὶ τὸ πνεῦμα τῆς χάριτος ἐνυβρίσας;
and who has insulted the Spirit of grace?

Ἐνυβρίσας is the nom. sg. masc. of the aor. act. ptc. of ἐνυβρίζω, "insult" (most EVV) or "outrage" (ESV; BDAG 342a; G. Bertram, *TDNT* 8:306; BGk. hapax; see esp. Koester 453). The obj. of the ptc. is τὸ πνεῦμα τῆς χάριτος, which is likely an allusion to Zech 12:10. Χάριτος could be an attrib. (or Heb.) gen. ("the gracious Spirit" [Bruce 262 n. 139; cf. REB]), possibly a descriptive gen. (implied with "Spirit of grace" [most EVV]), or even a subj. gen. ("the Spirit, the source of grace" [Cassirer]). Context indicates that πνεῦμα refers to the Spirit (although unclear in NAB).

This is the third ptc. governed by ὁ, indicating that the same individual (or perhaps group) is in view (Wallace 270–72; Ellingworth 538). The sg. ptc. may be generic or collective (BDF §139). All three aor. ptc. are global (Wallace 557). The cstr. ὁ + aor. ptc. can be used in "general expressions" (R 859), where the art. is generic. The joining of the three ptc. indicates that they are to be taken together to indicate a progression:

trampling; considering profane; insulting the Spirit. Together, the three ptc. add a "cumulative force to the argument" (Ellingworth 538)—the "greater" part of the *a fortiori* argument begun in v. 28. If rejecting the law of Moses had dire consequences, how much greater will be the consequences for the one who tramples the Son, profanes his blood (of the new covenant), and thus insults the Spirit? The issue in view is willful apostasy. As with the previous warning passages, the author switches from the first pers. to the third pers., suggesting that he may not have a specific individual or group in mind (also suggested by the use of the indef. pron. and the generic art. ὁ (Ellingworth 538); nevertheless, the warning is urgent and real.

VERSE 30

οἴδαμεν γὰρ τὸν εἰπόντα·
For we know the one who has said,

Γάρ grounds the previous discussion with a series of scriptural citations. Οἴδαμεν is the 1st pl. pres. (pf.) act. indic. of οἶδα. The ptc. (εἰπόντα) is subst., with God as the understood ref. The ptc. continues the use of speaking vbs. in Hebrews in conj. with Scripture. The author may have intended a double mng. of "know" (cf. Ellingworth 541)—both knowing God (e.g., ESV, NET, NIV; cf. Cockerill 491) and knowing that he has spoken (CEV, REB).

ἐμοὶ ἐκδίκησις, ἐγὼ ἀνταποδώσω.
Vengeance belongs to me; I will repay,

Ἐκδίκησις (-εως, ἡ) is "vengeance" (most EVV; "justice" [REB]; BDAG 301a; G. Schrenk, *TDNT* 2:442–46), although some EVV tr. the noun as an inf. ("to avenge" [NIV]) or a finite vb. ("I will take revenge" [NLT]). The position of ἐμοί is emph. (Cockerill 492 n. 45). The dat. indicates poss. ("mine" [ESV, NET, NIV]). Ἀνταποδώσω is the 1st sg. fut. act. indic. of ἀνταποδίδωμι (BDAG 87b; F. Büchsel, *TDNT* 2:169). The vb. is a double compound (ἀντί + ἀπό; "repay" [most EVV]; "pay them back" [NLT]). Ἐγώ in the nom. indicates emph. (BDAG 275a), although this is not captured in EVV (e.g., "I myself"). The citation is from the Song of Moses (Deut 32:35; also cited in 1:6). The precise wording differs from both the LXX and the MT, although it conforms with the citation in Rom 12:19 (see esp. Cockerill 492 n. 45). In the original context, God's vengeance was directed toward Israel's enemies, whereas here it is directed to his people, thereby indicating the true "enemy" status of those who deliberately reject Christ (cf. Cockerill 492; *pace* Attridge 296).

καὶ πάλιν·
and again,

Πάλιν introduces the citation from Deut 32:36 and links the two citations from Deuteronomy together (BDAG 752d). It draws attention to the second citation (Cockerill 493). Εἶπεν is understood elliptically from the first part of the v.

κρινεῖ κύριος τὸν λαὸν αὐτοῦ.
The Lord will judge his people.

The subj. of κρινεῖ is κύριος. The obj. of the vb. is λαόν, which is modified by αὐτοῦ. The citation from Deut 32:36 is here applied to new-covenant people of God who reject the gospel. As with the previous citation, the author has not disregarded the orig. context but rather underscores the seriousness of the sin of apostasy (*pace* Attridge 296). Alternatively, κρινεῖ could be tr. "vindicate" (NJB), offering encouragement to those who do persevere and anticipating vv. 32–34 (see esp. Cockerill 493).

VERSE 31

φοβερὸν τὸ ἐμπεσεῖν εἰς χεῖρας θεοῦ ζῶντος.
It is a terrifying thing to fall into the hands of the living God.

Φοβερόν is the nom. sg. neut. of φοβερός, -ά, -όν. Its usage in this v. forms an *inclusio* with φοβερά (v. 27; see comments there). Most EVV tr. the noun with the same English word in both vv. In the NT, this word only occurs in these two vv. and Heb 12:21 (Cockerill 494 n. 52). A vb. (e.g., "is" [most EVV]) is implied, with the subst. φοβερόν ("terrifying thing" [e.g., CSB]) functioning as a pred. nom. Its position is emph. (Lane 2:295). Ἐμπεσεῖν is the aor. act. inf. of ἐμπίπτω, "fall into" (most EVV; BDAG 324b). The expression is sometimes used as an appeal for mercy, whereas here it clearly refers to judgment (Ellingworth 543). Although not evident in EVV, the subst. inf. functions as the subj. of the implicit impers. vb. (e.g., "To fall . . . is a terrifying thing" [cf. R 1059, Wallace 660]). Χεῖρας (acc. pl. fem., "hands") is the obj. of εἰς, which is locat., although metaphorical. Θεοῦ modifies χεῖρας indicating poss. Θεοῦ is modified by ζῶντος (gen. sg. masc. of the pres. act. ptc. of ζάω, "living God" [most EVV]). See comments on 3:12 and 10:20. This v. offers a powerful summary of the two Scripture citations (cf. Attridge 296; Ellingworth 543).

FOR FURTHER STUDY

69. Apostasy in Hebrews (10:26–31)

Attridge, 168–69.
Barnett, P. W. *DLNT* 73–76.
DeSilva, David A. "Exchanging Favor for Wrath: Apostasy in Hebrews and Patron–Client Relationships." *JBL* 115 (1996): 91–116.
Marshall, I. Howard. "The Problem of Apostasy in New Testament Theology." *PRSt* 14/4 (1987): 65–80.
Ortlund, R. C., Jr. *NDBT* 383–86.
Schmidt, Thomas E. "Moral Lethargy and the Epistle to the Hebrews." *WTJ* 54 (1992): 167–73.

70. The Warning Passage in Hebrews 10 (10:26–31)

Gleason, Randall C. "The Eschatology of the Warning in Hebrews 10:26–31." *TynBul* 53 (2002): 97–120.
*Lewis, Thomas W. "And If He Shrinks Back (Heb 10:38b)." *NTS* 22 (1975): 88–94.
Proctor, John. "Judgement or Vindication?: Deuteronomy 32 in Hebrews 10:30." *TynBul* 55 (2004): 65–80.
Swetnam, James. "Hebrews 10:30–31: A Suggestion." *Bib* 75 (1994): 388–94.
Tanner, J. P. "For Whom Does Hebrews 10:26–31 Teach a 'Punishment Worse than Death?'" *Journal of the Grace Evangelical Society* 19 (2006): 57–77.

See For Further Study 12 (The Warning Passages in Hebrews)

71. Ecclesiology in Hebrews (10:25–31)

*Bockmuehl, Markus N. A. "The Church in Hebrews." Pages 133–51 in *A Vision for the Church: Studies in Early Christian Ecclesiology in Honour of J. P. M. Sweet*. Edited by Markus Bockmuehl and Michael B. Thompson. Edinburgh: T&T Clark, 1997.
Giles, K. N. *DLNT* 195–204.
McKelvey, R. J. *The New Temple: The Church in the New Testament*. London: Oxford University Press, 1969.
Motyer, Stephen. "'Not Apart from Us' (Hebrews 11:40): Physical Community in the Letter to the Hebrews." *EvQ* 77 (2005): 235–47.
Thompson, James W. "The Ecclesiology of Hebrews." *ResQ* 56 (2014): 137–46.

72. House Churches (10:25–31)

Blue, B. B. *DLNT* 91–95.
Filson, Floyd V. "The Significance of the Early House Churches." *JBL* 58 (1939): 105–12.
Harland, Philip A. *NIDB* 2:903.
Petersen, Joan M. "House-Churches in Rome." *Vigiliae Christianae* 23 (1969): 264–72.

HOMILETICAL SUGGESTIONS

The Reality of God's Judgment (10:26–31)

1. No Sacrifice Remains for Willful Sin and Ignorance (v. 26)
2. There Is Only Terrifying, Consuming Judgment (v. 27)
3. Judgment for Disregarding the Mosaic Law Was Severe . . . How Much Worse Will It Be Now? (v. 29a)
   (a) For those who treat the Son with disdain (v. 29b)
   (b) For those who treat his sanctifying blood as unclean (v. 29c)
   (c) For those who insult the Spirit (v. 29d)
4. PRINCIPLE: God's Judgment Is Real and Terrifying (vv. 30–31)
   (a) Vengeance is his alone (v. 30a)
   (b) He will judge his people (v. 30b)
   (c) This is a terrifying reality (v. 31)

3. *Bold Perseverance in the Midst of Suffering (10:32–39)*

STRUCTURE

This section transitions from warning to encouragement, as the author reminds his audience of their past actions as evidence of their true commitment to Christ (cf. the encouragement [6:9–20] following warning in 6:4–8 [see esp. Lane 2:296–97]). Note the shift to the second pers. as the author directly appeals to his audience. This passage also reflects a shift from hort. subjunc. to impv. (cf. 7:4), although it is unclear if this signifies anything more than a stylistic variation (Ellingworth 545). Lane (2:277 n. *kk*), however, suggests that the hort. subjunc. is more rhetorical and the impv. more specific in Heb.

The passage is anchored in the initial impv. (v. 32), the two corresponding indics. (v. 34), a prohibition (aor. subjunc. in v. 35), and two concluding indics. (v. 36 and v. 39). The Scripture citations in vv. 37–38 support the preceding appeal.

32 Ἀναμιμνῄσκεσθε δὲ τὰς πρότερον ἡμέρας,
ἐν . . . πολλὴν ἄθλησιν ὑπεμείνατε παθημάτων,
. . . αἷς φωτισθέντες
33 τοῦτο μὲν ὀνειδισμοῖς τε καὶ θλίψεσιν θεατριζόμενοι,
τοῦτο δὲ κοινωνοὶ τῶν οὕτως ἀναστρεφομένων γενηθέντες.
34 καὶ γὰρ τοῖς δεσμίοις συνεπαθήσατε
καὶ τὴν ἁρπαγὴν τῶν ὑπαρχόντων ὑμῶν μετὰ χαρᾶς προσεδέξασθε
γινώσκοντες ἔχειν ἑαυτοὺς κρείττονα ὕπαρξιν καὶ μένουσαν.
35 μὴ ἀποβάλητε οὖν τὴν παρρησίαν ὑμῶν,
ἥτις ἔχει μεγάλην μισθαποδοσίαν.
36 ὑπομονῆς γὰρ ἔχετε χρείαν
ἵνα τὸ θέλημα τοῦ θεοῦ ποιήσαντες κομίσησθε τὴν ἐπαγγελίαν.
37 ἔτι γὰρ μικρὸν ὅσον ὅσον,
ὁ ἐρχόμενος ἥξει καὶ οὐ χρονίσει·
38 ὁ δὲ δίκαιός μου ἐκ πίστεως ζήσεται,
καὶ ἐὰν ὑποστείληται,
οὐκ εὐδοκεῖ ἡ ψυχή μου ἐν αὐτῷ.
39 ἡμεῖς δὲ οὐκ ἐσμὲν ὑποστολῆς εἰς ἀπώλειαν
ἀλλὰ πίστεως εἰς περιποίησιν ψυχῆς.

VERSE 32

Ἀναμιμνῄσκεσθε δὲ τὰς πρότερον ἡμέρας,
Remember the earlier days

Δέ signals the transition from warning (vv. 26–31) to encouragement. It also urges a different "course of action" than the one outlined in vv. 26–31 (Lane 2:298; cf. "but" [ESV, NASB, NET], although untr. in some EVV). Ἀναμιμνῄσκεσθε is the 2nd pl. pres. pass. impv. of ἀναμιμνῄσκω: with pass., "remember" (NET, NIV), "recall" (ESV), "be reminded" (BDAG 68a). Πρότερον (acc. sg. neut) is the adv. form of the adj. πρότερος, -α, -ον. Here it functions as an adj. ("former" [ESV, NASB, NET], "earlier" [NIV; BDF §62], "previously" [BDAG 888d]) modifying ἡμέρας.

ἐν αἷς φωτισθέντες πολλὴν ἄθλησιν ὑπεμείνατε παθημάτων,
when, after you had been enlightened, you endured a hard struggle with sufferings.

The antecedent of αἷς is ἡμέρας. The prep. ἐν "marks the time within which" an event occurs ("when" [most EVV]; Ellingworth 545). Φωτισθέντες is the nom. pl. masc. of the aor. pass. ptc. of φωτίζω, "enlightened" (most EVV) (see comments on 6:4). The ptc. modifies ἀναμιμνῄσκεσθε temp. ("after" [most EVV]). The pass. implies divine activity. Ὑπεμείνατε is the 2nd pl. aor. act. indic. of ὑπομένω, "endured" (NASB, NET, NIV, BDAG 1039b–c); "remained faithful" (NLT). The vb. connotes the imagery of remaining on a battlefield (Ellingworth 546; "held firm" [REB]). Μένω and compounds are usually intrans., but here the vb. takes a dir. obj. (R 475). Ἄθλησιν is the acc. sg. fem. of ἄθλησις, -εως, ἡ ("struggle" in many EVV; cf. "contest"; "conflict" [NET, NIV]). It is the obj. of ὑπεμείνατε, and is modified by πολλήν ("hard" [ESV]; "great" [NASB, NIV], "harsh" [NET], "to being high on a scale of extent" [BDAG 847d]). Παθημάτων is the gen. pl. neut. of πάθημα, -ατος, τό, "sufferings" (most EVV). It is a gen. of content (e.g., "conflict of sufferings" [NASB: cf. BDF §167]), or perhaps a gen. of association ("in the face of sufferings," "with sufferings" [ESV; Wallace 128]), modifying ἄθλησιν.

Ἄθλησις freq. described an athletic contest in Hellenistic Jewish literature, often in conj. with ὑπομένω (e.g., 4 Macc; cf. BDAG 25a; BGk. hapax; Lane 2:298). Here it is understood figuratively (BDAG 25a), anticipating sim. athletic metaphors in 12:1–3. The historical background here is likely the persecution of Jews under Claudius in AD 49, although the persecution of Christians under Nero in AD 64 is also possible. The ref. here is not specific enough to identify a particular persecution, although it does suggest a plausible reason why the audience was tempted to pull away from their Christian faith.

VERSE 33

τοῦτο μὲν ὀνειδισμοῖς τε καὶ θλίψεσιν θεατριζόμενοι,
Sometimes you were publicly exposed to taunts and afflictions,

The correl. τοῦτο μὲν . . . τοῦτο δέ ("sometimes . . . at other times" [e.g., NIV; cf. BDAG 741b]) indicates "correspondence rather than contrast" (Ellingworth 546; cf. Lane 2:277 n. *mm*) and is an example of the adv. acc. (R 705; BDF §290[5]). It is less likely that this cstr. reflects two different groups: some publicly shamed and others who expressed solidarity (Cockerill 499; Ellingworth 546; *pace* REB; Koester 459; Lane 2:299). Θεατριζόμενοι is the nom. pl. masc. of the pres. pass. ptc. of θεατρίζω, "publicly exposed" (ESV, NET, NIV), "being made a public spectacle" (NASB), "exposed to public ridicule" (NLT), "put to shame," "expose publicly" (BDAG 446a;

G. Kittel, *TDNT* 3:42–43; BGk. hapax). The vb. is related to θέατρον, -ου, τό, "theatre," "spectacle" (BDAG 446a; Cockerill 499 n. 15). The ptc. is instr. ("partly by . . . partly by" [e.g., NASB; Cockerill 498]) or possibly circum. ("being . . ." [e.g., ESV]), modifying συνεπαθήσατε (v. 34). Some EVV tr. the ptc. as a finite vb. and treat the v. as a separate sentence (e.g., NET, NIV). The pres. is durative.

Ὀνειδισμοῖς is the dat. pl. masc. of ὀνειδισμός, -οῦ, ὁ, "insult" (NIV), "abuse" (NET), "reproach" (ESV), "humiliations" (NJB), "reviling," "disgrace," "affliction" (BDAG 710d; J. Schneider, *TDNT* 5:238–42). The word indicates verbal abuse (see esp. Cockerill 499–500; Koester 459). Θλίψεσιν is the dat. pl. fem. of θλῖψις, -εως, ἡ, "persecution" (NIV), "afflictions" (NET), "violence" (NJB), "tribulations" (NASB), "oppression" (BDAG 457b–c; H. Schlier, *TDNT* 3:139–40). The word signals physical abuse (e.g., "beaten" [NLT]; Attridge 298; see esp. Cockerill 500; Koester 459–60). The correl. τε καί indicates the close pairing of these two entities (Wallace 672; BDF §444), both of which are the indir. obj. of the pass. ptc. Both words have a rich LXX background (see esp. Ellingworth 546–47).

τοῦτο δὲ κοινωνοὶ τῶν οὕτως ἀναστρεφομένων γενηθέντες.
and at other times you were companions of those who were treated that way.

Γενηθέντες is the nom. pl. masc. of the aor. pass. ptc. of γίνομαι. Here it is virtually synonymous with εἰμί (cf. Ellingworth 548), with κοινωνοί functioning as a pred. nom. The ptc. is instr. ("by becoming" [e.g., NASB; Cockerill 498]) or possibly circum. ("being . . ." [e.g., ESV, NJB]). Like θεατριζόμενοι, some EVV tr. the ptc. as a finite vb., and treat the v. as a separate sentence (see above). Κοινωνοί is the nom. pl. masc. of κοινωνός, -οῦ, ὁ and ἡ, "partners" (ESV), "sharers" (NASB; BDAG 553d; F. Hauck, *TDNT* 3:797–809); the noun is tr. as an inf. in some EVV ("came to share with" [NET]). The noun is followed by the gen., which indicates the partner/sharer (e.g., ἀναστρεφομένων [BDAG 553d]). This noun indicates "support and solidarity" (Ellingworth 547; e.g., "stood side by side with" [NIV]). For example, prisoners depended on family and friends for food and other basic needs. Ἀναστρεφομένων is the gen. pl. masc. of the pres. pass. ptc. of ἀναστρέφω, "to be treated in such a way" (BDAG 73a; G. Bertram, *TDNT* 7:715–17). The author does not specify who is responsible for those who have been mistreated. The ptc. is subst. and is modified by the adv. οὕτως ("so" [ESV, NAB, NIV], "that way" [NET], "the same way" [NJB]).

VERSE 34

καὶ γὰρ τοῖς δεσμίοις συνεπαθήσατε
For you sympathized with the prisoners

The collocation καὶ γάρ "amplifies" the previous v. (Ellingworth 548), although καί is often untr. (but "in fact" [NET]). Συνεπαθήσατε is the 2nd pl. aor. act. indic. of συμπαθέω, "sympathize" (BDAG 958b; W. Michaelis, *TDNT* 5:935–36; only in Hebrews), "shared the sufferings" (NET), "had compassion on" (ESV), "showed sympathy" (NASB). Δεσμίοις is the dat. pl. masc. of δέσμιος, -ου, ὁ, "prisoners" (BDAG 219b), "those in prison" (ESV, NET, NIV). The dat. indicates accompaniment (Wallace 159). Although some early mss. read δεσμοῖς "chains", δεσμίοις best explains the origin of the var. rdgs. and is supported by important mss. (Metzger 600). Imprisonment often accompanied persecution (Ellingworth 548).

καὶ τὴν ἁρπαγὴν τῶν ὑπαρχόντων ὑμῶν μετὰ χαρᾶς προσεδέξασθε
and accepted with joy the confiscation of your possessions,

Although καί joins two equal syntactic clauses, it also signals a transition to the audience's own experience (Ellingworth 548). Προσεδέξασθε is the 2nd pl. aor. mid. indic. of προσδέχομαι, "accept" (most EVV), "receive" (BDAG 877a). Ἁρπαγήν is the acc. sg. fem. of ἁρπαγή, -ῆς, ἡ, "confiscation" (NET, NIV), "plundering" (ESV), "seizure" (NASB, REB), "forcible confiscation of property in a persecution" (BDAG 133c; see esp. Cockerill 501). Ὑπαρχόντων is the gen. pl. neut. of the pres. act. ptc. of ὑπάρχω; the subst. ptc. indicates "property" (ESV, NASB, NIV), "possessions" (BDAG 1029d), "belongings" (NET). The gen. is obj. and is further modified by ὑμῶν. Μετὰ χαρᾶς modifies the finite vb., indicating manner ("with joy" [NET], "joyfully" [NASB, NIV]). It marks "the typically NT paradox of joy in suffering" (Ellingworth 549).

It is not possible to correl. this v. with a specific historical event. It aligns well with Claudius's edict expelling Jews (including Jewish followers of Jesus) from Rome in AD 49 (see esp. Bruce 267–71; cf. Lane 2:300–301). For the chiastic structure of vv. 33–34, see Lane 2:299.

γινώσκοντες ἔχειν ἑαυτοὺς κρείττονα ὕπαρξιν καὶ μένουσαν.
because you know that you yourselves have a better and enduring possession.

Γινώσκοντες is the nom. pl. masc. of the pres. act. ptc. of γινώσκω. The ptc. is causal ("because" [most EVV]). Γινώσκω followed by the acc. and inf. (ἔχειν) reflects classical Gk. (with the mng. "to pass judgment" [BDF §397(1); cf. R 1036]), which is possibly in view here, although it is not reflected in EVV, which generally tr. the ptc. as "knew" [ESV, NET, NIV). The cstr. is uncommon in the NT (R 1103). The refl. pron. ἑαυτοῦ, -ῆς, -οῦ, is used with the second pers. ("yourselves" [most EVV]), and functions as the "subj." of the inf. (BDF §406[2]). The usage is emph. since the subj. is the same as the main vb. (cf. Attridge 300). Ὕπαρξιν is the acc. sg. fem. of ὕπαρξις, -εως, ἡ (BDAG 1029c). The noun has the same mng. as the cognate neut. subst. ptc. τὰ ὑπάρχοντα. The noun functions as the obj. of the inf. The sg. ὕπαρξιν ("possession" [ESV, NASB, NET]) contrasts with the pl. ὑπαρχόντων (Cockerill 503; Koester 461); *pace* "possessions" (NIV). The comp. κρείττονα (see comments on 1:4) modifies ὕπαρξιν, as does μένουσαν ("enduring" [most EVV]), "lasting" (NASB, NET, NIV), "abiding" (ESV), "more permanent" (NAB 1970). The usage of the ptc. here anticipates a sim. usage in 13:14. (See comments on 7:3.) Its position is emph. (Ellingworth 550).

This clause continues a major theme in Hebrews of setting one's hope on the age to come, rather than this one. It also anticipates the author's discussion of the patriarchs (Heb 11:8–16; cf. Cockerill 502).

VERSE 35

μὴ ἀποβάλητε οὖν τὴν παρρησίαν ὑμῶν,
So don't throw away your confidence,

Οὖν draws an inference from the reminder of what the audience has endured for the gospel (cf. Ellingworth 550). Ἀποβάλητε is the 2nd pl. aor. act. subjunc. of ἀποβάλλω, "throw away" (ESV, NASB, NIV; BDAG 107d), "abandon" (NRSV). Greek uses the aor. subjunc. instead of the impv. in second pers. prohibitions (Wallace 487). Παρρησίαν is the obj. of the impv. and is further modified by ὑμῶν. Most EVV tr. the noun the same way in v. 19 and v. 35. Together the two occurrences of παρρησία form an *inclusio*. See comments on 10:19. See also Cockerill 504.

ἥτις ἔχει μεγάλην μισθαποδοσίαν.
which has a great reward.

Παρρησίαν is the antecedent of ἥτις. The def. rel. pron. (ὅς) and the indef. rel. pron. (ὅστις) were no longer distinguished in Koine Gk. (BDF §293). The pron. could also have a causal sense ("because it has . . ." [NET; Lane 2:278 n. *tt*; R 728]). The obj. of ἔχει is μισθαποδοσίαν (acc. sg. fem. of μισθαποδοσία, -ας, ἡ). The same word occurred in Heb 2:2 (see comments there) with a neg. connotation (e.g., "punishment"); here the connotation is positive ("reward" [most EVV], "recompense" [NAB]). The anar. noun is qual. (Cockerill 504). Μεγάλην is a pos. ("great" [most EVV]) used as superl. to modify μισθαποδοσίαν. NIV tr. the noun as a vb. ("[confidence] will be richly rewarded"). Μεγάλην μισθαποδοσίαν anticipates the upcoming focus on the city of God (11:10) and the heavenly Zion (12:22–24).

VERSE 36

ὑπομονῆς γὰρ ἔχετε χρείαν
For you need endurance,

Γάρ continues the author's exhortation, now stated positively in contrast to v. 35 (Ellingworth 552). It is inferential rather than causal (Lane 2:278 n. *uu*). The obj. of ἔχετε is χρείαν (acc. sg. fem. of χρεία, -ας, ἡ, "need" [most EVV]). This noun is followed by the gen. (indicating content). Ὑπομονῆς is the gen. sg. fem. of ὑπομονή, -ῆς, ἡ, "endurance" (most EVV; BDAG 1039d; F. Hauck, *TDNT* 4:574–88; but tr. as a vb. in NIV [e.g., "to persevere"]). It forms an *inclusio* with ὑπεμείνατε in v. 32. The expression here suggests that the audience is lacking endurance (Ellingworth 553). The emph. on perseverance anticipates the examples of Hebrews 11, and esp. of Christ in Hebrews 12.

ἵνα τὸ θέλημα τοῦ θεοῦ ποιήσαντες κομίσησθε τὴν ἐπαγγελίαν.
so that after you have done God's will, you may receive what was promised.

Ἵνα followed by the subjunc. usually introduces a purpose clause, although here a "conceived" result may be in view (Lane 2:278 n. *vv*; Attridge 301; Ellingworth 553; R 998). The ptc. (ποιήσαντες) is temp. ("after" [many EVV]; "when" [ESV, NIV]). Τὸ θέλημα τοῦ θεοῦ is the obj. of the ptc. The ref. to θέλημα recalls the citation of Psalm 40 in Heb 10:7, 9. The main. vb. of the clause is κομίσησθε (2nd pl. aor. mid. subjunc. of κομίζω, "receive" [most EVV; BDAG 557d]). The obj. of κομίσησθε is ἐπαγγελίαν, which recalls the previous discussion in Hebrews 6 regarding the Abrahamic promises. The focus is on the "substance of the promise" (Koester 461); e.g., "what was promised" (most EVV).

VERSE 37

ἔτι γὰρ μικρὸν ὅσον ὅσον,
For yet in **a very little while,**

Γάρ offers the scriptural basis for the author's exhortation (Ellingworth 555). The expression ἔτι γάρ may reflect a "rephrasing of διότι ἔτι in Hab 2:3" (Ellingworth 555), which is cited next. The rest of the phrase is likely from Isa 26:20. The adv. ἔτι ("yet" [ESV, NASB]; "just" [NET, NIV]) together with μικρόν and the correl. pron. ὅσον is idiomatic: "soon" (BDAG 651a); "in a very little while" (NASB, NRSV; BDAG 729a; BDF §304).The rep. of ὅσον may reflect the LXX translator's attempt to imitate the Heb. (R 733; "soon, very soon now").

In Isaiah, this v. encourages withdrawal until the Lord's judgment passed; thus some have suggested that the audience may have viewed this v. as support for their own withdrawal (Lane 2:303–4). The ref., however, is certainly not obvious. Moreover, the temptation appears to have been to deny, not withdraw (Cockerill 508 n. 52). The lack of introductory formula for the citation in vv. 37–38 may have been for rhetorical effect (cf. Attridge 301). An introduction is added in some EVV (e.g., "as the scripture says" [GNB]).

ὁ ἐρχόμενος ἥξει καὶ οὐ χρονίσει·
the Coming One will come and not delay.

Ἥξει is the 3rd sg. fut. act. indic. of ἥκω ("will come" [most EVV; BDAG 435c]; cf. "will arrive" [NET]). Χρονίσει is the 3rd sg. fut. act. indic. of χρονίζω, "delay" (most EVV; cf. BDAG 1092a). The citation is from Hab 2:3b–4, although it has been modified by the author of Hebrews in several significant ways. LXX Hab 2:3 reads: ὅτι ἐρχόμενος ἥξει καὶ οὐ μὴ χρονίσῃ. First, the author added ὁ before ἐρχόμενος. In Habakkuk, the ptc. refers to a vision that would come, although the Gk. could suggest a person (see esp. Cockerill 507). So the author's addition of the art. makes the ptc. subst. and specifies a well-known messianic title—ὁ ἐρχόμενος ("the Coming One" [CSB, NLT]; cf. e.g., Matt 11:3; Attridge 302; Lane 304–5; Harris 259). The title is obscured with "he who is coming" (NASB, NET, NIV). The switch from the aor. subjunc. to the fut. indic. may possibly add emph. (Ellingworth 554).

VERSE 38

ὁ δὲ δίκαιός μου ἐκ πίστεως ζήσεται,
But my righteous one will live by faith;

Δέ indicates a transition (Ellingworth 556) more than a contrast. This v. continues the citation from Habakkuk 2 (see comments below). Ζήσεται is the 3rd sg. fut. mid. indic. of ζάω ("will live" [most EVV]). The subst. adj. δίκαιος ("my righteous one" [most EVV]) is the subj. of the vb. The prep. phrase is instr., "by faith" (most EVV).

καὶ ἐὰν ὑποστείληται,
and if he draws back,

For καί, see below. Ἐάν (εἰ + ἄν) introduces the prot. of a general cond. (BDF §§371[1], 454[2]; also known as a third-class cond.; see Wallace 696–99). Ὑποστείληται is the 3rd sg. aor. mid. subjunc. of ὑποστέλλω, "shrink back" (ESV, NASB, NET, NIV; BDAG 1041b; K. H. Rengstorf, *TDNT* 7:597–98), "turn away" (NLT). The word commonly denoted apostasy (Lane 2:306). The subjunc. is expected after ἐάν.

οὐκ εὐδοκεῖ ἡ ψυχή μου ἐν αὐτῷ.
I have no pleasure in him.

Εὐδοκεῖ is the 3rd sg. pres. act. indic. of εὐδοκέω. The neg. εὐδοκεῖ implies rejection (Lane 2:278 n. *ccc*): "have [no] pleasure in" (CSB); cf. BDAG 404c. The subj. of the vb. is ἡ ψυχή μου ("my soul" [ESV, NASB]). It could be a "Semitic periph. for ἐγὼ αὐτός" (Lane 2:278 n. *bbb*; T 3:43) as reflected in some EVV (e.g., "I" [most EVV]). The prep. phrase ἐν αὐτῷ is locat. The antecedent of αὐτῷ is ὁ δίκαιός μου.

In the continuation of the citation of Hab 2:3–4, the author transposes the order of the original text and quotes the second half of Hab 2:4 first. The LXX reads ἐάν ὑποστείληται, οὐκ εὐδοκεῖ ἡ ψυχή μου ἐν αὐτῷ, ὁ δὲ δίκαιος ἐκ πίστεώς μου ζήσεται. The author, however, cites the last part of Hab 2:4 first. He also switches μου from modifying πίστεως to δίκαιος, although this reading is found in some Old Gk. mss. (Attridge 302). This emphasizes "my righteous one," likely in anticipation of Hebrews 11 (Cockerill 511). He then cites the first part of LXX Hab 2:4 and adds καί (which may be adversative [Lane 2:305]), which effectively makes ὁ δίκαιος the subj. of ὑποστείληται and the antecedent of αὐτῷ. The restructuring of the LXX text enabled the author to draw out messianic, eschatological, and pastoral implications from the text, thus further exhorting his audience not to draw back, but to persevere, esp. in light of the certainty of Christ's return (cf. Cockerill 506–11). (See O. Palmer. Robertson, "'The Justified (by Faith) Shall Live by His Steadfast Trust': Habakkuk 2:4," *Presb* 9 [1983]: 52–71.) The author saw a connection between the assurance of vindication in Habakkuk and the fulfillment of that divine vindication in Christ (cf. Bruce 273), and used this to ground his exhortation to perseverance.

VERSE 39

ἡμεῖς δὲ οὐκ ἐσμὲν ὑποστολῆς εἰς ἀπώλειαν
But we are not those who draw back and are destroyed,

Δέ indicates a contrast with v. 38. A further contrast within the v. is indicated by οὐ(κ) . . . ἀλλά. Ἡμεῖς in the nom. indicates emph. (BDAG 275a), although this is not reflected in many EVV. Its initial position makes it "doubly emph." (Lane 2:278 n. *ddd*). This also marks a return to the first pers. (cf. v. 30).

Ὑποστολῆς is the gen. sg. fem. of ὑποστολή, -ῆς, ἡ, "the state of being timid, hesitancy, timidity" (BDAG 1041c; K. H. Rengstorf, *TDNT* 7:599; BGk. hapax); "the sort of people who draw back" (NJB), "those who shrink back" (ESV, NET, NIV). The noun is a cognate of ὑποστέλλω (v. 38). The gen. functions as the pred. of ἐσμέν (R 497) or as a gen. of relationship with υἱός understood (BDF §162[2]; cf. "of those . . ."/"belong to those" [ESV, NIV], "among those" [NET]). The connotation could be qual. (e.g., "we are not the sort of people who" [NJB; Ellingworth 557]) or descriptive of "two classes of people" (Cockerill 512). Ἀπώλειαν is the acc. sg. fem. of ἀπώλεια, -ας, ἡ ("destruction, ruin" [BDAG 127a]). Εἰς indicates result (BDAG 290c), as reflected in many EVV ("are destroyed" [ESV, NIV]; "are lost" [NRSV]).

ἀλλὰ πίστεως εἰς περιποίησιν ψυχῆς.
but those who have faith and are saved.

Ἐσμέν is assumed in this verbless clause (most EVV). Similar to ὑποστολῆς, πίστεως functions as the pred. (Wallace 44 n. 23; R 497). The use of πίστις recalls 4:2 and anticipates 11:1. The noun is tr. as a vb. in the NIV ("those who believe"). Περιποίησιν is the acc. sg. fem. of περιποίησις, -εως, ἡ ("preserving," "saving" BDAG 804c). Εἰς indicates result, as reflected in many EVV ("are saved" [NIV, NRSV]). Some EVV, however, are misleading (e.g., "to make our own life" [NEB]; "gain possession of their souls" [Weymouth]). Ψυχῆς (untr. in some EVV [e.g., NIV]) modifies περιποίησιν as an obj. gen. ("preserve their souls" [ESV, NET]).

As is freq. in Hebrews, the author draws the discussion to a close with a short, summarizing statement (see comments on 10:18). Attridge (304) also notes the alliteration of "p" (π) sounds in this v. In Hebrews, ὑπομονή and πίστις are closely related; see esp. Cockerill 504–6. The key themes of this passage (endurance, judgment, and faith) are all elaborated in Hebrews 11–12 (see Cockerill 514).

FOR FURTHER STUDY

73. Persecution in the First Century (10:32–34)

*Koester, Craig R. "Conversion, Persecution, and Malaise: Life in the Community for Which Hebrews Was Written." *HvTSt* 61.1–2 (2005): 231–51.
Kruse, C. G. *DNTB* 775–78.
Potter, D. S. *ABD* 5:231–35.
Reasoner, M. *DLNT* 907–14.

74. The Audience of Hebrews (10:32–34)

*Bruce, F. F. "'To the Hebrews' or 'To the Essenes'." *NTS* 9 (1963): 217–32.
*———. "Paul and Roman Christianity." Pages 379–92 in *Paul: Apostle of the Heart Set Free*. Grand Rapids: Eerdmans, 1977.
Cockerill, 16–23.
Dahms, John V. "First Readers of Hebrews." *JETS* 20 (1977): 365–75.
Ellingworth, 21–27.
Gray, Patrick. "Hebrews among Greeks and Romans." Pages 13–29 in Mason.
Koester, 64–79.
Lane, 1:*li–lx*
*Mason, Eric F. "The Epistle (Not Necessarily) to the 'Hebrews': A Call to Renunciation of Judaism or Encouragement to Christian Commitment?" *PRSt* 37 (2010): 7–20.
Murray, Robert. "Jews, Hebrews and Christians: Some Needed Distinctions." *NovT* 24 (1982): 194–208.
Rapske, B. M. *DLNT* 1063–68.
Tenney, Merrill Chapin. "New Approach to the Book of Hebrews." *BSac* 123 (1966): 230–36.

75. The Historical Setting of Hebrews (10:32–34)

Guthrie, George H. "Hebrews in Its First-Century Contexts: Recent Research." Pages 414–43 in *The Face of New Testament Studies: A Survey of Recent Scholarship*. Edited by Scot McKnight and Grant R. Osborne. Grand Rapids: Baker, 2004.
Lane, William L. "Social Perspectives on Roman Christianity during the Formative Years from Nero to Nerva: Romans, Hebrews, 1 Clement." Pages 196–244 in *Judaism and Christianity in First-Century Rome*. Grand Rapids: Eerdmans, 1998.
Walker, Peter. "A Place for Hebrews? Contexts for a First-Century Sermon." Pages 231–40 in *The New Testament in Its First Century Setting: Essays on Context and Background in Honour of B. W. Winter on His 65th Birthday*. Edited by P. J. Williams et al. Grand Rapids: Eerdmans, 2004.

HOMILETICAL SUGGESTIONS

Past Faithfulness as Encouragement for Present Perseverance (10:32–39)

1. Remember Past Faithfulness and Suffering (v. 32)
    (a) You and others with you were publicly bullied (v. 33)
    (b) You stood with those imprisoned (v. 34a)
    (c) You endured the confiscation of property (v. 34b)
    (d) Because you knew that you have better possessions (v. 34c)
2. So Don't Give Up Now! (v. 35a)
    (a) There is a reward that awaits you (v. 35b)
    (b) You can endure to receive the promise (v. 36)
    (c) The Messiah is coming (v. 37)
3. The Righteous Live by Faith, Not Shrinking Fear (v. 38)
4. You Do Live by Faith and Do Not Pull Back! (v. 39)

B. PAST EXAMPLES OF FAITH IN GOD'S PROMISES (11:1–12:3)

1. The Nature of Faith (11:1–3)

STRUCTURE

The key themes of endurance (ὑπομονή in 10:36) and faith (πίστις in 10:39) are now taken up in reverse order, with faith as the focus in Hebrews 11 (elucidating the Hab 2:4 citation in 10:38 [Cockerill 518]) and endurance in Heb 12:1–13 (Lane 2:312). The exhortations of Heb 10:19–39 shift to exposition in Hebrews 11 and back to exhortations in Hebrews 12. The numerous exemplars of Hebrews 11 culminate in the supreme example of Jesus in Hebrews 12. The rhetorical technique of *exempla* (exemplar lists) is found in Jewish (e.g., 4 Macc 16:16–23; Sir 44–50) and early Christian (e.g., 1 Clem. 17:1–19:3) literature, which had both apologetic and parenetic aims. See For Further Study 76 (Exemplar Lists and Rhetoric in Hebrews 11). The author's goal is to draw on past examples of faith to encourage sim. faithfulness in his present audience as well as to create solidarity with those who have gone before (Cockerill 516–17). The focus is on attesting God's faithfulness, as is also evidenced by the *inclusio* between 11:2 (ἐμαρτυρήθησαν) and 11:39 (μαρτυρηθέντες).

Although some have questioned the textual integrity of Hebrews 11 (often noting that the chapter could be removed with little disruption between 10:39 and 12:1), the arguments supporting such a claim are not compelling (see esp. Ellingworth 558) and the chapter is well integrated in Hebrews's overall argument, both logically and lexically.

The structure of vv. 1–3 is anchored on the finite vb. in each v., as indicated above.

1 Ἔστιν δὲ πίστις ἐλπιζομένων ὑπόστασις,
πραγμάτων ἔλεγχος οὐ βλεπομένων.
2 ἐν ταύτῃ γὰρ
ἐμαρτυρήθησαν οἱ πρεσβύτεροι.
3 Πίστει
νοοῦμεν κατηρτίσθαι τοὺς αἰῶνας ῥήματι θεοῦ,
εἰς τὸ μὴ ἐκ φαινομένων τὸ βλεπόμενον γεγονέναι.

VERSE 1

Ἔστιν δὲ πίστις ἐλπιζομένων ὑπόστασις,
Now faith is the reality of what is hoped for,

Δέ is transitional ("now" [most EVV; Ellingworth 564]). Ἔστιν in initial pos. with anar. preds. imitates formal definitions found in philosophical writings (Attridge 307; Ellingworth 564), although the v. is less a definition than "a summary of what faith *does*" (Ellingworth 566; Cockerill 520 n. 1).

Πίστις functions as a hook word, offering cohesion between this section and the last (esp. 10:38–39). The focus on faith indicates contextually that πίστις is the subj. of the sentence and ὑπόστασις the pred. nom., even though both are anar. (Wallace 44 n. 23). This is the third and final occurrence of ὑπόστασις in Hebrews (see comments on 1:3 and 3:14). In 1:3, it had an obj. sense (e.g., "real essence" [Bruce 277]), whereas in 3:14, the sense was perhaps more subj. (e.g., "conviction," "assurance"). The mng. here is debated. Many EVV suggest a subj. understanding: "assurance" (ESV, NASB; cf. Koester 472), or "being sure of" (NET). Among these, some see ὑπόστασις as the subj. counterpart to the obj. ἔλεγχος (e.g., Bruce 277) or argue that ὑπόστασις has both subj. and obj. aspects: "the confidence that what we hope for will actually happen" [NLT 2007]; cf. Koester 472). Yet the subj. mng. is not attested elsewhere (see esp. BDAG 1041a). Thus an obj. understanding is preferred: "reality" (Attridge 305; Cockerill 520; "objective reality," Lane 2:325–26), "realization" (NAB; BDAG 1040d), "substance" (REB), "guarantee" (NJB), "firm foundation" (Bruce 276). Cockerill (521) helpfully paraphrases: "Faith is living in accord with the reality of things hoped for." The subst. ptc. ἐλπιζομένων is an obj. gen., modifying ὑπόστασις. The pl. ptc. can be generalizing (e.g., "what is hoped for" [NAB]).

πραγμάτων ἔλεγχος οὐ βλεπομένων.
the proof of what is not seen.

The lack of conj. between this clause and the previous one suggests that both are to be understood as "definitions" of faith (cf. Ellingworth 566). Like ὑπόστασις, debated is whether ἔλεγχος (-ου, ὁ) has a subj. or obj. sense. Although many EVV tr. ἔλεγχος as "conviction" (ESV, NASB; cf. Bruce 277), such a mng. is not attested in extant literature (Attridge 310). Overall, an obj. sense is preferred: "proof" [CEV]; BDAG 315a; F. Büchsel, *TDNT* 2:476; Attridge 310; cf. "prove the existence of" [NJB]. Πραγμάτων is the gen. pl. neut. of πρᾶγμα, -ατος, τό, "things" (ESV, NASB; BDAG 858d–859a; cf. "realities" [REB]). The pl. can also be generalizing: "what" (NIV, NET). It modifies ἔλεγχος as an obj. gen. The neg. ptcl. modifies the adj. ptc. βλεπομένων, which in turn modifies πραγμάτων. The neg. ptcl. οὐ with ptcs. (instead of μή) is uncommon with ptcs. and may indicate that "the negative is clear-cut and decisive" (R 1137–38). It is "almost the equivalent of ἀ-privative" (BDF §426).

VERSE 2

ἐν ταύτῃ γὰρ
For by it

Γάρ grounds the preceding definition of faith in the numerous exemplars who were living demonstrations of it. The antecedent of ταύτῃ is πίστις in v. 1. The dem. could indicate "'by this' kind of faith" (Cockerill 522). The dat. πίστει (or prons. ref. to it) will become the primary means by which Hebrews 11 is structured (see comments on v. 3). Ἐν ταύτῃ instr. modifies ἐμαρτυρήθησαν.

ἐμαρτυρήθησαν οἱ πρεσβύτεροι.
our ancestors won God's approval.

Although the subst. adj. πρεσβύτερος (-α, -ον) often refers to a church elder or leader, here it refers to those who lived formerly, hence "ancients" (NAB, NIV), "ancestors" (CEV, NRSV; BDAG 862a; Cockerill 521–22; Ellingworth 568); "people of old" (ESV, NET, REB). It functions as the subj. of the sentence. Ἐμαρτυρήθησαν is the 3rd pl. aor. pass. indic. of μαρτυρέω. The pass. has the sense of gaining approval: "were commended for" (NIV), "won God's approval" (REB), "earned a good reputation" (NLT); cf. BDAG 618c; H. Strathmann, *TDNT* 4:497; Cockerill 523 n. 15; Koester 473. God is the implied agent (made explicit in some EVV, e.g., CSB) or their "attestation is conveyed through the Scriptures" (Koester 463; cf. Ellingworth 567). The aor. is global (Wallace 557). This is the fourth (of eight) occurrence of μαρτυρέω in Hebrews (7:8, 17; 10:15; 11:2, 4, 7[2x], 39): "in each instance the reference is to the witness of the biblical record" (Lane 2:330).

The mention of "ancestors" prepares for the numerous OT exemplars that follow. It is not clear why some of these individuals were selected. Most are not directly associated with faith in the OT. Even explicit ref. to the faith of some is not cited by the author (e.g., Gen 15:6 regarding Abraham [Attridge 306 n. 12]).

VERSE 3

Πίστει
By faith

The rep. of πίστει (eighteen times in Hebrews 11) is an outstanding example of the rhetorical device called *anaphora* (BDF §491). There are three options (see Lane 2:326 n. *h*) for the function of the dat. (cf. Lane 2:326 n. *h*): *instr. ("by faith" [most EVV; Cockerill 518]), manner ("in accordance with faith"), or causal ("because of our faith" [CEV]).

νοοῦμεν κατηρτίσθαι τοὺς αἰῶνας ῥήματι θεοῦ,
we understand that the universe was created by the word of God,

Νοοῦμεν is the 1st pl. pres. act. indic. of νοέω, "understand" (most EVV; cf. BDAG 674d). The first pers. pl. unites the author not only with the audience, but ostensibly with the OT exemplars as well (cf. Cockerill 525). The vb. is modified by πίστει. The acc. τοὺς αἰῶνας is the obj. of the vb. Here αἰῶνας (αἰών, -ῶνος, ὁ) retains the spatial understanding that it had in Heb 1:2 ("universe" [most EVV]; "world" [CEV], "worlds" [NASB, NET]; *pace* "ages" [NJB]). Κατηρτίσθαι is perf. pass. inf. of καταρτίζω (BDAG 526b). In Heb 10:5, καταρτίζω meant something like "prepare," which is possible here (NASB, NRSV), but the context suggests "created" (ESV), "formed" (NIV, REB). The inf. clause outlines the content of νοοῦμεν.

Ῥήματι (dat. sg. neut. of ῥῆμα, -ατος, τό, "word" [most EVV]) is instr. (see comments on 1:3). In Heb 1:2, the author asserts that the universe was made through the Son's agency; in 1:3, it is sustained by the Son's powerful word (τῷ ῥήματι τῆς δυνάμεως αὐτοῦ). Thus an allusion to the Son as the personified "Word" is unlikely; rather, this is a highly condensed summary of Genesis 1 (cf. Bruce 279–80; "at God's command," NIV, NLT).

εἰς τὸ μὴ ἐκ φαινομένων τὸ βλεπόμενον γεγονέναι.
so that what is seen was made from things that are not visible.

Εἰς with an art. inf. usually indicates purpose (Wallace 590–92), but here result is in view ("so that" [most EVV]; R 1003), a "consecutive εἰς" (Harris 90; Z §352). The cstr. is εἰς τό . . . γεγονέναι, although the number of embedded words (R 1070) and the word order are unusual (Moule 168). The cstr. further outlines the content of νοοῦμεν (indir. discourse [R 909, 1036]), although the cstr. directly modifies the inf. κατηρτίσθαι. The pf. in an art. inf. with εἰς is rare (R 1072), likely further indicating that this is a result clause (Attridge 315). The pf. is intensive (Wallace 574). The "subj." of the inf. cstr. is the art. βλεπόμενον. See comments on v. 1.

Φαινομένων is the gen. pl. neut. of the pres. pass. ptc. of φαίνω, "be visible" (most EVV). The neg. ptcl. μή likely modifies ἐκ φαινομένων (NET, NLT, NRSV; Attridge 315; Ellingworth 568), as the neg. adv. usually precedes the neg. word (R 423), although the force of the neg. is on the ptc. φαινομένων (BDF §433[3]; Attridge 315). Less likely, μή negates the entire inf. clause, or γεγονέναι (ESV, NASB, NIV; Cockerill 524; Lane 2:326–27 n. *k*). For the chiastic structure of this v., see Ellingworth 568.

The question arises as to whether this v. affirms the doctrine of creation *ex nihilo* (so Bruce 279; *pace* Attridge 316). While not denied, this is not an unambiguous statement of such and the focus is on the faith required to affirm "the unseen origin of the visible world" (Ellingworth 569; cf. Lane 2:332), particularly on God's word as the unseen agent (Koester 474). See Philip E. Hughes, "The Doctrine of Creation in Hebrews 11:3," *BTB* 2 [1972]: 64–77.

FOR FURTHER STUDY

76. Exemplar Lists and Rhetoric in Hebrews 11 (11:1–40)

*Baugh, Stephen M. "The Clouds of Witnesses in Hebrews 11." *WTJ* 68 (2006): 113–32.
Cockerill, 516–18.
Cosby, Michael R. *The Rhetorical Composition and Function of Hebrews 11: In Light of Example Lists of Antiquity*. Macon, GA: Mercer University Press, 1988.
*———. "The Rhetorical Composition of Hebrews 11." *JBL* 107 (1988): 257–73.
*———. "Hebrews 11 and the Art of Effective Preaching." *Covenant Quarterly* 48/2 (1990): 29–33,
Eisenbaum, Pamela M. "Heroes and History in Hebrews 11." Pages 380–96 in *Early Christian Interpretation of the Scriptures of Israel: Investigations and Proposals*. Edited by Craig A. Evans and James A. Sanders. *JSNTSup* 148. Sheffield: Sheffield Academic Press, 1997.
———. *The Jewish Heroes of Christian History: Hebrews 11 in Literary Context. SBLDS* 156. Atlanta: Scholars Press, 1997.

Lane, 2:316–23.
Miller, Merland Ray. "What Is the Literary Form of Hebrews 11?" *JETS* 29 (1986): 411–17.
Thompson, James W. "'Strangers on the Earth': Philosophical Perspective on the Promise in Hebrews." *ResQ* 57 (2015): 193–212.

77. Faith in Hebrews (11:1)

Attridge, 311–14.
Brawley, Robert L. "Discoursive Structure and the Unseen in Hebrews 2:8 and 11:1: A Neglected Aspect of the Context." *CBQ* 55 (1993): 81–98.
Bulley, Alan D. "Death and Rhetoric in the Hebrews 'Hymn to Faith'." *SR* 25 (1996): 409–23.
Culpepper, R Alan. "A Superior Faith: Hebrews 10:19–12:2." *RevExp* 82 (1985): 375–90.
Hamm, Dennis. "Faith in the Epistle to the Hebrews: The Jesus Factor." *CBQ* 52 (1990): 270–91.
Hartley, Donald E. "Heb 11:6—A Reassessment of the Translation 'God Exists'." *TJ* 27 (2006): 289–307.
Huxhold, Harry N. "Faith in the Epistle to the Hebrews." *CTM* 38 (1967): 657–61.
Rhee, Victor (Sung-Yul). "Chiasm and the Concept of Faith in Hebrews 11." *BSac* 155 (1998): 327–45.
———. "The Christological Aspects of Faith in Hebrews 3:1–4:16." *Filologia Neotestamentaria* 13 (2000): 75–88.
———. "Christology and the Concept of Faith in Hebrews 1:1–2:4." *BSac* 157 (2000): 174–89.
———. "Christology and the Concept of Faith in Hebrews 5:11–6:20." *JETS* 43 (2000): 83–96.
———. "Christology, Chiasm, and the Concept of Faith in Hebrews 10:19–39." *Filologia Neotestamentaria* 16 (2003): 33–48.
———. *Faith in Hebrews: Analysis within the Context of Christology, Eschatology, and Ethics*. New York: Lang, 2001.

78. Ὑπόστασις *(11:1)*

Hoerber, Robert G. "On the Translation of Hebrews 11:1." *Concordia Journal* 21 (1995): 77–79.
Köster, H. *TDNT* 8:572–89.
Smith, James D., III. "Faith as Substance or Surety: Historical Perspectives on Hypostasis in Hebrews 11:1." Pages 381–92 in *Challenge of Bible Translation: Communicating God's Word to the World*. Edited by Glen G. Scorgie, Mark L. Strauss, and Steven M. Voth. Grand Rapids: Zondervan, 2003.

HOMILETICAL SUGGESTIONS

Foundational Faith (11:1–3)

1. Faith Defined (v. 1)
    (a) The reality of our hope (v. 1a)
    (b) The proof of the unseen (v. 1b)

2. Faith Demonstrated by Those Who Have Gone Before (v. 2)
3. Faith Revealed in God's Creation (v. 3)
   (a) Created by God's word (v. 3a)
   (b) Created out of the unseen (v. 3b)

2. Preflood Faith (11:4–7)

STRUCTURE

Structurally, this section is divided by the three occurrences of <u>πίστει</u> (vv. 4, 5, 7). Following the first two, there is a general statement regarding faith in v. 6. A series of indics. are modified by either relative clauses, adv. ptc., purpose inf., or conjunctive clauses.

4 <u>Πίστει</u>
πλείονα θυσίαν Ἄβελ παρὰ Κάϊν προσήνεγκεν τῷ θεῷ,
δι᾽ ἧς ἐμαρτυρήθη εἶναι δίκαιος,
μαρτυροῦντος ἐπὶ τοῖς δώροις αὐτοῦ τοῦ θεοῦ,
καὶ δι᾽ αὐτῆς ἀποθανὼν ἔτι λαλεῖ.

5 <u>Πίστει</u>
Ἑνὼχ μετετέθη
τοῦ μὴ ἰδεῖν θάνατον,
καὶ οὐχ ηὑρίσκετο
διότι μετέθηκεν αὐτὸν ὁ θεός.
πρὸ γὰρ τῆς μεταθέσεως
μεμαρτύρηται εὐαρεστηκέναι τῷ θεῷ·
6 χωρὶς δὲ πίστεως
ἀδύνατον εὐαρεστῆσαι·
πιστεῦσαι γὰρ δεῖ τὸν προσερχόμενον τῷ θεῷ
ὅτι ἔστιν
καὶ τοῖς ἐκζητοῦσιν αὐτὸν μισθαποδότης γίνεται.

7 <u>Πίστει</u>
χρηματισθεὶς Νῶε περὶ τῶν μηδέπω βλεπομένων,
εὐλαβηθεὶς
κατεσκεύασεν κιβωτὸν εἰς σωτηρίαν τοῦ οἴκου αὐτοῦ
δι᾽ ἧς κατέκρινεν τὸν κόσμον,
καὶ τῆς κατὰ πίστιν δικαιοσύνης ἐγένετο κληρονόμος.

VERSE 4

Πίστει
By faith

See comments on 11:3.

πλείονα θυσίαν Ἄβελ παρὰ Κάϊν προσήνεγκεν τῷ θεῷ,
Abel offered to God a better sacrifice than Cain did.

The subj. of προσήνεγκεν (3rd sg. aor. act. indic. of προσφέρω, "offer"; see comments on 5:1) is Ἄβελ. The vb. is modified by πίστει. The obj. is θυσίαν (see comments on 5:1 and 7:27), which is further modified by πλείονα (from πολύς, -ή, -ύ), a comp. indicating "greater" ("of greater value" in some EVV [Ellingworth 571; Lane 2:335], but tr. "better" in many EVV). The author may have distinguished Abel's sacrifice from Christ's (e.g., κρείττοσιν θυσίαις in 9:23). The dat. θεῷ is the indir. obj. of the vb. Παρά with the acc. (Κάϊν) indicates comp. ("than"; Wallace 297 n. 10; 378; R 667). Both Ἄβελ and Κάϊν are transliterated from the Heb. and are indecl.; their syntactic function determines their case.

δι' ἧς ἐμαρτυρήθη εἶναι δίκαιος,
By faith he was approved as a righteous man,

The antecedent of ἧς is πίστει (so most EVV), not θυσία. Although θυσία is the closest possible antecedent, the overall focus on faith in Hebrews 11 argues against this (*pace* ESV). The prep. phrase δι' ἧς is instr. Although the instr. function of the prep. phrase (δι' ἧς) and the dat. (πίστει) is the same, the latter is reserved for introducing different exemplars in Hebrews 11. Like Heb 11:2, ἐμαρτυρήθη (3rd sg. aor. pass. indic. of μαρτυρέω) indicates approval ("commended" [ESV, NET, NIV], "received approval" [NRSV]). The agent of the pass. vb. is either God, or perhaps more likely, Scripture. The subst. adj. δίκαιος ("righteous" [most EVV]; *pace* "goodness" [REB]) functions as the pred. nom. of the equative εἶναι (BDF §405[1]), with Abel as the implied subj. Εἶναι indicates indir. discourse (R 1038). This use of the inf. with a pers. vb. such as μαρτυρέω is unusual (R 1085; BDF §405[2]). The designation of Abel as a righteous man is found in Jewish tradition (Attridge 316).

μαρτυροῦντος ἐπὶ τοῖς δώροις αὐτοῦ τοῦ θεοῦ,
because God approved his gifts,

Μαρτυροῦντος is the gen. sg. masc. of the pres. act. ptc. of μαρτυρέω; with the act. it can mean "approve" (so most EVV; "spoke well of" [NIV]; BDAG 618c). The gen. ptc. is causal (NET) or temp. (NIV, NJB). It forms a gen. abs. cstr., the "subj." of which is θεοῦ (see comments on 2:4). Less likely, the ptc. clause is instr. (ESV; Cockerill 527 n. 35; unclear in NASB). Δώροις is the dat. pl. neut. of δῶρον, -ου, τό, "gifts" (BDAG 267c), "offerings" (NET, NIV). Ἐπί means "concerning" (Koester 475–76).

καὶ δι' αὐτῆς ἀποθανὼν ἔτι λαλεῖ.
and even though he is dead, he still speaks through his faith.

Καί resumes the discussion of Abel's faith (R 724). Δι' αὐτῆς (its antecedent is πίστει) par. δι' ἧς in the first part of the v. The ptc. ἀποθανών is concessive ("even though" [most EVV; Ellingworth 573; Lane 2:327 n. *q*]). The adv. ἔτι ("still," most EVV) modifies λαλεῖ, the subj. of which is Abel. The pres. λαλεῖ is ongoing ("durative" [R 1111]). The implication of this clause is that Abel's faith in God (perhaps esp. God's justice) continues to cry out for divine vindication (cf. Ellingworth 573).

Alternatively, his righteous life of faith continues "to speak" through Scripture ("he still speaks to us by his example of faith" [NLT]; Cockerill 527–28 n. 37; Guthrie 376; cf. Attridge 317).

This v. draws on the account of Abel and Cain in Gen 4:1–10. The history of interpretation of this passage (esp. why Abel's sacrifice was acceptable and Cain's was not) is extensive (see the discussion in Bruce 281–83; Koester 475; Lane 2:333–36). (See also Richard S. Hess, *ABD* 1:9–10; K. G. Kuhn, *TDNT* 1:6–8; and esp. R. Walter L. Moberly, "Exemplars of Faith in Hebrews 11: Abel" in Bauckham, *Theology* 353–63.) The connection between Abel's offering and faith was likely suggested by the previous citation from Hab 2:4 in Heb 10:38 (cf. Bruce 283), although the Genesis account mentions neither Abel's faith nor his righteousness. The logic of 11:6 suggests that since Abel pleased God, he must have had faith (Bruce 283).

VERSE 5

Πίστει
By faith

See comments on 11:3. The causal understanding in the GNT is misleading: "it was faith that kept Enoch from dying."

Ἑνὼχ μετετέθη τοῦ μὴ ἰδεῖν θάνατον,
Enoch was taken away, and so he did not experience death.

Μετετέθη is the 3rd sg. aor. pass. indic. of μετατίθημι, "taken up" (ESV, NASB, NET; BDAG 642a; C. Maurer, *TDNT* 8:152–68). Like Abel and Cain, the name Ἑνώχ is indecl. and is transliterated from the Heb. Here Ἑνώχ is clearly the subj. of the pass. vb., and God is the implied agent. Ἰδεῖν is the aor. act. inf. of ὁράω (BDAG 280a). Here it means "experience" (e.g., "without passing through death" [REB]) understood as experiencing. Θάνατον is the obj. of the inf. The art. inf. here indicates result (Z §352; consecutive clause [Z §352]). The inf. clause interprets the mng. of the vb., which follows the LXX (Attridge 317; cf. Lane 2:336).

καὶ οὐχ ηὑρίσκετο διότι μετέθηκεν αὐτὸν ὁ θεός.
He was not to be found because God took him away.

Ηὑρίσκετο is the 3rd sg. impf. mid. indic. of εὑρίσκω ("be found" [most EVV]). It is a fixed expression in the LXX for "disappear" (Ellingworth 575). The CEV gives the wrong implication with "his body was never found." The conj. διότι introduces a causal clause ("because"; cf. BDAG 251c). In the restatement of the previous clause, the vb. is now act. (μετέθηκεν) with the subj. explicitly stated (θεός). The antecedent of αὐτόν (the obj. of the vb.) is clearly Enoch.

The author draws on the account of Enoch in LXX Gen 5:18–24, and quotes v. 24 here, following the LXX; the MT has "he was no more, because God took him." Additionally, the MT reads "Enoch walked with God" in v. 24, which was tr. in the

LXX as "Enoch pleased God," ostensibly to avoid the anthropomorphic image of God walking (cf. Lane 2:336).

πρὸ γὰρ τῆς μεταθέσεως μεμαρτύρηται εὐαρεστηκέναι τῷ θεῷ·
For before he was taken away, he was approved as one who pleased God.

Γάρ offers the basis for Enoch's being taken away. Μεταθέσεως is the gen. sg. fem. of μετάθεσις, -εως, ἡ, "removal" (NET; cf. BDAG 639a; see 7:12 and 12:27). The prep. phrase ("before the removal" [NET, TCNT], "before his assumption" [JB]) is tr. with a finite vb. in many EVV (e.g., CSB). The prep. phrase likely modifies μεμαρτύρηται (most EVV), although it could modify the inf. (e.g., GNB, NASB). Μεμαρτύρηται is the 3rd sg. pf. pass. indic. of μαρτυρέω. The pf. is intensive (Wallace 574). Εὐαρεστηκέναι is the pf. act. inf. of εὐαρεστέω, "please" (most EVV; BDAG 403c; W. Foerster, *TDNT* 1:456–57). Sometimes the vb. stem is not reduplicated in the pf., as is the case here (R 365). The vb. is followed by the dat. (θεῷ) and may reflect the underlying LXX in this allusion to Gen 5:24 (BDF §312[1]).

The fact that Scripture attests that Enoch pleased God was understood by the author to confirm Enoch's faith, as the next v. will make clear (cf. Cockerill 530). Enoch's life and "translation" generated extensive speculation in Jewish writings, such as 1 Enoch and Jubilees, but much less so in the NT (i.e., Luke 3:37; Jude 14). See Bruce 285; Ellingworth 573–74; 2:336–37.

VERSE 6

χωρὶς δὲ πίστεως ἀδύνατον εὐαρεστῆσαι·
Now without faith it is impossible to please God,

Δέ ("now" or "and" [most EVV]) introduces new information that is derived from the previous examples (cf. Ellingworth 576). The placement of v. 6 confirms the faith of both Abel and Enoch because they pleased God. It also prepares for the transition to the "future orientation of faith" that begins with the example of Noah (Cockerill 532). Χωρίς ("without") takes a gen. obj. (πίστεως). Ἀδύνατον is the nom. sg. neut. of ἀδύνατος, -ον, "impossible" (most EVV; see comments on 6:4). The adj. is pred. with an implied vb. and an impers. subj. ("it is impossible" [most EVV]). The complement of the pred. adj. is the inf. εὐαρεστῆσαι (aor. act. inf. of εὐαρεστέω, see comments on v. 5). In v. 5, this vb. was followed by θεῷ, which is implied here as well and is made explicit in most EVV (e.g., CSB). The aor. is global or possibly ingressive (Lane 2:327 n. *t*).

πιστεῦσαι γὰρ δεῖ τὸν προσερχόμενον τῷ θεῷ
since the one who draws near to him must believe

Γάρ grounds the general principle in the first part of the v. with an elaboration of faith (cf. Ellingworth 576–77). Πιστεῦσαι is the complement of the impers. δεῖ ("it is necessary"). The aor. is global (Wallace 557). The subj. of the inf. (different from δεῖ) is the art. προσερχόμενον (acc. sg. masc. of the pres. mid. ptc. of προσέρχομαι). (See comments on 4:16.) Many EVV treat the subst. ptc. as the subj. of the clause (e.g., CSB). Προσέρχομαι is followed by the dat. (BDAG 878b); here θεῷ. With the intrans. vb. προσέρχομαι, it is a "dat. of destination" (Wallace 147–48).

ὅτι ἔστιν καὶ τοῖς ἐκζητοῦσιν αὐτὸν μισθαποδότης γίνεται.
that he exists and that he rewards those who seek him.

Ὅτι indicates two affirmations that comprise the content of πιστεῦσαι. Ἔστιν in this context indicates existence ("exists" [most EVV]). Affirmations concerning the existence of God are found in both Jewish and Greco-Roman writings (see Koester 476). Καί joins the syntactically equal finite vbs. ἔστιν and γίνεται. The subj. of γίνεται is God, and its obj. is μισθαποδότης (-ου, ὁ, "rewarder" [ASV, NASB, Weymouth; BDAG 653b]; BGk. hapax). Many EVV tr. the unusual noun as a vb. (e.g., CSB). The cognate noun μισθαποδοσία occurs in Heb 2:2 and 10:35. It is possible that the author coined this word himself (cf. Ellingworth 577; Lane 3:338). Γίνεται functions par. to εἰμί in this v., with μισθαποδότης functioning as a pred. nom. Ἐκζητοῦσιν (dat. pl. masc. of the pres. act. ptc. of ἐκζητέω) is the indir. obj. of the verbal noun μισθαποδότης. The compound vb. may be intensive (e.g., "sincerely seek" [NLT], "earnestly seek" [NIV, Weymouth]). The antecedent of αὐτὸν is God. The pron. is the obj. of the ptc.

VERSE 7

Πίστει
By faith

See comments on 11:3. Here the dat. adv. modifies κατεσκεύασεν (see below).

χρηματισθεὶς Νῶε περὶ τῶν μηδέπω βλεπομένων, εὐλαβηθεὶς
Noah, after he was warned about what was not yet seen and motivated by godly fear,

Νῶε (indecl.) is the subj. of the ptcs. in this clause and of the finite vb. κατεσκεύασεν (see below). Χρηματισθείς is the nom. sg. masc. of the aor. pass. ptc. of χρηματίζω (with pass. "warned" [most EVV], "received a warning" [BDAG 1089b]). The ptc. is temp. ("after" [most EVV]), modifying κατεσκεύασεν. In addition to the warning, the vb. could suggest that God gave instructions for the ark as well (Ellingworth 578). Βλεπομένων is subst. ("what" or "things" [most EVV]; "events [unseen]" [ESV]). Μηδέπω is an "intensifying compound" (R 1173) formed by μηδέ + πω, an encl. mng. "up to this time," "yet" (BDAG 647c; BGk. hapax; "not yet" [most EVV]). It modifies βλεπομένων. The ptc. phrase is the obj. of περί ("about"). What was not yet seen for Noah was clearly the impending flood.

Εὐλαβηθείς is the nom. sg. masc. of the aor. pass. ptc. of εὐλαβέομαι. The pass. has a mid. force (R 334). The ptc. is either causal ("having been moved by godly fear" [Cockerill 532]), instr. ("with" [NET]), or *indicates manner ("in" [ESV, NASB, NIV]). There are three options for the mng. of this vb.:

1. Concern or attention: "good heed" (REB), "reverent regard" (NET), or "attentiveness to God's word" (Lane 2:339); "be concerned," "be anxious" (BDAG 407c).
*2. Reverence (NASB): "reverent fear" (ESV), "godly fear" (Cockerill 532), "holy fear" (NIV), "respect" (NRSV) (see discussion in Harris 65–66; [cf. BDAG 407c]). The view comports with the use of the cognate εὐλάβεια concerning Jesus in 5:7 (Attridge 319; Ellingworth 578; Koester 477).
3. Obedience (CEV, GNT, NLT): "took care" (NJB), "took heed" (Cassirer).

κατεσκεύασεν κιβωτὸν εἰς σωτηρίαν τοῦ οἴκου αὐτοῦ
built an ark to deliver his family.

Κατεσκεύασεν is the 3rd sg. aor. act. indic. of κατασκευάζω ("build" [most EVV], "construct" [ESV, NET], "prepare" [NASB], "erect," "create" [BDAG 527a]; cf. 3:3, 4; 9:2, 6). Κιβωτόν is the acc. sg. fem. of κιβωτός, -ου, ἡ, "ark" (most EVV). This is the same word used for the ark of the covenant in 9:4. The fact that a covenant was also associated with Noah's ark may have been understood by the author (Ellingworth 578). Although σωτηρία could mean "salvation" (NASB), here the sense is probably "deliverance" (NET) or "preservation." Εἰς indicates the purpose of building the ark, namely, the deliverance of Noah's family, with οἶκος understood as "family" (most EVV) or "household" (ESV, NASB). The prep. phrase is tr. as a purpose inf. in some EVV (e.g., "to save" [NIV, NJB, NRSV, REB]). Unlike 1 Pet 3:20, the author does not draw out a typological connection between Noah and his family and believers (Attridge 319).

δι' ἧς κατέκρινεν τὸν κόσμον,
By faith he condemned the world

For δι' ἧς, see comments on Heb 11:4. Although σωτηρία (or even κιβωτόν [ESV, NASB]) is the closest possible antecedent, the overall focus on faith in Hebrews 11 argues against this. Yet Noah's faith cannot be separated from building the ark (cf. Cockerill 533). Κατέκρινεν is the 3rd sg. aor. act. indic. of κατακρίνω, "condemn" (most EVV; "pronounce a sentence on" [BDAG 519a]; F. Büchsel, *TDNT* 3:951–52). The subj. of κατέκρινεν is Noah; the obj. is κόσμον, with humanity understood (Lane 2:328 n. *x*).

This v. may allude to later Jewish tradition that Noah was a "preacher of righteousness" to his generation (e.g., Sib. Or. 1.125–31; cf. 2 Pet 2:5; 1 Clem. 7:6; 9:4; see Koester 477), although it likely indicates that the flood vindicated Noah's faithfulness while simultaneously judging the rest of humanity (cf. Cassirer; Ellingworth 579; Lane 2:340).

καὶ τῆς κατὰ πίστιν δικαιοσύνης ἐγένετο κληρονόμος.
and became an heir of the righteousness that comes by faith.

Καί joins κατέκρινεν and ἐγένετο, suggesting that the outcome of Noah's faith was both the judgment of the world and his heirship (cf. Cockerill 533). Κληρονόμος (-ου, ὁ, "heir" [most EVV; BDAG 548b; see comments on 1:2]) is the pred. nom. of ἐγένετο. Δικαιοσύνης is the obj. gen. Κατά is causal ("that come by faith" [most EVV; Harris 158; BDAG 513a]) or indicates a standard ("according to" [NASB]).

Although the author does not draw typological significance from Noah (but see Cockerill 534), he clearly views Noah as one among a series of individuals from the past (culminating in 11:40) who partook of the same inheritance that he envisions for his audience (cf. Attridge 320). The statement in Gen 6:9 that Noah found favor in God's sight likely prompted the author to surmise his faith (Ellingworth 577).

HOMILETICAL SUGGESTIONS

Early Examples of Faith that Pleased God (11:4–7)

1. Abel (v. 4)
    (a) His offering pleased God (v. 4a)
    (b) His faith is still speaking (v. 4b)
2. Enoch (v. 5)
    (a) He was taken away by God without experiencing death (v. 5a)
    (b) He was found to have pleased God (v. 5b)
3. Noah (v. 7)
    (a) The warning about the flood produced godly fear (v. 7a)
    (b) By faith he built the ark (v. 7b)
        (1) His faith delivered his family (v. 7c)
        (2) His faith condemned the world (v. 7d)
    (c) His faith resulted in his being an heir (v. 7e)
4. Foundation Principle
    (a) Faith is necessary for pleasing God (v. 6a)
    (b) Faith acknowledges that God exists (v. 6b)

3. *The Faith of Abraham and Sarah (11:8–12)*

STRUCTURE

Structurally, this section is divided by the three occurrences of πίστει (vv. 8, 9, 11). Following each, there is a series of indics., modified by relative clauses, prep. phrases, or conj. clauses.

8 Πίστει
καλούμενος
Ἀβραὰμ ὑπήκουσεν ἐξελθεῖν εἰς τόπον
ὃν ἤμελλεν λαμβάνειν εἰς κληρονομίαν,
καὶ ἐξῆλθεν μὴ ἐπιστάμενος ποῦ ἔρχεται.

9 Πίστει
παρῴκησεν εἰς γῆν τῆς ἐπαγγελίας ὡς ἀλλοτρίαν
ἐν σκηναῖς κατοικήσας
μετὰ Ἰσαὰκ καὶ Ἰακὼβ τῶν συγκληρονόμων τῆς ἐπαγγελίας τῆς αὐτῆς·
10 ἐξεδέχετο γὰρ τὴν τοὺς θεμελίους ἔχουσαν πόλιν
ἧς τεχνίτης καὶ δημιουργὸς ὁ θεός.

11 Πίστει
καὶ αὐτὴ Σάρρα στεῖρα δύναμιν εἰς καταβολὴν σπέρματος ἔλαβεν
καὶ παρὰ καιρὸν ἡλικίας,
ἐπεὶ πιστὸν ἡγήσατο τὸν ἐπαγγειλάμενον.
12 διὸ καὶ ἀφ᾽ ἑνὸς
ἐγεννήθησαν, καὶ ταῦτα νενεκρωμένου,
καθὼς τὰ ἄστρα τοῦ οὐρανοῦ τῷ πλήθει
καὶ ὡς ἡ ἄμμος ἡ παρὰ τὸ χεῖλος τῆς θαλάσσης ἡ ἀναρίθμητος.

VERSE 8

Πίστει
By faith

See comments on 11:3.

καλούμενος Ἀβραὰμ
Abraham, when he was called,

The ptc. is temp. ("when he was called" [most EVV]), indicating time contemp. with ὑπήκουσεν ("he obeyed"). Ἀβραάμ (indecl.) functions as the subj. of the ptc. Abraham was previously referenced in 2:16 and 6:13–15.

ὑπήκουσεν ἐξελθεῖν εἰς τόπον ὃν ἤμελλεν λαμβάνειν εἰς κληρονομίαν,
obeyed and set out for a place that he was going to receive as an inheritance.

Ὑπήκουσεν is the 3rd sg. aor. act. indic. of ὑπακούω, "obey" (most EVV). Ἐξελθεῖν (aor. act. inf. of ἐξέρχομαι) indicates result (Wallace 592) and is ingressive ("set out," most EVV). It is sometimes tr. as a finite vb., which requires the addition of "and" (e.g., CSB). This same inf. occurs in LXX Gen 12:1. There are two options for understanding the inf.

1. It modifies ὑπήκουσεν, indicating the tangible evidence of Abraham's obedience. This is a more straightforward understanding of the syntax and is followed by several EVV (e.g., ASV, NASB, REB).
2. It modifies the ptc. καλούμενος, although this is a less natural reading of the Gk. (but see Cockerill 538 n. 8). This is followed by several EVV (e.g., ESV, NET, NIV, NLT).

Εἰς τόπον ("a place" [most EVV]; *pace* "a land" [REB], "a country" [GNT, NJB]) locat. modifies ἐξελθεῖν. The antecedent of ὃν is τόπον. Ἤμελλεν is the 3rd sg. impf. act. indic. of μέλλω. This vb. is important in Hebrews for pointing to eschatological realities (see comments on 1:14). Abraham is the understood subj. of λαμβάνειν, which complements ἤμελλεν. Context clearly implies that what was received by Abraham was given by God (cf. Ellingworth 582). Κληρονομίαν is the acc. sg. fem. of κληρονομία, -ας, ἡ, "inheritance" (BDAG 548a), although Genesis 12 does not describe the land as an inheritance (but cf. Gen 15:7; 22:17). See For Further Study 33 (The Promised Rest and Land Typology in Hebrews).

καὶ ἐξῆλθεν μὴ ἐπιστάμενος ποῦ ἔρχεται.
He went out, even though he did not know where he was going.

Καί coordinates ὑπήκουσεν and ἐξῆλθεν. Ἐπιστάμενος is the nom. sg. masc. of the pres. mid. ptc. of ἐπίσταμαι, "know" (most EVV) or "understand" (NET); cf. BDAG 380d. The neg. ptc. μή modifies ἐξῆλθεν, indicating concession. The adv. introduces a temp. clause, which modifies ἐπιστάμενος. The interr. implies the question "to what place?" The pres. ἔρχεται (ostensibly of the moment recorded in Gen 12) is retained (BDF §324), although it is tr. as an English past tense (most EVV).

The author draws generally on Genesis 12. Abraham's faith is explicitly stated in Gen 15:6, although the author does not cite that v. (unlike Rom 4:3–5; Gal 3:6–9). The emph. here is on Abraham's obedience to set forth. Although the author clearly knew that Abraham was called to go to Canaan, he does not use γῆ as is found in Genesis 12, but uses the ambiguous τόπος, thereby preparing for the revelation that the inheritance was not ultimately the land itself (cf. Lane 2:349). Κληρονομία recalls the important theme of inheritance in Hebrews.

VERSE 9

Πίστει
By faith

See comments on 11:3. The dat. modifies παρῴκησεν, indicating manner.

παρῴκησεν εἰς γῆν τῆς ἐπαγγελίας ὡς ἀλλοτρίαν
he stayed as a foreigner in the land of promise,

Παρῴκησεν is the 3rd sg. aor. act. indic. of παροικέω. The vb. followed by εἰς could mean "to migrate to" (BDAG 779c; Lane 2:344 n. *c*) or more likely "made his home . . . like a stranger" (NIV), "live as alien" (NASB), "make a temporary home" (Goodspeed), "stay as a foreigner" (BDAG 779b; *pace* "went to live" [ESV]). In LXX Gen 23:4, Abraham described himself as a πάροικος. For the social implications of living as a stranger in a foreign land, see Cockerill 537; Koester 485; see also K. L. and M. A. Schmidt, *TDNT* 5:841–50; 851–53.

Εἰς here has a locat. sense ("in" [R 593]), modifying παρῴκησεν. Ἐπαγγελίας (see comments on 4:1) is an attributive gen. (e.g., "the promised land" [NET, NIV]) modifying γῆν (see comments on 1:10). This is the only ref. to "the promised land" in the Bible. Moreover, like τόπος, γῆ is anar., possibly furthering the implication that the *land* was not the ultimate inheritance (Ellingworth 583). The conj. ὡς ("as" [BDAG 1104b]) introduces a comp. (Wallace 675). Ἀλλοτρίαν is the acc. sg. fem. of ἀλλότριος, -α, -ον. Although this adj. implied "strange" in 9:25, here it means "foreign" (BDAG 47c) and modifies γῆν. This is missed in some EVV, which tr. ἀλλοτρίαν as "foreigner," apparently modifying Abraham, but is captured in the NET ("as though it were a foreign country").

ἐν σκηναῖς κατοικήσας
living in tents

Σκηναῖς is the dat. pl. fem. of σκηνή, -ῆς, ἡ, "tent" (BDAG 928b). Although in 8:2 this noun referred to the tabernacle, here it refers to tents used by nomadic herders, such as Abraham and his descendants (W. Michaelis, *TDNT* 7:374–77). Ἐν is locat. modifying κατοικήσας (nom. sg. masc. of the aor. act. ptc. of κατοικέω, "live" [most EVV], "dwell" [NASB]). The ptc. is instr. or possibly indicates manner (Wallace 274–75). If παρῴκησεν is understood as "migrate to," then this ptc. would be circum. (Lane 2:344 n. *e*).

μετὰ Ἰσαὰκ καὶ Ἰακὼβ τῶν συγκληρονόμων τῆς ἐπαγγελίας τῆς αὐτῆς·
as did Isaac and Jacob, coheirs of the same promise.

Like Ἀβραάμ, Ἰσαάκ and Ἰακώβ are indecl. As the obj. of μετά ("with" [ESV, NET]), both names are in the gen. The adv. prep. phrase modifies κατοικήσας. Because this v. could be understood anachronistically (see below), some EVV tr. the beginning of the clause "as did" (e.g., NIV). Συγκληρονόμων is the gen. pl. masc. of συγκληρονόμος, -ον, "coheir" (BDAG 952c), "heirs with him" (ESV, NIV), "fellow heirs" (NASB, NET). The adj. is an appos. to both Ἰσαάκ and Ἰακώβ. This vb. is rare and is not used in the LXX of the patriarchs (Lane 2:350). Ἐπαγγελίας is an obj. gen. and recalls the importance of the Abrahamic promises in Hebrews (see 6:13–15). Αὐτῆς functions as an "identifying adj." (Wallace 349; BDAG 153d) modifying ἐπαγγελία (second attrib. pos.; see Wallace 306–307)—"the same promise."

This v. draws on the Abraham narrative (Genesis 12–25; but esp. LXX Gen 23:4). The ref. to Isaac alludes to Gen 26:25, and Jacob to Gen 25:27; 33:18–19; 35:21. In one sense, the ref. could seem anachronistic, since Isaac's birth is referred to in v. 11. The author, however, may have had LXX Gen 35:27 in mind, which mentions all three and uses παροικέω (elsewhere in the Pentateuch the three are freq. mentioned together [Ellingworth 583]). The author's point is to focus on the forward-looking faith that each demonstrated as they lived as nomads and foreigners in the land promised to them.

VERSE 10

ἐξεδέχετο γὰρ τὴν τοὺς θεμελίους ἔχουσαν πόλιν
For he was looking forward to the city that has foundations,

Γάρ introduces the reason why Abraham was able to live as he did in the land. Ἐξεδέχετο is the 3rd sg. impf. mid. indic. of ἐκδέχομαι, "look forward to" (ESV, NIV, NLT), "expect," "wait" (BDAG 300c). The connotation of "looking for" (NASB) is misleading. The impf. is durative, depicting the "ongoing" nature of the patriarchs dwelling in the land as sojourners. The subj. of the vb. is Abraham. The obj. is τὴν πόλιν, which is modified by the adj. ptc. ἔχουσαν. The obj. of the ptc. is θεμελίους (acc. pl. masc. of θεμέλιος, -ου, ὁ, "foundation" [BDAG 449a]; K. L. Schmidt, *TDNT* 3:63–64). The art. τούς may be emph. ("eternal foundations" [NLT], "firm foundations" [NET]; Lane 2:344 n. *g*); the author may have intended a contrast with the anar. τόπος and γῆ (Ellingworth 584).

ἧς τεχνίτης καὶ δημιουργὸς ὁ θεός.
whose architect and builder is God.

The antecedent of ἧς is πόλιν. The subj. of the verbless clause is θεός. Τεχνίτης is the nom. sg. masc. of τεχνίτης, -ου, ὁ, "architect" (NASB, NET, NIV), "designer" (ESV), "craftsperson," "artisan" (BDAG 1001c). This term was used widely of God in pagan, Jewish, and early Christian sources (Attridge 324). Δημιουργός is the nom. sg. masc. of δημιουργός, -ου, ὁ, "builder" (ESV, NASB, NIV), "maker," "creator" (BDAG 223a–b; W. Foerster, *TDNT* 2:62). The term is used by Philo for God as Creator (Attridge 324). Both nouns function as pred. noms. Neither term is used to describe God elsewhere in BGk. (Ellingworth 585–86). The position of θεός is emph. (Ellingworth 586). The v. alludes to several OT passages in which God is said to lay the foundations of Jerusalem (Ps 87:1, 5; Isa 28:16; 54:11). See also comments on 11:14.

VERSE 11

Πίστει
By faith

See comments on 11:3.

καὶ αὐτὴ Σάρρα στεῖρα
even Sarah herself, when she was unable to have children,

Σάρρα is transliterated from the Heb. and is possibly the subj. of this verbless clause (see discussion below). If so, then καί is ascensive ("even" [most EVV]). The pers. pron. is intensive (e.g., "Sarah herself" [R 686]). Στεῖρα (-ας, ἡ) is the nom. sg. fem. of στεῖρα. The noun refers to a woman incapable of having children, although some EVV tr. it as an adj. (e.g., "barren" [NET, NLT, NRSV]). It functions as the pred. In some early and important mss. this noun is omitted (e.g., 𝔓13^{vid} א A D^{2} 33; followed by ESV, NASB), although this was likely due to scribal error (Koester 487) and the noun is probably original.

δύναμιν εἰς καταβολὴν σπέρματος ἔλαβεν
received power to conceive offspring,

Technically, the subj. of ἔλαβεν could be either Sarah or Abraham (see discussion below). The obj. of the vb. is δύναμιν, which is modified by εἰς καταβολὴν σπέρματος, indicating purpose. Καταβολήν is the acc. sg. fem. of καταβολή, -ῆς, ἡ (BDAG 515a). The term generally means "foundation" (as in 4:3), but here the expression is idiomatic (e.g., "sowing of seed" [BDAG 515b; F. Hauck, *TDNT* 3:620–21]) and is associated with male procreation (e.g., "enabled to bear children" [NIV]). In EVV that consider Sarah the subj. of the v., some idea of conception in indicated (e.g., ESV, NASB, NET), although the expression is not attested with this mng. elsewhere.

καὶ παρὰ καιρὸν ἡλικίας,
even though she was past the age,

Context implies this phrase is concessive ("even though" [most EVV]). It modifies ἔλαβεν. Παρά here has the sense of "beyond" (R 616). Ἡλικίας is the gen. sg. fem. of ἡλικία, -ας, ἡ, "maturity" ("the normal age" [BDAG 436a]). The gen. modifies καιρόν. This phrase could apply to either Abraham's impotence or Sarah's postmenopausal state (see discussion below). The expression is used by Josephus with a postmenopausal sense (Lane 2:345 n. *n*). The author may have intended a double mng., since both were well beyond the time when they could produce offspring, although Abraham fathered children after Isaac.

ἐπεὶ πιστὸν ἡγήσατο τὸν ἐπαγγειλάμενον.
since she considered that the one who had promised was faithful.

Ἐπεί indicates cause or reason ("since" or "because" [most EVV; BDAG 360c]). Ἡγήσατο is the 3rd sg. aor. mid. indic. of ἡγέομαι, "consider" (most EVV; BDAG 434b). The obj. of the vb. is the subst. ἐπαγγειλάμενον (acc. sg. masc. of the aor. mid. ptc. of ἐπαγγέλλομαι, "the one who promised" [cf. BDAG 356b]). Πιστὸν ("faithful" [many EVV]; "trustworthy" [NET]) is the obj. complement. Depending on who is considered the subj. of ἔλαβεν, this is either a statement about Abraham's or about

Sarah's faith. On either view, the author links the ability to have children with a clear statement about either's faith.

There are numerous textual difficulties with this v. The text as it stands is rated {C} by the UBS committee. The expression *δύναμιν εἰς καταβολὴν σπέρματος ἔλαβεν* normally refers to males inseminating, not females conceiving (Metzger 602). Moreover, Abraham is clearly the subj. of the vbs. in v. 10 and v. 12 (and the referent of *ἀφ' ἑνός*), and could easily be understood as the subj. of the vbs. in v. 11 as well. Some also note that, unlike Abraham, Sarah's faith is not explicitly stated in Genesis (Ellingworth 588). In this case, *αὐτὴ Σάρρα στεῖρα* could be read as *αὐτῇ Σάρρα στείρᾳ* (BDF §194[1]; Attridge 325–36; Bruce 296; Ellingworth 588) and understood as a dat. of accompaniment—"by faith he [Abraham] also, together with barren Sarah, received power to beget" (Metzger 602). (Earliest mss. were uppercase without accents, so this is possible. There is, however, no extant mss. support for this option.) Alternatively, the UBS committee suggests that *αὐτὴ Σάρρα στεῖρα* is "a Hebraic circumstantial clause" and takes Abraham as the subj. of *ἔλαβεν*—"by faith, even though Sarah was barren, he [Abraham] received the power to beget" (Metzger 602; cf. Koester 488; Lane 2:344 n. *k*). Hebrews, however, does not evidence Heb. influence elsewhere (Ellingworth 587). Translations with Abraham as the subject include NET, NIV, NRSV.

On the other hand, *δύναμιν εἰς καταβολὴν σπέρματος ἔλαβεν* could be understood as Sarah receiving the power to receive Abraham's seed (Cockerill 544). The Genesis account indicates that Abraham was able to father a child before and after Sarah conceived Isaac and places the emph. on Sarah's barrenness. Thus if Sarah is the subj. of v. 11, the author is drawing out her faith to believe that she could conceive even if this is not indicated explicitly in Genesis (see esp. Cockerill 542–45). This view gives the most natural reading of the nom. *αὐτὴ Σάρρα στεῖρα*. Translations with Sarah as the subject include CSB, ESV, KJV, NASB, NJB, NLT, TNIV. See For Further Study 81 (Whose Faith—Abraham's or Sarah's?).

VERSE 12

διὸ καὶ ἀφ' ἑνὸς ἐγεννήθησαν,
Therefore, from one man . . . came

The inferential conj. *διό* ("therefore" [most EVV; BDAG 250c], "and so" [NIV]) draws on v. 11, and *καί* adds a further point (Ellingworth 590). The form *ἀφ'* (*ἀπό*) occurs before rough breathing. The antecedent of *ἀφ' ἑνός* is Abraham. The masc. pron. refers to Abraham ("one man" [most EVV]). The expression may allude to Isa 51:2. *'Εγεννήθησαν* is the 3rd pl. aor. pass. indic. of *γεννάω*, "came" (as in, "came descendants" [NIV], "were born descendants" [ESV], "children were fathered" [NET, EVV]). Some important mss. ($\mathfrak{P}^{46}$ A D* 33) read *ἐγενήθησαν* (*γίνομαι*) for *ἐγεννήθησαν* (*γεννάω*). The former coheres better with Sarah as the subj. of v. 11, and would give *ἀφ' ἑνός* the sense of "origin." If *ἐγεννήθησαν* is read, then *ἀφ' ἑνὸς* likely indicates agency (see esp. Cockerill 545 n. 31).

καὶ ταῦτα νενεκρωμένου,
—in fact, from one as good as dead—

The idiomatic καὶ ταῦτα can be tr. "in fact" (NET), "and that even" (BDF §425[1]), or "that is to say" (BDF §442[9]); it is an adv. acc. (R 704). The expression is a classical idiom (R 705) that is emph. (Ellingworth 590). The expression also indicates that the ptc. is concessive (R 1129; cf. Lane 2:345 n. *q*). Νενεκρωμένου is the gen sg. masc. of the pf. pass. ptc. of νεκρόω (R. Bultmann, *TDNT* 4:892–95). Although many EVV tr. the ptc. as something like "as good as dead," the ref. is to Abraham's apparent impotence ("from the point of view of begetting children was as good as dead" [Barclay]). The striking par. with Rom 4:19 probably suggests a "common tradition" (Ellingworth 590). The near impossibility of Isaac's birth—life coming from apparent death—could have contributed to the allusion to resurrection in v. 19 (cf. Koester 488).

καθὼς τὰ ἄστρα τοῦ οὐρανοῦ τῷ πλήθει
. . . offspring as numerous as the stars of the sky

The comp. conjs. καθὼς . . . ὡς are paired statements of the staggering number of Abraham and Sarah's descendants. In both phrases some subst. is implied (e.g., "descendants" [NIV]). Ἄστρα is the nom. pl. neut. of ἄστρον, -ου, τό, "star" (BDAG 146b), which is modified by οὐρανοῦ, as a partitive gen. Πλήθει is the dat. sg. neut. of πλῆθος, -ους, τό, here indicating a large quantity (BDAG 825c). The dat. indicates ref., although it is tr. as a comp. in many EVV (e.g., "as numerous as" [NIV], "as many as" [ESV]). This verbless clause alludes to Gen 22:17 (the first part of which was quoted in Heb 6:14), and perhaps Gen 15:5 and Exod 32:13.

καὶ ὡς ἡ ἄμμος ἡ παρὰ τὸ χεῖλος τῆς θαλάσσης ἡ ἀναρίθμητος.
and as innumerable as the grains of sand along the seashore.

Ἄμμος is the nom. sg. fem. of ἄμμος, -ου, ἡ, "sand." The noun is used fig. for something that cannot be counted (BDAG 54b). Χεῖλος is the acc. sg. neut. of χεῖλος, -ους, τό, "shore" (BDAG 1081d), which is further modified by the descriptive gen. θαλάσσης. The adj. prep. phrase παρὰ τὸ χεῖλος τῆς θαλάσσης modifies ἄμμος. The preceding art. indicates a second attrib. adj. cstr. Another modifier is indicated by the third occurrence of ἡ, which modifies ἀναρίθμητος (-ον), "countless" (NIV), "innumerable" (ESV, NASB; BDAG 71b; BGk. hapax). The rep. of the art. is unusual (BDF §269[5]; R 777). This verbless clause alludes to Gen 22:17 and 32:12.

FOR FURTHER STUDY

79. The Pilgrimage Motif in Hebrews (11:8–40)

Arowele, P. J. "The Pilgrim People of God (An African's Reflections on the Motif of Sojourn in the Epistle to the Hebrews)." *AsJT* 4 (1990): 438–55.

*Brown, Raymond. "Pilgrimage in Faith: The Christian Life in Hebrews." *SwJTh* 28 (1985): 28–35.

Cockerill, Gareth Lee. "To the Hebrews/To the Muslims: Islamic Pilgrimage as a Key to Interpretation." *Missiology* 22 (1994): 347–59.

DBI 462–64; 643–45.

Johnsson, W. G. "The Pilgrimage Motif in the Book of Hebrews." *JBL* 97 (1978): 239–51.

Olson, Stanley N. "Wandering but Not Lost." *WW* 5 (1985): 426–33.

*Perkins, David W. "A Call to Pilgrimage: The Challenge of Hebrews." *TTE* 32 (1985): 69–81.

80. Abraham in Hebrews (11:8–19)

Alexander, T. D. *NDBT* 367–72.

*Baird, William. "Abraham in the New Testament: Tradition and the New Identity." *Int* 42 (1988): 367–79.

Balzer, Jutta Leonhardt. *NIDB* 1:19–20.

Bockmuehl, Markus. "Abraham's Faith in Hebrews 11." Pages 364–73 in Bauckham, *Theology*.

Calvert-Koyzis, N. *DLNT* 1–6.

*Longenecker, R. N. "The 'Faith of Abraham' Theme in Paul, James and Hebrews: A Study in the Circumstantial Nature of New Testament Teaching." *JETS* 20 (1977): 203–12.

81. Whose Faith—Abraham's or Sarah's? (11:11)

*Bott, Nicholas T. "'And by Faith, Because Abraham Considered Him Faithful Who Had Promised, Sarah Herself Received Power to Conceive": A Reconsideration of Heb 11:11." *TJ* 32 (2011): 205–19.

Greenlee, J. Harold. "Hebrews 11:11: 'By Faith Sarah Received Ability'." *AsTJ* 54 (1999): 67–72.

———. "Did Sarah Have a Seminal Emission?" *BRev* 8 (1992): 35–39.

———. "Sarah's Faith or Abraham's?" *Notes* 4 (1990): 37–42.

Irwin, Joyce L. "The Use of Hebrews 11:11 as Embryological Proof-Text." *HTR* 71 (1978): 312–16.

van der Horst, Pieter W. "Sarah's Seminal Emission: Hebrews 11:11 in the Light of Ancient Embryology." Pages 287–302 in *Greeks, Romans, and Christians: Essays in Honor of Abraham J. Malherbe*. Edited by David L. Balch, Everett Ferguson, and Wayne A. Meeks. Minneapolis: Fortress, 1990.

Vennum, Eileen. "Is She or Isn't She?: Sarah as a Hero of Faith." *Daughters of Sarah* 13 (1987): 4–7.

HOMILETICAL SUGGESTIONS

The Faith of Abraham and Sarah (11:8–12)

1. By faith, Abraham obeyed God (v. 8)
   (a) He left everything known (v. 8a)
   (b) He set out for a place unknown (v. 8b)

2. By faith, he and his descendants lived in the promised land as foreigners (vv. 9–10)
   (a) Tents showed his outsider status; so also for Isaac and Jacob (v. 9)
   (b) Earthly tents do not compare with the foundations of God's city (v. 10)
3. By faith, barren Sarah was able to conceive (v. 11)
   (a) She was too old to conceive naturally (v. 11a)
   (b) She believed the One who promised (v. 11b)
4. The result of Abraham and Sarah's faith (v. 12)
   (a) It was against all appearances and normal human limitations (v. 12a)
   (b) It resulted in innumerable descendants (v. 12b)

4. The City of God and True Homeland (11:13–16)

STRUCTURE

This discussion elaborates the true nature of God's promise to Abraham concerning the land. It is anchored in five indics., the first of which is modified by four circum. ptcs.

13 Κατὰ πίστιν
ἀπέθανον οὗτοι πάντες,
μὴ λαβόντες τὰς ἐπαγγελίας
ἀλλὰ πόρρωθεν αὐτὰς ἰδόντες
καὶ ἀσπασάμενοι
καὶ ὁμολογήσαντες
ὅτι ξένοι καὶ παρεπίδημοί εἰσιν ἐπὶ τῆς γῆς.
14 οἱ γὰρ τοιαῦτα λέγοντες
ἐμφανίζουσιν ὅτι πατρίδα ἐπιζητοῦσιν.
15 καὶ εἰ μὲν ἐκείνης ἐμνημόνευον ἀφ' ἧς ἐξέβησαν,
εἶχον ἂν καιρὸν ἀνακάμψαι·
16 νῦν δὲ κρείττονος ὀρέγονται,
τοῦτ' ἔστιν ἐπουρανίου.
διὸ οὐκ ἐπαισχύνεται αὐτοὺς ὁ θεὸς θεὸς ἐπικαλεῖσθαι αὐτῶν·
ἡτοίμασεν γὰρ αὐτοῖς πόλιν.

VERSE 13

Κατὰ πίστιν ἀπέθανον οὗτοι πάντες,
These all died in faith,

Κατά here indicates manner (R 533; Ellingworth 592), whereas πίστει is instr. The switch here may be stylistic since πίστει is normally used to introduce a new exemplar, whereas this v. summarizes the previous section. The idea may be that these individuals died expecting the promised inheritance, but had not seen its fulfillment ("were still living by faith when they died" [NIV]; Ellingworth 592–93). The aor. ἀπέθανον is constative or summary (R 833). The antecedent of the dem. pron. οὗτοι is limited to Abraham, Sarah, Isaac, and Jacob, as those before them had not been given the divine promises. The pron. is modified by πάντες.

μὴ λαβόντες τὰς ἐπαγγελίας
although they had not received the things that were promised.

Μὴ . . . ἀλλά introduces correl. contrastive phrases ("not . . . but" [Wallace, 672]). Μή is the normal neg. used with a ptc. Λαβόντες is concessive ("although," CSB; but not indicated in many EVV [e.g., NET, NIV]). This is the first of four circum. ptcs. that modify ἀπέθανον.

Ἐπαγγελίας is the obj. of the ptc. Its usage recalls 4:1, but esp. 6:12–15 (see comments on 6:15). In 6:15, the sg. ἐπαγγελία was used in conj. with Isaac's birth—a promise that was fulfilled in Abraham's lifetime. (The sg. ἐπαγγελία is also used for that which believers anticipate inheriting [Cockerill 548].) The pl. ἐπαγγελίαι (here and 6:12) also includes the land promise, which was not fulfilled in Abraham's lifetime. This is reflected in many EVV (e.g., "the things that were promised" [CSB]).

ἀλλὰ πόρρωθεν αὐτὰς ἰδόντες
But they saw them from a distance,

Ἀλλά introduces a strong contrast (between not receiving yet seeing from afar). Although the classical adv. πόρρωθεν normally indicates a locat. sense of "from where" ("whence" [BDF §104(3)]), here it adds a temp. sense as well (cf. Ellingworth 593; even eschatological [Lane 2:356]), although this is not reflected in most EVV. Ἰδόντες is the nom. pl. masc. of the aor. act. ptc. of ὁράω, "saw" (most EVV). This is the second of four circum. ptcs. that modify ἀπέθανον.

καὶ ἀσπασάμενοι
greeted them,

Ἀσπασάμενοι is the nom. pl. masc. of the aor. mid. ptc. of ἀσπάζομαι, "welcome" (NASB, NET, NIV), "greet" (ESV; BDAG 144c). The ptc. is coordinate with ἰδόντες. Like ἰδόντες, this ptc. is often tr. in EVV as a finite vb. This may explain why several EVV understand πόρρωθεν as modifying ἀσπασάμενοι (e.g., "welcomed them from a distance" [NIV]). The obj. of this vb. is always pers. in BGk., so its usage could suggest that the author understood that "the heavenly city is primarily a community" (Ellingworth 594), anticipating 12:22–24. This is the third of four circum. ptcs. that modify ἀπέθανον, which is joined to the first two by καί.

καὶ ὁμολογήσαντες ὅτι ξένοι καὶ παρεπίδημοί εἰσιν ἐπὶ τῆς γῆς.
and confessed that they were foreigners and temporary residents on the earth.

Ὁμολογήσαντες is the nom. pl. masc. of the aor. act. ptc. of ὁμολογέω, "acknowledge" (ESV, NET), "admit" (NIV), "confess" (NASB; BDAG 708b). This is the final of four circum. ptcs. that modify ἀπέθανον, and is joined to the first three by καί. This fourth ptc. shifts the focus from what the patriarchs anticipated in the future to the circumstances that they endured in the pres. (cf. Cockerill 548 n. 43). Ὅτι introduces the obj. of the confession (understood as indir. discourse). The tense of the orig. discourse (εἰσίν) is retained in indir. discourse in Gk. (unlike English). Alternatively, the pres. could indicate "proximity" (Campbell, *Basics* 60) and a desire to connect the author's audience more closely with the OT exemplars (cf. Lane 2:346 n. *v*).

Ξένοι is the nom. pl. masc. of ξένος, -η, -ον. The subst. adj. has a wide semantic range: "strangers" (ESV, NASB, NET, NIV), "aliens" (some EVV; BDAG 684b; G. Stählin, *TDNT* 5:1–16). To die as a foreigner "in a foreign land was 'a pitiable fate' (2 Macc 9:28)" (cited in Koester 488; see also Koester 497). Παρεπίδημοί is the nom.

pl. masc. of παρεπίδημος, -ον. Like ξένος, the subst. adj. has a wide semantic range: "foreigners" (NRSV), "nomads" (NJB, NLT), "strangers" (NIV), "exiles" (ESV, NASB), "sojourners," "resident aliens" (BDAG 775d; H. Balz, *EDNT* 3:38b–c; W. Grundmann, *TDNT* 2:64–65). The latter adj. occurs in LXX Gen 23:4, describing Abraham (cf. LXX Ps 38:13). There is overlap in these terms (e.g., both terms are tr. as "strangers" in different EVV [e.g., NIV]). Indeed, they are probably best understood as an example of hendiadys (Lane 2:357). Both adj. are pred. Ἐπὶ τῆς γῆς modifies both ξένοι and παρεπίδημοί. Although γῆ can indicate either "land" or "earth," the contrast with "heavenly" suggests that the latter is meant ("earth" [most EVV; so Attridge 331; *pace* Lane 2:346 n. *w*]). The image of being sojourners on earth develops the pilgrimage motif already noted in Hebrews. See For Further Study 79 (The Pilgrimage Motif in Hebrews). This imagery has suggested to some that the author is drawing on Philonic and other Jewish ideas about earthly sojourners' "repatriation to their heavenly home" (Attridge 330). Yet the idea in Hebrews is not "repatriation" (cf. Koester 489) but rather the access that worshippers whose consciences have been cleansed by Jesus's blood now have (but which was previously unavailable) to God's presence.

VERSE 14

οἱ γὰρ τοιαῦτα λέγοντες
Now those who say such things

Γάρ draws a conclusion from v. 13 (Ellingworth 595). The subst. ptc. λέγοντες ("those who say"/"those who speak" [NASB, NET], "people who speak"/"people who say" [ESV, NIV]) is the subj. of ἐμφανίζουσιν (see below). The ref. could be the same as οὗτοι πάντες in v. 13, or it could ref. more narrowly to Abraham and Jacob, based on LXX Gen 23:4 and 49:9, respectively (Ellingworth 594). Τοιαῦτα is the obj. of the ptc. The correl. adj. is subst. ("such things" [most EVV]) or possibly an acc. adv. ("thus" [ESV]; "in such a way" [NET]). This v. introduces the author's "major premise" in Heb 11:13–16, namely that those who call themselves "foreigners" in the promised land must be seeking another location.

ἐμφανίζουσιν ὅτι πατρίδα ἐπιζητοῦσιν.
make it clear that they are seeking a homeland.

Ἐμφανίζουσιν is the 3rd pl. pres. act. indic. of ἐμφανίζω, "show" (NIV), "make [it] clear" (ESV, NASB, NET), "explain," "inform" (BDAG 326a). The subj. of the vb. is the subst. λέγοντες. The content of what the patriarchs "make clear" is introduced by ὅτι ("declarative ὅτι" [R 1034]). This vb. is not followed by ὅτι anywhere else in BGk. (Ellingworth 595).

Ἐπιζητοῦσιν is the 3rd pl. pres. act. indic. of ἐπιζητέω. The compound form is intensified (Lane 2:358; "have a strong desire for" [BDAG 371c]), although this is not reflected in EVV: "seek" (most EVV), "looking for" (NIV). This word recalls the earlier use of ἐκζητέω in v. 6, describing those who seek God (Cockerill 552). It also parallels the sim. images from ἐκδέχομαι (v. 10) and ὀρέγομαι (v. 16 [Lane 2:358]). The word order suggests that the vb. is emph. (Cockerill 552). The pres. either parallels such usage in indir. discourse or may be understood as "timeless" in the sense of indicating "the permanent record of Scripture" (Ellingworth 595). The obj. of the vb. is πατρίδα (acc. sg. fem. of πατρίς, -ίδος, ἡ), "fatherland" (TCNT), "homeland" (most EVV; BDAG 788b). The use of γῇ in v. 13 prepares for the revelation that this homeland was not on earth (Ellingworth 595). Thus the tr. "country of their own" (e.g., NASB, NIV) is unclear. This is the only place in Scripture where a "homeland" is understood as heavenly (see Ellingworth 595–96), but the term "homeland" could be misleading. The author is not talking about a region or country, but rather about a city. In the ancient world, one's identity was often closely bound to one's city of birth, where one held citizenship. This imagery is more likely what the author had in view (Cockerill 552). See also B. T. Arnold, *NDBT* 414–16; *DBI* 150–54; John E. Stambaugh, *ABD* 1:1043–48; H. Strathmann, *TDNT* 6:529–33; and Richard L. Rohrbaugh, "The City in the Second Testament," *BTB* 21 (1991): 67–75.

VERSE 15

καὶ εἰ μὲν ἐκείνης ἐμνημόνευον ἀφ' ἧς ἐξέβησαν,
If they were thinking about where they came from,

Καί introduces a development in the argument ("if indeed" [NASB; Ellingworth 597]), namely, the "major premise" in v. 14 is now supported by a minor one in v. 15, which is that the place that Abraham left (Ur) was not his true home either (Cockerill 552). The correl. μέν anticipates δέ in v. 16 to indicate a contrast (BDAG 629d). Εἰ with an aug. tense in the prot., and ἄν in the apod., identifies "an unreal case" (BDF §360[4]; R 921; second-class cond. [see Wallace 694–96]). The prot. presents a cond. understood to be false, which is signaled by a past tense vb. in Eng. ("if they were . . ." or "if they had been" [most EVV]).

Ἐμνημόνευον is the 3rd pl. impf. act. indic. of μνημονεύω. The vb. can mean "remember," but here the sense is more of "refer to" (Bruce 299 n. 120; Ellingworth 597; Lane 2:346 n. *z*), "thinking of" (ESV, NASB, NET, NIV), or "mean" (BDAG 655c). This vb. is followed by the gen. The remote dem. pron. ἐκείνης modifies an assumed πατρίδα (e.g., Ur) and functions as the obj. of ἐμνημόνευον ("that land" [ESV], "that country" [NASB]; but left untr. in many EVV). The antecedent for the rel. pron. ἧς is πατρίδα. Ἐξέβησαν is the 3rd pl. aor. act. indic. of ἐκβαίνω, "leave" (NET, NIV), "go out" (ESV, NASB), "come from" (BDAG 299a; BGk. hapax). This rare vb. is close in mng. to ἐξέρχομαι. The rel. clause ἧς ἐξέβησαν is embedded in the prep. phrase (ἀφ' before rough breathing; for the syntax of this cstr., see Wallace 480).

εἶχον ἂν καιρὸν ἀνακάμψαι·
they would have had an opportunity to return.

The clause represents the apod. of the "unreal" cond. begun in the beginning of this v. Εἶχον is the 3rd pl. impf. act. indic. of ἔχω, "they would have had" (most EVV). Although καιρός often indicates "time," here it is fig. understood as an "opportunity" (most EVV; Ellingworth 597). Ἀνακάμψαι is the aor. act. inf. of ἀνακάμπτω, "return" (most EVV; BDAG 65b). Ανακάμψαι is the complement of καιρόν ("a time for returning" [R 1062]).

VERSE 16

νῦν δὲ κρείττονος ὀρέγονται,
But they now desire a better place—

Δέ correlates with μέν in v. 15, indicating contrast ("but" [ESV, NET], "instead" [NIV]) between the reality that they sought and the unreal situation posed in the cond.; the adv. νῦν is thus logical, not temp. (Ellingworth 599; Lane 2:346 n. *dd*). The first part of this v. represents the conclusion of the author's argument begun in v. 14; namely, neither Canaan nor Ur was the patriarchs' true homeland, because their true "city home" is heavenly (Cockerill 553). Κρείττονος (see comments on 1:4) modifies an implied πατρίς ("a better country" [ESV, NASB, NIV], "a better land" [NET]; cf. BDF §241]). (The two-ending comp. uses the same form for modifying masc. or fem. subst.). Ὀρέγονται is the 3rd pl. pres. mid. indic. of ὀρέγω, "desire" (ESV, NASB), "aspire to" (NET), "long for" (NIV; BDAG 721d). The vb. is followed by the gen. (R 508). The pres. is timeless.

τοῦτ' ἔστιν ἐπουρανίου.
a heavenly one.

The expression τοῦτ' ἔστιν is fixed ("that is" [ESV, NET]; but left untr. in many EVV, or indicated with a dash) regardless of the antecedent (R 705). It further elaborates "the place" that the patriarchs desired. As with κρείττονος, ἐπουρανίου (ἐπουράνιος, -ον, "heavenly"; BDAG 388b) also modifies an implied πατρίς. As with the author's previous discussion of "heavenly" (see 3:1 and 6:4), the city to which the patriarchs looked is "real" and will not pass away; indeed it is "more real" than present realities (Cockerill 553).

διὸ οὐκ ἐπαισχύνεται αὐτοὺς ὁ θεὸς θεὸς ἐπικαλεῖσθαι αὐτῶν·
Therefore, God is not ashamed to be called their God,

The inferential conj. διό draws on the previous vv. and presents a gen. statement about faith. Ἐπαισχύνεται is the 3rd sg. pres. mid. indic. of ἐπαισχύνομαι, "be ashamed" (most EVV; BDAG 357d). (See comments on 2:11.) The first θεός is the subj. of ἐπαισχύνεται. Αὐτούς is the obj. of ἐπαισχύνεται, although the cstr. is unusual: "αὐτούς is redundant, anticipating αὐτῶν" (Ellingworth 599). Ἐπικαλεῖσθαι is the pres. pass. inf. of ἐπικαλέω, "to be called" (most EVV; BDAG 373b). If the vb. is understood as a mid., then the sense is that "God is not ashamed *to call himself* their God" (Lane

2:346 n. *ff*; italics original). The inf. complements ἐπαισχύνεται. The second θεός is the obj. of the inf. and is modified by αὐτῶν, indicating poss. The allusion is likely to the well-known designation "the God of Abraham, Isaac, and Jacob" (Lane 2:359).

ἡτοίμασεν γὰρ αὐτοῖς πόλιν.
for he has prepared a city for them.

Γάρ offers evidence to support the claim of the διό clause. Ἡτοίμασεν is the 3rd sg. aor. act. indic. of ἑτοιμάζω, "prepared" (most EVV; BDAG 401a). The obj. of the vb. is πόλιν. Αὐτοῖς is a dat. of adv. (BDF §188). For the origin of an eschatological city, see comments on 12:22–24. See also comments on 11:14.

HOMILETICAL SUGGESTIONS

The City of God, Our True Homeland (11:13–16)

1. The Patriarchs Saw the City from Afar (v. 13)
   (a) They died still believing, although they had not received the promise during their lives (v. 13a)
   (b) Their ongoing status as foreigners affirmed their ongoing faith (v. 13b)
2. What Their Faith Revealed (vv. 14–16a)
   (a) They were seeking a (heavenly) homeland (vv. 14, 16a)
   (b) They could have returned to their former (earthly) homeland (v. 15)
3. What Their Faith Achieved (v. 16b–c)
   (a) God is not ashamed to be called their God (v. 16b)
   (b) God has indeed prepared a city for them (v. 16c)

5. The Faith of the Patriarchs (11:17–22)

STRUCTURE

This section is structured around four occurrences of πίστει. The importance of Abraham is once again indicated by the narrative space allotted to him, which centers around three indics.; the first and third are modified by adv. ptcs. The remaining occurrences of πίστει are structured by short indic. statements about each of the patriarchs.

17 Πίστει
προσενήνοχεν Ἀβραὰμ τὸν Ἰσαὰκ
πειραζόμενος
καὶ τὸν μονογενῆ προσέφερεν, ὁ τὰς ἐπαγγελίας ἀναδεξάμενος,
18 πρὸς ὃν ἐλαλήθη
ὅτι Ἐν Ἰσαὰκ κληθήσεταί σοι σπέρμα,
19 λογισάμενος ὅτι καὶ ἐκ νεκρῶν ἐγείρειν δυνατὸς ὁ θεός,
ὅθεν αὐτὸν καὶ ἐν παραβολῇ ἐκομίσατο.

20 Πίστει
καὶ περὶ μελλόντων εὐλόγησεν Ἰσαὰκ τὸν Ἰακὼβ καὶ τὸν Ἠσαῦ.

21 Πίστει
Ἰακὼβ ἀποθνῄσκων
ἕκαστον τῶν υἱῶν Ἰωσὴφ εὐλόγησεν
καὶ προσεκύνησεν ἐπὶ τὸ ἄκρον τῆς ῥάβδου αὐτοῦ.

22 Πίστει
Ἰωσὴφ τελευτῶν
περὶ τῆς ἐξόδου τῶν υἱῶν Ἰσραὴλ ἐμνημόνευσεν
καὶ περὶ τῶν ὀστέων αὐτοῦ ἐνετείλατο.

VERSE 17

Πίστει
By faith

See comments on 11:3.

προσενήνοχεν Ἀβραὰμ τὸν Ἰσαὰκ πειραζόμενος
Abraham, when he was tested, offered up Isaac.

Προσενήνοχεν is the 3rd sg. pf. act. indic. of προσφέρω, "offer" (most EVV; see comments on 5:1). Some EVV add "as a sacrifice" (e.g., NIV). Moffatt's tr., "he sacrificed Isaac," is misleading. The pf. in ref. to an OT event may indicate "that this event still retains its (exemplary) mng." (BDF §342[5]) or it could be rhetorically emph. to underscore Abraham's faith. The subj. of προσενήνοχεν is Ἀβραάμ; its obj. is

Ἰσαάκ. The art. could indicate the case function of the indecl. Ἰσαάκ (R 760) or it could be anaphoric. Πειραζόμενος is the nom. sg. masc. of the pres. pass. ptc. of πειράζω, "test" (most EVV). The ptc. is temp., indicating time contemp. with the main vb. (e.g., "when he was tested"; cf. Lane 2:346 n. *ii*). The author does not state directly that God tempted Abraham (cf. Gen 22:1), but it is implied. For the history of interpretation of this v., see Ellingworth 600.

καὶ τὸν μονογενῆ προσέφερεν,
. . . and yet he was offering his one and only son,

Καί introduces a "more specific restatement" of the first part of the v. (Ellingworth 600) or is possibly epex. (Lane 2:346 n. *kk*). The incredulity that Abraham would be asked to offer Isaac is captured with "yet" in some EVV (NET). Προσέφερεν is the 3rd sg. impf. act. indic. of προσφέρω, "offer" (most EVV), "sacrifice" (NIV; see comments on 5:1). The impf. indicates "supplemental information" (Campbell, *Basics* 44) and that the action was begun but not completed (R 885; "conative" [BDF §327; Wallace 550–51]). This is expressed well in some EVV: "was ready to offer" (NRSV), "was ready to sacrifice" (Cassirer), "was willing to sacrifice" (CEV). The NJB is confusing: "he offered to sacrifice his only son."

Μονογενῆ is the acc. sg. masc. of μονογενής, -ές, "only" (ESV, NET, NLT), "one and only" (NIV; BDAG 658a; F. Büchsel, *TDNT* 4:737–41). The art. functions par. to a poss. pron. ("his one and only son"); "son" is understood from the context. The adj. is often mistr. as "only begotten" (e.g., ASV, KJV, NASB), but the root of the adj. is γένος ("kind" or "sort"), not γεννάω. Indeed, Isaac was not Abraham's "only begotten" son, but he was his "unique" (CSB) son due to his supernatural conception, and as the one through whom the promise would be transmitted to subsequent generations. The same adj. is used of Jesus (e.g., John 1:14), suggesting that Isaac may be a type of Jesus, God's unique ("one and only") Son (but see below).

ὁ τὰς ἐπαγγελίας ἀναδεξάμενος,
He received the promises

Ἀναδεξάμενος is the nom. sg. masc. of the aor. mid. ptc. of ἀναδέχομαι (BDAG 62b). The ptc. is subst. ("the one who received" [many EVV]), although it is tr. as a finite vb. ("receive") in some EVV (e.g., NET, REB). The obj. of the ptc. is τὰς ἐπαγγελίας (see comments on 6:15). The ptc. phrase is the subj. of προσέφερεν.

VERSE 18

πρὸς ὃν ἐλαλήθη
the one to whom it had been said,

The antecedent of ὅν is Abraham. Πρός indicates "to" here. Some EVV tr. the rel. clause as an independent clause (e.g., NET, NIV). The aor. ἐλαλήθη is global (Wallace

557–58). The pass. indicates that God was the one who spoke. A concessive idea may be inferred from the context (e.g., "even though" [NIV]).

ὅτι Ἐν Ἰσαὰκ κληθήσεταί σοι σπέρμα,
Your offspring will be traced through Isaac.

Ὅτι introduces the citation from LXX Gen 21:12 (*ὅτι recitativum*; BDF §397[5]; Wallace 454–55). *Σπέρμα* is the nom. sg. neut. of *σπέρμα, -ατος, τό*, "offspring" (ESV, NIV), "descendants" (NASB, NET; Ellingworth 602); but cf. "your seed will be traced" (CSB). It functions as the subj. of the vb. and is modified by *σοί*, as a dat. of poss. (BDF §189). *Κληθήσεταί* is the 3rd sg. fut. pass. indic. of *καλέω*, "be called" (NASB), "be named" (ESV), "be reckoned" (NIV). *Ἰσαάκ* is indecl., but is dat. as the obj. of *ἐν*. *Ἐν* indicates agency (BDF §191).

The author previously quoted Gen 22:17 (in Heb 6:14) concerning the divine promises, the citation here is from Gen 21:12. Although the "binding (or *Aqedah* from the Heb.) of Isaac" factored significantly in Jewish literature (see Lane 2:360), it is only referenced here and in Jas 2:21–23 in the NT (Bruce 302). The author follows the LXX in the citation (Ellingworth 601). Abraham's test to offer up Isaac was considered paradigmatic of faith in both Scripture and later Jewish literature (see refs. in Cockerill 555 n. 64).

VERSE 19

λογισάμενος ὅτι καὶ ἐκ νεκρῶν ἐγείρειν δυνατὸς ὁ θεός,
He considered God to be able even to raise someone from the dead;

Λογισάμενος is the nom. sg. masc. of the aor. mid. ptc. of *λογίζομαι*, "reckon" (REB), "consider" (ESV, NASB), "reason" (NET, NIV, NLT; BDAG 598a). The mid. voice emphasizes the *agent* (vs. the *action* [Wallace; Lane 2:347 n. *pp*). The ptc. is causal (Cockerill 556). Ὅτι introduces the content (indir. discourse) of Abraham's reckoning. *Καί* is emph. ("even" [most EVV; Ellingworth 602; Lane 2:347 n. *rr*]). The subj. of the clause is *ὁ θεός*, which is in emph. position (Cockerill 557). *Δυνατός* is the pred. of this verbless clause, which assumes *ἐστίν*. The use of *δυνατός* as a pred. recalls the use of the alpha privative *ἀδύνατος* in 6:4, 18; 10:4; and 11:6. *Ἐγείρειν* is the pres. act. infin. of *ἐγείρω*, "raise" (most EVV; BDAG 272a). The pres. may be gnomic (Lane 2:347 n. *qq*) or "of general statement," which is further supported by the lack of obj. for the inf. (Cockerill 556), although "people" (NASB) is the assumed obj. This is specified as Isaac in some EVV (e.g., "him" [NET]). The NIV tr. the prep. phrase as the obj. of the inf. ("raise the dead"). The inf. is the complement of *δυνατός*. *Ἐκ νεκρῶν* modifies *ἐγείρειν*, indicating source (Harris 104). The prep. phrase is "fixed" and is used of resurrection from the dead in the Gospels and Acts (see Ellingworth 602).

ὅθεν αὐτὸν καὶ ἐν παραβολῇ ἐκομίσατο.
therefore, he received him back, figuratively speaking.

The conj. ὅθεν could be *inferential, drawing a conclusion from vv. 17–19a ("therefore" [CSB; "for which reason"; BDAG 693a; BDF §451.6), locat. (e.g., "from there" [NASB, NET]), or par. to a rel. pron. ("from which" [ESV, NASB]; Lane 2:347 n. *ss*). Context supports any of the options. Καί is emph. or intensive ("even" [Ellingworth 602; Lane 2:347 n. *vv*]; "also" [NASB], or left untr. in many EVV). Ἐκομίσατο is the 3rd sg. aor. mid. indic. of κομίζω, "receive back" [most EVV; BDAG 557d]). The antecedent of αὐτόν, the obj. of ἐκομίσατο, is Isaac.

Παραβολῇ is dat. sg. fem. of παραβολή, -ῆς, ἡ. In 9:9, the noun was used in the sense of a "symbol" (see comments there), which also fits here ("as a symbol" [NAB]; "as a type" [NASB; Bruce 304 n. 151; Cockerill 557; Lane 2:347 n. *tt*]; cf. "considered symbolically" [Cassirer]; "by what was a parable of the resurrection" [Moffatt]). Ἐν παραβολῇ is also understood as an adv. (Moule 78): "figuratively speaking" (ESV, NJB), "in a manner of speaking" (NIV), "in a sense" (NET, NLT).

God's sparing of Isaac is understood here as a "type" of believers' resurrection (Koester 492): "Isaac, who embodies the many faithful descendants promised to Abraham, typifies their resurrection" (Cockerill 558). This v. also may suggest that Isaac was a type of Jesus, the "one and only" Son (cf. Ellingworth 602). Yet the focus here is on Abraham's faith, not Isaac's, so the typology is not as clear as some suggest (Cockerill 558). Abraham's reasoning concerning resurrection cannot be anchored in any OT or later Jewish reflection and thus likely reflects early Christian tradition (Ellingworth 602; *pace* Attridge 335).

VERSE 20

Πίστει
By faith

See comments on 11:3. Πίστει introduces a new exemplar—Isaac.

καὶ περὶ μελλόντων εὐλόγησεν Ἰσαὰκ τὸν Ἰακὼβ καὶ τὸν Ἠσαῦ.
Isaac blessed Jacob and Esau concerning things to come.

Καί is adversative, "also" (Attridge 336; cf. Ellingworth 604), although left untr. in many EVV (but cf. NASB). Εὐλόγησεν is the 3rd sg. aor. act. indic. of εὐλογέω, "bless" (most EVV; BDAG 408b). Ἰσαάκ is the subj. of the vb.; Ἰακώβ and Ἠσαῦ are the obj. Both arts. distinguish between the obj. and subj. of these indecl. proper names (R 788). The ptc. μελλόντων is subst. ("things to come" [NASB, REB]). Περί ("concerning") μελλόντων modifies εὐλόγησεν (*pace* NAB). The word order is unusual (Attridge 336).

The v. refers broadly to Gen 27:27–40 (cf. 28:1–5), and specifically v. 27. The "things to come" recalls the use of μέλλω with future salvation in 1:14 (see comments there). This connection is missed in some EVV (e.g., "invoked future blessings" [ESV], "concerning their future" [NET]). The author may have inferred Isaac's faith from the statement that Isaac pleased God in LXX Gen 48:15 (Koester 492). Whereas the previous vv. focused on "promise," vv. 20–22 focus on "blessing" (Cockerill 559).

The fut. focus of these vv., however, illustrates faith in the final fulfillment of God's promises (Cockerill 559). The inclusion of Esau appears to be problematic given Heb 12:14–17. Yet the author may intend a subtle warning: one who had been blessed was not able to receive that blessing because of his apostasy (Cockerill 560).

VERSE 21

Πίστει
By faith

See comments on 11:3.

Ἰακὼβ ἀποθνῄσκων
Jacob, when he was dying,

The ptc. ἀποθνῄσκων is temp. ("when/as he was dying" [most EVV; cf. R 827, 979]), modifying εὐλόγησεν (see below). The subj. of the ptc. is Ἰακώβ. The ptc. is likely an allusion to LXX Gen 48:21, and perhaps Gen 47:29 (Attridge 336)

ἕκαστον τῶν υἱῶν Ἰωσὴφ εὐλόγησεν
blessed each of the sons of Joseph,

Εὐλόγησεν is the 3rd sg. aor. act. indic. of εὐλογέω, "bless" (most EVV; BDAG 408b). Ἰακώβ is the subj. of the vb. Ἕκαστον is the obj. of the vb., which is modified by the partitive gen. υἱῶν (Wallace 85). Ἰωσήφ (indecl.) is gen., modifying υἱῶν for poss. The obj. of the vb. is ἕκαστον τῶν υἱῶν Ἰωσήφ.

καὶ προσεκύνησεν ἐπὶ τὸ ἄκρον τῆς ῥάβδου αὐτοῦ.
and **he worshiped, leaning on the top of his staff**.

Καί joins εὐλόγησεν and προσεκύνησεν. It is possibly epex. (Ellingworth 608). Προσεκύνησεν is the 3rd sg. aor. act. indic. of προσκυνέω, "worship" (most EVV). Προσκυνέω followed by ἐπί indicates worship in the LXX (Koester 493). Ἄκρον is the acc. sg. neut. of ἄκρον, -ου, τό, "top" (most EVV; BDAG 40a; R 775), which is modified by ῥάβδου ("staff" [most EVV]). Ἄκρον is left untr. in some EVV (e.g., NET). The tr. "head" is confusing (ESV). The connection between the prep. phrase (ἐπί . . .) and προσεκύνησεν is ambiguous, leading many EVV to supply an additional vb. for clarification (e.g., "leaning" [NASB]; "bowing in worship" [ESV]).

Jacob's blessing of both of Joseph's sons (Ephraim and Manasseh) is recorded in Gen 48:4–22. The citation is taken from LXX Gen 47:31. The LXX translators, however, apparently misread the Heb. word for "bed" as "staff." The MT suggests that Jacob leaned on his bed (indicating his weakened state [Attridge 336]). Although the LXX "staff" generated many allegorical patristic interpretations (see Attridge 336), the author does not attach such significance to the staff (see comments on 1:8). The staff may symbolize Jacob's "pilgrimage" (Cockerill 561 n. 92; cf. "his walking stick"

[CEV]). By focusing on Jacob blessing his grandsons, the author suggests the generational scope of the promises (Cockerill 561).

VERSE 22

Πίστει
By faith

See comments on 11:3.

Ἰωσὴφ τελευτῶν
Joseph, as he was nearing the end of his life,

Τελευτῶν is the nom. sg. masc. of the pres. act. ptc. of τελευτάω, "die" (BDAG 997b). The ptc. is ingressive, modifying ἐμνημόνευσεν (see below). This is well reflected in the CSB tr. The subj. of the ptc. is Ἰωσήφ. The clause likely alludes to Gen 50:26.

περὶ τῆς ἐξόδου τῶν υἱῶν Ἰσραὴλ ἐμνημόνευσεν
mentioned the exodus of the Israelites

Ἐμνημόνευσεν is the 3rd sg. aor. act. indic. of *μνημονεύω*. The vb. can mean "remember," but that sense would be anachronistic here, although it could suggest that Joseph "remembered" the Abrahamic promises, esp. regarding the land (Cockerill 563). Instead the sense is "recall" (JB), "thought about" (Moffatt), "refer to," or "reflect upon" (Attridge 336). The tr. "made mention" or "mentioned" (NASB, NET) may have the wrong connotation (e.g., mention in passing). Ἐξόδου is the gen. sg. fem. of ἔξοδος, -ου, ἡ (BDAG 350d), which here refers to the exodus and it does in the LXX. Some EVV add "from Egypt" (GNB, NIV). Υἱῶν modifies ἐξόδου for ref. Ἰσραήλ (indecl.) modifies υἱῶν for poss. The phrase τῶν υἱῶν Ἰσραήλ alludes to Gen 50:25 (Cockerill 563). As with previous uses of υἱῶν Ἰσραήλ, the term is inclusive (e.g., "Israelites" [CSB]). Depending on how the vb. is tr., περί is either tr. (e.g., "spoke about" NIV) or left untr. (e.g., NET).

καὶ περὶ τῶν ὀστέων αὐτοῦ ἐνετείλατο.
and gave instructions concerning his bones.

Καί joins ἐμνημόνευσεν and ἐνετείλατο. Cockerill notes the par. of the two περί phrases followed by the vb. (Cockerill 562). Ἐνετείλατο is the 3rd sg. aor. mid. indic. of ἐντέλλω, "give instructions" (most EVV; BDAG 339c). Ὀστέων is the gen. pl. neut. of ὀστέον, -ου, τό, "bones" (most EVV; BDAG 729c; but cf. "his burial" [NET, NRSV]). The clause alludes to Gen 50:24–25 (cf. Exod 13:19; Josh 24:32). The author understands Joseph's final commands concerning his bones as an example of remaining firm in his faith in God's promises of the "things to come," namely the (as yet future) exodus and conquest of Canaan (cf. Acts 7:9). See also Max Wilcox, "The Bones of Joseph: Hebrews 11:22," in *Scripture: Meaning and Method: Essays Presented to*

Anthony Tyrrell Hanson for His Seventieth Birthday, ed. Barry P. Thompson (Hull, UK: Hull University Press, 1987), 114–30; V. P. Hamilton, *NDBT* 606–8.

FOR FURTHER STUDY

82. Isaac in Hebrews (11:17–19)

Chilton, Bruce. *NIDB* 3:70–73.

Daly, Robert J. "Soteriological Significance of the Sacrifice of Isaac." *CBQ* 39 (1977): 45–75.

Martin-Achard, Robert. *ABD* 3:462–70.

Swetnam, James. *Jesus and Isaac: A Study of the Epistle to the Hebrews in the Light of the Aqedah.* AnBib 94. Rome: Biblical Institute, 1982.

Wood, J. Edwin. "Isaac Typology in the New Testament." *NTS* 14 (1968): 583–89.

HOMILETICAL SUGGESTIONS

The Faith of the Patriarchs (11:17–22)

1. Abraham's Extreme Faith (vv. 17–19)
   - (a) The extreme test of offering Isaac, his unique son (v. 17a)
   - (b) The extreme confidence in the promise of offspring (vv. 17b–18)
   - (c) The extreme faith that God could do the impossible (v. 19)
2. Isaac's Faith in Future Things (v. 20)
3. Jacob's Faith in the Future Generations (v. 21)
4. Joseph's Faith in the Future Occupation of the Land (v. 22)

6. The Faith of Moses (11:23–28)

STRUCTURE

The author has carefully structured the sections on Abraham and Moses. Each begins with four examples from each of their lives (vv. 8–12, 17–19 for Abraham, and vv. 23–29 for Moses), followed by three examples of those who came after them (vv. 20–22 for Abraham, and vv. 30–31 for Moses). This gives seven examples of faith associated with each paradigmatic figure (Cockerill 564). For the numerous pars. between these two sections, see Cockerill 565–66; 579. The structure of this section parallels the previous ones in Hebrews 11 with the use of πίστει followed by indics.

23 Πίστει
Μωϋσῆς γεννηθεὶς
ἐκρύβη τρίμηνον ὑπὸ τῶν πατέρων αὐτοῦ,
διότι εἶδον ἀστεῖον τὸ παιδίον
καὶ οὐκ ἐφοβήθησαν τὸ διάταγμα τοῦ βασιλέως.

24 Πίστει
Μωϋσῆς μέγας γενόμενος
ἠρνήσατο λέγεσθαι υἱὸς θυγατρὸς Φαραώ,
25 μᾶλλον ἑλόμενος συγκακουχεῖσθαι τῷ λαῷ τοῦ θεοῦ
ἢ πρόσκαιρον ἔχειν ἁμαρτίας ἀπόλαυσιν,
26 ἡγησάμενος* τὸν ὀνειδισμὸν τοῦ Χριστοῦ μείζονα πλοῦτον τῶν Αἰγύπτου θησαυρῶν
ἀπέβλεπεν γὰρ εἰς τὴν μισθαποδοσίαν.

27 Πίστει
κατέλιπεν Αἴγυπτον
μὴ φοβηθεὶς τὸν θυμὸν τοῦ βασιλέως·
τὸν γὰρ ἀόρατον ὡς ὁρῶν ἐκαρτέρησεν.
28 Πίστει
πεποίηκεν τὸ πάσχα καὶ τὴν πρόσχυσιν τοῦ αἵματος,
ἵνα μὴ ὁ ὀλοθρεύων τὰ πρωτότοκα θίγῃ αὐτῶν.

*The word order in this v. has been changed from the original Greek to make the syntax clearer, which is also reflected in most EVV. The original word order likely stresses the wealth of Egypt (see discussion below).

VERSE 23

Πίστει
By faith

See comments on 11:3. Πίστει modifies ἐκρύβη (see below).

Μωϋσῆς γεννηθείς
Moses, after he was born,

The ptc. γεννηθείς is temp. ("after he was born" [NIV]; "when" [ESV, NASB, NET]), indicating antecedent time to ἐκρύβη (see below). Μωϋσῆς (-έως, ὁ, "Moses") recalls the introduction of this paramount OT figure in 3:2 (see comments there).

ἐκρύβη τρίμηνον ὑπὸ τῶν πατέρων αὐτοῦ,
was hidden by his parents for three months,

Ἐκρύβη is the 3rd sg. aor. pass. indic. of κρύπτω ("was hidden" [most EVV; BDAG 571b]). Some EVV tr. this clause with the act. voice and Moses's parents as the subj. (e.g., NET, NIV). The aor. is constative (R 833). The implied subj. of the vb. is Moses. Πατέρων is the gen. pl. masc. of πατήρ, πατρός, ὁ. Although πατήρ often indicates "father," here the mng. is clearly "parents" (BDAG 786c). Αὐτοῦ modifies πατέρων for poss. Τρίμηνον is the acc. sg. neut. of τρίμηνος, -ον, "three months." The acc. neut. adj. functions as a temp. adv. modifying ἐκρύβη (BDF §243). Ὑπό followed by the gen. indicates the agency of the pass. ἐκρύβη (Wallace 433).

διότι εἶδον ἀστεῖον τὸ παιδίον
because they saw that the child was beautiful,

The conj. διότι introduces a causal clause ("because"; cf. BDAG 251c). The unexpressed subj. of εἶδον (3rd pl. aor. act. indic. of ὁράω) is Moses's parents. The neut. παιδίον reflects grammatical gender, not natural gender. The adj. ἀστεῖον (ἀστεῖος, -α, -ον, "handsome" [BDAG 145b]) modifies παιδίον as an obj. complement. This word derives from LXX Exod 2:2. The implication here is not just that Moses had a pleasing appearance (as suggested by "beautiful" [ESV, NASB, NET]), but rather that somehow he was extraordinary ("no ordinary child" [NIV; Lane 2:367 n. *c*; cf. "unusual" [NLT]). Despite much speculation in Jewish literature about Moses's appearance (see Lane 2:370), the author appears to follow the implication of Acts 7:20, that the baby was somehow pleasing to God. In secular literature, the word referred to good character (see Koester 501). As with Abraham, the author stays close to the OT text and does not engage later speculation (Cockerill 567–68).

καὶ οὐκ ἐφοβήθησαν τὸ διάταγμα τοῦ βασιλέως.
and they didn't fear the king's edict.

Καί joins εἶδον and ἐφοβήθησαν. Ἐφοβήθησαν is the 3rd pl. aor. pass. indic. of φοβέω. The vb. in the pass. has a trans. mng. (e.g., "fear" or "were not afraid" [most EVV]). The subj. of the vb. remains Moses's parents. The aor. is likely ingressive (Lane 2:367 n. *d*). Διάταγμα is the acc. sg. neut. of διάταγμα, -ατος, τό, "edict" (most EVV), "command" (BDAG 237c; NT hapax). The acc. indicates the obj. of fear (e.g., the edict). Βασιλέως is a subj. gen. modifying διάταγμα. By "king," the author of Hebrews clearly means the Pharaoh; βασιλεύς is used sim. in the LXX.

The focus on Moses's faith begins with his parents' faith. This v. refers to Exod 1:15–22; 2:1–2. The MT focuses on the midwives' fearlessness, not that of Moses's parents. Additionally, the MT indicates that Moses's mother hid him for three months. The author, however, follows the LXX, which says that his parents hid him. Their fearlessness can be inferred from the OT account (Koester 501).

VERSE 24

Πίστει
By faith

See comments on 11:3. Πίστει modifies ἠρνήσατο (see below).

Μωϋσῆς μέγας γενόμενος
Moses, when he had grown up,

Μωϋσῆς is the subj. of the ptc. The expression μέγας γενόμενος is idiomatic: "when he was grown up" (most EVV; BDAG 623d). The expression derives from LXX Exod 2:11. Acts 7:23 indicates that Moses was forty at this point.

ἠρνήσατο λέγεσθαι υἱὸς θυγατρὸς Φαραώ,
refused to be called the son of Pharaoh's daughter

Ἠρνήσατο is the 3rd sg. aor. mid. indic. of ἀρνέομαι, "refuse" (most EVV), "disdain" (BDAG 132d; H. Schlier, *TDNT* 1:469–71; cf. "renounce" [Ellingworth 611]). The inf. λέγεσθαι is the complement of ἠρνήσατο and introduces indir. discourse (R 1036). Υἱός is the obj. of the inf. It is modified by θυγατρός indicating poss., which is further modified by Φαραώ (indecl.), also indicating poss.

The account of Moses here has par. with Stephen's speech in Acts 7:20–44. Some have suggested that Moses's refusal involved legal denunciation of formal adoption by the Pharaoh's daughter, following Philo (*Moses* 1.49–51). More plausibly, Moses's defense of a Hebrew slave severed his association with Pharaoh's family. The language in this v. supports a personal decision rather than a formal renunciation (see Lane 2:371–72; cf. Cockerill 568). See also For Further Study 27 (Moses in Hebrews).

VERSE 25

μᾶλλον ἑλόμενος συγκακουχεῖσθαι τῷ λαῷ τοῦ θεοῦ
and chose to suffer with the people of God

Μᾶλλον is the comp. of the rare adv. μάλα, "very, exceedingly" (BDAG 613d). Here the expression μᾶλλον ἑλόμενος . . . ἤ can be tr. "he chose [the one] rather than [the other]" (most EVV; BDAG 614c). Ἑλόμενος is the nom. sg. masc. of the aor. mid. ptc. of αἱρέω. In the mid. the vb. means "choose" (most EVV). The mid. voice emphasizes the agent rather than the action (Wallace 415; Lane 2:368 n. *h*). Συγκακουχεῖσθαι is the pres. mid. inf. of συγκακουχέομαι, "be ill-treated" (NET), "be mistreated with" (ESV, NIV; BDAG 951b; BGk. hapax). The author may have coined this word himself (Attridge 340). The vb. is followed by the dat. (τῷ λαῷ), here an associative dat. (R 529; Wallace 160). Θεοῦ modifies λαῷ. Although the LXX account uses the term "the sons of Israel," the author changes this to "the people of God," thereby developing the solidarity that the author sees with God's people, both past and present (cf. Attridge 340; Ellingworth 612; see comments on 2:17). That Moses chose identification with God's people over worldly wealth (and reputation) offers a subtle, if not powerful, encouragement for the author's audience to do the same (cf. Cockerill 569; Ellingworth 612).

ἢ πρόσκαιρον ἔχειν ἁμαρτίας ἀπόλαυσιν,
rather than to enjoy the fleeting pleasure of sin.

Ἔχειν is the second complement of ἑλόμενος. Ἀπόλαυσιν is the acc. sg. fem. of ἀπόλαυσις, -εως, ἡ, "enjoyment" (BDAG 115c). It functions as the obj. of ἔχειν and is modified by πρόσκαιρον (πρόσκαιρος, -ον, "a short time" [NCV], "fleeting" [ESV, NET, NIV], "passing" [NASB], "temporary, transitory" [BDAG 881a]). Ἁμαρτίας modifies ἀπόλαυσιν as an obj. gen. or as an attributive gen. ("sinful advantages"). Many EVV tr. ἀπόλαυσις as a vb. (e.g., "to enjoy"; cf. Wallace 464), leaving ἔχειν untr. Several EVV tr. ἁμαρτίας ἀπόλαυσιν as "pleasures of sin" (e.g., ESV, NASB, NIV), which connotes sensuality ("having the good time that sin could bring" [CEV]) or luxury, but the tr. "have the benefit of" (BDAG 115c) or "advantage" fits the context better, particularly concerning the advantage that Moses could have had if he had not identified and suffered with the Israelites (see Cockerill 570).

VERSE 26

μείζονα πλοῦτον ἡγησάμενος τῶν Αἰγύπτου θησαυρῶν τὸν ὀνειδισμὸν τοῦ Χριστοῦ·
For he considered reproach for the sake of Christ to be greater wealth than the treasures of Egypt,

Ἡγησάμενος is the nom. sg. masc. of the aor. mid. ptc. of ἡγέομαι, "consider" (ESV, NJB, NASB), "regard" (NET, NIV). The ptc. modifies ἀπέβλεπεν (see below) causally. Ὀνειδισμόν is the acc. sg. masc. of ὀνειδισμός, -οῦ, ὁ, "reproach" (see comments on 10:33). Χριστοῦ modifies ὀνειδισμόν as an obj. gen. (R 500; cf. "for the sake of" [NIV]). Ὀνειδισμόν is the obj. of ἡγησάμενος. Πλοῦτον (acc. sg. masc. of πλοῦτος, -ου, ὁ, "wealth" [most EVV]) is the obj. of the ptc. and is modified by μείζονα (the comp. of μέγας, μεγάλη, μέγα, "greater"). Θησαυρῶν is the gen. pl. masc. of θησαυρός, -οῦ, ὁ, "treasures" (most EVV; BDAG 456c), or "storehouses" (Koester 503). The position of πλοῦτον . . . τῶν Αἰγύπτου θησαυρῶν at the front of the clause is emph. The granaries and wealth of Egypt were renowned. The gen. modifies πλοῦτον to indicate comp. (Wallace 112). Αἰγύπτου modifies θησαυρῶν as a gen. of source. Ὀνειδισμόν is the obj. of ἡγησάμενος. Μείζονα πλοῦτον is the obj. complement. The use of ὀνειδισμός may allude to LXX Ps 88:51–52. Cockerill notes how *μείζονα πλοῦτον* and *τὸν ὀνειδισμὸν τοῦ Χριστοῦ* "surround" *τῶν Αἰγύπτου θησαυρῶν*, thus emphasizing the magnitude of the comp. (Cockerill 571).

ἀπέβλεπεν γὰρ εἰς τὴν μισθαποδοσίαν.
since he was looking ahead to the reward.

Γάρ is causal. *Ἀπέβλεπεν* is the 3rd sg. impf. act. indic. of *ἀποβλέπω*, "look ahead" (NIV, NRSV), "look to" (ESV, NASB), "eyes fixed upon" (NET), "pay attention" (BDAG 107d; BGk. hapax). The compound (*ἀπό* + *βλέπω*) is probably intensive, and suggests that "Moses 'looked away' *from*" [his] present experience" (Lane 2:368 n. *l*). The impf. suggests a continuous or rep. action (cf. Ellingworth 615). The vb. is followed by *εἰς*, indicating the obj. (*μισθαποδοσίαν*) to which the subj. is looking. Here *εἰς* parallels the function of the dat. (R 594). *Μισθαποδοσίαν* occurred in Heb 2:2 (see comments there) with a neg. connotation (e.g., "punishment"); here the connotation is positive ("reward" [most EVV], "recompense" [NAB]).

Verses 25–26 are difficult to interpret. The author sees in Moses a type of Christ. Just as Moses forsook an immediate reward (wealth and prestige in Egypt) to suffer with his people in anticipation of a greater reward (the deliverance of God's people to the promised land), so also Jesus forsook joy to endure the cross for the greater reward of accomplishing God's purposes. These verses thus prepare for Heb 12:1–3. The author is not suggesting a preincarnate appearance by Christ to Moses (e.g., Bruce 311 n. 184), but rather that Moses understood from Scripture that his suffering was somehow in line with the suffering of the Lord's future anointed one (Cockerill 572; cf. "abuse suffered for the Christ" [NRSV]). If the author is drawing on Psalm 89 (LXX 88):51–52, he may have understood the psalm as prefiguring Christ's reproach, which he then applied to Moses's experience (Attridge 341; cf. Ellingworth 614, but refuted by Cockerill 572). The author's point is to offer further encouragement to persevere. Like Moses, the audience is to endure the reproach that Christ ultimately endured (Koester 502). The use of *ὀνειδισμόν* in v. 25 recalls *ὀνειδισμοῖς* in 10:33, where it was used in conjunction with the author's audience (Lane 2:374).

VERSE 27

Πίστει
By faith

See comments on 11:3. *Πίστει* modifies *κατέλιπεν* (see below).

κατέλιπεν Αἴγυπτον
he left Egypt behind,

Κατέλιπεν is the 3rd sg. aor. act. indic. of καταλείπω, "leave" (most EVV; BDAG 520d). The obj. of the vb. is Αἴγυπτον. Moses is the understood subj. An allusion to Abraham leaving his homeland is possible (Attridge 342).

μὴ φοβηθεὶς τὸν θυμὸν τοῦ βασιλέως·
not being afraid of the king's anger,

Φοβηθείς is the nom. sg. masc. of the aor. pass. ptc. of φοβέω. This vb. in the pass. has a trans. mng. (e.g., "fear" or "be afraid" [most EVV]). The subj. of the vb. remains Moses. The ptc. is circum. (R 1121), expressing coincident action (Lane 2:368 n. *n*). Μή is the usual neg. used with ptc. (BDF §426). Θυμόν is the acc. sg. masc. of θυμός, -οῦ, ὁ, "anger" (most EVV), "fury" (NAB), "wrath," "rage," "indignation" (BDAG 461d). Βασιλέως modifies θυμόν as a poss. gen. The acc. indicates the obj. of fear, namely the king's anger. As with v. 23, the "king" is the Pharaoh.

τὸν γὰρ ἀόρατον ὡς ὁρῶν ἐκαρτέρησεν.
for Moses persevered as one who sees him who is invisible.

Γάρ is causal, indicating why Moses was not afraid. Ἐκαρτέρησεν is the 3rd sg. aor. act. indic. of καρτερέω, "persevere" (NET, NIV, NRSV), "endure" (ESV, NASB; BDAG 510d; W. Grundmann, *TDNT* 3:617; NT hapax). The aor. is constative (R 833). The subj. of the vb. is Moses. Ὁρῶν is the nom. sg. masc. of the pres. act. ptc. of ὁράω. Although anar. ptcs. are not freq. subst., context confirms this function of ὁρῶν. Ἀόρατον is the acc. sg. masc. of ἀόρατος, -ον, "invisible" (most EVV). The adj. is subst. and is a circumlocution for God.

There is debate as to how to understand ὡς. It could be causal ("because he saw him who is invisible" [NIV]). Alternatively, it could be *qual. ("as though he could see[/saw] the one who is invisible" [NET, NRSV; "as if seeing" [NAB, Koester 504; BDAG 1104d]). The difference between the two is not significant. Related to the latter is whether this v. alludes to Moses's encounter with the burning bush (Exod 3:1–6 [Bruce 313 n. 198]), but this would be anachronistic if the ref. here is to Moses's first departure from Egypt (see below). Less likely is that the author drew on later traditions that emphasized Moses as a visionary (for examples, see Attridge 342). The author does not focus on Moses's visions, but rather his faith (Attridge 343), which is what the audience must emulate (Cockerill 575). The ref. could then be broadly understood as his "fixed habit of spiritual perception" (Lane 2:376).

Also debated is which departure from Egypt the author has in mind. Exodus 2:14 records that Moses was afraid after he killed an Egyptian foreman, but this fear is indirectly associated with his leaving Egypt in Exod 2:15. Both Philo and Josephus emphasize Moses's fearlessness with regard to Pharaoh (see Koester 503). The author may have drawn on this tradition to bracket discussion of Moses's life with his parents' fearlessness and his own (Lane 2:375). Such an interpretation would point to his first departure from Egypt. His second departure, the exodus, is apparently contradicted by reference to the institution of the Passover (v. 28), which happened before the exodus.

Yet the author has previously given a summary that could appear to be anachronistic. Such may be the case here as well (cf. Cockerill 574–75).

VERSE 28

Πίστει
By faith

See comments on 11:3. Πίστει modifies πεποίηκεν (see below).

πεποίηκεν τὸ πάσχα
he instituted the Passover

The mng. of πεποίηκεν is unusual: “kept” (most EVV; Wallace 582), “instituted” (TCNT, Weymouth; Cockerill 579), “celebrate” (CEV). Πάσχα (“Passover”) is indecl., but the art. indicates its function as the obj. of πεποίηκεν. The pf. may indicate that the Passover became “an ongoing institution” (BDF §342[4]). Cockerill notes that the pf. tense is reserved for the binding of Isaac (v. 17) and the institution of the Passover (v. 28).

καὶ τὴν πρόσχυσιν τοῦ αἵματος,
and the sprinkling of the blood,

Πρόσχυσιν is the acc. sg. fem. of πρόσχυσις, -εως, ἡ, “sprinkling” (most EVV). The expression alludes to Exod 12:22 and sprinkling blood on the doorposts (BDAG 887b).

ἵνα μὴ ὁ ὀλοθρεύων τὰ πρωτότοκα θίγῃ αὐτῶν.
so that the destroyer of the firstborn might not touch the Israelites.

Ἵνα followed by the subjunc. indicates purpose. Ὀλοθρεύων is the nom. sg. masc. of the pres. act. ptc. of ὀλοθρεύω (BDAG 703c; J. Schneider, *TDNT* 5:167–68). The ptc. is subst. (“the destroyer”). This expression derives from LXX Exod 12:23. It is used here abs. (e.g., “the destroyer might not touch the firstborn” [REB]), although many EVV take τὰ πρωτότοκα as modifying ὁ ὀλοθρεύων (e.g., “the destroyer of their first born” [e.g., CSB]). Θίγῃ is the 3rd sg. aor. act. subjunc. of θιγγάνω, “touch” (most EVV; BDAG 456d). Πρωτότοκα is the acc. pl. neut. of πρωτότοκος, -ον, “firstborn” (see comments on 1:6). The adj. is subst. The neut. is generalizing, including all firstborn human and animal males (cf. BDAG 894b). The antecedent of αὐτῶν is inferred to be τῷ λαῷ τοῦ θεοῦ in v. 25.

As with Heb 1:1, alliteration is used effectively (Πίστει πεποίηκεν . . . πάσχα . . . πρόσχυσιν . . . πρωτότοκα [Ellingworth 617]), but is difficult to bring out in English. The focus on Moses’s faith concludes with the institution of the Passover, to commemorate God’s deliverance from Egypt, *before* the actual exodus occurred.

HOMILETICAL SUGGESTIONS

The Faith of Moses (11:23–28)

1. Faith Surrounding His Birth (v. 23)
   (a) His parents recognized his uniqueness (v. 23b)
   (b) His parents hid him, not fearing the Pharaoh (v. 23a, c)
2. Faith Regarding His Privilege (vv. 24–25)
   (a) He refused the status he could have enjoyed in Egypt (v. 24)
   (b) He chose instead to suffer with God's people (v. 25)
3. Faith that Transcends Circumstances (v. 26)
   (a) He understood that present reproach to be greater than present rewards (v. 26a)
   (b) He understood that present reproach pointed to future reward (v. 26b)
4. Faith that Steps Out (vv. 27–28)
   (a) He left Egypt not fearing Pharaoh (v. 27)
   (b) He instituted the Passover believing that God would spare the firstborn of Israel (v. 28)

7. Faith during the Exodus and Conquest (11:29–31)

STRUCTURE

The final three examples to close off the focus on Moses are each structured the same way: the initial πίστει is followed by a finite vb., which is then modified by a rel. clause (v. 29) or an adv. ptc. (vv. 30, 31).

29 Πίστει
διέβησαν τὴν Ἐρυθρὰν Θάλασσαν ὡς διὰ ξηρᾶς γῆς,
ἧς πεῖραν λαβόντες οἱ Αἰγύπτιοι κατεπόθησαν.

30 Πίστει
τὰ τείχη Ἰεριχὼ ἔπεσαν
κυκλωθέντα ἐπὶ ἑπτὰ ἡμέρας.

31 Πίστει
Ῥαὰβ ἡ πόρνη οὐ συναπώλετο τοῖς ἀπειθήσασιν
δεξαμένη τοὺς κατασκόπους μετ᾽ εἰρήνης.

VERSE 29

Πίστει
By faith

See comments on 11:3. Πίστει modifies διέβησαν (see below).

διέβησαν τὴν Ἐρυθρὰν Θάλασσαν ὡς διὰ ξηρᾶς γῆς,
they crossed the Red Sea as though they were on dry land.

Διέβησαν is the 3rd pl. aor. act. indic. of διαβαίνω, "cross" (most EVV; BDAG 226b). The subj. of the vb. is understood to be "the people of God" (v. 25), already anticipated by αὐτῶν in v. 28 (Attridge 343; Ellingworth 618). This is made explicit in some EVV (e.g., "the people" [NIV]). Ἐρυθράν is the acc. sg. fem. of ἐρυθρός, -ά, -όν, "red" (BDAG 393c). The adj. modifies Θάλασσαν. The term "Red Sea" occurs regularly in the LXX, although MT has "Sea of Reeds" (e.g., Exod 10:19). Βαίνω is intrans., but the compound vb. is trans. followed by the acc. (R 800); "pass through" (NASB, NIV, NRSV; R 582–83; cf. Moule 55). Ξηρᾶς is the gen. sg. fem. of ξηρός, -ά, -όν, "dry land" (most EVV; BDAG 685a). The adj. modifies γῆς. Ὡς indicates an ellipsis of the vb. διαβαίνω ("as though *they were passing through* dry land" [NASB; BDAG 1104a]).

ἧς πεῖραν λαβόντες οἱ Αἰγύπτιοι κατεπόθησαν.
When the Egyptians attempted to do this, they were drowned.

Πεῖραν is the acc. sg. fem. of πεῖρα, -ας, ἡ. Together with λαμβάνω (here: λαβόντες), the idiom means "attempted to" (ESV), "tried to" (NIV). The antecedent of ἧς could be either θάλασσαν or ξηρᾶς γῆς. The rel. clause probably means something like "when they tried (to do) it [cross on the dry ground]" (BDAG 792d). The subj. of the ptc. is Αἰγύπτιοι (Αἰγύπτιος, -ία, -ιον, "Egyptian" [BDAG 25c]); the adj. is subst. Κατεπόθησαν is the 3rd pl. aor. pass. indic. of καταπίνω, "were drowned" (ESV, NASB, NIV). The compound prep. is intensive ("swallowed up" [GNT, Cassirer, NET; BDAG 524d; Attridge 344], "engulfed" [REB; Cockerill 583]).

This v. draws on Exod 14:13–30. The author ascribes faith to Israelites in crossing the Red Sea, and suggests that Egyptians died because of their lack of faith (Bruce 316). The miraculous event is recalled in Exod 15:1–21 (cf. Ps 106:9–12; Isa 43:16–17).

VERSE 30

Πίστει
By faith

See comments on 11:3. Πίστει modifies ἔπεσαν (see below). The author likely has both the people's faith and Joshua's (although not named specifically) in view here (Bruce 317). By not mentioning Joshua directly, the author begins a shift from individuals (Abraham and Moses) to the community of faith (cf. Cockerill 583). The author intentionally passes over the (unfaithful) wilderness generation.

τὰ τείχη Ἰεριχὼ ἔπεσαν
the walls of Jericho fell down

Ἔπεσαν is the 3rd pl. aor. act. indic. of πίπτω, "fall down" (most EVV). Normally a neut. pl. subj. takes a sg. vb., but not always (Wallace 400). Τείχη is the nom. pl. neut. of τεῖχος, -ους, τό, "walls" (BDAG 994a). Ἰεριχώ (indecl.) functions as a descriptive gen. (Wallace 79–80). The fortress at Jericho was believed to have been impenetrable (cf. Lane 2:378).

κυκλωθέντα ἐπὶ ἑπτὰ ἡμέρας.
after being marched around by the Israelites for seven days.

Κυκλωθέντα is the nom. pl. neut. of the aor. pass. ptc. of κυκλόω, "marched around" (NET, NIV), "been encircled" (ESV, NASB), "go around" (BDAG 574b). The ptc. is temp. ("after" [most EVV]), modifying ἔπεσαν. The assumed agent of the pass. vb. is the people of God, which is made explicit in some EVV (e.g., NLT). Ἑπτά is indecl. ("seven"); here it modifies ἡμέρας and is thus gen. sg. fem. Ἐπί followed by the acc. functions par. to an "acc. of duration" ("for seven days"; cf. Z §80). The v. alludes to Josh 6:1–21.

VERSE 31

Πίστει
By faith

See comments on 11:3. Πίστει modifies συναπώλετο (see below).

Ῥαὰβ ἡ πόρνη οὐ συναπώλετο τοῖς ἀπειθήσασιν
Rahab the prostitute . . . didn't perish with those who disobeyed.

Συναπώλετο is the 3rd sg. aor. mid. indic. of συναπόλλυμι, "perish with" (ESV, NASB), "be killed with" (GNT, NIV, NJB), "destroy with" (BDAG 996a: NT hapax). Like previous Heb. names, Ῥαάβ is indecl. Here it functions as the subj. of συναπώλετο. Πόρνη (-ης, ἡ, "prostitute" [most EVV] or "harlot" [NASB, RSV]) is an appos. to Ῥαάβ. Ἀπειθήσασιν is the dat. pl. masc. of the aor. act. ptc. of ἀπειθέω. The ptc. is subst. ("those who were disobedient" [ESV, NASB, NIV; BDAG 99d], "the disobedient" [NET], "[those] who refused to obey God" [NLT]). Although the cognate ἀπείθεια, -ας, ἡ, was used regarding the wilderness generation (Heb 4:6, 11), here the subst. ptc. refers to Canaanites. Yet it carries the same idea of disobedience, implying somehow that the residents of Jericho had heard the same news that Rahab had, yet they chose not to believe as she did (Cockerill 584–85 n. 79). The dat. is associative ("together with" [R 529; Wallace 160]).

The fact that Rahab was still associated with her family, indeed even acting on their behalf, could suggest that she was not a prostitute (cf. Lane 2:379), although this status is established in the OT and later tradition. The author's ref. to her may be for rhetorical effect: "if even a prostitute acted by faith, it would be disgraceful for the listeners to prove faithless" (Koester 505, paraphrasing Chrysostom).

δεξαμένη τοὺς κατασκόπους μετ' εἰρήνης
. . . welcomed the spies in peace and

Δεξαμένη is the nom. sg. fem. of the aor. mid. ptc. of δέχομαι, modifying συναπώλετο. The vb. often means "receive" (NRSV), but here "welcome" (most EVV) is better. The ptc. is causal. Κατασκόπους is the acc. pl. masc. of κατάσκοπος, -ου, ὁ, "spy" (most EVV [BDAG 527c]). Μετ' εἰρήνης indicates manner ("in peace" [NASB, NET]), modifying δεξαμένη. There may be an allusion to "shalom" as a greeting among the people of God (Bruce 315 n. 213) or a contrast with an expected war with Israel (Ellingworth 622). The position of εἰρήνης is emph. (Cockerill 585). Some EVV tr. μετ' εἰρήνης as an adv. (e.g., NIV).

Rahab is also used as a positive example in Jas 2:25 (cf. Matt 1:5). Rahab is the only woman apart from Sarah to be included by name in the *exempla* of Hebrews 11.

FOR FURTHER STUDY

83. Rahab in the NT (11:31)

Evans, M. J. *NDBT* 715–16.
Greenspoon, Leonard J. *ABD* 5:611–12.
Hanson, Anthony T. "Rahab the Harlot in Early Christian Tradition." *JSNT* 1 (1978): 53–60.
Mosser, Carl. "Rahab Outside the Camp." Pages 383–404 in Bauckham, *Theology*.
Wiseman, D. J. "Rahab of Jericho." *TynBul* 14 (1964): 8–11.

HOMILETICAL SUGGESTIONS

Faith in Exceptional Circumstances (11:29–31)

1. Faith that God Could Intervene in Nature: The Red Sea (v. 29)
   (a) The Israelites believed God could part the Red Sea (v. 29a)
   (b) The Egyptians did not (v. 29b)
2. Faith that God Could Bring Down Impossible Walls: Jericho (v. 30)
3. Faith that God Would Return a Favor: Rahab (v. 31)

8. A Multitude of Examples that Culminate in the Perfection Achieved by Christ (11:32–40)

STRUCTURE

This final section drops the familiar πίστει for διὰ πίστεως (vv. 33, 39), which forms an *inclusio* framing the section (Attridge 347). The author begins in v. 32 with six individuals presented in three pairings (as reflected above). These are followed by nine short clauses strung together without conjunctions ("asyndeton"), for rhetorical effect (BDF §494), although many EVV add punctuation per English convention. (The first six clauses have nine to ten syllables, further adding to the rhetorical effect [Ellingworth 624]—a "rhythmic barrage" [Koester 516].) Asyndeton gives the impression that the "list could be extended indefinitely" (Koester 516). These short clauses are further divided into three groupings (as reflected above). Clauses 2–8 each begin with the "ε" of an aug. aor. vb. (see comments below). The first major section (vv. 33–34) focuses on the period of the Judges and early monarchy. The next section (vv. 35–36) draws on the prophetic corpus and Maccabean history. The third section (vv. 37–38) draws broadly from multiple traditions. As is the case elsewhere, the author concludes with a summary in vv. 39–40. The function of vv. 32–40 is to highlight the persecution that believers can expect by drawing on past examples relevant to the audience's situation. See esp. Cockerill 585–600; Witherington 320–22.

32 Καὶ τί ἔτι λέγω;
ἐπιλείψει με γὰρ διηγούμενον ὁ χρόνος
περὶ Γεδεών, Βαράκ,
Σαμψών, Ἰεφθάε,
Δαυίδ τε καὶ Σαμουὴλ καὶ τῶν προφητῶν,
33 οἳ διὰ πίστεως
κατηγωνίσαντο βασιλείας,
εἰργάσαντο δικαιοσύνην,
ἐπέτυχον ἐπαγγελιῶν,

ἔφραξαν στόματα λεόντων,
34 ἔσβεσαν δύναμιν πυρός,
ἔφυγον στόματα μαχαίρης,

ἐδυναμώθησαν ἀπὸ ἀσθενείας
ἐγενήθησαν ἰσχυροὶ ἐν πολέμῳ,
παρεμβολὰς ἔκλιναν ἀλλοτρίων.

35 ἔλαβον γυναῖκες ἐξ ἀναστάσεως τοὺς νεκροὺς αὐτῶν·
ἄλλοι δὲ ἐτυμπανίσθησαν οὐ προσδεξάμενοι τὴν ἀπολύτρωσιν,
ἵνα κρείττονος ἀναστάσεως τύχωσιν·
36 ἕτεροι δὲ ἐμπαιγμῶν καὶ μαστίγων πεῖραν ἔλαβον,
ἔτι δὲ δεσμῶν καὶ φυλακῆς·

37 ἐλιθάσθησαν,
ἐπρίσθησαν,
ἐν φόνῳ μαχαίρης ἀπέθανον,
περιῆλθον ἐν μηλωταῖς, ἐν αἰγείοις δέρμασιν,
ὑστερούμενοι,
θλιβόμενοι,
κακουχούμενοι,
38 ὧν οὐκ ἦν ἄξιος ὁ κόσμος,
ἐπὶ ἐρημίαις πλανώμενοι καὶ ὄρεσιν
καὶ σπηλαίοις καὶ ταῖς ὀπαῖς τῆς γῆς.
39 Καὶ οὗτοι πάντες μαρτυρηθέντες διὰ τῆς πίστεως οὐκ ἐκομίσαντο τὴν ἐπαγγελίαν,
40 τοῦ θεοῦ περὶ ἡμῶν κρεῖττόν τι προβλεψαμένου,
ἵνα μὴ χωρὶς ἡμῶν τελειωθῶσιν.

VERSE 32

Καὶ τί ἔτι λέγω;
And what more can I say?

Καί introduces this rhetorical question (indicated by the interr. pron. τί, "what"), although it is sometimes untr. (Lane 2:381 n. *a*). The adv. ἔτι ("more" [most EVV]) modifies λέγω, which is a (deliberative) subjunc. (R 934; Wallace 467), although the form is the same as the indic. Καὶ τί ἔτι λέγω is a "common homiletical and literary idiom" found in Jewish literature to signal limited time (Lane 2:382). The intended effect of the rhetorical question may be: "What else can I say?" (CEV) or "Should I go on?" (GNT).

ἐπιλείψει με γὰρ διηγούμενον ὁ χρόνος
Time is too short for me to tell

Γάρ (postpos.) is usually second in a clause, although third position is possible (BDF §475[2]). Ἐπιλείψει is the 3rd sg. fut. act. indic. of ἐπιλείπω, "be too short" (REB), "fail" (ESV, NASB, NET; BDAG 375a; BGk. hapax). Διηγούμενον is the acc. sg. masc. of the pres. mid. ptc. of διηγέομαι, "tell" (ESV, NASB, NET, NIV), "describe" (BDAG 245b). The ptc. has cond. force: "time would fail me if I told" (Lane 2:38; Wallace 633). Με indicates the subj. of the ptc., which differs from the main vb. Many EVV tr. the pers. pron. as the subj. (e.g., "I do not have time" [NIV]).

This expression is a "rhetorical commonplace" (Attridge 347) found in CGk and Jewish literature (see Lane 2:382–83)—an example of paraleipsis (Koester 511). Its usage evinces the author's rhetorical skill (R 1126; cf. BDF §473[2]). This is the first occurrence of the first pers. sg. in Hebrews. The masc. ptc. probably rules out the possibility that the author was female (so most commentators). Wallace makes the intriguing suggestion that Hebrews could have been written by two people (Wallace 396–97 n. 11).

περὶ Γεδεών, Βαράκ, Σαμψών, Ἰεφθάε, Δαυίδ τε καὶ Σαμουὴλ καὶ τῶν προφητῶν,
about Gideon, Barak, Samson, Jephthah, David, Samuel, and the prophets,

These six Heb. names are all indecl. Προφητῶν indicates that the six previous objs. are gen., since all function as the obj. of the prep. περί, which with the gen. means "about" (or "of" [most EVV]). Τε καί joins the named individuals as a group, and the second καί adds a new element, "the prophets" (BDF §444[4]). The cstr. also aligns Samuel with the prophets.

The author switches from detailed discussion of an individual (e.g., Abraham and Moses) to a brief list of three pairs of individuals that span from the settlement to the early monarchy. In each pair, the *first* exemplar occurs chronologically *after* the second exemplar in the OT, with the more important member listed first (Ellingworth 623). This literary device "create[s] an image of a vast horde of exemplars of faith" (Attridge 347). For the third pair, the author places Samuel before the prophets, perhaps as the beginning of the prophetic line (Bruce 320). The reverse ordering and rapid mention without elaboration indicate that the list is merely representative (Cockerill 588).

The first four names are surprising since each demonstrated a significant *lack* of faith in his life. At some point, however, each attested faith in God, and perhaps offer commentary on the overall spiritual insensitivity during the time of Judges. These names may come from 1 Sam 12:11. Mention of Gideon refers to Judg 6:33–8:21, which records his defeat of the numerous Midianites with an army of only three hundred. Barak refused to go to battle without the prophetess Deborah (Judg 4:4–16), so perhaps his faith was as much a realization of hers as his own (Bruce 320–21). In any event, he (they) defeated the Canaanite Sisera (Judg 5:1–31). Samson (Judg 13:1–16:31) also seems unlikely, although Judg 13:25 presents his acknowledgment of God's spirit for his military victories (e.g., Judg 15:18). Jephthah prevailed against the Ammonites (Judg 10:6–11:32) and demonstrated his conviction that God would guide him. That feat, however, is usually overshadowed by the rash vow that led to his daughter's death (11:29–39).

The last two individuals are unsurprising. Samuel and David both appear in other Jewish *exempla* (see Lane 2:384–85). From this point forward, no individuals are named, although specific individuals are apparently in view at certain points. The predominant theme of "journeying" in both Abraham's and Moses's life may account for their extended treatment and for David's cursory treatment.

VERSE 33

οἳ διὰ πίστεως κατηγωνίσαντο βασιλείας,
who by faith conquered kingdoms,

The antecedent of οἵ is the list in v. 32. The rel. pron. functions as the subj. of κατηγωνίσαντο and the following series of finite vbs. The def. rel. pron. is used for the indef. one, ὅστις (BDF §293). The first grouping of three clauses concerns military and political victories accomplished "by faith" (Attridge 348). Each of the three vbs. is followed by a single obj. (Cockerill 588). This first clause could allude to any number of individuals, including any one of the six individuals just named. Κατηγωνίσαντο is the 3rd pl. aor. mid. indic. of καταγωνίζομαι, "conquer" (most EVV; BDAG 516b; E. Stauffer, *TDNT* 1:134–39; BGk. hapax). Γωνίζομαι is intrans., but the compound vb. is trans. followed by the acc. (R 477; Moule 37). The compound vb. is intensive (R 606). The pls. from here to v. 38 are "generalizing plurals" (Wallace 404). This aor. and those that follow are constative (Wallace 557–58). Διὰ πίστεως is instr. (par. πίστει), modifying κατηγωνίσαντο. Βασιλείας (acc. pl. fem.) is the obj. of the finite vb.

εἰργάσαντο δικαιοσύνην,
administered justice,

Εἰργάσαντο is the 3rd pl. aor. mid. indic. of ἐργάζομαι (BDAG 389c). Δικαιοσύνην is the obj. of the vb. The collocation may be tr. "administered justice" (most EVV; BDAG 247c). This clause may allude to the establishment of the monarchy. A sim. expression is used of David in 2 Sam 8:15 (Lane 2:386). Trying to identify a specific referent for this clause or any of the others, however, defeats the intent of the author, which is to present "an open-ended, innumerable host of the faithful" (Cockerill 586 n. 1).

ἐπέτυχον ἐπαγγελιῶν,
obtained promises,

Ἐπέτυχον is the 3rd pl. aor. act. indic. of ἐπιτυγχάνω, "obtain" (most EVV; BDAG 385c), "gain" (NET, NIV). The vb. is followed by the gen. obj. ἐπαγγελιῶν (R 509). The ref. is too general to align with any specific promise. It is unlikely that an allusion to the Abrahamic promises is intended. Each of the six individuals in v. 32 as well as many other individuals recorded in the OT received divine promises that were later fulfilled.

ἔφραξαν στόματα λεόντων,
shut the mouths of lions,

The next grouping of three clauses focuses on deliverance (Attridge 348; Lane 2:386). Each of these three vbs. is followed by an obj. with a gen. modifier (Cockerill 588–89). Ἔφραξαν is the 3rd pl. aor. act. indic. of φράσσω, "shut" (most EVV; BDAG 1065c), "close" (CEV, NAB), "stop" (Cassirer, ESV). Στόματα (acc. pl. neut. of στόμα, -ατος, τό, "mouths" or "jaws" [BDAG 947b]) is modified by λεόντων (gen. pl. masc. of λέων, -οντος, ὁ, "lion" [BDAG 593c]), indicating poss. This is clearly an allusion to Dan 6:1–28, although Samson (Judg 14:5–6) or David (1 Sam 17:34–37) could also be possible.

VERSE 34

ἔσβεσαν δύναμιν πυρός,
quenched the raging of fire,

Ἔσβεσαν is the 3rd pl. aor. act. indic. of σβέννυμι, "quench" (most EVV), "put out" (CEV, NAB; BDAG 917b). Δύναμιν is the obj. of the vb. and is modified by πυρός. EVV vary here: "power of fire" (ESV, NASB), "fury of the flames" (NIV), "raging fire(s)" (NAB, NET). The allusion here is to Shadrach, Meshach, and Abednego (Dan 3:18–50).

ἔφυγον στόματα μαχαίρης,
escaped the edge of the sword,

Ἔφυγον is the 3rd pl. aor. act. indic. of φεύγω, "escape" (most EVV; BDAG 1052c). Στόματα (acc. pl. neut. of στόμα, -ατος, τό, "edge" [most EVV; BDAG 947b]) is modified by μαχαίρης (gen. sg. fem. of μάχαιρα, -ης, ἡ, "sword"), indicating poss. See comments on 4:12. The unusual sense of στόμα as "edge" may reflect a Sem. idiom (Lane 2:387). The pl. indicates that swords often had two cutting edges (Koester 513). The allusion here could be to David escaping from Saul (1 Sam 17:45–47) or Absalom (2 Sam 14:15), Elijah from Jezebel (1 Kgs 19:1–18), Elisha from Jehoram (2 Kings 6:26–7:2), or even Jeremiah from Jehoiakim (Jer 26:7–24).

ἐδυναμώθησαν ἀπὸ ἀσθενείας,
gained strength in weakness,

The third and final grouping once again focuses on military victories (Attridge 348–49). Ἐδυναμώθησαν is the 3rd pl. aor. pass. indic. of δυναμόω, "gained strength" (NET), "pass fr. weakness to strength" (BDAG 263d). Ἀσθενείας is the gen. sg. fem. of ἀσθένεια, -ας, ἡ, "weakness" (most EVV; BDAG 142b). Ἀπό has a temp. sense here, "after" (BDF §209[4]). The "empowerment" is for battle and could refer to Gideon (Judg 6:1–8:35), Esther (Esther 7), or Judith (Judith 8). If healing is intended, then a ref. to Hezekiah is possible (Isa 38:1–8).

ἐγενήθησαν ἰσχυροὶ ἐν πολέμῳ,
became mighty in battle,

The vb. ἐγενήθησαν suggests an ingressive idea. The pass. may be a divine pass. Ἰσχυροί (nom. pl. masc. of ἰσχυρός, -ά, -όν, "mighty" [ESV, NASB, NET], "powerful" [NIV]) functions as a pred. adj. Ἐν πολέμῳ (dat. sg. masc. of πόλεμος, -ου, ὁ, "battle" [most EVV], "war" [ESV, NASB; BDAG 844b]) modifies ἐγενήθησαν ἰσχυροί, indicating ref. Again, any one of the previously mentioned individuals could be in view here, as could individuals during the Maccabean era (see Cockerill 590; Lane 2:387). The language here may reflect Sir 46:1 (Attridge 349).

παρεμβολὰς ἔκλιναν ἀλλοτρίων.
and put foreign armies to flight.

Ἔκλιναν is the 3rd pl. aor. act. indic. of κλίνω, "route" (NIV), "put to flight" (ESV, NET), "turn back" (NAB); cf. BDAG 550a. The vb. "has the nuance of breaking a military formation" (Lane 2:381 n. *j*). Παρεμβολάς is the acc. pl. fem. of παρεμβολή,

-ῆς, ἡ, "army" (BDAG 775a–b). Ἀλλοτρίων is the gen. pl. masc. of ἀλλότριος, -ία, -ον. As with 11:9, this adj. means "foreign" (BDAG 47c; cf. "belonging to another" [R 748]). The gen. is descriptive. The allusion is likely to Judith, who put foreign armies to flight, but also to later Jewish history (Lane 2:387).

VERSE 35

ἔλαβον γυναῖκες ἐξ ἀναστάσεως τοὺς νεκροὺς αὐτῶν·
Women received their dead, raised to life again.

This v. functions as the climax to the nine previous clauses (Cockerill 590), while also introducing the next major grouping (see comments above on structure). Γυναῖκες (nom. pl. fem. of γυνή, -αικός, ἡ, "women"; *pace* "wives" [NJB]) is the subj. of ἔλαβον; νεκρούς ("dead [people]") is the obj. The adj. is modified by αὐτῶν. Ἀναστάσεως is the gen. sg. fem. of ἀνάστασις, -εως, ἡ, "resurrection." Some EVV tr. this noun as a vb. (e.g., "raised to life" [NET; NIV adds "again"]). "Resuscitation" is more accurate, since each of the individuals raised to life would eventually die. Ἐκ (ἐξ before a vowel) indicates means (Harris 104–5).

The likely allusions here include the widow of Zarephath (1 Kgs 17:17–24 [Elijah]), the Shunammite woman (2 Kgs 4:17–37 [Elisha]). The ref. to women probably rules out an allusion to Genesis 22 (*pace* Attridge 349). The wording of this clause may have been influenced by LXX 2 Kgs 4:37 (Lane 2:388).

ἄλλοι δὲ ἐτυμπανίσθησαν οὐ προσδεξάμενοι τὴν ἀπολύτρωσιν,
Other people were tortured, not accepting release,

Ἄλλοι δέ introduces a "change of subj." within the sentence that extends from v. 32 to v. 40 (Lane 2:381 n. *k*). Δέ is left untr. in many EVV. This new group is characterized by those whose faith enabled them to endure torture and even martyrdom. Ἐτυμπανίσθησαν is the 3rd pl. aor. pass. indic. of τυμπανίζω, "torture" (most EVV; BDAG 1019d; NT hapax). The cognate τύμπανον (not found in BGk.) denotes a drum on a rack or stake (Attridge 349; Lane 2:388). The specific form of torture may have entailed "being stretched on a frame and beaten to death" (Bruce 325; see discussion in Koester 514; Lane 2:388–89; cf. "tortured on the wheel" [TCNT]). It could also refer to torture in general (Attridge 349; Cockerill 591). The allusion is likely to Eleazer (2 Macc 6:19, 28), who refused to eat (unkosher) pork and was thus tortured to death. It also alludes to the Maccabean mother and her seven sons who chose torture and death rather than break Torah (2 Macc 7:1–42).

Προσδεξάμενοι is the nom. pl. masc. of the aor. mid. ptc. of προσδέχομαι, "accept" (NASB, NET; BDAG 877a). The neg. ptc. is temp., indicating antecedent time to ἐτυμπανίσθησαν. In 9:15, ἀπολύτρωσιν had the sense of "ransom" or "redemption"; here the sense is of "release" (most EVV). (See comments on 9:15.) The neg. μή is often used with a ptc., but οὐ is not uncommon and may indicate that "the negative is clear-cut and decisive" (R 1137–38) or reflects CGk (BDF §430[3]). Some EVV tr.

the neg. ptc. "refuse" (e.g., NIV). All of these Maccabean martyrs could have avoided torture if they had been willing to recant, which would have given them "release" (see esp. 2 Macc 6:22, 30).

ἵνα κρείττονος ἀναστάσεως τύχωσιν·
so that they might gain a better resurrection.

Ἵνα followed by the subjunc. indicates purpose. Τύχωσιν is the 3rd pl. aor. act. subjunc. of τυγχάνω, "obtain" (NASB, NET, NRSV), "gain" (NIV); cf. BDAG 1019b. Ἀναστάσεως is the gen. sg. fem. of ἀνάστασις, -εως, ἡ, "resurrection." Κρείττονος (see comments on 1:4) modifies ἀναστάσεως ("a better resurrection" [most EVV]; but cf. "rise again to a better life" [ESV]). (The two-ending comp. κρείττονος uses the same form for modifying masc. or fem. subst.) A "better resurrection" likely hints at the distinction between physical resuscitation in the first part of the v. and the hope for eternal resurrection here. Although the OT does not present a clear understanding of resurrection (but cf. Dan 12:3), the hope for a final resurrection (often understood along the lines of Jews or "the righteous") began to emerge in STL (e.g., 2 Macc 7:9, 14, 23, 36). As the author will make clear in v. 40, eternal resurrection is only possible after the death and resurrection of Christ (cf. Bruce 325; Cockerill 591).

VERSE 36

ἕτεροι δὲ ἐμπαιγμῶν καὶ μαστίγων πεῖραν ἔλαβον,
Others experienced mockings and scourgings,

Ἕτεροι δέ introduces the next grouping in the sentence (vv. 36–40). Δέ is left untr. in many EVV. As with ἄλλοι, ἕτεροι refers to a large and somewhat vague group that contributes to the rhetorical effect of the *exempla*. This final grouping likely overlapped with some of the audience's own experiences (cf. Cockerill 592). This unspecified group is the subj. of ἔλαβον. Πεῖραν is the acc. sg. fem. of πεῖρα, -ας, ἡ. In v. 29, it had the act. sense of "attempt," but here it is more pass.: "faced" (NIV), "experienced" (NET; BDAG 792d; Attridge 350). Ἐμπαιγμῶν is the gen. pl. masc. of ἐμπαιγμός, -οῦ, ὁ, "mocking" (most EVV; BDAG 323b; C. Bertram, *TDNT* 5:635–36; NT hapax), "jeers" (NIV). Μαστίγων is the gen. pl. fem. of μάστιξ, -ιγος, ἡ, "flogging" (ESV, NET, NIV), "scourgings" (NASB; cf. BDAG 620d). Both gen. modify πεῖραν, as descriptive gen.

ἔτι δὲ δεσμῶν καὶ φυλακῆς·
as well as bonds and imprisonment.

The adv. ἔτι indicates an addition to the previous argument (BDAG 400 b–c), with πεῖραν ἔλαβον understood from the first part of the v. ("still others" [NKJV]). Δεσμῶν is the gen. pl. masc. of δεσμός, -οῦ, ὁ, "chains" (ESV, NET, NIV), "bonds" (most EVV; BDAG 219c). Φυλακῆς is the gen. sg. fem. of φυλακή, -ῆς, ἡ, "put into prison," "imprisonment" (ESV, NET, NIV). Both gen. modify πεῖραν, as descriptive gen. The allusion here could be to Jeremiah, who was placed in "stocks" (Jer 20:2), mocked (Jer 20:7–10), beaten, and imprisoned (Jer 37:15; 38:6–13). It could also refer to the seven brothers in 2 Macc 7:7, 10. Additionally, this v. could refer to members of the community who had experienced persecution (cf. Heb 10:32–35 [Attridge 350; Bruce 327; Cockerill 592]).

VERSE 37

ἐλιθάσθησαν,
They were stoned,

Ἐλιθάσθησαν is the 3rd pl. aor. pass. indic. of λιθάζω, "stoned" (most EVV; BDAG 595b). Tradition held that Jeremiah was stoned to death (Cockerill 593; Lane 2:390). The allusion could also be to the prophet Zechariah, stoned by King Joash (2 Chr 24:21–22), who is mentioned by Jesus in Luke 11:51.

ἐπρίσθησαν,
they were sawed in two,

Ἐπρίσθησαν is the 3rd pl. aor. pass. indic. of πρίζω, "saw in two" (most EVV; BDAG 863c; BGk. hapax). Still considered a generalizing pl., this ref. seems to have one individual, Isaiah, in view (Wallace 404–405). The apocryphal work *The Martyrdom and Ascension of Isaiah* (5:1–14) records that he was sawn in two with a wooden saw during Manasseh's reign. This horrific practice was continued in Roman times (Lane 2:390).

Many mss. add ἐπειράσθησαν ("they were tempted") either before or after ἐπρίσθησαν. Partly due to this inconsistent placement, the UBS adopted the shorter rdg. of ἐπρίσθησαν, with a {C} rating (Metzger 603–603). The longer rdg. is reflected in some EVV (ASV, KJV, NASB).

ἐν φόνῳ μαχαίρης ἀπέθανον,
they died by the sword,

Ἀποθνήσκω often means "die," but context suggests "put to death" (NASB, NIV), "murdered" (NET), "killed" (ESV). Φόνῳ is the dat. sg. masc. of φόνος, -ου, ὁ, "murder" (BDAG 1063d), although untr. in many EVV. Ἐν φόνῳ is instr. (R 534). Μαχαίρης (see comments on 11:34) modifies φόνῳ as a gen. of means. The two previous pass. vbs. and this intrans. vb. with an instr. prep. phrase underscore the powerlessness of the victims (Cockerill 593).

This likely refers to the prophet Uriah (Jer 26:23). It is unclear if the author also intended an allusion to John the Baptist (Mark 6:27) or James (Acts 12:2), both of whom were killed by the sword. General refs. to death by the sword include 1 Kgs 19:10; Dan 11:31–33.

περιῆλθον ἐν μηλωταῖς, ἐν αἰγείοις δέρμασιν,
they wandered about in sheepskins, in goatskins,

Περιῆλθον is the 3rd pl. aor. act. indic. of περιέρχομαι, "went about" (many EVV; BDAG 800c). Μηλωταῖς is the dat. pl. fem. of μηλωτή, -ῆς, ἡ, "sheepskins" (most EVV; BDAG 648a). Αἰγείοις is the dat. pl. neut. of αἴγειος, -εία, -ειον, "of a goat" (BDAG 25b). Δέρμασιν is the dat. pl. neut. of δέρμα, -ατος, τό, "skin," "hide" (BDAG 218d). Most EVV conflate the two appos.: "goatskins." Untreated animal skins were "the most primitive dress imaginable" and suggested "severe deprivation or asceticism" (Koester 515). The sheepskin probably alludes to Elijah and Elisha (2 Kgs 1:8).

ὑστερούμενοι, θλιβόμενοι, κακουχούμενοι,
destitute, afflicted, and mistreated.

Ὑστερούμενοι is the nom. pl. masc. of the pres. mid. or pass. ptc. of ὑστερέω, "destitute" (most EVV), "needy" (NAB), "homeless" (NJB); cf. BDAG 1043c. Θλιβόμενοι is the nom. pl. masc. of the pres. mid. ptc. of θλίβω, "afflicted" (many EVV), "persecuted" (NIV, NRSV), "oppressed" (NLT); cf. BDAG 457b. Κακουχούμενοι is the nom. pl. masc. of the pres. mid. ptc. of κακουχέω, "tormented" (NAB, NRSV), "mistreated" (ESV, NIV, NLT); cf. BDAG 502a (BGk. hapax). All three ptc. are circum., modifying περιῆλθον. These three "generalizing" ptcs. could apply equally to past exemplars or the present community.

VERSE 38

ὧν οὐκ ἦν ἄξιος ὁ κόσμος,
The world was not worthy of them.

The antecedent of ὧν is ἕτεροι (v. 36). The gen. is required by ἄξιος. The subj. of ἦν is the art. κόσμος. "World" (most EVV) refers to unredeemed humanity (Lane 2:392). Ἄξιος (-ία, -ον, "worthy" [most EVV], "too good" [NLT]) is the pred. The rel. clause is best understood as a parenthetical aside, as indicated in some EVV (ESV, NASB, NET).

ἐπὶ ἐρημίαις πλανώμενοι καὶ ὄρεσιν
They wandered in deserts and on mountains,

Πλανώμενοι is the nom. pl. masc. of the pres. mid. ptc. of πλανάω, "wandered" (most EVV; BDAG 502a). The ptc. is circum., modifying an implied περιῆλθον, parallels the final three ptc. of v. 37. Ἐπί with the dat. "has a primarily local sense of 'on' or 'upon'" (Harris 137), although trs. vary according to English usage (e.g., "in," "on"). The prep. governs the four following dat. nouns. Ἐρημίαις is the dat. pl. fem. of ἐρημία, -ας, ἡ, "desert" (most EVV; BDAG 391d). Ὄρεσιν is the dat. pl. neut. of ὄρος, -ους, τό, "mountain" (most EVV; BDAG 725a). The wilderness (desert) or mountains were places to which persecuted individuals often fled (Judg 6:2; 1 Sam 23:14 [see Koester

515]), although they were places of deprivation. Wandering may recall Abraham, and possibly Moses.

καὶ σπηλαίοις καὶ ταῖς ὀπαῖς τῆς γῆς.
hiding in caves and holes in the ground.

Σπηλαίοις is the dat. pl. neut. of σπήλαιον, -ου, τό, "den" (ESV), "cave" (most EVV; BDAG 938a), although some EVV tr. the noun as a ptc. (e.g., "hiding in caves" [NEB, NLT). Ὀπαῖς is the dat. pl. fem. of ὀπή, -ῆς, ἡ, "ravines" (NJB), "crevices" (NAB), "holes" (most EVV; BDAG 715d). The gen. γῆς ("ground" [most EVV], "earth" [ESV, NET]) is descriptive. The allusions could be to prophets (e.g., 1 Kgs 18:4, 13) or individuals in the Maccabean era (1 Macc 2:29–38; 2 Macc 6:11; 10:6).

VERSE 39

Καὶ οὗτοι πάντες μαρτυρηθέντες διὰ τῆς πίστεως οὐκ ἐκομίσαντο τὴν ἐπαγγελίαν,
All these were approved through their faith, but they did not receive what was promised,

The antecedent of οὗτοι comprises the entire previous list (vv. 4–38). The pron. is modified by πάντες. The expression recalls 11:13. (For additional par. between 11:13 and 11:39, see Ellingworth 634). Μαρτυρηθέντες is the nom. pl. masc. of the aor. pass. ptc. of μαρτυρέω. The pass. has the sense of gaining approval (see comments on 11:2). Most EVV tr. the vb. (nearly) the same in v. 2 and this v. Μαρτυρηθέντες here and ἐμαρτυρήθησαν in v. 2 form an *inclusio* around the *exempla* of Hebrews 11. The ptc. is concessive and the pass. indicates divine agency. Διά τῆς πίστεως forms an *inclusio* with διὰ πίστεως in v. 33. The art. in v. 39 refers back to the preceding *exempla* and can thus be tr. "their faith" (most EVV; Cockerill 597). The prep. phrase modifies μαρτυρηθέντες. These two uses of *inclusio*, together with the use of πίστει in vv. 4–31, underscore that each exemplar received divine approval for his or her faith (Cockerill 597). Ἐκομίσαντο is the 3rd pl. aor. mid. indic. of κομίζω, "receive" (most EVV; BDAG 557d). The aor. is constative (Wallace 557–58). The ref. to ἐπαγγελία recalls an important theme in Hebrews (see comments on 6:15). The Abrahamic promises (pl.) now converge and find their fulfillment in the "promise" (sg.) associated with Christ (e.g., "the promised inheritance" [NEB]; cf. Attridge 352). Some EVV tr. the noun as a rel. clause (e.g., "what was promised" [REB, ESV, NASB, NET]), which obscures the focus here on the singular promise in Christ.

VERSE 40

τοῦ θεοῦ περὶ ἡμῶν κρεῖττόν τι προβλεψαμένου, ἵνα μὴ χωρὶς ἡμῶν τελειωθῶσιν.
since God had provided something better for us, so that they would not be made perfect without us.

The first part of the v. is a gen. abs. cstr. (see comments on 2:4). Προβλεψαμένου is the gen. sg. masc. of the aor. mid. ptc. of προβλέπω. The mid. indicates "foresee"

(NAB), "plan" (NIV), "provide" (most EVV; BDAG 866c; NT hapax; Attridge 352). The subj. of the ptc. is θεοῦ. The obj. of the ptc. is κρεῖττόν τι ("something better" [most EVV]). This continues the important use of κρεῖττον in Hebrews (see comments on 1:4). Περὶ ἡμῶν means "for us" (most EVV).

Ἵνα followed by the subjunc. indicates purpose. Τελειωθῶσιν is the 3rd pl. aor. pass. subjunc. of τελειόω, "be made perfect" (most EVV; "reach perfection" [NJB, NLT]). The use of τελειόω continues an important theme in Hebrews (see comments on 2:10). This use of this vb. anticipates the cognate τελειωτής in 12:2. Χωρίς ("without") takes a gen. obj. (ἡμῶν). The ἵνα clause is likely epex., filling out the content of κρεῖττόν τι (Lane 2:392–93). This likely refers to the cleansed conscience and access to God that has been effected by Jesus's sacrifice (Cockerill 598), which ultimately enables the promised eternal inheritance (Heb 9:15) and anticipates 12:22–24.

FOR FURTHER STUDY

84. The Author of Hebrews (11:32)

Allen, David Lewis. "The Authorship of Hebrews: Historical Survey of the Lukan Theory." *CTR* 8 (2011): 3–18.

———. *Lukan Authorship of Hebrews*. Nashville: B & H Academic, 2010.

Anderson, Charles P. "The Epistle to the Hebrews and the Pauline Letter Collection." *HTR* 59 (1966): 429–38.

Black, David Alan. "Who Wrote Hebrews? The Internal and External Evidence Reexamined." *Faith and Mission* 18/2 (2001): 3–26.

*Borchert, Gerald L. "A Superior Book: Hebrews." *RevExp* 82 (1985): 319–22.

Burtness, James H. "Plato, Philo, and the Author of Hebrews." *LQ* 10 (1958): 54–64.

Cockerill, 2–10.

*DeSilva, David A. "The Epistle to the Hebrews in Social-Scientific Perspective." *ResQ* 36 (1994): 1–21.

Ellingworth, 3–21.

*Guthrie, George H. "The Case for Apollos as the Author of Hebrews." *Faith and Mission* 18/2 (2001): 41–56.

Havener, Ivan. "A Concerned Pastor." *TBT* 24 (1986): 223–27.

*Kistemaker, Simon. "The Authorship of Hebrews." *Faith and Mission* 18/2 (2001): 57–69.

Pitts, Andrew W., and Joshua F. Walker. "The Authorship of Hebrews: A Further Development in the Luke-Paul Relationship." Pages 143–84 in *Paul and His Social Relations*. Edited by Stanley E. Porter and Christopher D. Land. Leiden: Brill, 2013.

Pixner, Bargil. "The Jerusalem Essenes, Barnabas and the Letter to the Hebrews." Pages 167–78 in *Intertestamental Essays in Honour of Józef Tadeusz Milik*. Edited by Zdzisław J. Kapera. Cracow: Enigma, 1992.

*van Houwelingen, P. H. R. "Riddles around the Letter to the Hebrews." *Fides Reformata* 16 (2011): 151–62.

HOMILETICAL SUGGESTIONS

Endless Examples of Faith (11:32–40)

1. Faith Found in Unexpected (and Expected) Places (v. 32)
   (a) Unexpected: Gideon, Barak, Samson, Jephthah
   (b) Expected: David, Samuel
2. Remarkable Outcomes (vv. 33–38)
   (a) Justice administered, promises received (v. 33a–c)
   (b) Escaped persecution (vv. 33d, 34a–b)
   (c) Opposition overcome (v. 34c–e)
   (d) Unafraid of death: resuscitation to the hope of resurrection (v. 35)
   (e) Undaunted by extreme persecution; unrecognized in the world (vv. 36–38)
3. Things Are Not As They Seem (vv. 39)
   (a) They died apparently apart from receiving God's promise (v. 39)
   (b) But God had something better: perfection in Christ together with all God's people (v. 40)

9. The Example Par Excellence: Jesus (12:1–3)

STRUCTURE

Several factors indicate the shift to a new section, such as the switch from indics. to impv. forms and the shift from previous exemplars (11:1–40) to the audience's present experience. Yet Heb 12:1–3 is clearly linked to 11:39–40 (e.g., μαρτυρηθέντες in 11:39 and μαρτύρων in 12:1; ἡμῶν in 11:40 and ἡμῖν in 12:1). Moreover, the numerous exemplars of Hebrews 11 culminate in the supreme example of Jesus (Heb 12:1–2), with this single sentence in the Greek functioning as a "closing period" for the *exempla* in Hebrews 11 (R 432). Τοιγαροῦν (12:1) offers another link between 11:1–40 and 12:1–3 (Lane 2:407). See Lane 2:403–6 for the chiastic structure of 12:1–13. Hebrews 12:1–3 is structured around the hort. subjunc. τρέχωμεν (v. 1) and the impv. ἀναλογίσασθε (v. 3). Following this initial exhortation, the author presents the essential link between godly discipline and legitimate Sonship (vv. 4–11), which is followed by a concluding exhortation (vv. 12–13).

1 Τοιγαροῦν καὶ ἡμεῖς τοσοῦτον ἔχοντες περικείμενον ἡμῖν νέφος μαρτύρων,
ὄγκον ἀποθέμενοι πάντα καὶ τὴν εὐπερίστατον ἁμαρτίαν,
δι᾽ ὑπομονῆς
τρέχωμεν τὸν προκείμενον ἡμῖν ἀγῶνα
2 ἀφορῶντες εἰς τὸν τῆς πίστεως ἀρχηγὸν καὶ τελειωτὴν Ἰησοῦν,
ὃς ἀντὶ τῆς προκειμένης αὐτῷ χαρᾶς
ὑπέμεινεν σταυρὸν
αἰσχύνης καταφρονήσας
ἐν δεξιᾷ τε τοῦ θρόνου τοῦ θεοῦ κεκάθικεν.
3 ἀναλογίσασθε γὰρ τὸν τοιαύτην ὑπομεμενηκότα
ὑπὸ τῶν ἁμαρτωλῶν
εἰς ἑαυτὸν ἀντιλογίαν,
ἵνα μὴ κάμητε ταῖς ψυχαῖς ὑμῶν ἐκλυόμενοι.

VERSE 1

Τοιγαροῦν καὶ ἡμεῖς τοσοῦτον ἔχοντες περικείμενον ἡμῖν νέφος μαρτύρων,
Therefore, since we also have such a large cloud of witnesses surrounding us,

The syntax in this v. is complex, but it demonstrates the author's "elegant, genuinely oratorical word order" (BDF §473[2]) in which modifiers normally placed in close proximity are separated for effect. Τοιγαροῦν (τοί + γαρ + οὖν) is inferential, "therefore" (most EVV; BDAG 1009b). It occurs only here and in 1 Thess 4:8. (Τοί may be "the loc. of the indef. τί" [R 1154]). Καί is ascensive ("also" [untr. in most EVV]). The nom. ἡμεῖς is emph. (BDF §277; cf. Wallace 323) and anticipates τρέχωμεν (see below). The collocation τοιγαροῦν καὶ ἡμεῖς stresses what the audience already *has* (ἔχοντες), continuing a sim. emph. elsewhere in Hebrews (e.g., 4:14–15; 6:18–19;

8:1; 10:19 [Cockerill 602]). The first pers. is inclusive of the author and the audience (Wallace 398).

Ἔχοντες is causal ("since," most EVV) and modifies τρέχωμεν (see below). The correl. adj. τοσοῦτον (τοσοῦτος, -αύτη, -οῦτον; "so great" [ESV, NASB], "such a great" [NET, NIV], "such a large" [BDAG 1012c]) modifies νέφος (acc. sg. neut. of νέφος, -ους, τό, "cloud" [most EVV] or "host" [Cassirer; BDAG 670 b–c; BGk. hapax), which is the obj. of the ptc. Μαρτύρων (gen. pl. masc. of μάρτυς, μάρτυρος, ὁ, "witness" [most EVV]) is a descriptive gen., modifying νέφος. Περικείμενον is the acc. sg. neut. of the pres. mid. ptc. of περικεῖμαι, "surround" (many EVV; BDAG 803d). The ptc. is pred., modifying νέφος. The compound vb. περικεῖμαι is followed by a dat., ἡμῖν ("us" [R 542]). Some EVV tr. the ptc. as a finite vb. (e.g., "we are surrounded" [e.g., ESV, NET, NIV]).

A cloud was a common ancient metaphor for a crowd (Koester 522; cf. Attridge 354; Bruce 333). Here the ref. is to οὗτοι πάντες of 11:39, indicating vastness and unity (Lane 2:408). There are several aspects of μάρτυς that are relevant and may have influenced the author's word choice (summary based on Koester 522).

1. Μάρτυς could refer to a spectator at an athletic competition at a stadium or arena (Attridge 354; Ellingworth 638), in both Greco-Roman and Jewish literature (e.g., Wis 1:6). Yet here, the witnesses are clearly more than pass. spectators (Lane 2:408; Attridge 354–55; Koester 535)—they are "fans," cheering the audience on (Cockerill 602–603).
2. The μάρτυρες of Hebrews 11 attest to God's faithfulness and offer motivation for perseverance (Bruce 333; Lane 2:408; cf. BDAG 619b; H. Strathmann, *TDNT* 4:489–91).
3. The μάρτυρες have received approval from God (cf., 11:2, 39) for their faithfulness and are thus an example of what pleases God (Koester 522).

Understanding μάρτυς as "one who dies for one's faith" likely postdates the date of Hebrews, although the mng. of μάρτυς was in flux (Bruce 333–34). The focus here is on endurance, although 12:4 (and the final exemplars in Heb 11) suggest that martyrdom was a real possibility (Attridge 354; Lane 2:408).

ὄγκον ἀποθέμενοι πάντα καὶ τὴν εὐπερίστατον ἁμαρτίαν,
let us lay aside every hindrance and the sin that so easily ensnares us.

Ἀποθέμενοι is the nom. pl. masc. of the aor. mid. ptc. of ἀποτίθημι, "lay aside" (ESV, NASB), "throw off" (NIV), "get rid of" (NET; BDAG 124a). The mid. is indir., with the subj. "acting in relation to himself somehow" (R 804, 810). The ptc. modifies τρέχωμεν (see below) either as an attendant circumstance ptc., indicating action coordinate with the main vb. (Wallace 640–45), or having impv. force from τρέχωμεν (most EVV; Lane 2:398 n. *d*). Ὄγκον is the acc. sg. masc. of ὄγκος, -ου, ὁ. Its position is emph. (Ellingworth 638). This BGk. hapax has an athletic connotation, such as shedding excess body weight (Koester 522) or clothing (athletes often competed naked [Ellingworth 638; Koester 522; cf. "as an athlete strips for action" (Barclay)]), and thus is fig. understood as an "encumbrance" (NASB), "burden" (NAB), "weight" (ESV, NET; BDAG 689d; H. Seesemann, *TDNT* 5:41cf. Col 3:8). It could possibly be understood as excessive pride or one's reputation (Koester 522), but this is disputed (Attridge 355; H. Seesemann, *TDNT* 5:41). Πάντα, modifying ὄγκον, suggests that no specific "weight" is in view, but rather anything that would hinder faithful obedience to Christ ("everything that hinders" [NIV; cf. Lane 2:409]). Moreover, what could hinder one person may not hinder another (Bruce 336; cf. Cockerill 603). The audience was likely familiar with the use of extended athletic imagery for rhetorical effect (Cockerill 603).

The second obj. of ἀποθέμενοι is ἁμαρτίαν. Εὐπερίστατον (εὐ + περί + στατον) is the acc. sg. fem. of εὐπερίστατος, -ον, "so easily entangles" (NASB, NIV), "easily ensnaring" BDF §117(1), "clings so closely" (ESV, NET), "obstructing," "constricting," BDAG 410b; BGk. hapax. It is possible that the author coined this word; it occurs in later writings derived from this passage (Koester 522). The ptc. modifies ἁμαρτίαν (first attrib. pos., Wallace 618). The sg. art. ἁμαρτία suggests that sin in general is meant, not specific sins (Cockerill 604; Lane 2:409). The image is of a "bulky robe [that] impedes running" (Koester 522). The var. rdg. εὐπερίσπαστον ($\mathfrak{P}^{46}$ 1739; "easily distracting" [BDAG 410b]) is not likely orig. (Metzger 604).

δι' ὑπομονῆς τρέχωμεν τὸν προκείμενον ἡμῖν ἀγῶνα
Let us run with endurance the race that lies before us,

Τρέχωμεν is the 1st pl. pres. act. subjunc. of τρέχω, "run" (most EVV; cf. BDAG 1015b; H. Balz, *EDNT* 3:369b). The subjunc. is hort. (Wallace 465). The pres. is continuous (Wallace 518). Ὑπομονῆς is the gen. sg. fem. of ὑπομονή, -ῆς, ἡ (see comments on 10:36). The prep. phrase δι' ὑπομονῆς is instr. ("with endurance" [most EVV; R 583]), or possibly "attendant circumstance" (Ellingworth 639). Ἀγῶνα is the acc. sg. masc. of ἀγών, ἀγῶνος, ὁ, "race," most EVV (BDAG 17b; Lane 2:399 n. *g*). Προκείμενον is the acc. sg. masc. of the pres. mid. ptc. of πρόκειμαι, "lie before" (BDAG 871b). The ptc. is attrib., modifying ἀγῶνα (first attrib. pos., Wallace 618). The ptc. is temp., with both pres. and fut. implications. Τὸν προκείμενον ἡμῖν ἀγῶνα is a "fixed classical expression" for a race marked out by individuals (Attridge 355; cf. "marked out for us" [NIV]; cf. "set before us" [ESV, NASB]). Δι' ὑπομονῆς indicates that endurance, not speed, was paramount (cf. Attridge 355), even though races were often fairly short (Koester 522–23). This phrase anticipates v. 7 and recalls 10:36 (Attridge 356). The vb. takes a dat. obj. (ἡμῖν).

Race imagery is prevalent in the NT (e.g., Acts 20:24; 1 Cor 9:24; Phil 2:16; 2 Tim 4:7). See For Further Study 86 (The Metaphorical Imagery of Hebrews 12). The overall image is of reaching the final goal, not on competition with others (Ellingworth 639). Πρόκειμαι suggests that the race has been set before believers by God (Ellingworth 639; "the race for which we are entered" [REB]). For more on Greco-Roman athletic competitions, see Koester 534–37.

VERSE 2

ἀφορῶντες εἰς τὸν τῆς πίστεως ἀρχηγὸν καὶ τελειωτὴν Ἰησοῦν,
keeping our eyes on Jesus, the source and perfecter of our faith.

Ἀφορῶντες is the nom. pl. masc. of the pres. act. ptc. of ἀφοράω, "fixing our eyes" (NASB), "keeping our eyes fixed" (NET; BDAG 158b). Ἀφοράω followed by εἰς means "to look away from [the immediate surroundings] to" (Lane 2:399 n. *i*). The pres. is durative; the ptc. modifies τρέχωμεν indicating means (e.g., by "keeping" [NLT]). Some EVV tr. the ptc. as a finite vb. (e.g., "let us fix our eyes"). This likely alludes to the practice of athletes looking "to one who was seated in the place of honor" (Koester 523) or the necessity of keeping one's eyes fixed on the race course (Lane 2:410). The vb. is sim. to ἀποβλέπω used of Moses in 11:26 (Cockerill 610 n. 44). The obj. of the ptc. is Ἰησοῦν (last ref. in 10:19), which is placed at the end of the clause for emph. (Ellingworth 640; Lane 2:399 n. *j*). As was true in 2:9 and 6:20, ref. to Jesus stresses his incarnation, suffering, and death (Attridge 356).

Ἀρχηγόν is the first of two appos. of Ἰησοῦν, the second being τελειωτήν (acc. sg. masc. of τελειωτής, -οῦ, ὁ, "perfecter" [most EVV; BDAG 997a; G. Delling, *TDNT* 8:86–87; BGk. hapax]; cf. "the one who brings it to perfection" [Cassirer]). It is possible that the author coined τελειωτής as a par. for ἀρχηγός (but see N. C. Croy, "A Note on Hebrews 12:2," *JBL* 114 [1995]: 117–19). The single art. τόν for ἀρχηγόν and τελειωτήν indicates that they both refer to Jesus (Granville Sharp's rule [Wallace 274]). The placement of τῆς πίστεως indicates that the obj. gen. modifies both ἀρχηγόν and τελειωτήν (Lane 2:399 n. *k*). The position is also emph. (R 502; Cockerill 606). Τῆς πίστεως is best understood as obj. ("the faith" [cf. Ellingworth 640]). Less likely is a subj. sense, as implied in many EVV with "our faith" (Cockerill 606 n. 26). In 2:10 (see comments there), ἀρχηγός was best understood as "pioneer." Here Jesus is the pioneer who has gone before his brothers and sisters to the eternal inheritance. To "pioneer" is added the idea of "source [of faith]" (CSB; Attridge 356; cf. "author" [NASB, NKJV], "founder" [ESV]). Thus Jesus is both the obj. of faith and the supreme example of faith (cf. Koester 523). Together the titles indicate that Jesus is both the source and the one who brings faith to completion (cf. Lane 2:411). See For Further Study 18 (Perfection in Hebrews).

ὃς ἀντὶ τῆς προκειμένης αὐτῷ χαρᾶς
For the joy that lay before him,

The antecedent of ὅς is Ἰησοῦν. Προκειμένης is the gen. sg. fem. of the pres. act. ptc. of πρόκειμαι, "lie before" (NAB), "set before" (ESV, NASB, NIV; BDAG 871b). The rel. clause modifies ὑπέμεινεν (see below). Χαρᾶς (gen. sg. fem. of χαρά, -ᾶς, ἡ, "joy" [most EVV]) is the obj. of ἀντί. The mng. of ἀντί has generated extensive debate. Related to ἀντί is the nature of χάρα, so it is helpful to discuss both together. Although ἀντί has a wide range of mngs. (see esp. Harris 49–56; Wallace 367–68), there are two main options for Heb 12:2:

1. Substitution: "in place of" (Goodspeed), "instead of the joy" (R 574, BDAG 88a; Lane 2:399 n. *1*; 2:413–14). On this view, Christ substituted the joy that was his (e.g., his preincarnate, heavenly joy or perhaps some earthly joy) for the horrors of the cross. Some see a par. with Moses renouncing the wealth of Egypt (Heb 11:24–25 [Harris 55–56]). Supporting this view, *πρόκειμαι* has a present focus elsewhere in Hebrews (6:18; 12:1; BDAG 871b). Some cite the par. with 12:16, where Esau substituted his birthright for one meal.

*2. Reason: "for the joy" (ESV, NASB, NET, NIV), "because of the joy" (NLT), "for the sake of" (NAB, NJB, NRSV; Attridge 357; Cockerill 609 n. 38; cf. Bruce 339; Ellingworth 641, who admits "substitution" is also possible). On this view, Christ endured the cross for the joy placed before him. Greco-Roman texts refer to prizes "set before" athletes (Cockerill 639 n. 38; Koester 523–24; cf. "the joy in store for him as his recompense" [Cassirer]). This could parallel Abraham (11:13) and Moses (11:26), who both "looked forward" to what was promised. Thus the joy before Christ is that of perfectly accomplishing the cleansing of sinners' consciences and gaining their access to God. This joy is linked with Christ's exaltation. Some object to the idea of a "prize," but this imagery fits with the parenetic context of Hebrews 12 (Attridge 357), which is furthered with the use of *ὑπομένω* to describe Jesus on the cross (not found elsewhere in the NT) and the image of his despising the shame (Cockerill 609).

ὑπέμεινεν σταυρόν
he endured the cross,

Ὑπέμεινεν is the 3rd sg. aor. act. indic. of *ὑπομένω*, "endured" (most EVV; BDAG 1039b–c). The use of a cognate of *μένω* continues an important theme in Hebrews and heightens the exhortation to run *δι' ὑπομονῆς*. Μένω and compounds are usually intrans., but here the vb. takes a dir. obj. (R 475), which is *σταυρόν* (acc. sg. masc. of *σταυρός*, -οῦ, ὁ, "cross"). The anar. might be emph. (see Cockerill 609 n. 40).

This is the only ref. to the cross in Hebrews. Crucifixion was designed to be one of the most excruciating, prolonged, and shameful forms of death. It was reserved for the worst criminals. Roman citizens were exempt from this horrific practice. Yet Jesus chose to endure this type of death.

αἰσχύνης καταφρονήσας
despising the shame,

Καταφρονήσας is the nom. sg. masc. of the aor. act. ptc. of *καταφρονέω*, "despise" (most EVV), "scorn" (NIV), "disregard" (NET, NJB, NRSV; BDAG 529d). The compound vb. takes a gen. obj. (R 512). Αἰσχύνης is the gen. sg. fem. of *αἰσχύνη*, -ης, ἡ, "shame" (most EVV; cf. "disgrace" [REB; BDAG 30a]). This clause likely alludes to scorn and derision from passersby as Jesus hung on the cross (Koester 524; see comments on v. 3).

ἐν δεξιᾷ τε τοῦ θρόνου τοῦ θεοῦ κεκάθικεν.
and sat down at the right hand of the throne of God.

The language recalls the allusions to Ps 110:1 in Heb 1:3 and 8:1 (see comments there). Τέ joins "coordinate nonsequential items" (BDAG 993b). *Κεκάθικεν* is the 3rd sg. pf. act. indic. of *καθίζω*, "sit down" [BDAG 491d]). The pf. is emph. (Ellingworth 642; cf. Bruce 353 n. 44). The subst. use of the adj. *δεξιᾷ* (dat. sg. fem. of *δεξιός, -ά, -όν*, "right") assumes the subj. *χείρ* (made explicit in many EVV). The right hand was the place of honor (cf. NLT).

VERSE 3

ἀναλογίσασθε γὰρ τὸν τοιαύτην ὑπομεμενηκότα ὑπὸ τῶν ἁμαρτωλῶν εἰς ἑαυτὸν ἀντιλογίαν,
For consider him who endured such hostility from sinners against himself,

Γάρ draws an inference from the preceding vv. ("for," NASB; untr. in many EVV; BAGD 190a). *Ἀναλογίσασθε* is the 2nd pl. aor. mid. impv. of *ἀναλογίζομαι*, "consider" (most EVV), "think of" (NET, NLT, REB; BDAG 67c; NT hapax). *Ὑπομεμενηκότα* is the acc. sg. masc. of pf. act. ptc. of *ὑπομένω* ("endured," most EVV; see comments on v. 2). The pf. is likely emph., highlighting the "abiding ex. from the life of Jesus" (BDF §342[5]). The ptc. is subst. and refers to Jesus. The correl. adj. *τοιαύτην* (*τοσοῦτος, -αύτη, -οῦτον*; "so great, so large, so much" [BDAG 1012c]) modifies *ἀντιλογίαν* (acc. sg. fem. of *ἀντιλογία, -ας, ἡ*; BDAG 89d; H. Balz, *EDNT* 1:110a), "such hostility" (ESV, NASB), "such opposition" (NET, NIV). The placement of *τοιαύτην* is emph. (Cockerill 611 n. 46). *Ἀντιλογίαν* is the obj. of the ptc. *Ὑπό* has an ablative ("from") sense (R 635). (The "euphonic word play" between *ἀναλογίσασθε* and *ἀντιλογίαν* cannot be rendered in English [Lane 2:400 n. *t*]). This v. likely alludes to Jesus on the cross (Matt 26:45; Mark 14:41; Luke 24:7), although it could include general opposition to Jesus's ministry (e.g., Mark 2:23–3:6; 7:1–13 [Koester 525]).

The rdg. *ἑαυτόν* is rated {C} by the UBS committee ("against himself" [ASV, ESV, NASB, NET; Cockerill 611 n. 48). External evidence supports *ἑαυτούς* (א* D*) or *εἰς αὑτούς* (𝔓13.46 א2 Ψc 33 81 1739*) but the pl. rdg. is difficult to make sense of (*pace* Ellingworth 643–44; Lane 2:400 n. *u*). Thus the sg. rdg. was adopted, even with inferior mss. support (A P 104 326 1241 [Metzger, 604–605]). The pl. is adopted by KJV, RV, TCNT, Goodspeed; cf. Lane 2:416. The pron. is untr. in many EVV.

ἵνα μὴ κάμητε ταῖς ψυχαῖς ὑμῶν ἐκλυόμενοι.
so that you won't grow weary and give up.

Ἵνα followed by the subjunc. indicates purpose. *Κάμητε* is the 2nd pl. aor. act. subjunc. of *κάμνω*, "grow weary" (most EVV; BDAG 506d). The aor. is ingressive (Lane 2:400 n. *v*). The weariness could be physical, but is more likely spiritual or emotional exhaustion (Attridge 358). The dat. *ταῖς ψυχαῖς* is a dat. of respect (Lane 2:400 n. *w*) or is locat. ("in your souls" [NET; R 524]), although it is untr. in many EVV. *Ὑμῶν* indicates poss. It is unclear if ταῖς ψυχαῖς ὑμῶν modifies κάμητε (NET) or ἐκλυόμενοι (ASV, Cassirer). Its placement between the two vb. forms could mean that both are implied (Cockerill 613). Ἐκλυόμενοι is the nom. pl. masc. of the pres. pass. ptc. of ἐκλύω, "give up" (NET, NLT), "lose heart" (NASB, NIV, NRSV), "grow fainthearted" (ESV [BDAG 306d]). The ptc. indicates result (Wallace 639) or is circum. (R 1121), although it is tr. as a finite vb. in many EVV.

FOR FURTHER STUDY

85. Structure of Hebrews 12 (12:1–3)

Black, David Alan. "A Note on the Structure of Hebrews 12:1–2." *Bib* 68 (1987): 543–51.

*Horning, Estella B. "Chiasmus, Creedal Structure, and Christology in Hebrews 12:1–2." *BR* 23 (1978): 37–48.

Neamtu, Andrew. "An Exegesis on the Greek Text of Hebrews 12:2." *Faith and Mission* 16/3 (1999): 30–38.

Rhee, Victor. "Chiasm and the Concept of Faith in Hebrews 12:1–29." *WTJ* 63 (2001): 269–84.

86. The Metaphorical Imagery in Hebrews 12 (12:1–3)

Dautzenberg, C. *EDNT* 1:26–27.

Long, Thomas G. "What Cloud? What Witnesses?: A Preacher's Exegesis of Hebrews 12:1–2." *WW* 28 (2008): 349–57.

Sims, C. "Rethinking Hebrews 12:2." *IBS* 27 (2008): 54–88.

Sisson, Russell B. "Overcoming the Fear of Death: Physical Body and Community in Hebrews." *Scriptura* 90 (2005): 670–78.

87. Christ's Faithfulness in Hebrews (12:1–3)

Longenecker R. "The Foundational Conviction of New Testament Christology: The Obedience/Faithfulness/Sonship of Christ." Pages 473–88 in *Jesus of Nazareth: Lord and Christ: Essays on the Historical Jesus and New Testament Christology*. Edited by Joel B. Green and Max Turner. Grand Rapids: Eerdmans; Paternoster; 1994.

Richardson, Christopher A. *Pioneer and Perfecter of Faith: Jesus' Faith as the Climax of Israel's History in the Epistle to the Hebrews*. Tübingen: Mohr Siebeck, 2012.

Still, Todd D. "Christos as Pistos: The Faith(fulness) of Jesus in the Epistle to the Hebrews." *CBQ* 69 (2007): 746–55.

88. Perseverance in Hebrews (12:3)

deSilva, David A. *Perseverance in Gratitude: A Socio-Rhetorical Commentary on the Epistle "to the Hebrews."* Grand Rapids: Eerdmans, 2000.

Fuller, R. M. *DLNT* 1038–41.

Hauck, F. *TDNT* 4:581–88.

*Marshall, I Howard. *Kept by the Power of God: A Study of Perseverance and Falling Away*. London: Pater oster, 1995.

Peterson, Robert A. "The Perseverance of the Saints: A Theological Exegesis of Four Key New Testament Passages." *Presb* 17 (1991): 95–112.

Whitlark, Jason A. *Enabling Fidelity to God: Perseverance in Hebrews in Light of the Reciprocity Systems of the Ancient Mediterranean World*. Carlisle: Paternoster, 2008.

HOMILETICAL SUGGESTIONS

Eyes on Jesus! (12:1–3)

1. Let Us Run the Race! (vv. 1–2)
   - (a) Encouraged by those who have run it before us (v. 1a)
   - (b) Laying aside all hindrances (v. 1b)
   - (c) Running the race set out before each one (v. 1c)
   - (d) Keeping our focus on Jesus (v. 2a)
     - (1) The pioneer and completer of our faith (v. 2b)
     - (2) The one who endured the cross for the joy before him and despised its shame (v. 2b–c)
     - (3) The one now seated at God's right hand (v. 2d)
2. Consider Jesus! (v. 3a)
   - (a) Who endured such hostility (v. 3b)
   - (b) So that you do not grow weary (v. 3c)

C. PRESSING ON TO THE FUTURE CONSUMMATION (12:4–29)

1. Discipline and Legitimate Children (12:4–11)

STRUCTURE

The overall structure of this section is straightforward: after the initial exhortation (v. 4), Prov 3:11–12 is cited (vv. 5–6), exposited (vv. 7–11), and applied (vv. 12–13 [Cockerill 615]). The citation comprises two par. clauses (v. 5) and two clauses that form a simple chiasm (v. 6; see Lane 2:421). This is followed by a series of short clauses in v. 7 and a cond. in v. 8 (the dependent prot. is indented). Verse 9 comprises a sentence and a question, each of which begins with a long clause and is followed by a very short clause. The contrast between earthly fathers (οἱ μέν) and God the Father (ὁ δέ) continues in v. 10. The four prep. phrases in v. 10 depend on the sg. finite vb. ἐπαίδευον. The section concludes with a summary statement about discipline containing a contrast between its immediate pain and its long-term fruit.

4 Οὔπω μέχρις αἵματος ἀντικατέστητε
πρὸς τὴν ἁμαρτίαν ἀνταγωνιζόμενοι.
5 καὶ ἐκλέλησθε τῆς παρακλήσεως,
ἥτις ὑμῖν ὡς υἱοῖς διαλέγεται,
Υἱέ μου, μὴ ὀλιγώρει παιδείας κυρίου
μηδὲ ἐκλύου ὑπ᾽ αὐτοῦ ἐλεγχόμενος·
6 ὃν γὰρ ἀγαπᾷ κύριος παιδεύει,
μαστιγοῖ δὲ πάντα υἱὸν ὃν παραδέχεται.
7 εἰς παιδείαν ὑπομένετε,
ὡς υἱοῖς ὑμῖν προσφέρεται ὁ θεός.
τίς γὰρ υἱὸς ὃν οὐ παιδεύει πατήρ;
8 εἰ δὲ χωρίς ἐστε παιδείας
ἧς μέτοχοι γεγόνασιν πάντες,
ἄρα νόθοι καὶ οὐχ υἱοί ἐστε.
9 εἶτα τοὺς μὲν τῆς σαρκὸς ἡμῶν πατέρας εἴχομεν παιδευτὰς
καὶ ἐνετρεπόμεθα·
οὐ πολὺ [δὲ] μᾶλλον ὑποταγησόμεθα τῷ πατρὶ τῶν πνευμάτων
καὶ ζήσομεν;
10 οἱ μὲν γὰρ
πρὸς ὀλίγας ἡμέρας
κατὰ τὸ δοκοῦν αὐτοῖς
ἐπαίδευον,
ὁ δὲ
ἐπὶ τὸ συμφέρον
εἰς τὸ μεταλαβεῖν τῆς ἁγιότητος αὐτοῦ.
11 πᾶσα δὲ παιδεία
πρὸς μὲν τὸ παρὸν οὐ δοκεῖ χαρᾶς εἶναι ἀλλὰ λύπης,

ὕστερον δὲ καρπὸν εἰρηνικὸν τοῖς δι᾽ αὐτῆς γεγυμνασμένοις ἀποδίδωσιν δικαιοσύνης.

VERSE 4

Οὔπω μέχρις αἵματος ἀντικατέστητε
. . . you have not yet resisted to the point of shedding your blood.

Ἀντικατέστητε is the 2nd pl. aor. act. indic. of ἀντικαθίστημι, "resist" (most EVV; BDAG 88d). This vb. recalls ἀντιλογίαν in v. 3 (Ellingworth 645). Οὔπω ("not yet" [most EVV; BDAG 737b]) modifies ἀντικατέστητε. Μέχρι (μέχρις before vowels) is a marker that indicates measure, "to the point of" (most EVV; R 645; BDAG 644d). It is followed by the gen. (here αἵματος). The prep. phrase μέχρις αἵματος modifies ἀντικατέστητε. It implies "the shedding of [your] blood" (most EVV). Both the vb. and the prep. phrase suggest "an armed boxing match" or a wrestling match (Lane 2:417; cf. Cockerill 615, 618; Koester 525), both of which were often very bloody, or possibly a "military conflict" (Attridge 360). The expression could refer to the audience's resistance to sin (Koester 525), particularly regarding their response to public shame and ostracism (Attridge 360). Alternatively, the allusion could be to martyrdom (Lane 2:418; cf. "to the point of having to die for your faith" [Barclay], "given your lives" [NLT]), esp. if well-known passages about the Maccabean martyrs were in view (see Cockerill 618–19 n. 20). The severity of the situation is missed in the CEV: "none of you have yet been hurt."

πρὸς τὴν ἁμαρτίαν ἀνταγωνιζόμενοι.
In struggling against sin,

Ἀνταγωνιζόμενοι is the nom. pl. masc. of the pres. mid. ptc. of ἀνταγωνίζομαι, "struggle" (most EVV), "striving" (NASB [BDAG 86d; C. Dautzenberg, *EDNT* 1:26–27; NT hapax]). The ptc. modifies ἀντικατέστητε, indicating attendant circumstance (e.g., "in your struggle" [most EVV]). This vb. recalls the use of ἀγῶνα in v. 1 (Ellingworth 645). The ref. to ἁμαρτία in v. 1 in the context of race imagery could suggest a "subjective, inward struggle against sin," whereas in v. 4 (given the focus on opposition from sinners in v. 3), "sin" possibly refers objectively to any source of hostile opposition to the Church" (Lane 2:418–19; but challenged by Koester 526). Once again the author uses alliteration effectively (αἵματος ἀντικατέστητε . . . ἁμαρτίαν ἀνταγωνιζόμενοι [Attridge 360 n. 11]). The connection between this v. and Heb 10:32–34 suggests that the previous persecution that the audience endured did not (yet) involve martyrdom.

VERSE 5

καὶ ἐκλέλησθε τῆς παρακλήσεως, ἥτις ὑμῖν ὡς υἱοῖς διαλέγεται,
And you have forgotten the exhortation that addresses you as sons:

The clause could be taken as either a statement that continues v. 4 (e.g., "you have not resisted . . . and you have forgotten" [e.g., NASB, NIV, NRSV]) or as a question (e.g., "have you forgotten . . . ?" [NET, NJB, NLT, TNIV; Cockerill 620; Lane 2:401 n. *dd*]). A question has stronger rhetorical effect, but either is possible. Ἐκλέλησθε is the 2nd pl. pf. mid. indic. of ἐκλανθάνομαι, "forget" (most EVV). The compound vb. is intensive ("altogether forgetful" [Cassirer], "completely forgotten" [TNIV];" BDAG 305c; BGk. hapax; Ellingworth 646). The vb. is followed by the gen. (R 509). Παρακλήσεως can indicate either "encouragement" (NIV) or "exhortation" (most EVV), although both are probably in view here ("encouraging exhortation" [Ellingworth 647]). This is the same word that the author uses to describe his own address to the audience (13:22). The antecedent of ἥτις is παρακλήσεως. Διαλέγεται is the 3rd sg. pres. mid. indic. of διαλέγομαι, "inform," "instruct" (BDAG 232b). Notice again that Scripture "addresses" (most EVV) or speaks directly to the audience. The vb. is followed by the dat. (ὑμῖν). The comp. ὡς υἱοῖς underscores the true status of the audience (Ellingworth 647) and is pred. ("as sons" [ESV, NASB, NET; cf. NIV], "as children" [NLT, NRSV, TNIV]; cf. Koester 526).

The author grounds his exhortation in a citation from LXX Prov 3:11–12 (to which he added μου to υἱέ, underscoring the audience's status as sons and daughters [Cockerill 620–21]). The citation offers encouragement that suffering is an affirmation of the dignity of a legitimate child and the assurance of divine purpose behind difficult circumstances: "Sonship and suffering . . . go hand in hand" (Attridge 361).

Υἱέ μου, μὴ ὀλιγώρει παιδείας κυρίου
My son, do not take the Lord's discipline lightly

Υἱέ, the voc. of υἱός (modified by the poss. pron. μου) indicates dir. address ("my son" [most EVV]; "my child" [NRSV]). Ὀλιγώρει is the 2nd sg. pres. act. impv. of ὀλιγωρέω, "regard lightly" (ESV, NASB), "make light of" (NIV, NLT; BDAG 703b); cf. "disdain" (NAB), "scorn" (NET). The word occurs only in LXX Prov 3:5 and its citation here. The vb. is followed by the gen. (παιδείας [R 508]), which is modified by the poss. gen. κυρίου.

The mng. of παιδεία (-ας, ἡ) is debated. Some claim that παιδεία was nonpunitive in Greek thought (e.g., education, training), whereas it was punitive in Jewish thought (e.g., punishment, chastisement). This has been convincingly challenged (see esp. N. Clayton Croy, *Endurance in Suffering: Hebrews 12:1–13 in Its Rhetorical, Religious, and Philosophical Context* [Cambridge: Cambridge University Press, 1998]; cf. Koester 526–27). Overall, Hebrews suggests a nonpunitive, formative function for παιδεία ("discipline" [most EVV; BDAG 748d]; *pace* "the Lord punishes you" [CEV]). The goal is endurance not repentance in this passage (Koester 527; cf. Cockerill 617). This accords with Jesus the Son learning through suffering (Heb 5:8), which is also appropriate for God's sons and daughters (Cockerill 616). Four of the six NT occurrences of παιδεία occur in Heb 12:5–11 (cf. Eph 6:4; 2 Tim 3:16). See For Further Study 91 (Discipline).

μηδὲ ἐκλύου ὑπ᾽ αὐτοῦ ἐλεγχόμενος·
or lose heart when you are reproved by him,

Ἐκλύου is the 2nd sg. pres. mid. impv. of ἐκλύω. Most EVV tr. this vb. and the ptc. in 12:3 consistently; but cf. "faint" (NASB), "be weary" (ESV). Ἐλεγχόμενος is the nom. sg. masc. of the pres. pass. ptc. of ἐλέγχω, "reprove" (ESV, NASB), "rebuke" (NIV), "correct" (NET, NLT ; cf. BDAG 315c); *pace* "punish" (NRSV). The ptc. is circum. ("when" [most EVV]). Ὑπό followed by the gen. indicates the (ultimate) agency of the pass. (Wallace 433), which is here "the Lord." Many EVV tr. the pass. as an act. with "he" as the subj. (but cf. NET, NIV, NLT).

VERSE 6

ὃν γὰρ ἀγαπᾷ κύριος παιδεύει,
for the Lord disciplines the one he loves

Ἀγαπᾷ is the 3rd sg. pres. act. indic. of ἀγαπάω, "love" (most EVV). The subj. of the vb. is κύριος, with ὅν as the obj. The antecedent of ὅν is embedded within the rel. clause (Wallace 340; cf. Ellingworth 649). Παιδεύει is the 3rd sg. pres. act. indic. of παιδεύω, "discipline" (most EVV [BDAG 749b]).

μαστιγοῖ δὲ πάντα υἱὸν ὃν παραδέχεται.
and punishes every son he receives.

Δέ indicates "succession" to the next point (R 1184). Μαστιγοῖ is the 3rd sg. pres. act. indic. of μαστιγόω, "chastises" (ESV, NET), "punish" (NIV, NLT), "discipline" (BDAG 620d; C. Schneider, *TDNT* 4:515–19). The cognate μάστιξ, -ιγος, ἡ ("scourgings" [NASB]) occurred in 11:36, which is reflected in some EVV in this v. (e.g., "scourges" [NASB]). Πάντα υἱόν is the obj. of μαστιγοῖ, although some EVV tr. the phrase as a pred. of παραδέχεται (e.g., "accepts as a son" [NIV]). Παραδέχεται is the 3rd sg. pres. mid. indic. of παραδέχομαι, "receive" (ESV, NASB), "accept" (NET, NIV, NLT; BDAG 761c). Although this vb. may have eschatological implications, that is not the primary focus here (*pace* Ellingworth 650).

VERSE 7

εἰς παιδείαν ὑπομένετε,
Endure suffering as discipline:

The application of the Proverbs citation to the audience is an example of "parenetic midrash" (Lane 2:406). Ὑπομένετε is the 2nd pl. pres. act. indic. of ὑπομένω, "endure" (most EVV; BDAG 1039b–c). The form could be either indic. (ESV, NLT, NASB; Ellingworth 650) or impv. (NET, NIV, NRSV; Lane 2:421; Attridge 361–62). The context favors the impv. Some EVV supply an obj. for ὑπομένετε: ("trials" [NRSV], "hardship" [NIV], "suffering" [NET]), although none is stated in the Gk. Εἰς functions as a pred. acc., reflecting the underlying Heb. (Ellingworth 650): "endure hardship *as* discipline" (Harris 91; see esp. Lane 2:401 n. *jj*). It can also be understood as indicating purpose (ESV, NASB), particularly if ὑπομένετε is taken as an indic. The discipline in view is understood as God's discipline. The wording here is exceptionally terse, with the emph. on εἰς παιδείαν (Cockerill 622–23).

ὡς υἱοῖς ὑμῖν προσφέρεται ὁ θεός.
God is dealing with you as sons.

Προσφέρεται is the 3rd sg. pres. mid. indic. of προσφέρω, "treat" (ESV, NET, NIV, NLT), "deal with" (NASB); pass. in act. sense with dat. of pers. (BDAG 886d; W. Schenk, *EDNT* 3:177d). The comp. ὡς υἱοῖς is pred. ("as sons" [most EVV]; see comments on v. 5). The position of ὁ θεός is emph. (Ellingworth 650). This clause par. the opening part of v. 5 (Cockerill 623).

τίς γὰρ υἱὸς ὃν οὐ παιδεύει πατήρ;
For what son is there that a father does not discipline?

Γάρ introduces the conclusion to be drawn from the previous statement (Ellingworth 650). Both υἱός and πατήρ are anar. indicating "qual. force" (R 794; cf. Z §179). The anar. πατήρ may also indicate that anaphora is not intended (BDF §257[3]). The interr. pron. τίς modifies υἱός (Wallace 345–46). An impers. vb. is implied (e.g., "is" [NIV]). Paternal discipline is a significant biblical theme (e.g., Exod 12:26; 13:14; Deut 6:7; Prov 29:17; Eph 6:4). Παιδεύει is the 3rd sg. pres. act. indic. of παιδεύω, "discipline" (most EVV [BDAG 749b]).

VERSE 8

εἰ δὲ χωρίς ἐστε παιδείας
But if you are without discipline

Δέ develops the argument (Ellingworth 651). Παιδείας (gen. sg. fem.; "discipline" [most EVV]; see comments on v. 5). Some EVV tr. the noun as a vb. (e.g., "if you are not disciplined" [NIV]). Χωρίς ("without") takes a gen. obj. (παιδείας). Εἰ introduces a first-class cond., in which the prot. is assumed to be true for the sake of argument (Wallace 692–94). The rhetorical effect of the cond. strengthens the author's argument (cf. Cockerill 623).

ἧς μέτοχοι γεγόνασιν πάντες,
—which all receive—

The antecedent of ἧς is παιδείας. Πάντες ("all [legitimate children]") modifies μέτοχοι (μέτοχος, -ου, ὁ, "partakers" [NASB]; see comments on 3:1). The noun is followed by the gen. of the obj. shared (e.g., ἧς). The pf. γεγόνασιν indicates a general assertion (BDF §344). Many EVV miss the important use of μέτοχοι by translating the noun as a vb. (e.g., "all receive" [CSB]) or by leaving it untr. (e.g., "everyone undergoes discipline" [NIV]), although ESV attempts to capture it with "in which all have participated."

ἄρα νόθοι καὶ οὐχ υἱοί ἐστε.
then you are illegitimate children and not sons.

Ἄρα ("then" [most EVV]; although freq. untr.) introduces the apod. of the cond. νόθοι (νόθος, -η, -ον), "illegitimate" (most EVV [BDAG 675b; G. Schneirder, *EDNT* 2:470b; NT hapax]). The adj. is subst. (e.g., "illegitimate children" [ESV, NASB], "not legitimate" [NIV]; cf. "bastard" [NAB, NEB, NJB]). Καί is epex. (Ellingworth 652), further explaining νόθοι. Both νόθοι and υἱοί are pred.

The author wants to make clear that persecution and suffering do not indicate that God does not care or that believers are somehow out of God's will; indeed, such experiences confirm their true status (e.g., "true sons" [NIV]). Moreover, illegitimate sons could not receive inheritance (Koester 528).

VERSE 9

εἶτα τοὺς μὲν τῆς σαρκὸς ἡμῶν πατέρας εἴχομεν παιδευτάς
Furthermore, we had human fathers discipline us,

Εἶτα ("besides" [ESV, NET], "moreover" [NIV, NRSV], "furthermore" [NASB]) introduces a new aspect of the argument (BDAG 295c). A μὲν . . . δέ cstr. (with δέ sometimes omitted; see below) often indicates a comp. or contrast—here with another example of an *a fortiori* argument, arguing from the lesser (what is true of human fathers) to the greater (what is true of the heavenly Father). The impf. εἴχομεν could be habitual or customary (Wallace 548). Πατέρας is the obj. of the vb., which is modified by σαρκός as an attrib. gen. ("human fathers" [NIV, NJB], "human parents" [NRSV], or "earthly fathers" [ESV, NASB, NET]). Παιδευτάς (acc. pl. masc. of παιδευτής, -οῦ, ὁ, "instructor," "teacher" [BDAG 749a]; H. Balz, *EDNT* 3:3d) is a pred. acc., "a sort of apposition" (R 480; or an obj. complement), to πατέρας. Ἡμῶν modifies παιδευτάς for poss. The noun is tr. as a vb. (NET), freq. with ἡμῶν understood as the obj. (most EVV).

καὶ ἐνετρεπόμεθα·
and we respected them.

Καί links εἴχομεν and ἐνετρεπόμεθα in this clause. Ἐνετρεπόμεθα is the 1st pl. impf. mid. indic. of ἐντρέπω, "respect" (most EVV; BDAG 341b). An implied obj. αὐτούς is supplied by most EVV ("them").

οὐ πολὺ [δὲ] μᾶλλον ὑποταγησόμεθα τῷ πατρὶ τῶν πνευμάτων
Shouldn't we submit even more to the Father of spirits

The neg. adv. οὐ introduces a question that expects a positive answer (Lane 2:402 n. *uu*). Some EVV, however, tr. the clause as an implicit question (e.g., "how much more . . . and live!" [GNT, NIV]). The adv. πολύ strengthens μᾶλλον (comp. of the rare adv. μάλα, "very, exceedingly" [BDAG 613d])—"much more" (ESV), "all the more" (NET). Δέ occurs in some mss. due to μέν in the first part of the v.; it is probably not original (BDF §447[6]). Ὑποταγησόμεθα is the 1st pl. fut. pass. indic. of ὑποτάσσω, "submit" (most EVV; "be subject" [ESV]).

The expression "the Father of the spirits" may derive from LXX Num 16:22, 27:16 to indicate God's transcendence (see Cockerill 625). The art. before πνευμάτων could indicate poss. ("the God of our spirits" [NIV; Bruce 344 n. 80; Cockerill 625]). The expression intends a contrast with earthly fathers, although "Father of our spirits" (Moffatt) misses the allusion to God's transcendence. Also misleading is "Father of souls" (TCNT).

καὶ ζήσομεν;
and live?

Καί parallels its usage in the first part of this v. Ζήσομεν is the 1st pl. fut. act. indic. of ζάω, "live" (most EVV). There may be an allusion to Deut 30:11–20 here (Lane 2:424). The emph. on "life lived in enjoyment of God's blessings" in Proverbs is now understood as eternal life (Cockerill 625; cf. "live forever" [NLT]). NJB's "earn life" is misleading, as is "in order to learn to live" (Barclay). This v. anticipates the description of the heavenly Zion in 12:18–24.

VERSE 10

οἱ μὲν γὰρ πρὸς ὀλίγας ἡμέρας
For . . . us for a short time

Γάρ (untr. in some EVV) indicates why submission to God is better than submission to earthly fathers (Ellingworth 654). Μὲν . . . δέ contrasts the discipline of earthly fathers (οἱ) and God (ὁ). Both arts. function par. to pers. prons. (Wallace 212–13; BDF 250). Ὀλίγας (acc. pl. fem. of ὀλίγος, -η, -ον, "few" [BDAG 702d]) modifies ἡμέρας. Πρός often indicates "extension," as does the acc. ἡμέρας. "Day" indicates a limited time period, not necessarily a 24-hour period (e.g., "for a little while" [NET, NIV], "for a short time" [ESV, NASB], "for a few years" [NLT], "this short life" [JB]). The prep. phrase modifies ἐπαίδευον (see below).

κατὰ τὸ δοκοῦν αὐτοῖς ἐπαίδευον,
based on what seemed good to them . . . they disciplined . . .

Δοκοῦν is the acc. sg. neut. of the pres. act. ptc. of δοκέω, "seem." The use of a neut. subst. ptc. to indicate an abstract quality is unusual in the NT (R 1109). The idiomatic phrase is reflected in EVV: "as seemed good to them" (NET), "as they thought best" (NIV, REB); "at their discretion" (Cassirer; BDAG 255c). Ἐπαίδευον is the 3rd pl. impf.

act. indic. of παιδεύω, "discipline" (most EVV [BDAG 749b]). The impf. is customary or habitual (Wallace 548). The vb. is the cognate of παιδεία (see v. 5). The antecedent of αὐτοῖς (dat. of ref.) is "earthly fathers" (v. 9 [made explicit in NIV, NJB]).

ὁ δὲ ἐπὶ τὸ συμφέρον
but he does it for our benefit,

Ὁ δέ refers to God. Ἐπαίδευον is understood elliptically from the previous clause (Ellingworth 655). Συμφέρον is the acc. sg. neut. of the pres. act. ptc. of συμφέρω. The subst. ptc. indicates "benefit" (NET), "profit, advantage" (BDAG 960b); cf. "our good" (ESV, NASB, NIV), "our true welfare" (REB). Ἐπί indicates purpose (Harris 138).

εἰς τὸ μεταλαβεῖν τῆς ἁγιότητος αὐτοῦ.
so that we can share his holiness.

Εἰς with an art. inf. indicates purpose (Wallace 590–92). Μεταλαβεῖν is the aor. act. inf. of μεταλαμβάνω, "have a share in" (BDAG 639b). Many EVV tr. the inf. as a finite vb. (e.g., "that we may share" [most EVV]). The vb. is followed by the gen. ("a partitive dir. obj." [Wallace 132–33]). Ἁγιότητος is gen. sg. fem. of ἁγιότης, -ητος, ἡ, "holiness" (most EVV; BDAG 11d; H. Balz, *EDNT* 1:20a–b). This draws on a key idea that God's people should be holy as he is holy (e.g., Lev 19:2; 1 Pet 1:15).

VERSE 11

πᾶσα δὲ παιδεία πρὸς μὲν τὸ παρὸν οὐ δοκεῖ χαρᾶς εἶναι ἀλλὰ λύπης,
No discipline seems enjoyable at the time, but painful.

The first δέ joins this final, summarizing statement to the previous argument ("now" [NET, NRSV]; untr. in most EVV). The μὲν . . . (second) δέ cstr. indicates a contrast between pres. discipline (v. 11a) and fut. sanctification (v. 11b). The subj. of δοκεῖ is παιδεία (see v. 5), which is modified by πᾶσα. Many EVV take the neg. with παιδεία and not the vb. (e.g., "no discipline" [NIV]) or leave it untr. (ESV, NASB, NET). Εἶναι is the complement of δοκεῖ. Both χαρᾶς (χαρά, -ᾶς, ἡ) and λύπης (λύπη, -ης, ἡ; BDAG 605a) are pred. qual. gen. of εἶναι (R 497; BDF §165). They are tr. as adj. in many EVV: "joyful" (NASB, NET), "pleasant" (ESV, NIV); "painful" (ESV, NET, NIV), "sorrowful" (NASB). Χαρά here may form an *inclusio* with χαρά in 12:2 (Ellingworth 656). Παρόν is the acc. sg. neut. of the pres. act. ptc. of πάρειμι. The subst. ptc. means "the present" (BDAG 774a; G. Schneider, *EDNT* 3:36d). Πρός often indicates "extension," as does the acc. ("while it is happening," NLT; R 625]; cf. "at the time" [NET, NIV], "for the moment" [ESV, NASB]). Πρὸς τὸ παρόν modifies δοκεῖ temp.

ὕστερον δὲ καρπὸν εἰρηνικὸν τοῖς δι᾽ αὐτῆς γεγυμνασμένοις ἀποδίδωσιν δικαιοσύνης.
Later on, however, it yields the peaceful fruit of righteousness to those who have been trained by it.

The contrast between pres. discipline and fut. reward is signaled by δέ ("however" [NIV]). The neut. acc. ὕστερον (ὕστερος, -α, -ον) functions as an adv. ("later on" [NIV], "afterwards" [NASB; BDAG 1044b]). Ἀποδίδωσιν is the 3rd sg. pres. act. indic. of ἀποδίδωμι, "yield" (ESV, NASB), "produce" (NET, NIV). The subj. of the vb. is understood to be παιδεία. The obj. of the vb. is καρπόν ("harvest" [NIV], "fruit" [ESV, NET]).

Εἰρηνικόν (εἰρηνικός, -ή, -όν, "peaceful" [most EVV; BDAG 288c]) may allude to the OT concept of shalom, paralleling the concept of rest in Hebrews. Most EVV take the adj. as modifying καρπόν. Δικαιοσύνης ("righteousness" [most EVV]) is either epex. ("a result full of peace—namely, righteousness" [Weymouth]) or a *gen. of content ("the peaceful fruit of righteousness" [many EVV; Ellingworth 656]). Some EVV tr. the two modifiers (εἰρηνικόν, δικαιοσύνης) as par. (e.g., "harvest of righteousness and peace" [NIV]; cf. Ellingworth 656). Cockerill, however, notes that "righteousness" has been a thread running through the argument since the citation of Hab 2:4 in Heb 10:38 (cf. 11:4) and thus δικαιοσύνης is a gen. of source placed at the very end of this section for emph. (Cockerill 627–28). This thread is missed in some EVV (e.g., "harvest of an honest life" [NEB]).

Γεγυμνασμένοις is the dat. pl. masc. of the pf. pass. ptc. of γυμνάζω, "train" (most EVV; BDAG 208b; G. Schneider, *EDNT* 1:265b). The subst. ptc. is the indir. obj. of ἀποδίδωσιν. The vb. is another example of athletic imagery in Hebrews. The antecedent of δι' αὐτῆς is παιδεία. The prep. phrase is instr. ("by it" [most EVV]). Once again, the author concludes a section with a summary statement (e.g., 3:19; 8:13; 10:18 [Ellingworth 655]). The author combines both agricultural and athletic imagery in this v.

FOR FURTHER STUDY

89. God/God the Father in Hebrews (12:5–11)

Attridge, Harold W. "God in Hebrews." Pages 95–110 in Bauckham, *Theology*.
———. "God in Hebrews: Urging Children to Heavenly Glory." Pages 197–209 in *Forgotten God: Perspectives in Biblical Theology: Essays in Honor of Paul J. Achtemeier on the Occasion of His Seventy-fifth Birthday*. Edited by A. Andrew Das and Frank J. Matera. Louisville: Westminster John Knox Press, 2002.
Newman, C. C. *DLNT* 412–31.
*Peeler, Amy. "The Ethos of God in Hebrews." *PRSt* 37 (2010): 37–51.
Quell, G. *TDNT* 5:959–74.
Schrenk, G. *TDNT* 5.945–59; 974–1022.

90. Sonship in Hebrews (12:5–11)

Attridge, "Priesthood and Sonship," 146–47.
Lohse, E. *TDNT* 8:357–62.
Schweizer, E. *TDNT* 8:363–92.

91. Discipline (12:5–11)

Bertram, G. *TDNT* 5:619–25.

Fitzgerald, John T. "Proverbs 3:11–12, Hebrews 12:5–6, and the Tradition of Corporal Punishment." Pages 291–317 in *Scripture and Traditions: Essays on Early Judaism and Christianity in Honor of Carl R. Holladay*. Edited by Patrick Gray and Gail R. O'Day. Supplements to Novum Testamentum 129. Leiden: Brill, 2008.

Kingdon, D. P. *NDBT* 448–50.

Schneider, G. *EDNT* 3:3a.

Thiessen, Matthew. "Hebrews 12.5–13, the Wilderness Period, and Israel's Discipline." *NTS* 55 (2009): 366–79.

HOMILETICAL SUGGESTIONS

How to Endure Discipline (12:4–11)

1. Keep the Current Situation in Perspective (v. 4)
2. Do Not Forget the Exhortation that Confirms Legitimacy (vv. 5–6)
   - (a) Do not take divine discipline lightly (v. 5b)
   - (b) Do not be discouraged by divine discipline (v. 5c)
   - (c) Divine discipline is a sign of God's love and belonging to him (v. 6)
3. Endure Divine Discipline (vv. 7–11)
   - (a) God disciplines his children (v. 7a)
   - (b) Just as earthly parents discipline their children (v. 7b)
   - (c) If you are not disciplined, then you are not legitimate children (v. 8)
   - (d) We respected the imperfect discipline of our earthly parents (v. 9a)
   - (e) How much more will we benefit from the discipline from our heavenly Father? (v. 9b)
   - (f) There were short-term benefits from our earthly parents' discipline (v. 10a)
   - (g) There are much greater benefits from our heavenly Father's discipline (v. 10b)
4. PRINCIPLE: The Long-Term Benefits of Divine Discipline Are Not Evident During the Time of Discipline (v. 11)

Understanding Godly Discipline (12:5–11)

1. The Nature of God's Discipline (vv. 5–8)
2. The Analogy of Parental Discipline (vv. 9–10)
3. The Result of Godly Discipline (v. 11)

2. The Necessity of Community (12:12–13)

STRUCTURE

Verses 12–13 summarize the arguments of vv. 1–11. The two impv. (ἀνορθώσατε and ποιεῖτε) anchor the passage.

12 Διὸ τὰς παρειμένας χεῖρας
καὶ τὰ παραλελυμένα γόνατα
ἀνορθώσατε,
13 καὶ τροχιὰς ὀρθὰς ποιεῖτε
τοῖς ποσὶν ὑμῶν,
ἵνα μὴ τὸ χωλὸν ἐκτραπῇ,
ἰαθῇ δὲ μᾶλλον.

VERSE 12

Διὸ τὰς παρειμένας χεῖρας καὶ τὰ παραλελυμένα γόνατα ἀνορθώσατε,
Therefore, strengthen your tired hands and weakened knees,

Διό ("therefore" [most EVV]) is an inferential conj. (BDAG 250c) that both draws on 12:1–11 and points forward to 12:14–17. Ἀνορθώσατε is the 2nd pl. aor. act. impv. of ἀνορθόω, "strengthen" (most EVV [BDAG 86b]; ESV inexplicably tr. the vb. twice). The first obj. of the vb. is χεῖρας, "hands" (most EVV), which is modified by παρειμένας (acc. pl. fem. of the pf. pass. ptc. of παρίημι, "drooping" (ESV), "listless" (NET), "feeble" (NIV), "weaken" (BDAG 777d). The pf. is required as the vb. is defective (R 315). The second obj. of the vb. is γόνατα (γόνυ, -ατος, τό, "knee" [most EVV; BDAG 205b]). The noun is modified by παραλελυμένα (acc. pl. neut. of the pf. pass. ptc. of παραλύω, "weak" [ESV, NET, NIV], "shaking" [REB] "paralyzed" [BDAG 769c]). Both ptc. are adj. (BDF §97[3]).

The clause alludes to Isa 35:3–4—a word of encouragement directed to returning exiles, although the author may intend another allusion to a boxing match in which the exhausted fighter's hands droop and knees buckle (Cockerill 629).

VERSE 13

καὶ τροχιὰς ὀρθὰς ποιεῖτε τοῖς ποσὶν ὑμῶν, ἵνα μὴ τὸ χωλὸν ἐκτραπῇ, ἰαθῇ δὲ μᾶλλον.
and make straight paths for your feet, so that what is lame may not be dislocated but healed instead.

The obj. of ποιεῖτε is τροχιάς (acc. pl. fem. of τροχιά, -ᾶς, ἡ, BDAG 1017d), which is modified by ὀρθάς (ὀρθός, -ή, -όν, "straight paths" [most EVV; BDAG 722b; H. Preisker, *TDNT* 5:449–50; cf. "level paths" [NIV]). Τροχιά is "always plural and figurative" (Ellingworth 659). BDAG (1017d) notes: "make straight paths upon which one can advance quickly and in the right direction." NJB inexplicably adds "crooked":

"make your crooked paths straight." Τοῖς ποσὶν ὑμῶν could be instr. "with your feet" (Cockerill 630) or indir. obj. "for your feet" (most EVV).

Ἵνα followed by the subjunc. indicates purpose. Ἐκτραπῇ is the 3rd sg. aor. pass. subjunc. of ἐκτρέπω ("put out of joint" [ESV, NASB, NET], "disabled" [NIV], "dislocated" [NAB; BDAG 311b; Attridge 365]). The vb. could also mean "turn aside" (e.g., individuals who might be tempted to "turn aside" would be healed by the example of others who "walk straight" [Cockerill 630 n. 73]). The neg. ptcl. μή modifies ἐκτραπῇ. Χωλόν is the acc. sg. of χωλός, -ή, -όν, "what is lame" (ESV, NET ["*the limb* which is lame"]), "crippled" (BDAG 1093d). "The lame" (NIV) could imply people (e.g., CEV), but is less likely with the neut. Τὸ χωλόν is the subj. of ἐκτραπῇ. The sg. indicates a general application ("to any in your community" [Cockerill 630]). Ἰαθῇ is the 3rd sg. aor. pass. subjunc. of ἰάομαι, "heal" (most EVV; BDAG 465b). The pass. for both vb. indicates divine agency (Cockerill 630). Δὲ μᾶλλον means "instead" or "rather" (most EVV [BDAG 614b]).

This v. is an allusion to Prov 4:26, although the author has changed the vb. to pl. in his application of the citation to his audience (Lane 2:42).

HOMILETICAL SUGGESTIONS

We Don't Run Alone (12:12–13)

1. Strengthen Each Other's Hands and Knees (v. 12)
2. Straighten the Path So the Disjointed Can Be Healed (v. 13)

3. *The Shortsightedness of Esau (12:14–17)*

STRUCTURE

This section is bound to the previous section with εἰρήνη (cf. εἰρηνικόν in v. 11) and ἁγιασμόν in v 14 (cf. ἁγιότητος in v. 10 [Attridge 367]). The section is like a "prelude" that repeats early warnings and anticipates the final warnings in 12:14–29 (Attridge 366). The ref. to Esau offers a counterpart to 2:1–4, which cautions against drifting from God's word (Cockerill 632). Verses 14–16 comprise one sentence, dependent on διώκετε. Verse 17 consists of a summary of the account of Esau that echoes earlier warnings in Hebrews. See For Further Study 12 (The Warning Passages in Hebrews). For the overall structure of 12:14–29, see Lane 2:446.

14 Εἰρήνην διώκετε μετὰ πάντων καὶ τὸν ἁγιασμόν,
οὗ χωρὶς οὐδεὶς ὄψεται τὸν κύριον,
15 ἐπισκοποῦντες
μή τις ὑστερῶν ἀπὸ τῆς χάριτος τοῦ θεοῦ,
μή τις ῥίζα πικρίας ἄνω φύουσα ἐνοχλῇ καὶ δι᾽ αὐτῆς
μιανθῶσιν πολλοί,
16 μή τις πόρνος ἢ βέβηλος ὡς Ἠσαῦ,
ὃς ἀντὶ βρώσεως μιᾶς ἀπέδετο τὰ πρωτοτόκια ἑαυτοῦ.
17 ἴστε γὰρ
ὅτι καὶ μετέπειτα θέλων κληρονομῆσαι τὴν εὐλογίαν ἀπεδοκιμάσθη,
μετανοίας γὰρ τόπον οὐχ εὗρεν καίπερ μετὰ δακρύων
ἐκζητήσας αὐτήν.

VERSE 14

Εἰρήνην διώκετε μετὰ πάντων καὶ τὸν ἁγιασμόν,
Pursue peace with everyone, and holiness—

Διώκετε is the 2nd pl. pres. act. impv. of διώκω, "pursue" (NASB, NET, NRSV), "strive for" (ESV, NAB), "seek" (NJB); but cf. "make every effort to live in peace" (NIV). The pres. is continuous ("persistently strive for" [Weymouth]; Cockerill 633). The vb. has two obj.: εἰρήνην ("peace" [most EVV]) and ἁγιασμόν (ἁγιασμός, -οῦ, ὁ, "holiness" [most EVV; see comments on 12:10], "sanctification" [NASB]). The position of εἰρήνην is emph. (Ellingworth 661; Lane 2:432). Abstract nouns are often art. in Gk. (e.g., τὸν ἁγιασμόν [Wallace 249–50]). Εἰρήνην is anar., likely due to its emph. position. Both peace and holiness are depicted as obj. realities made possible by Christ, but which still need to be pursued by the community (Cockerill 634; Lane 2:449). Although the -μος ending indicates a process or action (e.g., "growth in holiness" [Weymouth]), the focus in Hebrews is more on what Christ has achieved for believers than the process by which believers are sanctified (although that is not excluded [Cockerill 634–35; Lane 2:450]).

Although μετά with the gen. can indicate "with," the sense here may be "in company with" (BDF §227[3]; *pace* most EVV). Πάντων likely ref. to other believers (cf. 13:24), with an emph. on harmony within the Christian community (Cockerill 634; Ellingworth 662; Lane 2:438 n. *b*). Taken together, the point is to "seek peace in company with everyone" (Lane 2:438 n. *b*) as the "objective basis of the solidarity of the community" (Lane 2:449; cf. "together with all pursue peace" [Cockerill 634]). Moreover, holiness would not be sought with nonbelievers. This v. may allude to Ps 34:14 (LXX 33:15 [Cockerill 633]).

οὗ χωρὶς οὐδεὶς ὄψεται τὸν κύριον,
without it no one will see the Lord.

The antecedent of οὗ is ἁγιασμόν (explicitly stated in NIV). Χωρίς ("without") takes a gen. obj. (οὗ) and always precedes the word it modifies except here (R 648; Harris 250–51). The subj. of ὄψεται is οὐδείς ("no one" [most EVV]). The obj. of the vb. is τὸν κύριον. "Lord" here probably refers to God, or possibly Christ, who is seated at God's right hand (Cockerill 635).

VERSE 15

ἐπισκοποῦντες μή τις ὑστερῶν ἀπὸ τῆς χάριτος τοῦ θεοῦ,
Make sure that no one falls short of the grace of God

Ἐπισκοποῦντες is the nom. pl. masc. of the pres. act. ptc. of. ἐπισκοπέω, "see to it" (ESV, NASB, NIV; cf. BDAG 379a), "be careful" (NJB). The ptc. either modifies διώκετε instr. (Cockerill 635) or continues an impv. force (Lane 2:451). It is followed by three "neg. purpose clauses" (par. to a ἵνα clause) that indicate the content of the warning (cf. Lane 2:438 n. *e*), each beginning with μή τις (see outline above). This expression may allude to Deut 29:18 (and likely 29:15–20), where μή τις occurs twice (Attridge 367 n. 25; Cockerill 635). Both this warning and the next one recall the neg. example of the wilderness generation in 3:7–4:11 (Cockerill 635).

Τις is the nom. sg. masc. of the indef. pron., which functions as the subj. in this clause. The neg. ptcl. μή modifies the indef. pron. (e.g., "no one" [NIV]). Ὑστερῶν is the nom. sg. masc. of the pres. act. ptc. of ὑστερέω, "come short of" (NASB, NET), "miss" (NIV), "fail to obtain" (ESV), "fail to reach" (BDAG 1043c). "Be deprived of" (NAB, NJB) has the wrong connotation. There may be an allusion to falling short in a race, thereby recalling the race imagery in 12:1–2 (Cockerill 637). The adj. ptc. modifies τις ("anyone who falls short" [Attridge 366]). The use of this vb. recalls its previous use in 4:1. The collocation indicates exclusion from something through one's own failing (Lane 2:439 n. *f*; BDAG 1043c) and probably suggests apostasy (Lane 2:452). Ὑστερῶν is intrans. Ἀπό indicates separation (BDF §180[5]). Τῆς χάριτος τοῦ θεοῦ is the obj. of the prep. Θεοῦ modifies χάριτος, indicating poss.

μή τις ῥίζα πικρίας ἄνω φύουσα ἐνοχλῇ καὶ δι' αὐτῆς μιανθῶσιν πολλοί,
and that no root of bitterness springs up, causing trouble and defiling many.

Μή τις introduces the second element in the three-part warning following ἐπισκοποῦντες. Some EVV repeat ἐπισκοποῦντες before this warning (e.g., CEV). Ῥίζα (nom. sg. fem. of ῥίζα, -ης, ἡ, "root" [most EVV]) is the subj. of ἐνοχλῇ (see below) and is modified by πικρίας (gen. sg. fem. of πικρία, -ας, ἡ, "bitterness" [many EVV; BDAG 813a; W. Michaelis, *TDNT* 6:124]). (NET takes μή τις as a ref. to a person who is like a bitter root that defiles. This fits the context but does not reflect the syntax.) The gen. could be attrib. ("no bitter root" [NAB, NIV; R 496]), "descriptive" ("root of bitterness" [ESV, NASB; Wallace 81]), or quality ("poisonous root" [NLT], "bitter, noxious weed" [REB; BDF §165]). Ῥίζα is modified by the indef. pron. τις ("any"), which is in turn modified by μή. Most EVV take μή with ῥίζα and leave τις untr. ("no root"). Φύουσα is the nom. sg. fem. of the pres. act. ptc. of φύω (BDAG 1070d–1071a). The adj. ptc. modifies ῥίζα and is modified by the adv. ἄνω: "grow up" (NIV), "spring up" (ESV, NASB, NET). Ἐνοχλῇ is the 3rd sg. pres. act. subjunc. of ἐνοχλέω, "cause trouble" (ESV, NASB, NET) "annoy" (BDAG 338d). NIV tr. the subjunc. as an inf. ("to cause trouble and defile"). Μή is used in expression of "apprehension" with the subjunc. (BDF §370[1]).

Καί joins the second part of this clause, although the subj. is no longer ῥίζα, but is instead πολλοί. Μιανθῶσιν is the 3rd pl. aor. pass. subjunc. of μιαίνω, "defile" (most EVV; G. Schneider, *EDNT* 2:427a), "corrupt" (NLT), "contaminate" (REB), "stain" (BDAG 650b); cf. "poison" (NJB). The subj. of this pass vb. is πολλοί ("many" [people] [many EVV]). The anar. could have an "inclusive nuance," indicating the community ("the rest of you" [Moffatt]; Lane 2:439 n. *i*). The antecedent of αὐτῆς is ῥίζα (*pace* "him" [NET]); the prep. phrase δι' αὐτῆς is instr. Many EVV tr. the pass. vb. as act. with πολλοί as the obj. and leave δι' αὐτῆς untr. (but cf. ESV, NASB, NET).

The author is drawing on Deut 29:18, although the wording differs from any extant LXX mss. (see esp. Cockerill 636 n. 19). It is possible that the author followed a different (no longer extant) textual tradition for this v. (Attridge 368). The author's reasons for alluding to a text that warns against the communal dangers of idolatry and breaking covenantal loyalty, however, are clear (Attridge 368). The ref. to bitterness may reflect what members in the audience felt due to persecution (Attridge 368). This danger is captured well with "poison a whole community" (JB) or "contaminate the whole community" (Barclay).

VERSE 16

μή τις πόρνος ἢ βέβηλος ὡς Ἠσαῦ,
And make sure that there isn't any immoral or irreverent person like Esau,

This is the third and final warning following ἐπισκοποῦντες (repeated in many EVV). The example of Esau offers a "fitting companion" to the example of the wilderness generation (Cockerill 635). Moreover, the allusion to Deut 29:15–20 is also fitting—the passage ends with "the description of one who flaunts God's covenant" (Cockerill 638), which is apt for Esau. Πόρνος is the nom. sg. masc. of πόρνος, -ου, ὁ, "immoral" (NASB, NET), "sexually immoral" (ESV, NIV), "fornicator" (BDAG 855a). Βέβηλος is the nom. sg. masc. of βέβηλος, -ον, "profane" (NAB), "unholy" (ESV), "godless" (NASB, NET, NIV; Cockerill 638), "worldly-minded" (NEB [cf. BDAG 173c]). The disjunctive conj. ἤ ("or") joins πόρνος and βέβηλος. Ἐστίν is implied (BDF §128[4]). The indef. pron. modifies both terms (e.g., "any immoral or irreverent person" [CSB]). Ἠσαῦ is indecl. but here is the nom. sg. masc.

ὃς ἀντὶ βρώσεως μιᾶς ἀπέδετο τὰ πρωτοτόκια ἑαυτοῦ.
who sold his birthright in exchange for a single meal.

The antecedent of ὅς is Ἠσαῦ. The rel. pron. is the subj. of the rel. clause. Ἀπέδετο is the 3rd sg. aor. mid. indic. of ἀποδίδωμι, "sold" (most EVV), "trade" (NLT [BDAG 110c]). Πρωτοτόκια is the acc. pl. neut. of πρωτοτόκια, -ων, τά, "birthright" (most EVV [BDAG 894b; NT hapax]). This word recalls the cognate πρωτότοκος in 1:6 (see comments there). The older son received a double share of the inheritance (Deut 21:15–17; cf. "his inheritance rights as the oldest son" [NIV]). Ἑαυτοῦ modifies πρωτοτόκια for poss. In Heb 12:2, ἀντί can indicate either reason or substitution; here substitution is clearly in view ("in exchange for" [Moule 71]; "in return for," "for the price" [Harris 50]). Βρώσεως is the gen. sg. fem. of βρῶσις, -εως, ἡ (BDAG 185b). The noun normally indicates "food," but with the adj. μιᾶς, the idea is of a meal (most EVV). The position of μιᾶς is emph. (Ellingworth 666; Lane 2:439 n. *n*) and pejorative—"a *single* meal" (most EVV; cf. "for only one meal" [CEV]). Βρώσεως could possibly be understood as a gen. of price (BDF §208[2]; Wallace 122).

This passage draws on Gen 25:29–34. Esau's action indicates how little he valued (indeed despised) his inheritance, the promised blessing. Genesis does not describe Esau as sexually immoral (yet this can be plausibly inferred from his marriage to two Hittite women), although this was prominent in later Jewish tradition (e.g., *Jub.* 25:1–8; Philo, *Virtues* 208–10 [see Attridge 369 n. 48; Bruce 350; Cockerill 638; *DBI* 244–45; U. Hübner, *ABD* 2:574–75]).

There is debate over whether the author intends literal sexual immorality (Moffatt, Cassirer, ESV, NIV; Bruce 350; Ellingworth 665; Koester 532) or apostasy (Attridge 369; Cockerill 639). The context, however, favors the figurative sense of πόρνος as someone who is unfaithful to God (Lane 2:454–55). The ref. to Esau is particularly fitting for the situation Hebrews addresses: "The addressees are similarly in danger of losing their association with the Firstborn (1:6) in the assembly of the firstborn (12:23)" (Attridge 369). See Amy Peeler, "The Warning of Esau: A New Look at Hebrews 12:12–17," *Journal of Theta Alpha Kappa* 29 (2005): 1–18.

VERSE 17

ἴστε γὰρ ὅτι καὶ μετέπειτα
For you know that later,

Ἴστε (2nd pl. pf. act. of οἶδα) reflects "literary Attic" (R319). The form could be either indic. ("you know" [most EVV]; R 360, 941; Lane 2:440 n. *o*]) or impv. (Wallace

[718], although the pf. impv. is very rare in the NT). Γάρ, however, suggests an indic. (Attridge 370 n. 56; Ellingworth 667). The cstr. ἴστε γάρ introduces "a well-known fact which will not be questioned" (Ellingworth 666), with ὅτι introducing the well-known content. Καί introduces a new point (Ellingworth 667), although it is untr. in most EVV. The adv. μετέπειτα ("later" [NET], "afterward" [ESV, NIV]; BDAG 642c; BGk. hapax) modifies θέλων.

θέλων κληρονομῆσαι τὴν εὐλογίαν ἀπεδοκιμάσθη,
when he wanted to inherit the blessing, he was rejected,

The subj. of θέλων is Esau. The ptc. is temp. ("when" [most EVV]). Κληρονομῆσαι (aor. act. inf. of κληρονομέω, "inherit" [most EVV; BDAG 547d]) complements θέλων. This exact language is not used in the Genesis account, but it recalls the important use of inheritance language in Hebrews (see comments on 1:2). Εὐλογίαν (acc. sg. fem. of εὐλογία, -ας, ἡ, "blessing" [most EVV; BDAG 409a]) is the obj. of the inf. Ἀπεδοκιμάσθη is the 3rd sg. aor. pass. indic. of ἀποδοκιμάζω, "reject" (most EVV; BDAG 110c). Although Esau remains the subj. of the pass. vb., the ultimate agent is God (BDAG 110c; BDF §130[1]). Again, this exact language does not occur in the Genesis account but fits well with the example that the author makes of Esau.

μετανοίας γὰρ τόπον οὐχ εὗρεν
. . . because he didn't find any opportunity for repentance.

Γάρ is explanatory, although it is untr. in many EVV. Εὗρεν is the 3rd sg. aor. act. indic. of εὑρίσκω ("find" [most EVV]), which is modified by οὐ (οὐχ before rough breathing). Τόπος often indicates "place" (e.g., 11:8; cf. NASB), but here it is fig.: "chance" (ESV), "opportunity" (NET [BDAG 1012a]). Τόπον is the obj. of εὗρεν. Μετανοίας is the gen. sg. fem. of μετάνοια, -ας, ἡ, "repentance" (many EVV; BDAG 640d; see below), which modifies τόπον as a gen. of purpose (BDF §166). The position of μετανοίας is emph. (Lane 2:440 n. *r*). The expression "place of repentance" is a well-established term referring to moral repentance (Cockerill 640), although this language does not occur in the Genesis account. The author may have intended an allusion to the warning in 6:4–6 (Attridge 370). Repentance indicates turning from sin, although some argue for "change of mind" (e.g., NAB, NIV), with the understanding that Esau was not able to change Isaac's mind, although he tried (for refutation of this view, see Cockerill 640; Koester 533).

καίπερ μετὰ δακρύων ἐκζητήσας αὐτήν.
even though he sought it with tears . . .

Δακρύων is the gen. pl. neut. of δάκρυον, -ου, τό, "tears" (most EVV; BDAG 211b). Μετὰ δακρύων modifies ἐκζητήσας, with a "metaphorical . . . idea of accompaniment" (R 611). Genesis 27:34 records that Esau cried out loudly and bitterly, but does not record his tears, although this is found in later Jewish tradition (Koester 533). Ἐκζητήσας is the nom. sg. masc. of the aor. act. ptc. of ἐκζητέω ("sought" [most

EVV; BDAG 302d]). The compound vb. may be intensive (e.g., "sought earnestly" [Weymouth]). The ptc., modifying εὗρεν, is concessive, which is confirmed by the conj. καίπερ ("although" or "even though" [most EVV; BDAG 497c; R 1129).

The antecedent of αὐτήν could either be μετανοία (closest) or εὐλογία, which is more consistent with the Genesis account (Cockerill 640–41; Koester 533; Lane 2:458; made explicit in some EVV [e.g., NET, NIV, NRSV]). Some argue that μετανοία fits with the author's appeal to Esau as a (neg.) example (Attridge 370; Ellingworth 668). But if μετανοία were intended, the pers. pron. would be αὐτόν not αὐτήν, because τόπον μετανοίας is a "fixed idiom" (Lane 2:440 n. *t*; cf. Cockerill 641). The example of Esau (and the wilderness generation) as someone who wants the blessing but has no desire for repentance fits the context of Hebrews well (Cockerill 641). The tr. "it" leaves this unclear in many EVV.

HOMILETICAL SUGGESTIONS

Pursue Peace and Holiness with Everyone! (12:14–17)

1. It Is Not Possible to See God Otherwise (v. 14b)
2. How to Pursue Peace and Holiness (vv. 15–17)
   - (a) By ensuring that others do not fail to receive grace (v. 15)
   - (b) By guarding against bitterness (v. 15b)
   - (c) By protecting against immoral and irreverent individuals like Esau (v. 16a)
     - (1) He devalued the things of God (v. 16b)
     - (2) He missed God's blessing (v. 17a)
     - (3) He was not repentant (v. 17b)

4. Earthly Sinai and Heavenly Zion Contrasted (12:18–24)

STRUCTURE

Verses 18–24 comprise another "periodic sentence" characteristic of Hebrews (see comments on 1:1), which sets out an extended contrast between Sinai (vv. 18–21; never explicitly mentioned) and Zion (vv. 22–24). The second parts of v. 20 and v. 21 are dependent on the clause indicated by the arrow. Two lists (containing seven items each) detail the contrast. (Some challenge that seven items are associated with Zion; see Attridge 372). Note the οὐ (v. 18) . . . ἀλλά (v. 22) cstr. The omission of the art. in these two lists is "striking" and characteristic of classical Gk. (Moule 114; cf. R 793). The anar. substs. stress the quality of the entities (Cockerill 647). Some suggest that the structure can be understood as a poem (see Lane 2:440 n. *u*).

18 Οὐ γὰρ προσεληλύθατε ψηλαφωμένῳ
καὶ κεκαυμένῳ πυρὶ
καὶ γνόφῳ
καὶ ζόφῳ
καὶ θυέλλῃ
19 καὶ σάλπιγγος ἤχῳ
καὶ φωνῇ ῥημάτων,
ἧς οἱ ἀκούσαντες παρῃτήσαντο
μὴ προστεθῆναι αὐτοῖς λόγον,
20 οὐκ ἔφερον γὰρ τὸ διαστελλόμενον·
κἂν θηρίον θίγῃ τοῦ ὄρους,
λιθοβοληθήσεται·
21 καί, οὕτω φοβερὸν ἦν τὸ φανταζόμενον,
Μωϋσῆς εἶπεν·
ἔκφοβός εἰμι καὶ ἔντρομος.
22 ἀλλὰ προσεληλύθατε Σιὼν ὄρει
καὶ πόλει θεοῦ ζῶντος,
Ἰερουσαλὴμ ἐπουρανίῳ,
καὶ μυριάσιν ἀγγέλων, πανηγύρει
23 καὶ ἐκκλησίᾳ πρωτοτόκων
ἀπογεγραμμένων ἐν οὐρανοῖς
καὶ κριτῇ θεῷ πάντων
καὶ πνεύμασι δικαίων
τετελειωμένων
24 καὶ διαθήκης νέας μεσίτῃ
Ἰησοῦ
καὶ αἵματι ῥαντισμοῦ
κρεῖττον λαλοῦντι
παρὰ τὸν Ἅβελ.

VERSE 18

Οὐ γὰρ προσεληλύθατε
For you have not come

The inferential γάρ indicates a new section, but one that grounds the exhortations in 12:14–17 (Lane 2:440 n. *u*). The effect is to encourage the audience that (unlike Esau) they have not come to Sinai but to Zion (Cockerill 642). The position of οὐ is emph. (Lane 2:440 n. *v*). Προσεληλύθατε is the 2nd pl. pf. act. indic. of προσέρχομαι, "come" (most EVV), "approach" (NAB; BDAG 878b–c). This vb. is a key term in Hebrews for a relationship with God (see comments on 4:16 and 12:22). The pf. tense indicates "heightened proximity" (Campbell, *Basics* 104), adding an intensity to the contrast and to the sense of what the audience risks should they not persevere in their faith. Previous occurrences of προσέρχομαι in Hebrews use the pres. tense.

This v. presents a terrifying description of Sinai, based on Exod 19:16–19; 20:18–21; and Moses's recollection in Deut 4:11 (where προσήλθετε occurs [Lane 2:459]). The author offers seven descriptions of Sinai, although the place is never stated explicitly, but may be inferred from ὄρει in v. 22. Some mss. add ὄρει after (or before) ψηλαφωμένῳ, but this inconsistent placement suggests it was added for clarification and is not orig. (Metzger 605). Some EVV (NASB, NIV) thus add "mountain" (cf. "Sinai" [REB], "physical mountain" [NLT]) to v. 18. The omission suggests that the location itself is unimportant (cf. Ellingworth 672). Indeed the contrast stresses the two options that confront the audience: unbelief, apostasy, and judgment, on the one hand, and belief, faithfulness, and blessing, on the other hand (Cockerill 643). Thus vv. 18–21 culminate previous warnings, whereas vv. 22–24 culminate previous assurances (Cockerill 644). Each description may be broadly understood as a dat. of place (R 536; cf. dat. of destination [Wallace 147–48]), although the first two appeal to touch, the next three to sight, and the final two to hearing (Cockerill 647).

ψηλαφωμένῳ καὶ κεκαυμένῳ πυρὶ καὶ γνόφῳ καὶ ζόφῳ καὶ θυέλλῃ
to what could be touched, to a blazing fire, to darkness, gloom, and storm,

The first descriptor, ψηλαφωμένῳ, is the dat. sg. neut. of the pres. pass. ptc. of ψηλαφάω (BDAG 1097d–1098a; H. Balz, *EDNT* 3:500a). Ψηλαφωμένῳ is a subst. ptc., "that can be touched" [NASB, NET, NIV], "palpable" [NEB], "tangible" [REB]). This word alludes to Exod 19:12, although it is not used in the LXX tr. The cognate noun occurs in Exod 10:21, the account of the ninth plague (of darkness), which may have influenced the author (Bruce 352 n. 123; Lane 2:460). Each occurrence of καί in this clause and the next v. adds the next item in the list.

The second descriptor, κεκαυμένῳ, is the dat. sg. neut. of the pf. pass. ptc. of καίω (BDAG 499c). The pf. pass. ptc. functions par. to verbal adj. with -τος endings (BDF §65[3]). Κεκαυμένῳ is either an adj. ptc. modifying πυρί (dat. sg. neut. of πῦρ, -ός, τό)—"blazing fire" (ESV, NASB), "burning fire" (NET), "flaming fire" (NLT), or κεκαυμένῳ is a subst. ptc. that is modified by πυρί as an instr. dat. ("burning with fire,"

NIV). Based on the par. to the subst. ptc. ψηλαφωμένῳ, the latter is preferred but there is little difference between the two options. Alternatively, but less likely, κεκαυμένῳ could be a subst. ptc., with πυρί and γνόφῳ as modifiers. The use of πῦρ forms an *inclusio* with πῦρ in v. 29. This somewhat odd image associates fire with darkness (Cockerill 648).

Γνόφῳ, dat. sg. masc. of γνόφος, -ου, ὁ, "darkness" (most EVV [BDAG 202c; NT hapax]), is the third descriptor. Some mss. substitute the more common σκότος for the rare γνόφος, perhaps because both words often occur together in the LXX (e.g., Exod 10:22; 14:20; Deut 4:11; 5:22 [Lane 2:441 n. *y*]). The less common term may have been chosen for euphony (γνόφῳ καὶ ζόφῳ [Lane 2:461]). Ζόφῳ, dat. sg. masc. of ζόφος, -ου, ὁ, "gloom" (most EVV; BDAG 429b), is the fourth descriptor. The poetic term may have been chosen "to intensify the foreboding imagery" (Attridge 373). (NAB combines the third and fourth descriptors, "gloomy darkness," but this is not supported by the syntax.) The fifth descriptor, θυέλλῃ, is the dat. sg. fem. of θύελλα, -ης, ἡ, "tempest" (ESV), "storm" (NAB, NIV), "whirlwind" (NLT, NASB, NET [BDAG 461b; NT hapax]). These first five descriptors clearly draw on LXX Deut 4:11 (note underlined words): καὶ προσήλθετε καὶ ἔστητε ὑπὸ τὸ ὄρος καὶ τὸ ὄρος ἐκαίετο πυρὶ ἕως τοῦ οὐρανοῦ σκότος γνόφος θύελλα φωνὴ μεγάλη.

VERSE 19

καὶ σάλπιγγος ἤχῳ καὶ φωνῇ ῥημάτων,
to the blast of a trumpet, and the sound of words.

Ἤχῳ is the dat. sg. masc. of ἦχος, -ου, ὁ, "sound," "noise" (BDAG 441c). Σάλπιγγος (gen. sg. fem. of σάλπιγξ, -ιγγος, ἡ, "trumpet" [BDAG 911d; H. Lichtenberger, *EDNT* 3:226a]) modifies ἤχῳ as a descriptive gen. Based on σάλπιγξ, many EVV have "blast." The LXX uses φωνή with σάλπιγξ, but the author likely used ἦχος since φωνή occurs in the next descriptor (Bruce 353 n. 125). The allusion is to Exod 19:16. This is the sixth descriptor of Sinai.

The seventh and final descriptor is φωνῇ (NASB) or "voice" (most EVV), which is modified by ῥημάτων ("words" [most EVV]). This descriptor alludes to Deut 4:12. The entire description of Sinai underscores the absence of God's presence (or rather his inaccessibility [Cockerill 643]), and amplifies the overwhelming divine presence in Zion. Sinai is reduced to a terrifying, auditory experience. Furthermore, the author implies that God was "not unambiguously present at Sinai" (Lane 2:460). For this reason, φωνῇ is better tr. as "sound" not "voice." Even "voice," however, stresses that the Lord was heard but not seen (Cockerill 649).

ἧς οἱ ἀκούσαντες παρῃτήσαντο μὴ προστεθῆναι αὐτοῖς λόγον,
Those who heard it begged that not another word be spoken to them,

The antecedent of ἧς is φωνῇ. The rel. pron. is the obj. of the ptc. οἱ ἀκούσαντες ("those who heard" [most EVV], "hearers" [ESV]). The subst. ptc. is the subj. of the rel. clause. (NRSV takes vv. 20–21 as parenthetical. Most EVV indicate no parenthesis; the difference is not significant.) Παρῃτήσαντο is the 3rd pl. aor. mid. indic. of παραιτέομαι, "begged" (most EVV; [BDAG 764b]). Προστεθῆναι is the aor. pass. inf. of προστίθημι. The acc. λόγον is the "subj." of the inf. Μὴ προστεθῆναι is the complement of παρῃτήσαντο and indicates indir. discourse. The idiom προστιθέναι λόγον τινί means "speak a further message to someone" (ESV [BDAG 885c]): "not another word be spoken to them" (NRSV), "no further word be spoken to them" (NASB, NIV), "to hear no more" (NET). In v. 25, this vb. means "refuse," which Koester (543) suggests for this v. On this view, μή is "pleonastic" (BDF §429). BDAG (764c), however, notes that the sense of "reject" occurs when the vb. is followed by the acc. as it is in v. 25, but not in this v. (Lane 2:462). The people's entreaty is a paraphrase of Exod 20:18–19 and/or Deut 5:23–25.

VERSE 20

οὐκ ἔφερον γὰρ τὸ διαστελλόμενον·
for they could not bear what was commanded:

Γάρ explains the previous clause. Ἔφερον is the 3rd pl. impf. act. indic. of φέρω. The sense is metaphorical: "bear" (most EVV), "endure" (ESV). The impf. offers background ("offline" [Campbell, *Basics* 62]) information that explains the people's fear. Διαστελλόμενον is the acc. sg. neut. of the pres. pass. ptc. of διαστέλλω. The pass. subst. ptc. means "what was commanded" (NET, NIV), "the command" (NASB [BDAG 236d–237a]); cf. "the order that was given" (ESV, NJB). The subst. ptc. is the obj. of ἔφερον.

κἂν θηρίον θίγῃ τοῦ ὄρους, λιθοβοληθήσεται·
If even an animal touches the mountain, it must be stoned.

The conj. κἄν ("if even" [most EVV; BDAG 507b]) introduces the prot. (κἂν θηρίον θίγῃ τοῦ ὄρους) of a general (concessive) cond. (BDF §374). Θίγῃ is the 3rd sg. aor. act. subjunc. of θιγγάνω, "touch" (most EVV [BDAG 455d]). The subj. of the vb. is θηρίον (nom. sg. neut. of θηρίον, -ου, τό, "animal" [most EVV]); cf. "wild animal" (Goodspeed), "beast" (ESV, NASB). The vb. takes a gen. obj. (R 508), τοῦ ὄρους ("mountain"). Λιθοβοληθήσεται is the 3rd sg. fut. pass. indic. of λιθοβολέω, "stoned" (most EVV [BDAG 595b]; cf. "stoned to death" [NIV, NRSV]). The agent of the pass. vb. is presumably the people. Λιθοβοληθήσεται is the apod. of the cond.

The clause is a paraphrase of Exod 19:12–13 (see Ellingworth 674). The author only mentions animals, "[b]ut the *a fortiori* inference to the case of a human being is obvious" (Attridge 373; cf. Ellingworth 675; Koester 543). The death sentence was necessary to preserve the mountain's sanctity. Stoning an animal (or human) meant that no other person would touch the offender and thereby risk the same punishment (cf. Cockerill 649). Some mss. add ἢ βολίδι κατατοξευθήσεται from Deut 19:13, which is reflected in some EVV (e.g., KJV, Moffatt).

VERSE 21

καί, οὕτω φοβερὸν ἦν τὸ φανταζόμενον,
The appearance was so terrifying

Καί is intensive (BDAG 495d): "in fact" (NET), "indeed" (ESV), "Moses himself" (NLT). Φανταζόμενον is the nom. sg. neut. of the pres. mid. ptc. of φαντάζω. The subst. ptc. indicates "the sight" (ESV, NASB, NIV, NLT [BDAG 1049a; NT hapax]), "the spectacle" (NAB), or "the scene" (NET). It suggests a theophany. Its position is emph. (Lane 2:441 n. *ee*). The art. indicates that φανταζόμενον is the subj. of the clause. Φοβερόν is the nom. sg. neut. of φοβερός, -ά, -όν (BDAG 1060d). The adj. is a pred. adj. The adv. οὕτω follows classical usage, "so terrifying" (NET, NIV), "so terrible" (NASB [BAGD 598]), "so frightening" (CEV). The author likely intended a connection with the last occurrence of φοβερός in Heb 10:31, which linked terror and God's judgment.

Μωϋσῆς εἶπεν· ἔκφοβός εἰμι καὶ ἔντρομος.
that Moses said, **I am trembling with fear**.

Εἶπεν introduces dir. discourse. Μωϋσῆς (indecl.) is the subj. of εἶπεν. Ἔκφοβος is the nom. sg. masc. of ἔκφοβος, -ον, "terrified" (NAB, NLT [BDAG 312b]; "full of fear" [NASB]). Ἔντρομος is the nom. sg. masc. of ἔντρομος, -ον, "trembling" (NASB, NLT [BDAG 341b]). The two adj. can be understood as a hendiadys ("trembling with fear" [NIV]), "shudder with fear" (NET).

There is no scriptural record of Moses being afraid at Sinai, but Deut 9:19 records Moses's fear of God's wrath over the golden calf incident (καὶ ἔκφοβός εἰμι διὰ τὴν ὀργήν). Later Jewish tradition, however, did present Moses's fear at Sinai (Koester 544). As is true elsewhere in Hebrews, the author was likely familiar with these accounts, which may also have influenced Acts 7:32 (see discussion in Lane 2:464). The effect is to heighten the fear and dread associated with Sinai, even for Moses, who is not mentioned again in Hebrews.

VERSE 22

ἀλλὰ προσεληλύθατε Σιὼν ὄρει
Instead, you have come to Mount Zion,

Ἀλλά introduces the contrast ("but" [most EVV], "now" [CEV]) to the description of Sinai in vv. 18–21 (see structural outline above). Προσεληλύθατε is the 2nd pl. pf. act. indic. of προσέρχομαι. Most EVV tr. προσεληλύθατε the same in v. 18 and this v. The word "proselyte" derives from the Gk. προσεληλύθατε; thus the author possibly intended an allusion to the audience's conversion (Bruce 355). But overall, the v. suggests that the audience has approached but has not arrived at Zion, which is consistent with the future-orientation of Hebrews (see comments on 1:14), including the promised rest (4:1–11), the city that Abraham saw from afar (11:13–16), the unshakable kingdom (12:28), and the city to come (13:14). At the same time, approach to the throne of grace is a present reality (4:14–16; 10:19–25). "At the end of your journey" (Cassirer) puts the emph. too much on realized eschatology. This passage is best understood as "already/not yet." The v. affirms the author's confidence that the audience has not apostasized but will persevere (cf. Cockerill 651). Although some see a Philonic/Platonic metaphysical distinction between earthly (Sinai) and heavenly (Zion), the author contrasts two covenants and their respective access to God.

Like Sinai, Zion is described by means of a series of dat. of place (R 536; cf. dat. of destination [Wallace 147–48]). The language in 12:22–24 is not drawn from one specific OT passage, but alludes to a variety of texts and images, both scriptural and extrabiblical. The emph. in this list is on joyous celebration in God's presence. The first descriptor is Σιών (indecl.), which is modified by the appos. ὄρει (dat. sg. neut. of ὄρος, -ους, τό, "mountain" ("Mount Zion" [most EVV]). The importance of Zion in biblical theology cannot be overstated. The convergence of Jerusalem, the temple, and Zion is freq. in the OT, with each considered the earthly dwelling of God (e.g., Pss 2, 110). In subsequent eschatological and apocalyptic speculation, Sinai and Zion were increasingly contrasted along earthly/present age and heavenly/age to come (respectively) planes. See For Further Study 92 (Sinai/Heavenly Zion [Jerusalem]). See also Attridge 374; Koester 544.

καὶ πόλει θεοῦ ζῶντος, Ἰερουσαλὴμ ἐπουρανίῳ,
to the city of the living God (the heavenly Jerusalem),

Καί is appos., "namely" (untr. in many EVV [cf. Lane 2:441 n. *gg*]), or explicative (Ellingworth 677). Zion is further modified by two appos., the first of which is πόλει, which is in turn modified by θεοῦ, which is further modified by ζῶντος ("city of the living God" [most EVV]). (For the expression θεοῦ ζῶντος, see comments on 3:12). This may also be an allusion to Deut 5:26. The expression "city of God" is rare (e.g., Psalm 46:4; 48:8).

Ἰερουσαλήμ (indecl.; L. Hartman, *EDNT* 2:176c–79c) is the second appos. to Σιών, which is indicated by parentheses in some EVV (e.g., CSB). Some EVV inexplicably reverse the order of the two appos. (e.g., NIV). Ἰερουσαλήμ is a transliteration of the Heb., although the Hellenized form, Ἱεροσόλυμα, is used in the Gospels, Acts, and Galatians (Ellingworth 678). It is further modified by ἐπουρανίῳ (ἐπουράνιος, -ον, "heavenly" [BDAG 388b]). The phrase "heavenly Jerusalem" (most EVV) occurs only here in the NT (cf. Gal 4:26; Rev 21:2) and nowhere in Jewish apocalyptic writings (Lane 2:466), but images of the heavenly Jerusalem or Zion occur in the OT (see esp. Isa 54:11–14) and NT (Rev 21:10–20; cf. 2 Bar 4:1–6). Whereas Mount Sinai was unnamed, Mount Zion is "triply designated" (Cockerill 650).

καὶ μυριάσιν ἀγγέλων, πανηγύρει
to myriads of angels, a festive gathering,

The second descriptor is μυριάσιν (dat. pl. fem. of μυριάς, -άδος, ἡ, "countless" [NAB], "innumerable" [ESV], "myriads" [NIV, "thousands upon thousands"; other

EVV, "ten thousands"] [BDAG 661b]). The gen. ἀγγέλων is descriptive. The expression μυριάσιν ἀγγέλων alludes to Deut 33:2 (and likely Dan 7:10; cf. Rev 5:11). Πανηγύρει (dat. sg. fem. of πανήγυρις, -εως, ἡ, "festal assembly" [BDAG 753d–754a; H. Balz, *EDNT* 3:9d; BGk. hapax]) is an appos. to μυριάσιν. Alternatively, the dat. could be locat. (e.g., "in festal gathering" [ESV], "in joyful assembly" [NIV], "in festal array" [cf. Bruce 352 n. 131]). Attempts to take πανηγύρει as a modifier of καὶ ἐκκλησίᾳ πρωτοτόκων (see below) do not reflect a natural reading of the Gk. (cf. Lane 2:441 n. *jj*). Some EVV take πανηγύρει with the following v. (e.g., "to the assembly and congregation of the firstborn" [NET]), although this counters the use of καί to introduce each descriptor. NIV retr. προσεληλύθατε at the beginning of this v.

A πανήγυρις was a "joyful festivity" in some Greco-Roman and Jewish literature (Attridge 375; Lane 2:441 n. *jj*; Koester 54), or simply a "plenary assembly" (see Ellingworth 679). The word "was used for civic festivals and athletic competitions, which drew people from all parts of the empire" (Koester 544). The image of joyful worship elaborates the mng. of σαββατισμός in 4:9.

VERSE 23

καὶ ἐκκλησίᾳ πρωτοτόκων ἀπογεγραμμένων ἐν οὐρανοῖς
to the assembly of the firstborn whose names have been written in heaven,

The third descriptor is ἐκκλησίᾳ, which is modified by the descriptive gen. πρωτοτόκων ("firstborn"). As with 2:12, here it refers to an "assembly" (ESV, NLT), "church" (NASB, NIV), or "congregation" (NET). Ἀπογεγραμμένων is the gen. pl. masc. of the pf. pass. ptc. of ἀπογράφω, "written" (NIV), "enrolled" (ESV, NASB, NET), or "inscribed" (BDAG 108c; E. Plümacher, *EDNT* 1:126b). "Names" (e.g., NIV, NLT) is inferred from the context. The adj. ptc. modifies πρωτοτόκων ("firstborn"). The ptc. is adv., modified locat. by ἐν οὐρανοῖς. The pl. "heavens" reflects Heb. usage. The lack of art. in prep. phrases is common (R 791).

Firstborn is an important theological term in Hebrews (see comments on 1:6). Here the firstborn (pl.) "share the inheritance (12:16) of the Firstborn par excellence (1:6)" (Attridge 375). The ref. contrasts the neg. experience of Esau, who despised his firstborn status and inheritance (Heb 12:14–17). This connection is obscured with "God's elder sons" (Goodspeed).

Some have suggested that ἐκκλησίᾳ πρωτοτόκων further modifies μυριάσιν ἀγγέλων. Several factors, however, argue against this. First, both ἐκκλησίᾳ (e.g., Deut 4:10, 9:10) and πρωτοτόκων (e.g., Exod 4:22–23) are used exclusively with the people of God in the OT (Lane 2:468). Moreover, the title πρωτότοκος is applied to Christ in 1:6, where he is clearly distinguished from angels (Cockerill 655). Second, ἀπογεγραμμένων is used in Scripture in conj. with humans, not angels (e.g., Isa 4:3; Dan 12:1; cf. Luke 10:20; Phil 4:3; Rev 3:5; cf. Ellingworth 680). See discussion in Lane 2:468–49. The word is also used in secular writing to record legal citizens (Koester 545). Additionally, each of the three terms (ἐκκλησίᾳ, πρωτοτόκων, and ἀπογεγραμμένων) occurs as designations of God's people, whom he delivered from Egypt (see Cockerill 654 n. 55).

καὶ κριτῇ θεῷ πάντων
to a Judge, who is God of all,

The fourth (and central) descriptor is κριτῇ (dat. sg. masc. of κριτής, -οῦ, ὁ, "judge" [most EVV]). Θεῷ is an appos. of κριτῇ. Πάντων (implied "people"; *pace* "things" [NLT]) modifies as a descriptive gen. This phrase could be tr. as "a judge, God of all" (e.g., CSB) or "God, judge of all" (most EVV). The word order here is intentional, and supports the first option (Attridge 376; Cockerill 656; cf. Moule 170). The position of κριτῇ is emph. (Lane 2:470), likely to contrast with the dread of judgment associated with Sinai. The image of God as judge recalls Heb 4:13 and 10:30. Here, God as judge is immediately followed by the presence of those made perfect and Jesus, mediator of the new covenant. Thus the emph. is on salvation and worshipful celebration in God's presence, made possible by Jesus.

καὶ πνεύμασι δικαίων τετελειωμένων
to the spirits of righteous people made perfect,

The fifth descriptor is πνεύμασι, which is modified by the descriptive gen. δικαίων (gen. pl. masc. of δίκαιος, -αία, -ον, "the spirits of the righteous" [most EVV; cf., NIV], "the spirits of the just" [NAB]; *pace* "good men" [REB]). This adj. recalls the citation of Hab 2:4 in Heb 10:38 as an indication of those who are pleasing to God (Lane 2:471). Τετελειωμένων is the gen. pl. masc. of the pf. pass. ptc. of τελειόω, "made perfect" (most EVV; see comments on 2:10). The adj. ptc. modifies δικαίων. The pf. tense is intensive (Campbell, *VA* 201). The identity of "spirits of righteous" is debated, but it most likely refers to believers who have died (both before and after) Jesus's advent and the perfection that he achieved (11:40; see also comments on 2:10). The designation refers to "the godly dead" in Jewish apocalyptic literature (Lane 2:470).

VERSE 24

καὶ διαθήκης νέας μεσίτῃ Ἰησοῦ
and to Jesus, the mediator of a new covenant,

The sixth descriptor is Ἰησοῦ, the position of which is emph. (cf. 2:9; 3:1; 6:20; 7:22; 10:19; 12:2; 13:20 [Lane 2:442 n. *nn*; Cockerill 658; Ellingworth 681]). The use of Ἰησοῦς continues the author's association of this name with Jesus's humanity and suffering (Attridge 376). Μεσίτῃ ("mediator" [see comments on 8:6]) is an appos. to Ἰησοῦ. Μεσίτῃ is modified by διαθήκης ("covenant," see comments on 7:22), which is modified by νέας (gen. sg. fem. of νέος, -α, -ον, "new"). The wording here recalls Heb 9:15. Most commentators view the switch from διαθήκης καινῆς to διαθήκης νέας as stylistic (Ellingworth 681; Lane 2:441 n. *oo*; cf. Attridge 376). This is the only place in BGk. where διαθήκης νέας occurs.

The ref. to Jesus as "mediator of a new covenant" offers a definitive contrast to Moses, the mediator of the old covenant, and heightens the contrast between the joyous celebration in the heavenly Zion and the terror of Sinai (cf. Lane 2:472). Moreover,

Jesus is positioned as the penultimate item of the list, with the means by which he mediated the new covenant (his blood) placed as the final element in the list (Cockerill 658).

καὶ αἵματι ῥαντισμοῦ κρεῖττον λαλοῦντι παρὰ τὸν Ἅβελ.
and to the sprinkled blood, which says better things than the blood of Abel.

The seventh and final descriptor is αἵματι, which is modified by ῥαντισμοῦ (gen. sg. masc. of ῥαντισμός, -οῦ, ὁ, "sprinkled" [most EVV; BDAG 903d]). Αἵματι is further modified by the adj. ptc. λαλοῦντι. Κρεῖττον ("better"; see comments on 1:4) is a subst. adj. that functions as the obj. of the ptc.: "something better" (NET), "a better word" (ESV, NIV), "better things" (REB). Some EVV (NASB) tr. κρεῖττον as an adv., "speaks better than." Παρά + acc. (τὸν Ἅβελ) indicates a comp. ("than"; Wallace 297 n. 10; 378; R 615, 667).

This clause is difficult to understand. The dir. ref. to sprinkled blood in the context of the new covenant recalls Christ's work outlined in Hebrews 9 and applied to believers in 10:22 (cf. Lane 2:473). The ref. to Abel is surprising given the focus on Sinai, and yet, the mention of Abel provides a fitting *inclusio* to the focus on faith and faithfulness in Heb 11:1–12:24 (cf. Ellingworth 682). Many thus see a contrast between the blood of Jesus and the blood of Abel (hence the addition of "blood" in the second part of the v. in many EVV), where the blood of Abel cries out for vengeance or vindication, whereas the blood of Jesus speaks of forgiveness and redemption (e.g., Bruce 361; Cockerill 659; Ellingworth 682; Lane 2:474; see esp. Koester 546 for a summary of main options). This understanding explains the var. rdg. παρὰ τὸ Ἅβελ in a few mss. (e.g., 𝔓[46] L), with τό referring to an implied αἷμα and as a poss. gen. ("the blood of Abel"). But the ref. to Abel in Heb 11:4 indicates that he "still speaks" through his faith, not his blood (cf. Attridge 377), although the author likely intended a distinction between how Abel "speaks" in 11:4 and how his blood speaks in 12:24 (Cockerill 658–59 n. 77). The best option is perhaps to understand that the blood of Christ has effected the new covenant and cleansed the believer's conscience, something which no blood shed under the former covenant could do. See Kevin B. McCruden, "The Eloquent Blood of Jesus: The Neglected Theme of the Fidelity of Jesus in Hebrews 12:24," *CBQ* 75 (2013): 504–20.

FOR FURTHER STUDY

92. Sinai/Heavenly Zion (Jerusalem) (12:18–24)

Casey, Juliana. "Christian Assembly in Hebrews: A Fantasy Island?" *TD* 30 (1982): 323–35.

DBI 572–74; 794; 980–81.

de Young, J. C. *Jerusalem in the New Testament: The Significance of the City in the History of Redemption and in Eschatology.* Kampen, Netherlands: Kok, 1960.

Dumbrell, William J. "Spirits of Just Men Made Perfect." *EQ* 48 (1976): 154–59.

Fohrer, G., and E. Lohse, *TDNT* 7:292–338.

*France, Richard T. "A Tale of Two Mountains: Mountains in Biblical Spirituality." *Rural Theology* 6 (2008): 117–25.

Levenson, Jon D. *ABD* 6:1098–1102.

*———. *Sinai and Zion: An Entry into the Jewish Bible*. Minneapolis: Winston, 1985.

MacRae, G. W. "'A Kingdom that Cannot Be Shaken': The Heavenly Jerusalem in the Letter to the Hebrews." Pages 98–112 in *Studies in the New Testament and Gnosticism*. Selected and edited by Daniel J. Harrington and Stanley B. Marrow. Wilmington, DE: Michael Glazier, 1987.

Mare, W. Harold. *ABD* 6:1097–98.

Newman, C. C. *DLNT* 561–65.

*Peterson, David. "The Spirits of Just Men Made Perfect (12:18–24)." Pages 160–66 in *Hebrews and Perfection: An Examination of the Concept of Perfection in the 'Epistle to the Hebrew.'* SNTSMS 47. Cambridge: Cambridge University Press, 1982.

Son, Kiwoong. *Zion Symbolism in Hebrews: Hebrews 12:18–24 as a Hermeneutical Key to the Epistle*. Paternoster Biblical Monographs. Waynesboro, GA: Paternoster, 2005.

93. Eschatology in Hebrews (12:18–24)

*Barrett, C. K. "The Eschatology of the Epistle to the Hebrews." Pages 363–93 in *The Background of the New Testament and Its Eschatology*. Edited by W. D. Davies and D. Daube. Cambridge: Cambridge University Press, 1964.

Beale, G. K. *DLNT* 330–45.

Brady, Cora. "The World to Come in the Epistle to the Hebrews." *Worship* 39 (1965): 329–39.

Caird, George B. "Just Men Made Perfect." *London Quarterly and Holborn Review* 191 (1966): 89–98.

Koester, 100–104.

Kreitzer, L. J. *DLNT* 856–75.

Mackie, Scott D. *Eschatology and Exhortation in the Epistle to the Hebrews*. WUNT 2/223. Tübingen: Mohr Siebeck, 2007.

Robinson, William Childs. "Eschatology of the Epistle to the Hebrews: A Study in the Christian Doctrine of Hope." *Enc* 22 (1961): 37–51.

Steyn, Gert Jacobus. "The Eschatology of Hebrews: As Understood within a Cultic Setting." Pages 429–50 in *Eschatology of the New Testament and Some Related Documents*. Edited by Jan G. van der Watt. WUNT 2/315. Tübingen: Mohr Siebeck, 2011.

Witherington, 185–90; 347–51.

HOMILETICAL SUGGESTIONS

Sinai and Zion Contrasted (12:18–24)

1. Seven Indications that God Is No Longer Present on Earthly Sinai (vv. 18–21)
    - (a) Untouchable (v. 18a)
    - (b) Blazing fire (v. 18b)
    - (c) Dark (v. 18c)
    - (d) Gloomy (v. 18d)
    - (e) Stormy (v. 18e)

- (f) Trumpet blast (v. 19a)
- (g) Sound of Words (v. 19b)
  - (1) The people were terrified (v. 19c–20)
  - (2) Even Moses was terrified (v. 21)

2. Seven Aspects of God's Glorious Presence in Heavenly Zion (vv. 22–24)
   - (a) The city of the living God, the heavenly Jerusalem (v. 22a)
   - (b) Myriads of angels in joyful worship (vv. 22b)
   - (c) The assembly of the firstborn (v. 23a)
   - (d) Judge, God of all (v. 23b)
   - (e) Spirits of perfected righteous ones (v. 23c)
   - (f) Jesus, the mediator of the new covenant (v. 24a)
   - (g) The sprinkled blood of forgiveness (v. 24b)

5. The Fifth Warning: Don't Miss God's Final Word (12:25–29)

STRUCTURE

The transition from exposition (vv. 18–24) to exhortation (vv. 25–29) is "abrupt" (Lane 2:474), an abruptness intensified by the lack of conj. (asyndeton) to introduce this new section (Attridge 379). The sharp exhortation not to reject God follows logically, however, after the dramatic depiction of what believers have (vv. 22–24 [Lane 2:475]). Cohesion between the two sections is found in the use of λαλοῦντι (v. 24) and λαλοῦντα (v. 25). The passage is structured around an impv. (v. 25), an indic. (v. 27), a hort. subjunc. (v. 28), and a verbless clause (v. 29).

25 Βλέπετε
μὴ παραιτήσησθε τὸν λαλοῦντα·
εἰ γὰρ ἐκεῖνοι οὐκ ἐξέφυγον ἐπὶ γῆς παραιτησάμενοι τὸν χρηματίζοντα,
πολὺ μᾶλλον ἡμεῖς οἱ τὸν ἀπ' οὐρανῶν ἀποστρεφόμενοι,

26 οὗ ἡ φωνὴ τὴν γῆν ἐσάλευσεν τότε,
νῦν δὲ ἐπήγγελται λέγων·
ἔτι ἅπαξ ἐγὼ σείσω
οὐ μόνον τὴν γῆν ἀλλὰ καὶ τὸν οὐρανόν.
27 τὸ δὲ ἔτι ἅπαξ δηλοῖ [τὴν] τῶν σαλευομένων μετάθεσιν
ὡς πεποιημένων,
ἵνα μείνῃ τὰ μὴ σαλευόμενα.
28 Διὸ βασιλείαν ἀσάλευτον παραλαμβάνοντες
ἔχωμεν χάριν,
δι' ἧς λατρεύωμεν εὐαρέστως τῷ θεῷ
μετὰ εὐλαβείας καὶ δέους·
29 καὶ γὰρ ὁ θεὸς ἡμῶν πῦρ καταναλίσκον.

VERSE 25

Βλέπετε μὴ παραιτήσησθε τὸν λαλοῦντα·
See to it that you do not reject the one who speaks.

Βλέπετε is an impv.: "see to it" (NASB, NIV), "see that" (ESV), "take care" (NET), "make sure" (NJB). The neg. adv. μή "is an expression of apprehension" (BDF §370[1]) that is usually followed by an aor. subjunc. This warning recalls the one in 3:12 (with a fut. indic.), also drawing on the neg. example of the wilderness generation. Παραιτήσησθε is the 2nd pl. aor. mid. subjunc. of παραιτέομαι; the mid. means "refuse" (ESV, NASB, NET, NIV) or "reject" (many EVV) when followed by the acc. (R 810; BDAG 764c; H. Balz, *EDNT* 3:23a). A neg. aor. subjunc. that follows an impv. indicates prohibition (cf. R 933). Together μὴ παραιτήσησθε indicate the "content" of the impv. βλέπετε (Lane 2:442 n. *rr*). The subst. ptc. λαλοῦντα ("the one who speaks") is the dir. obj. of παραιτήσησθε. The pres. continues the emph. in Hebrews on God speaking (cf. ESV, NASB, NET).

εἰ γὰρ ἐκεῖνοι οὐκ ἐξέφυγον ἐπὶ γῆς παραιτησάμενοι τὸν χρηματίζοντα,
For if they did not escape when they rejected him who warned them on earth,

Εἰ introduces the prot. of a first-class cond., which "indicates the assumption of truth for the sake of argument" (Wallace 690; R 922, 1160; BDF §372[1b]). Γάρ offers support for the warning in the first part of the v. (Ellingworth 684). Ἐξέφυγον is the 3rd pl. aor. act. indic. of ἐκφεύγω, "escape" (most EVV [BDAG 312a]). The subj. of ἐξέφυγον is ἐκεῖνοι, a ref. to the wilderness generation that recalls 4:2 (Attridge 379; made explicit in NAB, NLT). Ἐπὶ γῆς adv. modifies χρηματίζοντα locat. Its position is emph. (Lane 2:442 n. *vv*) and contrasts with ἀπ᾽ οὐρανῶν in the next clause. The contrast between earthly Sinai and heavenly Zion is here expanded to the entire earth and heaven (Ellingworth 685). Παραιτησάμενοι is the nom. pl. masc. of the aor. mid. ptc. of παραιτέομαι. Most EVV tr. the ptc. and subjunc. in the previous clause with the same Eng. vb. (see comments above). The sense here is "stronger" than the use of παραιτέομαι in v. 19 (Cockerill 662 n. 8); it implies repudiation (Attridge 380). The adv. ptc. modifies ἐξέφυγον temp., indicating contemp. time ("when" [most EVV]).

Χρηματίζοντα is the acc. sg. masc. of the pres. act. ptc. of χρηματίζω, "warn" (most EVV [BDAG 1089b]). The implied subj. is God. The vb. was used in conj. with Moses (8:5) and Noah (11:7). This v. parallels the warning in Heb 2:2–3. Each uses a first-class cond., followed by a question that applies the *a fortiori* argument to the audience, but the warning is more intense and the consequence more severe in this v. (see Cockerill 662–63).

πολὺ μᾶλλον ἡμεῖς οἱ τὸν ἀπ᾽ οὐρανῶν ἀποστρεφόμενοι,
even less will we if we turn away from him who warns us from heaven.

Πολὺ μᾶλλον (see comments on 12:9) introduces the apod. of the cond.—"how much less" (NET, NIV), "much less" (ESV, NASB). The v. presents another *a fortiori* argument characteristic of Hebrews. A form of ἐκφεύγω (e.g., ἐκφευξόμεθα, "we will escape") is understood elliptically from the prot. The nom. ἡμεῖς is emph. (BDF §277) and modifies the elliptical vb. It strengthens the contrast between the audience and ἐκεῖνοι (e.g., the wilderness generation). Ἀποστρεφόμενοι is the nom. pl. masc. of the pres. mid. ptc. of ἀποστρέφω (BDAG 123b). The ptc. is subst. and functions as an appos. to ἡμεῖς. It also has cond. force. Many EVV tr. ἀποστρεφόμενοι as a finite vb. (e.g., "if we turn away" [NIV], "reject" [ESV, NET], "turn our backs on Christ" [Barclay]). The art. τόν refers anaphorically to χρηματίζοντα in the prot. (Lane 2:442 n. *xx*), which is modified by the prep. phrase ἀπ᾽ οὐρανῶν. Many EVV make explicit the understood χρηματίζοντα and add an obj. (e.g., "from him who warns us" [CSB]).

The passage continues the emph. on God speaking in Hebrews. Some have suggested that the one speaking on earth was Moses (cf. NLT) and that God is the one now speaking from heaven. Yet allusions to the wilderness generation, the use of χρηματίζω (only used of God in the NT), and the allusion to Deut 5:23–24 (where God is the one speaking), all indicate that God is the speaker both "on earth" and "from heaven" (cf. Ellingworth 683; Lane 2:475–76). The contrast is not between speakers but rather modes of speaking (Attridge 380; Cockerill 661 n. 3).

In the passages concerning Sinai (e.g., Exod 19–20 and Deut 5), the entreaty that God speak no further (e.g., Heb 12:19) is not presented negatively; hence, the author in this v. appears to allude to the wilderness generation's repeated refusal to "hear God's voice" and thus to "harden their hearts," thereby recalling 3:12–19; cf. 2:1–4 (cf. Bruce 362–63). The clause may be understood as exclamation (GNB, NAB, NLT, NRSV) or a rhetorical question (NET, NIV, NJB). The effect is rhetorical: the author intends the audience to respond, "No, we are not those who turn away!" (Cockerill 663; cf. Koester 552).

VERSE 26

οὗ ἡ φωνὴ τὴν γῆν ἐσάλευσεν τότε,
His voice shook the earth at that time,

The antecedent of *οὗ* is *τὸν χρηματίζοντα* in v. 25. *Ἐσάλευσεν* is the 3rd sg. aor. act. indic. of *σαλεύω*, "shake" (most EVV [BDAG 911b; H. Balz, *EDNT* 3:224c]). The vb. is a "close synonym" of *σείσω* (see below [Cockerill 664]). The subj. of the vb. is *ἡ φωνή* (correctly tr. "his voice" in most EVV). The noun alludes back to v. 19 and perhaps also to the citation of Psalm 95 in Heb 3:7 (Ellingworth 685). *Τὴν γῆν* is the obj. of the vb. The correl. conj. *τότε* ("then" [NASB, NET], "at that time" [ESV, NIV]), *νῦν* ("now" [most EVV]) *δέ* continues the clear distinction that the author makes between the former and the new covenants (Lane 2:476). The rel. clause alludes to Exod 19:18, when God spoke at Sinai. Although this account does not record an earthquake, subsequent reflections on this event do (e.g., Judg 5:4–5, Pss 68:7–8; 77:18; 114:7 [Bruce 363 n. 195; Attridge 380 n. 32]).

νῦν δὲ ἐπήγγελται λέγων·
but now he has promised,

Ἐπήγγελται is the 3rd sg. pf. mid. indic. of *ἐπαγγέλλω*, "promised" (most EVV). *Λέγων* is redundant to *ἐπήγγελται*, which introduces dir. discourse. Whereas previously God's promise involved rest (4:1), the Abrahamic promises (6:13–15), the new covenant (8:6), and the eternal inheritance (9:15), here it involves the final judgment (Cockerill 664). Here the author brings "the art of combining warning and promise to perfection" (Cockerill 665).

Ἔτι ἅπαξ ἐγὼ σείσω οὐ μόνον τὴν γῆν ἀλλὰ καὶ τὸν οὐρανόν.
Yet once more I will shake not only the earth but also the heavens.

The adv. *ἔτι* ("yet" [ESV, NASB], left untr. in many EVV), together with the adv. *ἅπαξ* ("once more" [most EVV], "once and for all" [BDAG 97b]), modifies *σείσω*. The nom. *ἐγώ* is emph. (BDF §277). *Σείσω* is the 1st sg. fut. act. indic. of *σείω*, "shake" (most EVV [BDAG 918c]). The correl. cstr. οὐ μόνον. . . ἀλλὰ καί means "not only . . . but also" (BDF §479[1]).

The citation comes from Hag 2:6 and 2:21. Originally the oracle was spoken to Zerubbabel, Joshua, and the people as an encouragement at the (second) temple's dedication. The author makes several changes to LXX Hag 2:6. First, he adds "not only" and "but also" to stress the magnitude of the coming shaking (Koester 547). Second, he omits ref. to the sea and dry land, thereby focusing on earth and heaven (Lane 2:479). Third, he switches the word order: the LXX's τὸν οὐρανὸν καὶ τὴν γῆν become τὴν γῆν and τὸν οὐρανόν, which puts the latter in an emph. position (Lane 2:480). (For a comp. of the MT, LXX, and Hebrews, see Koester 547.) The image of a final, eschatological "shaking" is freq. associated with the Day of the Lord (Isa 13:13; Joel 2:10–11 [Koester 547; cf. Lane 2:479]). There are three time refs. in view in this v.: past (Sinai), present (what God has promised), and future (the final "shaking" [Lane 2:478]). The shaking of heaven as well as earth indicates "that this judgment is absolutely final" (Cockerill 666).

VERSE 27

τὸ δὲ Ἔτι ἅπαξ δηλοῖ [τὴν] τῶν σαλευομένων μετάθεσιν
This expression, "**Yet once more**," indicates the removal of what can be shaken—

The neut. art. τό introduces a key phrase from the Hag 2:6 citation ("this phrase" [ESV, NET], "this expression" [NASB], "the words" [NIV]; cf. Ellingworth 687; Wallace 238). Δέ continues the argument ("now" [EVV]). Δηλοῖ is the 3rd sg. pres. act. indic. of δηλόω, "indicate" (ESV, NIV), "denote" (NASB), "explain," "clarify" (BDAG 222d). The vb. introduces the author's exposition of the citation. Μετάθεσιν is the acc. sg. fem. of μετάθεσις, -εως, ἡ, "removal" (ESV, NET; Cockerill 667; cf. "removing" [NASB, NIV]), "passing away" (TCNT), "transformation" (BDAG 639a). Its use in Heb 7:12 suggests a transformation of the priesthood such that the old order is removed (Ellingworth 688). In Heb 11:5, the word describes Enoch's "translation" from earth to heaven (see comments below).

The ms. evidence is split regarding [τήν]. If original, it would suggest that μετάθεσιν had already been discussed (anaphoric use of the art.). On balance, the art. was likely added. Σαλευομένων is the gen. pl. neut. of the pres. pass. ptc. of σαλεύω (BDAG 911b). The ptc. is subst. ("what can be shaken" [NIV], "what is shaken" [NET], "things that are shaken" [ESV]). The subst. ptc. is an obj. gen. modifying μετάθεσιν.

ὡς πεποιημένων,
that is, created things—

Ὡς indicates "such as" (BDF §425[3]). The clause is appos. to τῶν σαλευομένων (Lane 2:443 n. *ccc*); "that is" (NET, NIV). The ptc. πεποιημένων is subst. and indicates "created things" (NET, NIV [BDAG 839b–c]; cf. "things that have been made"

[ESV]). The pf. pass. ptc. functions par. to a verbal adj. with a -τος ending (BDF §65[3]).

ἵνα μείνῃ τὰ μὴ σαλευόμενα.
so that what is not shaken might remain.

Ἵνα followed by the subjunc. indicates purpose. A neut. pl. (esp. inanimate objs.) often takes a sg. vb. (R 403). Σαλευόμενα is the nom. pl. neut. of the pres. pass. ptc. of σαλεύω, "shake" (see comments on 12:26). The ptc. is subst. and is the subj. of μείνῃ. The ptc. is neg. by μή.

Μένω is an important word in Hebrews (see comments on 7:3).The author's point is that, at the final judgment, those things that are part of God's created order and that have served their purpose in that context will be removed so that the permanent, final dwelling place (the city to come, the heavenly Jerusalem, the unshakable kingdom) is all that remains (cf. Cockerill 668).

VERSE 28

Διὸ βασιλείαν ἀσάλευτον παραλαμβάνοντες
Therefore, since we are receiving a kingdom that cannot be shaken,

Διό draws an inference from the previous v. Παραλαμβάνοντες is the nom. pl. masc. of the pres. act. ptc. of παραλαμβάνω, "receive" (most EVV). The idea is more of entering the kingdom than taking possession of it (Cockerill 670). The ptc. adv. modifies ἔχωμεν (see below), indicating cause ("since" [most EVV]). (Less naturally, ESV takes the ptc. as the complement of ἔχωμεν χάριν: "let us be grateful for receiving"). Βασιλείαν is the obj. of the ptc. Ἀσάλευτον (acc. sg. fem. of ἀσάλευτος, -ον) modifies βασιλείαν. The adj. is a cognate of σαλεύω and is formed with an α-privative prefix indicating "that cannot be shaken" (NIV), "unshakable" (NET), "enduring" ([BDAG 141a]). The position of βασιλείαν is emph. (Lane 2:443 n. *eee*).

Τὰ μὴ σαλευόμενα is now revealed to be an unshakable kingdom, the idea of which may have been drawn from both Hag 2:6–7 and Hag 2:21–22 (Cockerill 671 n. 46). The allusion here is probably to Hag 2:21, although Dan 7:14, 18 is also possible (Lane 2:484).

ἔχωμεν χάριν,
let us be thankful.

Ἔχωμεν is a hort. subjunc. Χάριν ("thanks," "gratitude" [NASB; BDAG 1080d]) is the obj. of ἔχωμεν. Although χάριν could be tr. "grace" (e.g., CSB), the context as well as the idiom ἔχω χάρις (BDAG 1080d) indicate that "gratitude" or "thankfulness" are in view (Cockerill 671–72 n. 47). Most EVV tr. ἔχωμεν as an equative vb. with χάριν as a pred. adj. (e.g., "let us be thankful" [NIV], "let us be grateful" [ESV]).

δι᾽ ἧς λατρεύωμεν εὐαρέστως τῷ θεῷ μετὰ εὐλαβείας καὶ δέους·
By it, we may serve God acceptably, with reverence and awe,

The antecedent of ἧς is χάριν. The prep. phrase δι᾽ ἧς indicates means ("by which" [NASB]). Λατρεύωμεν is the 1st pl. pres. act. subjunc. of λατρεύω, "worship," "serve" (BDAG 587c; see comments on 8:5). The dat. following λατρεύω indicates the one who is served (BDAG 587c), here θεῷ. The subjunc. is hort., even though it is in a rel. clause (BDF §377[3]; cf. R 955): "let us . . . worship" (NIV), "let us offer to God acceptable worship" (ESV). This is not reflected in some EVV (e.g., NASB). Εὐαρέστως is an adv. that modifies λατρεύωμεν ("acceptably" [NIV], "pleasing" [NET], "in an acceptable or pleasing manner" [BDAG 403d; BGk. hapax]). The cognate εὐαρεστέω occurs in 11:6, used to describe the faith that pleases God. Εὐλαβείας is the gen. sg. fem. of εὐλάβεια, -ας, ἡ, "reverence" (most EVV), "devotion" (NET [BDAG 407c]). The use of εὐλάβεια recalls its use in 5:7 with regard to Jesus (see comments there). Δέους is the gen. sg. neut. of δέος, -ους, τό, "fear" (NJB), "awe" (most EVV [BDAG 218c; NT hapax]). The two terms form a hendiadys: "with reverent fear" (Ellingworth 691), "godly fear" (Harris 65), although this is not reflected in EVV. Μετὰ εὐλαβείας καὶ δέους adv. modifies λατρεύωμεν indicating manner.

VERSE 29

καὶ γὰρ ὁ θεὸς ἡμῶν πῦρ καταναλίσκον.
for our God is a consuming fire.

Καὶ γάρ ("for even" BDF §452[3]; "for . . . indeed" [NET], "for" [many EVV], with καί untr.) offers the "final motivation" to serve God in v. 28 (Cockerill 673). Ὁ θεός is the subj. of this verbless clause, with πῦρ as a pred. nom. Καταναλίσκον is the nom. sg. neut. of the pres. act. ptc. of καταναλίσκω, "consume" (BDAG 522c; NT hapax); The compound κατα- is intensifying. The ptc. adj. modifies πῦρ ("consuming fire" [most EVV]), "devouring fire" [NET, NLT, REB]. The connotation of "destructive fire" (CEV) is probably misleading.

This v. alludes to Deut 4:24 (ὅτι κύριος ὁ θεός σου πῦρ καταναλίσκον; cf. Exod 24:17), in which Israel is warned not to forsake the covenant. The image recalls Heb 10:27, although there could be an allusion to Deut 9:3, where (more positively) fire consumes God's opponents so that his promises to his people can be fulfilled.

FOR FURTHER STUDY

94. The One Speaking (12:25)

Cortez, Felix H. "'See That You Do Not Refuse the One Who Is Speaking': Hearing God Preach and Obedience in the Letter to the Hebrews." *Journal of the Adventist Theological Society* 19 (2008): 98–108.

Smillie, Gene R. "'The One Who Is Speaking' in Hebrews 12:25." *TynBul* 55 (2004): 275–94.

95. The Unshakable Kingdom/Kingdom of God (12:27)

Goldsworthy, G. *NDBT* 615–20.
Kim, S. *DLNT* 629–38.
Thompson, James W. "That Which Cannot Be Shaken: Some Metaphysical Assumptions in Heb 12:27." *JBL* 94 (1975): 580–87.

96. The Fear/Judgment of God (12:29)

MacGregor, G. H. C. "The Concept of the Wrath of God in the New Testament." *NTS* 7 (1960–61): 101–9.
Seifrid, M. A. *DLNT* 621–25.
Stählin, G. *TDNT* 5:419–47.
Travis, Stephen H. *Christ and the Judgment of God: Divine Retribution in the New Testament*. Grand Rapids: Zondervan, 1987.

HOMILETICAL SUGGESTIONS

Do Not Reject the Voice of God Speaking! (12:25–29)

1. The Consequences for Rejecting This Voice (v. 25)
   (a) There were consequences when God spoke on earth (v. 25a)
   (b) How much greater will be the consequences as he speaks from heaven? (v. 25b)
2. The Power of God's Voice (v. 26)
   (a) Sinai shook when he spoke then (v. 26a)
   (b) But the entire universe will shake when he speaks at the end of the age (v. 26b)
3. The Final Shaking (v. 27)
   (a) All that is created will be shaken (v. 27a)
   (b) Only that which remains (with the Son) will not be shaken (v. 27b)
4. The True Kingdom (of the Son) Is an Unshakable Kingdom (v. 28a)
5. Our Response (vv. 28–29)
   (a) Gratitude (v. 28b)
   (b) Service to God (v. 28c)
   (c) For God's judgment is complete (v. 29)

VII. Exhortations and Offerings (13:1–21)

A. MORAL EXHORTATIONS FOR GOD'S PEOPLE (13:1–6)

STRUCTURE

Some speculate that Hebrews 13 was not orig. part of the epistle, and only later appended to an orig. "homily." Yet many textual and thematic links confirm the integrity of Hebrews 13. See also For Further Study 97 (The Integrity of Hebrews 13). The final series of exhortations divides between personal ethics (vv. 1–6) and church leadership (vv. 7–17). Heb 13:1–6 is structured around four pairs of exhortations (Cockerill 677–78) as indicated by the line spacing: the first pair (vv. 1–2) uses 3rd and 2nd pers. impvs.; the second pair (v. 3) uses a 2nd pers. impv. with two objs.; the 3rd and 4th pairs both have an implied vb. form with two objs. (aligned accordingly). This final pair is anchored with two OT citations, which are indented under the exhortations.

1 Ἡ φιλαδελφία μενέτω.
2 τῆς φιλοξενίας μὴ ἐπιλανθάνεσθε,
        διὰ ταύτης γὰρ ἔλαθόν τινες ξενίσαντες ἀγγέλους.

3 μιμνῄσκεσθε   τῶν δεσμίων   ὡς συνδεδεμένοι,
                 τῶν κακουχουμένων   ὡς καὶ αὐτοὶ ὄντες ἐν σώματι.

4 Τίμιος ὁ γάμος ἐν πᾶσιν καὶ
ἡ κοίτη ἀμίαντος,
    πόρνους γὰρ καὶ μοιχοὺς κρινεῖ ὁ θεός.

5 Ἀφιλάργυρος   ὁ τρόπος,
ἀρκούμενοι   τοῖς παροῦσιν.
    αὐτὸς γὰρ εἴρηκεν,
        Οὐ μή σε ἀνῶ οὐδ᾽ οὐ μή σε ἐγκαταλίπω,
6 ὥστε θαρροῦντας ἡμᾶς λέγειν,
        Κύριος ἐμοὶ βοηθός,
        [καὶ] οὐ φοβηθήσομαι,
        τί ποιήσει μοι ἄνθρωπος;

VERSE 1

Ἡ φιλαδελφία μενέτω.
Let brotherly love continue.

Φιλαδελφία is the nom. sg. fem. of φιλαδελφία, -ας, ἡ, "brotherly love" (ESV, NET), "love of the brethren" (NASB), "mutual love" (NAB, NRSV); BDAG 1055c; E. Plümacher, *EDNT* 3:424c). Μενέτω is the 3rd sg. pres. act. impv. of μένω. This is the only 3rd pers. impv. in Hebrews (Lane 2:507 n. *a*): "let . . . continue" (many EVV). The pres. is durative: "Keep on loving one another as brothers" (NIV).

The use of μένω (see comments on 7:3) provides a hook word to join this section to Heb 12:25–29 (cf. Attridge 385). It suggests that loving relationships within the Christian community are one manifestation of the "unshakable kingdom" (cf. Attridge 386; Koester 557).

Brotherly love was "highly esteemed" by both Greco-Roman and Jewish authors (cf. Bruce 369). Yet the idea of "brothers" and "sisters" outside one's immediate family was uncommon outside the Christian community (Attridge 385). Hebrews develops this further by proclaiming that believers have Christ himself as their brother (2:11–12, 17 [Ellingworth 694]).

VERSE 2

τῆς φιλοξενίας μὴ ἐπιλανθάνεσθε,
Don't neglect to show hospitality,

Ἐπιλανθάνεσθε is the 2nd pl. pres. mid. impv. of ἐπιλανθάνομαι, "neglect" (ESV, NASB, NET), "overlook," "care nothing about" (BDAG 374d). Many EVV add a complement to the vb. (e.g., "neglect to show" [ESV, NASB]). The tr. "do not forget" (NIV, NLT) weakens the intentionality of this exhortation. NJB tr. the neg. vb. as a positive: "always remember" (cf. GNB, NEB). The vb. is followed by the gen. only here in the NT (Ellingworth 695). Φιλοξενίας is the gen. sg. fem. of φιλοξενία, -ας, ἡ ("hospitality" [NET; BDAG 1058c], "entertain strangers" [NIV]).

Φιλαδελφία ("love of brothers") is joined with φιλοξενία ("love of foreigners") to indicate the scope of Christian concern (cf. Cockerill 679; Koester 563). The par. structure of the two clauses (noun followed by vb.) also links them (Cockerill 680 n. 13). Some EVV capture well the essence of φιλοξενία as "hospitality to strangers" (e.g., ESV, NASB, NLT). Both Jews and Gentiles considered such hospitality a virtue. Hospitality is a prominent NT theme. See For Further Study 98 (Hospitality in the Ancient World). The connotation of "entertain" (KJV) misses the necessity of hospitality in the ancient world.

διὰ ταύτης γὰρ ἔλαθόν τινες ξενίσαντες ἀγγέλους.
for by doing this some have welcomed angels as guests without knowing it.

Γάρ introduces the motivation for the impv. (cf. Cockerill 681). The antecedent of ταύτης is φιλοξενίας. The prep. phrase διὰ ταύτης is instr. (e.g., "through it" [NET], "by so doing" [NIV]), or possibly causal (e.g., "for thereby" [ESV], "because through it" [NET]). Ἔλαθον is the 3rd pl. aor. act. indic. of λανθάνω, "without knowing it" (most EVV), "without realizing it" (NLT), "escape notice" (BDAG 586b). Some EVV tr. the vb. as an adv. ("unknowingly" [NAB], "unawares" [ESV, REB]). Τινες is the subj. of ἔλαθον ("some" or "some people" [most EVV]). Ξενίσαντες is the nom. pl. masc. of the aor. act. ptc. of ξενίζω, "entertain" (ESV, NASB, NIV), "receive as a guest" (BDAG 683d). The supplemental ptc. modifies ἔλαθον (R 860), but the syntax reflects classical usage where the ptc. expresses the "chief idea" and the main vb. is "subordinate" (R 551; cf. BDF §414[3]). Thus many EVV tr. the ptc. as the main vb. and the main vb. as modifying the ptc. Ἀγγέλους is the obj. of the ptc. Lane (2:507 n. *c*) notes the paronomasia (play on words) in vv. 1–2 (φιλοξενίας—ἐπιλανθάνεσθε—ἔλαθόν—ξενίσαντες).

The allusion here is most likely to Abraham's hospitality to his three visitors (Gen 18:1–8; cf. Judg 13:3–22). The commands in vv. 2–3 may reflect Jesus's own teaching recorded in Matt 25:35–36 passed on by those who heard the Lord (2:1–4 [Lane 2:511]).

VERSE 3

μιμνῄσκεσθε τῶν δεσμίων ὡς συνδεδεμένοι,
Remember those in prison, as though you were in prison with them,

Μιμνῄσκεσθε is the 2nd pl. pres. mid. impv. of μιμνῄσκομαι, "remember" (most EVV [BDAG 652b]). The vb. takes a gen. obj. Prison conditions were often horrific, and prisoners depended on family and friends to provide basic needs. Δεσμίων is the gen. pl. masc. of δέσμιος, -ου, ὁ, "prisoners" (NASB [BDAG 219b]), "those in prison" (NET, NIV). Ὡς introduces a comp. The subst. ptc. is the obj. of the vb. Συνδεδεμένοι is the nom. pl. masc. of the pf. mid. ptc. of συνδέω. The ptc. is subst.: "as fellow imprisoned" [Cockerill 681 n. 20]). Most EVV tr. the ptc. with a finite vb.: "as if you were their fellow prisoners" (NIV), "as though you were fellow-prisoners" (BDAG 966d; NT hapax). This v. recalls the audience's own experience of imprisonment (10:32–34). See For Further Study 100 (First-Century Prisons).

τῶν κακουχουμένων ὡς καὶ αὐτοὶ ὄντες ἐν σώματι.
and the mistreated, as though you yourselves were suffering bodily.

Κακουχουμένων is the gen. pl. masc. of the pres. mid. ptc. of κακουχέω, "tortured" (NRSV; Cockerill 681–82), "mistreated" (ESV, NIV, NLT), "ill-treated" (NASB, NET); (cf. BDAG 502a; G. Schneider, *EDNT* 2:239c; BGk. hapax). This subst. ptc. is the second obj. of μιμνῄσκεσθε. As with the first part of the v., ὡς introduces a comp. Καί functions as an adv. ("also" [BDAG 495d]). Αὐτοί is an intensive ("you yourselves" [most EVV; BDAG 152c; Wallace 322]). Αὐτός can modify any pers. or gender in the nom. (BDAG 152c). The ptc. functions par. to συνδεδεμένοι. Ἐν σώματι either modifies an implied vb. (e.g., "suffer" [NIV], "torture" [NRSV]) or it is meant to underscore human "vulnerability to suffering and abuse" (Cockerill 682; cf. "in your own bodies" [NLT]; "for you are vulnerable too" [REB]). Some EVV (e.g., NIV) leave the prep. phrase untr. "In the body" (ESV, NASB, NJB) or esp. "in the one body" (JB) suggests the body of Christ, which is not likely here since that imagery does not occur elsewhere in Hebrews's use of *σῶμα* (cf. Cockerill 682 n. 25).

VERSE 4

Τίμιος ὁ γάμος ἐν πᾶσιν καὶ ἡ κοίτη ἀμίαντος,
Marriage is to be honored by all and the marriage bed kept undefiled,

The art. *γάμος* (-ου, ὁ, "marriage" [most EVV; BDAG 188d]) is the subj. of the first verbless clause in this v. Equative vbs. (e.g., *ἔστω*) are freq. omitted (R 395–96; cf. Attridge 387; Ellingworth 697). *Τίμιος* (-α, -ον, "be honored" [NET, NIV], "held in honor" [ESV, NASB], "be respected" [BDAG 1006a]) is a pred. adj. The position of the adj. is emph. (Lane 2:508 n. *i*). "Marriage is honorable" (NEB) is ambiguous. There are three options for *ἐν πᾶσιν* (cf. Cockerill 683 n. 28): instr. ("by all [people]" [most EVV]; cf. Lane 2:508 n. *j*), loc. ("among all" [ESV, NASB, NET]) and thus masc., or indicating manner with neut. *πᾶσιν* ("in every way" [Cassirer], "in all respects" [Ellingworth 697]). The effect of any of these options is the same.

Καί joins the two verbless clauses. The art. *κοίτη* (-ης, ἡ, "marriage bed" [most EVV; BDAG 554b]) is the subj. of the second verbless clause in this v. "Bed" is a euphemism for sexual intercourse within marriage (Attridge 387). The word often has neg. connotations, but is used positively here (Ellingworth 697). *Ἀμίαντος* (-ον) has a moral sense: "undefiled" (most EVV), "unpolluted" (Weymouth), "pure" (NIV; BDAG 54a). The same adj. was used to describe Jesus's high priesthood in 7:26. The adj. thus recalls the cleansing work of Christ in the life of the community (cf. Cockerill 683 n. 30).

The context is hort., as reflected in most EVV (e.g., "marriage must be honored" [NET]). This shift from the impv. in vv. 1–3 to verbless clauses in v. 4 adds "striking forcefulness" to two exhortations against actions that "destroy 'brotherly love'" (Cockerill 682–83).

πόρνους γὰρ καὶ μοιχοὺς κρινεῖ ὁ θεός.
because God will judge the sexually immoral and adulterers.

Γάρ grounds the previous exhortations (Ellingworth 698). The position of *ὁ θεός* is emph. (Lane 2:508 n. l). *Ὁ θεός* is the subj. of *κρινεῖ* ("judge" [most EVV]). *Πόρνους* is the acc. pl. masc. of *πόρνος*, -ου, ὁ, "sexually immoral" (NET, NIV), "fornicator" (NASB, NRSV). The adj. was used previously to describe Esau (cf. 12:13). *Μοιχούς* is the acc. pl. masc. of *μοιχός*, -οῦ, ὁ, "adulterer" (most EVV [BDAG 657b]). *Πόρνος* refers generally to sexual immorality, regardless of marital status, whereas *μοιχός* refers to adultery. The previous connection between sexual immorality and apostasy in Esau (12:14–17) and the covenantal foundation for marriage are underscored by the certainty of God's judgment on those who defile marriage (Cockerill 684).

VERSE 5

Ἀφιλάργυρος ὁ τρόπος,
Keep your life free from the love of money.

Like the two previous verbless clauses, context here indicates a hort. force (e.g., "keep . . . free from" [ESV, NIV]). The art. τρόπος (-ου, ὁ, "life" [ESV, NIV], "conduct" [NET]; BDAG 1017b; cf. "character" [NASB; Attridge 388]) is the subj. of the verbless clause. Ἀφιλάργυρος (-ον, "not loving money," "not greedy" [BDAG 157c; H. Balz, *EDNT* 1:183b]) is a pred. adj. Many EVV supply a neg. exhortation and tr. the noun without the alpha privative (e.g., "love of money" [e.g., ESV, NIV]).

The rep. of -ος endings as well as the alternation with -ους endings in vv. 4–5 offers "a sonorous effect" (Lane 508 n. *n–o*). Warnings against greed were common in Greco-Roman and Jewish writings (Ellingworth 699).

ἀρκούμενοι τοῖς παροῦσιν.
Be satisfied with what you have,

Ἀρκούμενοι is the nom. pl. masc. of the pres. pass. ptc. of ἀρκέω (BDAG 132a). In the pass. the vb. means "be satisfied" (GNT, NLT) or "be content" (ESV, NIV). The vb. takes a dat. obj. in the pass. (Ellingworth 699). Many EVV tr. the ptc. as an impv. The category of an independent or abs. ptc. is debated, so it is best to understand the impv. sense of the ptc. as a reflection of the hort. context (R 946; BDF §468[2]; *pace* Moule 179–80), while also modifying an implied ἔστω as an adv. ptc., indicating means (cf. Cockerill 685 n. 40). Παροῦσιν is the dat. pl. neut. of the pres. act. ptc. of πάρειμι. The neut. pl. ptc. denotes "possessions" (BDAG 774a); cf. "what you have" (most EVV).

αὐτὸς γὰρ εἴρηκεν·
for he himself has said,

The nom. αὐτός is emph. (BDF §277[1]), which is reflected in many EVV (e.g., "he himself"). Γάρ grounds the previous exhortations (Ellingworth 699). The pf. εἴρηκεν is likely extensive, emphasizing what was spoken (cf. Wallace 577). The subj. of the vb. is God. The collocation introduces the scriptural citation.

Οὐ μή σε ἀνῶ οὐδ᾽ οὐ μή σε ἐγκαταλίπω,
I will never leave you or abandon you.

Ἀνῶ is the 1st sg. aor. act. subjunc. of ἀνίημι, "leave" (ESV, NET, NIV), "fail" (NJB, NLT), "forsake" (NAB), "desert" (NASB [BDAG 82d]). Ἐγκαταλίπω is the 1st sg. aor. act. subjunc. of ἐγκαταλείπω, "forsake" (ESV, NASB, NIV), "abandon" (NET), "desert" (NJB; BDAG 273b). Οὐ μή followed by the aor. subjunc. indicates emph. denial, "never" (most EVV; cf. R 930; BDF §365[3]). Οὐδ᾽ (οὐ + δέ, which elides before a vowel [οὐ]) οὐ μή represents an uncommon triple neg. (R 1165). Alternatively οὐδ' may be understood as joining the two clauses, each of which has a double neg. (Cockerill 686 n. 45). The author may have intensified the LXX citation, which reads οὔτε μή (Moule 157). Alternatively, the text may represent a var. LXX rdg., which was also quoted in this form by Philo (Bruce 369 n. 8; Cockerill 686–87). The source of the citation is debated. It may derive from Josh 1:5, although Deut 31:6, 8 (cf. Gen 28:15) use the same vbs., but in the third pers. (Attridge 388). The citation also occurs in Philo, suggesting that both the author and Philo drew on an alternative LXX text (Attridge 388–89).

Sexual immorality and financial greed were freq. linked in Greco-Roman, Jewish, and Christian literature (Attridge 387). Both share a common root of not trusting God to provide and looking outside God-given boundaries for satisfaction. Both sins also eventually break Christian community. The alpha privative prefix of ἀφιλάργυρος and the root φιλ- recalls φιλαδελφία in v. 1 and φιλοξενία in v. 2 and underscores the contrast between "not love of money" and "love of brothers" and "love of foreigners" (Cockerill 685).

VERSE 6

ὥστε θαρροῦντας ἡμᾶς λέγειν,
Therefore, we may boldly say,

Ὥστε introduces a result clause. The "subj." of the inf. is ἡμᾶς. Θαρροῦντας is the acc. pl. masc. of the pres. act. ptc. of θαρρέω. Result is well expressed by BDAG 444b: "so we can say with confidence" (cf. NET; cf. NIV). The ptc. modifies λέγειν and may indicate manner ("with confidence" [NIV, NLT, NRSV], "confidently" [ESV, NASB]) or is circum. ("taking courage" [Cassirer]). The ptc. recalls previous exhortations regarding boldness (e.g., 3:6; 4:16; 10:19, 35 [Attridge 389 n. 77]). Elsewhere in Hebrews a scriptural citation is introduced with ref. to God speaking; the ref. here is unique in Hebrews (Ellingworth 700). The author invites the audience to confess its faith in God as a community (Cockerill 687).

Κύριος ἐμοὶ βοηθός,
The Lord is my helper;

Κύριος is the subj. of this verbless clause, with βοηθός (-όν, BDAG 180c) as the pred. adj. The adj. is subst. ("helper" [most EVV]). The imagery here recalls 2:18, 4:16 (Attridge 389). Ἐμοί is a dat. of poss. (correctly tr. as "my" in most EVV).

[καὶ] οὐ φοβηθήσομαι,
I will not be afraid.

Φοβηθήσομαι is the 1st sg. fut. pass. indic. of φοβέω, "be afraid" (most EVV [BDAG 1061c]; the vb. is always pass. in BGk. [BDAG 1060d]). The fut. reflects the LXX. The sense is durative (R 871). Καί appears in the LXX but may have been omitted by the author, or may reflect a different LXX rdg. (cf. Lane 2:509 n. *u*). Most likely it is not orig. (Ellingworth 701).

τί ποιήσει μοι ἄνθρωπος;
What can man do to me?

The interr. τί introduces a question: "what" (most EVV). The subj. of the question is ἄνθρωπος, the position of which is emph. (Ellingworth 701). Μοί is the indir. obj. of ποιήσει. The citation is from Ps 118:6 (LXX 117:6), the last of the Hallel ("praise") psalms, which would have been well known to the audience from Passover (Lane 2:520).

FOR FURTHER STUDY

97. The Integrity of Hebrews 13 (13:1–25)

Allen, David M. "Constructing 'Janus-Faced' Exhortations: The Use of Old Testament Narratives in Heb 13,1–8." *Bib* 89 (2008): 401–9.
Filson, Floyd V. *Yesterday: A Study of Hebrews in the Light of Chapter 13*. Naperville, IL: Allenson, 1967.
Lane, 1:*lxvi–lxviii*; 2:495–507.
Steyn, Gert Jacobus. "The Ending of Hebrews Reconsidered." *ZNW* 103 (2012): 235–53.

98. Hospitality in the Ancient World (13:1–6)

Barton, S. C. *DLNT* 501–7.
DBI 402–404.
Fitzgerald, J. T. *DNTB* 522–25.
Jipp, Joshua W. *Saved by Faith and Hospitality*. Grand Rapids: Eerdmans, 2017.
Koenig, J. *ABD* 3:299–301.
Pohl, C. D. *NDBT* 561–63.
Stählin, G. *TDNT* 5:17–25.

99. Ethical Imperatives in Hebrews (13:1–6)

Jones, Peter Rhea. "A Superior Life: Hebrews 12:3–13:25." *RevExp* 82 (1985): 391–405.
Lane, William L. "Unexpected Light on Hebrews 13:1–6 from a Second Century Source." *PRSt* 9 (1982): 267–74.
Smith, T. C. "An Exegesis of Hebrews 13:1–17." *Faith and Mission* 7 (1989): 70–78.
Thompson, James W. "Insider Ethics for Outsiders: Ethics for Aliens in Hebrews." *ResQ* 53 (2011): 207–19.

100. First-Century Prisons (13:3)

Koester, 564–65.
Rapske, B. M. *DNTB* 827–30.
Skinner, Matthew L. *NIDB* 4:615.
van der Toorn, Karel. *ABD* 5:468–69.

HOMILETICAL SUGGESTIONS

Ethical Imperatives for God's People (13:1–6)

1. Attend to Others (vv. 1–2)
   - (a) Love the people of God (v. 1)
   - (b) Show hospitality to strangers (v. 2)
2. Care for the Oppressed (v. 3)
   - (a) For prisoners as if you were imprisoned (v. 3a)
   - (b) For those mistreated as if it were you yourselves (v. 3b)
3. Protect Your Marital Pledges (v. 4)
   - (a) Honor marriage in every attitude (v. 4a)
   - (b) Honor marriage in every practice (v. 4b)
4. Be Content with What You Have (vv. 5–6)
   - (a) Do not love money (v. 5a)
   - (b) Focus on being satisfied with what you already have (v. 5b)
     - (1) Knowing that God will never abandon you (v. 5c)
     - (2) Knowing that the Lord helps and protects us (v. 6)

B. REMEMBERING CHURCH LEADERS (13:7–19)

STRUCTURE

The ref. to leaders (ἡγουμένοι) in v. 7 and v. 17 forms an *inclusio* that brackets the first part of this passage (Attridge 390–91). Three initial exhortations (underlined; vv. 7–9) are followed by an "explanatory paraenesis" in vv. 10–16 (Lane 2:526). The passage concludes with a series of four impv. (underlined; vv. 17–19).

7 <u>Μνημονεύετε</u> τῶν ἡγουμένων ὑμῶν,
οἵτινες ἐλάλησαν ὑμῖν τὸν λόγον τοῦ θεοῦ,
ὧν ἀναθεωροῦντες τὴν ἔκβασιν τῆς ἀναστροφῆς
<u>μιμεῖσθε</u> τὴν πίστιν.

8 Ἰησοῦς Χριστὸς ἐχθὲς καὶ σήμερον ὁ αὐτὸς καὶ εἰς τοὺς αἰῶνας.
9 διδαχαῖς ποικίλαις καὶ ξέναις μὴ <u>παραφέρεσθε</u>·
καλὸν γὰρ χάριτι βεβαιοῦσθαι τὴν καρδίαν,
οὐ βρώμασιν ἐν οἷς οὐκ ὠφελήθησαν
οἱ περιπατοῦντες.

10 ἔχομεν θυσιαστήριον ἐξ οὗ φαγεῖν οὐκ ἔχουσιν ἐξουσίαν οἱ τῇ σκηνῇ λατρεύοντες.
11 ὧν γὰρ εἰσφέρεται ζῴων τὸ αἷμα περὶ ἁμαρτίας εἰς τὰ ἅγια διὰ
τοῦ ἀρχιερέως,
τούτων τὰ σώματα κατακαίεται ἔξω τῆς παρεμβολῆς.
12 διὸ καὶ Ἰησοῦς . . . ἔξω τῆς πύλης ἔπαθεν
ἵνα ἁγιάσῃ διὰ τοῦ ἰδίου αἵματος τὸν λαόν.
13 τοίνυν <u>ἐξερχώμεθα</u> πρὸς αὐτὸν ἔξω τῆς παρεμβολῆς
τὸν ὀνειδισμὸν αὐτοῦ φέροντες·
14 οὐ γὰρ ἔχομεν ὧδε μένουσαν πόλιν
ἀλλὰ τὴν μέλλουσαν ἐπιζητοῦμεν.
15 Δι᾽ αὐτοῦ [οὖν] <u>ἀναφέρωμεν</u> θυσίαν αἰνέσεως διὰ παντὸς τῷ θεῷ,
τοῦτ᾽ ἔστιν καρπὸν χειλέων ὁμολογούντων
τῷ ὀνόματι αὐτοῦ.
16 τῆς δὲ εὐποιΐας καὶ κοινωνίας μὴ <u>ἐπιλανθάνεσθε</u>·
τοιαύταις γὰρ θυσίαις εὐαρεστεῖται ὁ θεός.

17 <u>Πείθεσθε</u> τοῖς ἡγουμένοις ὑμῶν καὶ
<u>ὑπείκετε</u>,
αὐτοὶ γὰρ ἀγρυπνοῦσιν ὑπὲρ τῶν ψυχῶν ὑμῶν
ὡς λόγον ἀποδώσοντες,
ἵνα μετὰ χαρᾶς τοῦτο ποιῶσιν καὶ μὴ στενάζοντες·
ἀλυσιτελὲς γὰρ ὑμῖν τοῦτο.

18 <u>Προσεύχεσθε</u> περὶ ἡμῶν·
πειθόμεθα γὰρ ὅτι καλὴν συνείδησιν ἔχομεν,
ἐν πᾶσιν καλῶς θέλοντες ἀναστρέφεσθαι.

19 περισσοτέρως δὲ παρακαλῶ τοῦτο ποιῆσαι,
ἵνα τάχιον ἀποκατασταθῶ ὑμῖν.

VERSE 7

Μνημονεύετε τῶν ἡγουμένων ὑμῶν,
Remember your leaders

Μνημονεύετε is the 2nd pl. pres. act. impv. of μνημονεύω, "remember" (most EVV [BDAG 655c]). The pres. is iterative ("continue to remember" [Lane 2:522 n. *a*], most EVV). The vb. recalls the synonym μιμνῄσκομαι in v. 3. The vb. takes a gen. obj. Ἡγουμένων is the gen. pl. masc. of the pres. mid. ptc. of ἡγέομαι. The subst. ptc. denotes "leaders" (most EVV [BDAG 434a]), "those who led you" (NASB). The term could apply to military, political, or religious leaders; however, it was used esp. for leaders within the Christian community in Rome (Attridge 391; Koester 559), although this usage could postdate Hebrews (Cockerill 689–90 n. 3). Ὑμῶν is poss.

οἵτινες ἐλάλησαν ὑμῖν τὸν λόγον τοῦ θεοῦ,
who have spoken God's word to you.

The antecedent of the indef. pron. οἵτινες is ἡγουμένων. The distinction between the def. and indef. rel. pron. was fading in Koine Gk. Οἵτινες is the subj. of ἐλάλησαν. The obj. of the vb. is τὸν λόγον, which is modified by the poss. gen. θεοῦ. The expression τὸν λόγον τοῦ θεοῦ recalls 4:12. Ὑμῖν is the indir. obj. of the vb. The clause could allude to 2:3 or could refer more generally to others who evangelized and preached to the congregation (cf. Koester 559).

ὧν ἀναθεωροῦντες τὴν ἔκβασιν τῆς ἀναστροφῆς
As you carefully observe the outcome of their lives,

The antecedent of ὧν is ἡγουμένων. Ἀναθεωροῦντες is the nom. pl. masc. of the pres. act. ptc. of ἀναθεωρέω, "reflect on" (NET), "consider" (ESV, NIV [BDAG 63c]). The pres. likely continues the iter. and possibly the impv. force of μνημονεύετε (e.g., ESV, NET, NIV). The ptc. modifies both μνημονεύετε and μιμεῖσθε, indicating means (Cockerill 690; cf. NASB, NJB). Ἔκβασιν (acc. sg. fem. of ἔκβασις, -εως, ἡ, "result" [NASB], "outcome" [most EVV; BDAG 299d]; H. Balz, *EDNT* 1:406c) is the obj. of the ptc. The word connotes a successful end to one's life (e.g., Wis 2:17; "how their lives ended" [NAB]); Koester 559; Lane 2:522 n. *d*]). In the context of Hebrews, this would imply these leaders' faithfulness to the end, but does not necessarily imply martyrdom (Cockerill 690; Koester 559). Ἀναστροφῆς is the gen. sg. fem. of ἀναστροφή, -ῆς, ἡ, "way of life" (ESV, NIV), "life" (NET), "conduct" (NASB), "behavior" (BDAG 73b). Ἀναστροφῆς modifies ἔκβασιν as an ablatival (source) gen. (R 514).

μιμεῖσθε τὴν πίστιν.
imitate their faith.

Μιμεῖσθε is the 2nd pl. pres. mid. impv. of μιμέομαι, "imitate" (NET, NIV), "emulate" (BDAG 651d), "follow the example of" (NLT). Context indicates that the art. is functioning par. to a poss. pron. ("their faith" [most EVV]; Cockerill 690). The tone of this v. suggests that these leaders may have died (implied with "former leaders" [Barclay, Weymouth]); thus, the audience is exhorted to consider their lives in their totality (Bruce 374–75). The v. recalls the exemplars in Hebrews 11, whose faith is also worthy of emulation. Any putative "crisis" of leadership is challenged by the command to "imitate" the faith of these leaders (Lane 2:528).

VERSE 8

Ἰησοῦς Χριστὸς ἐχθὲς καὶ σήμερον ὁ αὐτὸς καὶ εἰς τοὺς αἰῶνας.
Jesus Christ is the same yesterday, today, and forever.

The position of Ἰησοῦς Χριστός is emph. (Lane 2:522 n. *e*). This is the second (of three) occurrences of the compound Ἰησοῦς Χριστός in Hebrews (cf. 10:10; 13:21 [Lane 2:529]). As is common, an equative vb. (e.g., ἐστίν) is unnecessary (R 395). Αὐτός functions as an identifying adj. ("same"; Wallace 349) and as the pred. nom. The adv. ἐχθές means "yesterday" (most EVV [BDAG 419b]); the adv. σήμερον means "today" (most EVV). Εἰς τοὺς αἰῶνας ("forever" [most EVV], "to all eternity" [Cassirer], "the ages to come" [Weymouth]) recalls the sim. εἰς τὸν αἰῶνα in 1:8; 5:6; 6:20; 7:17, 21, 24, 28 (see comments on 1:8). The "center point" of the adv. modifiers, ὁ αὐτὸς, recalls the sim. affirmation in 1:12 (citing Ps 102 [Attridge 392]). Thus the v. affirms Jesus's divinity (Koester 560). Both the adv. and the prep. phrase modify the implied equative vb.

The adv. may correlate to Jesus's ministry (e.g., yesterday, he offered up his life [Heb 5:7]; today, he presents believers before the Father [Heb 4:15]; and forever, he intercedes [Heb 7:25]; so Bruce 375). More likely, however, "yesterday" refers to previous church leaders, and "today" correlates with present ones—but Jesus Christ is "forever" (so Lane 2:529–30; cf. Harris 95). The v. also anticipates the following exhortation (v. 9)—various teachings may come and go, but Jesus is forever (cf. Attridge 392; Bruce 375; Lane 2:528). There may be an inference that these leaders' faithfulness affirms the declaration in v. 8 and perhaps reflects the content of their preaching (Cockerill 690–91).

VERSE 9

διδαχαῖς ποικίλαις καὶ ξέναις μὴ παραφέρεσθε·
Don't be led astray by various kinds of strange teachings;

Παραφέρεσθε is the 2nd pl. pres. pass. impv. of παραφέρω. The vb. has a fig. sense here: "be carried away by" (NASB, NET, NIV [BDAG 772d]). The pass. is permissive (Wallace 441; Cockerill 692 n. 15). It is not clear from the pres. prohibition alone that the audience was to stop an action already begun (cf. Lane 2:522 n. *g*), although the abrupt shift from remembering former leaders to this exhortation does suggest a current threat to the community (cf. Cockerill 692–93; Lane 2:530–31). Thus the pres. is either iterative or durative (Ellingworth 707). Being carried away is the opposite of Christ's "constancy" (Koester 560).

The pl. διδαχαῖς occurs only here in the NT; it suggests "the polyvalent and polymorphous nature of human traditions" (Lane 2:532; cf. Koester 560; H. F. Weiss, *EDNT* 1:319d). Its position is emph., which suggests that the author has specific, contemporary "teachings" in view (Cockerill 692). The adj. ποικίλαις (dat. pl. fem. of ποικίλος, -η, -ον; "varied" [NASB], "diverse" [ESV; BDAG 842b–c]) modifies διδαχαῖς, as does ξέναις (dat. pl. fem. of ξένος, -η, -ον, "strange" [most EVV], "perverse" [Cockerill 694–95 n. 25], "outlandish" [REB]). The implication is that the teaching is foreign or contrary to the reality of the new covenant (Ellingworth 706–707). The two terms form a hendiadys (cf. Lane, 2:522 n. *h*): e.g., "various kinds of strange teachings" (CSB). The placement of this exhortation at the end of the epistle emphasizes the complete sufficiency of what the audience has in Christ (Cockerill 694–95). The contrast between the pl. "teachings" (v. 9) and the sg. Jesus (v. 8) recalls the sim. contrast drawn at the opening of the epistle (Heb 1:1–2), where ποικίλος also occurs. Once again, assonance is used effectively (διδαχαῖς ποικίλαις καὶ ξέναις [Lane 2:552 n. *h*]).

καλὸν γὰρ χάριτι βεβαιοῦσθαι τὴν καρδίαν,
for it is good for the heart to be established by grace

Γάρ offers the antidote to these strange, false teachings. Καλόν is pred. with an implied impers. vb. and subj. ("it is good" [most EVV]). Βεβαιοῦσθαι is the pres. pass. inf. of βεβαιόω, "strengthened" (most EVV [BDAG 173a]). This vb. was previously used in 2:3 (cf. 3:14; 6:16; 9:17) in conj. with those who orig. proclaimed the word of God to the audience (see Koester 560). The inf. is epex., further elaborating what is "good." Καρδίαν is the subj. of the inf. Throughout the epistle, the heart has been the place of rebellion or faith (Cockerill 695). The art. could indicate poss. ("our hearts" [NIV]). The dat. χάριτι instr. modifies βεβαιοῦσθαι ("by grace" [most EVV]).

οὐ βρώμασιν ἐν οἷς οὐκ ὠφελήθησαν οἱ περιπατοῦντες.
and not by food regulations, since those who observe them have not benefited.

Βρώμασιν is the dat. pl. neut. of βρῶμα, "food" (ESV, NASB [BDAG 184d]). The word previously had a neg. connotation (9:10), as it does here (Cockerill 695–96; Ellingworth 708). The dat. parallels χάριτι and instr. modifies βεβαιοῦσθαι, which is understood elliptically here. The neg. οὐ is unusual with an inf. (R 1162). The antecedent of οἷς is βρώμασιν. Ὠφελήθησαν is the 3rd pl. aor. pass. indic. of ὠφελέω, "benefit" (ESV, NASB, NET), "be of benefit to" (NIV), "be of use to" (BDAG 1107d). Περιπατοῦντες is the nom. pl. masc. of the pres. act. ptc. of περιπατέω. The metaphorical "walk" is rendered "observe" (NRSV), "participate in" (NET), "devoted to" (ESV), "so occupy with" (NASB). Some EVV tr. the ptc. according to the context (e.g., "eat" [NIV]). The subst. ptc. is the subj. of ὠφελήθησαν. Ἐν οἷς may have a double function of modifying οὐκ ὠφελήθησαν, either instr. or causally, while also modifying περιπατοῦντες in a locat. (metaphorical) sense (Ellingworth 708).

The "various strange teachings" are not elaborated, but the ref. to "food" could suggest contemp. "Jewish sacrificial meals" (Lane 2:532–35; "dietary laws" [JB], "ritual meals" [NET], "ceremonial foods" [NIV]) that paralleled sacrificial meals in the temple but were "conducted throughout the Roman world" (Cockerill 695). The teachings do not appear to be novel, since there has been time to observe their ineffectiveness (Lane 2:531). Gnostic practices are ruled out since most often involved abstention from certain foods (Cockerill 695–96 n. 32). In any event, the teachings challenged reliance on grace alone for the strengthening of one's heart for perseverance (cf. Lane 2:531).

VERSE 10

ἔχομεν θυσιαστήριον ἐξ οὗ φαγεῖν οὐκ ἔχουσιν ἐξουσίαν οἱ τῇ σκηνῇ λατρεύοντες.
We have an altar from which those who worship at the tabernacle do not have a right to eat.

Ἔχομεν continues the focus on what believers "have" in Hebrews (cf. Attridge 396 n. 83; Cockerill 696). (See comment on 12:1.) Θυσιαστήριον (acc. sg. neut. of θυσιαστήριον, -ου, τό, "altar" [most EVV; BDAG 463b]) is the obj. of ἔχομεν. This opening clause is the "thesis" of vv. 10–12 (Lane 2:537).

The antecedent of οὗ is θυσιαστήριον. The rel. pron. is embedded in the prep. phrase beginning with ἐξ, which modifies θυσιαστήριον. Λατρεύοντες is the nom. pl. masc. of the pres. act. ptc. of λατρεύω, "those who minister" (NIV), "those who serve" (ESV, NASB, NET). (See comments on 8:5.) The ptc. is subst. Σκηνῇ is the dat. sg. fem. of σκηνή, -ῆς, ἡ, "tabernacle" (most EVV [BDAG 928b]). The dat. modifies λατρεύοντες locat. Notice the embedding of the dat. within οἱ . . . λατρεύοντες. The entire collocation is the subj. of ἔχουσιν. The "worshippers" refers to contemporaries who continued to associate with the Levitical order, not believers (cf. Cockerill 697–98). This is indicated by the shift from the first pers. to the third pers. (Lane 2:539). Notice also the contrast between what believers have through Christ and what those who remain in the old order do not have (not limited to priests *only* [*pace* CEV, GNB, NLT]). The obj. of the vb. is ἐξουσίαν (acc. sg. fem. of ἐξουσία, -ας, ἡ, "right" [most EVV]). The language alludes to LXX Lev 6:30. Φαγεῖν is the obj. complement of ἐξουσίαν. It may also be understood as epex. Its position is emph. (Lane 2:523 n. *m*). It is likely understood fig., referring to participating in the benefits of Christ's sacrifice (see Cockerill 697–98; cf. Koester 570).

There are three main ways to understand the altar (following Koester 568–69).

*1. The cross and Christ's sacrificial death. By means of synecdoche (a part for the whole), the altar "encompasses multiple dimensions of Christ's death," which par. aspects of the Levitical system (so Attridge 396; Cockerill 697; Koester 568; Lane 2:538).

2. The heavenly sanctuary. This draws on 8:1, where Jesus is presented as the high priest in the heavenly sanctuary. Hebrews, however, does not indicate an altar in the heavenly sanctuary (Cockerill 696).
3. The Eucharist/Lord's Supper. Hebrews, however, makes no overt ref. to the Lord's Supper (Cockerill 696). Moreover, the association between the altar and the Lord's Supper postdates the composition of Hebrews (cf. Lane 2:538–39).

VERSE 11

ὧν γὰρ εἰσφέρεται ζῴων τὸ αἷμα περὶ ἁμαρτίας εἰς τὰ ἅγια διὰ τοῦ ἀρχιερέως,
For . . . those animals whose blood is brought into the most holy place by the high priest as a sin offering

Γάρ indicates that vv. 11–12 ground the statement in v. 10 (cf. Lane 2:539–40). The antecedent of ὧν (ζῴων) is "incorporated" within the rel. clause (see Cockerill 699 n. 47). The case of the rel. pron. has been "attracted" to the antecedent as well (R 718–19). The rel. pron. indicates that this clause is subord. to the next clause. Εἰσφέρεται is the 3rd sg. pres. pass. indic. of εἰσφέρω, "carry" (NIV), "bring in" (most EVV [BDAG 295c]). The subj. of the vb. is αἷμα. Ζῴων is the gen. pl. neut. of ζῷον, -ου, τό, "animal" (most EVV [BDAG 431c]). The generic ref. to "animals" both conflates the individual sacrificial animals (e.g., bulls and goats) and contrasts these sacrificial offerings with the sg. offering of Christ himself (Cockerill 699). Περὶ ἁμαρτίας is used in the LXX as "a technical expression" for sin offerings (Moule 63; see Harris 182–83; so most EVV; cf. "rite of expiation" [NJB]). As with the previous ref., ἅγια (acc. pl. neut.) refers to the inner chamber of the tabernacle (see comments on 9:12). Εἰς τὰ ἅγια modifies εἰσφέρεται spatially ("into" [most EVV]). The rep. of εἰς with a prefixed vb. (εἰσφέρεται) is common. Διὰ τοῦ ἀρχιερέως modifies εἰσφέρεται instr. ("by" [most EVV]). Ἀρχιερέως is the agent of the pass. vb., although some EVV (NET, NIV, NLT) tr. ἀρχιερέως as the subj. of the vb.

τούτων τὰ σώματα κατακαίεται ἔξω τῆς παρεμβολῆς.
[the bodies] are burned outside the camp.

The correl. use of ὧν . . . τούτων puts the focus on the second clause (Lane 2:523 n. *q*): "for [although] the blood of those animals is brought as a sin offering into to the tabernacle by the high priest, their bodies are burned outside the camp" (cf. NET). Κατακαίεται is the 3rd sg. pres. pass. indic. of κατακαίω, "burn" (most EVV), "consume" (BDAG 517b–c). Σώματα is the subj. of the vb. Παρεμβολῆς is the gen. sg. fem. of παρεμβολή, -ῆς, ἡ, "camp" (most EVV [BDAG 775a]; H. Balz, *EDNT* 3:38a).

The v. alludes to Lev 16:27–28, which prescribed that sacrificed animals had to be burned completely outside of the encampment. (For a comp. of this v. with LXX Lev 16:27, see Ellingworth 712–13).

VERSE 12

διὸ καὶ Ἰησοῦς,
Therefore, Jesus also . . .

Διό is an inferential conj. (BDAG 250c) that draws on the exposition in v. 11 both to introduce the comp. with Jesus (v. 12) and to prepare for the application to the audience (v. 13). The syntax is a bit unusual in that the ἵνα clause is embedded between the subj. Ἰησοῦς and the vb. ἔπαθεν (see below). The cstr., however, intensifies the ref. to Jesus (cf. Lane 2:523 n. *r*).

ἵνα ἁγιάσῃ διὰ τοῦ ἰδίου αἵματος τὸν λαόν,
so that he might sanctify the people by his own blood.

Ἵνα, followed by the subjunc., indicates purpose. The dependent clause modifies ἔπαθεν. Ἁγιάσῃ is the 3rd sg. aor. act. subjunc. of ἁγιάζω ("consecrate" [NAB, REB], "make holy" [NIV, NLT], "sanctify" [most EVV; BDAG 10a]). Λαόν is the obj. of the vb. and continues an important theme in Hebrews (see comments on 2:11). The identical adj. ἰδίου modifies αἵματος. The prep. phrase διὰ τοῦ ἰδίου αἵματος adv. modifies ἁγιάσῃ instr. ("by means of" [Harris 120]).

ἔξω τῆς πύλης ἔπαθεν.
suffered outside the gate,

Ἔπαθεν is the 3rd sg. aor. act. indic. of πάσχω, "suffered" (most EVV [see comments on 2:18]). Although most EVV tr. πάσχω as "suffer," the author of Hebrews uses this vb. consistently in conj. with Jesus's death (cf. Lane 2:523 n. *s*; "suffered and died" [NLT]). Πύλης (gen. sg. fem. of πύλη, -ης, ἡ, "gate" [most EVV]; BDAG 897b; R. Kratz, *EDNT* 3:196d; cf. "city gate" [NIV, NLT], *pace* "camp" [NET, NJB]) is the obj. of the prep. ἔξω. The prep. phrase adv. modifies ἔπαθεν locat.

The author draws a par. between the Day of Atonement sacrifices being burned outside the camp and Jesus's crucifixion "outside the city" (John 19:17–20); executions in general were carried out outside of towns and cities (Koester 570). The author's point is twofold: Jesus's death "fulfilled the intention of the Day of Atonement," and the ref. to "outside the gate" "involved the shame of exclusion from the sacred precincts" (Lane 2:542; cf. Cockerill 700–701).

VERSE 13

τοίνυν ἐξερχώμεθα πρὸς αὐτὸν ἔξω τῆς παρεμβολῆς
Let us then go to him outside the camp,

Τοίνυν draws an inference from the previous statement, "then" (many EVV), "therefore" (ESV), "so" (NASB, NLT [BDAG 1009c]). Ἐξερχώμεθα (1st pl. pres. mid. subjunc. of ἐξέρχομαι) is hortatory: "let us go out to" (NASB, NLT), "let us go to" (ESV, NIV). Πρὸς αὐτόν is locat. Other compounds of ἔρχομαι have indicated movement toward, whereas ἐξέρχομαι indicates movement from. Yet this is actually two sides of the same reality: believers are to go out of the old order and to approach and enter the new one (see comments below). Παρεμβολῆς (gen. sg. fem. of παρεμβολή, -ῆς, ἡ, "camp" [most EVV; BDAG 775a]) is the obj. of the prep. ἔξω ("outside" [most EVV]). The prep. phrase ἔξω τῆς παρεμβολῆς modifies ἐξερχώμεθα, indicating locat.

τὸν ὀνειδισμὸν αὐτοῦ φέροντες·
bearing his disgrace.

Φέροντες is the nom. pl. masc. of the pres. act. ptc. of φέρω, "bear" (most EVV). Its position is emph. (Lane 2:523 n. *w*). The ptc. modifies ἐξερχώμεθα, indicating manner. The obj. of the ptc. is ὀνειδισμόν (acc. sg. masc. of ὀνειδισμός, -οῦ, ὁ, "humiliation" [NJB], "stigma" [REB], "abuse" [NET, NRSV], "insult" [NAB], "reproach" [ESV, NASB], "disgrace" [NIV, NLT]). See comments on 10:33, 11:26. The author may intend a contrast between not being "borne" (παραφέρεσθε) by strange teaching, but rather "bearing" (φέροντες) Christ's reproach (Cockerill 703). Many EVV tr. this as a clause (e.g., "the disgrace he bore" [NIV]).

"Outside the camp" has been understood in several ways (summary based in part on Koester 570–571; see also Lane 2:544–46).

1. Leaving the material present for a transcendent world. For those who see a Philonic, middle Platonic background of thought for Hebrews, "outside the camp" entails rejecting bodily passions. But this background does not cohere well with Hebrews (see Cockerill 700).
2. Leaving the "sacred" to enter and serve in the "profane" world. The bifurcation between sacred and profane in Hebrews, however, is not based on geography; believers are fully sanctified by Christ's blood, regardless of their "location."

*3. Leaving Jewish practices and not retreating to them. Because Jesus is no longer "outside the camp," but is exalted at the right hand of the Father, going to him "outside the camp" means participating in the "shame and reproach" that Christ endured (Cockerill 701–702).

In any event, it must be stressed that the audience is not being urged to go "outside," but rather to go to Jesus, who is "outside." Moreover, "outside" is not "a location, but a social reality" of reproach for one's faith in Christ (Koester 576–77).

VERSE 14

οὐ γὰρ ἔχομεν ὧδε μένουσαν πόλιν
For we do not have an enduring city here;

Γάρ introduces the reasons why believers can go to Jesus and leave the camp (cf. Cockerill 703 n. 62). Πόλιν is the obj. of ἔχομεν and is modified by the adj. ptc. μένουσαν ("enduring" [NIV], "lasting" [most EVV], "permanent" [GNT, NJB, NLT]). The adv. ὧδε ("here") modifies ἔχομεν. The contrast between the city "here" and the "one to come" is indicated by οὐ . . . ἀλλά. This v. contrasts what believers already have (see comments on v. 13) with what they do not have (Attridge 399). There could also be a subtle refutation of the Roman claims that Rome was the "eternal city" (Koester 571).

ἀλλὰ τὴν μέλλουσαν ἐπιζητοῦμεν.
instead, we seek the one to come.

The compound ἐπιζητοῦμεν is intensified (Lane 2:358; "have a strong desire for" [BDAG 371c]), although this is not reflected in EVV: "seek" (most EVV), "look for" (NIV, NRSV), but "long for" (Weymouth). This word recalls its earlier use in 11:14, describing those who sought the city of God. Πόλιν is understood elliptically from the previous clause. Μέλλουσαν (see comments on 1:14) modifies "city," which is elliptically understood from the previous clause: explicit in many EVV (e.g., "the city that [or, which] is to come" [ESV, NASB, NET, NIV]). The art. stresses the certainty of this city (Cockerill 703). The important theological link to the heavenly Jerusalem is missed with "our permanent home" (NLT).

VERSE 15

Δι' αὐτοῦ [οὖν] ἀναφέρωμεν θυσίαν αἰνέσεως διὰ παντὸς τῷ θεῷ,
Therefore, through him let us continually offer up to God a sacrifice of praise,

Οὖν does not occur in many important early mss. It was likely added for clarity. It is included in square brackets and rated {C} (see Metzger 605), but is reflected in most EVV. The antecedent of αὐτοῦ is Ἰησοῦς (made explicit in NIV, NLT, REB). The adv. prep. phrase δι' αὐτοῦ modifies ἀναφέρωμεν for means. Its position is emph. (Lane 2:524 n. *z*). Ἀναφέρωμεν is the 1st pl. pres. act. subjunc. of ἀναφέρω, "offer" (NIV, NLT, NRSV) or "offer up" (ESV, NASB, NET [BDAG 75b]). The obj. of the vb. is θυσίαν (see comments on 5:1). Αἰνέσεως (gen. sg. fem. of αἴνεσις, -εως, ἡ [BDAG 27 b–c; H. Balz, *EDNT* 1:39d–40b; NT hapax]) is an epex. gen., further explaining θυσίαν, "a sacrifice of praise" (most EVV [Ellingworth 720; Lane 2:524 n. *bb*]). Διὰ παντός means "without ceasing" (Cassirer), "continually" (most EVV), and adv. modifies ἀναφέρωμεν temp., although NJB takes the adv. with θυσίαν ("an unending sacrifice").

τοῦτ' ἔστιν καρπὸν χειλέων ὁμολογούντων τῷ ὀνόματι αὐτοῦ.
that is, the fruit of lips that confess his name.

The expression τοῦτ' ἔστιν is fixed regardless of the antecedent (R 705). Here it introduces the metaphorical understanding of the sacrifice that is appropriate for believers (Attridge 400). It further elaborates θυσίαν αἰνέσεως. The descriptive gen. χειλέων (gen. pl. neut. of χεῖλος, -ους, τό, "lips" [most EVV; BDAG 1081d]) modifies καρπόν ("fruit" [most EVV]). Ὁμολογούντων is the gen. pl. neut. of the pres. act. ptc. of ὁμολογέω, "acknowledge" (ESV, NET, NJB), "give thanks to" (NASB), "profess" (NIV [BDAG 708b]). The vb. is followed by the dat., τῷ ὀνόματι αὐτοῦ (R 541). The ptc. adj. modifies χειλέων. There may be an allusion to the "name" of the Son in 1:4

(Cockerill 706). This v. alludes to LXX Hos 14:3. The expression "fruit of the lips" is "a Semitic figure of speech" (Lane 2:550).

VERSE 16

τῆς δὲ εὐποιΐας καὶ κοινωνίας μὴ ἐπιλανθάνεσθε·
Don't neglect to do what is good and to share,

Ἐπιλανθάνεσθε is the 2nd pl. pres. mid. impv. of ἐπιλανθάνομαι, which recalls its use in 13:2. Most EVV tr. the impv. the same in both vv. (see comments on 13:2). Εὐποιΐας is the gen. sg. fem. of εὐποιΐα, -ας, ἡ, "do good" (ESV, NASB, NIV, NLT), "well doing" (BDAG 410b; BGk. hapax). Κοινωνίας is the gen. sg. fem. of κοινωνία, -ας, ἡ, "to share with those in need" (NLT), "to share what you have" (ESV, NET), "to share with others" (NIV), "generosity" (BDAG 553b). The word has "financial connotations"—"partnership with other believers carried economic overtones" (Lane 2:552). The sg. art. governing both nouns is not an example of Granville Sharp's rule, but the art. does indicate that the two entities are closely related ("the second group is a subset of the first" [Wallace 287]). Ellingworth (721) calls them a "virtual hendiadys." The actions here expand on the exhortation regarding loving other believers in 13:1 (cf. Cockerill 707; Ellingworth 721).

τοιαύταις γὰρ θυσίαις εὐαρεστεῖται ὁ θεός.
for God is pleased with such sacrifices.

Γάρ offers motivation for the exhortation in the first part of the v. (cf. Cockerill 707 n. 84). Εὐαρεστεῖται is the 3rd sg. pres. pass. indic. of εὐαρεστέω, "be pleased" (most EVV [BDAG 403c]). Τοιαύταις (dat. pl. neut. of τοιοῦτος, -αύτη, -οῦτον) modifies θυσίαις ("such sacrifices" [most EVV]). The dat. indicates association or means (most EVV [R 532]). Less natural is a dat. of cause ("for God is pleased because of such sacrifices" [BDF §196; Lane 2:553]).

VERSE 17

Πείθεσθε τοῖς ἡγουμένοις ὑμῶν καὶ ὑπείκετε,
Obey your leaders and submit to them,

Πείθεσθε in the pass. means to "obey" (most EVV [BDAG 792b). The pres. is iterative (Lane 2:524 n. *gg*). It is followed by the dat. (BDAG 792b). The subst. ptc. ἡγουμένοις denotes "leaders." Ὑμῶν is poss. Ὑπείκετε is the 2nd pl. pres. act. impv. of ὑπείκω, "submit" (most EVV; BDAG 1030a; NT hapax). The vb. has the sense of submitting *to authority* (BDAG 1030a), which is brought out in some EVV (e.g., NIV), but is obscured in others ("give way to" [NJB], "defer to" [NAB]). An obj. is supplied in many EVV ("to them").

αὐτοὶ γὰρ ἀγρυπνοῦσιν ὑπὲρ τῶν ψυχῶν ὑμῶν
since they keep watch over your souls

Γάρ offers motivation for obeying and submitting to church leaders by recalling their task (Cockerill 708). Ἀγρυπνοῦσιν is the 3rd pl. pres. act. indic. of ἀγρυπνέω, "keep watch" (most EVV), "look after," "care for" (BDAG 16a). The word has the sense of vigilance and being alert to threats ("keep watch in defense of your souls" [Goodspeed]; cf. Cockerill 707 n. 91). The nom. αὐτοί is emph., both by syntax ("they themselves" [although left untr. in most EVV; BDAG 152c; Wallace 322]) and pos. (Lane 2:524 n. *ii*). Ὑπέρ with the gen. indicates "on behalf of," or "for the benefit of" (Harris 209). Τῶν ψυχῶν ὑμῶν implies concern for the "eternal welfare" of those entrusted to these leaders (Cockerill 708).

ὡς λόγον ἀποδώσοντες,
as those who will give an account,

Ἀποδώσοντες is the nom. pl. masc. of the fut. act. ptc. of ἀποδίδωμι. Ὡς does not indicate comp., but rather motive: "as men who 'with the thought that'" (BDF §425[3]). The fut. ptc. indicates "purpose or aim" (R 877) and possibly also cause (R 1128). The focus here is on the character of the leaders (Cockerill 707). As with 4:13, λόγον draws on the commercial realm of accounting (BDAG 600d). The expression is idiomatic: "as those who will give an account" (NASB).

ἵνα μετὰ χαρᾶς τοῦτο ποιῶσιν καὶ μὴ στενάζοντες·
so that they can do this with joy and not with grief,

Ἵνα followed by the subjunc. indicates purpose. Some EVV tr. the clause with an impv. force (e.g., "let them do this" [ESV, NASB, NET; cf. Lane 2:525 n. *ll*]). The dependent clause modifies ἀγρυπνοῦσιν. The subj. of ποιῶσιν is the leaders ref. in the beginning of the v. The antecedent of τοῦτο is probably the accounting required of leaders rather than their oversight (e.g., "their work" [NIV]), although the two are inextricably linked (cf. Cockerill 709 n. 95). Τοῦτο is the obj. of ποιῶσιν. Μετὰ χαρᾶς modifies ποιῶσιν, indicating manner ("with joy" [ESV, NASB, NET], "joyfully" [RSV, Cassirer]). Στενάζοντες is the nom. pl. masc. of the pres. act. ptc. of στενάζω (BDAG 942c; H. Balz, *EDNT* 3:272d). The ptc. modifies ποιῶσιν as a circum. ptc. Many EVV tr. the ptc. as an adj. par. to χαρᾶς and supply the prep. "with" (e.g., "with sorrow" [NAB], "with groaning" [ESV], "with complaints" [NET], "with grief" [NASB]).

ἀλυσιτελὲς γὰρ ὑμῖν τοῦτο.
for that would be unprofitable for you.

Γάρ gives the reason or motivation (Lane 2:556) for the preceding exhortation. The antecedent of τοῦτο is the preceding exhortation to obey and submit, understood generally. Τοῦτο functions as the subj. of the verbless clause. Ἀλυσιτελές is the nom. sg. neut. of ἀλυσιτελής, -ές, "unprofitable" (NASB [BDAG 48d; BGk. hapax]), "be harmful" (NRSV), "be of no advantage" (ESV, NET), "be of no benefit (NIV). The term has commercial or accounting connotations (Lane 2:525 n. *mm*) as well as eschatological ones (Cockerill 709). The adj. functions as the pred. of this clause. Ὑμῖν is a dat. of advantage. There may be hints in this v. of a strained relationship between the audience and their leadership, perhaps due to the "various strange teachings" (Lane 2:554–55).

VERSE 18

Προσεύχεσθε περὶ ἡμῶν·
Pray for us,

Προσεύχεσθε is the 2nd pl. pres. mid. impv. of προσεύχομαι, "pray" (most EVV). The pres. is iterative (Lane 2:525 n. *nn*) and suggests that the audience has been praying for the author (Ellingworth 725). Περί ἡμῶν modifies προσεύχεσθε.

πειθόμεθα γὰρ ὅτι καλὴν συνείδησιν ἔχομεν,
for we are convinced that we have a clear conscience,

Γάρ gives the reason for the preceding exhortation. Πειθόμεθα is the 1st pl. pres. pass. indic. of πείθω; the pass. indicates "be confident" (NAB), "be certain" (BDAG 792b); cf. "we are sure" (ESV, NASB, NIV). The declarative ὅτι (R 1035) indicates the content of the author's conviction. Ἔχομεν is the main vb. of the dependent clause. Συνείδησιν ("conscience" [most EVV]) is the obj. of the vb. (see comments on 9:9). The adj. καλήν usually means "good" (NASB), but here it has the sense of "clear" (most EVV). The switch to the first pers. pl. indicates that the author counts himself among the audience's leaders (Lane 2:556; cf. Ellingworth 722).

ἐν πᾶσιν καλῶς θέλοντες ἀναστρέφεσθαι.
wanting to conduct ourselves honorably in everything.

Θέλοντες modifies πειθόμεθα circumstantially ("wishing" [NAB], "desiring" [ESV], or perhaps causally ("since we strive to act" [Lane 2:522, 525 n. *pp*]). Some EVV tr. the ptc. as a coordinate finite vb. ("and desire to" [NET, NIV]). Ἀναστρέφεσθαι is the pres. mid. inf. of ἀναστρέφω. The vb. in the pass. means "conduct oneself" (NASB, NET [BDAG 72d–73a]; "to act" [ESV], "to live" [NIV]). The inf. complements θέλοντες. The adv. καλῶς ("honorably" [NASB, NIV], "rightly" [NET]) modifies ἀναστρέφεσθαι. Ἐν πᾶσιν modifies ἀναστρέφεσθαι, indicating manner ("in all things" [ESV, NASB], "in every respect" [NET], "in every way" [NIV]). The position of the prep. phrase is emph. (Lane 2:525 n. *rr*). This closing prayer request suggests that the author had a close relationship with his recipients and possibly a position of leadership.

VERSE 19

περισσοτέρως δὲ παρακαλῶ τοῦτο ποιῆσαι,
And I urge you all the more to pray

Δέ marks continuation (e.g., "and" [CSB], but left untr. in many EVV) in the author's appeal to his audience (Ellingworth 726). Παρακαλῶ is the 1st pl. pres. act. indic. of παρακαλέω, "urge" (most EVV). The use of the first pers. sg. is rare in Hebrews. Based on the use of ἡμῶν in v. 18 (which would be an unusual example of an epistolary pl.), Wallace argues that Hebrews may have been written by more than one pers. (Wallace 396–97 n. 10). Perhaps more likely, the pl. in v. 18 indicates individuals with whom the author was associated (Timothy?) but from whom he was temporarily separated (Cockerill 712 n. 11). Ποιῆσαι is the complement of παρακαλῶ. Many EVV make explicit what is implied in ποιῆσαι ("to do this" [ESV, NASB]), namely, "pray" (most EVV), drawing on προσεύχομαι in v.18. Περισσοτέρως is the adv. derived from περισσότερος, which is the comp. of περισσός ("abundant" [BDAG 806b]): "the more earnestly" (ESV), "especially" (NET), "particularly" (NIV), "all the more" (NASB). The adv. modifies either παρακαλῶ or ποιῆσαι. It underscores the urgency of the author's request (Cockerill 713 n. 20).

ἵνα τάχιον ἀποκατασταθῶ ὑμῖν.
that I may be restored to you very soon.

Ἵνα followed by the subjunc. indicates purpose. The dependent clause modifies παρακαλῶ . . . ποιῆσαι. Ἀποκατασταθῶ is the 1st sg. aor. pass. subjunc. of ἀποκαθίστημι, "be restored" (most EVV [BDAG 111d–112a]). The pass. suggests that God is the one who will restore the author to the audience (Koester 573). Ταχέως is the comp. of ταχύς, -εῖα, -ύ, "quick," from which is derived the comp. τάχιον, τάχιστα ("the sooner" [ESV, NASB], "more quickly" [BDAG 992b–c]), or elative ("very soon" [NET, NRSV, BDF 244(1)]). Some EVV tr. it as a simple pos. ("soon" [NIV]).

The request to be "restored" indicates that the author had previously been with the congregation, which renders implausible the suggestion that the author was anonymous to the orig. recipients of Hebrews. The reasons why the author was separated from the audience are not specified. The ref. to Timothy could suggest that the author had been imprisoned for his faith (Cockerill 714).

FOR FURTHER STUDY

101. The Altar, Strange Teachings, and Going "Outside the Camp" (13:9–16)

Attridge, 394–96.
Haak, Robert D. *ABD* 1:162–67.
*Isaacs, Marie E. "Hebrew 13:9–16 Revisited." *NTS* 43 (1997): 268–84.
Koester, Helmut. "'Outside the Camp': Hebrews 13:9–14." *HTR* 55 (1962): 299–315.
Sanders, James A. "Outside the Camp." *Union Seminary Quarterly Review* 24 (1969): 239–46.
*Saunders, Landon. "'Outside the Camp': Hebrews 13." *ResQ* 22 (1979): 19–24.
Schick, Edwin A. "Priestly Pilgrims: Mission outside the Camp in Hebrews." *CurTM* 16 (1989): 372–76.
Snell, Antony. "We Have an Altar." *RTR* 23 (1964): 16–23.

*Thompson, James W. "Outside the Camp: A Study of Heb 13: 9–14." *CBQ* 40 (1978): 53–63.
*Young, Norman H. "'Bearing His Reproach' (Heb 13.9–14)." *NTS* 48 (2002): 243–61.

102. Worship in Hebrews (13:15)

Aune, David D. *ABD* 6:973–89.
DBI 969–73.
Heil, John Paul. *Worship in the Letter to the Hebrews*. Eugene, OR: Cascade, 2011.
Madsen, Norman P. "The Place of Christ in Prayer." *SLJT* 27 (1983): 7–19.
*Peterson, David. "Further Reflections on Worship in the New Testament." *RTR* 44 (1985): 34–41.
*———. "Towards a New Testament Theology of Worship." *RTR* 43/3 (1984): 65–73.
Wu, J. L. *DLNT* 520–22.

HOMILETICAL SUGGESTIONS

Exhortations Regarding Church Leaders and Teaching (13:7–19)

1. Remember Those Who Have Led You (v. 7)
   (a) They brought you the Word of God (v. 7a)
   (b) Imitate their faith (v. 7b)
2. (Leaders May Be Gone but . . .) The One Who Never Changes (v. 8)
3. Reject Strange (Trendy) Teachings (vv. 9–10a)
   (a) God's grace alone grounds us (v. 9b)
   (b) Diets and regimes can't ground us (v. 9c)
   (c) We worship at the true altar, not accessible by those who practice earthly worship (v. 10a)
4. Let Us Therefore Go to Jesus (vv. 10b–14)
   (a) Just as sacrificed animal carcasses were disposed of outside the Israelite camp, so also Jesus was "disposed of" outside the city (vv. 10b–11)
   (b) This is why his blood sanctifies (v. 12a)
   (c) Like Jesus, we must go outside earthly norms (v. 13a)
   (d) Like Jesus, we must bear this rejection (v. 13b)
   (e) Like Jesus, our true home is not an earthly city (v. 14)
5. True Worship (v. 15)
   (a) Sacrifices of praise to God (v. 15a)
   (b) Confession of his name (v. 15b)
   (c) Doing good and sharing with others (v. 16)
6. Obey Those Who Are Leading You (vv. 16–19)
   (a) They will have to give an account for watching over you (v. 17a)
   (b) Don't grieve them in their ministry (v. 17b)
   (c) Pray for leaders who are temporarily absent, perhaps due to misunderstanding (vv. 18–19)

C. FINAL BENEDICTION (13:20–21)

STRUCTURE

The closing benediction is a standard feature of NT epistles. This benediction draws on language and imagery from throughout the epistle, making challenges to the integrity of these verses hard to defend. The author appears to have reworked conventional blessings and salutations (Cockerill 714). The force of the opt. in v. 21 grounds the opening prayer in v. 20 with an implied opt. The substan. ptc. ὁ ἀναγαγών is an appos. to θεός, and is aligned accordingly, as are the par. objs. of the ptc.

20 Ὁ δὲ θεὸς τῆς εἰρήνης,
  ὁ ἀναγαγὼν ἐκ νεκρῶν   τὸν ποιμένα τῶν προβάτων τὸν μέγαν
    ἐν αἵματι διαθήκης αἰωνίου,   τὸν κύριον ἡμῶν
                        Ἰησοῦν,

21 καταρτίσαι ὑμᾶς
    ἐν παντὶ ἀγαθῷ
    εἰς τὸ ποιῆσαι τὸ θέλημα αὐτοῦ,
    ποιῶν ἐν ἡμῖν τὸ εὐάρεστον ἐνώπιον αὐτοῦ διὰ Ἰησοῦ Χριστοῦ,
  ᾧ ἡ δόξα εἰς τοὺς αἰῶνας [τῶν αἰώνων], ἀμήν.

VERSE 20

Ὁ δὲ θεὸς τῆς εἰρήνης,
Now may the God of peace,

Δέ ("now" [many EVV]; left untr. in NAB, NIV) joins the final benediction with the prayer request in the previous section (Lane 2:558–59 n. *a*). The gen. indicates that God is the source of peace (Lane 2:560) or is a gen. of quality (BDF §165). Ὁ θεὸς τῆς εἰρήνης is an apparently uniquely Christian designation (Lane 2:560), which is esp. common in Pauline epistles. In this v., it likely recalls the exhortation to pursue peace in 12:14 (Attridge 405). The benediction assumes the opt. εἴη, likely drawing on the opt. in v. 21. Perhaps influenced by the first pers. in near proximity, NJB tr. this as first pers. ("I pray").

ὁ ἀναγαγὼν ἐκ νεκρῶν τὸν ποιμένα τῶν προβάτων τὸν μέγαν ἐν αἵματι διαθήκης αἰωνίου, τὸν κύριον ἡμῶν Ἰησοῦν,
who brought up from the dead our Lord Jesus—the great Shepherd of the sheep—through the blood of the everlasting covenant,

Ἀναγαγών is the nom. sg. masc. of aor. act. ptc. of ἀνάγω, "brought again" (ESV), "bring back" (NET, NIV), "bring up" (NASB [BDAG 61d]). The more common vb. used for resurrection is ἐγείρω, although ἀνάγω may recall ἄγω in 2:10 (Attridge 406). The word choice may reflect the author's emph. on Christ's exaltation, which presupposes his resurrection (Cockerill 715). This is the only dir. ref. to Jesus's resurrection in Hebrews. Ἐκ νεκρῶν locat. modifies ἀναγαγών. The adj. is subst. ("from the dead" [most EVV]).

The obj. of the ptc. is Ἰησοῦν, the pos. of which is emph. (Lane 2:559 n. *c*). This is reflected in some EVV by moving Jesus (together with "our Lord") toward the front of the clause (e.g., NIV). Τὸν κύριον ἡμῶν is an appos. of Ἰησοῦν. Ποιμένα is the acc. sg. masc. of ποιμήν, -ένος, ὁ ("shepherd" [most EVV]), which is modified by μέγαν. The rep. of the art. before the adj. is "sort of a climax in apposition" (R 777), or a "second attrib. pos." cstr. (Wallace 306–307). The use of μέγας recalls its use in 4:14, which describes Jesus as the great high priest (cf. 10:21). Προβάτων ("sheep") is a descriptive gen., modifying ποιμένα. The collocation τὸν ποιμένα τῶν προβάτων τὸν μέγαν is a second appos. of Ἰησοῦν. The entire cstr. (ὁ ἀναγαγών . . . Ἰησοῦν) is in appos. to θεός (Attridge 405). Διαθήκης modifies αἵματι as a descriptive gen. (most EVV) or possibly as an obj. gen. ("the blood that sealed an eternal covenant" [NJB]).

The mng. of ἐν αἵματι διαθήκης αἰωνίου is disputed. Most likely it modifies ἀναγαγών instr. ("through" [most EVV; cf. Ellingworth 728]) or is possibly casual (Lane 2:559 n. *b*). It indicates God's vindication of Jesus and the acceptance of his sacrifice as the basis of the eternal covenant (cf. Bruce 388). A sense of accompaniment does not cohere well with the rest of Hebrews (cf. Ellingworth 728; Lane 2:563). For διαθήκη, see comments on 9:16.

The shepherd imagery and much of the wording alludes to LXX Isa 63:11–14, which refers to Moses as a shepherd whom God has bought up from the sea (see pars. in Cockerill 716; Lane 2:561). The wording may also reflect Ps 81:10 (Cockerill 715 n. 32). Jesus as the Shepherd is esp. prevalent in John 10 and 1 Peter (2:25; 5:4 [see Lane 2:562]; for OT ref., see Cockerill 715 n. 33). The shift from the depiction of priest to shepherd may suggest the ongoing ministry of Jesus to lead his people to their intended destiny (Cockerill 716). See Craig S. Keener, *DLNT*, 1090–93; Steven W. Smith, "Jesus Christ, the Good to Great Shepherd," *SwJT* 56 (2013): 53–63.

The expression "eternal covenant" occurs in Isa 55:3; 61:8; Jer 32:40; Ezek 16:60; 37:26. The expression "encapsulates" the emph. on Christ's status as high priest and mediator of the new covenant in Hebrews (Cockerill 716). See Richard L. Mayhue, "Heb 13:20: Covenant of Grace or New Covenant? An Exegetical Note," *MSJ* 7 (1996): 251–57.

VERSE 21

καταρτίσαι ὑμᾶς ἐν παντὶ ἀγαθῷ εἰς τὸ ποιῆσαι τὸ θέλημα αὐτοῦ,
equip you with everything good to do his will,

Καταρτίσαι is the 3rd sg. aor. act. opt. of καταρτίζω (BDAG 526b). In Heb 10:5, καταρτίζω meant "prepare," which is closer to the sense here than "create" in Heb 11:3. The opt. indicates volition or "an attainable wish" (BDF §384): "may God equip." Many EVV make explicit the assumed opt. in v. 20 and then tr. καταρτίσαι as a coordinate (e.g., "make complete" [NRSV], "furnish" [NAB], "equip" [ESV, NASB, NET, NIV; so most commentators]). This is the only opt. in Hebrews. The obj. of the vb.

is ὑμᾶς. Ἐν παντὶ ἀγαθῷ modifies *καταρτίσαι* indicating instr. ("in every good thing" [NASB]; cf. "with" [ESV, NAB, NIV]). It functions as a summary of all the benefits that Hebrews has outlined concerning Christ's ministry (e.g., a cleansed conscience, access to God [Cockerill 717–18]). Εἰς with an art. inf. (ποιῆσαι) indicates purpose (Wallace 590–92). The subj. of the inf. is the same as that of the vb. *καταρτίσαι*, namely, "you." Τὸ θέλημα αὐτοῦ is the obj. of the inf. The antecedent of αὐτοῦ is θεός (v. 20).

ποιῶν ἐν ἡμῖν τὸ εὐάρεστον ἐνώπιον αὐτοῦ διὰ Ἰησοῦ Χριστοῦ,
working in us what is pleasing in his sight, through Jesus Christ,

Ποιῶν modifies *καταρτίσαι*, indicating instr., although many EVV leave this unspecified (e.g., "working"). Some EVV tr. the ptc. with the force of the opt. (e.g., "may he work in us" [NIV]). The dat. ἐν ἡμῖν is advantage or possibly locat. ("among us" [NRSV]). The adj. εὐάρεστον (εὐάρεστος, -ον) is subst. ("what is pleasing" [many EVV; BDAG 403d]). The cognate εὐαρέστως occurs in 12:28 and the cognate εὐαρεστέω in 13:16. Ἐνώπιον connotes "in the opinion of him" or "in the judgment of him" (BDAG 342d), which is suggested with "in his sight" (ESV, NASB), but is less clear with "before him" (NET), "to him" (NIV). Διὰ Ἰησοῦ Χριστοῦ modifies ποιῶν and is "comprehensive—means, manner, and cause" (Cockerill 718 n. 47), although most EVV tr. it instr. ("through Jesus Christ").

ᾧ ἡ δόξα εἰς τοὺς αἰῶνας [τῶν αἰώνων], ἀμήν.
to whom be glory forever and ever. Amen.

The antecedent of ᾧ is debated. In support of God is the opening "God of peace" (Ellingworth 731; Lane 2:559 n. *i*). Proximity, however, would support Jesus Christ (as reflected in most EVV; made explicit in CEV, GNT; Attridge 407). The author may have intended both, as a means of affirming once again Christ's deity (Cockerill 718–19). A form of εἰμί is often assumed in a doxology, although the sense of ascription is rendered well with "glory belongs to" (CSB) or "glory be ascribed" (Cassirer).

Εἰς τοὺς αἰῶνας [τῶν αἰώνων] recalls its use in 13:8. Τῶν αἰώνων is probably not orig. (cf. 13:8) and likely reflects scribal assimilation to other passages where the gen. modifier is attested (e.g., 1 Tim 1:17; 2 Tim 4:18). The UBS committee rated the rdg. {C} and enclosed it in square brackets (Metzger 606–607). It is reflected in most EVV, but omitted in some (NET) or placed in square brackets (NAB).

FOR FURTHER STUDY

103. Benedictions in the NT (13:20–21)

Cranfield, C. E. B. "Hebrews 13:20–21." *SJT* 20 (1967): 437–41.
*Jewett, Robert. "The Form and Function of the Homiletic Benediction." *AThR* 51 (1969): 18–34.
Mullins, T. Y. "Benediction as a NT Form." *AUSS* 15 (1977): 59–64.
———. "Greeting as a NT Form." *JBL* 87 (1968): 418–26.
Wu, J. L. *DLNT* 659–65.

104. Resurrection in Hebrews (13:20)

Cockerill, Gareth Lee. "The Better Resurrection (Heb 11:35): A Key to the Structure and Rhetorical Purpose of Hebrews 11." *TynBul* 51 (2000): 215–34.

Harris, Murray J. *Raised Immortal: Resurrection and Immortality in the New Testament*. Grand Rapids: Eerdmans, 1985.

Moffitt, David M. "'If Another Priest Arises': Jesus' Resurrection and the High Priestly Christology of Hebrews." Pages 68–79 in Bauckham, *Cloud*.

*Schrock, David Stephen. "Resurrection and Priesthood: Christological Soundings from the Book of Hebrews." *SBJT* 18/4 (2014): 89–114.

Travis, S. H. *DLNT* 1015–20.

Wright, N.T. *The Resurrection of the Son of God*. London: SPCK, 2003.

HOMILETICAL SUGGESTIONS

A Final Blessing (13:20–21)

1. To the Great God (v. 20)
   (a) He is the God of peace (v. 20a)
   (b) He brought Jesus back from the dead (v. 20b)
   (c) Our great Shepherd (v. 20c)
   (d) Whose blood inaugurated the eternal covenant (v. 20d)
2. May He Equip Us (v. 21)
   (a) With everything to do good (v. 21a)
   (b) Working in us through Jesus Christ to be pleasing in his sight (v. 21b)
3. To This One Be Glory Forever! (v. 21c)

VIII. Epilogue (13:22–25)

STRUCTURE

Final greetings and travel plans are standard features of NT epistles (for a comp. of Hebrews with other NT epistles, see Attridge 405). The fact that Hebrews starts as a sermon and ends as an epistle has generated much speculation. Perhaps the most satisfying explanation is that the author had hoped to preach the sermon in person but was not able to do so; thus he wrote it down and sent it as a letter (Cockerill 711). Suggestions that this ending was added to make Hebrews appear Pauline fail to explain why the epistle does not open as Pauline epistles do.

The epilogue structures around three impvs. and a final, short benediction. Each of the impvs. is further modified with either an indic. (vv. 22, 24) or a cond. (v. 23).

22 Παρακαλῶ δὲ ὑμᾶς, ἀδελφοί,
    ἀνέχεσθε τοῦ λόγου τῆς παρακλήσεως,
    καὶ γὰρ διὰ βραχέων ἐπέστειλα ὑμῖν.
23 Γινώσκετε τὸν ἀδελφὸν ἡμῶν Τιμόθεον ἀπολελυμένον,
        . . . ἐὰν τάχιον ἔρχηται
    μεθ᾽ οὗ . . .ὄψομαι ὑμᾶς.
24 Ἀσπάσασθε πάντας τοὺς ἡγουμένους ὑμῶν καὶ πάντας τοὺς ἁγίους.
    ἀσπάζονται ὑμᾶς οἱ ἀπὸ τῆς Ἰταλίας.
25 ἡ χάρις μετὰ πάντων ὑμῶν.

VERSE 22

Παρακαλῶ δὲ ὑμᾶς, ἀδελφοί, ἀνέχεσθε τοῦ λόγου τῆς παρακλήσεως,
Brothers and sisters, I urge you to receive this message of exhortation,

Δέ ("now" [NET], "but" [NASB]) joins this final section to the previous doxology, although it is untr. in many EVV. Παρακαλῶ is the 1st pl. pres. act. indic. of παρακαλέω, "urge" (most EVV; cf. "beg" [REB], "appeal" [ESV]). The use of the first pers. sg. par. its use in 13:19. As was true in 2:11, ἀδελφοί here is inclusive ("brothers and sisters" [*pace* ESV, NAB, NIV]). Ἀνέχεσθε is the 2nd pl. pres. mid. impv. of ἀνέχω.

The vb. often means to "bear with" (ESV, NASB, NET, NIV), or "put up with" (BDAG 78b; Attridge 408; Bruce 389), which would have rhetorically implied deference with the hope of "compliance" (Cockerill 720), so as to "listen willingly" (Lane 2:568; "to give a ready hearing" [Cassirer]). Some EVV miss this with "receive" (e.g., CSB). The second pers. impv. following the first pers. indic. is awkward in Eng.; thus many EVV use an inf. to tr. ἀνέχεσθε (e.g., CSB).

The expression τοῦ λόγου ("word" or "message" in most EVV) τῆς παρακλήσεως (παράκλησις, -εως, ἡ) refers to a sermon in Acts 13:15. Even with this designation, it is unlikely that Hebrews is the transcription of an actual sermon. Instead, it was composed to be read to the audience, which would have taken about an hour. The play on words between παρακαλῶ and παρακλήσεως (e.g., "I exhort you . . . word of exhortation") is often missed in EVV.

καὶ γὰρ διὰ βραχέων ἐπέστειλα ὑμῖν.
for I have written to you briefly.

The cstr. καὶ γάρ means "and/for in fact" (NET [Lane 2:566 n. *c*]), but is often tr. "for" (most EVV). Ἐπέστειλα is the 1st sg. aor. act. indic. of ἐπιστέλλω, which means to "inform or instruct by letter" (BDAG 381b) and is rendered "write" in most EVV. This is often designated an "epistolary aor." (R 845), although it is likely that the aor. simply indicates the contents of the epistle as a whole without ref. to the time of composition and time of reception. The vb. is followed by the dat. This exact collocation occurs nowhere else in the NT (Lane 2:566 n. *d*). In keeping with all of Hebrews, the author avoids the common γράφω (Cockerill 720 n. 56). Διὰ βραχέων (βραχύς, -εῖα, -ύ) adv. ("briefly" [most EVV]) modifies ἐπέστειλα. The use of διά to indicate manner is unusual (Lane 2:566 n. *e*). Βραχέων reflects a "literary convention" (Ellingworth 732). This is missed with "only a short letter" (CEV) or "brief exhortation" (NLT). This reflects a conventional statement (Koester 580).

VERSE 23

Γινώσκετε τὸν ἀδελφὸν ἡμῶν Τιμόθεον ἀπολελυμένον,
Be aware that our brother Timothy has been released.

Γινώσκετε is either indic. (CEV) or impv. ("take notice" [NASB]; cf. "you should know" [ESV, NET], "I want you to know" [NIV, NLT, NRSV]). The impv. is preferred because of the hort. context (Cockerill 720; cf. Ellingworth 733). The impv. implies that the audience did not know that Timothy had been released, whereas the indic. reminds them of something already known (cf. Cockerill 720). Τιμόθεον is an appos. of ἀδελφόν. Ἀπολελυμένον is the acc. sg. masc. of pf. pass. ptc. of ἀπολύω, "release" (most EVV; "set free" [NAB, NJB, NRSV]). Release from prison is implied (but made explicit in GNT, NLT). The ptc. modifies Τιμόθεον as a pred. (most EVV; R 910).

μεθ' οὗ ἐὰν τάχιον ἔρχηται ὄψομαι ὑμᾶς.
If he comes soon enough, he will be with me when I see you.

Ἐάν introduces a gen. cond. (third-class cond. [Wallace 696–99]), the contingency of which is expressed by the subjunc. (ἔρχηται). Τάχιον (see comments on 13:19) modifies ἔρχηται (most EVV tr. the adv. sim. in v. 19 and this v.). The obj. of ὄψομαι is ὑμᾶς. The antecedent of οὗ is Τιμόθεον. Μεθ' οὗ modifies ὄψομαι, indicating accompaniment.

In the absence of any further designation, this Timothy is undoubtedly the same one associated with Paul. This association does not indicate that Paul wrote the epistle, but that the author was known in the "Pauline network" (Cockerill 720–21). See For Further Study 106 (Paul and the Pauline Circle in Hebrews). Although there is no NT account of Timothy's imprisonment, it is certainly plausible. The v. suggests that the author anticipated seeing the audience imminently.

VERSE 24

Ἀσπάσασθε πάντας τοὺς ἡγουμένους ὑμῶν καὶ πάντας τοὺς ἁγίους.
Greet all your leaders and all the saints.

Ἀσπάσασθε is the 2nd pl. aor. mid. impv. of *ἀσπάζομαι* ("greet" [most EVV]). The first *πάντας* modifies *ἡγουμένους* (see comments on 13:7), which is further modified by *ὑμῶν*. The second *πάντας* modifies *ἁγίους*. The first part of this exhortation reinforces the exhortations in 13:7 and 17. The designation "saints" (most EVV; cf. "the holy ones" [NAB], "the Lord's people" [NIV]) was a common designation for believers (cf. Cockerill 721). The emph. on "all" suggests that the exhortation extends beyond the immediate house church addressed to the wider network of believers in Rome (cf. Cockerill 721).

ἀσπάζονται ὑμᾶς οἱ ἀπὸ τῆς Ἰταλίας.
Those who are from Italy send you greetings.

Οἱ functions par. to a dem. pron., "those" (most EVV; "the believers" [NLT]). The gen. *ἀπὸ τῆς Ἰταλίας* modifies οἱ as an ablative (separation). "Those from Italy" is ambiguous. It could either refer to Italians not living in Italy who sent their greetings to a group who was in Italy (e.g., "our Italian friends" [NEB]), or it could refer to Italians in Italy greeting a group not in Italy. The first option coheres better with the suggested background of the author addressing a house church in Rome, from which he was absent (cf. Attridge 410; Koester 481). Ἀσπάζονται is the 3rd pl. pres. mid. indic. of *ἀσπάζομαι* ("greet" or "send greetings" [most EVV]). Ὑμᾶς is the obj. of the vb.

VERSE 25

ἡ χάρις μετὰ πάντων ὑμῶν.
Grace be with you all.

This "standard" benediction has numerous par. in Pauline epistles (see esp. Cockerill 722 n. 70). Although some mss. add a concluding *ἀμήν*, early and important mss. do not. The UBS committee rates the ending without ἀμήν {A} (Metzger 607; *pace* ASV, KJV, RSV). Although numerous mss. add various subscriptions at the end of the epistle, textual evidence does not support any of these subscriptions (Metzger 607).

FOR FURTHER STUDY

105. The Genre of Hebrews (13:22)

Attridge, Harold W. "Paraenesis in a Homily (λόγος παρακλήσεως): The Possible Location of, and Socialization in, the 'Epistle to the Hebrews.'" *Semeia* 50 (1990): 211–26.
Ellingworth, 59–62.
Gelardini, Gabriella. "Hebrews, an Ancient Synagogue Homily for Tisha be-Av: Its Function, Its Basis, Its Theological Interpretation." Pages 107–27 in *Hebrews: Contemporary Methods—New Insights*. Edited by Gabriella Gelardini. Biblical Interpretation Series. Leiden: Brill, 2005.
———. "Hebrews, Homiletics, and Liturgical Scripture Interpretation." Pages 121–43 in Mason.
Lane, 1:*lxix–lxxxiv*.
*Lane, William L. "Hebrews: A Sermon in Search of a Setting." *SwJT* 28 (1985): 13–18.
McGehee, Michael. "Hebrews: The Letter Which Is Not a Letter." *TBT* 24 (1986): 213–16.
Swetnam, James. "On the Literary Genre of the 'Epistle' to the Hebrews." *NovT* 11 (1969): 261–69.
Wills, Lawrence M. "The Form of the Sermon in Hellenistic Judaism and Early Christianity." *HTR* 77 (1984): 277–99.

106. Paul and the Pauline Circle in Hebrews (13:23)

Bruce, F. F. *The Pauline Circle*. Grand Rapids: Eerdmans, 1985.
Garroway, Joshua. "A New Sort of Priest for a New Sort of People: Hebrews as an Interpretation of Romans." Pages 301–17 in *Portraits of Jesus: Studies in Christology*. Edited by Susan E. Myers. WUNT 2/321. Tübingen: Mohr Siebeck, 2012.
Thompson, James W. "The Epistle to the Hebrews and the Pauline Legacy." *ResQ* 47 (2005): 197–206.

HOMILETICAL SUGGESTIONS

Final Exhortations (13:22–25)

1. An Appeal to Receive the Message of the Epistle (v. 22)
   (a) A message of exhortation (v. 22a)
   (b) Briefly written (v. 22b)
2. An Appeal to Receive Timothy (v. 23)
   (a) Who has been recently released (v. 23a)
   (b) With whom the author hopes to come to the recipients (v. 23b)
3. An Appeal to Give Greetings (v. 24)
   (a) To the rest of the community (v. 24a)
   (b) From those with the author (v. 24b)
4. A Final Blessing (v. 25)

Exegetical Outline

I. Introduction: God's Final Revelation, the Son (1:1–4)
II. The Son: The Superior Mediator and the Perfect Human Being (1:5–2:18)
    A. The Son's Superiority to the Angels (1:5–14)
    B. First Warning: Heed the Revelation that Comes through the Son (2:1–4)
    C. The Humility and Glory of the Son, the Perfect Human Being (2:5–9)
    D. The Suffering, Solidarity, and Victory of the Son (2:10–16)
    E. The Perfected Son, the Merciful and Faithful High Priest (2:17–18)
III. The Son: His Faithfulness and Mercy (3:1–5:10)
    A. The Apostle of Our Confession, Even More Faithful than Moses (3:1–6)
    B. Second Warning: Listen to God's Voice While It Is Still Possible (3:7–19)
        1. The Lesson of the Wilderness Generation from Psalm 95 (3:7–11)
        2. The Psalm Applied to the Epistle's Audience (3:12–19)
    C. The Sabbath Rest of God That Remains (4:1–11)
    D. The Penetrating Nature of God's Word (4:12–13)
    E. Jesus the Son, the Great High Priest (4:14–16)
    F. The Son's Suffering as Qualifications for His Merciful Priesthood (5:1–10)
IV. Perseverance in the Promises (5:11–6:20)
    A. Prelude: It's Time to Grow Up and Move On to Maturity (5:11–6:3)
    B. Third Warning: There Is Only One Way to Be Renewed (6:4–8)
    C. The Conviction of Better Things (6:9–12)
    D. The Unchangeable Nature of God's Purposes (6:13–20)
V. The Son: The Superior High Priest (7:1–10:18)
    A. The New Order of Priesthood (7:1–28)
        1. Melchizedek and the Order of His Priesthood (7:1–10)
        2. The Aaronic and Melchizedekian Priesthoods Contrasted (7:11–19)
        3. The Superiority of the New Priesthood (7:20–28)
    B. The New Covenant (8:1–13)
        1. The Superior Ministry of Jesus (8:1–6)
        2. The Superior Covenant (8:7–13)
    C. The New Sanctuary and Sacrifice (9:1–10:18)
        1. The Limitations of the Old Order (9:1–10)
        2. The Eternal Redemption of the Son (9:11–14)

3. The Mediator of the New Covenant (9:15–22)
4. The Perfect Sacrifice (9:23–28)
5. Shadow and Reality, Sacrifice and Obedience (10:1–10)
6. The Finality of Christ's Sacrifice and Priesthood (10:11–18)

VI. Perseverance and Faith (10:19–12:29)
  A. Present Exhortations Based on Christ's Eternal Redemption (10:19–39)
    1. Approaching God's Throne and Meeting Together (10:19–25)
    2. Fourth Warning: The Reality of God's Judgment (10:26–31)
    3. Bold Perseverance in the Midst of Suffering (10:32–39)
  B. Past Examples of Faith in God's Promises (11:1–12:3)
    1. The Nature of Faith (11:1–3)
    2. Preflood Faith (11:4–7)
    3. The Faith of Abraham and Sarah (11:8–12)
    4. The City of God and True Homeland (11:13–16)
    5. The Faith of the Patriarchs (11:17–22)
    6. The Faith of Moses (11:23–28)
    7. Faith during the Exodus and Conquest (11:29–31)
    8. A Multitude of Examples that Culminate in the Perfection Achieved by Christ (11:32–40)
    9. The Example Par Excellence: Jesus (12:1–3)
  C. Pressing On to the Future Consummation (12:4–29)
    1. Discipline and Legitimate Children (12:4–11)
    2. The Necessity of Community (12:12–13)
    3. The Shortsightedness of Esau (12:14–17)
    4. Earthly Sinai and Heavenly Zion Contrasted (12:18–24)
    5. The Fifth Warning: Don't Miss God's Final Word (12:25–29)

VII. Exhortations and Offerings (13:1–21)
  A. Moral Exhortations for God's People (13:1–6)
  B. Remembering Church Leaders (13:7–19)
  C. Final Benediction (13:20–21)

VIII. Epilogue (13:22–25)

Grammar Index

C

R

S

Scripture Index

Hebrews